# HOLDING A GOOD THOUGHT FOR MARILYN

### 1926-1954 THE HOLLYWOOD YEARS

"…Marilyn whispered to me in that low, sexy voice that is natural with her: 'Hold a good thought for me.' She always says that when embarking on a venture. She feels much better when you tell her you will."
--friend and columnist Sidney Skolsky

Copyright © 2015 Stacy Eubank

All rights reserved.

ISBN: 0615715516
ISBN-13: 978-0615715513

# Holding a Good Thought for Marilyn
## 1926-1954 The Hollywood Years

Written, Edited and Compiled by
**Stacy Eubank**

Accompanied by Original Artwork by Stacy Eubank

# Dedication

This book is dedicated to my parents,
Joe and Norma Meador, who have both gone to be with the Lord.
My father, Joe B. Meador, was born in Matador, Texas.
He was a WWII veteran and after the war he majored
in Journalism at Texas Tech University.
He loved writing and always wanted to write a book.
He would have been very proud of my book.
My mother, Norma Jean Moore-Meador, was born in Floydada, Texas.
She endured a childhood that Charles Dickens could have appreciated.
Her mother died at home during her 8th birthday party of breast cancer.
She was then shuttled around from pillar to post
and was forever looking for her place in the world.
She, too, would have been proud for me.


I also dedicate this book to my son Bobby.
"I wish you the STRENGTH to face challenges with confidence,
along with the WISDOM to choose your battles carefully.
I wish you ADVENTURE on your journey and
may you always stop to HELP someone along the way.
Listen to your HEART and take risk carefully.
Remember how much you are LOVED.
I am so PROUD of you!"
--anon

**Honolulu Airport, Hawaii, January 29, 1954**

> Her face was sad and lovely with bright things in it,
> bright eyes and a bright passionate mouth,
> but there was an excitement in her voice
> that men who had cared for her found difficult to forget:
> a singing compulsion, a whispered "Listen,"
> a promise that she had done gay, exciting things
> just a while since and that there were
> gay, exciting things hovering in the next hour.
> — F. Scott Fitzgerald, *The Great Gatsby*

# Forward

Fifty years after Marilyn's death, researchers are finally penetrating the mysteries of her life. That life has long been obscured by the fixation on the part of many researchers solely with the circumstances of her death as well as by false claims on the part of many individuals—like Robert Slatzer and Jeanne Carmen—that they knew her well, when they were only acquaintances.

Among the Marilyn researchers Stacy Eubank stands out for her scholarly acuity, her determination, and her wisdom in thinking about the film star. She has spent hours, days, and finally years tracking down articles on Marilyn in movie fan magazines, newspapers, and general circulation magazines. She has scoured auction catalogues, gaining access to one of the major sources of information on Marilyn, before the auction items disappeared into private collections.

Stacy put her research together into a large compendium of primary sources, which I had the privilege of using when I wrote my recent biography of Marilyn. Without Stacy's help, I could not have completed the book I have written. She has now distilled and expanded that compendium into a stand-alone biography of Marilyn. It is written with verve and grace, and it is filled with unique insights. It deserves attention as a major work in the biographical tradition regarding Marilyn. .

I salute Stacy as an accomplished scholar and a fine human being, whose work should be recognized and read.

Lois Banner, Professor, University of Southern California
Author: *MM Personal: From the Private Archive of Marilyn Monroe* and *Marilyn, The Passion and the Paradox*

# Acknowledgements

First and foremost I need to thank my husband, Bruce, and my son, Bobby, without whose unwavering support and patience, I would not have been able to devote the time required to produce this book. Bruce has helped with proof-reading, editing and was instrumental in helping me to organize my thoughts. Being a history teacher, his point of view was taken into consideration for the historical background to the information I had on Marilyn. I appreciate both of the men in my life. Their confidence in me, and in this undertaking, has given me wings and enabled me to go beyond my fears.

I could not have asked for a better experience than being a research assistant for Dr. Lois Banner, Phd, on her two books on *Marilyn Monroe: MM Personal: From the Private Archive of Marilyn Monroe* and *Marilyn, The Passion and the Paradox.* Lois is a gifted writer and she had become a good friend. Her heart is large and generous and she not only opened herself, but her home to me. We had many adventures together as we sought out Marilyn's various homes in and around Los Angeles, some of her old haunts and the Rockhaven Sanitarium where Marilyn's mother lived…and we also gave Penny McGuiggan her last adventure. I was afforded an opportunity to meet many people who are important in the Marilyn community through Lois, specifically Greg Schreiner and Scott Fortner of the Marilyn Remembered Fan Club who sponsor Marilyn's Memorial Service on August 5th of each year at the Westwood Memorial Park; Michelle Justice of All About Marilyn; Hollywood Museum President and Founder Donelle Dadigan; and Margaret Barrett of Heritage Auctions, Beverly Hills. Lois and I spent many hours discussing the life of Marilyn Monroe and without this commiseration on her life my book would have not been as rich in thoughtful details.

I am currently a moderator on Everlasting Star, a community of the best writers and thinkers on Marilyn Monroe. My fellow members have given me a richer understanding of Marilyn's life through their postings of rare photographs, documents and research. I'd like to thank Melanie Claisse, from France, who founded and owns the site. She has a generous heart. My special thanks to Scott Fortner (themarilynmonroecollection.com) from Los Angeles, who sponsors the Everlasting Star community. I hesitate to mention any by name, for fear of leaving someone out, but I would be remiss not to acknowledge the contribution that Celia from Spain; Jeannette Lindgreen from Las Palmas de Gran Canaria; Nina Gehn from German (www.marilyn-online.de); Jily from Australia; Suus Marie from the Netherlands; Merja Pohjola from Tampere, Finland; Christine Heas from France; Lasse Karlsson from Aland; Roksana from Russia; and I would like to thank these authors and the contribution they have made to my knowledge of Marilyn: Tara Hanks, *The MMM Girl: Marilyn Monroe, by herself;* Michelle Morgan, *The Marilyn Monroe Address Book, Marilyn Monroe Private and Undisclosed and Marilyn Monroe Private and Confidential;* Eric Woodard-Monroe, *Hometown Girl*; and Jim Parsons who is currently writing the story of Marilyn and photographer John Florea.

I want to thank my brother, Dr. Joseph Meador, PhD, of Austin, Texas, for clarifying Kundalini Yoga for me, its practice and its symbolism. Joseph is a Teacher at The Ambrosia Society in Austin, Texas. He also teaches at Flower of Life Healing Ministry in Austin, Texas, is on the Faculty of Yoga Philosophy and the founder and a Yogi at Anandamaya Yoga Institute.

Cathy Lindstrom, Executive Director of the Castroville Artichoke Festival, Inc., provided me with the rarest of information concerning Marilyn's stint as The Artichoke Queen in 1948. For more information about attending this historic festival, call (831) 633-2465.

My sincere gratitude is extended to Jerry Haendigis, who helped me with the correct information on Marilyn's radio appearances. He is not only a learned historian of Old Time Radio, but a very nice man. You can access his web site, Vintage Radio Place, by going to www.OTRS.com.

Dennis Bitterlich of the UCLA University Archives helped me gather information on Marilyn's participation in the UCLA Prom of 1952.

I am grateful to the Milton Greene Archives, and Joshua Greene, Sonni Strenke and James Penrod in particular. The beautiful images of Marilyn that were taken by Milton Greene are being restored so that future generations will be able to see the incredible photographs and share in the magic that existed between Marilyn and Milton. I am indebted to them for the rare information they provided about Marilyn's sittings with Milton. You can access their site by going to www.archivesmhg.com

I want to thank Taylor White for designing the cover of my book using a photograph that was gifted to me by my dear friend Lois Banner.

**5% of the Net Profits from the sale of this book will go to the**
# Korean War Veterans Memorial Foundation, Inc.

The Korean War Veterans Memorial Foundation, Inc., is a non-profit, tax exempt foundation chartered in the District of Columbia as a 501. C. 3. Foundation. Donations made to the Foundation are justified as a tax deduction by the donor.

The goal of the Foundation is to raise an endowment fund to support preservation of the Memorial and/or future renovations as may be necessary.

Your generous support of the campaign to raise funds will be of great value to the goal of ensuring proper and perpetual maintenance of this Memorial. Though the generation that fought that war are Forgotten Warriors----- their Memorial should not suffer the same fate!

You may make your tax deductible donation online at Paypal to:
General Richard G. Stilwell Korean War Veterans Memorial Foundation, Inc.

You may mail your tax deductible donation to the address below:
Korean War Veterans Memorial Foundation, Inc.
10301 McKinstry Mill Road
New Windsor, MD 21776-7903

 

Marilyn had this to say about the GIs in Korea. "Two years ago I flew to the Orient to repay a debt. In the early part of my career I'd had several small roles, without much success. Then letters began pouring in from Korea. My fan mail jumped abruptly from less than 50 letters a week to more than 5,000. My studio was so impressed they began to give me wonderful parts. I felt I owed those boys something for what was happening to me; and I wanted to repay them in the only way I knew how--with a personal appearance tour. There will never be another audience like this one in Korea." Marilyn also told the press, "This trip is the climax to everything in my career. I never felt like a movie star until I came over here. I sort of feel the guys over here were responsible for a lot that happened to me. They are very close to my heart. It was so wonderful to look down and see a fellow smiling at me."

Ben Hecht posed this question to Marilyn, "What's the happiest time you've ever had?" Without hesitation she replied, "It was the time last month when I sang to the soldiers in Korea. There were thousands of them. It was a very cold afternoon, and it was snowing. All the soldiers sat in their winter uniforms. I appeared in a décolleté evening gown, bare back, bare arms. And I was so happy and so excited that I didn't know it was cold or snowing. In fact, the snow never fell on me. It melted away almost before it touched my skin. That was my happiest time—when the thousands of soldiers all yelled my name over and over."

# Preface

I have labored for nearly 15 years on the making of this book. I started out to make a chronology of the various events in Marilyn's life. Those notes, over 1,200 pages long, became the impetus for this book. My dear friend, Dr. Lois Banner, PhD, also had access to my notes for her books on Marilyn. I became, like the Apostle Paul, a "seed picker." I have a large collection of vintage magazines, I own and have read every major book written about Marilyn Monroe, I own a large collection of Auction Catalogs and I have access to a vast array of newspapers. Also, my association with the Everlasting Star community has given me much opportunity to learn about Marilyn's life. I feel a debt to all of the writers and historians who have gone before and originally collected these facts about Marilyn. To quote Sir Isaac Newton, "They may be giants and we may be pigmies, but we stand on the shoulders of giants and we see farther." I appreciate the vantage point that these writers have given me and I could not have done this work without their efforts.

I labored under the question: if you gathered all the facts you could about someone, can you really come to know them. I collected dates and facts from magazines and newspapers, from auction catalogs and biographies written about Marilyn, and from various interviews with her. Because I have dedicated years to the study of Marilyn's life it is easier to weed through various articles and interviews. I especially like the vernacular and the tone of the vintage columnist of the 40s and 50s. Their voices have been silenced as the years pass and I wanted to have them heard again. Many were given to hyperbole and inflated facts, but if you know what to look for you can find hidden gems there.

As far as coming to know Marilyn, she steps out of the shadows, and despite her "dumb blonde" image, she emerges as a woman who had a clear vision of her path in life and a dogged determination to succeed in it. Her chosen profession of acting was fraught with hardships and perils, and the odds of her making it were slim. Yet, she not only was successful, but abundantly so. She is revealed as smart and savvy in her dealings with the men in charge of Hollywood. It took the feminist movement a long time to appreciate her. She was in the thick of things as a woman in a man's world and continued to battle sexism even as a major movie star in Hollywood. Despite her sex-bomb image, she also has hidden middle class values which contribute to endearing her to the public. She was very much a part of her time, yet, ahead of it. She was a student of life and of acting in particular and sacrificed many necessities to be able to study at the feet of great acting teachers like Phoebe Brand, Morris Carnovsky, Helena Sorrell, Natasha Lytess, Michael Chekhov, and Lee Strasberg.

There is no one in Hollywood who compares to Marilyn. The new versions of the Hollywood Starlet have nothing in common with her. They lack her desire to become a legitimate actress through study and content themselves with their lack of decorum and an absence of morals and manners, running lose on the streets of Hollywood wasting their youth.

There is also no one who compares to her capture of the world's attention. She is unique and reigns in the Hollywood pantheon secure and without challenge. The depth of her beauty is still unmatched and she remains the blonde that all others are compared to.

# Chapters

**Chapter One…..14**
A Foundling in the City of Angels

**Chapter Two…..22**
Life With Mama

**Chapter Three…..31**
It's a Hard Knock Life

**Chapter Four…..53**
The Marrying Kind

**Chapter Five…..61**
A Big Slice of Blonde Cheesecake

**Chapter Six…..87**
The Hardest Working Starlet in Town

**Chapter Seven…..109**
A Pretty Panhandler

**Chapter Eight…..133**
Paying Her Dues

**Chapter Nine…..174**
The Making of a Star

**Chapter Ten…..192**
Stalled On the Launching Pad

**Chapter Eleven…..220**
Heavenly Body

**Chapter Twelve…..263**
Riding the Publicity Rocket

**Chapter Thirteen…..352**
Sex Bomb

**Chapter Fourteen…..436**
Mrs. DiMaggio and the Boys

**Chapter Fifteen…..470**
Becoming "The Girl"

**Chapter Sixteen…..510**
Birth Pains of the "New Marilyn"

# Chapter One
## A Foundling in the City of Angels

"The nightingales are sobbing in the orchards of our mothers.
And hearts we broke long ago, have long been breaking others."
W.H. Auden

**1**926 was a banner year for the Golden State of California and the Los Angeles Basin in particular. The movie industry was going gang busters and the economy was thriving. "Talkies" were just around the corner, soon to eclipse the great silent movies. 1926 gave birth to Orange Julius, Central Casting, and a fatherless girl named Norma Jeane Mortensen. She was born in the city of Angels, on the first day of June, at 9:30 on a sunny Tuesday morning. She began her life under inauspicious circumstances at the Charity Ward of the Los Angeles General Hospital. 36 years later her life would end under the exact opposite of circumstances, because by then she had become the most famous woman in the world, Marilyn Monroe.

Norma Jeane's mother, Gladys Pearl (Monroe) Baker, was a young woman of 24 who was employed as a film cutter at a Motion Picture Laboratory, Consolidated Films. Norma Jeane's father was listed on her birth certificate as Edward Mortenson, 29. His occupation was listed as a baker on the birth certificate, but in reality he held a job as a meter reader for the Southern California Gas Company. The full name of the child was listed as, baby Norma Jeane Mortenson. On June 5, 1926, Norma Jeane's birth certificate was filed with the California State Board of Health, Bureau of Vital Statistics, No. 7791.

Gladys took the name of her first husband, Jap Baker, instead of using Mortensen. The name of Gladys' husband, whom had filed divorce papers on her in May 1925 for desertion, was actually spelled Mortensen, with an "e." The seemingly innocent misspelling of the last name would cause Gladys no little trouble in 8 years. The divorce between Gladys and Mortensen would not be final until 1928. Norma Jeane's real father is considered by most reliable research as C. Stanley Gifford, Gladys' day supervisor at Consolidated Films. He refused to acknowledge paternity of the infant and Gladys broke off the affair.

Many speculate that Gladys named her baby after screen actress, Norma Talmadge and Jean Harlow. It is a logical conclusion considering that Talmadge and Harlow were two of the most elegant and glamorous film stars of that era, but what few people realize is that Harlow changed her name and began her film career after the birth of Norma Jeane. The truth of the baby's name may not have been so glamorous. It is more likely that Gladys named her baby after a little girl, Norma Jean Cohen. She had been a housekeeper for Harry and Lena Cohen, in Louisville, Kentucky in 1923. Gladys had moved to Kentucky in search of her son and daughter after her first husband had kidnapped them and fled from California. She located them in Kentucky, but declined to reestablish custody because she realized that they were enjoying a better life than the one she could have provided. Gladys continued working for the Cohen family until her increasingly strange behavior had frightened the little girl and she was dismissed. Possibly still emotionally attached to the little girl, she now found a way to fill that emptiness by naming her own daughter Norma Jeane. Although, the name Norma was a popular one for girls in 1926, whatever the reason it was chosen.

Norma Jeane lived with her mother, Gladys, at 5454 Wilshire Blvd, in Los Angeles and slept in a dresser drawer, as Gladys had no crib for her. This seemingly strange substitute sleeping arrangement for her baby was in fact a rather shrewd solution to Gladys' poor financial situation. Photographer Earl Theisen worked at Consolidated Films during that time remembers Gladys. "Gladys Baker worked in the print department of Consolidated. Later she was a cutter at RKO. I never met Mortenson. I never even heard of him. I remember when Norma Jean was born we all took up a collection at Consolidated to pay for the hospital and doctor's expenses. Gladys was flat broke." Later on, Theisen would take beautiful photos of Marilyn for *Look* magazine. Hollywood was a small town and there would be many in the industry who would remember Gladys and the young Norma Jeane. Stanley Gifford was not among the contributors, much to Gladys' disappointment.

Taking into consideration her future mental health issues, credit must be given to Gladys for realizing she was unable to take proper care of her infant by herself. When Norma Jeane was only a little over a week old, Gladys' mother, Della M. Grainger, found a family across the street from where she lived who were willing to take Gladys and Norma Jeane in. On June 11, 1926 Wayne and Ida Bolender allowed Gladys and Norma Jeane to share a room in their home at 459 E. Rhode Island St., in Hawthorne, CA. Wayne was a letter carrier and Ida a housewife. Hawthorne was known as "Between the City and the Sea," and was located in the Los Angeles Basin. It was a relaxing time away from the city and it's cares for Gladys. As she recovered from the birth and her work schedule increased, Gladys was pulled back into the city and left Norma Jeane in the care of the Bolenders.

Gladys moved in with her friend and co-worker, Grace McKee, whom she met while working at Consolidated Films. They had lived together in 1923 and would now live together again. Grace was a vibrant woman by all accounts and chose to turn her attention to shy Gladys. A casual observer might think the pairing an odd one, but Grace and Gladys complimented each other and as strange as it was, the relationship worked.

Getting back and forth to Hawthorne would be easy for Gladys. The Red Car Line was Southern California's mass transit system connecting the urban areas to the outlying suburban and rural areas. It enabled one to travel from Los Angeles to Hawthorne in about 1/2 an hour, as it was a little over 12 miles away. Gladys would have had easy access to visit her baby at the Bolenders, and in fact did spend more time than is commonly believed with Norma Jeane. In the very least she spent the weekends in Hawthorne with her. There are a series of photographs of Gladys and Norma Jeane at El Segundo beach with her brother Marion, his wife Olive and their daughter Ida Mae. Norma Jean and Ida Mae have pictures taken together at the beach that day. The two will become close friends when Norma Jeane moved in with the family in 1938.

Gladys did bond with her young daughter and tried her best to be a good mother. She would dress Norma Jeane in her finest and take her to work and show her off. In turn, Norma Jeane loved to spend time with her mother and her friends. It was very hard at that time to be a single mother, factoring in work and time with your child, but Gladys had a helper in Grace McKee. Whatever strength Gladys had can be attributed to the bolstering influence of her friend, and both shared in the fantastic notion that Norma Jeane would be a movie star. Sometimes a dream has a better chance if shared by two. The French call it Folie a Deaux or a shared madness.

The Bolender's took in foster children for the money it brought in, but also because they loved children and the desire to provide a home for less fortunate children grew naturally out of their faith. They raised all the children within the parameters of an evangelical Christian faith. To outsiders, it might seem strict and harsh. While the Bolenders disciplined Norma Jeane with spankings at times, it was not out of the norm for that day. To those who have grown up in such homes, it can be compared to raising flowers in a green house. The influence of the outside world is kept to a minimum and the flowers are indulged with loving care. In order to guarantee the proper growth, plants are sometimes pruned. Discipline was applied in order to ensure that the child mature in a godly fashion. Such was the early childhood of Norma Jeane. Ida Bolender said, "We treated her like our own child because we loved her." There is no evidence to support the accusations of later press writers and journalist, and even Marilyn herself, that she was raised in a sadistic household where religious fanaticism ruled. Instead, the very opposite is true, the middle class sensibilities that were a large part of Marilyn's personality were first cultivated with the Bolenders. Later on they were rarified by the loving influence of her dear Aunt Ana Lower, and the family of Chester and Doris Howell.

On December 6, 1926, Della Grainger and Ida Bolender take Norma Jeane to be baptized at Amiee Semple McPherson's Foursquare Gospel Church. In the tradition of the Calvinistic belief system, a child is born with the stain of original sin; hence, the baptism of infants cleanses them from this inherited sin. Even though Ida Bolender wasn't a member of the Four Square Gospel Church, this Calvinistic notion was much in line with her Moody Baptist theology.

In 1923, Sister Amiee opened the 5,300-seat Angelus Temple in Echo Park. It marked the beginning of the International Church of the Foursquare Gospel. This was to be Norma Jeane's first brush with fame. It was in May of 1926 that Sister Amiee disappeared in the surf while swimming at Ocean Park. Thousands of her devoted worshipers and the media were transfixed by the drama. Five weeks later she was found in Arizona declaring that she had been kidnapped. She later confessed to being in a lover's hideout in the Hollywood Hills. She was welcomed back by her faithful followers and resumed business as usual.

Norma Jeane also grew up attending the various churches of those closest to her. The Christian Evangelical church, The Foursquare Gospel church and The Christian Science church would all have a hand in shaping her young psyche. Salvation and sin, love and grace, and God, Jesus and the Holy Spirit were conversations she would have been familiar with. She would go around singing *Jesus Loves Me* to anyone who would listen. This early spiritual environment set her moral compass and later in life it would wound her sensitive conscious, giving her pains of guilt over some of her decisions.

In the spring of 1927 Gladys actually moves in for a brief time with her mother Della when she becomes concerned about her mother's mental health. In July, Della attempts to smother Norma Jeane while the child is napping. This is a story that Marilyn said she clearly recalls. The period prior to your first childhood memories is termed childhood amnesia, and it is generally accepted that it has its offset at about 3 1/2 years of age, on average. Traumatized children experience an offset of childhood amnesia at a later age. With Marilyn being just a year old, coupled with her traumatic childhood, it makes it unlikely that the memory is her own. It makes more sense that someone intervened in the situation and she had been told what had happened. But in later interviews Marilyn will be adamant that she does remember that far back. When shown a photo of herself as a baby she will say, "I'm about six months old...I guess you're not supposed to remember that far back, but I do...I remember green grass, a long dress over my feet, being pushed backward in a wicker go-cart."

False memories can carry the same impact as real memories, and the episode becomes a strong childhood event for Norma Jeane. It is chilling to think that Marilyn's future sleep problems can be traced back to this summer afternoon.

On August 4th, the hottest month in the Los Angeles Valley, Della attempted to violently break into the Bolender's home to see Norma Jeane. Ida and the children are horrified and Della was apprehended by the Police and confined to the Norwalk State Hospital. Della dies on August 23rd from complications of myocarditis, an inflammation of the heart. The cause of her summer breakdown is still not completely understood. One can only imagine the bewilderment of the little girl inside the eye of this emotional hurricane.

Norma Jeane grew up with 5 "siblings," Mumsey, Alvina, Noel, Nancy, and Lester. She and Lester were quite close because of the few months' difference in ages. Lester came to live at the Bolenders two months after Norma Jeane was born. The Bolenders officially adopted Lester. They were often referred to as "the twins." A few photographs survive of the two children and one cannot fail to appreciate the bonds that exist between them. A letter survives from Ida Bolender to Lester's mother Pearl, written in 1927. It reads in part, "Little Norma Jean is with me. She is the baby girl I had when Lester came. They have great times together. Lots of people think them twins. I dress them alike at times and they do look cunning. . . They are full of mischief and keep me busy."

Norma Jeane was not a shy child while living at the Bolender home. Marilyn will later describe herself as a mischievous child who could be aggressive at time with the other children. She remembers pushing Nancy against a stove and another time pushing Lester off a toy car. But childhood is filled with moments where you are king of the hill or someone else is. She also remembers telling her school teacher that her mother and father were in fact dead. The teacher, in reaction to the sad story, treats Norma Jeane was a bit more tenderness than her other pupils. This will be her first taste of handling her own publicity to elicit a desired effect. It will work again for her when she has to fend for herself in the Hollywood jungle.

Norma Jeane spends the next three years uneventfully with the Bolenders in the bucolic setting of Hawthorne. By all accounts she had a pleasant childhood with the Bolenders. She entertained herself with hopscotch, learned to play the piano, and listened to her favorite radio shows, "The Green Hornet" and "The Lone Ranger." Her imagination flourished and she had a rich fantasy life. When she felt comfortable with people, she was outgoing and adventuresome.

By Marilyn's own accounts in later stream of consciousness writings taken from her own journals, she and Ida had somewhat of a tenuous relationship. At one point Ida had discovered Norma Jeane touching herself and harshly reprimanded her, even going so far as to tell her that people who did such things would go to hell. Masturbation at that time was deemed abnormal behavior and forbidden. Attached to it were all kinds of dire consequences such as blindness and madness. As an adult, Marilyn would rebel against this memory of childhood exploration and the extreme guilt attached to it as the result of Ida's reaction.

While not a financially wealthy family, the Bolenders prospered in the things that matter to a child. Norma Jeane had all of her material needs met and most importantly, her emotional needs were satisfied while in the Bolender home. She wasn't allowed to call Ida, "Mother" because she had a Mother, instead she called her "Aunt," and she called Wayne, "Daddy." Ida sewed clothes for her and the other children. Norma Jeane was fortunate to have this period of stability.

On October 24, 1929, while Gladys was at work, a fire broke out in her department at Consolidated Films. The buildings were rocked with explosions and toxic fumes from the burning celluloid film filled the air. She was able to remain calm and led the other workers in her department to safety, out of the burning building. Gladys was hailed as a heroine. The fire consumed the entire building. There was one death and $6 million dollars in damage. Consolidated had to move its company to Santa Monica. Gladys tried commuting, but it was too burdensome and so she quit and started to work at Columbia Studio. Grace and Gladys would move in together at 6228 De Longpre Ave.

In the summer of 1930 neighbor Julian Arnold Smith takes a candid snapshot of Norma Jeane running through the sprinklers at his home. She was only wearing a pair of frilly pantaloons as she and her playmates ran through the cool shower. Norma Jeane and the other Bolender children had come over to visit Julian. When Norma Jeane moved in June of 1933, her friend only saw her one other time when she visited the Bolender's. He did, however work with Norma Jeane's future husband, Jimmy Dougherty, as a policeman in Los Angeles. Julian's father, however, had occasion to see Marilyn on the studio lot, as he was an actor and even played an extra in *River of No Return* in 1953.

In 1930, the census indicates that both Gladys and Norma Jeane were living with the Bolenders again. Starting on September 28, 1930, Norma Jeane attends pre-school classes at the Hawthorne Community Sunday School, starting in the Cradle Roll class and ending in the Beginners Department. Having been prepared for grade school, Norma Jeane attended the Ballona Elementary and Kindergarten School, in Hawthorne, in September 14, 1931 thru June 17, 1932. It was later renamed the Washington Elementary School. Norma Jeane attended Kindergarten here. There is a photograph of her with her Kindergarten class. She is sporting a short bobbed haircut and a determined expression.

Lester and Norma Jeane used to walk to school together followed by Norma Jeane's dog Tippy. Tippy was a Boston terrier mix Wayne had found on one of his postal routes and Norma Jeane's constant companion. Norma Jeane's 2nd grade music teacher, Evelyn Gawthrop said she was a timid girl who loved to sing, and had a beautiful voice. She made good grades and was always dressed neatly. She played well with the other children. Mrs. Gawthrop said that Lester and Norma Jeane's parents bought each of them an instrument, the "parents" being Wayne and Ida Bolender.

On March 27, 1932, Norma Jeane participated in the Sunrise Chorus at the Hollywood Bowl Easter Sunrise Service. On Easter Sunday the Los Angeles Basin was filled with events honoring the day. Pageants, programs and re-enactments were attended by thousands in the Evangelical capital of California. The Saturday before the ceremony the children rehearsed their maneuvers in forming a cross onstage. People who had participated in the Saturday morning Lilly processional on the grounds of the Hollywood Bowl gathered to watch the rehearsal. Mabel Miller Barnhart, the chairman of the Living Cross feature, had arranged an Easter egg hunt for the children. After the rehearsal 500 Easter eggs were passed out to the children from a giant nest constructed in a nearby glen. They were given out by members of the junior auxiliary of the Hollywood Women's Club.

On Easter Sunday, at 5:30am, a new "Sunrise Fanfare" was heralded in by a trumpeter corps on the hill tops surrounding the Hollywood Bowl; this signaled the Sunrise Chorus who sang anthems at the break of dawn. Hugo Kirchhofe, pioneer Los Angeles choral leader, led the Sunrise Chorus of 300 children whose ages ranged from 8 to 18. The Sunrise Chorus also enacted The Living Cross. The children stood on stage in formation of a cross and on cue took off their black capes and unveiled their white robes. Norma Jeane was slow to remove her cape and for a brief moment became a little black spot on the cross. A photograph of the event shows that she quickly disrobed and blended in with the other children and the cross was pure white. Yet this event will make a memory that Marilyn will carry with her throughout her life. The failure to disrobe from her black cape becomes fixated and exaggerated in her memory to the point that she narcissistically thinks she ruined the Living Cross by being a black spot on it. It is a grandiose conclusion and comes from a neurosis entrenched by the harrowing events in her early life. She will tell this story often in interviews and confides the shame it brought her to Arthur Miller. "We all had on white tunics under the black robes and at a given signal we were supposed to throw off the robes, changing the cross from black to white. But I got so interested in the people, the orchestra and the hills that I forgot to watch the conductor for the signal. And there I was-- the only black mark on a white cross. The family I was living with never forgave me."

Approximately 40,000 people attended this event which was broadcast over the Columbia Network. What Norma Jeane doesn't realize is that she will live in a beautiful home close by the Hollywood Bowl the next year.

In the spring of 1933 Norma Jeane develops a case of whooping cough. The number of whooping cough cases reached its peak in 1934 with more than 260,000 reported cases nationwide. Norma Jeane would have had a cough and a runny nose, followed by weeks of rapid coughing that ended with a whooping sound. Gladys was so concerned for Norma Jeane's health that she moves back into the Bolender home to take care of her.

In late spring of 1933 Norma Jeane's dog, Tippy, was run over by a car. Norma Jeane found the body of her beloved companion before it could be disposed of. She was said to have been so traumatized that she developed a stutter after this painful experience, but other factors in 1934 may have actually contributed to this speech impediment. Norma Jeane's school closed temporarily due to damage by an earthquake. Gladys mulled these events over in her mind and decided that maybe it was time to care for Norma Jeane herself.

# Chapter Two
## Life With Mama

"Los Angeles was a town populated with the walking dead--without hope--and right around the corner the movie moguls made dreams by the reel loads to delude a nation--to delude the sick, sick world."
George Miller

In the middle of the Great Depression, on May 23, 1933 Gladys regained custody of Norma Jeane and they shared her small apartment in Hollywood on Afton Place with an English family, George, Maud and Nell Atkinson. Norma Jeane was finally living with her mother and the two became bonded during this short sweet time together. Marilyn will tell Ben Hecht ruefully, "My mother found another couple to keep me. They were English people, and needed the five dollars a week that went with me. Also, I was large for my age and could do a lot of work."

Gladys and Norma Jeane started their new life off in an adventurous spate of sightseeing in Hollywood and surrounding areas in Southern California. Most things were only a short ride away on the Red Line, but Gladys had purchased a new Plymouth Sedan, so instead they drove around enjoying the sites of Southern California. The new car cost around $500 and the payment was $27.00 a month. Gladys must have been feeling very optimistic to take on this debt. A car means many things to different people, but most of the time it can be traced back to a yearning for freedom and independence. The summer of 1933 was stacking up to be a time for Gladys to act on her impulses and regain some of the freedom that fate had robbed her of.

On the 4th of July Gladys took Norma Jeane and Lester Bolender to Catalina Island on board the SS Catalina, affectionately known as "The Great White Steamer." The Steamship carried upwards of 2,000 people at a time and the trip took a couple of hours, costing $2.25 for a round trip ticket from Los Angeles. One can imagine the excitement as the trio crossed the 26 miles to the beautiful Channel Island.

"To board the Catalina during its heyday was to enter a world of luxurious leather settees and gleaming teak. On the upper deck people danced to swinging big bands. Magicians and clowns entertained passengers. On the lower deck youngsters played hide and seek among the lifeboats, and couples found hidden spots where they could be alone. ... Residents fondly remember the rituals with which the ship was greeted as it approached the island: Speedboats would circle the ship, water skiers slicing through its giant wake. Closer to shore, children swam out to dive for coins passengers tossed into the bay. People in Avalon gathered to sing as passengers stepped off the ship that docked near the center of town."

Lester remembers Norma Jeane frolicking on the dance floor, spinning round and round as people gather to watch the exuberant little girl.

Once there, they would stroll along the Paseo de El Enchanto and see a Spanish village full of shops. There was a glass shop, candle makers, a Mexican cafe and even a Puppet Show. There was a plant that made colorful Catalina pottery that the public was invited to tour. The Avery on the Island boasted the "largest bird cage in the world." The fountain in the marketplace had the day's catch on display nearby. Creatures from the deep could be found hanging by their tails providing added excitement for the children. The Harbor was an excellent place to see celebrities who were anchored there. At dinnertime chimes rang out from the hillsides. The place to be at sundown was the Casino. It had a circular ballroom that is built over the water. Marilyn will have her own memories of watching her mother dance to the strains of the orchestra. She was up past her bedtime and shared in her mother's abandonment of the cares and conventions of society, at least for this one night.

Gay's Lion Farm, about 13 miles from Los Angeles in El Monte, California, was another fun destination for Gladys and Norma Jeane. African Lions were trained for the movies, and MGM had even used a couple of them for their iconic introduction to their movies. While watching the lions perform, Norma Jeane wonders if the lions have trouble making peace with their natural instincts and their trained behaviors. She wonders if people feel the same way. It is all a little confusing for the thoughtful girl.

Hollywood was full of tea rooms, comparable to our coffee bars of today. You could go and see the stars while sipping tea and eating sandwiches. Hollywood Boulevard was full of shops and restaurants. One can imagine the pair window shopping and strolling down the Boulevard.

By far, the outings that had the deepest impact on Norma Jeane were going to see movies. Gladys and Grace would take her to see the stars arriving for the various premiers. Norma Jeane loved the movies and Gladys would use them as a safe place to stash Norma Jeane while she was at work. She would sit for hours, enraptured by the flickering pictures, the gay, glamorous stars, and on occasion the prologues at Grauman's Chinese Theater. She loved the monkeys that were once kept outside in the courtyard. Here the dream was born in her young mind to be a movie star, not an actress, that dream would come later. Yet, Norma Jeane felt a twinge of guilt seeing a movie because of the strict upbringing at the Bolender's. They frowned on going to the movies.

Marilyn will later remember, "The first family I lived with told me I couldn't go to the movies because it was sinful. I listened to them say the world was coming to an end, and if I was doing something sinful when it happened, I'd go down below, below, below. So, the few times I was able to sneak into a movie, I spent most of the time that I was there praying that the world wouldn't end."

Marilyn was once quoted as saying, "I used to think as I looked out on the Hollywood night — there must be thousands of girls sitting alone like me, dreaming of becoming a movie star. But I'm not going to worry about them. I'm dreaming the hardest." She came by dreaming naturally, for Gladys' dream for her and her daughter was a big one, a home of their own. Marilyn recounts to Ben Hecht the moment when Gladys told her about the new home. "One day my mother came to call. I was in the kitchen washing dishes. She stood looking at me without talking. When I turned around I saw there were tears in her eyes, and I was surprised. 'I'm going to build a house for you and me to live in,' she said. 'It's going to be painted white and have a backyard."

The urban sprawl of the growing Los Angeles Basin spread unchecked throughout the 1920s. The Great Depression slowed the growth, but did nothing to stop it. Movie Stars of the time grew weary of the increasingly cheap storefronts and the urban decay that started to accumulate in Hollywood. They fled to the outskirts in Beverly Hills and new developments like Whitley Heights in North Hollywood.

Many previous biographers glossed over the home Gladys purchased for herself and Norma Jeane, describing it as a small white bungalow. Dr. Lois Banner was the first to fully realize what a grand home it actually was and to appreciate the location. Three years earlier the home had been broken into and the burglar made off with $1500 worth of furs, jewels and clothing from then occupant, Mary A. George, proving the neighborhood was an affluent one.

On August 23 Gladys made a down payment of $750 on a $5000 property, formerly owned by Daniel and Nadine Whitman. She had secured a loan from the New Deal Home Owners Corporation in the summer of 1933. It was established under President Franklin D. Roosevelt and its purpose was to refinance home mortgages currently in default to prevent foreclosure. She bought her home through the California Title Mortgage Co. This was an ambitious act for a single mother in the middle of the Great Depression. Not only was the debt she incurred great, but the home was not a modest dwelling. Aerial photographs dating from that time show established trees shading the property at 6812 Arbol Drive. It was a large 4 bedroom home. It sat on a big shady lot and had a welcoming grand entrance in the front, with a portico supported by columns and a big porch in the backyard. Gladys scoured auctions for furniture and her prized possession was a piano that once belonged to Frederic March. She fantasized Norma Jeane playing it in the living room by the glowing fireplace. The home was situated on a cul-de-sac that skirted Hollywood's elite neighborhoods and the Hollywood Bowl itself. In fact, it was so close to the Hollywood Bowl that you could hear the performances at the Bowl outside on your lawn or through an open window. It nestled up against Whitley Heights and it's bounty of movie stars and the important people in Hollywood. The best glimpse of the home can be seen in the 1966 documentary, *The Legend of Marilyn Monroe*.

A.H. Weil, an auctioneer selling another property on the street, 6826 Arbol Drive, for Benjamin Brodsky, a "motion picture magnet," described the neighborhood. "Arbol Drive is right at the entrance of the Hollywood Bowl; this is just a few hundred feet from the intersection of Highland Avenue and Cahuenga Avenue." He described the house he was selling as, "set amid surroundings which suggest the English countryside, yet within two minutes' drive of Hollywood Boulevard." The lot was described as, "50 feet frontage by 60 feet in the rear. It is 126 feet in depth on one side and 123 feet in depth on the other. It has fruit trees, including avocado, orange and cherry."

Grace begged Gladys not to buy the house as she feared the ongoing strike of sound men and the sympathy walkout of other unions at Columbia would put their jobs at risk and they might be laid off. But Gladys paid no attention to her warnings. Gladys was intent on having a place for all of her children, Jackie, Berniece and Norma Jeane. Supposedly, the strike did affect their jobs and Gladys was even photographed crossing the picket line with another woman and climbing the fence at Columbia to get to her job.

Marilyn remembers this time in her life, "My mother bought furniture, a table with a white top and brown legs, chairs, beds and curtains. I heard her say, 'It's all on time, but don't worry. I'm working double shift at the studio, and I'll soon be able to pay it off." "It was a pretty little house with quite a few rooms. But there was no furniture in it, except for two cots that we slept on, a small kitchen table, and two kitchen chairs. The living room was entirely empty, but I didn't mind. It was a very pretty room. After several weeks my mother came home from work in a truck. I watched two men carry in the first furniture she had bought for our house. It was a wonderful-looking white piano. It was put in the living room. There wasn't any piano bench. It just stood there by itself. Neither my mother nor I could play. But it looked very beautiful to me...I always remembered the white piano. I saw it in my mind every night as I grew up." "You'll play the piano over here, by the windows,' my mother said, 'and here on each side of the fireplace there'll be a love seat. And we can sit listening to you. As soon as I pay off a few other things I'll get the love seats, and we'll all sit in them at night and listen to you play the piano."

According to Marilyn's sister Berniece, it was a black Franklin Grand piano. She remember seeing Marilyn and her daughter, Mona Rae, playing "Chopsticks" on it when they came for a visit in 1946 and the piano was still in Ana Lower's home. It was painted white sometime before 1953. Marilyn told Ben Hecht that after she found it as an adult she had it painted white and new strings. In photographs taken in 1953 for a biography by Sidney Skolsky, Bob Beerman snapped her playing her beloved piano, and it was white. Skolsky commented that the piano had been given a facelift. She had the piano moved to her apartment in New York that John Moore decorated in monochromatic shades of white in 1957.

When Marilyn had her beloved piano moved to New York Amy Greene did not share her sentiments. In an interview with Norman Mailer, he says, "she goes on and on about how ugly the piano is, tacky. 'She was in love with this thing. It wasn't even white, it was honey-colored. To her, it represented such elegance, such chic, such class. It was ugly, it sounded terrible. She had never played it. She just put flowers on it, and pictures. It had no line, it was stubby; it did not have the right curvature or the right leg height.'" The piano was Marilyn's *Velveteen Rabbit* and like in the classic story, people who didn't understand what it was to "be real" would never understand a child's love. And that was what Marilyn had for her mother's relic, a child's love.

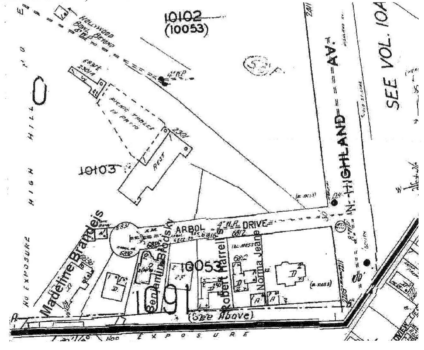

As you turned onto Arbol Drive the homes in the cud-de-sac were all located on the left side, as across the street were picnic areas and parking for the Hollywood Bowl. The first lot remained vacant and was never built on. Gladys' home was the next lot and the first house on the street. Norma Jeane's next door neighbors were Robert and Wilhelmina Harrell. Mr. Harrell was a lawyer and Mrs. Harrell was described in the *Los Angeles Times* as a Society Matron. They had a son, Bobbie, who was close in age to Norma Jeane. There appears a photo in the *Los Angeles Times* of a Halloween party given for the Bobby and his friends in 1935. Norma Jeane had moved by then, but it helps to imagine the kind of neighborhood she lived in. Norma Jeane would attend the Selma Street School while living on Arbol. Perhaps she and Bobbie were school mates.

Children's author, Madeline Brandeis, lived at the end of the cul-de-sac. She wrote the popular children's series, "Children of America," and "Children of Other Lands." She was actively writing during the time Norma Jeane lived on Arbol. Her home was described as, "a charming old Spanish home on the hill at the entrance to the Hollywood Bowl."

Norma Jeane's home was adjacent to the Whitley Heights development which was built in the style of a Spanish-Moorish village. On a Sunday stroll Norma Jeane and her mother crossed Highland Avenue and wandered around the sidewalks of Whitley Heights. Many times they were accompanied by Grace McKee, who was becoming a prominent figure in Norma Jeane's life. For the cost of a 2 mile stroll one saw the homes of the most glamorous people in Hollywood and the added possibility of glimpsing Carole Lombard, Jean Harlow, Theda Bara, Rudolph Valentino or Maurice Chevalier going about their daily lives.

Marilyn remembers being infatuated with movie stars and Jean Harlow in particular at about this age. "I was fascinated by Jean Harlow. I had white hair--I was a real towhead--and she was the first grown-up lady I had ever seen who had white hair like mine. I cut her picture out of a magazine, and on the back of it was the picture of a man. I pasted his picture in a scrapbook--just his picture. There was nothing else in the book. It was Clark Grable."

For the price of a quarter and a short walk Norma Jeane had only to go to Grauman's Chinese Theater to see her idol, Jean Harlow, in *Dinner At Eight*, which opened in October. That Autumn she would have had the opportunity to see *I'm No Angel* with Mae West and featuring a young Cary Grant; The World Premiere of *The Bowery* with George Raft; and *The Private Lives of Henry VIII* with Charles Laughton. The future Marilyn would tell that the movie she most enjoyed was *Cleopatra* with Claudette Colbert. Sitting in the flickering darkness of the theater Norma Jeane builds a dream of claiming her own place up on the luminous screen. She will one day work with many of the actors she watches.

   Marilyn will remember her first day at the Selma Street School as a sad adventure. "I'll never forget my first day of school. I'd been living with an English family at the time. When they were lucky, they worked at the studios as extras and bit players. The first day of school they said they were sorry, but I'd have to go by myself because they were working. I'd been scared all of my six years, but that day I hit a new low. The other kids had a mother or a father with a nice comforting hand to hold on to while they registered. I was alone...When the teacher asked me why my mother didn't come with me, I just hid my face and bawled." In another interview Marilyn recalls being told, "Go down two blocks, turn left and keep going till you see the school."

   In order to help pay the rent Gladys leased out part of the house to an English family, the Atkinson's, George, Maude and daughter Nell. All three were employed as actors. George was George Arliss' stand-in, Maude played bit parts, and Nell was a stand-in for Madeline Carroll. It needs to be noted that Gladys had shared the Afton Place apartment with them before moving into her home, and that they were always counted in the equation of her home purchase, and this might have been the other voice in Gladys' head when Grace discouraged the whole affair.

   In October, shortly after acquiring her home, Gladys learned that her grandfather, Tillford Hogan, had committed suicide, and her son Jackie had also died in an automobile accident. Marilyn will relate the death of her half-brother to her agent Harry Lipton. She will tell him that Gladys screamed at her, 'Why couldn't it have been you? Why couldn't it have been you?'

It is also during this time that Norma Jeane will recall being molested by a man who rented a room at her home. From all the evidence and Marilyn herself, it doesn't appear that she was actually raped, but the fondling and inappropriate behavior carries with it the same weight of guilt and shame. It is not clear if it was George Atkinson or another man, possibly another boarder. Marilyn's later description fits George Atkinson, but Marilyn names a Mr. Kimmell who is a boarder. Norma Jeane tried to tell on him, and as a result she was slapped and told not to tell lies about the star boarder. If it was during this time, Gladys needed the financial security provided by the man, more than the trouble Norma Jeane's allegation would bring. It could be this traumatic event, and not the killing of her dog, that led to Norma Jeane's stutter.

   The Atkinson's would remain in her life, on and off until early in her marriage in 1942. She would stay with them while at the Arbol House, and again after they had moved into a nearby apartment. They would be on the list of visitors to the Orphanage when Norma Jeane was there, and she would attend Nell's baby shower shortly after her marriage in 1942.

There is another event that connects Arbol Drive to her molestation. Marilyn recalls her first love, "I never daydreamed about love, even after I fell in love the first time. This was when I was around eight. I fell in love with a boy named George who was a year older. We used to hide in the grass together until he got frightened and jumped up and ran away. What we did in the grass never frightened me. I knew it was wrong, or I wouldn't have hidden, but I didn't know what was wrong."

It is possible she is remembering an experience with a neighbor on Arbol and misnamed him. There was an open field with a picnic area across the street from her home. Children often explore sex, but it is usually at an older age. Norma Jeane could have been acting out this unusual sexual activity because she had been molested. One of the tendencies of children who have been sexually abused is that they engage in sexual play earlier than would be normal and engage in more elaborate sexual displays. Marilyn would admit to having had sexual feelings since she was a small child. This all goes together to make the likely location of her molestation at the Arbol home.

*Little Women* open at The Chinese at Christmas time. The book was a favorite of little girls and one wishes that Norma Jeane got to see the movie with Katherine Hepburn.

On Christmas a suitor of Gladys', Harry C. Wilson, remembers taking the pair to see the Santa Claus Lane Parade on Hollywood Boulevard. He lifted Norma Jeane up on his shoulders so that she could get a better look. In 13 years Norma Jeane herself would be riding on a float in this very parade. Mr. Wilson remembers when he took them home there was a decorated Christmas tree in the house, and Norma Jeane sang to them before going to bed. He claimed to be in love with Gladys and wished to marry her. But that was not to be.

# Chapter Three
## It's a Hard Knock Life

"Happiness was what she devoured on the screen: sleeping in a
bed by herself on sheets that were changed every day; fresh
orange juice for breakfast; Clark Gable kissing the back of your neck.
She lived in a simple world of deprivation and despair.
She imagined happiness to be just as simple."
Aljean Meltsir

On New Year's Day 1934 a flood of mythic proportion struck the Crescenta Valley in the Los Angeles Basin. Weeks before the flood, wildfires raged in the San Gabriel Mountains, setting the stage for the great flood. The flood disaster in Crescenta Valley was so horrendous that Woody Guthrie wrote a song about it and called it, *Los Angeles New Year's Flood.* Approximately 1400 people died. You don't have to personally experience a disaster to be effected by it. A localized tragedy has a very large impact which radiates out through the towns and the state itself, especially one like this was, with a high death toll.

For someone with Gladys' fragile emotional health, the wildfires and the New Year's Day Flood must have carried with it an ominous foreboding of things to come. Gladys had a grab-bag of stressors to choose from. The stress of being a single mother and being a homeowner coupled with a loss of income from the strike at the studios; the death of her grandfather by his own hand; the residual guilt from losing custody of her first two children, and now the death of her son in an automobile accident, leaving her dream of reuniting her children forever crushed; the possibility of Norma Jeane's molestation; and the natural disaster looming around her all worked together to create a perfect storm of incidents that gave rise to an break with reality in Gladys' mind.

In January she had a complete psychotic breakdown. She was found underneath the staircase in a psychotic state, laughing and crying. The Atkinson's called Grace McKee who advised them to call the authorities. Norma Jeane was told to stay upstairs, but she couldn't help but hear the commotion caused by her mother. They removed Gladys from her home in view of all the neighbors. She was taken to a rest home in Santa Monica for several months and would then be transferred to LA County General Hospital's psych ward. On January 15th, Gladys was adjudged insane by the Superior Court of the Los Angeles County. The dream that Gladys had for her and Norma Jeane ended that cold winter day in 1934. Norma Jeane would forever suffer from the loss of her Mother. Her ability to feel safe in the world and trust others would be seriously effected and she would experience difficulty handling stress and disappointments in the years to come. She would suffer from the rending of her attachment bond with her mother and consequently she would have trouble in her adult relationships. Understanding these early traumas help to explain why many times she acted out as an adult.

Alice Miller, in her book *The Drama of the Gifted Child*, writes that a child without a mother "…would remain without a mirror, and for the rest of [her] life would be seeking this mirror in vain." It could also go that if the mother was mentally ill, the mirror would be forever cracked, and looking into that broken mirror would prove a terrifying vision.

Edward Mortensen, who was listed on Norma Jeane's birth certificate as her father, was subpoenaed by the State Welfare Board. He didn't even realize that Gladys had a child, or that he was listed as her father. He was working now as a repairman for the Southern California Gas Company. He was unable or unwilling to care for Norma Jeane, and never pursued a relationship with her, although, he did contact Gladys at Norwalk State Hospital where she was institutionalized in January of 1935. In that winter she actually made plans to escape with him. Gladys was apprehended, but the staff didn't understand that Mortensen was alive, because they had him mixed-up with the Edward Mortenson who was killed in a motorcycle accident. They thought she was hallucinating about her dead ex-husband and must certainly be delusional. It was a pitiful comedy of errors that ended up costing Gladys her freedom and Norma Jeane her mother. Shortly after that she was transferred to Agnews State Hospital in San Jose.

Mortensen later told a counselor at the gas company that Gladys had abandoned him before he knew she was pregnant and she had never contacted him about the birth of the baby. He remembered that she was wild and beautiful. Upon his death in 1981 many documents relating to Gladys and Marilyn were found in his apartment, including Norma Jeane's birth certificate and newspaper clippings of her as Marilyn Monroe. Yet, in his lifetime he never surfaced claiming to be her father, even though he had obviously taken an interest in her from afar. When the State Welfare Board contacted him about Norma Jeane in 1934 he denied paternity and refused to become involved with her affairs. Marilyn herself confessed to Hedda Hopper in 1953 about what she thought of Mortensen as her father. "I never called myself Mortensen at any time because Mr. Mortensen was not my father. He proved that to the satisfaction of the authorities, and for that reason, he had no financial responsibility for me."

Norma Jeane was taken care of by the Atkinson's who boarded at the Arbol home. If George Atkinson was the person who had previously molested Norma Jeane, it doesn't seem that the incident repeated itself, at least from Marilyn's memories. George Atkinson worked as the stand-in for George Arliss who was making *The House of the Rothschilds* during this time. It would open in March of this year at The Chinese. While the film was in production George Atkinson would have been busy on the set and away from the home.

Grace had found out somehow that the Atkinson's weren't treating Norma Jeane well, which is to say she was unsupervised much of the time. Marilyn herself recalls how she used to sit out by the side of the road and pretend to sell cigarettes and whiskey bottles to passersby. "My next foster parents gave me empty whiskey bottles for playthings. With them, and with empty cigarette packages, I played store. I guess I must have had the finest collection of empty whiskey bottles and empty cigarette packages any girl ever had. I'd line them up on a plank beside the road, and when people drove along I'd say, 'Wouldn't you like some whiskey?' I remember some of the people in the cars driving past my 'whiskey' store saying, 'Imagine! Why, it's terrible.'"

Norma Jeane would later tell Elyda Nelson, her sister-in-law, "Day after day I'd dress the 'dead soldiers' in little wisps of cloth and call them 'my babies.' And when I grew up, I understand one thing a lot of parents couldn't. They'd give beautiful dolls to their children who in turn would ignore them and play with little beaten up characters made of rubber with the painted eyes gone. To me, those whishey bottles were real dolls, and I think that most parents should pay more attention tto what's in a childs mind than they do to the pretty things they can buy to influence that mind."

Given the upscale residents on Arbol Drive, she probably was a spectacle. The Atkinson's didn't mistreat Norma Jeane, they were just a free spirited family with lax rules and it was not the proper environment to raise a little girl in. Despite this, the Atkinson's were allowed to visit her and take her out when she was in the Orphanage. After Grace sold the Arbol home they moved to another home close by on Glencoe Way and remained residents of North Hollywood. They never did permanently return to England as so many biographers have them doing. The evidence to the contrary is overwhelming. George, Maude and Nell were on the visitor list at the Orphanage for Norma Jeane in the fall of 1935. George acted in several movies after they left the Arbol house. Nell got married in 1939, and in 1942 Norma Jeane wrote to Grace McKee that she attended a baby shower for Nell. In March of 1944, Maude died and was interned at Forest Lawn. The newspaper article stated that she was a retired actress and a 25 year resident of Southern California.

Marilyn will later recall of this bittersweet time in her life, "Mother had a nervous breakdown, fell seriously ill, and had to be taken to the hospital. All the furniture disappeared. The white table, the chairs, the beds, and white curtains melted away, and the grand piano, too. The English couple disappeared also...I never forgot the white painted house and its furniture."

While driving through Hollywood after her marriage in 1942 with her sister-in-law Elyda Nelson, Norma Jeane pointed out "a beautiful white house high in the hills" and said, "I lived there once, before mother was ill. It was beautiful. The most wonderful furniture you can imagine. A baby grand piano, and a room of my own. It all seems like a dream."

The Bolenders did not have room to care for Norma Jeane, so Grace found the family of one of Norma Jeane's schoolmates to care for her, the Giffen's. Harvey worked for RCA as a sound engineer. He and his wife Elsie were the parents of a schoolmate of Norma Jeane. They took Norma Jeane into their home and cared for her despite having three children of their own. The Giffen's got along so well with Norma Jeane that they offered to adopt her, but Gladys refused to let them. She was determined to never play the role of *Stella Dallas* again, being on the outside looking in at her children. She was determined to stay in Norma Jeane's life. The Giffen's were heartbroken because they had become quite attached to Norma Jeane. While in their care they took her to have her portrait taken at The Broadway Studio in Hollywood. The negatives would be kept on file there under H-31806. In the surviving image of Norma Jeane, the hand tinted portrait shows the loving care that Harvey and Elsie lavished on her. They were placed on her visitor list at the Orphanage in the fall of 1935.

Grace's co-worker, Reginald Carroll and his wife also offered to adopt Norma Jeane. Again, Gladys wouldn't hear of it. He will later say of Gladys and Norma Jeane, "When I knew her she was a negative cutter at Consolidated. She was a cute blonde, kind of short, and a lot of fun when she wanted to be. She usually kept to herself. I remember Marilyn as a dark-haired child, skinny and frightened. Timid, that's the word. I never met Mortenson."

On March 25, 1935, Grace applied to become the Guardian of Gladys' estate. It would be case No. 149502, in the Matter of the Estate of Gladys P. Baker, Incompetent. In the

Petition for Appointment of Guardianship, Grace had to inventory and provide a statement of Gladys's Assets. They included $60.00 cash in the bank, a $90.00 unendorsed insurance check, a 1933 Plymouth Sedan which had an outstanding balance of $250.00, (Grace would have the car repaired and drive it until she sold it on August 6, 1936) a small radio which was valued at $25.00 and had an outstanding balance of $15.00, and a Franklin Baby Grand Piano which had an outstanding balance of $230.00. Grace was reimbursed $35.50 for money she had already spent on the estate. She was represented by her attorney, J.P. Patterson. Grace was made the legal Guardian on April 4th.

By all accounts, Grace did truly love Norma Jeane and tried to care for the child to whom she owed no blood allegiance. She not only obtained guardianship of Gladys and her sad little estate, but for Norma Jeane as well. It is established in court records that Grace tended to Norma Jeane and saw to it that she had the material things she would need. It will always be a mystery, though, why Grace didn't have Norma Jeane live with her instead of placing her in all the foster homes. Still, Grace will become one of the earliest influences on young Norma Jeane's life, and it would be Grace's voice that remained to whisper in her ear that she would someday be a great movie star. Grace also served as her first publicity agent, telling anyone who would listen about the destiny of this young girl. Yet, Grace did nothing and used none of her connections at the studio to make this happen. Was Grace a master manipulator who gained something from arranging and rearranging Norma Jeane's life?

On May 22, 1935 a check for $25.00 was issued to Mrs. Atkinson for the care of Norma Jeane. This was the last time Norma Jeane was in the care of the Atkinson family. Before the Arbol home had been sold the Atkinson's moved to an apartment not too far from the location of the home on Glencoe Way. In an interview with Jane Corwin for *Photoplay* magazine, March 1954, Marilyn described living with the Atkinson's in their home on Glencoe Way. "They lived in a crowded little flat in an auto court near the Hollywood Bowl."

On June 1, 1935 In an Inventory and Statement of Assets filed with the court, No. 149502. Gladys's estate had assets totaling $5849.75. Money in the bank, $6.75, Insurance checks received, $210.00, Gifts from friends, $43.00, Plymouth Sedan, $350.00, Franklin Baby Grand Piano, $225.00, Radio, $15.00, home on 6812 Arbol St., $5,000.00. Grace sold the Arbol Drive home for $4838.07 on June 26, 1935.

Grace finally moves Norma Jeane in with her at her Lodi Place apartment and she lives there until Grace gets married. The apartment was across the street from the Hollywood Studio Club. One can imagine Norma Jeane spending her free time watching the young actresses come and go at the Hollywood Studio Club and Aunt Grace pointing out that someday she would be an actress and live there. In a little over 10 years, she would live there as up and coming starlet Marilyn Monroe. It is while living at the Lodi St. apartment that Norma Jeane overhears Grace's friends warn her about caring for this child with her family history of mental illness.

Grace marries Erwin "Doc" Goddard on August 10th and Norma Jeane lives with them for approximately a month before going into the orphanage. Marilyn will later say of this incident, "'What happened next in my life I don't think I can ever forget. My mother's best girlfriend was my legal guardian and I was living in her home at this time, but when she remarried all of a sudden the house became too small and someone had to go. You can guess who that someone was. One day she packed my clothes and took me with her to her car. We drove and drove without her ever saying a word that afternoon. When we came to a red brick building she stopped the car and we walked up the stairs to the entrance of the building. At the entrance there was this sign and the emptiness that came over me—I'll never forget. The sign read: Los Angeles Orphans Home, and I began to cry, 'Please, please, don't make me go inside. I'm not an orphan, my mother's not dead. I'm not an orphan, my mother's just sick and can't take care of me.' And as I was crying and protesting I can still remember they had to use force to drag me inside the place. I may have been only 9 years old, but something like this, you never forget!' Marilyn learned later that the woman who put her in the orphanage, Aunt Grace, cried all day afterward. She said Aunt Grace promised to take her out as soon as possible and used to visit her often. 'But when a little girl feels lost and lonely and thinks that nobody wants her, it's something she doesn't forget as long as she lives. I think I wanted more than anything in the world to be loved. Love to me then and now means being wanted. When my Aunt Grace put me in that place, the whole world around me crumbled. It seemed nobody wanted me, not even my mother's best friend.'"

Grace Goddard was granted a court order to sell Gladys's personal property on September 4, 1935. One of the things she sold was the Franklin Baby Grand Piano for $235.00, to her Aunt, Ana Lower, which was $10.00 in excess of the appraisal value. Norma Jeane buys back her piano from Ana Lower, in February of 1945, for $10.00. One of the things Grace did not sell was the Plymouth Sedan, but Doc Goddard would buy it in August of 1936, just to keep things legal.

On September 9th the *Los Angeles Times* ran an article about the Columbian Drama League at Columbia Studios. They were going to perform the Broadway stage hit, *Up Pops the Devil*. Grace McKee is listed in the cast. With Norma Jeane safely tucked away, maybe Grace was going to make a final grasp for her own dream of stardom.

On September 13, 1935, Grace takes Norma Jeane to the Los Angeles Orphan's Home, 815, N El Centro Ave, Hollywood, where she became child number 3463. The Orphanage was just a few walking blocks from Grace's old apartment on Lodi Place. Grace would tell Norma Jeane that she placed her in the Orphanage because of financial hardships that she and Doc were having. It is a hard sell, because she was reimbursed for any expenses for Norma Jeane by the estate. So, whether Norma Jeane was with them or at the Orphanage, Grace got reimbursed. Still it was in the middle of the Great Depression and there was not much money to go around. The most likely reason was that the County Welfare Department had a condition that a child with a parent in an institution had to be placed in the orphanage prior to a change in guardianship from the parent to another adult, i.e. Grace Goddard. Grace applied for guardianship on February 26, 1936, five months after Norma Jeane was placed in the orphanage and she left the orphanage in October 1936, thus completing her year as required. It is the most logical explanation, but a hard one for a child to understand. While in the Home Norma Jeane was watched over very closely by Grace.

If Marilyn was bitter about Grace's decision to place her in the Home, she doesn't give any indication in this account of life with Aunt Grace. "At times she took me to live with her. When she ran out of money and had only a half-dollar left for the week's food, we lived on stale bread and milk. You could buy a sackful of old bread at the Holmes Bakery for 25 cents. Aunt Grace and I would stand in line for hours waiting to fill our sack. When I looked up at her she would grin at me and say, 'Don't worry, Norma Jeane. You're going to be a beautiful girl when you grow up. I can feel it in my bones.' Her words made me so happy that the stale bread tasted like cream puffs...Grace, my new guardian, had no money and was out looking for a job all the time, so she arranged for me to enter the Orphan Asylum--the Los Angeles Children's Home Society...It wasn't till later that I realized how much she had done for me. If not for Grace, I would have been sent to a State or County institution where there are fewer privileges."

When she walked through those ominous doors, she was nine years, three months and twelve days old. At first she refused to enter the Orphan's Home because she insisted that she wasn't an orphan because her mother was alive. After that bitter introduction to the Home, Norma Jeane settled into the routine quite well. This was not the hard-knock-life so often portrayed her biographers. The orphanage was run with as much affection and care as possible. Norma Jeane made friends, remained close to the people in her life, and depended upon Grace Goddard to provide extra support and affection.

Jim Henaghan wrote in 1952 that "Marilyn, according to the supervisors of the Los Angeles Orphan Home Society, was almost a model child. She gave little trouble, and worked in the Home pantry for a wage of five cents a month without complaint—and showed real gratitude when she was promoted to the kitchen as a dishwasher at ten cents a month."

Marilyn shared additional memories of her time at the orphanage with Mr. Henaghan. "It seemed very big, but maybe it wasn't—maybe I just remember it as big. We lived in two dormitories, one a large room and the other smaller. We got to the small room on the merit system, and all of the girls tried very hard to get there. I don't know why, because, after all, it was still the orphanage. We went to school at a public school a couple of blocks away. We all wore gingham dresses—of different colors, but all the same style. Probably the hardest thing I ever had to do in my life was go to that school, because once in a while I'd hear another kid say, 'She's from the Home,' and I knew I was different—and I didn't want to be different. I was just shy and scared. At one time, just after school started in the fall, three boys in my class liked me. And then they found out I was from the Home—and it was terrible."

"'Norma Jeane's behavior is normal and she is bright and sunshiny,' reads an early report on her in the dossier at the orphanage. 'The school reports on her are good. She is quiet. She sleeps well and eats well. She is well behaved. Her grades are good. She participates in all activities. She is cooperative.' This is supported by Margaret Ingram, superintendent of the Home. And according to the institution's records, Mrs. Goddard had visited the girl every week. 'She brought her clothes and presents often. She felt badly about not being able to give Norma Jeane a home. She seemed to be very devoted to her.'"

Yet, there were happy memories of going to school. Norma Jeane and the children from the orphanage would walk together to and from the Vine Street School. She seemed to fit in with the other children at the Home and made new friends. She enjoyed playing softball and other group games. One of her early boyfriends, also from the Home, Bob Lampert, gave her a ring from Woolworth's that he had stolen for her.

An ironic nugget in Norma Jeane's life is the constant reminder of her mother in the RKO water tower she could see through her window sill. She was quoted as saying, "at nights when all the kids were asleep, I'd perch on the dormitory window sill and look across at the RKO water tank with 'RKO' in big letters and light shining like a Hollywood premiere. 'My mother used to work there,' I'd whisper. 'Someday, I'd like to be a star there.'"

Grace bought Norma Jeane a coat in October from the Broadway Department Store for $18.16.

On October 15 and 16 the Los Angeles Orphans Home held its traditional ingathering of fruits, groceries and canned goods donated by the community. The board of managers and directors met with the generous visitors and showed them through the home. The *Los Angeles Times* declared that there were 104 orphans and abandoned children living at the orphanage. The newspaper also showed a photo of several orphans eating bread and jam that had been donated. One can only imagine what Norma Jeane felt as the visitors toured the facility after dropping off their donations, gawking at the poor orphans with gazes that combined curiosity with pity.

There survives a photo taken during Norma Jeane's time of a Halloween Party in the lunch hall.

Grace wrote a letter Mrs. Dewey at the Los Angeles Orphan's Home on December 4th, referring to Norma Jeane as "little Norma Jeane Baker." Grace didn't want Ida Bolender to visit Norma Jeane again and to instruct people who might have her on an overnight visit that Ida was not to have any contact with the child. Grace felt that Ida unduly upset the child. She gives permission for Elsie or Harvey Giffen, Maude, George or Nell Atkinson and Norma Jeane's Aunt Olive Monroe or her mother, Mrs. Martin to see her or take her out as they wished. Grace adds that she is to be contacted to grant permission for anyone else who wants to visit Norma Jeane. She listed her work phone, Hollywood 3181, or her home phone, Granite 4288, as contact numbers.

Mrs. Dewey, of the Los Angeles Orphans Home Society, responds to Grace's letter on December 6th. She tells Grace that Ida Bolender had visited Norma Jeane recently and that she didn't seem the same since her visit. She tells Grace how much Norma Jeane loves her. When she has misbehaved Norma Jeane tells Mrs. Dewey that she wouldn't ever want Aunt Grace to find out about it.

Norma Jeane's time at the Home had a bit of misbehaving attached to it, but it is not certain that Aunt Grace ever found out about it. Jim Henaghan tells of Norma Jeane, "being a member of a 'crash-out party,' but only because she was too frightened to refuse. To a nine-year-old it was a desperate adventure, with a bleak world the other side of a high hedge the only promise. But it had something to do with freedom, so the girls risked it. The escape was well planned, the youngsters thought. Nap time was H hour. Led by a 'tough' youngster, Marilyn and her pals slipped through a back window of the institution and set out across the wide lawn for the street. Sighting a couple of office workers, however, they scurried under the building and sat in the damp darkness, trembling in terror. Eventually, urged on by threats and tottish imprecations by their leader, they made a break for it. They didn't make it—and were herded back to their naps in disgrace by Home employees."

Whether it was this elaborate escape or another one, there is an incident of Norma Jeane being returned to the supervisor after an attempt to run away. She thought she would be punished and was prepared for the worst. Instead, something happened that would remain with her forever. "The superintendent remarked how pretty Norma Jeane looked. Taking out her own powder puff, she gently patted it across the youngster's shiny nose. The little girl looked up, baffled by this unexpected kindness. 'No one ever before had noticed my hair, or my face—or even me—I guess. For the first time in my life I felt loved.'" She was allowed to wear the powder for the remainder of the day.

Marilyn will tell Isabel Moore, "No one ever told me I was pretty when I was a little girl. All little girls should be told they're pretty, even if they aren't."

Grace took Norma Jeane clothes shopping a couple of times in December.

On December 18th the children were entertained at the Orphanage by "acting dogs, clowns, magicians, marionettes, dancers, Indians, acrobats, and singers in vaudeville" as the Federal Theater Project put on a show. The Federal Theater Project was made up of unemployed entertainers.

At Christmas time the RKO studio invited the children from the Orphanage to visit the studio. The children were also taken to the Army and Navy Club for a big Christmas party sponsored by the Los Angeles chapter of the National Association of Cost Accountants. By most accounts the Orphanage party was a happy time for the children with many trees and presents. Each little girl was given an imitation pearl necklace. Marilyn would later recall with exaggerated memories of only being given an orange.

Grace filed a Petition for Guardianship of Minor on February 26, 1936. She paid $7.00, for which she was reimbursed by Gladys's Estate. Grace also paid .50 for a Verification of Petition for Guardianship, for which she was also reimbursed. In March, Grace paid $50.00 to hire attorney J.P. Patterson to file the Petition and Appearance in regarding Guardianship of the person of Norma Jeane Baker, minor child of the incompetent. Grace paid the Orphans Home $15.00 a month for Norma Jeane's board and keep. Grace was awarded guardianship of Norma Jeane on March 27th.

Grace sent Norma Jeane a birthday card on June 1$^{st}$ for her 10th birthday and on the next Saturday took her to an ice-cream parlor.

Norma Jeane receives a citizenship certificate from the Vine Street School. It was presented to Norma Baker for "her excellent record in citizenship during the current semester." It was signed by Lydia M. Bensen, and dated June 19, 1936.

The last payment to the Orphanage is on June 21, 1936, per Grace's records. On September 28, 1936 Grace files for a reimbursement for her expenses for Gladys, Norma Jeane and the estate, starting March 25, 1935. Further reimbursement records by Grace reveal that she requested a reimbursement for Norma Jeane's living expenses starting in October 1936. In 1955 the then Superintendent of the Los Angeles Orphans' Home Society, Margaret Ingram told Ezra Goodman what they recommended to Grace Goddard, "We recommended finally that she had had enough of group living and needed some family life. Some children don't respond as well as others to the environment of the home. We do all we can to give them affection and individual attention, but it doesn't always work."

Marilyn would visit the orphanage as an adult. Three different visits are listed in the visitor's log books starting in 1947. It seems she retained some fondness for the place where she had spent a year of her young life. Marilyn will say, "I understand how the kids feel. A little kindness means a lot, even from a stranger."

Norma Jeane came to live with Grace and Doc in October at 3107 Barbara Court in the Hollywood Hills. Grace also made a promise to Gladys that she would take Norma Jeane out of the institution and after a year's time, and she kept her promise. Grace had lost her job at Columbia and life was hard for her and Doc, yet she took in Norma Jeane.

Marilyn will later recall the hard times she and Grace endured during the Great Depression. "Everything seemed to go wrong for Aunt Grace. Only bad luck and death ever visited her. But there was no bitterness in my aunt. Her heart remained tender and she believed in God. Nearly everybody I knew talked to me about God. They always warned me not to offend Him. But when Grace talked about God she touched my cheek and said that He loved me, and watched over me. Remembering what Grace had said, I lay in bed at night crying to myself. The only One who loved me and watched over me was someone who I couldn't see, or hear, or touch. I used to draw pictures of God, whenever I had the time. In my pictures He looked a little like Aunt Grace, and a little like Clark Gable."

Grace has photographs taken of Norma Jeane in December, the cost was $5.41. She also purchased her some shoes, a purse, a sweater, and a meal for $6.20. She got her some miscellaneous items totaling $5.57. She purchased a scrapbook for Norma Jeane, $2.00., and had her coat altered, $2.50. Grace gave Norma Jeane $10.50 spending money to buy Christmas Gifts. Grace also bought Gladys slippers and clothes, totaling $11.51. She also bought Norma Jeane a coat at Kay Co., costing $11.28.

In January 1937, Grace bought Norma Jeane some miscellaneous items, $4.00, had her shoes repaired, $1.36, bought her some bedroom slippers, $1.40, and also bought her a hair treatment at a salon, $6.00.

According to a final assessment document in her file at the orphanage, dated February 20, 1937, they concluded that Norma Jeane was "anxious and withdrawn" and she had a tendency to stutter. It was also noted that she "is also susceptible to a lot of coughs and colds." It was recommended that while she was sick she needed to be treated with "much reassurance and patience" or she became frightened. The document also recommended that she be placed with a "good family."

Grace bought Norma Jeane clothes from Sears-Roebuck in April. They included dresses, $3.84, sun suits, $1.85, a coat, $6.13, shoes, $3.04, miscellaneous items, $5.30, and also paid for shoe repairs, $9.15. In May, she bought her some new shoes, $4.42, and underwear and drugs, $6.00.

In October 1936 Norma Jeane enters the Lankershim School, 5250 Bakman Ave, in North Hollywood.

Grace decides that for the sake of her marriage, she needs to find another living arrangement for Norma Jeane. In November of 1937 Grace was reimbursed from the Estate of Gladys, $280.00 for the care of Norma Jeane from October 1936 until November 1937. Grace was paid for 14 months at $20.00 per month.

Grace would send Norma Jeane to live with her Aunt Olive Monroe, and her daughters Ida Mae who was close to Norma Jeane's age, and her other daughter Olive and son Jack. Also living there was Olive's mother, Ida Martin. These were not strangers to Norma Jeane and they also lived in North Hollywood. They had been part of her life, albeit on the periphery, since she was an infant. She would stay there for 9 months. These were simple people who had little money and were left in a hard situation when Olive's husband, Marion, disappeared in 1929. Olive had tried to get him declared dead so the family could get benefits, but it would be 1939 until benefits would start. They took Norma Jeane in, mainly, for the money she brought in, along with a feeling of familial obligation. A freeway runs where the home once stood. Similar homes remain in the neighborhood to give on an idea that the home was quite small. Norma Jeane had to share a small bed with Ida Mae. In a later magazine article Marilyn dramatically remembered, "When I was poor, I always had to sleep with a female relative in a bed too small and too uncomfortable."

Norma Jeane will not have to go to a different school which helped maintain some kind of stability in her life. She had an almost two mile walk to school with her cousins. Marilyn will remember making up stories in her mind as she walked through vacant lots on her way to school. Norma Jeane would win first place in high-jumping while at the Lankershim School. It was here where she became known as "Norma Jeane the Human Bean," due to her height and thin frame. It is not unusual for girls that age to be taller than the boys. Pictures taken of Norma Jeane around this age show a gangly looking girl who is more plain than pretty. Later, Marilyn would recall the nick-name and shame it fostered within her fragile self-esteem. "'I was never happy in grade school--I went to lots of them in different neighborhoods. I always felt in the way; I stuttered and the others made fun of me; they all had their own little groups and I didn't know how to go about pushing my way in. They called me 'Norma Jeane-the Human Bean.' Her eyes clouded as she voiced those painful reminiscences."

Marilyn told Hedda Hopper in an interview in May of 1952, "I was tall for my age and scrawny and my hair was short and rather thin and scraggly. We'd talk, as kids do, about what we were going to be when we grew up. One girl was going to be a nurse, another, a school teacher; but when I said I was going to be an actress, they'd all laugh. The boys used to yell, 'Norma Jeane--string bean!' and they thought it was so funny that I wanted to be an actress that after a while I didn't talk about it anymore. But I thought about it a lot. I'd be the fairy prince or the king in the class plays when I wanted to be the beautiful princess with the long golden hair. Somehow they thought I looked like a boy. I was straight up and down.'"

Gerry Grissman remembers Norma Jeane from the fifth grade, as he sat next to her. He said. "She was a quiet little girl and didn't flirt with any of the boys and none of the boys gave her any special attention. Marilyn may be beautiful now, but in the fifth grade she was very plain looking."

While there she and became close to her cousin Ida Mae. The girls engaged in make believe games that took up most of their time. Once they tried to make wine in a discarded washtub in the front yard. They dreamed of running off to San Francisco and finding Ida Mae's father. Later Marilyn would tell stories of having to bath in dirty bathwater, but sharing bathwater was not an uncommon practice and wasn't used as punishment. There was a mentally challenged woman who lived across the street whose family kept her mind occupied with movie magazines. When she had finished with them they were given to Olive and after she was through Marilyn and Ida Mae devoured the stack of paper dreams. Marilyn would be the resident expert when it came to movie stars, given her mother and Grace's occupations and she could speak from authority when Jean Harlow, Carole Lombard, Robert Taylor or Fred Astaire appeared in print. After all, the Sunday strolls in Whitley Heights gave her stories to share about their mansions and brief sightings. She can tell them of watching movies at Grauman's and of the monkeys housed in the forecourt. In 12 years she will start to appear along with some of the movie stars in the magazines. The Marx Brothers, Bette Davis, Barbara Stanwyck, Ginger Rogers and Cary Grant will eventually share screen time with her. Even though she doesn't realize it, her life will not be spent in these sad little houses on lots more dirt than grass.

All told, Norma Jeane's relatives did the best they could do for Norma Jeane. They had little money, but gave to her in other ways. Grandmother Martin told stories of pioneer life that thrilled the girls. She was not the doting grandmother you think of today. It was a different era and she came from an even earlier one where children were seen, but not heard. Yet she did have a measure of love for Norma Jeane as evidence in the fact that when she was older and out of their care Norma Jeane sent Mrs. Martin a photo of herself signed, "To My Darling Grammy, Always Lovingly, Norma Jeane."

In March of 1938 there was a major flood that affected the area. Photographs show people in small boats navigating the submerged streets. Norma Jeane was moved for a short time to live with the family of John and Ruth Mills.

According to Bebe Goddard, Norma Jeane was moved shortly after that to Grace's brother's home. Bryan, Lottie and Geraldine Atchinson lived at 1826 East Palmer Ave. Norma Jeane would again attend the Vine Street School, at least for a little while. Mr.

Atchinson made furniture polish which he sold to various hardware stores in the area. Each Saturday they would pile into the front seat of the Chevrolet and fill the backseat with furniture polish and make the rounds of the Hardware stores in the area. Marilyn will recall Mrs. Atchinson hollering to her while she finished her breakfast to get going and lock the door behind her.

The Monroe's continued to receive support payment for the care of Norma Jeane through August of 1938 at $30 a month. Presumably the payments were continued as an act of charity on Grace's part to help Norma Jeane's relatives recover from the devastation from the great flood.

Norma Jeane lived with Grace and Doc Goddard for a short time until an unfortunate incident happened. It is during this time that Doc drunkenly went into Norma Jeane's bedroom during the night and gave her an intimate kiss. She ran frightened from the room and told Grace about the incident. It was easy to see that she was not safe in this environment and another place needed to be found. She was moved again in September of 1938 to live with Grace's Aunt, Ana Lower at 11348 Nebraska Ave, West Los Angeles, or Sawtelle. This was a life changing event in the young girl's life. Deprived of a mother's love for so long, she would now reap the benefit of being taken care of by a woman who had an exceptionally good heart. Aunt Ana became the custodian of Norma Jeane's tender psyche and as often happens when older women are coupled with young girls, each receives from the other the thing that they need most. They find that they are not so different from each other. Due to age and circumstance they have been marginalized from the faster paced movers-and-shakers. Sequestered on the outskirts of the hustle and bustle of busy lives, these two refugees of progress join forces. Norma Jeane's long vigil of dreary days and lonely nights is over and she will reap the rewards of living with such an affectionate woman and finding that she does have a place, however small, in this world. Aunt Ana will hold her through the bad times and uplift her with spiritual teachings. In the end, Marilyn will be tethered to Aunt Ana's influence for the rest of her life.

Marilyn remembers Aunt Ana reassuring her during this time, "It doesn't matter if other children make fun of your clothes or where you live. It's what you are that counts. You just keep being your own self. That's all that matters…Live each day and take things as they come. Face everything, work hard at the things you want to accomplish, and you will have nothing to fear. Maybe you don't think so right now, but you will find out later that I'm right." Marilyn will later say that, "I have never been clothes crazy. Aunt Ana's good sense cured me of that."

Norma Jeane is also reunited with a piece of her own history, her mother's piano. The piano will always hold a special place in her heart as it is one of the few surviving remnants of her childhood with her mother.

The Sawtelle district grew up around a Veterans Home and its hospital and cemetery. Sawtelle also had a large population of Nisei farmers who owned nurseries and florist shops. There was an underlying network of Japanese businesses that supported these two industries, making the area quite unique. When she lived with Arthur Miller and in 1962

when she owned her own home, Marilyn loved to putter around in her garden. Surely the influence of the Nisei farmers must have played a small part in her love of gardening.

It is during this period, when Marilyn was 12 that she learns that she has a half-sister, Berniece Baker-Miracle and a little niece Mona Rae. Norma Jeane begins to correspond with her sister. In an interview with Hedda Hopper at the end of 1952, Marilyn clears up how Berniece came into her life. "'I do have a half-sister, though—a very nice girl who lives in Florida. I met her through Mrs. Ana Lower, one of my guardians and the woman who came closer to giving me a true mother's love than anyone else in the world.' 'How did that happen?' Mrs. Lower located Berniece, her half-sister, Marilyn said, when she herself had no idea at all where she was. 'Two years ago,' Marilyn recalled, 'she came here to Hollywood to meet me. She is a lovely person. We have the same mother, but different fathers. It seemed strange to meet when we were already fully grown, but we liked each other on sight.'"

Norma Jeane was introduced to a family that would become a part of her life for the next few years, Chester and Doris Howell, and their daughters, Jane, Doralee and Loralee. She called them Uncle Chet and Aunt Doris. Ana Lower and Doris were acquainted and Norma Jeane was often asked to baby sit the twins. She became a "Mother's Helper" to Doris and was a frequent visitor to their home at 432 Bentley in West Los Angeles. Chester was the senior partner at the law firm of Dixon, Howell, Westmoreland and Newman. Doris was frequently in the Society columns hosting parties for the Westwood Village Rotary

Club and other events. Norma Jeane went on vacations with the family, and in fact there is footage of a teenage Norma Jeane at the beach with Doralee and Loralee and Jane. She romps in the waves with them and turns cartwheels on the beach. Jane mimics her as they cartwheel toward the camera, the twins running to catch up. Waving to the camera we glimpse her tenderness and charm. Jane remembers Norma Jeane as very compliant, not really able to voice her opinion. They would sit on the stairs and Jane would ask, "What do you want to do?" Norma Jeane would reply, "I don't care. What do you want to do?" Jane would always end up making the decision. When Norma Jeane was older, she would have her dates pick her up at the Howell home. She would drive Chester crazy spending hours putting on makeup in the bathroom. She loved the family very much. Doris hosted Norma Jeane's wedding and reception at their beautiful home and the twins, Doralee and Loralee participated as flower girls. Norma Jeane continued to attend the parties for the University girls that Doris gave into the early 1950's, when she was Marilyn Monroe. The Howell family was a source of strength and stability for the adolescent Norma Jeane, and their influence and contribution is highly overlooked by most of her biographers. The sense of pride and belonging that being included in a family brought to her cannot be overestimated. She was a sweet girl with a soft voice and the Howells did not find it hard to love her.

Norma Jeane attends Ralph Waldo Emerson Jr. High School for 7th, 8th and 9th grades. The school was in West Los Angeles. While she was still the new girl at Emerson, she was befriended by Bob Muir, who was a year older and a grade above her. He helped her retrieve some papers that had blown away from her. She soon became friends with the rest of the kids he hung around with. Her own classmates will shun her, perceiving her shyness as being "stuck-up." In reality she is morbidly withdrawn and insecure until she feels at ease

Marilyn remembers she preoccupied herself with movies during this time. "In junior high school, I was completely movie-struck. I used to go see movies I liked three or four times when I could afford it. Ginger Rogers was my favorite. A girl who lived across the street subscribed to several of the fan magazines and she would give me all of the pictures of Ginger. I had several dozen of her portraits pinned up around my room." There survives a signed portrait of Ginger Rogers that was sent to Norma Jeane. It reads, "To Norma Jean Baker Sincerely Ginger Rogers 1939."

A boy who had several classes with Norma Jeane remembers her as being a "giggly" sort of girl who often wore a powder blue suit to school. He said she was friendly and pretty. Ron Underwood, another boy in her class recalls that she signed her yearbook, "To a super fellow. I really don't know you, but I think you are." About Norma Jeane herself, Mr. Underwood states, "As I recall, she was an attractive blonde, with well-coiffed hair. She was always neat and well groomed, very often in plain clothes. She was somewhat shy and withdrawn, and seemingly had few friends."

A kind remembrance of Norma Jeane is given by one of the girls in her school, Marion Losman-Zaich. "I only passed Norma Jeane in the halls of Emerson Jr. High and she smiled and said 'Hi' to me, even though I never knew her. I did not see her too often at school and when I did she seemed to be alone. After she was married she moved two blocks from me and we never crossed paths. A close friend of mine went to see an acquaintance and was told by him that Marilyn had just left and had had a most intellectual conversation with her. It's unfortunate that she had such an unhappy childhood. I think, had it been different, her life would not have ended so soon."

The perception of her being "wild" begins here in Jr. High School. It is during this time that she becomes aware of her body and its effects on people around her. "I wasn't aware of anything sexual in their liking for me and there were no sex thoughts in my mind. I didn't think of my body as having anything to do with sex. It was more like a friend who had mysteriously appeared in my life, a sort of magic friend. One of her classmates, Tom Ishii (Dshee) remembered that she, "talked loud--so everyone considered her to be wild."

One of the girls in her class, who also attended University High with her, Sally Kosack, remembers her in an unusually harsh light, "She was a tramp. No taste--would wear plaid skirts with a print blouse. No friends--off by herself most of the time. She was horrible in both Jr. High and High School. Stand-offish--did not associate with others. A tramp--even the fellows at school didn't go off with her. She must have had fellows away from school. She thought she was a real big shot--Better than everybody else--They had families; She didn't. She was homely--dressed tacky--plump. Norma Jeane didn't have the brains to become Marilyn Monroe. Someone had to guide her." After getting all of this off her chest, she reflected that, "Maybe she was insecure and the kids just thought that she was stuck up."

This gives an indication of how she was thought of and treated by the girls in her school classes and later, how the women of America came to view her early in her career.

Marilyn will recall with sadness this lonely time in her life, "At 12 I looked like a girl of 17. My body was developed and shapely. But no one knew this but me. I still wore the blue dress and the blouse the orphanage provided. They made me look like an overgrown lummox. I had no money. The other girls rode to school in a bus. I had no nickel to pay for the ride, rain or shine, I walked the two miles from my 'aunt's' home to the school. I hated the walk. I hated the school. I had no friends. The pupils seldom talked to me, and never wanted me in their games. Nobody ever walked home with me, or invited me to visit their homes. This was partly because I came from the poor part of the district, where all the Mexicans and Japanese lived. It was also because I couldn't smile at anyone...In school the pupils often whispered about me and giggled as they stared at me. They called me dumb and made fun of my orphan's outfit. I didn't mind being thought dumb. I knew I wasn't."

A different estimation of her is given by Norma Jeane's Science teacher, Mabel Ella Campbell, who recalls her famous student, "She was a youngster who looked as if she wasn't well cared for. Her clothes separated her a little bit from the rest of the girls. She was like a little girl, not well developed as some of the youngsters were. She just seemed like a nice child. Not very outgoing. Not very vibrant."

Norma Jeane's grades were not impressive during her time at Emerson. She did, however, excel in the Journalism class she took. Her name appears in the school newspaper, *The Emersonian*, where she contributed to the "Features" column. Norma Jeane was chosen by her Journalism class to be the Secretary. The major obstacle she faced in school was her acute shyness and almost morbid fear of speaking in public. She nearly failed her Rhetoric and Spoken Arts class because of her stuttering, first mentioned in the Orphanage document of February 20, 1937. What was once an occasional manifestation of her anxiety, now became more pronounced and threatened to handicap her success in school and later as an actress.

In February of 1939 the students at Emerson Jr. High School take standardized test in various subjects. Norma Jeane scored a 77 on her reading test and a 72 on her arithmetic test.

On her birthday Grace took Norma Jeane to visit Gladys in a boarding house in San Francisco, CA. By all accounts, the visit didn't go well, as Gladys was unaffectionate and distant.

She may have been average in academics, but on June 31st Norma Jeane is given an award for serving as a member of the School Safety Committee.

Steve Cronin identifies a little known fact in Norma Jeane's young life. Her neighbor is future actor Howard Keel, who lived across the street from Ana Lower, and she develops a serious crush on him. "She has admitted to only one infatuation, a crush on a neighbor boy who today is making quite a name for himself in pictures, one Howard Keel of MGM." In an interview with Hedda Hopper, we learn this, "'How about the story that you used to live across the street from Howard Keel and had a terrible crush on him?' 'True,' Marilyn said. 'He was Harry Keel then. I was about eleven or twelve, and he didn't even know I was alive.'"

Marilyn comments about her first crush. "I remember my first 'romance.' He was 22 and I was not yet 14. He lived across the street from me, and I know now that I was just a kid as far as he was concerned. I should have known that from the way he would pat me on top of the head when he came home and I happened to be standing near the fence on his side of the road. But I didn't. To me he was the center of my thoughts, my feelings, my whole world. One day he came out of his house and was already in his car when he noticed me (there I was hanging around again!). 'Ask your Aunt Ana if you can come along. It's a good picture.' Aunt Ana, who was my guardian, and who liked him, said yes, and I flew out to join him. When I sat down beside him my heart was pounding, my head in a whirl, and an inner voice kept whispering to me, 'You shouldn't have gone. You won't know how to conduct yourself. He will never bother with you again.' That voice was right. I not only tried to act like an older girl and failed, but I was too far affected by being out with him to even act my own age. I was gawky. I was giggly. I was stupid. When I had been sitting too long in the car without saying anything I got nervous. Not being able to think of an idea of my own, I read an advertising sign we passed, read it aloud and mispronounced practically every word! When he made a driving error and I should have kept my mum till the incident was forgotten, I laughed and earned an annoyed look. When we pulled up in the parking lot of the theater and he was coming around to open the door on my side, I not only opened it myself first, but closed it again quickly so he could open it after all! When we got inside my feet went rubbery and he had to save me from stumbling a half dozen times. And all through the picture I was in a daze. He still said hello after that night, but no more smile, no invitations, not even a pat on the head! I cried off and on for weeks and that was the first time I thought—'Who'd ever marry me?'"

Marilyn will reveal to Ben Hecht that she had fooled Keel into thinking that she was 18 instead of 13 by what she wore and her skill in makeup. It seems it didn't take him long to uncover the truth.

Sometime between 13 and 14, Norma Jeane shows up in school wearing a sweater. She remembers the sensation she created and the change it made in her social life. "I arrived at school just as the math class was starting. As I walked to my seat everybody stared at me. It was a very tight sweater. At recess a half dozen boys crowded around me. They made jokes and kept looking at my sweater as if it were a gold mine. I had known for some time that I had shapely breasts and thought nothing of the fact. The math class, however, was more impressed. After school four boys walked home with me, wheeling their bicycles by hand. I was excited but acted as if nothing unusual were happening. The school and the day became different after that. Girls who had brothers began inviting me to their homes, and I met their folks, too. And there were always four or five boys hanging around my house. We played games in the street and stood around talking under the trees till suppertime. I wasn't aware of anything sexual in their new liking for me and there were no sex thoughts in my mind. I didn't think of my body as having anything to do with sex. It was more like a friend who had mysteriously appeared in my life, a sort of magic friend."

Socially, Norma Jeane hangs around her gang of upper-classmen friends. That September she goes on a hike with her school chum, Bob Muir and his friends. After the hike, the group returns to Bob's home, where Norma Jeane is introduced to his mother, Dorothy. Her memories of Norma Jeane were, "that she was shy, possibly thirteen years old, and just a trifle dazed at being accepted as a peer by boys and girls who were all at least one year older." Norma Jeane visited their home regularly for the next several years. Dorothy remembers that she laughed and talked without apparent reservation, at the same time carefully avoiding anything personal. Norma Jeane and the other girls spent hours in the Muir living room playing Monopoly or trying to teach the boys to dance. The record of choice was "Begin the Beguine." Norma Jeane showed a talent for dancing. It is of interest that in 1949, when Marilyn posed for her nude calendar, Tom Kelley would play "Begin the Beguine" to get her in the mood.

On February 7, 1940, Grace Goddard's attorney, J.P. Patterson, filed a Final Accounting and Petition for Discharge of Guardian, for the estate of incompetent, Gladys P. Baker. Grace is reimbursed for expense incurred since her last reimbursement on September 28, 1936.Grace and her lawyer were each paid $325.00 for their administration of the estate of Gladys P. Baker.

Norma Jeane goes with the Muir family and friends to Green Valley Lake, in the San Bernardino Mountains, to do some sledding on February 25. Before taking off in the family's Packard, the girls, Norma Jeane and Betty Dugger, drew straws to determine who got to ride in the rumble seat. Betty won the chance to sit in it going up to Green Valley, and Norma Jeane got to ride in the rumble seat coming back. Near dark, the snow started to mix with rain, causing ice to form. Everyone piled back into the car, with Norma Jeane sandwiched between the two boys, Bob Stotts and Bill Heiss, in the rumble seat. They pulled a tarp up over their heads to fend off the rain. Down the mountain made treacherous by the ice and debris that had collected on the road, the car made its way. Suddenly, a rock tumbled down the mountain, crashing against the hood of the car. No one was hurt, but all were frightened because of the close call, everyone except the three in the rumble seat. They were unaware of what had just happened. When told by Mrs. Muir, Norma Jeane gamely replied, "My head's too hard. That old rock would have bounced off and wouldn't have left a dent."

Although Norma Jeane was living with Aunt Ana, she was listed in the 1940 census on April 4th as living with Doc and Grace Goddard at 11336 Nebraska Ave. They also listed a 79 year old widowed lodger as living with them as well. Ana Lower was listed as the head of her household and had a lodger, a 49 year old Minnie Price, a cook and housekeeper, listed as living with her.

In May Norma Jeane was a member of the Emerson Girls Glee Club. She will also accompany the Muir family and friends to the desert to view the wildflowers, hike and have a picnic.

On June 20, 1941, Emerson Jr. High School issued its annual, *The Emersonian*. It featured class photos and a centerfold of the 1941 graduating class. This was to be her first centerfold. In the school newspaper, of the same name and date, she appears in the section titled, "A Peek Into the Future." Ironically her current sex appeal was remarked upon, "Norma Jeane Baker will one day be the smiling and beaming Chairman of the Beverly Hills home for Spinsters."

Norma Jeane was one of the class members chosen to be in a "Class Alphabet." At her own suggestion, she was listed under "M, Mmmm: Norma Jeane Baker." This was her own way of poking fun at herself for her stuttering. In later years the Press would refer to this label in an entirely different context, when she would be touted as "Marilyn Monroe, Fox's Mmmm Girl." Norma Jeane also contributed a small article about the results of a survey titled, "What is Your Favorite Type of Girl?" It is interesting to note that she found that, "...53 percent of the gentlemen prefer blondes as their dream girl."

Six days later Norma Jeane Graduated Emerson Jr. High School, West Los Angeles. She signed the back of classmate Nathan Langford's class picture. Her inscription said, "Here's wishing you loads of luck to a 'keen' fellow! -- Norma Jeane Baker." It is interesting to note the boldness of her signature. The "B" in Baker practically takes over the text of her inscription. Norma Jeane's panoramic class photo was labeled at the bottom in her handwriting, "Belongs to Norma Jeane Baker."

After graduating Jr. High, Norma Jeane moves back in with the Goddard's for a short while in their new home, 14743 Archwood St., in Van Nuys. Ana Lower had gone back east for a while. Norma Jeane had a good relationship with Doc's children Bebe and Fritz, but Nona was often mean to her. Doc had been transferred to West Virginia. He and Grace came to the sad conclusion that they could not take Norma Jeane with them when they left California. Aunt Ana's declining health wouldn't permit her to care for Norma Jeane again. Chester and Doris Howell were approached concerning adopting her, but they felt they could not take on the extra burden of another child, as they had three already.

Grace was acquainted with Ethel Dougherty, as they often talked over the back fence, and knew that she had a son, Jim, who would make Norma Jeane a perfect husband. The two women conspired to get Norma Jeane and Jim married. It was either marriage for Norma Jeane or back to the orphanage or foster care.

Jim Dougherty was friendly with the Goddard family and even made blueprints of Doc's inventions. Jim was working the graveyard shift at Lockheed and Norma Jeane and Bebe used to come to the house and wake Jim up on their way home from school and he would drive them home.

Norma Jeane attended Van Nuys High School, for the first semester of 10th grade, September of 1941 thru February of 1942. Grace gave her a weekly allowance of $1.50, along with any necessities she might need. Marilyn remembers her short stint as a High School student. "My arrival in school with painted lips and darkened brows, and still encased in the magic sweater, started everybody buzzing. And the buzzing was not all friendly. All sorts of girls, not only 13-year olds, but seniors of 17 and 18, set up shop as my enemies. They told each other and whoever would listen that I was a drunkard and spent my nights sleeping with boys on the beach....But I couldn't feel angry with the scandal-makers. Girls being jealous of me! Girls frightened of losing their boy-friends because I was more attractive! These were no longer day dreams made up to hide lonely hours. They were truths! They disliked me more and more as I grew older. Now, instead of being accused of stealing combs, nickels, or necklaces, I was accused of stealing young men...Why I was a siren, I hadn't the faintest idea. I didn't want to be kissed...The truth was that with all my lipstick and mascara and precocious curves, I was as unsensual as a fossil. But I seemed to affect people quite otherwise."

When Jim first met Norma Jeane he felt she was much too young for him, but his ideas about her rapidly changed. Grace had a note pinned to Jim's pillow asking him to take Norma Jeane to the dance and to find a date for Bebe. By the time of Norma Jeane's first date with Jim, at the Dance at Adel Precision Products Co. Christmas Party, he fell hard for her. They began to date exclusively and he broke it off almost immediately with his current girlfriend, who was Queen of the Santa Barbara Festival. Despite her young age, he sensed a maturity beyond her years. And she made him feel, "like a big-shot."

Jim had been student body President at the Van Nuys High School. He had appeared in school plays with then unknown Jane Russell, a fellow classmate. He also played football. Norma Jeane had developed a crush on Jim so it wasn't hard for Grace and Ethel to continue push the relationship toward its ultimate conclusion. As the romance continued, they would sometimes double-date with Bebe Goddard and her beau.

While dating Norma Jeane and Jim would often go on Sundays to Ventura County to visit his sister Elyda. She lived close to Lake Sherwood where Jim liked to fish and they also rowed around the lake in a boat or went hiking. Although Norma Jeane wasn't an avid outdoorsman, she gamely participated in these activities.

When the Goddard's left for West Virginia in late 1942, Norma Jeane moved back in with Aunt Ana Lower who's health seemed to stabilize enough to care for her again. Marilyn will say in a later interview, "…it seemed almost as if I hadn't been away." She attends University High School for the 2nd semester of 10th Grade, February thru June. She and Jim continue to date. They would sometimes park on a street just off Mulholland Drive and make out. They are finally talked into marriage because of Norma Jeane's tenuous living circumstances and the chance that she might have to go into another foster home.

Jim proposed to Marilyn without anyone's knowledge. She said yes, but asked him to take back the rings he had bought. She thought they were too expensive. She chooses a more modest set.

At the annual family picnic at Lake Sherwood Rev. Lingenfelder was there and was delighted to be asked to officiate the marriage, especially when he learned that it would be on the same day, June 19$^{th}$, as his own marriage. Jim played the guitar and serenaded Norma Jeane during the day. She brought six lemon pies to the event and said they were her mother's recipe and Jim's favorite.

Marilyn will later say of her marriage to Jim, "When I was sixteen and a senior in high school, I was so lonely and unsure of myself I imagined that an older boy who was headed for the War was the answer for me....I learned that good intentions alone can't turn a girl into a successful wife. The truth is we both were simply far too young and too ignorant of the possibilities of love. We didn't understand each other. I'm not the outdoor type, and today would say so. But then I attempted to go fishing and hunting like the pal he wanted. I just never could get any fun out of killing anything. Our chief trouble, however, was that we were too unacquainted with our own selves to choose a life partner with discernment."

Marilyn will tell Milton Shulman, "I wasn't in love with him. That was the last thing I had in mind. But he was very kind and I didn't want to go into another home. And I was astonished and flattered at being asked."

Marilyn will tell Hedda Hopper, "It's hard to define reasons for something as emotional as marriage—especially if you're as young as I was. But I suppose you could say that having a home of my own had something to do with it. But there were other considerations—just being in love with love, or sex, or whatever you want to call it. We both realized soon that it wasn't going to be a success."

Marilyn's memories of her marriage will take on a bitter tone in later years, "I didn't have a crush on him, although he claimed I did in a story he wrote about us. The truth is the people I was staying with moved East. They couldn't afford to take me because when they left California they'd stop getting the twenty dollars a month the county or the state was paying them to help them clothe and feed me. So instead of going back into a boarding home or with still another set of foster parents, I got married."

# Chapter Four
## The Marrying Kind

"I kept thinking of all the years in the orphan's asylum and in foster homes. Of all the time when I was afraid of what the next day might bring. I knew if I married, that I wouldn't have to worry about that. You don't send married women to foster homes."
Marilyn Monroe

On June 7th Jim Dougherty and Norma Jeane rented a small apartment with a Murphy bed at 4524 Vista Del Monte St. in Sherman Oaks. A week before the wedding Norma Jeane had moved some of their bridal shower gifts into the small home that would be their new residence. Marilyn stated that it was Aunt Ana who designed and made her wedding gown. She also added, "I was so proud on my marriage certificate to be called her niece!"

The June 12, 1942 edition of the *Westwood Hills Press*, "Social Activities" column, written by Meredith Overpeck, carries an article about the nuptials of Norma Jeane Baker and Jim Dougherty. The headlines read, "Norma J. Baker to marry James E. Dougherty on Friday...Wedding will be solemnized in the home of Mr. & Mrs. Chester Howell, at 8:30 O'clock. Miss Norma Jeane Baker, niece of Mrs. E. Ana Lower, of 11348 Nebraska Ave., Westwood, will become the bride of James Edward Dougherty, son of Mr. and Mrs. Edward Dougherty, of Van Nuys, on Friday evening, June 19, at 8:30 O'clock. The wedding will be solemnized in the home of Mr. and Mrs. Chester Howell, 432 South Bentley Ave, West Los Angeles."

The day before the wedding, Norma Jeane's Aunt Ana gave her a book on a bride's responsibility to her husband. It was a modest manual on the sexual relationship between a husband and wife. Although, she had been molested as a child, she was a virgin when she married Jim Dougherty. Even after reading the enlightening material, she was very nervous about her role as a bed partner to Jim. Jim acknowledges her fears, "She was terrified of being alone with me, and I learned later that she had asked Grace Goddard if she could be married and be 'just friends' with her husband." Marilyn would say later about her fears, "I was frightened of what a husband might do….It wasn't fair to push a frightened teenager into marriage—what did I know about sex? My Aunt Ana brought me a book with hints for a bride-to-be and I told Aunt Grace I didn't feel confident about being a good wife…I thought I was too young. Later, after marriage, I've been told Jim said I was a responsive bride, a perfect bride in every respect—except in the cooking department!"

Norma Jeane's marriage to Jim Dougherty took place on June 19, 1942, at the home of Chester and Doris Howell, 432 South Bentley Ave, West Los Angeles, at 8:30pm; The ceremony was performed by Benjamin Lingenfelder, a minister for the Christian Church of Torrance, CA, and a close friend of the Dougherty family. He was an avid hunter and often accompanied the Dougherty men on hunting trips. Aunt Ana provided the music for the ceremony and was accompanied by soloist, Florence Andre. Chester Howell walked Norma Jeane down the aisle. Jim's brother Marion was the best man, a friend of Norma Jeane's from High School named Lorraine Allen, was her Maid of Honor. The ring bearer was Jim's nephew Wes Kanterman, his sister Billie's son, and the Howell's twin girls, Loralee and Doralee, were the ribbon stretchers. Wayne and Ida Bolender, and all their children were among those in attendance, by special request of Norma Jeane. A bit of drama was added by the attendance of the sister and brother-in-law of Jim's former steady girlfriend, Doris Drenen. The wedding portraits were taken by Axel Fogg. A small reception, with 75 people attending, was held after the ceremony in the dining room. Norma Jeane's mother Gladys, her sister Berniece and niece Mona Rae, and Grace Goddard were not in attendance.

Norma Jeane decided at the last minute not to through the wedding bouquet. "She raised her arm and exclaimed, 'To heck with that! I'm taking these flowers home to press and keep.'"

After the reception at the Howell's, Jim and Norma Jeane were taken to the Florentine Gardens in Hollywood, where Jim drinks too much and Norma Jeane watches when he is invited to get up on stage and dance with the chorus girls. According to Jim she becomes angry with him and accuses him of, "making a monkey out of yourself." On their wedding day, Jim was 21 and Norma Jeane had just turned 16.

Norma Jeane's nervousness about fulfilling her marital obligations led her to spend much time in the bathroom. Jim proved to be persuasive and she not only submitted to her husband's advances, but in time, he would define her as, "a most responsive bride."

Norma Jeane and Jim go to Lake Sherwood in Ventura County and spend their honeymoon fishing. There are surviving photographs of the young bride with her fishing license pinned to her blouse. She appeared to love the outdoors as much as Jim did, but in truth she was not an outdoor girl. Too insecure to let on, she gamely cleaned and cooked the catfish that Jim caught, sometimes even making sashimi out of them.

Of Norma Jeane's outdoor prowess, Jim had this to say, "She did everything I wanted to do. I don't think she ever really liked to fish or hunt, but she went along with me willingly. I gave her a .22 rifle and taught her to be a pretty good shot. For a long time we kept an empty shotgun shell that she had nicked right through the middle from a distance of fifty feet."

The marriage license of James Edward Dougherty and Norma Jeane Mortensen was filed on June 22nd with the State of California, County of Los Angeles, file No. 9953. The Certificate was signed by witnesses Marion E. Dougherty residing at Van Nuys, and Lorraine Allen, residing at Los Angeles, as well as the signature of the person solemnizing marriage, B. H. Lingenfelder.

The June 25th edition of the *Los Angeles Times* ran this column about the newlyweds, "Dougherty's Will Live in Van Nuys...Van Nuys will be the new home of Mr. and Mrs. James Edward Dougherty (Norma Jeane Baker) upon their return from a wedding trip. Marriage vows were exchanged by the young couple last week 8:30 o'clock ceremony in the Westwood Hills' home of the bride's uncle and aunt, Mr. and Mrs. Chester E. Howell, 432 S. Bentley Ave. The bride is the niece of Mrs. E. Ana Lower, also of Westwood Hills. Mr. Dougherty is the son of Mr. and Mrs. Edward Dougherty of Van Nuys." Norma Jeane's life seems to be overrun with aunts and uncles.

Although, the couple didn't live in Van Nuys until 6 months their marriage, they did remain close to Jim's family in Van Nuys. Jim and Norma Jeane continued to live at 4524 Vista Del Monte St. until December. Sometime in October, Jim and Norma Jeane help Jim's sister, Elyda Nelson, who recently had a baby. Norma Jeane had spent many days helping Elyda take care of her son Larry while she was pregnant and it doesn't take her long to get comfortable handling her new born nephew, Denny. She would spend the day helping the new mom, and then Jim would pick her up at night. Although, she was a little disconcerted about the prospect of being pregnant, Norma Jeane nonetheless was adamant that she wanted to have a baby, and the first one she hoped would be a boy.

Sometime that autumn, Norma Jeane wrote to Grace a newsy letter listing her wedding gifts, drawing a diagram of their home and telling her about her new role as a bride. She starts the letter thanking Grace for writing to Gladys and "explaining things about Stanley G. I'm sure she understands now." Norma Jeane also closes with a post script inquiring how to get in contact with Stanley Gifford. Gladys told Grace that Stanley Gifford was Norma Jeane's real father. Grace had confided it to her before her marriage. Grace even told her that her father wanted to adopt her when she was a year or two old, but that Gladys didn't let him because she hated him so. From the moment Norma Jeane found out, she made a resolution to contact him, never considering that this news might not be as well received as it had been for her. Marilyn will later say of learning that Gifford was her father, "The things that shocked me most when I was older were finding out when I was 15, that I was an illegitimate child, and finding out when I was 16 and sort of pushed into marriage, about the facts of life."

It seems that autumn was a nostalgic time for Norma Jeane and she attends a baby shower for the former Nell Atkinson. She confesses that she "had a nice time."

By Jim's own account she was an excellent wife. "She was a wonderful housekeeper and didn't have a lazy bone in her body. She darned socks and sewed on missing buttons like a veteran housewife. She banged ears a lot with the neighbors, but she never took out so much time that our apartment didn't look like a professional cleaning crew had just gone through it."

Jim will also say that she hated to be teased and he had to be careful when teasing her not to carry it too far. Presumably she got enough teasing at school to last her a lifetime. It should be noted that her other two husbands Joe DiMaggio and Arthur Miller had laconic and somber personalities that would most likely produce no teasing toward her. Yet, those who knew her maintain that she had a wicked sense of humor and loved to laugh.

In December Jim and Norma Jeane moved into the Dougherty home at 14747 Archwood St, Van Nuys, CA, until the home sold. This was close to the home where Norma Jeane had lived with Grace and Doc Goddard at the end of 1941. Jim continued to work at Lockheed where he works with his friend and fellow co-worker Robert Mitchum.

In 1954, while filming *River of No Return*, Mitchum told Marilyn that "he had heard all about her long before she was in the movies. He explained that he had worked next to a rugged, red-headed guy in an aviation plant. 'This guy,' said Mitchum, 'was always telling me about the beautiful blonde doll he was married to. How he couldn't wait to finish work to get home to her. Showed me and the other guy's snapshots of her. Good lookin chick, I never knew it was you until I read his article. And here I am playing hero to my former pal's ex-wife. That's one for the Small World Department."

In 1961 Mitchum remembers the teenage Marilyn to Earl Wilson. "I really think she is a great dame. I've known her since she was 15....Her first husband, Jim Dougherty, was my partner at Lockheed when we were sharper operators. He used to carry a picture of her around when she was 15 or 16. He would hold up the picture and say, 'This is my old lady. That's a picture of her waiting at home for me." Bob said then she was quite a model, judging by the picture which he still remembered. 'First time I met her was at a Lockheed dance. Frank Sinatra was singing at the Palladium, probably with the Dorsey Orchestra.' 'Was she already a sexpot?' 'I was too beat to even think about girls.'"

On February 16, 1943 Norma Jeane wrote a letter to Grace resuming the idea of making contact with Stanley Gifford. It seems that finding out about her father gave her a purpose to look forward to. Jim remembers her placing a phone call to Gifford, who promptly hung up on her. Gifford ran the Red Rock Dairy in Hemet, CA. Norma Jeane was devastated by this callous response. Yet, she would make several attempts to contact him in the coming years, each time as unsuccessful as the last. This wound in her psyche would never heal and would become part of the impetus that would drive her indefatigable ambition. She was determined to make him take notice of her. The cruel irony is that while she gained the attention of the world, her father never acknowledged her existence, even after her death.

Natasha Lytess told Ezra Goodman that she and Marilyn made another attempt to see her father. "Monroe and she drove out to a Southern California community because Monroe wanted to try to see her father, whom she had never met. 'We went to this farm. Marilyn tried to contact him from the area. She called him three times and finally got through to him. He refused to see her. His voice sounded cold and cruel. He said, 'I have a family and children.' He took her phone number and said he'd contact her in Los Angeles and never did.' Lytess said Monroe had known about her father for a long time and had finally worked up the courage to try to see him. 'Marilyn once told me that Grace McKee Goddard had told her that her father wanted to adopt Marilyn when she was a year or two old, but that Marilyn's mother didn't let him because she hated him so. Grace also told Marilyn that she looks a lot like her father."

After the home sold, Jim and Norma Jeane live on Bessemer Street, Van Nuys, CA. It is not long after this that Jim joins the Merchant Marines and leaves for basic training in San Diego. Norma Jeane is left alone in their little bungalow, but Jim buys her a collie, that she named Muggsy, to keep her company. Norma Jeane and Aunt Ana purchase a War Bond on April 23, in the amount of $25.00.

Jim returns from basic training and by that fall he is assigned to the Maritime Service Training Base on Catalina Island. He will teach ocean safety to the recruits there. The Dougherty's make the move to Catalina with their dog Muggsy in tow. Catalina had changed since Norma Jeane was there as a child. Military boats now bobbed in the water at the piers in the harbor where the yachts of the rich and famous once were moored, and twin antiaircraft guns had been mounted in front of the famous Avalon Casino ballroom for defensive purposes.

Sfc Robert Lightfoot was attending the cooks and bakers school for the US Maritime

Service while Norma Jeane and Jim lived on Catalina, and recalls seeing Norma Jeane on the island. "'When Miss Mmmm visited her husband she was always accompanied by a huge shepherd dog. She was the main reason I got my first pair of eyeglasses fitted. When I'd glance at Miss Monroe my eyes just didn't seem to focus properly.' The actress usually wore shorts and a halter on her visits."

Jim and Norma Jeane rented the second floor of a wooden framed building on the corner of Metropole and Beacon, overlooking Avalon Harbor. She managed to keep herself occupied. Along with keeping her apartment and dog well groomed, she lifted weights, and played with neighborhood children. She had made a couple of girlfriends, the wife of the master-at-arms of the Maritime Service cafeteria, Mrs. Lynn White and a neighbor, Mrs. Jim Patton.

Jim hosted poker parties at their apartment, and Norma Jeane greeted the guest and served sandwiches and then retired to her bedroom to read or listen to the radio. She and Jim spent weekends at beach luaus. The Avalon Theater hosted boxing matches every Friday evening and the USO also used the Theater to host its shows. When not being used as a classroom for Maritime Service Men, the Avalon Casino hosted dances on special occasions in the famous circular ballroom. Every Saturday there was a street dance in Avalon where servicemen and locals danced to the music of the Maritime Service Band. Norma Jeane and Jim took advantage of the dances and legend has it that she was a living doll when she dressed up for these events.

Young Norma Jeane is nothing less than a sensation on Catalina. Her choice of revealing outfits coupled with her amazing figure never cease to draw admiring glances and comments from the men stationed there, much to Jim's chagrin. Marilyn spends a good portion of her time walking Muggsy around Avalon. It is while walking her dog that Norma Jeane finds that the men on the base now have an excuse to come close and talk to her. Instead of creating a barrier between his wife and the men, he has unwittingly given them a reason to boldly approach her in the guise of being interested in her dog. It is impossible for her to keep her blossoming sexuality at bay, for she is a vision here on Catalina. She doesn't yet understand the power she has and for the moment she is at a loss to explain the commotion she creates while walking Muggsy down the street. She is both apprehensive and intoxicated by her power over men. She is an apprentice goddess refining her craft.

Norma Jeane corresponds with her half-sister Berniece. On the 12th of February she mentions living on Catalina Island with Jim and also tells Berniece a little history behind the island and of a trip she took with her mother there when she was a little girl. "I don't know if you have ever heard of Catalina Island, being from the East, but it was (in peace time) a very beautiful summer resort. It's an island out her all by itself, about 30 miles from L. A. Harbor. My mother brought me over for the summer when I was about seven years old. I remember going to the Casino to a dance with her, of course I didn't dance, but she let me sit on the side and watch, and I remember it was way after my bedtime too. But anyway, what I'm getting at is that at Christmas time, the Maritime Service held a big dance at the same Casino and Jimmie and I went. It was the funniest feeling to be dancing on that same floor ten years later, I mean being old enough and everything. Oh it's hard to explain the feeling I had."

During the time she spent on the channel isle, she becomes nothing less than the embodiment of Botticelli's Venus, emerging a full grown woman from the frothy sea off Catalina Island. And it takes just a light breeze of fate to bring our Aphrodite back to the mainland and closer to finding her dual purpose, which will be to arouse passion and to inspire contemplation by her beauty. It will be a spring like no other when our heroine will softly tread on her path to immortality. She arrived in Avalon a girl and she will leave a full bodied woman.

In the March of 1944 Norma Jeane moves in with Jim's mother, Ethel Dougherty, at their new home at 5354 Hermitage St., North Hollywood, when Jim is transferred to a new post in Southeast Asia.

Norma Jeane writes a letter to Janice Wright on April 13. She was a friend who lives in Sandy, Utah. Norma Jeane complains to her about her loneliness while Jim is away in the service.

Jim's mother, Ethel, gets Norma Jeane a job at Radioplane Company, Metropolitan Airport, Burbank California. Norma Jeane started working on April 18, 1944, and her occupation was as an inspector of parachutes, and she started at a salary of .70 cents an hour. She lists her nearest living relative as Gladys Pearl Baker, San Francisco. Her Social Security number is 563-32-0764. Her phone number is listed as sunset 1-8814. Her clock number is 302-B. She lists her address as 5354 Hermitage Street.

Norma Jeane begins her work career as the most famous "Rosie the Riveter," of them all. She is good at her job and receives a raise on May 22, to .75 cents an hour. By June 10th, she was transferred to Doper-Brush, meaning she applied the dope, a kind of glue/sealant to the fuselages. This job was less tedious than packing and inspecting parachutes. It seems she didn't have her mother's ability to withstand a repetitive and monotonous job, but one thing was now similar, the smell. Marilyn would comment to Ben Hecht that the RKO sign made her remember her mother bringing her to work with her as a film cutter and how the small office she worked in smelled of glue. It is possibly this early association with an unpleasant smell will contribute to her habit of literally bathing in perfume when she is a star.

Ethel Dougherty tried to tell her that the fumes would ruin her beautiful hair. Ethel arranged a transfer for Norma Jeane and David Conover will photograph her working on helping to assemble Radioplane OQ-3 Target Drones, not in the Dope room.

When she posed for photographer Douglas Kirkland in November of 1961, Marilyn will tell him how she used to frequent the movies when she worked on the assembly line. She would go and sit in the back row and lose herself in the glamour onscreen and it helped pass the time while Jim was away.

Norma Jeane receives a telegram from her husband the day before her birthday on June 1st it read, "Darling on your birthday, I send you a whole world of love."

On June 15, 1944 Norma Jeane was also elected the first "Queen of Radioplane." The girl who sold the most tickets for the first company picnic would be named "Queen." The picnic was held at Balboa Park in San Diego, California. Norma Jeane didn't even bother selling any tickets. To her surprise, the men in her department sold the tickets for her and she was named "Queen of Radioplane." She was so happy, she burst into tears. There is a surviving photograph of Marilyn at that company picnic. She is seated on the grass with fellow workers, Bernadette Walsh, Muriel Sundom, Marg Dolan, and an unidentified woman. Norma Jeane looks every bit the Queen. *The Radio Static* company newsletter gives Norma Jeane a paragraph concerning her participation in an effort to increase War Bond sales. The unexpected support from the men would happen again to her in a few years as she begins her bid for stardom. She will have one thing in her favor as she battles the studio heads, the support from the men in the Korean War. She will never fail to give them homage in the coming years for the debt she felt to them.

Also on June 15th she writes Grace a letter. In it she mentions her time at Radioplane. "I am working 10 hrs. a day at Radioplane Co., at Metropolitan Airport…the work isn't easy at all for I am on my feet all day and walking quite a bit. I was all set to get a Civil Service Job with the army, all my papers filled out and everything set to go, and then I found out I would be working with ALL army fellows. I was over there one day, there are just too many wolves to be working with, there are enough of those at Radioplane Co. without a whole army full of them. The Personnel Officer said that he would hire me but that he wouldn't advise it for my own sake. So I'm back at Radioplane Co. and am pretty content.

She gets another raise on August 21 and is now making .80 cents an hour. *The Radio Static* company newsletter, August 31, 1944, mentions Norma Jeane and her award for making a useful suggestion about the operation of the machinery. She was awarded a gold button and a certificate for excellence on the job. Along with her button she was given a $50.00 War Bond. Her good fortune only engendered resentment for her among the women she worked with. This will provide Norma Jeane motivation to pursue her modeling career when it presented itself at the first of next year.

In October Norma Jeane takes her first trip across the country when she visits her sister, Berniece, in Detroit where she lives with her husband, Paris and daughter, Mona Rae. While there they visit the Minor's Bird Sanctuary in Kingsville, Ontario, Canada. This is the first time Norma Jeane has left the country, and the first of two visits she will make to Canada. During the trip East, Norma Jeane also visits Doc and Grace Goddard in Chicago, Illinois where Grace worked at a film lab. She sends Berniece a postcard to thank them for the visit on October 28. Norma Jeane also sends a postcard from Chicago to her friend, Catherine "Cathy" Staub, from Oceanside, California. In December Norma Jeane writes a letter to Grace and mentions the visit to Chicago and the film lab where she worked. Jim will remark of her trip, "She took every cent out of the account when she went to visit the Goddard's."

During Christmas Jim sends her $100 to get a coat. Not only did she spend the $100, but she took another $200 out to buy a coat. This was not appreciated by Jim.

# Chapter Five
# A Big Slice of Blonde Cheesecake

"Her sexuality...the lever by which she might move the world."
--Maurice Zolotow

Norma Jeane got a raise at her job on January 15th. She is now making .85 cents an hour. She uses some of her new found money to buy her mother's beloved Franklin Grand Piano from Ana Lower for $10.00, on February 10th. In 1999, pop-singer Mariah Carey would buy the piano for $662,500, at the Christie's Auction of Marilyn's personal belongings.

Jim comes home on his first leave after nearly a year's absence. Norma Jeane gives her marriage one last try when her husband returns. She looks radiant and happy in a photograph taken during the time.

In early March Norma Jeane writes a letter to Berniece. She tells her of a week-long vacation she and "Jimmie" spent in Big Bear Lake, CA, at the Ember Lodge. According to Jim they enjoyed their time at the mountain resort. "There was snow on the ground and I remember there was one couple who tried to teach us how to ski. Once I made a jump and went in head first and Marilyn thought I was hurt and got hysterical trying to dig me out again. One night there she ordered a Tom Collins, and then another one. It was the first time I'd seen her drink at all, and I didn't like it. I kept swallowing her drinks to keep them away from her, and the only result was that I had too many. Then one night I got into a blackjack game with some college girls who were there, and Marilyn gave me the big old green eye and went upstairs. When I went up later she was in bed and crying. And then we had another argument about having children. She was still only lukewarm toward the idea." Upon returning to Los Angeles Jim soon returns to duty and Norma Jeane goes back to her uneventful life at Radioplane.

In the spring of 1945 Norma Jeane's modeling career was jump-started when a photographer, David Conover, on a morale boosting "Rosie the Riveter" assignment for the Army, discovered Norma Jeane at her job. Capt. Ronald Reagan of the U.S. Army's 1st Motion Picture Unit assigned Conover to take still pictures of women in war work. The war with Japan was still raging on with no end in sight and cheesecake was still in high demand. The stills photographer, Conover, along with men in the moving picture division, headed to Radioplane Corp., in Van Nuys, Calif., owned by Reagan's friend and fellow actor, Reginald Denny. The Army maintained a photographic headquarters at the Hal Roach Studios. Norma Jeane had just resumed working upon returning from her trip back East. When the photographers discovered her they exclaimed, "Where have you been?" They encouraged her to come outside for a picture taking session, but she refused so as not to inflame the situation with the other ladies. She told them, "Can't. The other ladies here in the dope room will give me trouble if I stop doing what I'm doing and go out with you." They got special permission for her to go outside with them. She remembers they posed her "rolling ships." Conover, who was taking the stills that day photographed her, while still inside, helping to assemble the Radioplane OQ-3 Target Drone, which was used for military gunnery practice. Despite her quote she had not worked in the Dope Room since her transfer. She was wearing a green, short sleeved blouse with tweed pants. He photographs her first in this green blouse. She looks a little nervous in these photos, smiling broadly and squinting into the sun. He gives her a camera for a prop in order to occupy her hands and try to relax her. Her hair hangs in thick brown ringlets that indicate she put much thought into her looks before coming to work. Realizing that the blouse was doing nothing for her he asked her if she has a sweater and she runs to put it on, adding another swipe of crimson lipstick on her full lips. The transformation from little girl to woman is remarkable. When she has on the red sweater that hugs her breasts, she radiates an immediate erotic wave of energy that the camera picks up. Her skin is flawless and photographs like pink alabaster. Conover takes a few shots from below, to make her breasts look larger. He will realize after developing the film that her face does not photograph well from that angle. He does manage to take one fabulous image. It is a classic pin up pose of her looking over her left shoulder. The red sweater provides the color the shot needed and also complements her red smiling lips. In this photograph she gets everything right. Her smile is perfection, as is the positioning of her head and body; it all comes together in that one magnificent image. It is as if she instinctively knows she needs just one photograph to come from this sitting that will be the foundation upon which she will build her career. She will learn to manage her smile in the coming months. Although, she had much to learn about positioning herself to take advantage of the light as it highlights the planes of her face, and how to form expressions that will achieve the maximum effect, she has proved that she is already superb. It is a seminal moment for Norma Jeane. With this one frame of film she will start her journey into history. This unsure girl in the green blouse has just morphed into a siren in red, and she has just been discovered, and will in time, and with much hard work, become the most photographed woman in the world.

 Conover had the film developed and in a couple of weeks shows the photographs to Norma Jeane at her home. She is once again living with her Aunt Ana Lower in West Los Angeles, but in a private apartment attached to the main house. She will say of this time in a later interview, "I went back to live with Aunt Ana. I always felt that I had a home with her. She made me feel that way."

 Although, she is not yet a refined beauty, there is an unmistakable quality in her portraits that hints at the fame that is to come. There is no reason that she should have photographed so well and every reason to believe that she would only improve with time and hard work. Norma Jeane had that rare gift, the camera not only adored her, but her images had a flesh-like quality that made her approachable to the viewer. This created an instant familiarity. It is this quality that people will respond to. It is important to remember that this image was first focused at men, but before long, the world itself would come to adore her. Billy Wilder said of her, "The day a photographer took a picture of her, she was a genius." She is a curious student of photography and what makes a great image. It will not be too long before she will be an expert at transmitting her image to a piece of film, and in effect, to the world.

 We can imagine our tender heroine embarking on her fabled quest armed with just her honeyed smile. F. Scott Fitzgerald must have had a premonition of such a moment when he wrote these lines in, *Tender is the Night*. "She smiled at him, making sure that the smile gathered up everything inside her and directed it toward him, making him a profound promise of herself for so little, for the beat of a response, the assurance of a complimentary vibration in him." Not only does the photographer pick up on the promise behind her smile, but men who see her photographs will start to respond to it. Before he develops his film, Conover will feel a gut response to this young model that will tell him, in no uncertain terms, "this girl has it."

"When David Conover passed by where I was at work, he said, 'You're a real morale booster. I'm going to take your picture for the boys in the Army to keep their morale high.' First he took pictures of me in my overalls. When he discovered I had a sweater in my locker, he asked if I would mind wearing it for more pictures. 'I want to show the boys what you really look like,' he said. Those pictures he took of me were the first that ever appeared in publication. They were used in Army camp newspapers, including *Yank* and *Stars and Stripes*." In these first images she did not pose in her beloved white suspender shorts. She only posed in the green blouse and the red sweater. She will tell Florabel Muir in a 1952 interview, "'I wasn't exactly a fool,' she says now. 'I was aware that I was attractive to men. The fellows used to whistle at me and one time the foreman moved me behind a partition so I wouldn't distract the men near me.'" Marilyn will say of sweaters in the future, "Sweaters are like life. You get nothing out of a sweater that you don't put into it."

A curious myth surrounds Norma Jeane's appearance on the August 2, 1945 edition of *Yank* magazine. In truth she never appeared in the Conover photos on or in *Yank* magazine. In a quote from *War Time Press*, "There have been many questions about an August 2, 1945 issue with Marilyn Monroe on the cover and an article about "Women in Industry" with her being pictured in it also. This issue with her was never printed. This hoax has been perpetrated by several Internet websites that cannot produce the claimed issue. Although, the "Women in Industry" was written, it appears in the December 22, 1944 issue without a picture of Marilyn Monroe or Norma Jeane Dougherty." There was no August 2$^{nd}$ edition. The August 3, 1945 edition of *Yank* featured a photo on the cover of a Carrier Catapult framed with its 5 inch guns. And nowhere inside is an article about women in industry or a picture of Norma Jeane.

Norma Jeane makes the reckless decision to concentrate full time on her modeling career. She quits the security of her job at the Radioplane Co. on March 15, 1945. Her records at the company indicate that she was an above average employee and such impulsiveness didn't sit well with Jim's mother.

Jim was soon relegated to the periphery of Norma Jean's life and each visit home he sensed a widening gulf between them. He tries at first to go along with her modeling career, but before long he makes sure she knows that his wife will be a full time homemaker and mother.

Buoyed by the experience with Conover it didn't take long for Norma Jeane to find work and she poses for Lee Bush of the Schwartz Studio in Los Angeles and signs a model release on May 18, 1945. This was her earliest known modeling assignment. She smiled beneath a mass of curly brown hair in the photo at the beach. She wore her own two-piece Catalina swimsuit with a hand painted seagull motif on the bottoms while posing. She will wear this swimsuit in numerous other photographs as a model.

Norma Jeane writes to Grace on June 4th and tells her about being approached while at work to do some modeling by David Conover. "The first thing I knew the photographer had me out there taking pictures of me. They all asked me 'where the H___ I had been hiding?' They took a lot of moving pictures of me, and some of them asked for dates (naturally I refused.) After they finished with some of the pictures an army corporal by the name of David Conover told me he would be interested in getting some color still shots of me. He used to have a studio on 'the Strip' on Sunset Boulevard. He said he would make arrangements with the plant supervisor if I would agree, so I said okay. He told me what to wear, what shade of lipstick, etc., so the next couple of weeks I posed for him at different times. He said all the pictures came out perfect. Also, he said, I should by all means go into the modeling profession, that I photographed very well and that he wants to take a lot more. Also, he said he had a lot of contracts he wanted me to look into…He is awfully nice and is married and is strictly business, which is the way I like it."

David Conover took a two week furlough on July 4, 1945, granted by the Captain of the 1st Motion Picture Division Unit, to go on an extended modeling shoot with Norma Jeane through the Mohave Desert, Mount Whitney, Death Valley and back through Hemet, California. It is here that we first become acquainted with her white suspender shorts. Marilyn, who referred to them as her "overalls," will later utter this bon mote about them, "putting a girl in overalls is like having her work in tights—if a girl knows how to wear overalls." In one of the sexiest images he has her posing with ski poles dressed in her red sweater and white suspender shorts. The image has movement because of the play of her jutting breast and the confines of her suspender shorts. Yet, in contrast to the blatant sexuality, her face is the face of a modest girl; sweet, innocent and detached from what her body was offering. In a relatively short amount of time she is learning the skills of a good model. In 5 more months Norma Jeane will be escorted on a similar journey through the West and by a much greater photographer, Andre de Dienes. But for now she is content with the things an average photographer could teach her.

Conover will be transferred shortly, but before he goes he shows the photographs of Norma Jeane to his friend, photographer Potter Hueth, whose studio was at Pico Boulevard and Fairfax. She modeled for Hueth, posing at his studio several nights a week. He shared the photos with Emmeline Snively of the Blue Book Modeling Agency. An appointment to meet the lovely young model was quickly set in motion.

Despite the Potsdam Declaration on July 26, which threatened "prompt and utter destruction," Japan ignored the threat and kept to their rigid agenda of war. An atomic bomb, Little Boy, was dropped on the city of Hiroshima on August 6th, followed by Fat Man, an atomic bomb on the city of Nagasaki on August 9th. The world entered the Atomic Age and nothing was ever to be the same. Japan would surrender on August 15 and officially signed the Instrument of Surrender on September 2nd. That Norma Jeane began her career at the explosive end of such a horrific war was a foreshadowing of things to come, for she would become the most famous pinup of the Atomic Age, and would forever change Hollywood's notion of a sex symbol. She would annilate any competition, past or present, and the lingering effect of her beauty would become the touchstone for Hollywood glamour that all actresses will be measured against.

On August 2$^{nd}$, 1945, Potter Hueth accompanies Norma Jeane on her interview with Emmeline Snively at the Blue Book Model Agency, which was located at the iconic Ambassador Hotel on Sunset Blvd.

In a 1943 article Miss Snively condenses the 5 essential things needed to be a good model. "1. A good disposition, for she will have to work with temperamental people under difficult circumstances. 2. Good health, because it will be reflected in a clear skin, sparkling eyes and hair that looks alive. 3. A structurally good face. Perfect teeth and large eyes are priceless assets. 4. A reasonably good figure, preferably between 5 feet, 2 inches, and 5 feet, 7 inches. 5. Adequate training in makeup, hair styling, posing and taking camera direction." Beauty, interestingly enough, was not listed in Miss Snively's qualifications.

Miss Snively's first impression of Norma Jeane was, "She was a round faced girl with an astonishing bust which made her size 12 dress look too small. I saw this cute girl and said, 'quick, give me your picture. I think I can get you some modeling jobs.' Marilyn had a wiggly way of walking and the name Norma Jeane Dougherty. My records show her qualifications--size 12, height 5'6", 36 bust, 24 waist, 34 hips. Blue eyes and blonde hair.

Her hair was a dirty blonde. She put down on her application that she 'did a little singing.' She wasn't much interested in clothes. Usually our girls furnish their own wardrobes, but hers was very limited. She had on white dress with a green yoke, which on her looked terrific, though models usually don't choose white clothes. It accentuated her bust and brought attention to her figure. It was tight across the front. She also had a teal blue suit, man-tailored, that didn't do a thing for her. She wore it for some airline ads for which she got $25."

Miss Snively confided to Maurice Zolotow about the young girl who showed up in her office. "When ushered into Miss Snively's office, Norma Jeane started to sit down after the agent greeted her, but Miss Snively said, 'My dear, please walk to the door and back.' Norma Jeane didn't walk well—too unevenly. The hair was bad. A 'California blonde'—light on top and dark underneath. Needed a good coiffure. Should cut it short and bleach it. But the smile was friendly, the legs marvelous, the bosom excellent, and there was a general air of sweetness about her. 'Potter Hueth's been saying the nicest things about you,' Miss Snively said. 'I can see how true they are. Do you want to be a model?' Norma Jeane knew how to be shy and humble when she had to. 'I don't know,' she said. 'I thought I could be one and then—I mean, s-seeing all those pictures of the models, I don't know if I'm beautiful enough. But if you would g-give me a chance, I'd like to try.' 'Try—that's the spirit, honey. If you've got the will power to work hard, you've got to be a success, because you've got one thing, honey, and it's one of the rarest gifts in this world, and that's charm, charm's what you've got.'"

Miss Snively's first impressions of Norma Jeane had nothing to do with her innate sexiness. "Actually, Marilyn was so naïve, so sweet, and so eager to succeed that my heart went out to her at once…I asked Marilyn about her background and she confessed (again shyly) 'I sing a little. That's all.' She had no ambition to become an actress, unless, of course, it was a secret desire. She did have a pleasant personality, what we call an All-American girl kind of personality—cute, wholesome and respectable. There was no sultry sexiness about her except that her clothes were a little too tight across the chest. That sex buildup was to come much later, although I did realize immediately that Marilyn would never do as a fashion model. Most fashion models are tall, sophisticated-looking and slim-chested. Marilyn was none of these. The first day Marilyn attended classes, I knew she would do alright, because she aroused the good nature in people. She would walk in and in her cute, high voice and say 'Hello everybody.'' Everyone would answer, 'Hello.' There was something arresting and sincere about the girl's personality. When I introduced her to a photographer, she would look him straight in the eye and cling to his every word. She was sincerely eager. She made everyone she talked to feel as if he were the only guy in the world. She did this naturally without design or premeditation…I knew at once that Marilyn was a fair and honest and very fine girl, and I decided to get her a much work as I possibly could. I sent her out to audition for some *Montgomery Ward* catalogue work. She didn't make the grade, but she wasn't discouraged. 'Maybe I'll do better next time,' That's what she said, and those words really typified her spirit. It was upbeat all the way…Marilyn had no one. Only herself. I guess it was because of this that I took a strong interest in the girl. I concentrated on her. She gobbled up every bit of instruction. She was wonderful on had positions, body positions, and simply great when it came to make-up. But I just couldn't do anything with her fashion modeling, probably because of her cute figure and her walk…In 1946, however, Marilyn and I decided to do the best with what she had. Her two great photogenic virtues back then were her 'cutie' figure and her face."

In an interview in 1954 Miss Snively summed up meeting Norma Jeane a little differently. "She first came into my office in August of 1945.' Miss Snively said. 'A photographer who had been doing some shots of her in the aircraft plant where she worked brought her in. Right away I was crazy about her and thought she had great possibilities. She was so sweet and fresh and had wonderful blue eyes and a gorgeous figure. She needed training, though. I paid for her course and she paid me back later. She had only one dress, a white think with a horrid orange and green yoke. But on her it looked good. First thing we tried to do was change that horrible walk. That wiggle wasn't good for fashion models, but it was Marilyn and we couldn't change it. I'm glad now, of course.'"

Despite her flaws, Miss Snively had a witch's intuition about what made a good model and she shrewdly observed Norma Jeane had possibilities. She offered her a three month long modeling course at the agency and Norma Jeane was touched by this affirmation of her talent as a model and agreed.  Norma Jeane was told that she could work out the $100 tuition for the modeling course. She took fashion modeling classes taught by Gavin Beardsley, make-up and grooming classes with Maria Smith, and artistic posing classes taught by Miss Snively. Miss Snively suggested that Norma Jeane specialize in pin-up work because she was "bosomy in bathing suits," and not well suited for fashion work. Norma Jeane would have a shaky beginning at the Blue Book. She will have to retrain herself to lower her smile and angle her head in order to become more photogenic. Once learned, these lessons will serve her well and she will be known as a superb model. In the future she will be known for her tremulous smile, as she consciously arranges her lips into pleasing configurations. It will be her trademark and a rudimentary starting point for all who will imitate her.

A picture of her in her red sweater taken by David Conover will grace the pages of *The Models Bluebook 1945*.

In a newspaper article in 1954, Miss Snively again tells her first impressions of Marilyn. "When Marilyn first came to see me in 1945, she had a wiggly way of walking and the name Norma Jeane Dougherty. My Records show her qualification—size 12, height 5'6", 36 bust, 24 waist, 34 hips. She had one white dress with a green yoke which accentuated her bust and brought attention to her figure. It was tight across the front. Her face was too round and her hair was so frizzy it couldn't be managed. Her nose was too long and her smile cast shadows, besides this she smiled too high and it made deep lines around her nose."

Ah, her nose and her smile. Miss Snively remembers that, "New York editors complained that Marilyn's nose was too long, that her smile cast shadows. She smiled too high, that's what was wrong, and it made deep lines around her nose. We taught her how to bring her smile down and show her lowers." "New York picture agents weren't too sold on her. Magazine art directors pointed out her bad angels. Nevertheless, the photographers themselves, from rank amateur to famous professional were confident of her national appeal. They were sold on her vibrant personality, coloring, and on her clean scrubbed 'American Girl' looks."

Photographer Earl Leaf quotes Miss Snively on Norma Jeane's smile, "She smiled too high, that's what was wrong, and it made deep furrows around her nose. We taught her how to smile down and talk or laugh with her lower jaw. Compare the pictures of her smiling today with the old ones and see the difference."

Miss Snively would write, "Studio photographers did wonders with Marilyn's nose. When publicity stills first came out on my ex-student, I was sure that a little plastic surgery had been done on her nose. It seemed to photograph smaller than it used to. Photographers who had shot Marilyn said the same thing. Their photographs of her in 1945 had been rejected by magazines because 'Marilyn's nose was too large and her smile too high.' By smiling too deeply, Marilyn was accentuating the lines around her nose, thus highlighting what was not a very good nose--too broad and too curvy. I've made inquiries, and the truth is that Marilyn still has the nose she was born with. She's not happy with it and has talked from time to time about altering it. But as yet she's done nothing about it. Cameramen at the studio say it gives them no trouble since Marilyn has learned how to bring her smile down and concentrate on her lower lip. I'm glad she's mastered this trick because I was the first one who suggested she do exactly that. Nowadays when Marilyn poses for photographers the accent is usually on her figure, not her nose. But it wouldn't surprise me if she submitted to plastic surgery."

Marilyn's later photographs indicate more than makeup made the subtle changes in the shape of her nose. It appears that the bridge of her nose was narrowed and straightened and the tip of her nose refined. In November of 1950 Johnny Hyde paid for Marilyn to have surgery to strengthen her chin by Dr. Michael Gurdin. His partner, Dr. Pangman, admitted to having performed the rhinoplasty on the tip of her nose, creating a more refined look.

Despite all this criticism on her photographic appeal, it is as if Norma Jeane is guided by some unwavering narcissistic notion that someday she will be great. She made good use of her time by taking home the black and white shots and the discarded color ones. She studied them for hours, trying to learn from the mistakes she made. This is the first reported evidence of her drive and determination to be successful. Few models will study themselves and use their negative photos to actually improve their skills as a model. Norma Jeane was fearless when it came to bettering herself. Later, her publicity photos will owe a debt to all the hours she poured over these early images of herself. As a result of her diligence she will often control the shoot by posing herself so that every shot will become useable.

Not only will New York advertisers not see her potential, but when Marilyn is a major star columnist Sheilah Graham, looking back on her early modeling photographs, will be shocked by how she came across. "And now I know why Marilyn Monroe always smiles in her photographs. I've just seen some old serious poses of her in Joe Franklin and Laurie Palmer's, *Marilyn Monroe Story*, and the glamour doctrine doesn't even look pretty in them. Look at any star's photographs before her or she became important and you sometimes wonder how they became stars. Even Marilyn's famous figger didn't photograph as good then as it does now."

Her dark curly hair does nothing for her and her still untrained smile causes deep shadows between her lips and nose as she smiles with an unopened mouth, and yet photographers are intrigued enough to want to use her. Miss Snively remembers, "Some of her first pictures with me were taken on location. Her hair was so frizzy that the photographer covered it with a bathing cap. The bathing suit pictures were sold to some Canadian magazines."

Her first job as a model for the Blue Book Agency was for Larry Kronquist who was shooting publicity shots for the interior of a new Douglas Aircraft at American Airlines. Kronquist met Norma Jeane at the Ambassador Gardens to approve her for the shoot. This would lead to Norma Jeane's first appearance on the cover of a magazine on January 1946. Miss Snively remembers that, "Kronquist always meant to use her outdoors with a surf board to show off her healthy 'good looks,' but just never got around to it."

Photographer Paul Parry remembers his first introduction to Marilyn. "'I was sitting in my office chinning with a couple of other fellows one day when this girl--her name was Norma Jeane Dougherty then--came in and asked if I thought she could be a model. I'll never forget it, because she was wearing a pink sweater--and the other two fellows just fell right off their chairs. Could she!' Her first check for modeling for Parry was a huge sum at the time, $15, and Marilyn was sure she was on the road to riches. However, lovely as she was, modeling was a hard grind. One advertising manager, as a matter of fact, called Parry down for using her in a fashion layout, contending that she would never amount to anything as a fashion model."

Parry will go on to photograph Marilyn for a calendar top that would be used in 1953. She posed in a cowboy hat, kerchief and was holding a bottle of Mission Orange Drink, "the California Sunshine Flavor." The calendar wouldn't be released until 1953 and her name was prominently displayed by her face, as she bore no resemblance to her new persona. Maybe Mission Beverages was trying to cash in on the Marilyn Monroe calendar racket that had taken the country by storm.

Norma Jeane posed for John Randolph, a Powers model and actor who had turned to photography. Miss Snively says he "was one of the first color cover photographers of note to use Marilyn. His photo taken during the winter of 1945, shows her with her dark, curly hair. Later on as she improved and her hair was changed, John tried some outdoor action ideas again, in color of course." He captures the quintessential California girl, albeit a brunette, in an early session with Norma Jeane who wore a dark two piece swimsuit. The photo is erroneously credited to Bruno Bernard in several of his books.

Potter Hueth and Bob Farr worked together to shoot covers on speculation. This is when the photographer doesn't pay a fee to the model and she furnishes her own clothes or costume and time. If the photos sell, the model receives a percentage of the sale. They posed the inexperienced model in country settings as the suggestive farmer's daughter. They also took photos of her with a Dalmatian and another with a Great Dane. In these images she is improving and is starting to appear more comfortable being photographed. Her face is relaxed and the positioning of her body is getting more graceful. The Great Dane photo was actually picked up and used as a calendar top called the Dame and the Dane. Yet despite Hueth and Farr's continued confidence in Norma Jeane's all-American, healthy good looks, the magazine editors in New York were still reluctant to use her.

While on location at a turkey farm for the "farmer's daughter" shoot, Marilyn loses her engagement ring. She is quite heartbroken back home as the evening progresses. Norma Jeane and Jim go back to the turkey farm the next day and retrace her steps. Against impossible odds, she finds her ring.

It is during this time that Norma Jeane totals their little Ford V-8 car. "I guess I must have been dreaming again because I drove head-on into a street car. You should see our poor car. It's completely demolished…All I have is a bump on the head. I guess it's a miracle that I'm alive."

Norma Jeane appears in her first screen-test for the Blue Book Modeling Agency on September 2, 1945. Norma Jeane offers the camera her awkward beginning skills as a model and the camera gives her back in return, a stunning image of her potential impact hidden in a mass of curly brown hair. She wears her Catalina two-piece with the seagull motif in this test and also her red sweater.

Beginning on September 3, 1945 Norma Jeane worked as a hostess for 10 days at the Pan Pacific Auditorium for the Industry on Parade Show, modeling for the Holga Steel Company. Norma Jeane made $10 a day and used this money to pay off her tuition to Miss Snively, and in doing so, impressed Miss Snively with her determination and ambition. This was much more than just a show about office equipment, since World War II had begun, the labor force in America had been called on to ramp up production of War goods, and to stay on the job until victory was won. This Industry on Parade was kicked-off by the first postwar Labor Day Parade since Pearl Harbor and people were invigorated, having just come off the victory of wars in both Europe and Japan. The American labor force was ready to flex its postwar muscles. There was a massive CIO organized parade at 2:30pm, leading up to the Industry on Parade Program at the Pan Pacific Auditorium. The Show was "a preview of "things to come" in the world of industrial achievements." There were more than 1950 exhibitions showcasing products and advancements for the housewife as well as the businessman in postwar America. On September 8th, there was a beauty contest to choose Miss Industry of 1945. The contestants were made up of the demonstrators from the various booths. Whether or not Norma Jeane took part in this competition is not known. It is known that if she did, she did not win. Miss Snively did not enter her in beauty contests because she was married. Possibly, the fact that she was once Queen of Radio Plane buoyed her confidence enough to compete, with or without Miss Snively's approval.

Interestingly enough in with the surviving photos showing a sweet-faced, wholesome girl standing in the Holga Steel Co. booth in her white dress with the green yoke, she seems a bit self-conscious. Then there are a couple of photographs showing her in a strapless evening gown, posing provocatively by a filing cabinet, possibly what she wore if she competed in the beauty contest. She is aware of the camera and her body as she poses, tilting her head for the best effect. There is a distinct change in her demeanor in the photos at the Holga booth. She started out sweet and demure and towards the end of the ten days we see she is relying on her innate sexuality to attract businessmen to her booth. What she lacked in competition skills, she more than makes up with her child-like eroticism, and men are quick to notice. If she had competed the next year, she would have been a shoe-in, as the judges were well acquainted with her as a model. They were Earl Moran, calendar artist, and Paul Parry and Larry Kronquist, both cover girl and fashion photographers, and all will have worked with Norma Jeane.

    Miss Snively remembers her at the Industry on Parade exhibition, "Marilyn was the hostess in a booth. She was a wow. She was kind of a breathless little girl….She was the little-girl-next-door type when she was with us.'

    In the winter of 1945 Miss Snively made this observation about Norma Jeane. "She still seemed a scared, pretty, lonely little kid who wore mostly fresh white cotton dresses and wanted somebody, somewhere, to think she was worth something." She was about to meet a photographer whose interest in her would match her desires and would give her the professional boost she needed.

    Norma Jeane has her first sittings with Andre de Dienes on November 20th and 26th. De Dienes documents her early beauty in much the same way Milton H. Greene will do with Marilyn at the pinnacle of her fame. The photographs he will take of her now and in 1949 and 1952 will define her as one of greatest beauties that ever sat for a still camera. They both share in the responsibility for this remarkable collection of images. For, if not for her beauty and innate cleverness at posing herself, and his expertise with a camera, they would be just another series of situational pictures of a sweet girl. He takes her to Paradise Cove, a semi-deserted beach, north of Malibu. He had requested a model for a bathing suit session and Miss Snively sent him Norma Jeane. She arrives at his apartment and changes into her bathing suit for his approval. He is smitten at once and can't wait to work with her. He remembers, "…she was sent to his apartment in Hollywood's famed Garden of Allah by a model agency. 'There came this lovely little girl in a pink sweater and checkered slacks. I fell right away in love with this girl. In my subconscious I wanted to marry this nice young girl. What was wrong with that? I was a nice young boy myself.'"

    He will later write of his association with the young Norma Jeane. "One day in 1946, when I was in Hollywood on business, there came a knock at my door. When I opened it I was confronted by a pretty young girl, fresh looking, carrying a large hatbox and wearing a tight pink wool sweater. In the hatbox, it developed, there was a bathing suit and nothing more. But in the young lady's head there were a great many things, including a quiet, preserving ambition. She had long, curly dark-blonde hair, I remember (it has been lightened many shades since then), and she introduced herself to me: 'I am Norma Jean Daugherty,' said this pink-sweatered vision, 'and I hope you can use me for modeling.' She had been sent by the Blue Book Model Agency, and after a brief conversation I arranged to use her for a series of photographs to be taken a few days later. That was my introduction to the girl who became Marilyn Monroe, and I think you might be interested in the kind of a girl she was then. Norma Jean—excuse me, Marilyn—was a good-natured, happy type of person. She was almost always in a good mood, sincere, enthusiastic, eager to work. She had a delightful laugh and was the picture of youth and health. I was to take hundreds of pictures of her over the next seven years."

According to *Parade* magazine, de Dienes has four steps when photographing a beautiful girl. "1. He has to find the right girl. 2. He has to visualize situations that will bring out her beauty. 3. He has to find the right scenic background and the proper clothes. And, 4. He has to experiment with different conditions of light and shade." He uses a 35mm for fast action, a 2 ¼ x 2 ¼ reflex for posed shots and a big view camera for wide angle effects.

Norma Jeane was paid $20 on November 20th and $30 on November 26th for her modeling fees by Andre de Dienes. He posed her in a two piece swimsuit at the beach; with braids in the middle of a highway; in jeans and a tied-up shirt in front of an old barn; and in a pinafore with a lamb. Even though she is still a curly headed brunette, she radiates something indefinable in these earlier images. Her skin had a creamy glow that created an aura around her, and she photographs more beautiful than she actually was at this time. It is as if the fates were giving a hint of her exceptional gifts yet to come. It did not escape de Dienes attention. He is a good enough photographer to know that she will only get better with time, and he is narcissistic enough to think that only he has the talent to draw out her beauty. After developing the images, he becomes one of the first professionals to become infatuated with her.

The December 1945 issue of *Movieland* magazine carried an ad with a brunette Norma Jeane modeling the "Hollywood Star Suit" from Arnold's of Hollywood. It was made of Shetland wool and would only set you back $16.98. Despite her failure to make it as a model for catalog work, this fashion shot, not cheesecake, marked her first appearance in a magazine, albeit an ad.

Andre de Dienes has another photo sitting with Norma Jeane in December of 1945, which lasted for nearly a month. They traveled through California, Arizona, Nevada, and Oregon. They stayed at the Furnace Creek Inn at Death Valley, CA. They then passed through Las Vegas, NV to re-fuel the car as they went through Southern California, and into Arizona. While they stopped at Yosemite overnight, Norma Jeane insisted that de Dienes rent two small cabins. Andre surprised Norma Jeane by buying her an entire winter wardrobe at the Gift Shop at the Lodge. They drove through San Francisco to Portland, where they had a short visit with Norma Jeane's Mother. Then continuing to Mt. Hood, Oregon, they stayed at the Government Lodge where they become lovers. de Dienes had tried since the beginning to seduce Norma Jeane and she finally gave in to his advances in a snowy cabin in Oregon. On this trip, Andre made some of the loveliest photos taken of her. They have become classic images of a charming young woman who was destined to define sexuality for an entire generation. Andre de Dienes writes a $300.00 check on December 20, 1945 to Norma Jeane for her modeling fees for the three week trip. He leaves for New York with Norma Jeane promising to marry him when he returns.

In 1953, De Dienes remember his beautiful model, "We made trips to the seashore, the desert and up in the high mountains where I photographed her in the snow. What a pleasure it was to work with this girl. It is difficult to put most models in the mood to work let alone to get something worth photographing. But Marilyn was always ready to jump out of the car and pose any place, any time—hot or cold, comfortable or uncomfortable. If something went wrong she apologized. She loved to be photographed and she was born for it. I told her that I would make her the world's most photographed woman. Without a doubt she is. This girl was never dull, never tired. She made you feel good and above all was quick to respond to suggestions and photographic ideas. In those first years I photographed her for what she was—a clean, wholesome American girl, untouched by fame, fortune or false ways. I wanted those pictures to be young, innocent, sweet, unsophisticated even to her long hair. And they were."  De Dienes again reflects on Norma Jeane in an article from 1962, "This girl got up at the crack of dawn to do her hair. She was never late. That was an idiosyncrasy Hollywood gave her. If I told her to be up at 7, she would be up at 5. I would go to her cabin and she'd tell me, 'I'm doing my hair.' She was sweet. Beautiful. Her beautiful smile. Her laughter. And she was frail—frail mentally and physically. As soon as she finished her work she would hop back in the car and fall asleep. This girl had no business in show business. She was a sensitive, sweet little girl."

It seems that Jim had planned to come home for the holidays and was none too happy when Norma Jeane announced that she would be out of town on a photo assignment. If he knew how de Dienes pressed her to pose nude and have sex with him, he would have been livid. During her modeling years Jim was still in her life, albeit on the periphery, and he had a husband's jealousy of the new men in Norma Jeane's life.

Norma Jeane starts 1946 on a high note when the January issue of *Douglas Airview* magazine was finally published. This was an in-house magazine for the airline industry and it featured her on a shared cover and in the article about the new Douglas DC-4 Flagship for American Airlines. This is her first appearance on the cover of a magazine, not a national publication and it is not a solo appearance, but it is a beginning. Norma Jeane wears own her teal colored, man-tailored suit in the cover photo that Miss. Snively aptly said, "did nothing for her." She also demonstrates the sleeping compartments of the plane, dressed in a black negligee' for some of the photos, and a robe and bunny slippers were added for others. She will also wear the black negligee for pin up artist Earl Moran in a later session.

Norma Jeane was hesitant to get her hair straightened and bleached initially because she thought it would look fake and cheap. Another reason she was hesitant is that she realized that once she started the process she would have to keep it up and how could she afford it?

Miss Snively promised her, "'Look, darling,' I told her, 'if you really intend to go places in this business, you've just got to bleach and straighten your hair, because now your face is a little too round and a hair job will lengthen it. Don't worry about money. I'll keep you working.'"

Norma Jeane's natural hair was too kinky for commercial use and clients hinted that it too closely resembled black hair. In order to sooth the clients fears, her naturally curly hair needed to be straightened so it would appear soft and silky. As fate would have it, in February of 1946 Norma Jeane was chosen by Raphael Wolff for a national shampoo ad. He hired Marilyn with the understanding that she would have something done to her hair. He paid for the straightening and bleaching. Mrs. Snively remembers how fortunate this was for Norma Jeane, "And her hair! It was so curly and frizzy. It grew so curly it couldn't be managed. When she bent over, nothing happened; not a hair moved. We wished she could get her hair straightened, but she couldn't afford it. Then along came a national shampoo ad that required both a straight permanent and then a soft permanent at the ends of her hair for shaping."

The African American newspaper, *The Pittsburgh Courier*, on September 8, 1962, featured a column by Marguerite Cartwright and she mentions Marilyn's problems with her hair. "A woman who was interviewed and credited with being one of the first to discover the popular blonde star, described her as being a "summer blonde" with her hair being "really too curly." Then, as near as I can remember, she added, "When she would hold her hair down, the curls would remain where they were. We took to straightening her hair and she liked the effect and wore it that way until she died." Somehow I found this memory of the star rather intriguing." It seems that black women had found something in common with this pale woman that they could sympathize with.

"The photos for the Frank and Joseph crème shampoo were never used. We sent Marilyn to Hollywood hair stylist Frank and Joseph who had their color technician, Sylvia Barnhart, transform the skittish model. First a straight permanent to make the hair more manageable, then a regular permanent at the ends after shaping. Then the hair was bleached and Marilyn emerged the golden blonde you know today." Zolotow gives the ultimate statement of her transformation. "She was uneasy when she first saw herself in the mirror. It wasn't the 'real me.' Then she saw it worked." Ed Rees aptly states of her transformation, "It was first-rate advice. With her new blonde hair and that startlingly pink and white complexion, Norma Jeane looked like something carved out of ice cream." "Miss Barnhart remembers that Norma Jeane actually thought the lighter color would bring out her eyes, which it did."

The photographs taken at the H. Maier Studios survive and show a young woman who is more polished and restrained than the younger photos Norma Jeane had posed for at the start of her modeling career. She was learning her lessons well. Norma Jeane did appear in a local hair show modeling a beautiful hairstyle designed by Sylvia Barnhart for the Frank and Joseph Salon. The cold set permanent wave was very popular now and Miss Barnhart won her first award with the wave enhanced up-do and color treatment she designed for

Norma Jeane. A surviving photo taken by a photographer from H. Maier Studios shows the team from Frank and Joseph, including Miss Barnhart, in front of sparkling letters announcing, "The Wave," and surrounding an elegant looking Norma Jeane sitting in the stylist chair.

Joseph Jasgur took a portrait of Marilyn and a man that was intended for a shampoo ad. Her hair was lighter and straightened so it was after she had gone through her initial transformation.

Norma Jeane's career picked up after she changed her hair color and hair style, and had learned the secret of lowering her smile. Potter Hueth and Bob Farr were able to sell more of her photographs on speculation and she gained a lot of exposure by doing this.

Douglas Airview, March 1946, featured Norma Jeane in a magazine back cover, using a photo from the January 1946 issue. It appeared as an ad for the new Douglas DC-6.

Marilyn also did some modeling for the Erwin Steinmeyer Studios in Los Angeles. She was photographed by Hal Bloom modeling various pieces of wardrobe, including dresses, shorts and halter tops on the grounds of the Ambassador Hotel. These photographs are not well known, giving weight to the thought that they were never actually used in print, but remained as transparencies in the studio for some 60 years, until it was realized who the young woman in the images was.

Norma Jeane had a sitting with Joseph Jasgur on March 6, 1946. Emmeline Snively, at the Blue Book Model Agency, asked him to take some photographs of Norma Jeane. She arrived wearing a pink sweater, plaid pedal-pushers, and a beret. She posed in the alley behind his studio and then watched with him as the negatives developed in his dark room.

Before she went back to The Blue Book Agency, he took her to eat a hamburger because he felt she was too thin.

Miss Snively remembers that Jasgur didn't find Marilyn sexy at all, and in fact he said that she was too skinny. He wasn't overwhelmed with her until much later when he wrote his memoirs. Then he, like so many others, remembers the beauty and talent that only he saw in the young Norma Jeane. He remembers in his book that he found her overweight. All one has to do is look at his photographs of Norma Jeane to see that she was not overweight, and that Miss Snively's memories are accurate. According to Jasgur himself, he took Norma Jeane to a few movies where he was more interested in trying to get to first base than what was showing on the screen.

Marilyn would make this observation two years before her death about what was expected from some photographers. "When I started modeling, it was like part of the job. All the girls did. They weren't shooting all those sexy pictures just to sell peanut butter in an ad, or get a layout in some picture magazine. They wanted to sample the merchandise, and if you didn't go along, there were twenty-five girls who would. It wasn't any big dramatic tragedy. Nobody ever got cancer from sex." Norma Jeane navigated the hostile waters of the modeling business with a disarming innocence backed up with a shrewd mind. It will prepare her for the brackish waters she will have to contend with when she becomes a starlet in Hollywood.

Norma Jeane first poses for calendar illustrator Earl Moran on March 8th. She will model for Moran, off and on for the next few years. He takes some lovely nudes of her to use as references for his calendar work. They weren't intended to be made public and he kept their existence hidden until after her death. Her body is in superb condition and it is obvious she is continuing the weight training she started in Catalina. Joseph Jasgur takes a photograph of Marilyn modeling for Moran, he is illustrating the calendar top, "Bus Stop," with Norma Jeane in character standing nearby.

Moran claims she is a natural for calendar work. In fact, Norma Jeane is a natural for cheesecake photography. The idea behind cheesecake is the unreality of the situation the girl finds herself in and the ability to suspend disbelief by her pose and expression. She is in on the joke. Her skirt has blown up or has been caught on a nail, exposing her panties. Oops! Whoops! Wink! Moran referred Norma Jeane to several acquaintances. She continued to model for Earl Moran and others, while concentrating on getting her acting career going. Once, when she came to Moran's studio her shoes were completely worn out. He gave her a pair that another model had left in the studio and she gratefully wore them home. When she achieved some success with her acting career, she gave Moran the dress she wore while filming *Asphalt Jungle* in 1949.

Fox photographer Frank Powolny said, "a pin-up picture must combine three things to be a success: It must have wholesomeness, sex appeal and be different from the usual poses. A pin-up is good proportion to the amount of imagination it stimulates. If it suggests more than it reveals, it is memorable." He should know, he snapped the iconic photograph of Betty Grable that established her as "The Pin-Up" during WWII.

On March 10th Joseph Jasgur photographs Norma Jeane atop the Don Lee Towers TV Station, overlooking the Hollywood sign. He and posed her in comic situations wearing a plaid shirt and jeans. She uses a telescope and a bow and arrow as props. She also poses in her sweater and plaid pants. If any good photos came out of this session it is due to her skills as a model. Jasgur insisted on photographing her from a low angle because of her weak chin, which was an incorrect angle to choose. Most of the photos he took of her on the first day and today on their second sitting are from this low angle, and while he is trying to compensate for her weakness, he sacrifices her beauty.

She models for calendar artist Earl Moran again on March 11$^{th}$. The next day Norma Jeane poses for Richard C. Miller in the first of their sessions. This would be the start of some of the most gorgeous color photos of the young beauty. Miller would pick up Norma Jeane at her Santa Monica home and take her to the underdeveloped Valley to shoot her. She was paid a $10 modeling fee.

Miller and Norma Jeane first went to his friend Gene Hanson's place and he posed her by a Sycamore tree, and other pastoral settings. He frames her within the bounty of nature's beauty and she is stunning. He photographs her as a fisherman complete with a red fishing hat full of fishing flies. She wears a few colorful plaid blouses and also a Polynesian print midriff and yellow skirt, as these were to show off the magnificent beauty of color film. She was meant for Technicolor. Her creamy complexion was a perfect complement to the colorful clothes and props she posed with. They also went to Santa Monica Beach where she posed in various two piece swimsuits until men started to gather and Miller realized that it was becoming uncomfortable for her. According to Miller the beach session was halted and they finally ended up at a farm in the San Fernando Valley where he again posed her in colorful clothing with a barn and split rail fencing as her props. Miller was so enamored of one of the photos he took of Norma Jeane that he entered it in *Cosmopolitan* magazine's contest, "My Favorite Picture." He was disappointed when the photo of Norma Jeane sitting on a wooden fence, dressed in a striped shirt and red cowboy hat wasn't chosen, but it didn't lessen his faith in her. He even took her home to his family to have dinner on a couple of occasions. He had a fondness for her sweetness and compliance and he found her a joy to photograph.

Things seem to be looking up for Norma Jeane as she signs a contract at National Concert Artists Corporation upon the recommendation of Miss Snively. As incredulous as it sounds, it seems that she had become overexposed during her first year as a model and was having problems finding work. Even Richard C. Miller hesitated to use her at first because she had done so much print work and was worried that the magazines he usually sold photographs to wouldn't want to use her. She gave her address as 11348 Nebraska Ave. This was a one year contract and Helen Ainsworth signed as resident manager for the Agency. Harry Lipton wouldn't officially be assigned as her agent until July 23, 1946. By then, Norma Jeane would be hired by Twentieth Century Fox Studio.

When Norma Jeane walked in to the agency she dropped her hat box and all its contents, minus a hat, spilled across the floor. After Lipton helped gather her belongings, a flustered

Norma Jeane sat for an interview with him and Helen Ainsworth. She was signed, not for her obvious assets alone, but rather Miss Ainsworth, despite a nervous beginning, saw a look in her eyes that told her that she had possibilities, and that it was backed by determination. Norma Jeane was assigned to Lipton because he handled all newcomers. They would work together for the next five years.

Harry Lipton gives an insight into the real Marilyn and her deep-seated insecurity and loneliness. Norman Rosten will also tell of similar phone calls even after Marilyn was an established star. She was known to a call at all hours of the night if the urge hit her and it symbolized her trust in you as a friend. "We became friends very quickly. Specifically, we became friends at 12:57 one morning some months after we met in Helen's office. I do not know how long the telephone rang before I woke up. I got out of bed and groped for the receiver. 'Hello,' I said sleepily. 'Hello,' Marilyn said, a little uncertainly. I was completely awake. 'Marilyn. What's wrong?' There was a moment of silence. 'I was just lonely, sort of. I just wanted to talk to somebody.' That was the first of many midnight telephone calls, the first of many nights when I awoke to hear Marilyn's lonely or frightened voice. She had accepted me as her friend, and when she offered her friendship to someone, all her wariness fell away, to be replace by a loyalty that was complete and unwavering."

Norma Jeane goes to Zuma Beach with Joseph Jasgur on March 18th. He photographs her in a stripped two piece bathing suit that was a very popular swimsuit in 1946, as many models and starlets had been photographed in it. Again, she has a telescope and bow and arrow for props. He photographs her drawing hearts in the sand. The images that capture her beauty are of her sitting in the sand because he shot her from a high angle. The most remarkable thing about this series of photographs happened 41 years later. Jasgur was making some prints from the session on the beach and thinks he sees that Norma Jeane had 6 toes on her left foot. He deduced that she later had the extra toe surgically removed. This is completely untrue. All one has to do is look at early photos of Norma Jeane to see her foot is completely normal.

Norma Jeane again goes to Zuma Beach with Joseph Jasgur on March 23rd. He had also invited the members of a local production of *The Drunkard*, to join them. Another Blue Book Model that day was Mary Lou Massey, who often went on assignments together with her. Norma Jeane wears one of her favorite swimsuits, a Catalina two-piece with hand-painted seagulls on the bottom. It is the same one she wore in the photograph by Lee Bush back in 1945.

It is interesting to note the differences in Joseph Jasgur's photographs of Norma Jeane compared to the ones she had taken with the other early photographers such as Andre de Dienes, Potter Hueth, Bob Farr, John Randolph, Paul Parry, William Carroll, Laszlo Willinger or Richard C. Miller. Jasgur's photos are the least flattering she will have taken of her during her early years as a model. Her clothes seem ill fitting, except for her bathing suits, her hair and makeup are not flattering, and her poses are disingenuous. In her work with the other aforementioned photographers, she is radiant and comes across, in the least, as very commercial. Jasgur's photos are only interesting now in retrospect because he photographed her at the start of her modeling career. They will not be used as publicity photos of her in newspapers or magazines. He is one of the few lensman she will fail to connect with.  It is in the spring of 1946 that Norma Jeane ended her personal and professional acquaintance with photographer Joseph Jasgur. He will have one more session where she is one of a group of models for The Blue Book Models. The last time he will photograph her was at a distance while she was riding on a float with other hopeful starlets in "The Santa Clause Lane Parade" in November of 1946.

Richard C. Miller photographs Norma Jeane again on March 26th.  He takes a series of gorgeous pictures of her on the beach in Santa Monica in a red candy-stripped two piece, a white/pale pink two piece and a color blocked two-piece, both by Catalina and in a yellow bikini that she will become famous for. Miller had borrowed some swimsuits from the Catalina swimsuit company and Norma Jeane falls in love with the white/pale pink two-piece. She asks to keep it for a modeling shoot the next day and promises to return it. One only has to look at all the photographs she wore the suit in to realize that she changed her mind and kept the swimsuit.  It seems she also kept the yellow bikini and in the future photographer Anthony Beauchamp will sing its praises. Norma Jeane and Miller pose for a photo together taken by Chuck S.

*Colliers* magazine carries an ad for the new Douglas DC-6 featuring Norma Jeane, in their March 30th issue.

Gladys moves in with Norma Jeane in April while she is still living with Ana Lower in West Los Angeles. Norma Jeane has little time to spend with her mother as her modeling career is off to a stellar start. Gladys was not happy that Marilyn was posing for sexy pictures and she was starting to appear on the cover of men's magazines instead of respectable ladies magazines. The start of Norma Jeane's modeling career left little room for Gladys to be proud, but it won't be long before the publications that Gladys has high regard for will start to use images of her lovely daughter. In fact, she will be on the cover of *Family Circle* this month. Being ladylike was very important to Gladys and Marilyn never lost touch with this characteristic and she will harbor a polite and cultured affect in her interviews after 1952.

Gladys will start to see the success that Norma Jeane is having and will even make a trip to the Blue Book Agency to see Miss Snively. She recalls Gladys as, "an attractive woman, prim and proper, wearing a small hat and white gloves. 'She introduced herself as Norma Jeane's mother. Her reason for coming, she said, was simply to think me for what I was doing for her daughter.'"

On April 4th, Richard C. Miller photographs Norma Jeane at the Sheraton Town House Pool. She brings back the Catalina two-piece she wore for him at the beach and puts it to good use for this shoot. She will also wear a black swimsuit, and a red striped two piece. To demonstrate color film she wears a color striped towel on her head in one shot. A daring blue halter sundress makes its first appearance in this session with Miller. This dress will later show up, as will the two-piece she did not return, in films in August for the Blue Book Modeling agency.  The early color film compliments Norma Jeane and she radiates a

Technicolor beauty in Miller's photos. The next day he photographs Norma Jeane as a hunter. She is posed in a hunting cap aiming a bolt-action hunting rifle, and in another with binoculars. In still another pose, she wears a Bandana and holds a Colt Woodsman, Semi-Automatic .22 pistol. She looks out of character in these photos, but now they have a rather kitschy appeal.

Her modeling career is paying off. Norma Jeane has her first national and international solo covers in these April magazines, and is featured in a couple of ads. These magazines had a large public following.

April 8, 1946: *Time* magazine carries Norma Jeane's ad for the new Douglas Aircraft DC-6, "Off to a flying start."

April 13, 1946: *Leader* magazine, an English publication, has Norma Jeane on the cover. This becomes Norma Jeane's first solo appearance on the cover of a magazine. The photo was taken in 1945 by Andre de Dienes.

April 20, 1946: *Colliers* magazine carries an ad for the new Douglas DC-6 featuring Norma Jeane.

April 26, 1946: *Family Circle* magazine features Norma Jeane on its cover. This becomes Norma Jeane's first solo appearance on a U.S. national magazine. It is a sweet photo of her and a lamb taken by Andre de Dienes. When she was interviewed for a two-part article in *Family Circle*, May and June 1953, she told the interviewer, Harry Evans, "There is something you don't know--I'm sure you don't because it was so long ago--and it wouldn't be important to anybody, really, but me, but if I could only tell you what it meant at the time! The first cover picture I ever posed for was for *Family Circle*! Of course you won't remember, but I was carrying a lamb. It's among the first things in my scrapbook. And if you could have seen me running around showing it to all my friends. You can't know the encouragement that job gave me. Or what the money meant. For years I've wanted to thank somebody. So, thank you."

Marilyn would later say, "It was the first published picture of me. It was a cover on *Family Circle* magazine (at that time it was given away free.) The lamb I was holding had to die, it was a twin and its mother wouldn't nurse it. It seems a sheep only wants one kid at a time. So, I had ambivalent feelings, as you can see. My face looks a little distorted--half smiling, half sad."

She ends the month of April with another session with Richard C. Miller on April 30th. He had a small studio at his home and he photographed her there as a bride, a sweet photo in an organdy blouse and a choker, and as a skier and in a ski lodge. The ski lodge photo where Miller posed her in a red sweater enjoying a cup of cocoa is often erroneously credited to Bruno Bernard. She wore her own wedding dress and she used Margaret Miller's white Bible in the bride photo. The bride photo made the cover of *Personal Romance* in June of 1947. The next time they would work together would be on March 12, 1950. By then, her name would be Marilyn Monroe and she would have a new look to go with her new name. Miller used a special technique called Carbro printing for making his color prints. It was not complex, but labor intensive, and the results are seen in his amazing images of Norma Jeane.

In the summer of 1946 William Carroll needed a model for a color advertising counter-card to display at his film processing and printing laboratory in Los Angeles. His mother, who worked in his office, called to tell him about some slides that photographer Potter Hueth was showing her of a girl who she thought would be perfect for the ad campaign. Carroll came to see the slides. The girl turned out to be of Norma Jeane. The slides had recently been taken by Hueth's friend, David Conover. Carroll liked her "girl-next-door appeal" of the model and Hueth gave him Norma Jeane's phone number. Carroll called and arranged an appointment to pick her up and take her to Castle Rock in Malibu for the shoot. Carroll remembers that Norma Jeane was on time and he photographed her all day, breaking for lunch at a local hamburger stand. The best photos were achieved in the afternoon. He drove Norma Jeane home and paid her the modeling fee of $20 for the day's work. When he calls the Blue Book Agency to use her again, Norma Jeane's fee had gone up to $50, and he refused to pay this amount. He never saw her again. Carroll didn't realize that she had transformed herself into Marilyn Monroe until 1968. He came across a box of slides marked, "Norma Jean" while moving. After looking closely at them he realized that they were of a young Marilyn Monroe. He stored them away until 1987 when he was reading an auction catalog containing some of David Conover's photos of Norma Jeane and realized their worth. Carroll auctioned off 96 color slides and 6 black and white prints at Christies in 1988. The images sold for $53,955. Not bad for his $20 investment in an unknown model. Carroll remembers, "She was alive. She was the kind of person who, if she walked through here, you'd say, 'holy smoke.' You'd turn around twice, then you'd turn around again. Her smile, her freshness, her genuineness."

In these images of William Carroll, Norma Jeane is improving her skills as a model. The success of these lovely images is shared by both the photographer and his model. Carroll frames her with great skill in each photograph. She doesn't compete with the background images of surf and cliffs. He uses the tricks of a good photographer and never shoots her full frontal and center frame. Her legs appear long, her bosom is high and her face is the essence of girl-next-door sweetness. At this point she is still only as good as the photographer and she will learn many valuable lessons from this sitting with Carroll. It won't be long before she will eclipse the photographers she poses for and gain the marketable knack of making any shot usable.

Lazlo Willinger will take full advantage of her red and white stripped two-piece and take several photos of Norma Jeane at the beach and at his studio. She, as Norman Mailer so aptly puts it, "looks like a ripe peach, bursting before one's eyes." It is interesting to note that Willinger finds her "rather uninteresting" until she poses for the camera, then her passive persona transforms into a show of light and energy that suits itself effortlessly to the medium of film.

Norma Jeane has a partial cover of the May 1946 issue of *U.S. Camera.*

Norma Jeane finally takes action on her failing marriage and on May 14th she moves in with Minnie Willette, Grace Goddard's Aunt, at 604 S 3rd Street in Las Vegas, NV, in order to establish residency to gain her divorce from Jim Dougherty. She had recently learned that no major studio would want to waste their time and effort on a young woman who was married, and could possibly become pregnant. She was required by law to live in Las Vegas until September 13th, in order to meet the demands of the divorce decree.

Norma Jeane writes Emmeline Snively, of the Blue Book Modeling Agency, a letter from Las Vegas on May 25th. She mentions riding Trigger and dining with Roy Rogers and his crew at the Last Frontier Hotel. They are there for the Helldorado Rodeo which ran from the 23rd to the 26th. Also she inquires about the photographers Richard C. Miller, Paul Parry, John Randolph and Laszlo Willinger.

Jim Dougherty will later recall that he and Norma Jeane once met Roy Rogers in a Van Nuys western clothing store, where Jim had gone to buy some boots. Jim recalls Roy kidding with Norma Jeane as he tried on his boots.

Norma Jeane appears on the cover of two magazines in June. Norma Jeane's cheesecake career is jump-started with her appearance on the cover of *Laff* magazine. She is identified as Norma Jeane Dougherty. *Laff* was a magazine intended for male readership. Her cover appearance would allegedly spark the interest of Howard Hughes and compel Twentieth Century-Fox Studios to quickly sign Marilyn to a contract.

*Pageant* magazine also featured her on the cover and a paragraph on the index page. "Vivacious 19 year old Norma Jeane Dougherty was working in an aircraft factory when she was asked to pose for office War Department pictures. She has been modeling ever since. Norma Jeane likes the outdoor life and cooking for her Coast Guard husband. Photographed for *Pageant* by Andre de Dienes."

In an unrelated article she is photographed at her graduation from the Blue Book Modeling School. She is in a couple of group photos of the beautiful "grads," then has one by herself, holding the June edition of *Pageant* showing her on the cover. "Wearing a chartreuse midriff bathing suit, Marilyn hits the cover of *Pageant* magazine in June, 1946. Photo shows how she has changed from early frizzy hairdo to a smoother coiffure and improved smile." The photo was credited to Bill Harvey. She wears the white Catalina two-piece she has yet to return.

Norma Jeane will be treated at the Las Vegas General Hospital with a bad infection of her mouth after having four wisdom teeth extracted. She was only out for one day before she was once again hospitalized, this time with measles. Her time in Las Vegas has not started well.

It is during this spate of bad health that Jim cuts off Norma Jeane's allotment. Jim remembers Norma Jeane snapped at him, "How could you possibly cut me off like that?" And he replied, "You don't pay for anything when you're not getting it."

Author, Michelle Morgan, introduces us to a person long hidden in the shadows of Marilyn's past, Bill Purcel. After Norma Jeane recovered from her hospital stays she meets Bill Purcel, who worked at a local service station. Purcel was visiting with a neighbor and spotted Norma Jeane standing on the porch of Miss Willette's home. They have an instant friendship and he takes her to all the local recreational areas, such as Mount Charleston,

Lake Mead and the Hoover Dam. They spent nearly every day together doing some activity. They traveled to Utah and visit Bryce Canyon and Zion National Park where, much to Norma Jeane's delight, she was recognized by some women as a cover girl.

Purcel even took Norma Jeane home to meet his family and have dinner. She had an uncanny ability to win over other people's mothers, and Mrs. Purcel was no exception. After meeting Norma Jeane the first time she has an urge to mother her. It was hard to resist Norma Jeane's sweetness, especially when it came wrapped in such loveliness, and Mrs. Purcel, like writer Carl Sandberg, will be impressed by Norma Jeane's willingness to help with the dishes without being prompted to do so.

In July Norma Jeane appeared inside two magazines. *Douglas Airview* magazine features a photo of Norma Jeane in their article about the DC6 Sleeper-plane. Norma Jeane is shown in her night gown stretching out in one of the births. The photos were taken by Larry Kronquist in 1945 for the in-house publication for the airline industry.

Norma Jeane also made an appearance in the S*tars and Stripes* military newspaper and was featured in a side bar photo wearing some magazines in which she appears on the cover. The photo is captioned, "Cover-ed Girl...Norma Jeane Dougherty, comely Los Angeles girl, rang the bell by appearing on the cover of five national magazines this month. Editors inspirations: Blonde hair, blue eyes and perfect shape." This captioned photo also made its way into the mainstream media. This photo would be transmitted by *NEA Wire Services* in newspapers all over the country giving Norma Jeane valuable exposure. Hollywood studios would be interested in a girl like this who generated her own publicity.

Actually she appeared on a total of 4 magazine covers in the photo, and not any were in the month of July. *Family Circle*, April 26, 1946, *U.S. Camera*, May 1946, and *Laff* and *Pageant*, both June 1946. A love affair between this pretty girl and America's GI's was sparked and through the alchemy of their lust and her desire to succeed, Marilyn will be transformed into a phenomenon when the Korean War breaks out.

Marilyn will later remember her modeling career with writer Pete Martin, "I had appeared on five magazines covers. Mostly men's magazines.' What, I asked, did she mean by men's magazines? 'Magazines,' she said, 'with cover girls who are not flat-chested. I was on *See* four or five months in a row. Each time they changed my name. One month I was Norma Jean Dougherty--that was my first husband's name. The second month I was Jean Norman. I don't know what all names they used, but I must have looked different each time. There were different poses--outdoors, indoors, but mostly just sitting looking over the Pacific. You looked at those pictures and you didn't see much ocean, but you saw a lot of me. One of the magazines I was on wasn't a man's magazine at all. It was called *Family Circle*. You buy it in supermarkets. I was holding a lamb with a pinafore. I was the one with the pinafore. But on most covers I had on things like a striped towel. The towel was striped because the cover was to be in color and the stripes were the color, and there was a big fan blowing on the towel and on my hair."

Upon establishing her six-week residency in Nevada, Norma Jeane initiates divorce proceedings against Jim Dougherty. On the 4th of July, 1946, Jim received a "Dear John" letter from Norma Jeane's lawyer she had retained while in Las Vegas, C. Norman Cornwell, announcing that she had filed for divorce. Jim had no clue that Norma Jeane was making plans to divorce him, and was near Shanghai, on the Yangtze River and had been shopping for gifts to bring back to her.

The next day Norma Jeane filed for divorce in Las Vegas. Case #31146, Dept. No. 1, in the 8th Judicial District of the State of Nevada, in and for the County of Clark. Complaint: Plaintiff complains of the defendant and for cause of action alleges, "....That since marrying the defendant has treated the plaintiff with extreme cruelty (mental in nature) all without cause or provocation on the part of the plaintiff; and that plaintiff's health is and was thereby and therefrom impaired."

Marilyn will tell Ben Hecht, "I had been sort of a 'child bride.' Now I was sort of a 'child widow.'"

Before she returned to Los Angeles Jim Dougherty remembers calling Marilyn while she was in Las Vegas establishing residency. He got the number from Aunt Ana. "I asked the operator for the number and waited for the click on the other end of the line. Her voice came over, low and purring, not at all like the voice I remembered. 'Hello,' I said. 'Norma Jeane?' 'Oh, hello, Bill,' she said. I think she used the name Bill…" 'This is Jim,' I said. 'Oh, Jim,' she said without even a ripple. 'How are you?' 'What the devil happened to your voice?' I said. 'It doesn't sound like you.' She told me they wanted her to keep it low, that it sounded better that way."  Could the Bill be Bill Purcel?

Norma Jeane makes a risky return to Los Angeles on July 18$^{th}$, as she had to stay for the full 6 weeks in Las Vegas to establish residency for her divorce.  She took Bill Purcel up on his offer to drive her home. Her car broke down in Baker and they waited hours for it to be fixed. The weary travelers finally made it to San Bernardino, where they found a park. They soaked their feet in the water and eventually parted ways. Bill had to be back in Las Vegas for work, and Norma Jeane drove the rest of the way to Aunt Ana's. Their parting was bittersweet and she welled up with sadness at the thought of losing her summer love.

In the summer of 1946 Norma Jeane's sister, Berniece, and her daughter Mona Rae, come to Los Angeles for a visit. Gladys is reunited with both of her daughters and her granddaughter. The visit last nearly three months.

The *New York Sunday Mirror* newspaper supplement carries an article, "Beauty and the Beach." Norma Jeane was photographed by Andre de Dienes. Norma Jeane appeared balancing on a volleyball, captioned, "Evidently Norma Dougherty doesn't like to sit on damp sand."

During her time with the Miss Snively and the Blue Book Modeling Agency Norma Jeane had immersed herself in not only how to be a great model, but what it takes to be a great photographer. She learned lessons from both the viewpoint of a model and also the photographer. The knowledge of angles, light, shadows, posing, etc., will serve her well in the coming years. Sidney Skolsky commented on her skills in posing for photographer Bob Beerman. "I was in Marilyn's apartment that evening when your photographer arrived. I was listening to Marilyn play her guitar and sing. Then I watched the photographer shoot a layout. It's quite a job posing for pictures. The average reader picking up a magazine might say, 'Oh, another picture of Monroe,' and flip the page. Well, it took from nine until a little past midnight to get those pictures. Marilyn's performance impressed me. She not only knew the best angles, but she knows the best angles for the photographer. She knew if the light was casting a shadow across her. She was aware of minute details, such as what part of her thigh the blanket should cross. She even combed her hair so it would look uncombed. She doesn't leave it to chance that photographs of her will be interesting."

Whitey Snyder will second this notion of Marilyn as a great model. "Most women expect to look good in any pose. Marilyn knows her best angles and she uses them. I've known only a few women who are as wise as to what is good for them. They are Loretta Young, Marlene Dietrich, Claudette Colbert and Joan Crawford."

On July 24th, Norma Jeane signs a photo release for Bruno Bernard, a Hollywood glamour photographer. She will pose for him and like many others who knew her he will take more credit than is his for her career.

In a 1961 interview with Jim Anderson, Bernard seems have bitter memories of Marilyn, despite his book that celebrates her. "She was about 16, a cute little kid with long brown hair, a lovely smile and a tight red sweater. She wanted to know if I could take a sexy picture of her. I said, 'What do you want with a sexy picture? You're the girl-next-door type!' The only thing she had which you would recognize now were some curves, but those aren't a particularly rare commodity in Hollywood. But I took the pictures, showed them to a talent scout at $20^{th}$ Century-Fox, and they agreed to use her for cheesecake pictures. When her contract ran out, they sacked her because she wasn't worth the $120 a week they were paying her. Then a press agent fell in love with her and got her an acting contract. She couldn't act, she had a screechy voice and was impossibly stiff. Yet out of this girl, Hollywood's army of beauticians, technicians and publicity agents manufactured the very prototype of glamour, the epitome of desire. Now take that photograph. Who could have dreamed that a sweet, young girl like that, completely innocent of any acting talent, could have become the successor to Lana Turner and Jean Harlow…As Hitler said, repeat a lie over and over again and eventually people will believe it. Give the right press agent a girl—any average girl—and he can create a myth." Ouch!

# Chapter Six
## The Hardest Working Starlet in Town

"I didn't go into movies to make money. I wanted to become famous so everyone would like me, and I'd be surrounded by love and affection."
Marilyn Monroe

**H**arry Lipton represented Norma Jeane on behalf of the National Concert Artist. Later, when he had left movies to run a Hollywood candy store he had this slightly bitter comment about her, "One thing that Marilyn was never careless about was her career. She studies harder than anyone I have ever known. And she had a curious faith in herself, even when no one shared it….Marilyn has a fantastic quality--it's an electricity she turns on. She brings out the desire in people to help her, to protect her, to mother and father her. It's not a sex thing at all. She's playing a role--this sex thing. Marilyn has played everything up to a point and then dropped it and gone on to something new. She has a gift for timing. She has milked people and things dry."

Lipton accompanied Norma Jeane to Twentieth Century-Fox Studio on July 25th, 1946, to see Ivan Kahn, head of Fox Studio's Talent Department. She then had her first interview at Fox with Ben Lyon, who recruited new talent for the studio and was head of casting. He asked Norma Jeane to read a portion of the script, *Winged Victory*. After the reading he invited her to return for a screen-test on August 14th. Marilyn remembers, "It was a warm day. I wanted to wear something that would look different from the other girls, who were waiting, something to catch his eyes. So I wore something cool. I guess he walked up to me right away because I looked the coolest of them all."

Lyon has this vivid memory of first meeting Marilyn. "Before I actually tell you how Marilyn entered my life I must describe my office to you because it has a direct bearing on the story. That office was, without a doubt, one of the most beautiful rooms I have ever been in. The walls were dark leaf green, the settee was Chinese red, the lamps chartreuse, and the curtains Scots plaid. It sounds awful when you describe it cold like that but when you saw it altogether it really was something…The girl who walked through that door took my breath away…That dark green wall, the striving colors of that office of mine, made the perfect setting for her golden hair, peaches-and-cream complexion and the simple little flowered cotton dress she was wearing—an inexpensive dress but nicely cut and very nicely filled out. The girl's entrance to my office was a picture I shall never forget. Maybe if my office had been in any other color or if Marilyn had worn black the effect would have been different and the whole story never would have happened."

Ben Lyon called columnist Louella Parsons about meeting Norma Jeane. He told her, "She had a good face. You can tell with some faces--the way the flesh sits on the bones; the planes and angles--that they'll photograph well. And she was real blonde, a rarity. In addition, there was the way she moved." Later in Marilyn's career Miss Parsons confronted Mr. Lyon about his claim that Norma Jeane was a natural blonde. He stated, "She is a natural blonde. I didn't make the mistake. Nature did."

Ben Lyon will tell Milton Shulman, "She impressed me with her youth, beauty, charm and ambition."

Things are moving fast for Norma Jeane, she is given an option to sign with 20th Century-Fox and it will be based on her upcoming screen-test. Ben Lyon sends George

Wesson a request to sign Norma Jean Dougherty to a contract with Twentieth Century-Fox Studios. Her agent is listed as Harry Lipton NCAC. "Will you please draw up an optional contract on Norma Jean Dougherty. We agree to make a test of her then within ten (10) days after she completes the test, we agree to advise her whether or not we intend to exercise the option: 6 months--20 out of 26 weeks--$150.00. Miss Dougherty's home address and phone number are: 11348 Nebraska Ave, W. Los Angeles - AR 3-2487."

The test will be scheduled for August 14th. Bill Purcel was visiting Marilyn during this time and actually helped her learn her lines for the upcoming screen-test.

Ben Lyon takes Norma Jeane to lunch on the 28th of July. The next day, July 29th, Hedda Hopper gives Norma Jeane her first mention in a "Gossip Column," and includes a tidbit given to her by Emmeline Snively. "Yes, Howard Hughes is on the mend. Picking up a magazine, he was attracted by the cover girl and promptly instructed his aide to try and sign her for pictures. She's Norma Jean Dougherty, a model."

Miss Snively remembers giving Norma Jeane this boost, "What happened was this. Howard Hughes had been in a plane wreck in Beverly Hills and had been in an iron lung for some time. One day I got a call from him that he was interested in a girl on the cover of a certain magazine--it was *Laff* for August 1946. I released a story to Parsons and Hopper that Hughes must be on the mend, as he had asked to see a girl who's on a magazine cover about a movie contract. Hughes never met her. But Fox tested and signed her. I've heard all kinds of rumors about her start, but they're not true. Marilyn's not that kind of girl."

August holds promise for the last days of Norma Jeane. She is featured on the cover of two magazines, *Laff* magazine cover, where she uses the name Jean Norman, and *Salute*.

August also finds Norma Jeane joining six other models at the Ambassador Hotel in Los Angeles. The models are used for a talk show about photography techniques. It was hosted by the KFI Radio station. A surviving photograph, taken by Gene Lester, shows Norma Jeane sitting with the other models, one of whom is actress Joan Caulfield. Both she and Norma Jeane would study with Michael Chekhov in a few years. Film footage shows Norma Jeane standing in line with the other models. She is dressed in a blouse and skirt. Norma Jeane is also filmed at the swimming pool relaxing with other Blue Book Models and she even garners a few close-ups. She is dressed in a daring halter dress that crosses in wide strips of material across the bodice. She is finally shown sitting on a stool in her Catalina two-piece, once again she is shown in close-ups that show off her luscious features. The film was shot by Leo Caloia. The footage was originally two films titled, *Seven Sirens* and *Model Maids*. One of the films announces, "Introducing the Famous Blue Book Models of Hollywood." According to the 1948 brochure they were directed by Emmeline Snively. The surviving images give a glimpse of the "flesh impact" that Norma Jeane had with the moving camera. She is no less than stunning in these fleeting images. The footage would end up being offered for sale in 1948 by World in Color Productions. The blue halter dress and the Catalina two-piece were originally worn by Norma Jeane for a Richard C. Miller shoot in the spring of 1946.

Even though she will be hired by Fox, Marilyn and other girls from the Blue Book participate in publicity photos for the Blue Book Model Agency. Her hair is a bit longer and blonder in these photographs. Marilyn wore her two-piece Catalina swimsuit, and posed with a lifesaving ring with the Blue Book Model Agency written around it. Joseph Jasgur photographed this series of images.

   Things at the studio are progressing. The sound and photographic test of Norma Jeane Dougherty, supported by Bob Cornell, were made on August 14, at Twentieth Century-Fox. It was a silent test filmed on the set of a just completed Betty Grable movie, *The Shocking Miss Pilgrim*. They first used black and white film, and then some color film leftover from the movie is used.

   Norma Jeane is introduced to the man who will conduct her screen-test, Leon Shamroy, a legendary award winning cinematographer who played cameraman for the test. Shamroy will remember later, "When I first watched her, I thought this girl will be another Harlow--and I still do. Her natural beauty plus her inferiority complex give her a look of mystery….She was a scared little girl then and she's a scared little girl now. Don't believe those stories you hear. She's a good girl… She is Jean Harlow. Period." "Marilyn has the kind of glamour that explodes right into the camera lens. She's so pyrotechnical she practically curls the edges of the film. You name the angle—she does the most with it, and for it. What more could a cinematographer ask?"

   Despite his glowing remarks of the young Norma Jeane, by 1955 Shamroy will come to another, far more cynical, conclusion about her. "When you analyze Marilyn, she is not good-looking. She had a bad nose, bad posture and her figure is too obvious. She has a bad profile--hers is a phony sex. In order to be sexy, you don't have to shake your behind. Sex is not a physical thing. It is something inside you."

She also meets makeup artist, Allen "Whitey" Snyder; director Walter Lang; and costume designer Walter LeMaire. The screen-test is almost over before it begins as Norma Jeane requires Whitey Snyder to give her a heavy makeup application, amid protest from Snyder. When she walks onto the set, cameraman Leon Shamroy sees that her makeup photographs grotesquely and calls for Whitey to reapply it for her. Norma Jeane is humbled and quickly realizes her mistake. She submits herself to Whitey's artistry, which she will trust, even after she's dead. For in time she will exact a promise from Snyder to do her makeup for her funeral. Whitey will become a life-long friend and confidant of Marilyn's.

Whitey Snyder reveals how he does Marilyn's makeup, "Basically, Marilyn's makeup is very thin. It begins with a lotion to seal the pores. This is left on and it dries. Then a very light base--the exact color of her skin--goes on. The very light base allows the natural skin color to come through, and all that is left to do is blend in eye shadow and rouge. Her preferences in lipstick color are light pink and coral, with variations depending on the lighting or scene. The eyes are accentuated with brown pencil, although her eyes are very beautiful anyway, and she has long naturally dark eyelashes. Then, a light mascara is applied, and the makeup is finished."

As Marilyn Monroe, she will work with the people in this group numerous times as they help to cultivate and perfect her image for the movies. In the coming years she becomes even closer to the intimate group of people who function as underpinnings to her image. Whitey performs the chief role as her make-up artist, with various stylist creating her hairstyles and others hovering over her body. She keeps them close to her when she makes a film. They understand her and she needs them to help her transform into the celluloid confection that lights up the screen. Norman Mailer refers to them as her "coven," and with the screen magic they wrought, he is not too far off.

Bill Purcel waits with Aunt Ana at her home on Nebraska St. for Norma Jeane to return from her screen-test, and when she returns, it is with good news...they like her. That is, they like everything but her name.

On August 22, Ben Lyon helps Norma Jeane to pick out her new name, Marilyn Monroe. Marilyn comes from Ben's acquaintance with actress Marilyn Miller. He was once engaged to her, and now in Norma Jeane, he found someone who closely resembled her. Monroe was chosen because it was the family name of Norma Jeane's mother. She will now be known only as Marilyn Monroe, except on legal documents. When she marries Joe DiMaggio in 1954 she will appear as Norma Jeane DiMaggio on the marriage license and her passport. On March 12, 1956, she will have her name changed legally to Marilyn Monroe. In a bit of irony, on June 29, 1956 she would become Marilyn Miller, when she wed playwright, Arthur Miller.

Earl Wilson interviewed Ben Lyon about naming Marilyn. He ran the story on June 12, 1953, "Meet The Man Who Named Marilyn Monroe...Dear Marilyn (Monroe, of course!): I thought maybe you'd like to know I ran into the bloke that named you. Ben Lyon was telling me about it at dinner at Siegi's. Ben and his wife Bebe Daniels, the once-great

American movie stars are now radio stars here and among the most popular people in London. 'I think it was late summer '46,' Ben said. 'I was casting director at 20th Century-Fox in Hollywood when she came in looking for work. She was peaches and cream'--he's talking about you honey--'and I said, 'I'm going to make a test of you this afternoon.' We had a rule against shooting tests in Technicolor. It was worth your job. I chanced it. It came out great and Zanuck saw it and we signed her at $75 a week, with options for seven years. But I said to her, 'About your name...' It was Patricia Jean Doherty or something. We went through the casting directory and couldn't hit on anything. I finally said to her, 'I know who you are. You're Marilyn!' I told her that once there was a lovely actress named Marilyn Miller and that she reminded me of her. 'But what about the last name?' Marilyn finally said to me. 'My grandmother's name was Monroe and I'd like to keep that.' I said, 'Great! That's got a nice flow, and two Ms should be lucky.' That's how she got her name and it's never come out.' So then, Marilyn, I said to him, 'How did you happen to compare her to Marilyn Miller?' 'Oh,' he said, 'well back in the days of 1925, before I knew Bebe, I was engaged to Marilyn Miller.'"

While making *There's No Business Like Show Business*, Marilyn was photographed with Ben Lyon at the studio. Marilyn autographed the photo, "Dear Ben, you discovered me, you named me, and you believed in me when no one else did. Love, Marilyn"

According to Marilyn, she appeared in a parade shortly after changing her name and she was asked for her autograph by some kids. She had no idea how to spell her new name, so she asked someone standing next to her. It's a sweet story and bolsters her legendary naiveté as she navigates her way through the dangers of Hollywood.

Norma Jeane is signed by Twentieth Century-Fox to a Standard Contract on August 22nd. Grace Goddard countersigned the contract for Norma Jeane as her legal guardian. But according to California law, she needn't have bothered, for a married person 18 and older were considered emancipated. Her contract was a seven-year optional, without exclusions, exceptions or emendations. Marilyn started out at $75.00 a week. Her Fox publicity number will be F999. This will appear on all her publicity photos taken at Twentieth Century-Fox studios. It is interesting that they are numbered in sequential order, e.g. F999-S-1, F999-S-2, and so forth. By 1953 her tally of publicity photos would reach the 400s with no end in sight.

Marilyn has navigated the "chutes and ladders" world of modeling and in a little over a year's time has become a motion picture actress at a major studio. Miss Snively was to say of her most famous student, "She'd not only 'arrived'—she'd set a new record for the course." "People often ask me how she got there. I tell them not her wiggle or her sexy look or her mouth open, but a combination of that and luck and fortitude."

*Look* magazine photographer Earl Theisen remembers photographing Marilyn early in her career. "I remember a series I shot with Marilyn, oh back in 1946 or 1947. I picked her up at her place and I saw a big book on the human anatomy open and all marked up, and I said, 'what was the idea,' and she said, 'I'm studying the bone structure of the body. Your body does what your bones do. Did you know that?' Anything she does is calculated and is based on a more scientific knowledge of the human body than anybody has except doctors. She's built kind of like a sex machine. She can turn it on and off. I've seen her turn the sex machine into operation. I'll focus on her, get ready to shoot, and then looking in the finder, I can actually see the sex blossoming out, like it was a flower. If I'm in a hurry and want to shoot too quickly, she'll say, 'Earl, you shot it too quick. It won't be right. Let's do it over.' You see, it takes time for her to create this sex thing. And don't let anybody tell you it's in her hips or in her bosom. I'll tell you where it's located. It's in her mind. That's where it is."

Earl Theisen had a history with Marilyn that began all the way back to 1926. He worked at Consolidated Films, the same studio where her mother Gladys had been a film cutter. He remembers her birth and that Gladys' co-workers took up a collection to help pay for the doctor and other cost. Given the small town nature of Hollywood back then, it is reasonable to assume that he mentions the story to Marilyn, who would have appreciated someone sharing a good memory about her mother. He takes some beautiful photos of a young Marilyn in a pastoral setting, wearing a blue gossamer gown.

Shortly after signing with Twentieth Century-Fox, Harry Lipton called photographer Ed Clark and told him he knew a girl who was a 'real tomato.' Clark remembers that he had a sense that she was going to make it big. Marilyn and Clark worked together for two weeks. She styled her own hair, while Clark applied her makeup and photographed her around town. Clark would continue to photograph Marilyn during the next few years as she matured into her stardom.

In the late summer of 1946 Marilyn meets another contract player, Tommy Zahn. He was a lifeguard who was dating Darryl Zanuck's daughter, Darrylin, and was signed to a contract. Zahn would take Marilyn to Malibu beach where they would tandem surf. He remembers that she was in top physical shape, which was due in large part to her weight lifting routine and running. He really liked her. He took her out later in winter for some surfing and he was impressed that she was unfazed by the cold water. Marilyn became acquainted with the surfing community and spent much of her free time at the beach. This is an overlooked part of Marilyn's past and is one that marks her as a quintessential Californian girl. Anthony Summers and Dr. Lois Banner deserve mention as the ones who found this rare information on this little known aspect of Marilyn as part of the Southern California surfing community. Dr. Banner even found a rare photo of a young Marilyn at a luau at "Cap" Watkins house on Malibu beach. "Paradise Cove surf-agenarian Cal Porter is certain this is Norma Jean Baker, and the location is far west Malibu. 'I am told by the fellow who owns and lives on the property now that this photo was taken at a beach party at Santa Monica lifeguard captain George Watkins' old place at Nicholas Beach near Zero Point, north Malibu.'" In 2007 Dr. Arthur T. Verge, former lifeguard and history professor at El Camino College, spoke at the Ocean Park Library. He recalled Tommy Zahn and Marilyn's relationship. He said, "She dated Tom Zahn, and she was crazy about him. He's the only man who ever ran away from Marilyn Monroe. She would wear a disguise and visit him down at the boat station." Also, "He stayed friends with her for the rest of her life." Years after her death, while working together on *Baywatch*, they were out in a boat and Zahn stopped the motor and told Verge, "'She wanted fame, and she got it, but she paid the price for it.' Then he just started the boat up again,"

The September issue of *Popular Photography* magazine ran an ad for *Albumcolor Prints*, featuring a lovely young model, our Norma Jeane, photographed by Richard C. Miller.

On September 5th, *Variety* entertainment newspaper mentions Marilyn Monroe for the first time in the "New Contracts" column.

Norma Jeane returns to Las Vegas to appear for the court hearing on her divorce from Jim Dougherty on September 13th.

Case No. 31146 in the Eighth Judicial District Court of the State of Nevada, Clark County, filed July 5, 1946. Complaint for divorce: Extreme Mental Cruelty that has impaired the Plaintiff's health. Plaintiff, Norma Jeane Dougherty vs. Defendant, James Edward Dougherty.

Court Transcripts of Norma Jeane's hearing before Hon. A. S. Henderson, District Judge, Las Vegas, Nevada, 2:00pm. Norman Cornwall, Esq., Attorney for the Plaintiff. Norma Jeane Dougherty was sworn and testified as follows:

Name: Norma Jeane Dougherty

Address: 604, S. 3rd St.; Las Vegas, NV

Mr. Cornwall: Your name is Norma Jeane Dougherty?

Norma Jeane: Yes.

Mr. Cornwall: Is James Edward Dougherty, the defendant in this action, your husband?

Norma Jeane: Yes.

Mr. Cornwall: Where do you live, Mrs. Dougherty?

Norma Jeane: 604 South Third Street, Las Vegas, Nevada.

Mr. Cornwall: When did you first come to Las Vegas, Nevada to live?

Norma Jeane: May 14th, 1946.

Mr. Cornwall: Have you been physically present and actually domiciled in Las Vegas, Nevada each and every day from May 14th, 1946 to including at least July 5th of this year, when this complaint was filed?

Norma Jeane: Yes.

Mr. Cornwall: And when you come to Nevada May 14th, 1946 was it your intention to make your home and permanent place of residence?

Norma Jeane: Yes.

Mr. Cornwall: Has that been your intention since then?

Norma Jeane: Yes.

Mr. Cornwall: Is it your present intention?

Norma Jeane: It is.

Mr. Cornwall: You intend to remain her permanently or for at least an indefinite period of time?

Norma Jeane: That's right.

Mr. Cornwall: Have you read the Complaint which is on file in this action?

Norma Jeane: Yes I have.

Mr. Cornwall: And are all the allegations therein contained true?

Norma Jeane: Yes.

Mr. Cornwall: You have alleged that your husband treated you with extreme cruelty without just cause or provocation on your part. Will you tell the Court some of the acts upon which you base this cruelty charge?

Norma Jeane: Well, in the first place, my husband didn't support me and he objected to my working, criticized me for it and he also had a bad temper and would fly into rages and he left me on three different occasions and criticized me and embarrassed me in front of my friends and he didn't try to make a home for me.

Mr. Cornwall: Did that conduct on his part continue over a considerable period of time?

Norma Jeane: Yes, it did.

Mr. Cornwall: And did it grow better or worse?

Norma Jeane: Worse.

Mr. Cornwall: What effect did this have on your health?

Norma Jeane: It upset me and made me nervous.

Mr. Cornwall: So much so that you cannot live with him under the conditions and enjoy good health?

Norma Jeane: Yes.

Mr. Cornwall: Is reconciliation possible?

Norma Jeane: No.

After deliberating a short time, Judge Henderson announced, "A decree is granted," and sealed the decision with the crack of his gavel. Norma Jeane was now free to pursue her career. In a few weeks, Jim would countersign the divorce papers. Judgment Roll was signed for Marilyn's divorce on October 2, 1946. Her divorce was listed in Judgment Book-29, page 340-1.

It is interesting when Marilyn has her first scenes in *The Misfits*, and the subject of divorce is discussed, the whole thing could be summed up, like Roslyn says in the movie, "Why can't I say he was just never there?"

Back in Los Angeles the alliance of women surrounding Marilyn…Gladys, Grace and her sister Enid, Aunt Ana, Marilyn, Berneice and Mona Rae meet for dinner at Clifton's Pacific Seas to celebrate Marilyn's new found freedom. Doc Goddard was friends with the owner Marvin Kramer so the group was treated with a little extra attention. Even Gladys' mood was uncharacteristically buoyant this evening and she finds it easy to smile. Marilyn initiated a toast, "to the future." She made the same toast directly to Gladys, "to the future, Mother," and she smiled and toasted her daughter. A Polynesian band and singing girls added a celebratory mood as well. Marilyn sprang to her feet and took center stage in front of the microphone without having to be asked when the girls went into the audience for volunteers. Like Karaoke bars of today the patrons sang in amateurish fashion and everyone loved it. All except Marilyn, she sang *Blue Hawaii* with so much feeling and emotion that there was a pregnant pause in the show. Most of the other participants wandered back to their seats. But Gladys was spellbound and couldn't take her eyes off her daughter and she was said to have had a beautiful smile throughout Marilyn's performance. This is the same song made famous by Elvis Presley in 1961 in a movie of the same name. It was written by Leo Robin and Ralph Rainger in 1937 for the movie *Waikiki Wedding*, where it was sung by Bing Crosby.

This will be the last victory the group will share together. Fate and commitments conspire to separate them. Berneice had thoughts of moving to Los Angeles to be closer to Gladys and Marilyn, and had almost convinced her husband, but he changed his mind and wanted Berneice and Mona Rae to come home to Florida. Marilyn will become driven with a single minded desire to become an actress and will have little time to spare for family. Gladys will get restless and eventually move out from Aunt Ana's apartment with Marilyn. Yes. Their time together was short, but this gathering was a sweet culmination of Norma Jeane's fondest desire, to be reunited with her family. And that it turned out that they were all women, that was fine too, as there has always been a mysterious power in a gathering of women. The final missing piece of her family puzzle will be to find her father. She will search the rest of her life in vain, trying to fill that hole left by an absent father.

Jim will see Marilyn one more time when he gets back to Los Angeles and comes by the apartment at Aunt Ana's to sign the divorce papers. According to Jim, Marilyn offers to still be intimate with him, despite being divorced. But according to Arthur Miller, Jim demands that she sleep with him in order for him to sign the papers. The truth is somewhere in the middle. The papers were signed and no hard feeling remained.

What can be said of Marilyn's marriage to Jim was that it lasted for a little over four years. From all accounts she seemed to work at making a go of it, at least in the early years, and they had a happy and quiet uneventful life together. When he was called to active duty and had to leave her alone it is quite possible that it triggered some latent fear of being abandoned, reminding her of all the starts and stops of her childhood. To help endure the hours she went to work, and then she discovered modeling and the power of her sexuality. That the lure of modeling and motion pictures caused the end of their marriage cannot be disputed. During Jim's absences she will eventually began to be unfaithful to him. Her promiscuity could be the direct result of feelings of abandonment. It doesn't excuse it, but helps to make her motivations understandable. As she kicks loose the restraints of intimacy that hold a marriage together, it becomes easier for her to form new attachments while becoming unattached to her husband. Marilyn had most likely picked up this attitude of "free love" from the European photographers she worked with, Lazlo Willinger, Bruno Bernard and especially Andre de Dienes. "Free love" was originally a 19th century concept that meant that you were free to choose a monogamous sexual partner and you were also free to end the marriage or relationship when love had run its course. The term will eventually evolve in the 1960s and 70s to mean casual sex. Even before the end of WWII there was a releasing of the mores and traditions surrounding marriage and sexuality. The Kinsey Reports on male sexuality will be released in 1948. With the release of the female sexuality study in 1953 there would begin to be a shift in the perception of sex in America.

In regards to sexuality Marilyn would take a definite step away from her middle class upbringing. Hers would be a cautionary tale of free love and the inherent risks involved. She was lucky to have navigated the sexual swamps and cesspools of Hollywood and have actually emerged to become a public figure. Yet, she carried in her the memories of those years where she gave her self away for little in return and they will continue to haunt her dreams. She will later reflect that Goya's paintings contain images that she sees in her own dreams.

Still, this must have been a liberating period in Marilyn's life. She is at last free to make her own choices. No more foster parents or a husband to monitor her behavior. She makes the decision for herself to become an actress and to sign with 20th Century-Fox. How grown-up she must feel, no longer a waif shunted around by the capricious whims of others.

Andre de Dienes returns home from New York. While in New Mexico he calls Marilyn who tells him not to come back with intentions to marry her. She explains that yes, she is now divorced, but she is an actress now and there is no room for a husband in her life. This is one of her first independent decisions she has made since being emancipated by her divorce. He responds by being overcome with jealousy and driving out to Los Angeles as fast as he can. By the time he got there his emotions were spent and he had no choice but to forgive her.

In late September 1946 Marilyn accompanies Andre de Dienes to San Diego to visit the San Juan Capistrano Mission. He takes some casual photos of her sitting by a fountain. In these photos she wears little makeup and her hair is worn down. She looks fresh and innocent even though the studio had begun to refine her look. She posed again for him at a beach. She furnished her Catalina two-piece and he requested that she braid her hair and asks her to apply makeup. These are the first professional photos he takes of the newly named Marilyn Monroe. Her transformation has begun and her hair has a radiant blonde sparkle. She seems more sophisticated and self-assured as she poses on the beach. They buy an oriental statue and end up taking it to San Francisco to be appraised by a dealer in Chinese art that Andre knows. It ends up that the statue and the small figures enclosed in it are quite valuable. Marilyn keeps a little wooden Buddha figure and allows Andre to take the more valuable pieces.

Norma Jeane Dougherty is issued a Temporary Automobile Pass to Twentieth Century-Fox Studio lot on November 1st. The license number is 93-R-583. It is signed by Ben Lyon.

NBC sponsored the annual "Santa Clause Lane Parade" down Hollywood Boulevard on November 22, 1946. The stars of NBC shows entered floats in the parade. This was a tradition in Hollywood and in fact, Marilyn had attended the parade when she was a girl. This year Fibber McGee and Molly rode with Santa, who was played by veteran actor William McGinnis. Celebrities included Jack Benny, Rochester, Kay Kyser, Phil Harris, Red Skelton, Frank Morgan, Dennis Day, Roy Rogers and Gene Autry. An interesting bit of trivia, Gene Autry, who rode his horse Champion in the parade, heard children shouting

"Here Comes Santa Clause," and this gave him the idea for a new Christmas song. He would go on to co-write the classic "Here Comes Santa Claus" in 1948. The parade changed its name in 1978 to "The Hollywood Christmas Parade," as it is known today.

The "Alan Young Radio Show" had its own float with Fox starlets provided by Ben Lyon. Marilyn was one of the starlets chosen to ride on the Alan Young float. She and the other starlets carried signs which read, "We want Alan Young, and Vice-Versa." In a surviving photograph taken by Joseph Jasgur, Marilyn is shown dressed in a sweater and skirt, wearing a beret. Mr. Young viewed the parade from a window on the float and noticed Marilyn because she smiled more than any of the other starlets. After the parade, some of the cast members and the starlets go to the Brown Derby. Marilyn and Alan Young, brought together by their innate shyness, spend the evening sitting together. He invites her to a cocktail party the following evening at Conrad Janis' home. She accepts his invitation.

On November 23rd, Alan Young comes by Ana Lower's home to pick up Marilyn. She identifies Miss Lower as her grandmother. He also noticed several Christian Science books and a photo of the "mother-church" in Boston. He revealed that he, too, was raised as a Christian Scientist. He visits with Miss Lower until Marilyn is finally ready to leave. She feels a connection with him and in the car becomes rather animated, telling him about her religious experiences with the Christian Scientist. She told him that once she had been hit by a streetcar as a child and walked away unhurt, no one even called a doctor. While going to the cocktail party they ran into a heavy fog. Alan turned the car around and they ended up at his home to call for directions. Marilyn was naturally suspicious until he revealed that he lived with his parents. His parents were simple people, and he was concerned by the reaction his mother might have to Marilyn's tight red sweater. He left the room to compose himself. When he came back Norma Jeane and his mother were discussing Christian Science. It ended up that Marilyn had charmed his mother and she didn't want her to leave. They then made their way to the cocktail party. Alan felt that she was uncomfortable with the other people at the party, so they left early. When he dropped Marilyn off, he was hesitant to kiss her. All he could think about was Marilyn and his mother discussing religious books, so he just gave her a kiss on her cheek. They never dated again but she did appear on his radio show.

Marilyn is quick to read a situation and act accordingly. She will be sweet and differential when needed. Yet, with Charlie Chaplin, Jr., she is giggles in bed. She is not necessarily false. Her past has taught her to make judgments like quick-silver in order to survive.

On December 17, 1946 Louella Parsons reported, "Charlie Chaplin, Jr. with Marilyn Monroe at Slapsy Maxie's to see Martha Raye. She came and sat with them." Martha Raye's show consisted of a burlesque troupe, of which she was the comedic cornerstone, and in her first nightclub performance in 11 years she was getting rave reviews. Miss Raye was also starring in Charlie Chaplin's upcoming film, *Monsieur Verdoux*. It is only natural that she would extend such favors to his son and his beautiful date.

In December, Marilyn, June Haver and Peggy Ann Gardner are sent on a publicity shoot at the Darrin Motor Car Co., to promote the new Kaiser-Frazer car. B & B Publicity arranged the photo shoot. Fake snow was brought in for the event. One of the children was 10 year old Carl Barks whose father was a co-owner of the B & B Publicity firm. Existing photos show Marilyn with Santa in the Kaiser-Frazer car designed by Harold "Dutch" Darrin, aka Darrin of Paris. In another photo she and the other actresses are helping Santa hand out treats to kids, and in the last photo the kids are getting ready to throw snowballs at Marilyn. She is wearing her white form-fitting suspender shorts she has worn for David Conover's photo and a sweater. She also wears a mink coat on loan from the Twentieth Century-Fox studio. Darrin first met Darryl Zanuck when he came to Hollywood in 1939 and they became friends. He then designed many cars for stars including Clark Gable and William Powell

Twentieth Century-Fox Studio issues its first press biography of Marilyn on December 30, 1946. Studio publicist Jet Fore wrote the first studio bio of Marilyn, under the name of the head of Fox's publicity team, Harry Brand. 20th Century-Fox, for years put out an official biography of her that said Marilyn's father had died when she was a baby. Fore told this in 1983, "'It was made up because Marilyn wanted it that way. She told me her father was dead.' Fore said he later heard that her father had abandoned her mother, and was under the impression that Miss Monroe was illegitimate. 'That's what we all thought. It's in several books.'" Fore tells John Maynard a little different story in 1956. "She was always frank with us about this and we in turn were perfectly honest with the press. They understood, and made no mention of it. A child of love is a victim of circumstance, nothing more. Oh, we did invent a father who got killed in an accident, but what would you do? Besides, nobody had to buy it."

The bio also gives Marilyn's age is given as 18 instead of 20. It is here that the baby-sitter story gets its birth. The biography reports several things. One is that she is being given six months of "intensive grooming" before she gets the chance to be in a movie. Another is that she was adopted by Mr. and Mrs. E.S. Goddard. And, interestingly enough, it does not mention her marriage to James Dougherty at 16.

In late December of 1946 Jim Dougherty saw Norma Jeane/Marilyn for the last time. His family was planning a New Year's Eve party and they needed a phonograph. He remembered that he and Marilyn had owned one. He went over to her apartment. "She met me at the door and when I called her Norma Jeane, she told me her name had been changed to Marilyn Monroe…the Monroe from her grandfather's name. I asked if I could borrow the phonograph and she said no, that she needed it to practice her dancing lessons. I began to burn on the way home, and I think it was then that the torch went out. It had been a cold day, standing there on the doorstep and I'd got the feeling that I was begging. All my longing turned to anger."

Marilyn goes back to the old orphanage neighborhood when she moves into the Hollywood Studio Club, 1215 N Lodi Place, Hollywood. It is across the street from Grace Goddard's old apartment. She lives in room #307, a semi-private room. She has come full circle in her life, but she is in a better place now.

In the near future, Ben Lyon will advance her $15 from his own money to pay for two weeks back rent at the Studio Club. He will later say that Marilyn is one of the few people who ever paid back a loan to him.

1947 started by having Marilyn featured in the *Jantzen Wholesale Swimwear Catalogue*, modeling the "Double Dare" swimsuit, and the "Temptation" swimsuit. She rode on a Float in the Tournament of Roses Parade in Pasadena, California, with several other Twentieth Century-Fox starlets on January 1, 1947. January 3rd has her on the cover of the program for the Official opening of *Ken Murray's Blackouts 1947*. She is featured on the program/magazine cover in an Earl Moran pin-up of her as a sexy version of "Little Red Riding Hood." This was a program for Ken Murray's vaudeville review show, which was wildly popular in Los Angeles. Marilyn will have future associations with Ken Murray, thanks to Earl Moran, as she becomes more popular.

*Laff* magazine also features Marilyn on the cover in January, using the name Norma Jeane Dougherty. She signs a copy for hairstylist Sylvia Barnhart. "To Sylvia, Thanks a million for everything. You're really wonderful. Love always, Norma Jeane."

Norma Jeane Dougherty aka Marilyn Monroe finally signs a standard one year contract with her agent, Harry Lipton who was now at the Elsie Cukor-Lipton Agency on January 10, 1947 and agrees to pay them 10% of her earnings. She discharges the National Concert and Artists Corporation as her agents. Marilyn also signs a power of attorney giving the agency the permission to collect all compensation that is owed to her. It enables them to endorse and deposit her checks into an account and retain all monies owed and a 10% commission. Then the balance would be forwarded to her account. Lipton was forever trying to encourage Marilyn to be more responsible with her money. She would have to learn a few hard lessons before taking his advice.

On January 18th Marilyn Andre de Dienes comes by her home, only to learn that it was all over between them. Marilyn gave him a leather bound copy of the Christian Science book, *Science and Health With Key to the Scriptures* by Mary Baker Eddy. It was sweetly inscribed to him. Andre took this as her "Dear John" letter to him, as she still refused to marry him. "On the flypage was the inscription, in careful, school-girlish handwriting: 'Dearest Andre. Line 10 and 11 on page 494 of this book is my prayer for you always. Love, Norma Jeane.' The lines she had referred to were: 'Divine love always has met and always will meet every human need…since to all mankind and in every hour, divine love supplies all good.'" De Dienes will go on to say, "Only it didn't work, for her."

De Dienes made some interesting remarks about her, "'She was a go-getter,' he said. 'She had a terrific figure. I photographed her a great deal from the rear--in fact, too much so. Her fanny was always sticking out.' Dienes said that Monroe's present success would not have come about if she had not co-operated so wholeheartedly with many photographers. 'In fact,' he said, 'no girl can succeed in this business unless she poses for any Tom, Dick and Harry photographer. She was always enthusiastic and appreciative with photographers.'" He ended by saying, "Marilyn is not sexy at all. She has very little feeling toward sex. She is not sensuous. Since she is not the slave of sex, her work comes first."

1947 is when Marilyn gets her first big publicity buildup. On January 30th Fox runs a story about her, "Baby Sitter Lands in Films...She didn't know it at the time, but when an 18-year-old blonde baby-sitter walked into a 20th Century-Fox talent scout's home the other night she was on the road to possible stardom. The baby sitter, Marilyn Monroe of West Los Angeles, isn't a baby sitter anymore. She was assigned to a contract that appraises her possibilities so greatly that she will be groomed for dramatic work for a year before being assigned a role. Marilyn, a native daughter, attended University and Van Nuys High Schools."

Fox will keep releasing the fabrication to the press each month. By June the story-line changes from a talent scout to a casting director and by then they have found a casting director with two twin boys, and a daughter, to photograph with Marilyn. The photos were taken by David Cicero. Marilyn had this to say about this campaign. "Publicity made up a story about how I was a baby sitter who'd been babysitting for the casting director and that's how I was discovered. They told me to say that, although it strictly wasn't true. You'd think that they would have used a little more imagination and have had me at least a daddy sitter."

The studios generated a massive amount of publicity on this unknown starlet. She had yet to be in a movie when the wheels of the publicity machine printed the first stories of Marilyn Monroe. They capitalized on her youth and unspoiled attractiveness. She was likable, she was wholesome, and she was childishly cute. Her willingness to engage the viewer set her apart from other pin ups. She generated an intimacy that crossed over the boundary of the printed page. The ripe fruit of her blossoming beauty was her sexuality. She had the approachability of the girl next door and the potent honey of her loveliness upped the ante. With the help of the press she found a conduit more powerful than girlie magazines. With every pump of the paper boy's arm, she came directly into homes and in direct contact with the American public. Her photos didn't pass unnoticed. Her smiling image aroused emotions, good and bad. Women envied her and men were aroused by her, yet both wanted to offer her protection from something even they could not name. She was like a beautiful doe, without threat. She was becoming a household name, and a reference point where sexuality was measured from. Whether she appeared in the guise of a baby-sitter, posed in a bustle swim-suit, frolicked on the beach with her dog, or beamed from the headlines as a starlet, the public took note. And when the public takes note the cash registers ring.

Marilyn's contract with Fox was renewed on February 10th and she received a pay increase to $150 per week. Marilyn will receive another big publicity push when she is featured on the cover with an article in *Parade* magazine on February 16th. *Parade* was a Sunday newspaper supplement and had a wide readership. "Cover Girl...Marilyn Monroe's Movie Career Stems From Magazine Cover Pages." The next day Marilyn signs an agreement with Twentieth Century-Fox Studio in order for her to appear on the *Lux Radio Theatre*, February 24.

Marilyn makes her first appearance on radio when she has a small part on the *Alan

*Young Radio Show* on February 21st. The title of the show is "McPherson Fortune." Marilyn will also pose in a publicity still for the episode with Alan Young and Bill Thompson. All are dressed in kilts and Marilyn is playing a bagpipe. After her appearance Alan wouldn't see Marilyn for another five years, until he chanced to meet her while she was filming *Clash by Night* in 1952.

Marilyn appears on the Lux Radio Theater on February 24$^{th}$, in a presentation of *Kitty*, starring Paulette Goddard. Marilyn makes a guest appearance during the intermission to help sell "Lux" soap. John Milton Kennedy is the announcer.

This is an important audio recording of Marilyn, because it is the first time we get to hear her voice. It is interesting how natural and unaffected Marilyn's speaking voice was at this time. This is the raw talent that she started with. In later years she takes on a slightly English sound. It is probably due to the influence of people like British Helena Sorrell at Fox, and later the European Natasha Lytess. She has yet to make a motion picture. It will be June before she starts work on her first film, *Scudda Hoo, Scudda Hay*. It is easy to imagine the earnestness which she pours into this performance. Much like "the Girl" in *Seven Year Itch* will stand by Dazzledent toothpaste long after the cameras have stopped rolling, it wouldn't be surprising to find that Marilyn actually used "Lux" flakes herself.

Charles Chaplin, Jr. gave Marilyn an autographed portrait of himself. "To Marilyn, with sincerest hopes that you become a great actress. Feb. 28, 1947, Charles Chaplin, Jr."

The protectors of public decency for the film industry have noticed Marilyn. She will have an increasingly combative relationship with them as they try to restrain her sexuality and put a stop to her provocative attire. She once joked that, "they worried if a girl had cleavage. They should worry if she didn't." Jack Lait, Jr., reported on March 3rd, "The Hollywood and Vine whistle boys are eager for a gander at 20th-Fox's new find, Marilyn Monroe, ever since they learned that the Johnston office censored 24 of the first 32 publicity photos she posed for." Her first photos for Fox were a series of Marilyn in the Catalina two-piece swimsuit that she didn't return to the company. F999-S-22 is the earliest known publicity photo still in existence.

In April 1947 the publicity department will start running a series of photographs of Marilyn in a two piece swim suit with a bustle. It will run throughout April in newspapers across the country and be a rousing success. As innocuous as this all sounds, these were very popular photos of Marilyn and just racy enough to draw a closer look in a newspaper. You must remember that the bikini was invented in July of 1946 and was still considered scandalous. What Marilyn wore in her early career was a two-piece swimsuit. The difference in the two-piece and the bikini is the amount of coverage of the midriff, and in particular, the belly button. As long as the bottoms covered the navel, everything was fine. But changes were in the wind and Marilyn seemed to find herself riding the crest of the bikini. Lazlo Willinger comes the closest to photographing her in an actually bikini. It is interesting that even wearing these swimsuits she poses in such a way as to hide her belly button, using her arm to block the pesky navel, when the photos start to appear as magazine covers in late 1949. Marilyn's navel first saw print in the February 1950 issue of *Laff*, in a cover credited to Bruno Bernard.

*Acme Photo Service* shows another photo of Marilyn in the bustle swim suit, "Marilyn Monroe, Hollywood actress, drew so much fan mail when she posed for newspapers in a bathing suit that Charles LeMaire, studio wardrobe director, designed a special job for her to wear when posing for pictures. The suit, which has Hollywood mermaids clamoring for copies, has a provocative feature--a perky bustle in the back. It is made of ivory silk faille printed in red roses and green leaves. Form fitting tights are covered by a full sash which ties in the back into the oversize bustle."

On April 4th columnist Harold Heffernan revealed that Marilyn and Colleen Townsend had replaced director F. Hugh Herbert's daughters, Diana and Pamela, in *Scudda Hoo, Scudda Hay*. Heffernan revealed that as writer, as well as director of *Scudda Hoo, Scudda Hay*, his daughters urged him to write bit parts for them. He complied, but the boys in the front office decided to test Marilyn and Miss Townsend instead.

On April 10th Marilyn will be featured in Nat Dillinger's "Inside Hollywood" photo column in an image that has her playing tennis. "Marilyn Monroe, once her High School "Oomph Girl," is walloping the daylights out of those tennis balls. Marilyn soon will debut in *Scudda Hoo, Scudda Hay."*

Marilyn was invited on April 15th to the Hollywood Post No. 43 of the American Legion's annual ceremony honoring "Studio Starlings." Marilyn was also featured in the program, along with 16 other starlets. She was referred to in the program as the 'Oomph' girl of Emerson Junior High School."

May features two new concepts for publicizing Marilyn that the Fox Publicity department generates in an attempt to create interest in her among the nation's press. The first is Marilyn skiing on the sand in a Jantzen color-blocked two-piece, called the "Eye-Catcher," and the second is series of her romping on the beach with her black and white spaniel wearing the same swimsuit. The "Eye-Catcher" was designed for Catalina by RKO stylist, Edward Stevenson.

June finds her on the cover of *Personal Romances* magazine. It is a photograph by Richard C. Miller, taken in April 1946 where she is wearing her own wedding dress.

Marilyn moves to a new place, 131 S. Avon St, in Burbank. She will live here until November.

Marilyn begins studying at the Actors Lab with Morris Carnovsky and Phoebe Brand, his wife. She will study here until the Lab is forced to close because of loss of funding because of supposed ties to Communism in 1949. She studied speech with Margaret MacLean and elementary acting with Phoebe Brand. The Actors Lab was a West Coast extension of The Group Theater in New York. The acting methods of Konstantin Stanislavski were transformed into an American acting technique later to be known as "the method." An actor personalized his experiences and used them to create the character he is playing. The actor did exercises that taught them how to observe and internalize human emotions and actions, even animal behaviors. The more an actor knows about himself, the better an actor he would become. Much of Stanislavski's peculiar language was used, "sublimation," "affective memory," "the living part." You don't have to look hard for the reason this school appealed to Marilyn. For someone so bereft of education as she was, being a part of this kind of training, and the esoteric lexicon that went with it, would have given her a sense of validation that she was at long last learning. But to make the picture complete, Marilyn also needed a savant to her acolyte. She never seemed to connect with Carnovsky or Brand, and for that matter, they with her. Miss Brand recalls Marilyn at the Actors Lab, "I never knew what to make of her. I didn't know what she thought of the work. She didn't tell me what her acting problems were. But she came to classes on time and did all her assignments conscientiously. Frankly, I never would have predicted she would be a success. I remember her for her beautiful long blonde hair, which was usually in need of a good combing. I tried to get through to her and find out more about her, but I couldn't do it. She was extremely retiring. What I failed to see in her acting was her wit, her sense of humor. It was there all the time--this lovely, comedic style, but I was blind to it."

The Actors Lab was located behind Schwab's Drugstore. Shelley Winters and Dorothy Dandridge were also studying there at the time and Marilyn befriended both actresses. She would hang out at Schwab's before or after classes, often times with Shelley Winters.

It is also at Schwab's that she befriends columnist Sidney Skolsky. Marilyn will end up driving him to his appointments, as he didn't drive. He will in turn, keep her name in the press. Slolsky will tell of Marilyn's desire to become an actress. "Back in the beginning, she wanted to be a movie star more than anything else. 'It's something precious,' she told me once. She formed a cup with the palms of her hands, looked at them longingly and said, 'I don't want to lose a drop of it.' She always doubted that she'd make it, but the motor inside her was self-winding and it kept driving her."

June heralds in her movie career as Marilyn's first film, *Scudda Hoo, Scudda Hay*, begins production. Marilyn will play Betty, a girl friend of the lead, Rad McGill, played by June Haver. A small scene remains of Betty greeting Rad on the steps of the church. A young Natalie Wood is also in the scene. All the rest of Marilyn's scenes were cut out of the film. To commemorate her start in films, Grace Goddard gives Marilyn an antique Elgin pocket watch, and has her initials engraved inside.

Enroute to location shoots, Marilyn shares a car with Rose Steinberg, a script supervisor. Miss Steinberg engages her in conversation. Marilyn asked her how she can become a star. They talk about the road to stardom and this prompts Miss Steinberg to give her a book, *As a Man Thinketh*. She tells Marilyn that reading this book should help her realize the power of positive thinking. Marilyn gratefully accepted the book and advice with great interest. Like Miss Snively, Miss Steinberg is struck by Marilyn's determination and drive.

Marilyn signs an amended contract with 20th Century-Fox because she had turned 21 on June 1st. In the state of California an 18 year old married woman was considered emancipated so Grace Goddard's co-signature wasn't needed in the first place. Maybe she had included Grace as a kindness to her.

June 1st also finds her on the cover of the *Sunday World Herald,* (Omaha, NB), a Sunday supplement. She appears in a photo by David Cicero on the cover as a baby sitter watching over twin baby boys. It is captioned, "The pretty sitter is sitting pretty. Marilyn Monroe is in motion pictures because she was a baby sitter." She is shown inside the magazine rehearsing with Helena Sorrell at her home. In another she appears in a gown in front of a movie camera. This photo is often said to be of her screen test, but most likely it was not. In the last photo the little girl Marilyn is playing dolls with is identified as Joanne Metzler.

Although, British transplant Helena Sorrell worked for Twentieth Century-Fox as the head dramatic coach and by developing the young talent that arrived at the studio, she also conducted private classes in her Beverly Hills home. Miss Sorrell was adamant that a girl must have these characteristics to insure a screen career: "1. Ability to concentrate; 2.Good diction; 3. Good posture; and 4. Poise and self-assurance. Inability to concentrate is the greatest fault of all young screen aspirants....'Sloppy diction is a tremendous fault,' Miss Sorrell adds, 'and girls are the worst offenders. They talk without opening their mouths,' she explains. 'No lip reader in the world could understand what they are saying. This construction of the lips and jaw causes a tightness that produces a nasal tone. It's a big job to teach them to relax their jaw muscles.'....Another fault is a bad walk, says the dramatic coach. 'Girls, particularly, walk from the knees instead of from the hips. Their posteriors are not tucked under as they should be,' Miss Sorrell says. 'This produces a swayback line that is awkward and ugly.'....Beauty and personality may get you into motion pictures, but they won't keep you there."

The *United Press Wire Service* is also starting to realize that photos of Marilyn make good copy and picked up the baby sitter story again and ran three separate items in June about her with photos by David Cicero.

Helena Sorrell arranged for Marilyn to meet photographer Bill Burnside, who represented the J. Arthur Rank Organization in Hollywood, at the studio of Bruno Bernard. Marilyn was posing for glamour photos when they arrived. Burnside remembers, "She was pretty, but not beautiful by the standards of the day, and did not seem particularly adept at posing."

Marilyn met with Miss Sorrell and Burnside afterward for dinner and he remembers that she was dressed in a sweater and tweed skirt. She didn't interact with either of them until Miss Sorrell told her that Burnside had helped Vivien Leigh get the part of Scarlett O'Hara in *Gone With the Wind*. After that, her personality changed as she wanted to know if he had met Clark Gable and a barrage of questions followed. She revealed her obsession with Gable, even going so far as to always carry his photo with her.

Burnside remembers Marilyn, "She prattled away over dinner at the little things that filled her life. Never once did she mention her career or ask Helena's advice or mine. She was always about two hours late for appointments. Charming, because her apologies were always really sincere. Unusual, for her thought process were impossible to follow with a logical, compartmentalized mind. She varied from gay to grave with infinite and exquisite abandon....Once I knew her better I decided Marilyn was something special. For her part, she had her own private life which she did not share with me. Never easy to get to know.

Constantly on the defensive, she also walked very much alone. While not frigid, she was so insecure that sex seemed out of place. A kiss took weeks to achieve. She did not like to be touched, and that merely enhanced the prominent remoteness of her breasts. I could not think of sexual conquest by force, wrestling on a couch or in the back of a car. One could only wait and hope. More likely, it was her shyness combined with her sense of insecurity that provoked a curious amalgam of beauty and sex that set her apart from the usually rapacious starlets of the time. She wasn't dumb. She was dumb like a fox. Her love of poetry, which she read avidly and wrote quite well, her desire for learning and her appreciation of the outdoors. Music she loved and she sat for hours on the floor of the living room playing records. Her taste were very catholic, favorites of the day-- Crosby, Sinatra and traditional jazz. She was a beautiful dancer, either alone or in one's arms moving with rhythm and fluidity. Our encounter was a brief two-year affair."

Burnside was intrigued with her and they began an affair which ended when he spent time in Argentina on a photographic assignment. Before leaving he arranged for Marilyn to be photographed by great photographer Paul Hesse, at his beach house in Malibu sometime during the summer of 1947. They arrived one and a-half hours late. Mr. Hesse's immediate, and unfortunate, reaction was, "Darling, You're too fat." Marilyn burst into tears and in an attempt to placate her Burnside took her down to the beach and photographed her in casual attire, a blue top and red shorts. The photos showed her sitting in the sand and playing in the surf. Years after her death, these will be discovered and are among the most revealing glimpses into the rare beauty of the young Marilyn Monroe. He also would take some lovely professional publicity photos of Marilyn. He tried to submit her photos to the J. Arthur Rank Organization in order that they might sign her up. They agreed with Mr. Hesse that she was too plump. But as they say, "hind-sight is 20-20," and looking at these images of Marilyn cavorting on the beach proves once and for all that our "Darling" was not too fat. Years later, Bill Burnside, still flabbergasted that they didn't sign her, remembers, "But they didn't know her. If I took her to a restaurant, however flash, the waiters were ready to jump to her bidding. She had it all right, the star quality, at the age of 20 or 21."

On June 8th the *Stars and Strips* military newspaper ran an article that covered 2 half-pages titled, "Pass That Bottle, Baby." It featured photos by David Cicero of Marilyn as a babysitter and the one with Helena Sorrell.

On June 11th, The Greater Los Angeles Press Club was established with a grand opening at the Case Hotel. Their newsletter was titled the *8-Ball*, and Marilyn was chosen as their first "8-Ball Girl." She would again be chosen as their "8-Ball Girl" in 1953. She was photographed this day for the *Los Angeles Times* by R.O. Ritchie.

Marilyn participated in Twentieth Century-Fox Studio's Annual Golf Tournament and Dance at the Brentwood Country Club on July 20th. She was photographed on the golf course wearing her Mabs of Hollywood "Hourglass" swimsuit. She also had a publicity picture made with Henry Fonda.

On July 25th the tourism board in Las Vegas, Nevada started an Air Taxi from Burbank to "Lucky Las Vegas," and the best part...the round trip in the DC-3's was free. Hedda

Hopper even drove to Las Vegas and met with the movie stars that were brought in to hype the event and wrote about it in her column on July 26th. The Flamingo was the late gangster Bugsy Siegel's "Monte Carlo in the desert." It had been in financial trouble and was recently sold to Sanford Adler, who also owned the El Rancho. In order to attract gamblers, he had a group of starlet's parade around the Hotel grounds, where they were photographed by the pool. The starlets were also in attendance in the showroom as legendary Las Vegas showgirls entertained the audience. They then worked as shills in the casino, sitting at the gaming tables and playing with the house's money. Marilyn was one of these starlets. There is a surviving photograph of her at the pool, surrounded by a group of young men. She is wearing her Mabs of Hollywood "Hourglass" swimsuit that she was photographed steadily in throughout 1947.

Marilyn finished July out in the production of her second movie which started on July 30th. *Dangerous Years* had Marilyn playing Evie, a waitress at the Gopher Hole. She had one small scene. She was loaned out from 20th Century-Fox to the Sol Wurtzel Productions studio and was compensated $125 for one week of work.

In his syndicated column on August 2nd, Harrison Carroll mentions this bit of gossip, "Town's Newest-Twosome: Dave Street and Marilyn Monroe at the Somerset House."

On August 3rd Marilyn represented Fox in another charity golf tournament, the Third Annual Frank Borzage Motion Picture Golf Tournament at the California Country Club, located on Motor Ave, between Pico and Washington. The tournament benefited the Damon Runyon Cancer Fund. Bob Hope, Bing Crosby, Clark Gable and Jack Benny were among the participants. This was her last professional duty to the studio before she was let go. Marilyn was assigned to the featured pairings at 12:40 of John Carroll, Ken Murray, Edgar Kennedy and Walter Daniels as their starlet score-keeper. She meets John Carroll's wife Lucille Ryman, head of talent at MGM. She is befriended by the Carrolls and they take enough interest in her to sign her to a contract in December, which will pay for her living expenses and her acting lessons. She was spotted by photographer Ed Baird, who took some candid pictures of her. She looked radiantly happy this day in her pink cashmere sweater and white shorts.

Miss Ryman tells Florabel Muir about meeting Marilyn, "I liked Marilyn when I first saw her, but I felt terribly sorry for her, too. She came to a party at my house on Sunday afternoon. I don't remember who brought her, if I ever knew. All the girls were disagreeable to her, but the men flocked around like buzzing bees around flowers. Reason enough for the gals not like her, huh? I gave her advice and lent her money. She impressed me with her sincerity. She is a good girl--I can't emphasize that too much. With her charm and beauty it would have been easy for her to get all the money she needed from roving-eye males, but she wouldn't have it that way." Marilyn told this about Miss Ryman in *American Weekly*, November 21st, 1952. "'Marilyn,' she said, 'you have talent.' I could have kissed her. Not Marilyn you have a figure, but Marilyn you have talent. 'Now don't be discouraged,' she went on. 'You can't expect everything to happen overnight. In the meantime count on me to be your friend.' She really proved herself by tangibly helping, giving me $25 a week."

Marilyn herself commented on this period of her life, "Most of what I did while I was at Fox that first time was pose for stills."

If you weigh her movie appearances alongside her photographic ones, her movie career carried no weight.

# Chapter Seven
## A Pretty Panhandler

"We sat in drugstore counters. We sat in waiting rooms. We were the prettiest tribe of panhandlers who ever overran a town. And there were so many of us! Beauty contest winners, flashy college girls, home grown sirens from every state in the union. From cities and farms. From factories, vaudeville circuits, dramatic schools, and one from an orphan asylum."
Marilyn Monroe

**D**espite all her success in generating publicity for herself, Twentieth Century-Fox Studio dropped her option on August 25th and she received her last paycheck in August 31st. Soon after her dismissal, Marilyn applies for Unemployment Compensation from the State of California.

Tommy Zahn, Marilyn's surfing companion and friend, thinks that Darryl Zanuck was unhappy with their growing relationship. Zanuck intended Zahn to marry his daughter Darrylin, not Marilyn, so when that appeared to not be happening, he got rid of both of them.

Marilyn herself says that Fox let her go because they found her unphotogenic. "Mr. Zanuck feels that you may turn into an actress some time, but that your looks are definitely against you." She remembers thinking at the time, "It wasn't only that I'd been fired. If they had dropped me because I couldn't act it would have been bad enough. But it wouldn't have been fatal. I could learn, improve, and become an actress. But how could I ever change my looks? And I'd thought that was the part of me that couldn't miss…I hated myself for having been a fool and had illusions of how attractive I was. I got out of the bed and looked into a mirror. Something horrible had happened. I wasn't attractive. I saw a coarse, crude-looking blonde. I was looking at myself with Mr. Zanuck's eyes. And I saw what he had seen—a girl whose looks were too big a handicap for a career in the movies."

According to Harry Lipton, Marilyn's agent, she was heartbroken over her firing, she cried and cried. Then, she recovered her composure and told Harry, "After all, it doesn't matter. It's all a case of supply and demand." But, lucky for Marilyn that the men of America, and especially those that will serve in Korea, demanded what she could supply.

Lipton remembered escorting her to a party in the early part of 1947. A wealthy man had offered her some expensive gifts in exchange for an evening with her. She grabbed Lipton and left the party. He had never seen her so upset. He recalls, "I suddenly realized that she was only 20 years old. For all her sensuous face and figure, she was only 20 years old."

He told her that she would learn. To which she replied, "I have to learn a lot of things. And they," her hand swept around the car, including in its movement wealthy admirers, studio executives, and film critics, "don't think I will. But I'll learn."

Marilyn came to an epiphany during this lean period, "It was then that I realized that an actress must act." She would concentrate on her thespian studies in a way few actresses ever had. She also had this to say, "I had vague notions about the motion picture business, but I wasted my first Hollywood break because I was too shy to ask necessary questions. Now I realize you can't find out too much about any business." "Fortunately, it dawned on me that it must be my own fault that I was failing. I wanted to act, but I wasn't skilled in the craft I wanted to get into. I began budgeting every spare dollar for dramatic lessons. I determined to hang on, black as my prospects looked. I was pretty discouraged many times, to be quite honest. I became a photographic model, barely managing to eat until at last I got another break here at 20th in a very small roll...I had to admit to myself that I wasn't sufficiently trained to deserve a chance in pictures. I had to do something about the fundamentals of acting before I was ready for another studio call. I'm grateful to Hollywood for teaching me that life is a road to finding one's self. I had forced into starting to think about my qualifications as an actress. Then my shortcomings stood out so plainly to me that I at last knew where I stood and why."

After she is fired from Fox she comments about her emotional state. "But there was something that wouldn't let me go back to the world of Norma Jeane. It wasn't ambition or a wish to be rich and famous. I didn't feel any pent-up talent in me. I didn't even feel that I had looks or any sort of attractiveness. But there was a thing in me like a craziness that wouldn't let up. It kept speaking to me, not in words, but in colors—scarlet and gold and shining white, greens and blues. They were the colors I used to dream about in my childhood when I had tried to hide from the dull, unloving world in which the orphanage slave, Norma Jeane, existed. I was still flying from that world and it was still around me."

It is interesting that she talks about her inner voice speaking to her in colors. In many Eastern religions a person's chakra's, their source of energy, is revealed in colors. Each chakra has a specific color and role. Scarlet is the color of the root chakra and is thought to connect the person to a sense of spirituality. Green is the color of the $4^{th}$ chakra and is the seat of love, compassion and healing. Blue is the color of the $5^{th}$, or throat chakra. It is the seat of communication, self-expression and contemplation. White, or as Marilyn described it, a "shining white," represents the $7^{th}$ or crown chakra. Gold represents the enhancement of the true self in the development of the psyche.

Marilyn recalls the self-evaluation this experience had begun in her. "I knew how third-rate I was. I could actually feel my lack of talent, as if it were cheap clothes I was wearing inside. But how I wanted to learn! To change, to improve! I didn't want anything else. Not men, not money, not love, but the ability to act. With the lights on me and the camera pointed at me, I suddenly knew myself. How clumsy, empty, uncultured I was! A sullen orphan with a goose egg for a head. But I would change."

When people are presented with a glimpse of their true identity it can be a revelation, a moment of clarity. For one so bereft of any strong identity in her life, this moment of self-discovery becomes the sure place she uses as the foundation of her identity. She will always claim that she wants to be an actress, not just a movie star, but a skilled and accomplished actress. It will be important to remember this as her life unfolds. It will become the touchstone she uses to guide her decisions and, make no mistake, no one will stand in her way. Her road will be littered with family, friends, lovers and husbands, but she will cling to this idea that her true self, her essential nature is wrapped up in being able to act. It is ironic that people of little identity are attracted to a career that demands that they forfeit their true selves and become something entirely different. She is searching for an identity that by its very definition she will have to learn to fragment in order to succeed, and yet, at the same time, she will have to remain intact. This is where the danger comes in. It is a gamble and she is willing to roll the dice of her true self upon the chance of her future accomplishment. It seems that Marilyn was becoming surer of herself as she progressed as an actress. "I spent my salary on dramatic lessons, on dancing lessons and singing lessons. I bought books to read. I sneaked scripts off the set and sat up alone in my room reading them out loud in front of the mirror. And an odd thing happened to me. I fell in love with myself…not how I was, but how I was going to be. I used to say to myself, 'What the devil have you got to be proud about, Marilyn Monroe?' and I'd answer, 'Everything, everything.'"

Columnist Fred Harris remembers meeting Marilyn during this time. "To understand more fully, come with me back a few years, when Marilyn Monroe was a struggling starlet who had just had her option dropped and was living in a furnished room. A photographer friend of mine had had an assignment to do some 'cheesecake' photos (regular starlet stuff) of Marilyn and decided that since he had nothing better to do he might as well follow through. I went along for the ride, mostly. A hoarse voice answered our knock. Marilyn was in bed with a heavy cold. She looked like anything but a glamorous symbol of sex and she apologized for not being able to go out for the pictures at the beach. We sat and talked to her for a couple of hours, just killing time, but one thing she said stuck in my memory, 'One of these days the same studio which let me go will ask me back. And this time it will be as an accepted personality.'

Ironically, Marilyn appeared in a *CP Wire Service* newspaper article on August 25th, with words of wisdom by talent scout, Ivan Kahn, titled, "The Road to Fame in Hollywood; Only One in 25 Succeeds, Says Talent Scout...The luck element which sometimes keeps people from a career despite talent once in a while throws others into a screen career without any effort on their part. An example is Marilyn Monroe. She was a babysitter who happened to "sit" for a studio executive and was offered a test without asking for it."

During this period it is reported that Marilyn used to hang out at the Roosevelt Hotel and people watch. Some biographers insist that it is during this lean time that she worked as a call girl, or in the least made ends meet by soliciting men. There are rumors, but no clear evidence that she engaged in this practice. If she traded sexual favors with men it would be, at the least, a pragmatic calculation on her part to further her career, and they would have been powerful men who had the influence to help her. She was by no stretch of the imagination a common prostitute, trolling the streets for men. Before one judges her, it would be well to remember that she is just 21 years old and without a family to guide her as she makes her way through this lair of dragons that was Hollywood.

Marilyn would tell Florabel Muir, "This would be a very uninteresting world if there weren't any wolves. A girl has to learn how to handle them or she'll run into a bushel of trouble. There are many types of wolves. Some are sinister, others are just good-time Charlies trying to get something for nothing, and still others just make a game of it. I find the latter type interesting. If you are born with what the world calls sex appeal, you can either let it wreck you or use it to advantage in the tough show business struggle. It isn't always easy to pick the right route….Whether a girl survives a pack of wolves depends entirely on her. If she is trying to get something for nothing she often winds up giving more than she bargained for. If she plays the game straight she can usually avert unpleasant situations and she gains the respect of even wolves."

August comes to an end and she finally appears on the cover of a magazine as Marilyn Monroe when she graces the front of *Laff's* September issue. She also appeared on the cover of *True Experiences* magazine.

As an eager student of her craft, Marilyn will pick up the payments herself at the Actors Lab when Fox stops paying for her lessons. On September 21st Marilyn went on a casting call for *Glamour Preferred,* a stage production at the Bliss-Hayden Theatre, advertised in the *Los Angeles Times*. She landed the second lead in the play which was a "lighthearted spoof of Hollywood," and made her debut on October 12th.

In late summer/early fall Marilyn was photographed by *LIFE* photographer Loomis Dean on the set of Clifton Webb's movie, Twentieth Century-Fox's *Sitting Pretty*. She did not appear in the film, but she was a friend of Webb and had dropped by to see him or Webb might have invited her to the set for a chance of some extra work. She is seen sharing a big box of candy with Webb and another actress. Around a dozen photos remain, but none of them made it into the *LIFE* article. The other actress in the photos, Laurette Luez, would appear with Marilyn again in the October 10, 1949 edition of *LIFE* magazine, photographed by Philippe Halsman, "Eight Girls Try Out Mixed Emotions." Miss Luez would also appear inside the front cover of *Modern Man*, November 1953, still trying to jump-start her career. Marilyn appeared in the magazine in a 6 page photo essay by Andre de Dienes, and her career was in full throttle.

Webb will become one of her biggest supporters, remaining close to her throughout her career. Webb was quoted as saying, "Clifton Webb swears she'll one day develop into the biggest femme star ever to hit Hollywood. 'And not because she's so all-fired talented, but because she work so hard,' he says. 'Why it's nothing for Marilyn to put in a twelve-hour day on the set and go over her next day's lines with her drama coach until all hours.'" Webb will give an astute observation of Marilyn in a 1955 magazine article, saying that, "she is very sweet, very serious. She likes to talk about the theatre and the kind of thing that makes people tick. She is intense and completely straightforward. She reads all the time. She is in complete earnest towards her career. Ambitious and anxious to know her job. This girl, when she was making very little money, spent practically every cent she made on various coaches. Now she will work all day, go to her little flat for a little bit of dinner on a tray, and then work with her coach on the next day's scenes. And often they will work until early morning."

Louella Parsons reported on September 24th, "Alice Faye's brother, Charlie, and Marilyn Monroe are really an item. Their favorite spot is the Seacombers in Malibu."

Columnist Nat Dallinger published a captioned photo on September 25th of Marilyn and George Jessel dining at the Mocambo nightclub. On the 29th Harrison Carroll commented, "George Jessel didn't lose any time after his fight with Tommye Adams. He was at the Mocambo the next night with Marilyn Monroe." George Jessel was an actor who had transformed himself into a producer of musicals at Twentieth Century-Fox. As was her habit, Marilyn was quick to recognize those who could help her career and she would remain close to Jessel until she attained star status in 1952. Jessel had a great faith in her talent and even though she had been dropped by Twentieth Century-Fox, he still invested himself in her career, as will become evident during her stint at Columbia.

It seemed that Fox might not have appreciated her acting abilities, but nevertheless they did appreciate her photogenic qualities as Marilyn was featured in *Screen Guide* magazine's October 1947 issue in the "Hollywood Merry-Go-Round...Three Starlets From *Mother Wore Tights* Get An Off-Season Sun Tan." There are a couple of photos of Marilyn with two other starlets. They are captioned, "Sun lamps will do the trick, when even California weather gets a bit chilly for outdoor tanning. Donna Hamilton smoothes more lotion on Marilyn Monroe's back. Donna tunes in soft music for Marilyn and their hostess, Marjorie Holliday, also from 20th Century-Fox." A close-up photo of Marilyn is captioned, "Fair-skinned Marilyn has to make her sun-lamp sessions short. She is in Betty Grable's *Mother Wore Tights*."

There is no documentation that proves Marilyn actually appeared in this movie, although, it is possible given the fact that she was a starlet at the time and may have appeared in it uncredited. Neither Donna Hamilton, nor Marjorie Holiday is credited as having been in the movie either. It is interesting to note that Marjorie Holiday will go on to appear, albeit uncredited, in *Don't Bother to Knock* as a switchboard operator, as a cashier in *O'Henry's Full House*: *The Cop and the Anthem*, and as a secretary in *Monkey Business*. Donna Hamilton will be photographed with Marilyn for a postcard advertising the Postmasters Convention in Los Angeles on October 12-16. Miss Hamilton will go on to publish the *Paris Gazette*, an English language tabloid. It seems once again, that Marilyn will be the only break-out star in this group of starlets.

The Los Angeles County Orphanage was keeping track of its most famous ward and one of the social workers talked to Grace Goddard. They then quote Grace and made the last notation in the file of Norma Jeane Baker on October 4, 1947. "Norma Jeane Baker has great success in pictures and promises to be a star. She is a very beautiful woman and is now acting as Marilyn Monroe."

Marilyn again finds herself in the gossip column on October 8th when Louella Parsons revealed, "John Carroll's new chick is Marilyn Monroe, Twentieth actress."

On October 11th, she once again linked with John Carroll in a story by Patricia Clary on Hollywood's young starlets. "A dozen or so 16- and 17-year-old glamour girls basked yesterday in a blaze of cafe society worship from the movie colonies richest and handsomest men...Every season numerous beauties make their debut in movie cafe society. They go out every night with movie stars and refer intimately to Darryl, Dore and Louis. (Less beautiful Hollywoodites call them Mr. Zanuck, Mr. Schary and Mr. Mayer.) But by next season, they will have been around for centuries. No one knows where they go, and no one cares...This season's bistro debutantes--some of whom will go on to stardom and some of whom will disappear--include Marilyn Monroe, former baby-sitter, who went out with almost everyone and now has settled with actor John Carroll..." Ouch!

In January of 1947 Los Angeles had been rocked with the murder of Elizabeth Short. It was a gruesome crime and the body was found dismembered in a suburban front yard. Miss Short would forever be known as "The Black Dahlia." Months later, the city was still reeling from the brutal attack. *The Los Angeles Times* ran a steady stream of articles on the disturbing murder which didn't slow down until July, but the effect on the psyche of Los Angelians was to last much longer.

Harry Lipton tells the story of a frightening event in Marilyn's life which occurred that November. She was just 21 when this happened and living alone in a small bungalow on Avon Street in Burbank. "It had begun that afternoon. She finished a bit part in a movie, and she had hurried to get dressed when she was through because someone had promised her a ride to Hollywood Boulevard. After she was dropped off there, she tried to get a cab. Then she realized that she had left her purse at the studio. Not quite sure what she should do, she saw a policeman at the next corner. She walked up to him and told him the story. 'You don't have any money?' he asked. She felt in her pockets--and found the $75 check from the studio, her pay for the part. 'There's a department store a block down,' he said. 'Maybe they'll cash it for you.' Then he smiled. 'I'll show you where it is.' The cashier at the store, probably impressed by the policeman, asked Marilyn for her name and address and cashed the check. Marilyn thanked the policeman and took a cab home. She was very tired. She opened a can of soup, and when she finished it, she went to bed. She had been asleep for hours when she awoke to the noise of somebody trying to pry open her bedroom window. She lay motionless, hoping that she was dreaming. But the noise went on, then the screen ripped as someone tore it with a knife. She sat up in bed and forced herself to look at the window. In the dim glow of the street light, she saw the face of the policeman who had helped her that afternoon. Breathless with fear, she put on a robe and crept from her bed to the back door. She ran to the next house, tearing her robe on a hedge. As she banged on their door, she kept thinking that she was safe. The porch light turned on. 'Who is it?' a man's voice asked. Marilyn was sobbing. 'I live next door. There's a man...' 'Who is it?' a woman's voice asked. 'Some girl.' 'There's a man...he's trying to get into my apartment. Let me in. Please let me in.' The man started to unlock the door. There were whispers, then the woman's voice again. 'Sorry. We don't want to get involved.' Marilyn went back to her apartment and called Harry Lipton. He called the police, then went over to her apartment. From her description, they knew who the man was, and he was apprehended. After the police left and Lipton left, Marilyn spent the night in an all night movie theater.

The next day the editor of the local Burbank newspaper wanted to take a picture of Marilyn in her negligee to run with the story. A reporter camps out on her doorstep. In a panic, she calls Lucille and tells her what is happening and she immediately picked up Marilyn and she stays with the Carrolls for a short time.

Given the context of the Black Dahlia murder, her vulnerability as a single young woman living alone in Los Angeles really got to Marilyn and she became completely unnerved after her attack. Lipton remembers how much the incident frightened her. "For a long time, she was afraid to live alone. And for a longer time--when we had dinner together after an interview or went to an early preview--she looked over her shoulder at the empty night, searching it. But it was not the man who had done the worst damage. It was the people next door who 'didn't want to get involved.' They brought back bitter memories of Norma Jeane Baker and the childhood when nobody wanted to get involved and no one cared what happened to her."

Lucille invited Marilyn to live in the 3rd floor of their suite of apartments at The El Palacio Apartments, Apt F., 8491-8499 Fountain Ave, West Hollywood. Marilyn's friend, Dorothy Dandridge, will live in this same apartment complex in 1965 when she dies of an overdose. Hollywood was a small town with many coincidences.

Marilyn stayed rent free and had a $25 a week spending allowance. She spends the weekends with the Carrolls on their ranch in Northridge, where she feels safer, but before too long, she was able to relax and enjoy her new independence. Marilyn recalled, "It was just wonderful. It was the first nice place I'd ever had, and I felt really independent and sure that something good was going to happen to me."

Despite the gossip items in the paper about Marilyn and her husband, Lucille didn't seem to mind. She seemed to be able to calculate the damage Marilyn could do to her marriage verses her ability to succeed as an actress, and deemed her worth the risk. Miss Ryman will later recall to Florabel Muir about Marilyn, "Under Marilyn's baby-doll kitten exterior, she is tough and shrewd and calculating or she wouldn't be where she is today."

It is also during this time that she renews her relationship with Sam and Enid Kneblecamp, Grace Goddard's sister. She often stops by and has coffee with Enid. When she will be between homes she will stay with them for short periods of time.

October 12th thru November 2, 1947 Marilyn appears at the Bliss-Hayden Playhouse in the play *Glamour Preferred.* She alternated her role with another actress. Marilyn invited her agent Harry Lipton to attend and she was met after the performance by Hunington Hartford, a multimillionaire. This impressed Lipton more than her acting did.

On December 4th John Carroll signed Marilyn to a personal management contract which was later voluntarily withdrawn. Marilyn's address was listed as 4215 Rowland Street, Burbank California, which was different from the address of the Carroll's apartment where she had been living. She would be paid $100 a week. Her salary as an actress would be paid to John Carroll, with 10% going to Harry Lipton her agent. This contract was in effect from December 4, 1947 thru February 29, 1948. Carroll ends the contract with this paragraph, "I agree to use my best efforts to guide and counsel you to the end that your professional career will be furthered and enhanced."

*The Los Angeles Times* reported on December 5th that Harry Haden, of the Bliss-Hayden Theater, is now in rehearsals for *Penny Wise*. The cast included Marilyn and it was due to open at Christmastime.

Jimmie Fidler's syndicated column on December 11th mentions an interesting incident concerning Marilyn. "...the other evening, a starlet named Lila Leeds, deciding that a glamour girl named Marilyn Monroe was talking too ardently with Steve Crane, straight-armed Miss Monroe and then swung a haymaker at Steve."

Miss Leeds was also managed by Lucille Ryman and, like Marilyn, had at one time been taken in by the Carrolls. She would be caught up with Robert Mitchum in a drug bust that would end her career, yet Mitchum would be able to rise above it. Things were different back then for men and women.

Marilyn had been seeing Charles Chaplin, Jr. during the year and at Christmas he gave her a number of dresses. Even though their relationship soon ended, they remained close friends.

It is in the early part of 1948 that Marilyn once again moves from 4215 Rowland into a small house on Franklin Ave, in Hollywood. It is also early that year that John Carroll and Lucille Ryman introduce Marilyn to shady businessman Pat Di Cicco and he invites her to be one of the girls at a party given at Joseph Schenck's Owlwood Estate. Di Cicco was a friend, of sorts, to Schenck, a powerful executive at Twentieth Century-Fox. He provided girls for Schenck's parties, which were well known for having the "best food and the best whore's in town." Di Cicco was once married to actress Thelma Todd, and also to heiress Gloria Vanderbilt whom Marilyn will become friends with in 1955.

Marilyn is befriended by Joseph Schenck. She later recalls, "I could love Joe for his wisdom and kindness alone. He looks on me as a child. I treasure his knowledge so much I could sit at his knee like a child….He was full of wisdom like some great explorer. I also liked to look at his face. It was as much the face of a town as of a man. The whole history of Hollywood was in it."

Louella Parsons gives an insight to Joseph Schenck's support for Marilyn and Darryl Zanuck's blindness to her talent. "It should have been quite easy for him to get her career into high gear at that studio. It wasn't. The reason was Darryl Zanuck, then head of production at Fox. No matter what Joe tried to tell him about Marilyn, Zanuck insisted that she was not the material of which stars were made. He admitted that she was beautiful, nothing more. He felt that at best she would be a 'starlet,' an all-encompassing term that meant little and someone who looked attractive posing for cheesecake art for promotion purposes. He maintained that she could not act, and that he didn't believe she would ever learn. And, despite Joe's importance and prestige, Zanuck would not be budged. Joe, however, felt that Darryl was wrong. He continued to push for Marilyn, told her that despite Zanuck she would someday be a star. Yet, even in those days Marilyn hoped, but she did not believe. She was grateful for everything Joe did for her, but when so little came of it she was not surprised. 'He was very kind to me, always treated me like a lady and gave me excellent advice.' To which Joe added, when I told him this, 'Advice which she never took.'"

Marilyn is taken in by Joseph Schenck, and even lives at times in his guest cottage. According to both she and Schenck, their relationship was purely platonic. Ezra Goodman quoted Schenck on his relationship with Marilyn. "Joseph Schenck, at 76, a massive, balk, Beverly Hills Buddha, received me in his feudal manor off Sunset Boulevard. His eyes were half closed. He had been ill. She spoke slowly and laboriously. Had Schenck been sort of a father to Monroe? 'She used to come here quite often for dinner. I think she liked to eat. We have good food here. No, I never had any romantic thoughts about Marilyn and she never had any such thoughts about me. But it make me appear very old if you say I'm a father.'"

Marilyn told Maurice Zolotow that her relationship to Joseph Schenck was not sexual. "Get this straight, Mr. Schenck and I were good friends. He gave me encouragement when I needed it. He didn't do anything for me. He let Mr. Zanuck run the studio the way Mr. Zanuck wanted to run it. I know the word around Hollywood was I was Joe Schenck's girlfriend, but that's a lie. The only favor I ever asked him, Mr. Schenck, was later, when I was back at Twentieth I wanted a decent dressing room, and I asked him about it, and he put in a good word for me and I got a good dressing room. I never asked him to help me get good parts at Twentieth, and he didn't. He knew how I felt about it, that I wanted to succeed on my talent, not any other way, and he respected my feelings. I went to his house because I liked Mr. Schenck and I liked his food and it was better than the Studio Club food. I didn't mean to imply the Studio Club had bad food. I mean, let's say, that Mr. Schenck's cook was just better than their cook."

Studio rumors have a different story. George Seaton, a writer at Fox, asked Marilyn to come to his office one day at 3:00 after she was back at Fox. She said she couldn't make it at 3:00, as she always goes to Mr. Schenck's office at that time. "But don't worry,'" she said. "I'm always done by 3:20."

Orson Welles remembers Marilyn as she navigated the treacherous Hollywood landscape during her early career. One incident stands out in particular, Marilyn was at one of these parties when a man came up behind her and pulled down her dress, exposing her breasts, then began fondling them in front of everyone. Marilyn's reaction, Welles recalled, was to laugh, then pull up her top. One can only imagine how Marilyn really felt. It is small wonder in the years to come that she will have a fair amount of animosity against the big men at the studios in Hollywood. Incidents such as this will contribute not only to her rage at the men in power, but will also explain the lack of respect Hollywood executives in general had toward her. Her youthful indiscretions will not be forgotten by the men who controlled Hollywood and as Norman Mailer so eloquently put it, "She will pay in the future for being a girl who could once be had."

Marilyn will say of this time spent among the rich men of Hollywood, "The men liked to show off to each other and to the kibitzers by gambling for high stakes. When I saw them hand hundred and even thousand dollar bills to each other I felt something bitter in my heart. I remembered how much twenty-five cents and even nickels meant to the people I had known, how happy ten dollars would have made them, how a hundred dollars would have changed their whole lives. When the man laughed and pocketed the thousands of dollars of winnings as if they were wads of tissue paper, I remembered how my Aunt Grace and I had waited in line at the Holmes Bakery to buy a sackful of stale bread for a quarter to live on a whole week. And I remembered how she had gone with one of her lenses missing from her glasses for three months because she couldn't afford the fifty cents to buy its replacement. I remembered all the sounds and smells of poverty, the fright in people's eyes when they lost their jobs, and the way they skimped and drudged in order to get through the week. And I saw the blue dress and white blouse walking the two miles to school again, rain or shine, because a nickel was too big a sum to raise for bus fare. I didn't dislike the men for being rich or being indifferent to money. But something hurt me in my heart when I saw their easy-come, easy-go thousand dollar bills."

Marilyn makes this eloquent quote about this time in her life, "In Hollywood a girl's virtue is much less important than her hairdo. You're judged by how you look, not by what you are. Hollywood's a place where they'll pay you a thousand dollars for a kiss, and fifty cents for your soul. I know, because I turned down the first offer often enough, and held out for the fifty cents."

One person she met at Schenck's home was columnist Louella Parsons. Parsons was to remain a supporter of Marilyn after she became a star. "I remember the first time I had met her, just as she was starting her sensational climb, at a party at Joseph Schenck's home. The dress she wore was cut too low and she looked like a siren—until she opened her mouth. Then I realized what a shy, ill-at-ease girl she really was, despite all her lush, sexy beauty."

In this period between 1948 and when she made *The Asphalt Jungle*, Marilyn was involved with many men in Hollywood, in various relationships. Those that can be verified are Bill Purcel, John Carroll, George Jessel, Joe Schenck, Pat DiCicco, Dan Cahn, Mikey Rooney, Fred Karger. Lester Cowan and Johnny Hyde. Others who claimed to have had an affair with her during this time are Milton Berle and James Bacon. Norman Mailer contends that it is these years that bring some kind of horror into her later life. At this point she was just one of many girls making the rounds in Hollywood. It has been well established that the men of Hollywood conducted themselves like Sultans with an unlimited harem of young girls. If she traded sexual favors with photographers to persuade them to release her image to the magazines, how many favors did she engage in to get her image on a piece of celluloid? One hopes that such acquaintances were few and far between for our heroine.

In January she is featured in *Popular Photography* magazine in a full page photograph by Andre de Dienes playing in the snow.

*Dangerous Years* was released on January 16, 1948. Although, this was actually the second movie Marilyn made, it was released first and contains her first speaking part. Marilyn wrote a letter to her sister Berniece on February 6th, adding this post script, "P.S. Has "*Dangerous Years*" played down there yet. I'm in it but for heaven's sakes don't blink your eyes you might miss me in it."

Marilyn wrote her address as 11348 Nebraska Ave. West Los Angeles, California, but crossed that out and wrote 1711 N. Stanley instead.

Marilyn's agent, Harry Lipton, remarked on this period of her life when she had numerous changes of address, "She moved around like a flea on a girdle."

Marilyn was reclaiming a pattern that was started in her youth. Her unstable home life as a child had robbed her of a strong identity. As a result, it was easier to move when the notion struck her, easier to pull up roots and make a fresh start. To stay in a permanent location courted ambivalence and a tendency for her decision making to become sluggish.

She needed to be able to think fast as opportunities came her way. She could indulge in lazy days when she became famous. In a strange way, Marilyn's childhood had prepared her for this kind of lifestyle.

She makes the pages of *Holiday* magazine in February. "That Lovable Garment...The Bathing Suit, Past and Present." Marilyn is a featured model in two photos. One of her suits is a green velvet number designed by Margit Fellegi for Cole of California. It features a bow-tie bra and shirred trunks, and it is separated for a two-piece effect. Marilyn will wear that suit again when she makes publicity photos while at Columbia.

On February 20th, she was the recipient of one of the oddest titles with she was crowned the Castroville Artichoke Festival Queen. According to the Festival, "It all began when Jim Seedman and Stan Seedman decided to put on a 'diamond' promotion in their respective jewelry stores. Jim owned Carlyle's Jewelry Store in Salinas (California) and Stan owned a jewelry store in Hollywood. They were also partners in both jewelry stores. "Stan happened to have a diamond salesman from Los Angeles who also worked as a part-time movie star promoter. When the Seedmans decided to have their major diamond sale, they took advantage of this connection and opted to have a starlet who would help with the promotion of their sale. The starlet they originally lined up was Noreen Nash. She cancelled out at the last minute, so the promoter/diamond salesman picked a young, up-and-coming blonde, with a stage name, Marilyn Monroe.

Stan Seedman then brought her to Salinas for a week of public relations for the diamond sale in Salinas. She stayed in Salinas at the old Jeffery Hotel. As things developed, they ended up with a free day on Thursday. Stan went to the Thursday meeting of the Kiwanis in Salinas. He sat next to Randy Barsotti, who was the manager of the local Bank of America branch. Stan mentioned to Randy that he was hosting this starlet and they had a free day. Randy suggested that he and Stan take her to visit his friends at Cal Choke for a photo session. They did. They took some photos of her with some of the chokes and some of the growers. Randy suggested that they call her the Artichoke Queen, and it stuck! Likely, they had no idea that this beauty would attain legendary status. Luckily for us, she did--and the legend continues."

The jewelry store ordered only 200 photographs of Marilyn for her to autograph, but they soon ran out and they quickly sent someone for more photos. By the week's end they had given out over 1,000 photos of Marilyn. The Salinas' Police Department assigned two patrolmen to direct traffic in front of the store when Marilyn was there. Marilyn selected the winning name in a drawing at the Vogue Theatre for a $250.00 diamond ring. She wore a full length gown with a plunging neckline. The Vogue theatre played two movies that day, *Carnival in Costa Rica,* a musical starring Dick Haymes and Vera-Ellen, and *Backlash*, a film-noir starring Jean Rodger and Richard Travis. The ticket stub had the logo for Carlyle's Jewelers in the upper left corner, complete with a sparkling diamond. The rest of the ticket read, "Carlyle's Jewelers, 362 Main Street, Salinas, Calif., Presents a Beautiful...Coronation Diamond Ring. To Be Given Away FREE From the Stage of the Vogue Theatre, Friday Evening, Feb. 20 -- 8:00 p.m. Winner Must Claim Award Within 2

Minutes. Employees of Carlyle's or Vogue Theatre and Their Families Not Eligible to Participate."

The event was memorialized in the local paper with Marilyn, some local business men, and of course, artichokes. Castroville, California claims the title of "The Artichoke Capitol of the World," and in the Franco Hotel in Castroville, they paid homage to the first "Artichoke Queen" by naming a bar after her, *The Norma Jeane Club*. Also, every year "The Annual Artichoke Festival" is held in Castroville, and they still offer tribute to the first legendary Artichoke Queen of California.

Noreen Nash, the starlet who canceled, married Dr. Lee Siegel in 1942. He was Fox's on-lot physician who treated Marilyn. They would both be in the 1952 film, *We're Not Married*, but they didn't share screen time.

Back in Los Angeles Joseph Schenck used his influence to get Marilyn seen at Columbia. He asked Columbia's head mogul Harry Cohn to consider hiring Marilyn. At the same time and in possible collusion, Harry Lipton asked Max Arnow, a talent executive at Columbia, to view Marilyn's screen test she had made at Fox. Shortly after, Cohn consulted with Max Arnow about his evaluation of her worth. Arnow then involved acting coach, Natasha Lytess, who also reviewed Marilyn's screen test. Though not impressed, she agreed to meet with her. After a couple of weeks working with Marilyn, Natasha noted her progress on a report card that Arnow viewed. He told Natasha that she was wasting her time, and too much of it, with Marilyn and she should drop her. Natasha asked Arnow permission to prepare Marilyn for an audition at Columbia. Arnow consented and they worked on a drama piece, *They Knew What They Wanted*, with Marilyn paying for the lessons herself. Marilyn will be tested at Columbia upon the weight of Schenck's endorsement, which was hard to ignore. Beyond anyone's expectations, Marilyn is very good in the part of the girl in *They Knew What They Wanted*. Natasha and Marilyn's hard work had paid off and she is signed by Columbia Studio on March 9th at a starting salary of $125 a week. She was quickly starring in a film, albeit, a B-movie, and she was given special attention by being assigned an acting coach, a vocal coach and dance instructions. All this attention for a starlet, newly signed by the studio. Norman Mailer aptly said, "maybe Schenck knew where some bodies were buried." Edwin P. Hoyt shares a similar feeling about Marilyn at Columbia. "Joseph Schenck was a power in Hollywood, and it might be that Harry Cohn, head of Columbia Pictures, would have accommodated him by placing 'Schenck's girl' in a second lead in a cheap movie. The loss to Columbia would be negligible no matter how badly it turned out. The truth is clouded…Had it not been for Natasha Lytess, Joseph Schenck, or whoever exerted the influence on Columbia Pictures producer Harry Romm to use Marilyn Monroe in *Ladies of the Chorus*, her movie career might have ended in 1948. She was beautiful, but she was getting nowhere."

Natasha Lytess will become her mentor and acting coach. Miss Lytess had been a student of the German theater master Max Reinhardt. Marilyn will maintain a close relationship to Natasha until she moves to New York in December 1954. Natasha's first impression of Marilyn wasn't very flattering, "'That voice!' My ears couldn't take it." "She wiggled nervously into my Hollywood office, dressed in a red frock of knitted wool that hugged her thighs. It was cut very, very low. Clearly, she was not wearing a bra...She perched hesitantly on the brink of a chair, clutching an untidy brown paper parcel. Her face was as wooden as a ventriloquist's dummy. I saw her nose had a lump on its tip, which she had tried to disguise with heavy make-up. When she spoke, her voice was like a knife clattering on a cafeteria plate...a girl with dyed pale yellow hair, a petulant mouth which moved nervously, and a body...a gauche, vacuous-faced girl dressed like a trollop." "I was not impressed. She was inhibited and cramped; she could not say one word freely. Her habit of speaking without using her lips was unnatural, obviously superimposed. Her voice was a piping sort of whimper. "I strove to get her to let go, to say things freely, to walk freely, to know that relaxation brings authority. These new sensations, to a girl suffering from acute insecurity, were the difference between existing underwater and coming alive" "What struck me was that she was very, very closed. She was so much in a shell, she couldn't talk. She was very, very unhappy. I felt she had a dire need of what I had to offer."

Later, Natasha's view of her first meeting with Marilyn is somewhat tempered. "Marilyn had it, has it. She should be thankful to God and seek the help beyond me--and she will. But the material problems of this girl! She was frightened when I met her, because she needed money for clothes and food. And fear is not good in Hollywood. Here they can smell it, and the egos feed on it. But under the fear and frantic desire I saw much more. Marilyn was pretty, yes--with all the physical 'tools' of an actress. But beyond these I believed I sensed much more....'And what did you see in the face of Marilyn?' I prompted. 'First the burning ambition to be worth-while. Backed by unrelenting sincerity. Her sincerity made me her friend, and the faint glimpse of her gifts that shone through the fear and worry convinced me that she could be good--very good--in this business. If there were enough time. But no. Directors tried to hurry her. She could not be hurried. She's not that kind. She is neither precocious--is that a proper word?--nor is she an apt pretender, a clever faker. Nor is she the sly diplomat, the good fellow who allows physical privileges to flatter men of importance."

It doesn't take Natasha long to realize that underneath the cheap packaging is a girl who has the will to become a great actress. They form an unlikely alliance, this "trollop" and the educated European. Hollywood can be forgiven for not taking them seriously. It becomes the first of Marilyn's dependent alliances with her acting coach. She will never outgrow this need for reassurance.

Upon some success as an actress for Marilyn, Lytess will not take credit. "All I taught her was to open up and let go of her voice and body and not telegraph her emotions ahead of time."

Marilyn also has a fateful meeting with Fred Karger, who becomes her voice coach and lover. This will be the first significant relationship of Marilyn's adult life. An interesting side-note to these relationships is that Natasha lived at 1306 1/2 Harper Avenue, just a few houses down from the Karger's home at 1312 Harper Avenue. How convenient for Marilyn.

Although by the year's end their affair will be finished, Marilyn and Fred did leave a lasting memento of their work together, a 12-inch acetate disk of *How Wrong Can I Be*. The handwritten label gives this information, "Fred Karger at the piano, Manny Klein on the trumpet, vocal by Marilyn Monroe." The moody ballad was written by Fred Karger and Alex Gottlieb. Marilyn does her best to give the tune a torchy, seductive flair. "How wrong can I be, If my heart says to me a love like ours never dies. How wrong can I be, when it's sure plain to see that a heart never lies." The song was never released. The music and lyrics were handwritten on three pages of Holograph Musical Manuscript paper. It is interesting that credit is given to Terry Meredith and Fred Karger on the sheet music, and not to Fred Karger and Alex Gottlieb, as indicated on the acetate disk. The sheet music had a handwritten note referring to Marilyn. "Marilyn Monroe sings this beautiful song in the key of 'C.'"

Marilyn was superb at manipulating the Hollywood columnist and reporters. To court their favors meant that your name was mentioned by them in their syndicated columns, giving you publicity you couldn't buy. And in Hollywood, publicity is everything. She might have been uneducated, but she had street smarts, as this incident indicates. Louella Parsons gives Marilyn a plug in her syndicated column on March 13th. "Marilyn Monroe, formerly with Twentieth Century-Fox, was sweet enough to call me and tell me that I am responsible for the best break she has had--the lead in *Ladies of the Chorus* at Columbia.

Well, I have news for her. I'm sure it was her blonde beauty and talent that turned the trick and not the few plugs I've given her in the column. She is such a pretty girl. *Ladies of the Chorus* will be made as an independent by a New York stage producer, Henry Romm, and released through Columbia. The background is the burlesque stage around the turn of the century and I hear the costumes are an eyeful."

Marilyn commences doing research for her role as a burlesque dancer and enlists the aid of photographer, Bruno Bernard. He takes her to watch on of his best models, Lili St. Cyr, perform her restrained and elegant version of striptease at the Florentine Gardens. For all her research, the usual bumps and grinds were not allowable by the movie censors. Even when she was in production on *Gentlemen Prefer Blondes* in late 1952, a memo was sent down to restrain the bumps and grinds in the *Little Girl From Little Rock* dance number.

Ana Lower dies on March 14, 1948. Marilyn had lived with her on and off while she was in Jr. High and in High School and as a young adult. She was one of the few people that Marilyn trusted and that she had developed a close bond with. Aunt Ana had guided her down the path of Christian Science and forever transformed her mind with its tenants. In some very real way, she had begun to heal the scars in Norma Jeane's psyche with Mary Baker Eddy's guided thoughts and prayers. Whatever goodness inhabited her inmost being can be traced back to this loving older woman. Aunt Ana had given her a book called *The Potter*. She inscribed it, "Marilyn, dear, read this book. I don't leave you much except my love. But not even death can diminish that, nor will death ever take me far from you."

Marilyn made this comment about what she had learned from her beloved Aunt Ana. "I became interested in Christian Science because, for a time, I lived with a wonderful woman who was a practitioner. I only wish I'd been mature enough at the time to learn more from her. But I do know that faith brings healing and that the belief that illness is error has a calming, healing effect. If only I had more time to devote to quiet prayer and meditation, I know I could prevent myself from going into emotional tailspins."

After Miss Lower's death Marilyn will comment, "I was left without anyone to take my hopes and troubles to. I was miserable." Marilyn will find in Anne Karger, Fred Karger's mother, a woman to fill the void in Marilyn's affections. Marilyn will come to regard "Nana," as she calls her, in much the same way she did Aunt Ana. They will remain close for the rest of Marilyn's life. Marilyn will spend much time at her home and they will go on picnics together with Mary, Fred's Sister. Marilyn will be lifelong friends of the Karger women. Marilyn nicknames Mary, "Buddynuts." Marilyn will visit on and off with Anne and Mary for the rest of her life and they were personally invited by Joe DiMaggio to attend her funeral on the basis of her friendship with them.

Maybe the death of her Aunt Ana and Marilyn's ensuing loneliness prompted her to write to Berneice. In her letter she mentions her mother, "I haven't heard from Mother nor do I write her, in fact all I know is that she is somewhere in Oregon. She and I can't seem to be very close due to no one's fault. I wish it could be different but someday I hope to be able to help her out a little, right now it's rather difficult for me, contract or no contract."

*Action!,* April 1948, an in-house magazine for Twentieth Century-Fox Studio has

Marilyn featured in two photos in an article about a studio production called, "Strictly For Kicks!," in which she participated. The variety show had a four day run plus a one-night holdover by popular request. Approximately 50 employees worked behind the scenes to make the show a success for the 75 members of the cast. Colleen Townsend, who also had a bit part in *Scudda Hoo Scudda Hay*, performs in the variety show. Publicist Jet Fore, who wrote her studio biography for Twentieth Century-Fox, participated behind the scenes. Marilyn performs in three dance numbers choreographed by Mitzie Mayfair Henderson, with original songs written by Charles Henderson. The purpose of the show was to showcase Fox's new talent. In one of Marilyn's dance numbers she is in cut-out wedges, wearing a two-piece swim suit and holding a parasol. The swimsuit she is wearing is the same two-piece bustle suit designed by Charles LeMaire she wore for Fox publicity photos in April of 1947. She also performs another song and dance for a stage full of the press called, *I Never Took a Lesson in My Life*, in the black gown designed by Jean-Louis that she will wear in *Ladies of the Chorus*. Marilyn replaced another starlet, Diana Herbert in this number. She had replaced Miss Herbert earlier in her career in *Scudda Hoo Scudda Hay*. In her third number she wears her own gold lame' gown she wore for Earl Moran photos, and that she will wear in *Love Happy*.

    Her participation in this Fox Talent Show is odd, given that she is currently under contract to Columbia Studios, which is revealed by her Jean-Louis gown. One explanation of her appearance in this production is that it is a testament to how much the people behind the scenes at Fox liked her. She is also being guided by the unseen hand of George Jessel, producer of Fox musicals. It was thought that if she appeared in this variety show one of the movers-and-shakers at Fox might see her and re-sign her. Although, she had the support of the employees, and a powerful benefactor in George Jessel, once again the executives failed to see her potential. It would take them two more years before they re-signed her. Meanwhile, she will fare no better at Columbia.

    On April 8th Marilyn participates in a private Hair Fashion showing at the Wilshire Ebell. The Helen Hunt Salon put on this show featuring twenty five famed motion pictures beauties, each wearing an original Helen Hunt coiffure. Rita Hayworth, Lucille Ball and Ann Miller were among the actresses featured in the show. Marilyn will also be featured in the June issue of *Movie Life* magazine modeling a hairstyle from the show. "Another variation of the new and more feminine page-boy (note the absence of harsh lines) is shown by Marilyn Monroe. These hair-dos modeled by Columbia players at the Wilshire Ebell, were created by Helen Hunt, studio hair stylist."

    Production started on April 22nd for *Ladies of the Chorus,* filming on Stage 9 and will last 10 days. Designer Jean-Louis dressed Marilyn in this movie. He would work with her in the later part of her career on *The Misfits* and the uncompleted, *Something's Got To Give*. He will also design her iconic nude soufflé "Happy Birthday" gown she wore to serenade President Kennedy. Helen Hunt styled Marilyn's hair and Clay Campbell, head of the makeup department, designed her makeup. Marilyn played Peggy Martin, a burlesque performer. This was the first movie where she got the chance to sing and dance. She has three musical numbers, *We're the Ladies of the Chorus, Anyone Can See I Love You,* and *Every Baby Needs a Da-Da-Daddy*. Marilyn's love interest in the film was Rand Brooks. He will go on to say, "I think the moment I am most proud of is having given Marilyn Monroe her first screen kiss."

According to her agent Harry Lipton, she rehearsed her dance routine from 8:00 in the morning until 10:00 at night with dance coach Jack Doyle. She fell and cut her leg during rehearsals, but kept on until she learned her part. She was determined to be believable in her role as a dancer. Already, Marilyn's dedication to her craft was evident.

Milton Stein, a press agent at Columbia, invites entertainment reporter James Bacon to meet Marilyn. Mr. Bacon will write about Marilyn throughout her career and will like many others, allege that they had an affair.

Marilyn will make the most of her time while at Columbia. Like at Fox, she will make use of the photographers at the studio. Photographs of her taken during her Columbia days will continue to be used for the next few years in publications. As is her habit, she will take the singing, dancing and acting lessons seriously. Those that have a chance to work with her will not fail to give her credit for her determination and drive.

In early May Marilyn is featured in newspapers across the country in a plaid taffeta bra and ruffled skirt, with black satin shorts, called "The Swish." It was a swimsuit designed by iconic California swimsuit designer Rose Marie Reid. Miss Reid got a big boost when she introduced a metallic swimsuit and Columbia bought one for Rita Hayworth to pose in. From then on the studio kept a ready supply of Reid's latest creations to use for publicity purposes. Marilyn will be used as a model for Reid in several outfits this summer and they will fill the nation's newspapers. Marilyn will later credit Reid almost as much as Mother Nature for her pin-up popularity.

May 1948 finds Marilyn associated with various men around town. In Walter Winchell's syndicated column, May 15th, he mentions that, "Ron Randall and Marilyn Monroe are hotter than Citation and Coaltown."

On May 26, 1948 Marilyn attends the premiere of *The Emperor's Waltz* at the Paramount Theater in Hollywood with Mickey Rooney. She and Rooney were photographed by Frank Worth as they entered the Theater. The film was co-written and directed by Billy Wilder, and starred Bing Crosby and Joan Fontaine. Marilyn would go on to have two of her best movies directed by Billy Wilder, *Seven Year Itch* and *Some Like it Hot*. Of all the movies she made, these two represent the Marilyn the public loved and adored. Afterward, there was a supper party at the home of Henry Ginsberg. *The*

*Emperor's Waltz* was the first televised Hollywood premier on station KTLA.

June has Marilyn out on the town, attending the star-studded opening of *George White's Scandals* at the Florentine Gardens with George Jessel on June 3rd. *The Toledo Blade* newspaper, June 14th, featured pictures of Marilyn and George Jessel. Also attending were Celeste Holm, Mr. & Mrs. Jackie Coogan and Mr. & Mrs. Donald O'Conner. Marilyn will star in *All About Eve* with Celeste Holm and later in *There's No Business Like Show Business* with Donald O'Conner.

Still, Marilyn's career is sufficiently stalled to have her move back to the Hollywood Studio Club a week later, on the 9th. She shared room #334 with Clarice Evans. In an interview published in the November 21 & 28, 1954 editions of the *Los Angeles Times* newspaper, Miss Evans reported on living with Marilyn.

Miss Evans remembers being in the shower when Marilyn moved into her room. She recalls Marilyn's blonde hair and a white, wrap-around sports coat she wore. Marilyn moved in her large book collection, her luggage and an enormous professional hair dryer. Marilyn will be photographed in her apartment when she is a successful starlet and will still have the hair dryer. Marilyn seemed to need this dryer as Miss Evans noted that she washed her hair frequently and would nestle under the machine with a good book. She also moved in with a bathroom scale and a leather portfolio embossed with her name. Marilyn brought along a bicycle that she later gave to Freddie Karger's daughter. The day she moved in, Marilyn had an acting lesson and a singing lesson in the afternoon. The telephone in the hall rang constantly with calls for Marilyn. The room had only one bed, so Marilyn slept on a cot down the hall in the girl's dormitory. Miss Evans would sneak a hard-boiled egg from the dining room and wake Marilyn up with breakfast. When making a movie Marilyn was in bed by 9:30. Miss Evans also noted that Marilyn never complained or appeared depressed about her career. When she was dropped by Columbia Studios she reacted by reading her Christian Science Handbook and the next day she continued to look for work pounding the pavements of Hollywood.

On June 16th, Marilyn attends the opening of the musical revue, *Lend An Ear*, at the Las Palmas Theatre in Hollywood. She is photographed sitting with Bill Eythe and Bill Callahan. William "Bill" Eythe was the producer and director of *Lend An Ear*, and also had a part in the production. Bill Callahan was a Broadway actor who had participated in Fox's New Talent Showcase, *Strictly For Kicks*, with Marilyn in March. Carol Channing was one of the actresses in *Lend An Ear*. Miss Channing would go on to success in the Broadway show *Gentlemen Prefer Blondes* as Lorelei Lee.

On June 23rd Marilyn is featured in newspapers modeling a one-piece metallic bathing suit designed by Rose Marie Reid.

Fred Karger arranges some dental work for Marilyn. Dr. Walter Taylor arranges for Marilyn to wear a retainer to correct her slightly protruding front teeth. He does not charge her for this work. To him it might have been a small thing, but to Marilyn it fixed a noticeable flaw in her appearance and that was an enormous gift. Dr. Taylor had a history of violence and his antics were often in the newspaper. His second wife divorced him this spring because of it. Despite his personal turmoil, Marilyn befriended the orthodontist, who suffered from alcoholism. Marilyn was not one to forget a kindness. In the years to come she maintained contact with him and visited him the day he succumbed to pneumonia in the Veteran's Hospital in her girlhood neighborhood of Sawtelle.

*See* magazine, July 1948, features Marilyn in, "The Vanishing Swimsuit." It featured a photo of Marilyn in the bustle swim suit from back in April of 1947, courtesy of Charles LeMaire of Fox.

In July Columbia released a classic cheesecake image by Robert Coburn. It featured Marilyn dressed as an Indian maiden, sitting on a block of ice. Columbia also sent out this blast to accompany it, "The Iceman Cometh…and, our guess is, the butcher, the baker, the lawyer—well, why go on? Beauteous Marilyn Monroe, who might be playing an Indian maid trying to keep cool, is in shape to attract plenty of attention. And that is exactly what she did when she was doing work at an aircraft plant during the war. Her model proportions caught the alert eye of an Army photographer, who displayed her photogenic qualities in bond-selling exploitation at home and morale-building among the troops overseas. A modeling career soon led to movie offers, with Columbia Pictures giving her a first real break as ingénue lead in *Ladies of the Chorus*." Unlike Fox, Columbia stuck to her real story, no baby-sitter was needed to boost her to stardom.

On July 6th Jack Lait reported, "Mickey Rooney is currently going with Marilyn Monroe, which ain't bad going." Then on July 9th he reported, "Joe Kirkwood, Jr. is supposed to be Marilyn Monroe's property, but Cathy Downs has been doing a bit of claim-jumping." Fred Karger introduced Marilyn to Kirkwood and she will go on to assist him in his trick golfing act for a short time. Cathy Downs and Marilyn will pose in *LIFE* magazine in 1949 for Phillipe Halsman. Shortly after that Miss Downs will become Mrs. Joe Kirkwood, Jr. This was possibly Columbia's way of generating interest in Marilyn, but being named with several men at a time makes her appear a little tawdry.

Marilyn used cheesecake as a way to keep her image in front of the public. It is death to an actress to become unfamiliar. On July 6, 1948 the AP *Wire Service* runs a photo of Marilyn sitting atop a piano, modeling a two-piece suit created by Jean Louis for her role in *Ladies of the Chorus*. She also has a poolside session at The Town House Hotel posing in a bathing suit. On July 28th *The Toledo Blade* has Marilyn prominently featured in a 3/4 page photo by Robert Coburn of Columbia Studio. She is dressed as an Indian maid keeping cool by sitting on a block of ice. On August 8th Marilyn again models for Rose Marie Reid in a sun-suit. It is a delustered satin bra and shorts, and Marilyn poses with a racket on a tennis court. In mid-August a picture of Marilyn exercising by Columbia stills man Edward Cronenwerth is used to illustrate a newspaper article on fitness by Alicia Hart. Another newspaper piece during the same time featured a photo of Marilyn, by Cronenwerth, exercising in conjunction with an article by Josephine Lowman on the benefits of exercise. This will become a popular photo session. In one version Marilyn wears a sweater and shorts and in another a swimsuit. After careful consideration the poses Marilyn uses in the photographs are actually Yoga asanas. The wire services love to use them and they will start to appear in magazines before too long.

Marilyn is still hard at work perfecting her acting skills. If the studios won't use her, she would make her own opportunities. She appeared in the production of *Stage Door* at the Bliss-Hayden Theater August 15th thru September 12th. In a 1975 interview, Lela Bliss recalled Marilyn's experiences at the Bliss-Hayden: "She could have played anything. We never had any struggle about parts with her -- she was always happy to play what you cast her in."

In September Marilyn moved in with Fred Karger and family for 3 weeks, 1312 Harper Ave, West Hollywood, saying that she was homeless. Fred finds out that she still has a room at the Studio Club, and demands that she move back in to it.

Marilyn's friend, Bill Purcel, moves to Los Angeles to attend school. Although, she was involved with Fred Karger, she and Purcel would meet often for lunch or other casual events. They even went on a classic California outing, the grunion run.

Purcel took Marilyn to a production of *Madame Butterfly*, which played at the Hollywood Bowl on September $3^{rd}$ and $4^{th}$. Afterward, he noticed that Marilyn was subdued and sad. He attributed this to her participation at the Bowl in the Easter Sunrise service as a child and the traumatic occurrence in her mind that she forgot to turn her robe from black to white. But there were other reasons that the Hollywood Bowl could have produced such a downfall of despondency. The home she shared with her mother on Arbol was just a stone's throw away and music from the Bowl would drift in the night air and make its way to their home. You literally had to pass by it to get to the parking lot. Also, it was there that her mother was forever taken from her. Such memories were almost impossible for her to control. The subject matter of *Madame Butterfly* could have also reminded her of her mother, who was also abandoned by the father of her child and became sole caretaker. Yet, in the opera, the father returns to reclaim the child. Marilyn's father would never be reconciled with her, and she would always be fatherless.

On September 8, 1948 Marilyn's option was dropped by Columbia Studio. She had a name for this period in her life when she was dropped by Fox and Columbia, "pulling myself up and slipping back."

Rumor had it that Marilyn had refused the advances of Harry Cohn. She remembers being told, "'…I had just finished working in a musical entitled *Ladies of the Chorus*. Friends who had seen the rushes told me that all was well, and I was further enthused when I was informed I was up for an important role in one of the studio's forthcoming major productions. Naturally I was terribly excited about it and I took great pains to dress as attractively as I knew how for the important meeting at which I was to be given the good news. Luck was with me, I thought. I was happy as I entered the office, and waited patiently until the man in charge spoke. He looked at me for a long moment, and then said, 'Miss Monroe, we believe in you, and think you'll go far. But at the moment, we have nothing for you at this studio.' Then he added that my option had been dropped, and the meeting came to a sudden end. Prior to all this, I had had a contract for a year at $20^{th}$ Century-Fox, but I felt that didn't count because I had played only one small role which was finally cut out of the picture. But the Columbia contract was different. I was sure that my big opportunity had come. Now everything crashed in a big heap! I went back to modelling to earn my living, and at the same time, I started doing some serious thinking. You're not fired twice without a good reason, I thought, and if I kept this up, it could get to be a demoralizing habit! There more I thought about it, the more I realized that perhaps there was a blessing in disguise somewhere in my failures. An actress hates not to act, but there's more to it than her mere desire to emote before the cameras. Maybe she can't act, and she's told the studio has nothing for her just to let her down gently. I came to the conclusion that I knew very little about acting, and it was up to me--and me alone--to do something about this important lack. If I wasn't a good actress, I concluded, then it was about time I made some drastic alterations. I searched out dramatic coach Natasha Lytess, and enrolled with her for a series of lessons. To pay for this, I continued with my modeling, and I studied very hard whenever I had free time during the day and in the evening."

The first person she went to with the bad news was Anne Karger. She advised Marilyn "to go to church. It's good. You'll get some comfort from it." Marilyn went to St. Victor's Catholic Church and spent three hours in contemplation. It is after that when she went to Lytess and fell apart emotionally. Lytess recalls, "I'll never forget the day she came to tell me that her option had been dropped by Columbia. True, it's a wrenching moment for any young actress, but not often have I seen a human so dispirited as Marilyn was. She tried to be brave about it, but the tears kept breaking through."

Natasha Lytess remembers, "...when her contact at Columbia expired, she was dropped. Never have I seen a human so disconsolate. And again the fear. She had saved but little of the weekly wage of $75. I told her she must come back to me, and we would work together always. I said, 'My dear, I know your true substance. You can be an actress.' And she said, 'It is more than that, Natasha. I must be an actress.'"

Sometime in the fall of 1948 photographer, Tom Kelley, remembers seeing a tearful Marilyn standing on Sunset Plaza Drive, near the LaRue restaurant, talking to a policeman while an older man was yelling at her. There was a crowd of by-standers looking on. It seems while on her way to the audition, she rear-ended the man's car. Her car suffered damage which made it unable to be driven. After the commotion, Kelley approached Marilyn and inquired about her situation. She told him she was late for an audition and now had no way to get there. He gave her $5.00 for cab fare and his business card. She promised to pay him back. He remembers Marilyn as, "Blonde and lovely, appearing even younger than her twenty-one years; She was wearing a dress that was too tight and heels that were too high..." In April of 1949 Marilyn will have her first sitting with Tom Kelley, and begin a professional relationship that will propel both of their talents into legend with the Red Velvet sittings.

On September 21, 1948 Marilyn participated in the Los Angeles Ladies of the Press of Theta Sigma Phi, "Fashionations" luncheon and fashion show in the Embassy Room of the Ambassador Hotel at 12:30. Emmeline Snively remembers this event "After Marilyn Monroe was under contract, the studio loaned her out to model in a benefit fashion show at the Ambassador. She came back to our studio, and we gave her some free advice--to brush up on her fashion modeling. I saw that fashion show, and do you know she was still a lousy fashion model?....This was in 1948." The show was first publicized on August 12th, while Marilyn was still under contract. She was most likely booked for it when she was dropped from Columbia, and just decided to go ahead and participate. It is possible that Marilyn didn't mention to Miss Snively that she had recently been dropped by Columbia, and it's understandable.

On September 23, 1948, *The Long Beach Press Telegram* used a photo of Marilyn from *Ladies of the Chorus* to illustrate an article on skin massage. The caption read, "Keep That Smile--Don't stop laughing just because you develop crow feet. Your smile is probably as becoming to you as actress Marilyn Monroe's, but do keep those lines softened with creams."

Another popular series of photographs taken during her time at Columbia was a makeup and hair session with Clay Campbell and Helen Hunt and the photos started to appear in newspapers across the country after she was dropped by the studio. There are also a series of solo photographs of Marilyn applying her own makeup under the tutelage of Mr. Campbell.

The *San Antonio Express* newspaper, September 30th, uses a photo of Marilyn applying makeup to accompany an article by Josephine Lowman. "Why Sacrifice Beauty? If you are allergic to most lipsticks, you will be able to find a nonallergy product which will cause you no trouble and give the same fine results obtained by actress Marilyn Monroe."

On October 8, 1948 Marilyn wrote a check to Gene and Harry's Service for $3.67. She first wrote the amount wrong and crossed it out, before writing in the correct amount. It was written on her account at the Bank of America, Sunset and Laurel branch which was to be her bank until she moved to New York in January of 1955. She also wrote a check for cash in the amount of $3.00 on October 16th.

The *Motion Picture Herald* newspaper on October 23rd gave a review of *Ladies of the Chorus*, This was Marilyn's first printed review.

# Chapter Eight
## Paying Her Dues

"Hollywood has given us the 'It Girl,' 'Oommph Girl,' 'Sweater Girl,' and 'The Body.' Marilyn Monroe now becomes the 'Mmmm Girl,' and like her 'Whistle Girl' competition of the past, is destined to become a star of importance according to her advance notices."
Daily Independent Journal

*The Los Angeles Times* newspaper column, "Movieland Briefs," features a blurb about Marilyn on October 25th. It goes on to say that she will have a leading role in *Love Happy*, being shot now, and will probably be signed by Artists Alliance Inc., Lester Cowan's studio. Marilyn received $500 for her screen appearance, $100 to pose for promotional pictures, and undisclosed monies for appearing in a promotional capacity on various radio shows for *Love Happy*.

Although, Johnny Hyde was supposed to have introduced Marilyn to Lester Cowan for the job in *Love Happy*, by Marilyn's own account she never met Hyde until 1949. According to Maurice Zolotow's biography, which was released in her lifetime, Marilyn was lunching at the Schwabadero, the name that Sidney Skolsky had given to the diner in Schwab's Drugstore. (It was a play on the word Trocadero, a famous night club.) A starlet sitting next to her told her they were casting a sexy blonde for a bit-part in a Lester Cowan production at RKO. The girl had tried out and had been turned down. Marilyn called Cowan and made arrangements to test for the part with him and Groucho Marx. Cowan and Marx were sufficiently impressed with Marilyn. Cowan even went the extra mile to heavily promote her for a film she spoke only two lines in. He tries to interest *LIFE* and *Look* magazines in her and she even does a few radio spots.

Marilyn plays Detective Sam Grunion's client, and a perfect foil for Groucho's leering comedy. Marilyn's look for the film was designed by hairstylist, Scotty Rackin, and make-up artist, Fred Phillips. Credit for the design of her gown was given to Grace Houston, but Marilyn had owned and used the gown in several modeling photos and in the 20th Century-Fox production, "Strictly for Kicks" in March of 1948. The film suffered from financial problems from the start. Shaky finances and marketing problems delayed the release of the film for a year. In retrospect, Marilyn's appearance is the only memorable thing about the movie, other than the fact that it was the last movie the Marx Bros. made.

In an interview in 1963, Groucho describes his encounter with Marilyn. "I want to tell you about Marilyn Monroe. We did one picture in which she had a bit part. She got $100 dollars for one day's work. Now imagine how long ago this was. And ah, Lester Cowan, who was producing the picture, he called me up, because I was going to do the scene with Marilyn. He called me up. He said we should come over to the studio tomorrow, to his office, because we're going to try out three girls for the part in this picture. I think it was called *Love Happy*, a terrible picture. So, uh, I sat there with Lester and the three girls were there. I was introduced to them, and he said, 'now the first girl, walk'. And she walked across. It was nice. 'Now,' he said, 'the second girl walk.' And she did it too. And then he said to the third one, 'now you walk across.' He said, uh, 'well, which one do you like the most?' I said, 'are you kidding? How can you take anybody except that last girl? The whole room revolved when she walked.' It was Marilyn Monroe. She got $100 dollars. We quit shooting at five, and she got $25 dollars extra for going to a couple of gas stations. They were plugging some kind of gas or something, which was part of the picture or something.

She got $25 dollars extra...for...they took snapshots of her from six to eight. She was a wonderful girl, really; a very nice girl."

Groucho commented to Erskine Johnson about Marilyn in *Love Happy*. "It was Groucho who picked Marilyn Monroe in 1949 for her first film bit role in *Love Happy*. Miss Wiggle Hips had only a brief scene with Groucho, but he fondly remembers, 'I could hardly remember my dialog. But it didn't worry me because her body was a big improvement over the dialog.'"

Marilyn is featured in a wire photo riding an antique bicycle on November 4th. "Riding high is cute Marilyn Monroe, Columbia Pictures starlet, as she tries out the 'Columbian'—ultra fashionable bicycle built in 1875. The rare bike will be one of many thousands of priceless items on display at the second annual Pacific Coast Antiques Show, which opens a 5 day run at the San Francisco Civic Auditorium next Tuesday." In May Marilyn's image would also be used to advertise the Pacific Coast Antiques Show in Los Angeles.

On November 5, 1948 Lester Cowan writes a letter to Mr. Grad Sears of the United Artist Corporation concerning Marilyn and her involvement in the upcoming film *Love Happy*. "….In addition I have just signed a young girl who is a real find. I put her in a few scenes with Groucho and the *LIFE* magazine photographer [J.R. Eyerman, se] who was on set immediately took her to the gallery and shot thirty-five portraits of her for a *LIFE* cover. Her name is Marilyn Monroe and she has the Lana Turner-Ava Gardner type of appeal. She sings and dances better than Betty Grable I intend to co-star her in my next film, "*THE CUSTOMER IS ALWAYS RIGHT*." You will be reading a lot about her as beginning immediately we are going to give her a big campaign including a trip to New York in January and visits to some key cities in connection with the film….Our radio campaign in addition to intense plugging to make our title song "*LOVE HAPPY*" a hit includes guest shots with credit on Approximately twenty-five major TC network shows. These guest shots involve Groucho, Chico, Massey, Hutton and Monroe. Included are the Crosby and Jolson shows, Jimmy Durante, Louella Parsons, Burns and Allen, etc.…."

Photographer J.R. Eyerman, who was assigned to *LIFE* magazine's Los Angeles office took portraits of Marilyn and also photographs for a photo essay concerning the things she does to prepare herself as an actress. Eyerman was accompanied by *LIFE's* Los Angeles correspondent, Carlton McKinney. In each she wears the gold dress, first revealed in *Strictly for Kicks* in March of 1948. We can only imagine Marilyn's cautious gratitude at being chosen for this kind of buildup. After being let go by Fox and Columbia, we can well imagine that she was a bit suspicious of such a promotion.

Eyerman photographed her during her ballet class taught by Nico Chariss and taking acting lessons from Natasha Lytess. Nico's future ex-wife will be the elegant dancer Cyd Chariss, who will go on to star with Marilyn in her last, uncompleted film, *Something's Got to Give*.

Marilyn was also photographed taking a lesson from voice coach to the stars, Phil Moore, at the Champagne Room of the Mocambo nightclub. In the scenes from the nightclub she wore the gold dress. She wore a collared knit shirt and skirt for the recording set. Marilyn sang *Embraceable You*. Moore stressed really believing the words she was singing in order to convey the meaning to your audience. After the rehearsal, Moore played back her singing on an acetate disc, much to her delight. Even though these shots were scripted, Marilyn manages to look earnest in them, not to mention lovely.

Marilyn was most fortunate indeed to have such a talented musician as Phil Moore as her vocal coach. He was a renowned jazz composer and arranger, and had done arrangements for Harry James, Woody Herman, Bob Crosby and Duke Ellington. He also worked as an accompanist and musical director for Hazel Scott, Georgia Gibbs, and the great musical stars, Dorothy Dandridge and Lena Horne. Moore founded the Singers Workshop in Hollywood to help aspiring vocalists. Fox would use his talent to help prepare Marilyn for *Gentlemen Prefer Blondes*.

In an interview with *Bold*, January 1954, Marilyn commented on her improvement as a singer through working with Phil Moore. "I'll always be grateful to Phil. I discovered through his efforts that there is more to carrying a song than mouthing words in time to music. Most important, he gave me confidence in my own vocal ability and made me realize that people would be willing to listen as well as look at me. Marilyn has no illusions about her voice. 'I don't try to kid myself about it,' she says. 'I do think though that if you can put some feeling into a song, you don't need a spectacular voice. I try my best to feel what I'm singing by painting word images. For instance, if a song is about loneliness, I think of a stretch of desolate beach with a solitary figure staring out to sea. I do the same thing with a love ballad, putting myself in the place of the girl and forcing myself to feel her problem is my problem and her happiness is my happiness. I learned from Phil that true feelings for a song come not only from your voice but in the gestures you use. I try to put my whole body into a song. A twist of the head, a clasp of the hands, a slight shiver may convey more feeling in a song sometimes than all of the lyrics.'"

Steve Cronin chronicles Marilyn's early involvement with Phil Moore. "With modeling proving to be a pretty tough racket, even for a girl with all of Marilyn's attributes, she decided to branch out into the entertainment field. It has never been publicized, but she started taking lessons in vocalizing and stage comportment from Phil Moore, the famous jazz musician who has coached many stars in stage and café technique. She tried hard but never got anywhere."

Eyerman would also take some other stunning photographs of the young Marilyn Monroe, many of which were never published at the time. In these images her blossoming beauty is clearly seen. If Hollywood would be slow in recognizing her talent, the photographers would not. The intended photo-essay of Marilyn never appeared in *LIFE* magazine. By April 1949, *LIFE* had changed its mind and photographer, giving the job to Philippe Halsman. Eyerman's portraits of Marilyn first appeared in the July 1949 issue of *Movie Play* magazine, not exactly *LIFE*.

Marilyn appeared in the November 1948 issue of *Holiday* magazine which carries an ad for Argoflex Camera and features a photo by Andre de Dienes. *The Long Beach Press Telegram* newspaper, November 5th, carries a Columbia publicity picture of Marilyn applying make-up to illustrate the article, "Women with Sensitive Skin Should Use These Cosmetics," by Josephine Lowman.

November also had her going back to modeling to make ends meet. Marilyn commented during an interview of such a setback. "Of course people said, 'Why don't you go and get a job in a dime store?' But I don't know; once I tried to get a job at Thrifty's and because I didn't have a high school education they wouldn't hire me. And it was different really-- being a model, trying to become an actress, and I should go into a dime store?"

On November 16$^{th}$ Marilyn goes back to her old standby, modeling, and signs a model-release contract with illustrator Earl Moran. She agreed to pose for the fee of $10-an-hour. Marilyn listed her home as 1215 Lodi Place, which was the address of the Hollywood Studio Club.

Marilyn will tell Maurice Zolotow how grateful she was to calendar illustrator Earl Moran. "Earl saved my life many a time. He liked to paint me with different-colored hair. Sometimes he gave me red hair, sometimes brown or brunette. I was his favorite model. He did illustrations for short stories a lot. I was able to use my acting experience in striking a good pose and holding it for him. I helped him bring out the emotions of the scene he was painting."

Three days later on November 19th Marilyn signs a model release for the Ideal Publishing Co. For the use of her picture in *PERSONAL ROMANCES* or *INTIMATE ROMANCES*. Once again Marilyn gave her address as 1215 Lodi Place and her phone number as GL-3166.

Starting in late November the press starts to carry an article about Marilyn being signed to do *Love Happy*. Columnist Jay Carmody advised his readers that the "Girl to be on the lookout for is Marilyn Monroe, who has just been signed to an acting contract by independent Producer Lester Cowan. Mr. C's press department describes Miss Monroe as a 'young Bergman-like person." The full article released by Cowan reads as follows, "Hollywood's newest Cinderella story stars a beautiful, 20-year-old Los Angeles girl, Marilyn Monroe, who was signed to a long-term contract by Producer Lester Cowan, it was announced today. A young Bergman-like person, Miss Monroe's road to stardom starts in Producer Cowan's forthcoming Marx Brothers-Ilona Massey-Vera Ellen-Marion Hutton film-comedy, *Love Happy*, which will be released early next year by United Artists. She makes her bow in the Groucho Marx sequences, which were just completed in Hollywood. Making Miss Monroe's film fortune even more spectacular is her youthful years, 18 of which she passed as a ward of the state of California. Immediate plans for her next screen appearance have been concluded by Mr. Cowan. She will be cast for an important supporting role in his next production, *The Customer's Always Right*."

Marilyn had an uneventful start to December. *Ladies of the Chorus* was released on December 2nd. But it generated no great interest in her. She attended a Christmas Eve party at the home of Marilyn Maxwell. On January 5th, 1953, Bob Thomas reported, "Two Marilyn's Provide Some Confusion...Five years ago, Marilyn Maxwell tossed a Christmas eve party at her Hollywood apartment. Among those present was another blonde, lovely but uninvited. Miss Maxwell met the girl and was struck by the similarity of their names. 'Is that your real name?' she asked. 'Oh, yes,' replied the blonde. 'And do you plan to go into the movies?' 'I certainly hope to.' 'Gee, maybe you'd better change your name then. It might get confusing.' The other blonde, who was actually born Norma Jean Baker, didn't change her professional name. She still calls herself Marilyn Monroe. She is much better known

now, thanks to a well circulated calendar pose, among other things. And, as her hostess predicted five years ago, the confusion between Marilyn Maxwell and Marilyn Monroe is considerable. 'I was the only Marilyn in pictures until she came along,' said Miss Maxwell. 'I suppose she is subject to the same confusion, but people often call me inadvertently 'Miss Monroe.' My answer is: 'No. I'm the Marilyn with clothes on.' Miss Maxwell added that she is subject to ribs from her friends. A pair of school chums even sent one of the Monroe calendars--but with Maxwell's head pasted on it. Despite the confusion, Miss Maxwell said she isn't peeved with the other Marilyn. 'I think she has done a great deal of good for the movie industry,' said Miss Maxwell...'She is just what the business needed--someone to put some glamour and magic back into Hollywood--I think we have gone too far in promoting stars on the 'girl next door' level. We need to return to excitement and allure of the days when Garbo was a reigning star.'"

   On Christmas Marilyn gave Fred Karger an expensive engraved watch even as their affair comes to an end. She had it engraved simply, 12.25.48, so he could wear it even if he is with a new woman. It will take Marilyn over two years to pay for this extravagant token of her affection. Despite their breakup, and possibly at the urging of his mother, he helped Marilyn get a job with Joe Kirkwood, Jr., as an assistant in his trick golf routine.

Marilyn agreed to go on an extended publicity trip back East, starting in June, to promote *Love Happy*. Supposedly she thought it would make Fred Karger miss her, but her plan didn't work.

A letter from Sam Kerner to Lester Cowan regarding Radio Tie-Ups, February 1, 1949, "….Marilyn Monroe..is set for Skippy Hollywood Theatre--March 28$^{th}$ which is pre-recorded…Zeke Manners March 8$^{th}$, "Stars Over Hollywood"-date to be determined.. "Meet the Missus"-April 1$^{st}$." "Giveaway Shows….Meet the Missus will give away three bottles of "*Love Happy*" perfume. This will involve two plugs per week throughout the entire month of March."

On February 6th, the "Stars in Your Eyes," newspaper column reported, "Marilyn Monroe and Joe Kirkwood, Jr., are planning a 12-week stage tour in the East and Midwest." Joe Kirkwood, Jr., an actor and trick golfer needed a sexy girl to assist him in his trick golf routine. Fred Karger had talked Kirkwood into hiring Marilyn as his assistant. Their initial show was at the Veterans Hospital in her old Sawtelle neighborhood. Marilyn was too nervous to hold the ball steady and Kirkwood found it almost impossible to hit it. He quickly replaced Marilyn with a tee and their plans to tour came to an end. Kirkwood later found fame as *Joe Palooka*.

On February 8th, Lester Cowan wrote a letter to Groucho Marx and had this to say about Marilyn. "…*LIFE* Magazine has approved a cover on Marilyn Monroe and a story which assumes she has a bit in the picture. Immediately the cover appears, I have been planning to send her on a publicity tour to principal cities in advance of the film. Her immediate future is in our hands."

Still in need of cash and not relying on her movie career, Marilyn looks for work in the fringes of movies. In late February, while auditioning girls for his upcoming shows at the Hollywood Palladium in March, Benny Goodman gives a listen to Marilyn croon, *How Deep is the Ocean*. His advice to her is, despite her beauty, she has no future in show business and suggests she just go home. Buddy Greco was a vocalist and pianist for the band and remembers Marilyn's audition. He will remind her of it when they meet in July 1962 at the Cal Neva Casino. She was no Dinah Shore, but Marilyn had worked with two outstanding vocal coaches and did an acceptable job singing in *Ladies of the Chorus*. One wonders what Benny Goodman didn't see in her. In 1952 Louella Parsons reported that, "…she tried to get a job with Benny Goodman's band after she was dropped by Columbia Picture, and the great Goodman himself complimented her singing. However, she didn't get the job." Her voice will only improve with time, so that by 1953 people will find it hard to believe that she actually did her own singing in *Gentlemen Prefer Blondes*.

While on a modeling assignment in Palm Springs with Bruno Bernard, Marilyn meets Johnny Hyde at the Racquet Club pool. He made no great impression on her and she dismisses the memory of meeting him. Later that evening at the home where she is staying, the owners give a party to which he comes. Hyde reminds her that they met earlier in the day. By now she knows who he is and is struck by the great respect people have for him in that he is one of the most powerful talent agents in Hollywood and works for the renowned William Morris Agency. Marilyn recalls meeting him, 'I first met Johnny while I was still living at the Studio Club. I met him at a friend's house and he called me the next day and invited me to lunch. After that I spent a great deal of time with him—until his death.' They begin to talk and he shows her a world of possibilities that he can provide to her. "We talked and Johnny was marvelous, he really was. He said I would be a very big star. I remember laughing and saying it didn't look like it, because I couldn't make enough to eat three squares. He explained something to me that I had not realized before--that if you are a star it is hard to find little roles. They either have to give you a star part, even if it isn't big, or nothing."

Arthur Hornblow, Jr. comments, "Only one man was responsible for making her a star. That man was Johnny Hyde. He had faith in her when she was a starlet and a damn unimportant starlet. When you had Johnny in your corner, you had a pipeline to the guys who really count in Hollywood. He made this town Marilyn Monroe conscious. He did more than blow her trumpet, he taught her how to dress and talk to people and make the right contacts. It's the old story of Trilby and Svengali, and it's the same old plot, because Svengali can make a star out of Trilby, but he can't make her fall in love with him."

Later, as a star, Marilyn rejects the idea that she was a just a puppet as a starlet. "Johnny Hyde was wonderful, but he was not my Svengali. Natasha Lytess was not my Svengali. I'm no marionette for anybody and never have been."

Back in Los Angeles Johnny Hyde convinces Lester Cowan to let him see the rushes of her walk-on in *Love Happy.* He is sufficiently impressed and will sign her to a contract with William Morris. He will be the catalyst that helps launch Marilyn Monroe to stardom. He will end up leaving his wife for her, but although, she moves in with him, Marilyn will refuse to marry him. He tells her that he has a bad heart and will be dead soon, and she will be a rich woman, yet she refuses to marry him. Edwin P. Hoyt declares that, "She was not a rich man's whore; she was a courtesan of the old school. She traded favors for Johnny Hyde's influence, knowing exactly what she was doing."

Marilyn's desire to become a great actress supersedes any other motivation that she might have.  At one point in her career, she will tell her lawyer that she isn't interested in money, she just wants to be wonderful. Hollywood would never quite grasp this fundamental truth about Marilyn. There wasn't a materialistic bone in her body. She did not equate money with power; rather she thought that being talented as an actress was real power.

Al Tamarin of United Artist was sent a letter from Bill Chaikin, who worked for producer Lester Cowan. "We need your help and cooperation, again, on two big breaks coming up on *"Love Happy."* *LIFE* is going to do two more stories in connection with the picture. The first story is on Marilyn Monroe, who plays a small part in the picture. The story has already been completed on this and sent on to the New York office. We are supposed to get the cover with Marilyn, besides an inside story. Please follow up on this and see that *LIFE* is serviced with anything they need. Also, do whatever you can to see that we do not lose the picture credit. If you can ascertain when this layout will be used, please let me know as soon as possible...."

She was in *LIFE* magazine, but not on the cover and not an exclusive article as Cowan had hoped for. It seems that *LIFE* had scrapped many of the photos taken in November 1948 by J.R. Eyerman and instead of an exclusive article about her, she was hidden in a photo essay about struggling young starlets in Hollywood, photographed by Philippe Halsman. The Eyerman photos released years after her death show a starlet on the brink of stardom and there is a palpable feeling in these photographs that she has "It," and has it in spades. In the *LIFE* article which would come out in October, she stands out from among the other hopefuls like a vibrant rose in a bouquet of wild flowers.

The spring issue of *Film Humor* magazine features Marilyn on a partial cover. *Movie Stars Parade,* March 1949, features Marilyn in an article, "Beauty: Best Shape Ever," featuring her doing various exercises. The photos were the series taken by Edward Cronenwerth when she was at Columbia Studios.

On March 2, 1949, Marilyn signs a contract with the William Morris Agency. She will primarily be represented by Johnny Hyde. She would be represented by Abe Lastfogel, John Hyde, Sam Weisbord and Moe Sackin. They would charge her 10% for their services. Marilyn lists her address as 1215 Lodi Place, which is the address of the Studio Club.

On March 13th, Marilyn moves out of the Studio Club and into room #350 at the Beverly Carlton Hotel, 9400 W. Olympic Blvd, Beverly Hills, CA. Her phone number will be CRstvw-5-5221. With Johnny Hyde's help she is moving up in the world of Hollywood. She will never live at the Hollywood Studio Club again. She says goodbye to old neighborhoods and hello to the glittering world of Hollywood.

On March 14th Lester Cowan sends a telegram to Bill Chaikin concerning Marilyn. "....We have shot final color shots for cover *Look* Magazine article, entire piece is completed and will be sent East probably tomorrow. Will write Tess Michaels to follow up. Please show *LIFE* Magazine the picture so we can get Marilyn Monroe layout...." Marilyn never made the cover of Look magazine in 1949.

*Riders of the Whispering Pines* is released on March 15th. There is a photo of Marilyn from *Ladies of the Chorus* used as a prop in the film, and to which Gene Autry serenaded with *Hair of Gold.*

April proves to be a very fortuitous month for Marilyn. She will be photographed by two of the best photographers in their fields, master lensman Philippe Halsman and famed calendar shutterbug Tom Kelley. April also finds her back in the studio of Earl Moran for more cheesecake posing on April 8th and the 26th. She receives a $15 modeling fee for each session. Marilyn gives her address as 1301 N. Harper. This is the new address for Natasha Lytess, who, by this time, had moved across the street from her old home at 1306 1/2 Harper Ave.

Marilyn will also appear in two magazines, keeping her in the public eye. *Movie Life* magazine features a photo of her, "Fabulous Dept. (Marilyn Monroe Models Ermine Bathing Suit,)" for *Love Happy*. *Picture Show* magazine has her in an article, "Suits Makes Beauts," featuring 10 models, including Marilyn, wearing swim suits. Marilyn's photo is captioned, "Bustle Back Beauty Suit." Once again Fox's old 1947 swim suit publicity photo makes an appearance.

In early April Marilyn has her first sitting with renowned photographer Philippe Halsman. In it, "Eight Girls Try Out Mixed Emotions" for an upcoming edition of *LIFE* magazine which would be published on October 10, 1949. *LIFE* editor Gene Cook invited the girls to pose for the magazine. According to Halsman, Marilyn was shy and withdrawn and only successfully accomplished the task of being embraced by a lover. Looking back at the photos of Marilyn which appeared in *LIFE*, she is far and away the most beautiful girl of the eight, and she has a certain sensual innocence that will define her in years to come. In later years, Marilyn will recall this about the experience, "I wanted to be a model, but they only wanted to use me on men's magazines and in bathing suits, that kind of thing. Philippe Halsman took this shot (a close-up of Marilyn laughing,) and it was the first time that only my head was being photographed. He was shooting a lot of girls registering various emotions--anger, fear, sorrow, happiness, etc. Philippe was so pleased and so encouraging. He said, 'Come to New York--most models can't act, but you can...' I didn't go, but I was thrilled by his encouragement."

Despite what Marilyn would remember in later years, Halsman's memory of her is entirely different. "I had just finished photographing a vivacious red head named Lois Maxwell, who, of the entire group, showed the greatest promise. After her came a little blonde named Marilyn Monroe. She was painfully shy, and wooden in her actions. Her desire to be as provocative as possible and her fear of showing too much of her figure were waging a constant tug of war. In my four-part test she was unaffected by my inaudible joke, she was rather unafraid of the invisible monster, and she registered her enjoyment of the most delicious drink on earth by simply gulping it down. Only when she tried to embrace and kiss the invisible lover did Marilyn become an inspired actress. She gave a performance of such realism and intensity that both she and I were utterly exhausted...Marilyn was so pent-up inside, so high-strung, she couldn't act out simple bits like enjoying a make-believe drink. But her tenseness seemed to assist her in really emotional situations like love-making and tantrums. At times she would relax, her true self would come to the surface, and she would perform well... I went back to New York, and--except for the one picture in which she made love--forgot about Marilyn Monroe."

Halsman again recalls the situation with Marilyn. "I remember that one of the girls was an artificial blonde by the name of Marilyn Monroe and that she was not one of the girls that impressed me the most. She acted well only when she was in the arms of the fabulous lover. Even there, she was not the best, because there was a freckled redhead who acted it out with such passion that even photographing the group of eight actresses together, the blonde was the one who always made me wait. She was constantly dreaming, arranging her skirt, adjusting her blouse, and never ready. She impressed me as being very self-conscious and insecure."

Grace Goddard contacts Marilyn to tell her that her mother married John Stewart Eley, an electrician from Los Angeles, on April 20th. They would remain married until he passed away from heart ailments on April 23, 1952.

On April 28th Marilyn had been sent to photographer Tom Kelley to model for a *Pabst Beer* ad. He remembers Marilyn's appearance, "Marilyn came in one Saturday afternoon. There wasn't anything in particular to distinguish her from the scores of other would-be models. Her hair was now reddish-blonde, worn long, curly and fluffed around the face, a style popular in the late 1940's. Her skirt was tight. Her blouse was very low-cut. She wore high-heeled shoes, ankle strapped. Her mouth was made up like Joan Crawford's, old-style, and she kept on moistening her lips." Kelley's wife, Natalie, helped Marilyn change for the photo shoot. Wearing her Rose Marie Reid swim suit, Marilyn posed for over an hour, holding a beach ball up in the air. He remembers that she never complained and refused to take a break when offered. The resulting Pabst poster was entitled, "Swimming." Marilyn was paid $30 for the day's work.

John Baumgarth, head of the Baumgarth & Sons Calendar Company, made one of his twice yearly trips to Hollywood to find models for his calendars. He had seen the photos of Marilyn in a bathing suit and sailor cap hanging in Tom Kelley's office. He told him he would like to use her for one of their artistic nude calendars. Kelley made a proposal to Marilyn to pose for "artistic nude color shots." She turned him down, telling him of her intentions to become a serious actress. Baumgarth claims he was the one who suggested that Kelley's wife be present during the shoot to make the offer more acceptable to Marilyn.

On Mother's Day, May 8th, Marilyn sent Anne Karger a card. She will never lose the connection with Fred Karger's mother, Anne. Marilyn will remember her with a gift or card on each birthday and Mother's Day until her death.

*The Los Angeles Times* featured a photograph of Marilyn, on May 24th, posing with a Victorian miniature chair to publicize the Fourth Annual Pacific Coast Antiques Show at Pan-Pacific Auditorium. She is also photographed riding an antique bicycle that doesn't make it into the papers. In these it appears that Marilyn is wearing her beloved angora sweater.

May turned out to be a slow month for Marilyn and Johnny Hyde was out of town attending Rita Hayworth's wedding. Without Johnny Hyde's influence she makes a decision that will one day come to haunt her and threaten the career she has worked so hard for. Towards the end of the month she reconsiders Tom Kelley's proposal to pose nude, and submits to his request to pose naked on a background of red velvet for one-fifth of a second, resulting in the "shot seen 'round the world." Marilyn called and spoke with his wife, Natalie, on May 25$^{th}$, almost a month after her first session with Kelley for Pabst Beer. She told Natalie that she had changed her mind about posing for nude photos and scheduled the appointment for 7:00pm, Friday, May 27th.

Marilyn could not have picked a better photographer for her nude portrait. Tom Kelley believed that "art—good art—is the key to what he says and how he says it." Kelley had immersed himself in the study of classic art since he was an apprentice to a Long Island society photographer. "He has gone to museums to observe good art, read books about art, watched for it in the everyday things he has seen…A good sense of art is needed to determine the balance of colors, the composition of the picture, the key of the lighting. Kelley sometimes works for hours to obtain just the right balance and lighting to get the exact feeling he wants." Kelley himself said, "I work very hard on a picture. If I have an important job I give it a lot of thought. I sleep on it. I think it out as best I can."

On May 27, 1949 Tom Kelley made a notation in his date book indicating that the session was for John Baumgarth & Sons. It was business as usual for him. He had photographed many a hungry model for calendars and this day seemed like all the rest. How wrong he was, for the photos he would take of this unassuming girl would be destined to become some of the most famous images in popular history. Marilyn arrived at the studio wearing blue jeans, with a rolled cuff, a low-cut blouse and red high-heels. Natalie asked her to change into a loosely fitting robe, so as to reduce the marks on her skin caused by her clothing. She then applied her make-up and combed out her hair. Kelley put on *Begin the Beguine*. This was a song that Norma Jeane had taught the boys to dance to as a girl back in Jr. High, and now in the full measure of her womanhood, she will use it to influence men by the lascivious image she will present to the world, and she will use this piece of film to full effect to launch her career as the greatest sex symbol of the Twentieth century. It was a gamble to use something so volatile to pin your dreams on. She will never fully get out of the shadow of its impact. Marilyn will employ it to gain the attention of the world and yet, once it was out, the genie will be nigh to impossible to put back in the bottle. Her desire to become a legitimate actress will always be colored by this red velvet. She took off her robe and reclined, and once she became comfortable on the soft fabric, something phenomenal happened. It was as if she went through an inner change so radical as to alter the waves of energy emanating from her. She was no longer a timid model. She became an enchantress, a luscious nymph from one of Bouguereau's paintings, abandoning herself to erotic pleasure like Psyche in the arms of Cupid. After three hours of shooting her from various angles, they were finally done, and Kelley was awe struck at this young woman. He knew from his professional experience that this was a rare session, a gift from the gods. It would take almost three years to prove him right.

Kelley would tell Maurice Zolotow in 1955 about photographing Marilyn. "'How long did it take?' 'About three hours. I must have stood about 10 feet above her. She was lying on the floor. I'll tell you something. A lot of people don't know there are two Monroe calendars. One is titled Golden Dreams and the other is A New Wrinkle…the big seller is Golden Dreams. A New Wrinkle is more artistic. It has plastic symmetry but the public doesn't seem to appreciate plastic symmetry, I guess. They want golden dreams.' 'How fast was the exposure time?' 'One-fifth of a second, the lens set at f18.' 'Was the radio playing?' 'It wasn't the radio. It was a phonograph. I had Artie Shaw's record of *Begin the Beguine* playing. I find *Begin the Beguine* helps to create vibrations. The thing about Marilyn is she's got more vibrations than any other woman I ever photographed. I shot about 20 poses that night. I sold two of them.' 'What happened to the other 18?' 'The negatives just disappeared on me. Somebody—I don't know who—broke in here and stole them.'"

This was actually the tamer of the two sessions, and during this session, she posed in such a way that no pubic hair showed, as standards of public decency did not allow such things to be published. Mr. Kelley took 6 poses for the calendar company. Yet, after the first session, he used another camera and took more photos of a nude Marilyn, unrestricted. Years later she asked him for transparencies from this last sitting to show Joe DiMaggio. She never returned them and by the time Kelley got them back, they were in unusable condition.

After Marilyn got dressed, Tom, Natalie and she went to Barney's Beanery for a bite to eat. During their meal, Marilyn revealed to Tom their first meeting. He had not recognized her as the girl to whom he had loaned cab fare to in 1948. Marilyn then claimed that part of her motivation for posing nude for Kelley was her way of saying "thank you" for his past kindness. She signed her calendar release as "Mona Monroe." Marilyn would see him occasionally throughout the coming years, visiting his studio on Seward Street in Hollywood, and even having her portrait made by him in the early years of her stardom.

This sitting produced the iconic "Red Velvet" images. Marilyn was paid $50 for the night's work. The Baumgarth & Sons Calendar Company of Chicago paid Kelley $500 for the pose, "Golden Dreams." The Western Lithograph Company paid Kelley $250 for "A New Wrinkle." Baumgarth released "Golden Dreams" on a calendar top for 1951 to lack luster business. When Marilyn hit fame in *Clash by Night* and she began to be recognized as the girl on the calendar, they ramped up production and suffice it to say, it was a success. But the real success was the Western Lithograph version, "A New Wrinkle," which was issued in 1952 and this becomes her iconic calendar image and was even printed in Marilyn's cover issue of *LIFE* magazine in April of 1952.

According to Karl Weindel, Baumgarth's president, "We didn't know what we had. We didn't know who she was. But I'll tell you one thing: That picture is 'arty.' It isn't dirty. Our objective was to make artistic-type calendars." Baumgarth & Sons got a release granting full rights to use the model's name and photograph for any purpose they saw fit.

Marilyn's pinup also helped to establish Chicago as a center of pinup activity. Springboarding out of this was a young magazine publisher, Hugh Hefner. He would start a magazine in 1953 that would establish the standard for soft-core pornographic publications, *Playboy*. Marilyn's nude, "Golden Dreams," would grace the first issue as the centerfold.

In an ironic interview with Earl Wilson in 1959, Marilyn recalls her nude calendar and gives advice to young actresses about posing nude. "Marilyn Monroe bounced into a taxi recently behind pale sunglasses, with a scarf covering her hair, and without makeup. 'Lady, you're BUILT! In my spare time I do photography,' the hackie chattered. 'I think you should do a nude calendar.' 'WHAT!' protested the coy, but curvy customer. 'I beg your pardon!' 'Don't knock it lady,' argued the cabbie. 'Look what it did for Marilyn Monroe. It might do the same for you.' Aglow with health, happiness, beauty—and sex appeal—Marilyn told me that story in an interview a few days ago, adding that she hopes the hundreds of girls now posing nude aren't doing so because they think it's a guarantee of success. Or because they're taking her as a 'sexample.' Marilyn…expressed doubt about ever 'doing a Brigitte Bardot' in pictures herself. Not that she respects B.B. less…she respects us American men more. 'No, it's not a change of attitude…I just would want these girls to be aware of what they're doing' Now she was on the floor, but sitting up on her knees. 'There was a starlet who was being taken advantage of,' she said. 'I told her 'You don't need to do that.' And she said, 'But look at you.' 'She didn't UNDERSTAND,' Marilyn frowned. 'I had to take care of bills…it was to eat…and for just room and board…or going back to work in a factory…I had signed a fake name and the photographer had told me I would never be recognized…I just say,' she rolled her eyes toward the ceiling, 'that the girl who thinks this is going to make her a success will be disappointed and disillusioned. There isn't any short cut. You may have to work harder to overcome it.' With a tinkly laugh she cried, 'I was saving one of my calendars for my grandchildren—and somebody stole it!'….Would YOU ever do a nude scene in a movie?...'Well, I don't think it's necessary,' she smiled. 'However, for Miss Bardot, I don't see anything wrong with it, either…I WAS considering it. For a picture about Goya. Not the one they just did. Another one. But just to appear nude for nudity's sake…I think the American male is healthier than that. He doesn't NEED that. I've heard that some men like a little left to their imagination. Either way, I'm not frowning down on it, I also feel it's alright for everybody to do everything they want to do…About the nude posing,' she said, 'there's not really any money in it. Just the $50 that saved my life.'"

Years later, Tom Kelley remembers the "Shot Seen 'Round the World…When I shot that picture in the latter part of 1949, I knew I was going to get a good picture. But I think she knew more than I did that something was going to happen with it. She had a kind of intuitive sense about her life...When I finished the calendar shooting with my 8x10 camera, I took my small camera and told her, 'Now I want you to move around and don't worry about anything,' and I shot four rolls of 120 size film and practically every exposure showed her fully, frontally nude. Now she had a body like, well, you know the artist Varga and how he idealizes women? When he draws a figure, there really isn't anyone who has that kind of figure. But Marilyn was the closest I have ever seen. Her calves, waist, bust, shoulders, everything seemed to be the right proportion; one of the greatest bodies I've ever seen.' Kelley's eyes sparkle at the remembrance. 'Today, those pictures would be worth a fortune because of the legend she is.' But a sigh comes from Kelley. For the second time in his dealings with Marilyn Monroe, fortune was to be a fleeting thing. 'I had those transparencies in my desk for a long, long time. One day she came in and I pulled them out to show to her. She said, 'Oh, Joe (DiMaggio) would love these,' So I let her have them to show him and I never got them back.' Kelley almost got them back. About a year ago the attorney for the last actress' estate petitioned the court for permission to destroy the transparencies. 'I got an attorney to get a restraining order because we believed these were my pictures which she had never returned. So after about three months we finally viewed them in the presence of both attorneys, and they were mine. But the transparencies were so faded it was like looking through a piece of glass. They were absolutely unusable. Otherwise, I had visions of a lot of money.'….When I shot that picture in the latter part of 1949, I knew I was going to get a good picture. But I think she knew more than I did that something was going to happen with it. She had a kind of intuitive sense about her life."

In 1955 "Golden Dreams" was featured in the book, *Studies of the Nude Figure*. The art-minded text eulogized the classic aspects of Marilyn's pose. "'Golden Dreams' is certainly the most famous nude photograph ever made. It has appeared on thousands of calendars and has been the subject of newspaper stories throughout the world. It placed the name of the model--Marilyn Monroe--on every man's lips. Yet in all the excitement one important factor has been overlooked. 'Golden Dreams' is a beautiful illustration by itself--Marilyn Monroe or no Marilyn Monroe. This is not to say that Marilyn did not help. Certainly the model regardless of her prominence is of the utmost importance in photographic art. Technically the photograph observes the rules of placement and composition yet is not hampered by them. There is a strong feeling of action, due partly to the dominance of the diagonal traversing the picture area from upper right to lower left. The line is not rigid, but S-shaped, the traditional line of beauty. The extension of the model's right arm serves to break the line in a dramatic fashion and also balances the mass formed by the head and the arm. The gracefully folded legs act as a solid base for the composition, giving it added strength. Color wise, the illustration is simple. It is predominantly a study in two colors, the delicately rendered flesh tones and the brilliant red of the background (which matches the tips of the breast.) To relieve the red, the golden hair adds a third shade, but does not change the basic color pattern. However, despite the emphasis on red--the strongest of all colors--the photograph is not garish. To create his famous illustration, photographer Tom Kelley placed his strongest light to the right of the camera. A weaker fill-in bulb near the lens prevented unattractive solid-black shadows. A third light illuminated the hair. When she posed for this history-making shot, Marilyn Monroe never dreamed her name would someday be synonymous with glamour. A struggling would-be actress a week behind on her room rent, she needed the modeling fee. 'Tom Kelley didn't think anyone would recognize me,' she recalls. 'My hair was long then. But when the picture came out, everybody knew me.' However, Marilyn claims, 'I am not ashamed of it. I have done nothing wrong.'"

June turned out to be a month of changes for Marilyn. She would be featured in *Leatherneck* magazine in a full page pin-up as "Pin-Up of the Month." This was a publication for the United States Marine Corps. By way of pin-up photos she is immersing herself in the consciousness of the men in the military so that when the Korean War breaks out she is the natural choice as the golden girl of their dreams.

Marilyn, ever developing herself as an actress, reads a script with fellow Actors Lab student Clark Gordon. She is very nervous during the reading and he helps to calm her nerves by telling her to hold on to him as she reads. Afterwards she tells him she doesn't know how to thank him for his help. He suggests that they go across the street to *Coffee Dan's* for a cup of coffee. She tells him that she has a meeting with Johnny Hyde. He realizes who Johnny Hyde is and that it is important for her to attend. He calls her a couple of days later, but finds that she has moved in with Johnny. She moved in with Johnny Hyde at his home on 718 N. Palm Drive, in Beverly Hills, but still maintains her room at the Beverly Carlton Hotel, in keeping with her independent nature.

Marilyn is scheduled to participate in the *Photoplay Dream House Give-Away Promotional Tour* in conjunction with the nationwide tour for *Love Happy*. Stars of the movie, Ilona Massey, Vera-Ellen, and Marion Hutton were originally scheduled to go on the tour, but by June plans had changed and Marilyn went in their place. She traveled by train to New York City, Chicago, Rockford, Detroit, Cleveland and Milwaukee before abandoning the tour and returning home to Los Angeles in early August, much to producer Lester Cowan's chagrin. She would be paid $100 per week while she was on the publicity tour. Marilyn described her experience on *Love Happy* as, "My first job of any importance, as far as promoting Marilyn Monroe was concerned…Actually it was a walk-on and it was all over in less than a hundred feet of film. I just walked across the stage while Groucho leered. It was the first time I had ever been out of the State of California. I did press interviews and charity shows for $100 a week."

On June 1st, her 23rd birthday, the itinerary for her publicity tour is scheduled. Barney Rossen sends Al Tamarin of United Artist a telegram. "Have written Fred Joyce today as follows: Marilyn Monroe will leave Hollywood June 10th and will arrive Chicago on Sunday June 12th at 1:45 pm Central Standard Time. She will travel on Super Chief Train Number 18, Roomette Number 6, Car 183. She has signed personal appearance contract for three weeks commencing on or about June 11th Copy of Which was sent you today."

*The Rockford Register*, Rockford, Illinois, is already promoting her visit by running a picture of her in the ermine bikini. She will make a three-day personal appearance and wake-up this sleepy town. "Pretty Marilyn Monroe, in Hollywood, wears this ermine number in a new movie with the Marx Brothers and on her it looks good." She did not actually wear the bikini in the movie.

The first stop for the *Love Happy* Tour arrives in Rockford, Illinois, not Chicago as previously scheduled, on June 12th. The decision to host the premier of the film in Rockford was arrived at after a survey of the community during May by Hollywood producers and United Artist film distributors. Also, helping to make choice was the decision of the U.S. Marine corps to film a marine short in Rockford. *LIFE* magazine cinched the deal after they selected Rockford as a "typical American city." If Rockford was good enough for the Marines and *LIFE* magazine, it surely was good enough for *Love Happy*. After arriving, Marilyn joined the local press at a supper buffet at the Faust Hotel. She gives her age as 21 and surprises the press by preferring milk to coffee. The press sees her as an innocent, a babe in the woods. In fact, she was 2 years older than she let on and had been navigating the Hollywood jungle since she was 19. She was savvy and cunning to have survived the modeling racket and the Hollywood studios at so young an age and without any real protection, and yet, she is also delicate and fragile, and that is what people first respond to. She will never lose this vulnerability, and she is not necessarily false. In an unfamiliar situation she disarms people by her need to be taken care of, by her frailty and her tenuous demeanor.

Margaret Parton, who wrote an article on Marilyn for the *Ladies Home Journal* in March of 1961, aptly describes the paradox of meeting Marilyn. "...a sense of a sick little canary instead of a peacock. Only when you pick it up in your hand to comfort it...beneath the sickness, the weakness and the innocence, you find a strong bone structure and a heart beating. You recognize sickness and you find strength." Marilyn would tell Florabel Muir, "I'll tell you something. I don't feel sorry for myself now. Don't get me wrong. One thing I learned was to rely on myself and I guess the sooner one does that in this world the better off one is. I don't expect too much from anybody, so I'm never disappointed."

The next day was a hectic one for Marilyn. She appears in the local paper, *The Rockford Register Republic* in a Rose Marie Reid taffeta two-piece she had worn in last year's publicity poses, and poses with two lifeguards, Ruth Perkins and Don Casey, as she helped open the Fairgrounds Pool. There was a one column interview with Marilyn printed alongside the photo. The press found her, "as a pretty, unspoiled youngster who would prefer a chocolate soda to caviar." Later in the afternoon it began to rain. She is photographed in a sweater and shorts posing sitting in a window, and in another she is engaged in a rainy publicity stunt with a Harpo impersonator, who is holding an umbrella for her. The photos make the front page of the *Rockford Morning Star* the next day. Along with the photos, an interview spanning 1 1/2 columns is included. Marilyn is again pointed out as not one to drink or smoke. She likes to write short stories, poetry, sketch, paint and design. Laurence Olivier and Joan Crawford are her favorite actors. She predicts a bright future for fellow actor Montgomery Clift. She hopes to one day be on the legitimate stage. Finally, her idea of an evening off is to spend it quietly at home or go to the movies. It seems that while she is in the American Heartland she is less the Hollywood Movie Star and instead has traded the brazen image for the sensibilities of the All American Girl. Though, not totally dishonest, it once again demonstrates her chameleon like skill at blending into the situation she finds herself in. Kudos to her hard knock life.

June 14th was Flag Day and Marilyn's day started early as she participated with the local Elks Club by putting a flag in the street holder in front of Owens, Inc., a sportswear shop. The photo appeared on page 13 of the *Rockford Register Republic*. (On the 19th, the *Rockford Register* will run a photo of Marilyn in a polka-dot two-piece, furnished for her by Owens, Inc.) Later that morning she tours the Children's Home of Rockford where she signs autographs and has her picture taken with the children, which appears in the local newspaper. She wore one of her wool suits and gloves with a large corsage of flowers, which she will wear to the premier. Later that night at the theater, she was signing autographs behind a counter in the back of the lobby. She made the front page of the *Rockford Morning Star* holding 3 year-old Vivian Johnson and signing an autograph for her. *Love Happy* ran for two showings a day.

On the 15th, Marilyn made a live radio broadcast promoting *Love Happy* at the State Theater. Marilyn gamely signed autographs in the lobby for the next three days. After the movie, she would make a brief appearance onstage. Marilyn later recalled, "I felt guilty about appearing on the stage when I had such an insignificant role in the film, but the people in the audiences didn't seem to care."

On January 11, 1952, Hal Nelson of the *Rockford Morning Star* remembers Marilyn's visit to Rockford with fondness, "In June of 1949, we dropped in on a Sunday night buffet supper at which Marilyn Monroe was hostess. We had never previously heard of Marilyn Monroe. She hadn't heard of us, either. Marilyn had been sent to Rockford by United Artist as a publicity stunt for the premier of a new Marx Brothers movie, *Love Happy*, at the State Theater. It was a fair movie, not good, not bad. It was up to Marilyn to help draw a crowd to the State. As part of the buildup, Arthur Granquist, State Theater manager, arranged a buffet supper in the Faust hotel. Newspapermen and women were invited. It was a very enjoyable party. We managed to wrangle a break for ourselves. At the supper table, we sat at Marilyn's right. And we monopolized her pretty unfairly as far as the rest of the guest were concerned. But she didn't seem to mind too much….We liked Marilyn. She wasn't just another Hollywood beauty. She had a fresh charm about her. She acted as though she really liked us, too. Newspaper people can usually tell. She was co-operative about posing for pictures. And photogenic. As a result she got quite a bit of publicity during her three day stay in Rockford. Charlie Ayres, who interviewed her, described Marilyn as 118 pounds of blue-eyed, blonde loveliness. It wasn't only newspapermen who liked Marilyn. There were long lines in the State Theater lobby each afternoon and evening. Men and women and kids. Waiting for Marilyn's autograph. She almost wore out her fingers signing her name.

We stopped by at the Theater the last night Marilyn was in Rockford. She thanked us for the publicity, the kind things we'd said about her. We told her she deserved them all. That we felt she'd go far in Hollywood. We predicted she'd hit stardom. She held our hands in hers. And smiled a little wistfully. It's tough to get to the top in Hollywood she told us seriously. But you'll make it, we assured her. After that, we didn't see or hear anything of Marilyn for two years. We'd look for her name in movie cast but never find it. Then one day last summer we saw *Asphalt Jungle*. And there, unexpectedly, was Marilyn on the screen again. Her undulating walk, her baby stare were bright spots in one of the better movies of the year. Marilyn didn't have a big role, but apparently it was enough."

Hedda Hopper revealed in her column on the 16$^{th}$, "Marilyn Maxwell telephoned from Rockford, Ill., where she is on a personal appearance for *Love Happy*, the Marx Brothers picture. 'Just passed through your home town, Dixon,' she said. 'What press agent dreamed up this?'" It seemed Marilyn Maxwell was right about the trouble with two Marilyn's in Hollywood. Hedda mixed up these two Marilyn's, but by this time next year, she wouldn't be making this mistake again.

By June 17th, the tour makes it to Chicago. Marilyn is interviewed in the Pump Room in the Ambassador East Hotel, on the 18th. Marilyn will visit Chicago and the Pump Room again on her Publicity tour for *Some Like It Hot* in 1959.

*Chicago Tribune* newspaper features Marilyn on June 20$^{th}$, in the entertainment column, "Tower Ticker," by Savage, "Short snortin' the town: Marilyn Monroe, that oddity among Hollywood blondes, a native daughter, is one of the chase-ees in the Marx Brothers' picture *Love Happy*--formerly, *Blondes Up*. The picture had its test run the other day at the State Theater in Rockford, Ill., and Marilyn was sent along by the studio to add glamour to the occasion. The Rockford city water department had torn up the street in front of the theater, but when it learned of Miss Monroe's imminent arrival, workers hastily threw up a pontoon bridge (must be some ex-Seabees among 'em!) across the impassable pavement gape and labeled it: 'For Marilyn's little feet, only!' Toll charge to Marilyn was the autographing of the water workers' shovels. Yesterday, catching her breath at the Pump Room, she reflected, 'They had a bigger opening in the street outside than we had inside!'"

The tour arrives in New York City on June 20th. Marilyn had packed three wool suits for her trip back east, thinking it didn't get hot in New York. A press agent quickly comes up with a plan to photograph her with three fake ice cream cones as she exits the train. In one photo she is also carrying an electric fan. A summer dress is purchased for her off the rack at Macy's and she will wear it the rest of the trip. She will also wear it for Earl Moran when she comes back to Los Angeles.

While on the train to Warrensburg, NY, for the *Photoplay* Dream House, photographer Charles Carbone, working for *Photoplay* magazine, snaps photos of Marilyn and her companions and at the home of Miss MacAllister, winner of the Dream House.

The *Love Happy* Tour arrived in Warrensburg, New York, on June 21st and presented keys to a new home, fully furnished, to the winner of the *Photoplay* Dream House contest, Virginia MacAllister and her son Rusty. The ceremony was memorialized in the November issue of *Photoplay* magazine. After the ceremony *Photoplay* hosted a cocktail party at the Colonial Arms of Warrensberg.

*Photoplay* editor at the time, Adele Whitely-Fletcher, remembers meeting Marilyn for the first time, "My first glimpse of Marilyn came as I waited, others bound for the Dream House presentation, at the gates of an early morning train to Albany. Across the vast marble stretches of Grand Central Station came United Artist' publicist, Tess Michaels. She was almost running, her eyes on the big clock that showed one minute to train time. Beside her was Marilyn Monroe, the starlet she'd promised to bring to the presentation ceremonies. At the sight of her my heart sank. I wondered how her shoulder-length hair, bleached to a straw color, and her shirred pink sun-dress, cut almost as low in front as in back, would be received in the little upstate town for which we were bound. When we were introduced, Marilyn smiled but had little to say. Tess whispered, 'I'm sorry to be so late, but I couldn't get her started. She kept fussing with her hair and make-up. She's painfully shy.'...Hours later, as we stepped from the car in which we'd driven from the Albany station to the little town and hotel where the Dream House luncheon was to be held, Marilyn tugged at my hand and stuttered, 'P-please w-walk with m-m-me to the p-p-powder room!' Her dress had been badly stained at breakfast when a coffee cup overturned, and she hadn't had time on the train to wash it. Standing nude, except for her high-heeled sandals, she rinsed the spot out of her dress and slip and she even rinsed her scanty panties. She had no need of the falsies she sometimes was said to wear. 'I c-can almost wr-ring them dry,' she promised when she saw me looking at her rinsing the panties--and then at my watch. Carelessly, we hadn't locked the powder room door. In barged a townswoman. She took one look at Marilyn, gave a couple of horrified clucks and backed out, slamming the door behind her. 'What's she so cross about?' Marilyn wanted to know. She was so bewildered she forgot to stutter. In many ways Marilyn was unbelievably naive. She did not have the faintest inkling of the scandalized buzz that woman's description of her would immediately set off all over town. It was then, I guess, that I became her champion."

On February 22, 1956, Marilyn had lunch at the apartment of Fleur Cowles and Miss Whitley-Fletcher was there also. She said of Marilyn that there had not been a time when she had not been able to count on Marilyn's cooperation and friendship. Marilyn replied, "But how could I do otherwise--after that trip we went on, remember...when that prize house was presented to a contest winner way up in New York state? She was a war widow, with a little boy, remember? And she was on crutches because she'd had a skiing accident. I'll never forget how we saw Monty Woolley--beard and all...He was getting on the train at Albany when we got off. Remember? And remember that nice steward in the diner? We did send him the autographed pictures, I hope...Oh, I remember we did. And that man who handled the broadcast of the presentation ceremonies...Wasn't he wonderful at handling crowds?"

There were over 500 spectators who watched Mrs. MacAllister and her son receive the keys to their new home that day. Adele Fletcher, officials from the National Retail Lumber Dealers Association, radio and pressmen, and, of course, Marilyn, Don DeFore, Donald

Buka and Lon McAllister, were on hand for the festivities. The newspaper reported that "the four movie stars who came to Warrensburg for the ceremonies were besieged all afternoon by autograph seekers and amateur shutterbugs."

Back in New York, Marilyn is interviewed by Earl Wilson for his column on June 24th. Wilson remembers the occasion in a 1958 column, "Nine years ago this month I interviewed a girl who'd never had a N.Y. story done about her. Fred Joyce, then a Hollywood publicist, tipped me off to her potentialities." The interview takes place at her hotel, the Sherry-Netherland.

In a column in 1975 Wilson revealed more about how the interview came about. "In 1949, a press agent up in the Bronx almost begged me to interview an unknown actress. I resisted because she was a nonentity. She *was* a nonentity….One of the press agents for the Shorehaven Beach Club, Spencer Hare, said to me back in 1949 that she'd never had a New York interview. I yielded. I happened to need a column, to tell the truth. A year later that blonde nobody was so famous that I was lucky to get to see her when I went to Hollywood. She had several scrapbooks. My interview with her was the first pasted in. I never told her how close I was to saying, 'No, she's a nobody. I won't interview Marilyn Monroe."

Marilyn stayed up late to prepare for the interview, but she really need not have bothered, for Earl Wilson didn't take her or the interview very seriously. The article was published in his column on July 28. Earl would later give a glimpse into the early Marilyn, before fame was beating down her door. "At that time, Miss Monroe was so unknown that no reporter wanted to interview her, and no photographer could be aroused to take her picture. The press agent had to arrange to get the pictures taken himself. And Miss Monroe, when I talked to her, was shy, and modest, and didn't say anything especially quotable. The fact is, I wasn't much impressed about her as a great beauty or siren--I thought of her more as a nice young girl being 'oversold.'" Earl dismissed her as having no "claim to any acting genius." Yet, three years later when he met Marilyn again, he formed a different opinion and became a huge supporter of hers. He also said of the interview, "To me it seems now so very long ago—actually only 1949—that I was induced, on a dull Saturday, to interview a blonde starlet nobody else in New York would bother seeing. MMMMmmm was already her publicity gimmick. She was supposedly a sexpot, but to me she was colorless and wooden. Four or five years later, when she was the biggest thing in the country, I had to wait an hour or two for her to primp when I dropped around to her Hollywood house. Would she remember me? 'Oh, here's the interview you did—the first one—I kept it in my scrapbook!' she said, all out of breath about it, when she eventually wriggled and slithered out."

Earl Wilson devoted a single sentence to Marilyn in his column on June 27th. "Marilyn Monroe, 'The Mmmm Girl' is here exploiting *Love Happy*--and herself..." That same day *New York Daily Mirror* Column by Sidney Fields published her photo along with an encouraging prediction for her future success in movies.

Three days later, on the 30th, Walter Winchell gave Marilyn this blurb in his column,

"Celebs about Town...Marilyn Monroe, the star of *Love Happy*, on her initial visit to the Big Town."

Marilyn shares her own memories of arriving in New York in an article in *This Week Magazine*, December 17, 1960, "I was on tour to promote *Love Happy*, in which I had a bit part...I didn't get paid until I started to sue. I had never been to New York; I thought it was always cold there. So I came in all wool--in the middle of summer! It was so hot that I spent all the rest of my visit in a cotton dress Lester Cowan got in a wholesale house."

In his syndicated column, on July 5, 1956, Leonard Lyons shared memories of this time in Marilyn's life, "...Now she's front-page news here, this actress whose first trip to N.Y. was to help exploit, a movie in which she had one brief scene. She got $100 a week for this promotion job, she told me. 'I had a big suite in the afternoon, to meet the exhibitors. And later that night I was moved to a tiny room.' She wasn't upset about the change to smaller quarters. The studio hadn't canceled her right to order room via room service. 'Caviar for breakfast. It's the first thing I remember of New York,' said Miss Monroe...'I used to walk to a cafeteria near Grand Central for coffee, alone.' she said. From room-service caviar to cafeteria coffee. She still goes to cafeterias, but in disguise."

Marilyn was housed in the Sherry Netherland Hotel on Fifth Ave., across from Central Park's main entrance. She will stay here again in August of 1951 during her trip to New York.

While in New York City, Marilyn met discount dress manufacturer, Henry Rosenfeld, who becomes a good friend. She had been invited to the El Morocco nightclub and while there Rosenfeld spied her and invited her to join him. He will give her financial advice in the future, offer to marry her in 1955 and be one of the last people she will call days before her death.

Marilyn also runs into an old acquaintance, Andre de Dienes. He holds no grudge that she refused to marry him, and insists that she accompany him to Jones Beach where he creates some of the most enduring images of her young beauty. Marilyn later had this to say about a photograph taken on the beach, "This was the same hot summer in New York...Andre de Dienes took this at Jones Beach. I still had my slave bracelet. What I'm actually doing in this photo is dancing by myself. My arms are up to embrace an imaginary partner. But note my hair was a shade lightened, because it always went dark in black and white."

During this session on the beach he will take, in his words, "the sexiest picture I ever took…My native land is Hungry, a country noted throughout the world for the beauty and allure of its women, yet I regard this picture of Marilyn Monroe as the sexiest picture I have ever taken. The reason is obvious: Marilyn herself. From an artistic standpoint, her face and figure are the most perfectly balanced ever presented to a camera. In addition to this asset, Marilyn has great vitality, and she radiates a magnetism that has never needed 3D to reach out to an audience. I have known Marilyn since 1944, when she was a pretty teen-ager whose quick imagination and high-intelligence made her a valuable model. She has always been a delight on a difficult setting: her good temper never failed no matter how weary she became, and she was always, as you Americans say, a lady. Agents and talent scouts are trying to find her equal, but they'll fail."

July had Marilyn featured in two magazines, both in connection with *Love Happy*. *Movie Teen* magazine featured her in an article, "Tomorrow's Stars." "Marilyn Monroe is a Californian making good without experience on Broadway or any other stage...her current release is *Love Happy*."

*Movie Play* magazine featured a one-column article with two photos of Marilyn by J.R. Eyerman, "Marilyn Monroe, a newcomer to the movie cameras, plays an important role in the new Marx Bros. film, *Love Happy*. There's no lack of feminine charmers in the United Artists' pic, for in addition to Marilyn the movie features Vera Ellen, Ilona Massey, and Marion Hutton...blonde charmers all!" Marilyn was also featured in *US Camera* magazine in an ad for EMDE Aluminum Protectochrome Mounts.

It seems the *Love Happy* tour retraced its earlier stops and July finds the tour back in Chicago for a charity baseball game. Marilyn makes the front page of the *Chicago Herald American* on July 9, 1949. Her photo is captioned, "It'll Be a Lovely Game With Marilyn Monroe As Bat Girl, She'll Be Joined By Others--And Every One A Big Star." Marilyn is shown holding six bats. She and her companions were in town for the Film Stars World Series Baseball game at Wrigley Field to benefit the City of Hope, the Motion Picture Relief Fund and the *Herald-American* Benefit Fund. Bob Hope, Milton Berle and a roster full of comedians and movie stars entertained the crowd. The event was billed as a Triple Header with the 4th Annual Prep All-Star Baseball Game and the 2nd Annual Old Timers Diamond Classic being played that day as well. Marilyn was photographed at the game with Joe Murphy, Chief Lt. in Andy Frain's Ushers which were used for crowd control in Chicago, and with several participants of the games. There is also a short film of Marilyn in the dugout.

Marilyn meets Chicago White Sox power hitting outfielder, Gus Zernail. "Gus remembered that she was "such a nice girl." "She asked a bunch of questions about baseball...she was really interested in the game." Zernial said that he was perplexed later when they made her look less than wholesome in many of her films." Mr. Zernail will reunite with Marilyn in 1951 in a publicity picture for the White Sox Training Camp in Pasadena, which will be instrumental in introducing her to Joe DiMaggio.

Marilyn will also be reunited with Alan Young, Joe Kirkwood, Jr., Adele Jergens, and a few others she would share screen time with in the future. Participating in the game was Jane Russell, Marilyn's future co-star in *Gentlemen Prefer Blondes*.

Roddy McDowell also took part in the baseball game and afterward he and Marilyn spent the evening together at Ricketts Restaurant, where they were photographed by Arthur Meyers. According to McDowell, he and Marilyn ended the evening by playing strip poker in his hotel room. Marilyn had worked with Roddy when they were both with Columbia Studios in 1948. She was an off camera dance partner to "pace" him through his routines. He found her very shy and withdrawn, and although he liked her, he was unwilling to be drawn in by her neediness.

The *Love Happy* publicity tour stopped in Detroit and movie critic, Tony Weitzel recounts the rare details. "Once, when I was in Detroit a friend of mine named Fred Joyce came to town to ballyhoo a Marx brother movie. It was not necessary to see the movie because the same things always happened to Groucho and Chico and Harpo. So, to prevent utter critical boredom Fred had brought along a cuddly young lady who had a 30-second role in the picture…He produced this little blonde $75-a-week broad, and it was July and we wanted a picture so we had her put on a bikini and pose lying on a 300-pound cake of ice until one side of her lovely torso was pale blue. The picture made the front pages in the midst of a heat wave and we used the little gal's name. She was somebody called Marilyn Monroe."

Marilyn was extremely tired of being on the road. The constant attention she received from local photographers was almost too much for her to bear. She spent her days promoting *Love Happy* and her nights talking long distance to Natasha Lytess and Johnny Hyde. Marilyn would travel on to Milwaukee and cut the tour short, returning home to Los Angeles for some much needed rest.

The last stop on the tour was Milwaukee, Wisconsin. While there she was brought to the *Milwaukee Journal* for an interview with Raymond E. McBride. He noticed that she was at ease around men, unlike other starlets who had dropped by the newspaper office. He found her unselfconscious, even allowing the interview to continue when she was primping in the photo studio, combing her hair and checking her makeup. Of course, he noticed her figure and her striking beauty. She posed for photographs for a staff photographer, John Ahlhauser. He remembers that Marilyn was a very capable model, knowing how to make the most out of both the photographer's time and film. Mr. McBride commented to her press agent, "'That is one of the prettiest girls you've ever brought around here.' 'That,' he said, 'is what girls are supposed to look like.'"

On July 17th the *Milwaukee Journal* ran the item of Marilyn's visit and her photo. "The latest starlet to drop into Milwaukee is Marilyn Monroe, who is featured in the new Marx Brothers comedy, *Love Happy*, which by no coincidence will open here Aug 6. Miss Monroe is 21 years old and a Los Angeles native whose real name is Norma Jean Dougherty. And what's wrong with her real name? 'Too long,' she said. Miss Monroe was hired by the Howard Hughes outfit after her picture appeared on five magazine covers in a month. She played the lead in *Ladies of the Chorus* for Columbia and shares the feminine honors in the Marx opus with Ilona Massey and Vera-Ellen. In the United Artists picture, Marilyn chases Groucho Marx which is certainly a new twist."

Syndicated columnist Earl Wilson gave Marilyn a big publicity boost by devoting his entire column to her on July 28th. This would be her first extensive interview as an actress. "New Type Of Hollywood Girl…Over the years, Hollywood has joyously given us its 'It Girl,' its 'Oomph Girl,' its 'Sweater Girl,' and even 'The Body'--and they've all become big movie stars. Now we get the 'Mmmm Girl.' Miss Marilyn Monroe still wasn't quite sure what an 'Mmmm Girl' has to do when I talked to her. 'But I'm sure none of the girls ever got hurt by being called such names,' she said. Miss Monroe is probably right. They don't get hurt, but they get mighty tired, even sick of the tags. Miss Monroe, who is practically an unknown, is a 21-year-old, long-haired blonde from Van Nuys, Cal. She has a nice flat waist that rises to an (mmmm) 36 ½ bra line. She also has long pretty legs. 'But why do they call you the 'Mmmm Girl?'' I asked her. 'Well,' she said, doubtless remembering it like the press agent told her to. 'It seems some people couldn't whistle so they went, 'Mmm.'' 'Why couldn't they whistle?' I said. 'Well,' she said, 'some people just can't whistle.' 'Maybe they couldn't whistle because they had their mouths full of popcorn,' I suggested. Personally, we think the whole thing was dreamed up by the publicist--but the fact remains that these appellations (get HIM!) have helped make a few girls pretty famous. Annie Pie Sheridan, the 'Oomph Girl' told me once she was sick to death of oomph, and she was a good enough actress to make people forget she was ever the 'Oomph Girl'. The 'Mmmm Girl' starts out, candidly, without any claim to acting genius.

She was working as a typist in a factory in California a couple of years ago when The Big Thing happened. 'I only did 35 words a minute and didn't do them very well, so they gave me a job inspecting parachutes,' she says. 'One day some photographer came in and they said, 'where have you been hiding?'' Very soon after that her picture was in magazines and a Howard Hughes scout phoned her, but by this time she was already signed by 20th Century-Fox, 'They gave me a bit part in a picture but cut it out,' she says. So she left there. One day she met Louis Shurr, the Hollywood agent who keeps a lot of mink coats for emergencies, and without so much as offering her a mink coat. He suggested she go to see Producer Lester Cowan. Groucho Marx was there, too. 'Groucho said, 'You get behind me and walk like I do.' Groucho did a girlish swagger, very much exaggerated. 'I did it, and they said, 'you start tomorrow.''

Marilyn makes the cover of *Glamorous Models* magazine in August.

Marilyn chose not to participate in the *Love Happy* premier in Milwaukee on August 6th. She went AWOL and returned to Los Angeles. This put Lester Cowan in a bad spot, as he didn't have anyone there to promote the movie. He managed to bring in Vera-Ellen to fill in for Marilyn. In the newspaper ad for the *Love Happy* premiere in Milwaukee Marilyn is nowhere mentioned. It is easy to understand his frustration, given the big buildup he had given her. Her perceived disloyalty will sever her relationship with him. Back in Los Angeles she tried in vain to contact Lester Cowan, who refused to return her calls. Even though his anger is understandable, he should have been glad that she gamely stuck out the monotonous *Love Happy* Tour as long as she did.

Erskine Johnson will say of her experiences with *Love Happy*, "When Groucho Marx chased Marilyn in *Love Happy*, he chased her to stardom without knowing it. She went on tour to help ballyhoo the picture, met the press, did TV and radio shows and lassoed enough publicity to interest Fox studio in casting her as a dancing girl in *Ticket to Tomahawk*. But it was Marilyn's role of a sultry doll interested in an older man in *Asphalt Jungle* that melted the candy bars in theater lobbies."

Marilyn bounced back quickly and thanks to Harry Lipton and old acquaintances, Ben Lyon, George Jessel and Joseph Schenck, she was cast in 20th Century Fox's *Ticket to Tomahawk*. Marilyn received a call from Fox asking her if she could dance. She told them yes and they asked her to report for filming. Darryl Zanuck comments about this in the November 3, 1970 edition of *Look* magazine. "One day a great friend of mine, Joseph M. Schenck, brought over to my home in Palm Springs this very beautiful girl, who was also on the plump side. I didn't jump up and say, 'Oh, this is a great star,' or anything like that. Later on, Joe said, 'If you can work her in some role or something, some, you know, supporting role, do so.' I did, but I didn't think that I had found any gold mine. John Huston gave her a hell of a good role in *The Asphalt Jungle*. Jesus, she was good in it. I thought it must have been the magic of Huston, because I didn't think she had all that in her. But then I put her in *All About Eve*, and she was an overnight sensation."

Marilyn has a modeling session with Earl Moran on August 4th. He referred her to Ken Murray who was looking for new talent for his "Blackouts" show. Marilyn had graced the cover of the 1947 program for "Ken Murray's Blackouts," which was illustrated by Moran, and she had met Murray two years ago when she was a caddy for a celebrity golf tournament, as he was part of the same pairing as John Carroll. It seems that one of the agents at the William Morris agency, Charles Wick, also told Murray about Marilyn.

Murray was taking his very successful vaudeville review, "Ken Murray's 'Blackouts'" to New York. Marie Wilson, who was one of the headliners in the show, wasn't going. Trying to find a replacement for Marie wasn't easy. He had interviewed many girls and agreed to see Marilyn. Mr. Murray remembers the episode a little differently than Earl Moran, "However, one of the most beautiful young hopefuls who applied is worthy of more than a passing mention. She was sent to me be a friend, Charles Wick, who was with the William Morris office at the time. Into my dressing room walked the most unusual girl I had ever seen. She was blonde, beautiful and buxom. When she talked she had the manner of a startled bird. She read the script in a low husky voice. I seriously considered giving her the job, but she failed the last exam. The most perfect 36 still doesn't fit perfectly into the perfect 39. But I was so fascinated with this girl that I called my wife and said, 'Honey, there's a girl down here I'm not going to hire, but I want you to come and see her. She's sort of a caricature of a movie star. I think she'll be great in pictures.' Bette was intrigued by my request. It was the only time I had ever called her to come down and see a girl I was auditioning. Bette came down with her girlfriend and they sat and watched the audition. She had an accompanist, and she sang some songs in a throaty voice. They agreed that she was one of the most fascinating people they'd ever seen. But in the end, I had to tell her I couldn't take her. She was terribly upset. She wanted badly to go East with us. But by the time we came back to Hollywood this girl had made quite a name for herself. I called her and said, 'Well, I saved you from a fate worse than death. Aren't you glad you didn't go to New York with us?' Her initials are M.M.--and I don't mean the candy."

Marie Wilson will dispute Murray's version, telling Sheilah Graham that Marilyn didn't get the job because the costumes were too long, but that everything else was a perfect fit.

On August 8th, a photo of Marilyn at the Jones Beach Pool by Wee Gee, hits the newspapers.

By August 15th Marilyn is busy with production on *Ticket to Tomahawk*, Twentieth Century-Fox. Marilyn had the part of Clara, one of the showgirls in this western. *Tomahawk* was co-written by Mary Loos and her husband, Richard Sale. Loos was the niece of Anita Loos, the author of *Gentlemen Prefer Blondes,* and was married to Richard Sale, who happened to be the director. Loos would say after filming that Marilyn was going to be famous. "She was going to be a great star someday because she had all the wrong things that make a star."

*Ticket to Tomahawk* will be Marilyn's first time to work with Musical Director Lionel Newman. Newman and Marilyn had a few dates back in 1946 when she was a starlet at Fox. "They would go to dinner and then often call David Boutolph, a composer. Marilyn would sit quietly in a chair reading, while Newman and Boutolph played backgammon." When she makes her great musicals at Fox, he will play an important part in helping shape her career. Charles LeMaire, who created her bustle swim suit in 1947, will design the costumes. Marilyn renews her friendships with Fox crew members. They have always thought of her as one of their own.

On August 17th, *NEA Wire Service* ran a column, "Beauty Hints," by Alicia Hart, which featured a captioned photo of Marilyn at the Jones Beach swimming pool, taken by Wee Gee. "A daily swim, indoors or out, helps starlet Marilyn Monroe keep her figure trimmed for the camera's revealing lens." Another variation of the same picture was captioned, "Coming Out Party -- After a quick plunge, Marilyn Monroe seems to be emerging from both the pool and her bathing suit. One more dip and that neckline should be plunging down around her ankles."

Marilyn appears in *Kyron Way Diet Tablets* national newspaper ad in a photo by cheesecake photographer Laszlo Willinger starting in late August of 1949. "Screen beauties can't be fat--and no one needs to be!...Marilyn Monroe lovely screen star...appearing in the latest Marx Bros. smash hit, *Love Happy*...If you want slim, youthful lines like Miss Monroe and other stars, start the *KYRON* way to slenderness today!"

Marilyn will also be featured on the fall 1949 edition of the *So-Rite Fall Fashions* catalog. This is one of her last forays into fashion modeling. She is identified on the cover and connected with *Love Happy*. The photo was taken by Peter Fland and she looks lovely and elegant in a sweater, a leopard print coat and a hat by Mad Caps.

*Ticket to Tomahawk* took Marilyn away for five weeks of location shooting in Durango, Colorado. She became sick during filming, most likely from altitude sickness. She demanded that the doctor give her a large prescription of penicillin, despite his protest. She broke out in a rash as a result of her own prescription.

While on location, Marilyn participated in a charity baseball game between the local team in Durango and Twentieth Century-Fox studio workers. She came up with a bit to entertain the crowd. After batting, and on her way to first base, her pants fell down, revealing black lacey underwear. The stunt was a hit, of course. The money raised was donated to a local hospital.

Ann Baxter, who starred in *Ticket to Tomahawk,* did not have fond memories of Marilyn during the filming. She remembers that Marilyn took to wearing a V-necked angora sweater, without a bra. She wore it so often that people began to wonder if she slept in it. Miss Baxter also remembers that she was seen with a different crew member every night at the greasy spoon where the cast ate. When not working, Marilyn and her two roommates slept in between filming and all day on Sundays, or they took turns calling Hollywood on the only pay phone in town. These are bitter memories by Miss Baxter and ultimately unfounded if you look at her participation in several events for charity, and the fact that she was sick during the production.

Marilyn will also go on to share screen-time with Ann Baxter in *All About Eve*. She will make another movie with Dan Dailey in 1954, *There's No Business Like Show Business.* This is also the first of three films Marilyn would make with Rory Calhoun. The other two being, *How to Marry a Millionaire*, and *River of No Return.*

While in Durango, Colorado, Marilyn visited the Trimble Hot Springs Resort and Spa. She is photographed with some fellow cast members in the Lounge. Reportedly Marilyn loved the amenities there and savored a dip in the hot springs.

When Marilyn returned to Los Angeles, Jack Kramer, manager of the Kiva Theater in Durango, Colorado, sent her a photograph taken of a production she appeared in while on location in Durango making *Ticket to Tomahawk*. The photo show Marilyn lined up onstage with several other actors, some of whom were also in the cast of *Ticket to Tomahawk*. The photo is signed, "To Marilyn Monroe, a starlet now in the eyes of the studios, a very bright star now in the eyes of the people of Durango."

In his syndicated column, September 23rd, Jimmie Fidler writes, "As far as actress Marilyn Monroe is concerned, *Ticket to Tomahawk* should be entitled '*The Girl With the Green Face.*' Allergic to high altitudes she's been on the sick list most of the time since the troupe arrived in Colorado for location work."

Back on level ground in Hollywood in late September, Marilyn meets Rupert Allen, a *Look* magazine editor and writer, who will go on to become one of her earliest confidante's and eventually her publicist. He will introduce her to Milton Greene in 1953. Allen would remain in that position until November of 1960, when *The Misfits* completed shooting. He then took a position as Grace Kelly's personal publicist in Monaco.

In October Marilyn is featured in a *Photoplay* magazine fashion article, "On the Fashion Goal-Line." She is shown modeling a coat and suit for the upcoming football season. *Teen Age Diary Secrets* magazine has her on the cover with no follow up article inside. These magazines are the last using Marilyn as a simply a model. From now own she will be featured on the strength of her up and coming star power. Marilyn Monroe is about to burst onto the national consciousness.

On October 10th, the *LIFE* magazine article she participated with in April is finally released. "Eight Girls Try Out Mixed Emotions." Marilyn was featured in the article with seven other hopeful starlets, Lois Maxwell, Suzanne Dalbert, Ricky Soma, Laurette Luez, June Nigh, Delores Gardner and Cathy Downs. Photographer Philippe Halsman photographed the girls as they reacted to seeing a monster, hearing a joke, embracing a lover and tasting a drink. Cathy Downs would shortly marry actor/golfer Joe Kirkwood, Jr., Marilyn's one time trick golfing partner. This was the second time Marilyn posed with Laurette Luez. Miss Luez posed in August of 1947 with Marilyn and Clifton Webb for publicity pictures by Loomis Dean for *Sitting Pretty*.

Louella Parsons broke the news about Marilyn's part in *Asphalt Jungle* on October 28th. This is an early quote by Marilyn and an insight into how Hollywood was marketing her at the time, as a humble, girl next door who grew up an orphan. "It's good to hear anyone as thrilled as Marilyn Monroe when she telephoned to say she has the biggest part of her life in *Asphalt Jungle*. She was breathless when she said, 'I am grateful to Joseph Schenck, who gave me my first part in the movies. I am grateful to Mr. Johnny Hyde who signed me. I am grateful to Mr. John Huston for accepting me. I am just grateful to everyone,' said Marilyn. Marilyn was brought up in an orphan's home and has turned out to be one of the sweetest girls I know."

An early believer in networking, Marilyn's courting of influential people was starting to pay off. She was able to get the part through Lucille Ryman, who worked at MGM, and Johnny Hyde. Miss Ryman remembers trying to get Marilyn cast in the role. "When John Huston was casting *The Asphalt Jungle,* I read the script he had written and I knew that the role of Angela Phinlay was tailored for Marilyn. I told John about her. 'You're nuts,' he said. 'Look I wrote this screen play and I know a lot better than you do the sort of girl I want for the part.' 'Well, I kept on arguing with John until finally he gave in and agreed to test Marilyn just to get me out of his hair. And the minute he saw her on the screen he knew that I was right and hired her on the spot.'"

Marilyn told Barbara Berch Jamison during an interview in 1953 about auditioning for *Asphalt Jungle*. "No director has ever been able to tell her how to project herself—'how to make myself—uh—sexy. It just seems to happen anyway. Mr. Huston, now, when I first read for him I was so scared I shook. I'd studied my lines all night but when I came in to read I just couldn't relax. He asked me to sit down but there were only straight-backed chairs all around the room so I asked him if I could sit on the floor—just to get comfortable. But I was still nervous so I asked if I could take off my shoes. 'Anything,

anything,' he said. Then I read for him—and I was sure I was awful—but before I had a chance to say anything he kind of smiled and said I had the part, all right.' She tucked her bare feet under her. 'Then he said I'd probably turn into a very good actress—which is really what I want to be."

*The Asphalt Jungle* is in production during October and November. No time is wasted getting Marilyn in front of the stills camera. She is memorialized by photographer Ed Clark, who has shot her many times in the past. For *The Asphalt Jungle*, Marilyn appears with an elegant up-do and a chic dress that captures a self-control that her cheesecake photos lack.

Marilyn plays Angela Phinlay, the mistress of a lawyer who is tangled up in a crime. Marilyn later said that she made it "by the skin of her teeth."

Sydney Guilaroff was listed as the hair designer for this film. It is for this movie that Marilyn starts to sport a new hairstyle. Gone are the long blonde curls, and in its place is a new, more refined style. It is a sleek page boy in the manner of Lana Turner. In fact she will soon be touted by the press as a usurper to Lana's sweater girl throne.

Guilaroff remembers that Arthur Hornblow called him prior to Marilyn's test and told him to make her more "ladylike." Marilyn arrived and was almost overcome with nerves. Charlie Schram applied her makeup. Guilaroff cut and styled her hair into a modified pageboy, leaving plenty of movement in her hairstyle. As she was sitting under the hairdryer Guilaroff surveyed his assistants on their take on Marilyn. Their common opinion was, "nice looking, but nothing special." He felt far differently. He even went as far as taking over her screen test. He claims to have "recruited the best cinematographer I could find and personally made sure the lighting was perfect." He coached her from a distance in the darkness. Marilyn wore a sweater over a white shirt. The test lasted for almost 30 minutes. The last 5 minutes was devoted to close-ups. When John Huston saw the test he exclaimed, "What vulnerability—sexy without being crude or coarse."

Despite her refined hairstyle Marilyn is still unsure she has what it takes to get the role. James Bacon remembers running into Marilyn during her audition for *Asphalt Jungle*. "Possessor of one of the world's most famous figures, she was headed for the interview wearing falsies. I tried to tell her in a nice way that she looked grotesque—like a chiffonier with the top drawer pulled out. But Producer Arthur Hornblow was more direct. He ordered her to remove the artificial padding before continuing with the interview. 'She did, and displayed a perfect figure that needed no artificial help. She got the part, but I have always thought her appearance in falsies that day was the all-time height of insecurity."

In another column Bacon recalls that John Huston actually took the falsies out of Marilyn's bodice.

Producer Arthur Hornblow recalls the young Marilyn and takes credit for giving Marilyn the role, "It was a role with impact. The kind that comes along once every ten years. When Marilyn came in to read for the part, I must confess that she didn't read very well, but she had something--it's hard to define--some inner quality that made me pick her.' Hornblow speaks with some authority for it was he who picked the then-unknown blonde and cast her as Louis Calhern's girlfriend in '*Jungle.*' It was a small role, but it touched off the most fabulous career in recent movie history."

Tom Davidson relates an anecdote about Marilyn's allure on screen. "It seems some MGM studio big-wigs were running *Asphalt Jungle* in a private projection room deep in the basement of the lot's main building, where a dozen or so screening parlors are situated. Suddenly there was confusion on the screen, and one of the executives pushed a button stopping the picture. When the projectionist came in to see what the matter was, the executive was puzzled. 'There must be something the matter,' he said, 'The film doesn't make sense. There's something wrong with the continuity.' The projectionist flushed. 'I'm sorry,' he stammered. 'It's those other projectionist. They must have stolen reel four again.' 'For what?' asked the executive. 'Well, sir.' Said the projectionist, 'every time I turn my back those guys swipe reel four and run it over and over so they can get another look at that dame. They can't seem to get enough of her.'"

Julie Paul gives a succinct description of Marilyn at this point in her career. "Hollywood was intrigued, as was the rest of the country, when Marilyn burst into view as a rich lawyer's mistress in *Asphalt Jungle*. Sultry, not too pretty, but sexy in a restrained manner, smartly directed and knowingly photographed, she came across the screen with such physical impact that discerning fans knew a star was born."

It is during the filming of *The Asphalt Jungle* that John Huston introduces Marilyn to a young Truman Capote, whom she will befriend when she moves to New York in 1955.

Shelley Winters remembers that after the wrap party for *Asphalt Jungle,* Marilyn, bolstered by her accomplishment as an actress, made a phone call to Stanley Gifford in the hopes of finally having a relationship with her father. He told her not to contact him again.

When MGM failed to offer Marilyn a contract, Sydney Guilaroff offered his services to her for any future readings and test. He said her got her a drive-on pass at MGM and instructed his staff to give her the star treatment. This promise by Guilaroff would come in handy when she tests for *All About Eve.*

All of Marilyn's hard work on the *Love Happy* Tour are reduced to a few photos in the November issue of *Photoplay* magazine and the article, "Dream House Contest: A Home in Warrensberg, New York" by Jackie Neben. "...Early on the morning of the house-warming, a special car attached to the New York Central's crack Empire State Express left New York with a party of very special people to help make the party a success. Many of them were people you'd know--whether you saw them in Hollywood, your own home town, or in Warrensburg, New York, the site of the Dream House. They were Don DeFore, Lon McCallister, Donald Buka and Marilyn Monroe."

Marilyn is featured in photos posing with Dream House winner, Virginia MacAllister and her son Rusty, and the other guests from Hollywood. They posed along with the trappings of a well-furnished dream home: Dirlyte flatware, a Thor Automagic Clothes Washer, a Lane Cedar Chest, a Bissell carpet sweeper, and a Norge Refrigerator.

Miss MacAllister remarried and gained success in New York City as a writer for soap operas, including *The Guiding Light* and *The Young and the Restless.* Rusty was adopted by

Miss MacAllister's new husband and changes his last name to McDonnell. He will become a successful stockbroker in California. He has few memories of Marilyn's visit.

On November 17th Marilyn accompanies Johnny Hyde to Dana and Mary Andrews 10th wedding anniversary party. Mr. Andrews remembers Johnny bringing his date along. "So this girl came. I must say she didn't look very attractive, and she didn't have anything to say, and nobody paid any attention to her. All of the other people were well known-- directors, people like Preminger, people I worked with. It was not a large Hollywood-type party, a party where I didn't know anyone personally. They were all close friends. And everyone said about this girl, "Who the heck is she?" with a sort of derogatory expression on their faces. I said, "Oh, it's some friend of Johnny Hyde's." I went over and tried to engage her in conversation and didn't have much luck. She seemed shy. I thought, this is very peculiar, for her to be with Johnny Hyde, who's quite a man of the world. If you'd been at that same party two years later, everybody would have been trying to talk to her. Her name was Marilyn Monroe. This is the way Hollywood is. The girl was there; she was just the same as she is now, more or less, yet they weren't able to see it. Johnny Hyde saw it. He's the one who got her into pictures."

Columnist Brandy Brent reveals that Marilyn and Johnny Hyde were among the celebrity audience at Danny Thomas' opening night at Ciro's on November 23rd.

Marilyn borrowed $200 from the William Morris Agency on December 27th.

Johnny Hyde is busy keeping her in the public eye. He takes her to dine regularly at Romanoff's. She is on the cusp of fame. Her old stand-by, modeling, has served her well during the last year. Johnny Hyde will perform his greatest act of servitude for her by convincing 20th Century-Fox to again put her under contract, and then fighting for roles for her that will make her career flourish. Marilyn is Johnny Hyde's date at the annual New Year's Eve Party given by producer Sam Spiegel at his Beverly Hills mansion, 702 North Crescent Drive. Until *Asphalt Jungle* is released in June of 1950, Marilyn will rely on publicity from *Love Happy* and *Ticket to Tomahawk,* along with a few other small items to keep her name in the headlines.

Marilyn is in *Earl Moran's The Girls of 1950* calendar by Baumgarth Calendar Co. She is featured in 6 of the 12 months. Photographer Bernard of Hollywood publishes his book of cheesecake art titled, *Pin-Ups by Bernard of Hollywood* in 1950. A full page photo features a not quite blonde Marilyn in her yellow bikini, although she is not credited by name.

Marilyn appears in her only TV Commercial. It is for the *Royal Triton Oil Company*. She coos, "This is the first car I ever owned. I call it Cynthia. She's going to have the best care a car ever had. Put Royal Triton in Cynthia's little tummy...Cynthia will just love that Royal Triton." She is reunited in this commercial with Joe Kirkwood, Jr. She was directed in this commercial by the legendary film maker, Hal Roach. On June 10, 1953, columnist Erskine Johnson reported that the commercial was playing on the east coast. Presumably they were cashing in on Marilyn's growing fame, even though her "look" had changed since filming the commercial.

In 1950 *Topps Flip Book Card* featured photos of Marilyn and Groucho from *Love Happy*. Marilyn appeared in a two piece bathing suit. Another card book that was produced was, *Flip-O-Vision* presents 'Mr. Missed Her Kisser,' with The Marx Bros. The booklet features Marilyn, Chico Marx and Harpo Marx. Marilyn, who is also dressed in a two piece bathing suit, loses to Chico in a numbers game and leans over to kiss him. They play again and this time Chico loses and goes to kiss Marilyn, but in classic Marx Bros. style, Harpo sticks his head in the way. The third card book produced was "Flip-O-Vision presents 'Love Happy' with Harpo." Marilyn once again appears in a two piece bathing suit with Harpo. He pulls his familiar gag of putting his leg into Marilyn's hand. The *Flip-O-Vision* books worked by making the characters seem to move when you flipped through the pages.

Wardrobe tests for *The Fireball* were conducted on January 5, 1950. The costumes in the film were designed by Rich and Staub. However, in one scene Marilyn wore her own sweater dress. She would wear this dress again in the films *All About Eve, Home Town Story* and in a screen test for the film *Cold Shoulder*.

On January 24, 1950 columnist, Edwin Schallert, reported that Marilyn will have the second feminine lead in *The Challenge* with Mickey Rooney. *The Challenge* was the original name of *The Fireball*.

*The Fireball* was in production in January and February of 1950 through Thor Productions, released through Twentieth Century-Fox. Marilyn plays Polly, a Roller Derby groupie in love with Johnny Caesar, played by Mickey Rooney. Marilyn meets Agnes Flanagan, a hairdresser. Miss Flanagan will work with Marilyn on and off throughout the rest of her career. Agnes will style Marilyn's hair for her 1962 sitting with George Barris and will assist Sydney Guilaroff in styling Marilyn's hair for her funeral.

Marilyn attended the "Players Ball" at the Panteges Theater with friend Mickey Rooney to publicize their upcoming roles in *The Fireball*. Photographer Joseph Jasgur had a chance to talk to her that night. Jasgur was on assignment for the *Hollywood Citizen-News*. Mickey Rooney arrived with Marilyn on his arm. Jasgur recognized her immediately. He called to her. She looked at him with no recognition. He later had a chance to speak to her and she blew him off. He asked her if she didn't remember the guy whose pictures made Zanuck sit up and take notice of her. She responded by saying that she did not know him. There must be more to the story for her to react in such a way, but we only have Jasgur's version to go on, she, on the other hand, never mentioned him again. For him to have suggested that his were the photos that launched her career gives insight to just what might have turned Marilyn off.

Her magazine appearances have slowed down. She made the cover of *Laff*, again, and will appear on the cover of the February/March issue of *Man to Man*.

On the 18th she borrows $150.00 from the William Morris Agency.

Dorothy Manner devotes a large photo and a bio of her modeling days to Marilyn in her column on February 19th. The photo accompanying the article was taken in Durango, Colorado when Marilyn was there to film *Ticket to Tomahawk*. At some point she performed with members of the cast at a theater there. She is shown in her angora sweater, shorts and wearing a cowboy hat. "If you were just born to be a model and then get in the movies, it doesn't matter much where you start. Take Marilyn Monroe--born Norma Jeane Dougherty. Norma Jeane was working in an aircraft plant in her native Van Nuys, California, when an Army photographer came out to the factory to take pictures to promote bond buying during the war. The first thing he spotted was Norma Jeane clad in bandanna, coveralls and toting a welder's torch. First, he whistled--and then he said: 'Young lady, wipe that smudge off the end of your nose and get over by that plane. You are now a model in the service of Uncle Sam's Army!' And although, Norma Jeane stuck to her welder's bench until the war's end, the San Fernando Valley blonde had her eye on a new and exciting career. With VJ-Day, she doffed the coveralls and tied herself to a Los Angeles photographer. Of the 10 portraits he made of her, five hit magazine covers. That's how little movie starlets are born--particularly if they are as beautiful, blonde, blue-eyed and luscious looking as our girl, Marilyn. She came by the Marilyn Monroe title by way of a casting director who superstitiously believed the initials M.M. are lucky for blondes--as witness the careers of Marilyn Miller and Marilyn Maxwell. 'Let's call you,' he suggested, hesitating just a minute, 'Marilyn Monroe.' Her first movie contract was at 20th Century-Fox, where she made *Scudda Hoo, Scudda Hay*, and she did two pictures at Columbia before getting her really good break, the dumb but gorgeous blonde menace in *Asphalt Jungle* for John Huston at MGM. She lives with an aunt in West Los Angeles and still sees her old high school pals from Van Nuys and University High Schools. She prefers mature men to boys of her own age. In fact, the rumor is around that she may marry her agent, popular Johnny Hyde, who brought Rita Hayworth to world fame. In the vital statistics line, Marilyn is of Welsh, English and Irish descent, weighs 118 pounds and stands five-feet-six inches."

On February 22nd, publicity is focused on an upcoming film, *Right Cross*. Columnist Edwin Schallert reveals that Marilyn will appear with in it with Dick Powell. Despite this early publicity, the film wouldn't go into production until August.

*Love Happy* was finally released on March 8th. For all her hard work on the pre-production and publicity, it fell flat. Even the chaotic energy of the Marx Bros. couldn't save it.

On March 12th Richard C. Miller photographs Marilyn as she tries out for a role in *The Corn is Green* with the Player's Ring Theater on Sunset. She didn't get the part, but Miller did get some lovely images of her involved in the audition process.

It is during this period that Marilyn receives this insightful view into her inner-self by writer William Saroyan. "No, you're a loner, Marilyn, and you'll always be alone." Even without knowing the context of the statement, we can say with certainty that Marilyn suffered from this feeling of isolation and loneliness all of her life. Saroyan was in Los Angeles to produce and direct a play he had written, *The Son*, at the Circle Theater. It starred Marilyn's good friend, Sydney Chaplin. She may have even tried out for a part in the play, or Chaplin could have invited her to see his performance and then invited her to meet Saroyan.

Marilyn had a screen test for *Eve All About*. She asked Sydney Guilaroff to supervise her hair and makeup for the test, taking him up on his offer. He wanted to handle the negotiations with Fox and she agreed. He demanded $5000 to supervise her beauty demands. He thought by doing so Fox would take notice of Marilyn. Fox accepted his offer. He created a hairstyle that was lighter in color and in an elegant up-do. After her test Darryl Zanuck told him, "Sydney, I think we've got a star here."

On March 27th Marilyn signs with Fox to do *All About Eve* for $500.00 a week, with a one week guarantee. *Asphalt Jungle* and *All About Eve* will be her breakout roles. After seeing her in *All About Eve*, Darryl Zanuck will be impressed enough to sign her to a contract at 20th Century-Fox. But until then, she gamely plugs along without the protection that a major studio provides.

Using her uncanny intuition for picking an ally she garnered the attention of columnist Sydney Skolsky. "I had known Marilyn long before *All About Eve*, but it was during the filming of this picture that we became really buddy-buddy. I don't believe I know of another actress who works as hard or as intensely at her career as Marilyn, and I know many hard workers. She is working as hard to day to maintain her position as she did in the days when she was climbing. In those days I would go for long walks or long auto rides with Marilyn and I'd listen to her talk. Mainly she talked career, and great conflict was going on inside her. She'd say that she'd keep working and that nothing—do you hear?—nothing would stop her from becoming a movie star. Then in the next breath she'd express doubt that she'd make it."

On April 4th Costume test for *All About Eve* were held. The wardrobe was created by Charles LeMaire. Iconic Hollywood designer Edith Head dressed Bette Davis for the film. Miss Head never worked with Marilyn, but had this to say about her, "I met Marilyn socially several times, and we always talked about clothes. She was extremely knowledgeable about fit and fabric, which surprised me. I never thought she looked especially comfortable in what she wore. Every designer who worked with her cinched her and harnessed her. Marilyn was a free spirit who should have been dressed in such a way that she would be able to forget about her clothes. When a woman is sexy, she knows it and she doesn't need clothes that constantly remind her."

In another interview, Miss Head recalls, "Marilyn Monroe had the look of utmost softness, like a Persian kitten. It was a clinging helplessness look, very unconscious, very appealing. That was the time of form fitting fashion, with tightly belted waist and tightly fitted pushed-up bust. With full skirts that fluttered around the legs. It was a much more feminine look than in the 1940's."

*All About Eve* begins filming at Twentieth Century-Fox in early April. Marilyn plays Miss Caswell, a gold-digging actress trying to climb up the ladder to success. Marilyn was very fortunate to have a part in a great film such as this. It also proved that she could hold her own in a cast of top stars. An interesting and revealing memory about Marilyn at this time is given by director Joseph L. Mankiewicz, when he noticed that she was reading a book of poems by Rainier Maria Rilke. "I asked Marilyn if she knew who he was. She shook her head. 'No. Who is he?' I told her that Rilke had been a German poet, that he was dead...and asked her how the hell she came to be reading him at all, much less that particular work of his. Had somebody recommended it to her? Marilyn replied, 'You see, in my whole life, I haven't read hardly anything at all. I don't know how to catch up. I don't know where to begin. So what I do is, every now and then I go into the Pickwick and just look around. I leaf through some books, and when I read something that interest me, I buy the book. Is that wrong?'"

According to Natasha Lytess, she introduced Marilyn to Rilke, and specifically, *Letters to a Young Poet* and *The Brothers Karamazov*. Marilyn signed a copy of *Wisdom of the Sands* by Antoine de Saint-Exupery to Natasha. "Because I met you, I'm learning."

Marilyn will also explain her love of reading to John Florea. "Photographer Johnny, another long-time friend, when to her house one day to photograph her for a mag layout. Her found her reading von Clausewitz' ponderous tome *On War*. 'Why the devil are you reading that?' Johnny demanded in astonishment. 'Well,' she said thoughtfully, 'I don't always understand all I read in these books, but they make me think. They keep by brain going, even if I don't absorb all I read. And if I keep on, maybe I will understand it all someday.'"

Marilyn also said of her habit of reading, "There is so much I don't know. I keep on buying books, quiet deep books. And I read them."

This is the first film that Marilyn will be in with Thelma Ritter. They will also act together in *As Young as You Feel* and *The Misfits*. Marilyn will work for the first time with body makeup artist, Bunny Gardel. Miss Gardel will join the inner circle of Marilyn's artisans who labor to create the Monroe myth. Although Gladys McCallister was listed as the hairdresser for the film, Marilyn submitted to the services of Mr. Guilaroff. Grady Johnson was the publicist working with her on this film.

George Sanders wrote about his memories of working with Marilyn in *All About Eve*. "Marilyn played a very dumb would-be actress. Even then she struck me as a character in search of an author. I am delighted she found Mr. Miller eventually. She was very beautiful, very inquiring and very unsure--she was somebody in a play not yet written, uncertain of her part in the over-all plot. As far as I can recall she was humble, punctual and untemperamental. She wanted people to like her. In the circumstances it is not surprising that Marilyn soon got together with the glittering future we all foresaw for her. I lunched with her once or twice during the making of the film. I found her conversation had unexpected depths. She showed an interest in intellectual subjects which was, to say the least, disconcerting. In her presence it was hard to concentrate. What made me sure that Marilyn would eventually make it was that she so obviously needed to be a star. Marilyn is said to have spent her childhood in an orphanage and with foster-parents. She had been neglected and unloved. Nobody took any notice of her until, at the age of 15, she put on a sweater. Once a woman puts on a sweater she has, as it were, a joker up her sleeve. To a girl with Marilyn's background--and foreground--to be a film star meant to be universally loved."

Marilyn's publicity was a well-oiled machine at Fox. They used a team of people to construct and broadcast publicity about their creations. "Everybody in the studio publicity department worked on her. The picture division, the magazine division, the fan magazine division, the planters who plant the columnists, the radio planters, and so forth. Then, when you make a motion picture, a 'unit man' or 'unit woman' is assigned to cover it's shooting, and he or she handles publicity for that film alone. In addition, the whole department works on the same picture. Our department is highly specialized, but each specialist makes his contribution to the personality we're creating in the public's mind. The unit man is not always the same for a certain star's pictures. Sonia Wilson's been unit woman on Monroe pictures, and Frank Neal's been a unit man on her pictures, but Roy Craft has been her unit man more than anyone else. Roy likes her. He gets along with her fine."

Marilyn will work with one of the Fox publicity team, Julian Myers, for the first time. He will recall that one of his best days ever was waking Marilyn up for an appearance before thousands of troops. He affirms that although, Marilyn was by far the sexiest actress on the lot, the publicity men all had a crush on a woman who worked in the legal department. In his opinion Harry Brand made a smart decision having Roy Craft supervising her career.

In an article that appeared in June of 1953, Bill Tusher reveals "The Mystery Man in Marilyn Life…Roy Craft was an assistant art editor at 20$^{th}$'s publicity department. When they signed Marilyn on the heels of her triumph in *Asphalt Jungle*, she was sent to the gallery to be photographed. Roy was assigned to handle her sittings. They hit it off well from the start. I what I think will pass for the understatement of the year, Roy told me that he took an interest in her. Marilyn liked Roy because he was not a con man and she leveled with him from the first day. She returned his confidence in her by having confidence in him, and Roy simply gravitated into the job of becoming Marilyn Monroe's Man Friday. Roy has a genuine respect not only for her abundant beauty, but for her wit, intellect, sincerity—and good conduct! This may come as a bombshell, but she doesn't even drink. Roy spent three hours with her at the Players Restaurant on Sunset Strip, where he interviewed her for the studio biography. When he returned to the lot, Craft told fellow publicity men, 'She's the first girl in the business who ever game me a lump in my throat and a gleam in my eye at the same time.' The reason for the lump in his throat was Marilyn's disarming honesty. In that first interview, Marilyn told Roy that her mother was living and had been in a State Hospital. She also told him of her first short-lived marriage, and of the fact that she had modeled. It was not because of evasion, but only because she attached no importance to it that Marilyn did not specifically mention the calendar photos which were destined to make her name—and unencumbered image—a household word.'…'When Marilyn first came to the studio,' Craft explained, 'we treated hers as a story of a pretty girl, not an expose. Nowhere in the basic biography which I wrote was it ever stated that her mother was not living, or that Marilyn had not been married. Naturally, there was no reason to make an issue of either.' Roy maintains that there wasn't the slightest practice of deception in the publicity about Marilyn being an orphan. 'It's a matter of record that she spent one and a half years in an orphanage, and that she was farmed out to eight to twelve different families as she grew up,' Craft said. 'When that happens, you've been raised as an orphan.'"

Craft will tell Zolotow about using Marilyn's past. "I thought it would do her more harm than good. It wasn't until 1952 that we played the orphan bit for all it was worth. By then, she was becoming a solidly established sex symbol, and the story of her unhappy childhood got space because it was a terrific switch." In a another interview, a studio aide, which was probably Craft, was quoted as saying on Marilyn being born out of wedlock, "She was always frank with us about this, and we in turn were perfectly honest with the press. They understood, and made no mention of it. A child of love is a victim of circumstance, nothing more. Oh, we did invent a father who got killed in an accident, but what would you do? Beside, nobody had to buy it."

Craft will write of working with the early Marilyn. "My interest in the Monroe story is valid. I did not 'invent' the on-stage Marilyn Monroe, but I did help expose her to public view. Marilyn was her own creation, and the role she assumed—the breathless, naïve sex image—was the product of her own facile mind and ingenious, if not ingenuous, imagination. I knew both Monroes, the real one and the public one, and it was sometimes difficult to tell them apart, for like any good artist she lived her part except in rare moments of privacy. I first met Marilyn as a bit player in *All About Eve*. I had worked for a time as a *LIFE* magazine correspondent in Hollywood and this had led me to some publicity work. I had some theories on publicity pictures and Marilyn, aggressively ambitions, cooperated fully. She was always late (her later 'lateness' was not an affectation of stardom, but a persistent emotional thing), but she put thought and humor into every sitting and the photographers were delighted."

Craft will say of Marilyn in another interview, "When I handled Marilyn, in her happy days, she was extraordinary. Now Marilyn, I remember her as a bright, terribly bright woman, with a great sense of humor to her. She was entirely different from the dumb blonde she played on the screen. And she was so captivating with the press. I could take her to New York or Seattle and have four interviews back-to-back and she would delight each of the four people. Each would get a different story and a different anecdote. She was simply masterful at this. During those five happy years with her, before her disintegration and then her death, she was consummate in her abilities. To me, Marilyn created Monroe, and I thought her great charm was comedy, a classic comedienne. Of course, I have a deep loyalty to Marilyn."

Marilyn will say this about publicity. "It's good for me, mostly. It keep my name and face in the papers. The publicity boys at the studio are right about how important that is. They're my buddies, those publicity guys. They're hard and tough and they growl at you ninety percent of the time, but if you try to understand their job and their problems—well, pretty soon you get to know them as swell guys. They have been wonderful to me.'"

*Ticket to Tomahawk* held its world premiere in San Francisco at the Fox Theatre on Market and Ninth. Although in town to film *All About Eve*, Marilyn didn't attend.

Marilyn finally has a little press, on April 30th, *The Waterloo Daily Courier* newspaper captioned photo. "Marilyn Monroe, appearing in the 20th Century-Fox Technicolor production *A Ticket to Tomahawk*, takes her jewelry from her miniature Lane Cedar Chest during a visit to New York. The Lane miniature chest is an exact duplicate of those to be presented next month to High School Graduates by Hurwich Furniture Co." The photo is from the *Photoplay* Dream House Tour she was on in June of 1949.

After a dry spell of a couple of months, Marilyn is featured in four magazines. Two of the magazines are *Glance* and *True Experiences*. The *Glance* magazine cover and inside front cover featured Marilyn before her movie success. "Another Glance at Norma Dougherty, The Cover Girl...The loverly version, emerging from the water to pause for a pose on the diving board of our front cover is Norma Jeane Dougherty. Norma, a native Californian, an all-around athlete, and promising movie star, first gained recognition when she won the title of Queen of Aircrafts. After that 20th Century-Fox signed her to a contract, renamed her Marilyn Monroe, and presented her to an appreciative audience. Now, our cover beauty is slated for fame, according to photographer Richard Miller of Guilemette, who is responsible for our front cover Kodachrome."

*True Experience magazine* cover and article, "I'm A Modern Day Cinderella...Do I look happy? I should--for I was a little child nobody wanted. A lonely girl with a dream--who awakened to find that dream come true--I am Marilyn Monroe...read my Cinderella story."

Despite her film appearances, Marilyn was still living hand to mouth. She borrowed $25.00 from the William Morris Agency on May 2nd.

On May 8th, Marilyn was chosen as the "Star of the Week" of the *Chicago Daily Tribune*. A short bio accompanied her photo.

# Chapter Nine
## The Making of a Star

"I guess I had known it all the time. I knew I belonged to the public and to the world, not because I was talented or even because I was beautiful, but because I had never belonged to anything or anyone else. The public was the only family, the only Prince Charming and the only home I had ever dreamed about."
Marilyn Monroe

**J**ohnny Hyde negotiated a six month contract for Marilyn on May 11, 1950. Zanuck, after seeing her in *Asphalt Jungle* and in the rushes of *All About Eve,* was encouraged to hire her. It took some time because Marilyn wanted it in her contract that Natasha Lytess was to be hired to accompany her on the sets of all her upcoming films and this slowed down the negotiations. Natasha Lytess would say of Marilyn's demand to have her hired at Fox, "Let me tell you that to get me into this studio and continue our association, Marilyn walked over corpses. Important corpses!"

In an interview with Louella Parsons published on April 1, 1951, Marilyn reveals that she told Darryl Zanuck this concerning her firing by Fox in 1947, when she re-signed with Fox, "Do you know what I told Mr. Zanuck. I told Mr. Zanuck that I should have been fired. I was no good. I was so scared I couldn't say a thing." Zanuck told Marilyn, "Things are very different around here now. You have a three-dimensional quality having to do with sex, very reminiscent of Harlow." It seems that Zanuck couldn't see past her sexuality and view her as an actress. Marilyn would say in an interview a few months before her death, "Zanuck signed me to a contract because he said I had a third dimension—and this was before 3-D. He said I had something, but he didn't know what it was."

Hyde would be in her corner until his death, seeing to it that her contract was honored in full and that she would get the right kind of roles to make her stardom a sure thing. Her contract would be renewed on December 11th, just a week before his death.

Marilyn rented a 1947 Chevrolet Sedan on May 12th, and would drive this until she purchased a car on July 5th.

A photo session she has on May 17th will document her transformation from model to movie star. Earl Leaf photographs Marilyn in the backyard of Johnny Hyde's Beverly Hills mansion and in his home. Leaf remembers taking these images of her. "Marilyn was always a most cooperative model. I was touched by her eagerness to please. When I had finished taking all the pictures needed for my layout, she remained insistent that I be completely happy with her. 'Is there anything else, Earl?' she asked. 'Want me to climb a tree or something like that?'" Some of the photos will appear in an article in the *Chicago Daily Tribune* on August 20th. Marilyn's image is being cultivated by the teams of beauty experts at 20th Century-Fox, and it shows. These are some of the most beautiful photographs taken of a youthful Marilyn. She appears more refined and confident. She wears little makeup and is utterly charming, posing in a two-piece swim suit, a tight fitting blouse and shorts and in a lovely summer dress. In some of the photos Marilyn has her little Chihuahua, Josefa, who was an early birthday present from Joseph Schenck.

Alice Craig Greene gives us a glimpse into Marilyn at this time and her potent brand of innocent sexuality. "I was at the Cock and Bull bar, Hollywood's unofficial press club, with a bunch of guys most impervious to feminine charms. Hollywood's press agents, editors, photographers, fan writers and publicity men, the crew that builds or breaks the stars, have seen the most famous; beautiful, desirable women in all the world, under all circumstances, from all angles. And they're understandably hard to impress. In walked the world's most disillusioned editor-writer, Tommy Carlyle, escorting a little gal who looked vaguely familiar. She wore a simple white, high-necked blouse, and a dark, plain, tailored skirt. Her face had a disarmingly sweet, pensive quality at first glance. But another quality, call it sex appeal, leaped out so the whole room lighted up. Suddenly through the bored, blasé group, you heard buzzing, 'Who's that?' and 'Wow!' Through the girl certainly wasn't dressed for display or glamour projection, and nothing in her manner was flamboyant or aggressive, the wolf whistles howled as the bunch suddenly became simply eager males. When Tom brought her to us, I saw a dazed, adoring look even in his eye, and I knew this was something really special. He introduced her. 'Marilyn Monroe—a new chick out at Fox—bit parts—just finished a pretty fair deal in an unreleased thing at Metro—*Asphalt Jungle*—doing George Sanders' girlfriend in *All About Eve*.' Then we knew why she looked familiar. We'd spotted her in press previews of the new pictures. We'd had art from the studios on her. While the crowd moved in around her, Tommy bent down and said, 'I've done stories on every big star in this town. Every gal whose publicity says she's Miss Sex herself! But I never had a single one of these females really excite me till this one. Besides,' he added, 'she's got a mind!' Monroe has, without effort, the intangible quality of desirability. Simply by being, she reached out and created dreams and fantasies in the minds of men. You knew they'd be fighting to write about her, photograph her, tell the world about her.'"

Bob Thomas mentions Marilyn in his column on May 19th. Later on he will devote more space and ink to her growing popularity. "Remember the name Marilyn Monroe. She does a scene in *Asphalt Jungle* that is the sexiest since Harlow. Now she's due for a star build-up at 20th-Fox. The gal is blonde, doesn't smoke, dislikes nightclubs and wants to be a dramatic actress." Mr. Thomas is the first columnist to link Marilyn to the iconic Jean Harlow, but will certainly not be the last.

Harold Heffernan devoted his column to Marilyn on June 17th. "Miss Monroe in Comeback at Age 21...*Asphalt Jungle* Role Paves the Way." This was an important column for Marilyn and it is one of the few times she embraced the studio generated story that she had her start as a baby sitter. She is identified in the article as being only 21 years old, when in fact she had just turned 24. "The one factor that keeps Hollywood out in front as the most unpredictable, exciting place in the world is the periodical ascent of flashing new personalities to captivate the paying public. Latest of these is a voluptuous blonde named Marilyn Monroe. Virtually unbilled and unidentified in a current movie, *Asphalt Jungle*. Marilyn's breath-taking appearance immediately piques fandom's curiosity and imagination. Not since the brief introduction of another tempestuous blonde, Shelley Winters, three years ago, in *A Double Life*, has a newcomer stirred so much interest. Oddly enough—or maybe not when you understand what goes on behind Hollywood's political iron curtains—Marilyn was allowed to get away from the studio, MGM, that gave her this sensational debut. Quickly enough, $20^{th}$ Century-Fox grabbed her—and there she is finishing her most important assignment, a role with Bette Davis in *All About Eve*. Only 21 years old, a native of Los Angeles, orphaned since early childhood, Marilyn is not unfamiliar with being booted around. She has become hardened to it. Her story is one of struggle, hunger and perseverance—a sort of female Horatio Alger epic. She did all sorts of strange odd jobs to keep going with her drama lessons. One of these paid off. She did a chore of baby-sitting one night—and found herself guarding the offspring of a talent scout. It wasn't the payoff, but it did start her on her way up the film-career ladder. And she managed to cling to the precarious steps in spite of many brushoffs. Audiences seeing *Asphalt Jungle* are referring to Marilyn as 'another Lana Turner.' She has much the same sensuous brand of blonde appeal and a provocative figure. Marilyn is definitely against the look-alike comments. 'I don't like it a bit when they say I resemble Lana Turner,' she said. 'It isn't right to trade on another's fame. Besides, I think I have looks and personality of my own.' Darryl F. Zanuck, head of 20$^{th}$ Century-Fox, must have concurred on that score, for just the other day, after viewing her performance in *All About Eve*, he placed her under long-term contract. Reports around the lot are that she will carry the star role in her next film there and get a tremendous publicity buildup. Marilyn's own life story possibly outdoes anything the script writer ever dreamed up. She was making barely enough money to survive—and putting half of what she earned into dramatic lessons—when MGM let her wear Cinderella's golden slipper for a few weeks while she played one of the top roles in *Asphalt Jungle*. While working in that one, the news seeped out that here was one of the most exciting new personalities to hit the town in years. Producers, directors, studio executives dropped in to watch and, as Metro stalled, 20$^{th}$ Century-Fox slipped in and bagged the prize. Once before Marilyn had worked for the Zanuck studio. At that time, the consensus was that she was 'too beautiful' for films—that her tantalizing looks always stole the scene from the character she played and the plot. 'That was what they told me,' she said, 'but I know better. After I was dropped, I worked at anything I could—modeling, babysitting, small roles—and took half the money I earned for dramatic lessons. I knew I couldn't act—that people were saying, 'Here's another pretty girl, but what can she do?' I went without meals to pay for some of the lessons. I'm glad I did.' That kind of determination, which she masks behind blue eyes and a low, gentle voice, may stem from the long struggle she has had. The humility she has—unusual for an actress—also may have come out of the same battle. Marilyn's father died in an automobile accident a year after her birth. A short time later her mother became so desperately ill that she couldn't look after her. She was taken in during the next few years by this and that good-hearted family, and finally adopted by old friends of her parents. Born in Los Angeles, she has lived here all of her life. In high school everyone told her she should be in the movies, but she never gave the idea much thought. She hoped to become a photographer specializing in animals—kittens and pups. The necessity of earning a living took her, however, into other fields. She worked as a secretary at a defense factory and there the United States Army 'discovered' her. The first roles she played were for Army training films. She later became a photographer's model and had her face on most of the magazine covers, but Hollywood—which has signed up many another cover girl—continued to pass her by. 'It was the baby-sitting that did it,' she said. 'When the modeling business was bad, I'd ask to baby-sit for neighbors and friends. One family would tell another, and I didn't know I was working for a talent scout and his wife until he asked me to make a test.' That was when 20$^{th}$ Century-Fox signed her for the first time. The only roles she got were bit parts, and she wasn't surprised when the studio dropped her at the end of the first year. 'At 18 I was on my way in the movies,' she said modestly. 'By 19 I was a has-been. Now at 21 I'm making a comeback.'"

The *Asphalt Jungle* was released on June 20th. Earlier, at its Hollywood premiere, Marilyn did not attend, but her former husband, Jim Dougherty did. He was working for the police department and was one of the officers used for crowd control.

Still financially strapped, Marilyn borrowed $800.00 from the William Morris Agency on June 24th and another $300.00 on the 26$^{th}$ and finally she borrowed $10.00 for a traffic violation on the 27th.

Photographer Anthony Beauchamp was in Hollywood for his honeymoon with wife Sarah Churchill in the summer of 1950. She was the daughter of Winston Churchill. Beauchamp was on assignment for *LIFE* magazine to take a series of photos of promising young actresses who might become stars. Beauchamp was interviewing girls in his room at a hotel in Beverly Hills. Johnny Hyde arranged for him to meet Marilyn. He remembers meeting her for the first time,

"At that time I was interviewing hundreds of girls in my search for a dozen or so pretty faces for the magazine, and when I heard of Marilyn's story up to that time it differed very little from that of many other would-be starlets. In other words her life story was typical of many other pretty girls in Hollywood. But however much Marilyn may have seemed at first to resemble the others she had only been in the room for a few minutes before I realized that there was something quite different about her--something that distinguished her from all the others. I seemed to have sensed that here was something unique--that here was someone the like of whom the screen had not known certainly since the days of Jean Harlow. It was with that in mind that I decided at once that I should feature Marilyn-- almost unknown as she was then--in my new series. So I arranged with Johnny Hyde a series of photographs of Marilyn. In the meantime Sarah and I moved into the large ocean- side house belonging to Bebe Daniels and Ben Lyon, and appropriately enough Marilyn was the first person I photographed there. Whether the fact that Ben Lyon discovered her, coupled with the fact that the pictures were taken in his house, worked as a charm I don't know, but those pictures of Marilyn had a phenomenal success. Marilyn arrived with a publicity man and a trunk full of glamorous evening gowns, furs and jewels--plus the usual props necessary to the build-up she was getting from the studio. I decided to take pictures of her on the terrace of the house, and after having completed a number of pictures of her in evening gowns we sat down on the terrace for a drink. Marilyn seemed to be a very quiet little girl and said very little during the session. She did what was asked of her with a nice smile, and gave all the cooperation that one could wish. But there was little sign of 'big-star' personality. As the three of us sat chatting on the terrace I notice that Marilyn had opened a hat box. She took out of the box what appeared to be two broad yellow ribbons held together by a piece of string. 'What's that,' I asked her, 'ribbons for your hair?' 'Oh, no,' she said, 'this is a bikini. I made it myself. I don't like bikinis usually--they conceal too much.' Then in a very quiet little voice she asked: 'Would you like to take my picture in it?' I noticed that the publicity man was looking very pale and slightly desperate. 'Now, Marilyn,' he said, 'you know perfectly well you can't possibly be photographed in a thing like that, the studio would go crazy.' He was very apprehensive, but realizing that this would be the Marilyn picture to end all Monroe pictures I gave the publicity man another large drink. I told him that I would like to take the pictures of Marilyn in her home-made bikini, but that they would not be published before they had been shown to and approved by Twentieth Century-Fox. With the publicity man thus calmed, and with a very large drink to soothe his nerves, I told Marilyn to go and change. She disappeared for a moment and came back in a most explosive swimsuit, which could only be described as a parody of a bikini. In fact it consisted of nothing more than the two broad yellow ribbons. One of them, encircling her neck and held down by a piece of string, made a not very serious effort to conceal the two renowned upper features of her anatomy which many people feel should not be concealed at all. The second rather broader ribbon was attached to another piece of string to form the remainder of her costume. There she was, Venus de Milo clad in ribbons and string. I poured the publicity man yet another large drink, then one for Marilyn--and then one for myself, I needed it. It was only then, when she was virtually unclad, that Marilyn's true personality emerged. Someone has called her 'just a shy exhibitionist,' and how true is that description. In her home-made bikini she was quite a different girl. She became animated; she talked with a delightfully unconscious humor, and with almost flamboyant self-assurance. In fact it was difficult to stop her talking. Her sparkling personality, bottled up in clothes, had emerged bubbling and effervescent as soon as she had discarded them in favor of her bikini. Anything that Marilyn left unsaid was most eloquently enlarged upon by her anatomy. During the next two weeks I devoted many days to obtaining a full series of Monroe pictures...From all our conversations and as I got to know Marilyn better, I became quite aware that Marilyn is neither a highbrow nor a dumb blonde--she is just a badly educated and intellectually naive girl with a fanatical desire for culture...During those days on the Californian coast when I took the series of Marilyn pictures, some of which have been published all over the world, I discovered that she had no fear in front of the camera. She is particularly sure of herself, and meticulously aware of every angle, of every arched muscle and strand of hair and even of her eyelashes. In many ways she is the perfect model and it is not for nothing that she has become a pin-up queen. But although she is a perfect model, it is not always easy to take a perfect picture. Sometimes it is quite difficult to take a good one and Marilyn knows it. She has a bump on the end of her nose which discourages profile shots and I noticed that when she was disturbed or had been talking about unhappy events it was most difficult to get a good picture, but if Marilyn is content and happy she glides into a perfect pose with the rhythm of a ballet-dancer. Almost instinctively her mouth opens, her lips glisten with moisture, and her body tenses gracefully as the shutter drops."

In an interview with Mr. Beauchamp this was revealed this about shooting Marilyn, "Beauchamp had suggested that Miss Monroe bring her own posing costume, thinking that she'd bring a new Dior creation. Instead she arrived with two items so scanty that they made a bikini suit look like a cassock."

These photos of Marilyn in her bikini, still considered very risqué, would not be published until 1952 and would shock the public and Fox.

Propelled by her newfound success, Marilyn puts herself in nearly $6000 in debt in July. On July 1st she bought a 1950 Pontiac Coupe Sedan from Beverly Motor Co., Inc. for $2529.69. A few days later she purchased car insurance from Jack L. Manor, Inc., Auto Insurance. She listed her address as 1301 N. Harper Ave, which was Natasha Lytess's home. When she wasn't living with Johnny Hyde, she actually resided at an apartment near Natasha Lytess's home. She rented a small apartment at 1309 N Harper from Michael DiMucco and paid $135 a month. But she will use Miss Lytess' address on her checks to distance herself from interested fans. She takes out a loan from California Bank for the amount of $4000. It seems Marilyn wasted no time in getting in debt after her new contract with Fox. This is an indication of the faith she had in herself after her success in *Asphalt Jungle* and *All About Eve*.

Marilyn received her first real support from the men who made her a star, not the ones in Hollywood, but the men in the Korean War. On July 7th the *INS* ran a captioned photo of Marilyn, an early Fox publicity photo in her Mabs of Hollywood "Hourglass" swimsuit, "Blonde, Beautiful and Curvaceous, say men of the Marine First Division in choosing actress Marilyn Monroe their 'Miss Morale.' She recently visited the Leathernecks before they left for Korea." On July 21st *ACME* Wire Service featured a photo of her captioned, "Hip-Hip-Hooray...Blonde and Shapely Marilyn Monroe, who visited Leathernecks of the First Marine Division before they embarked for the Korean war area, has been dubbed, 'Miss Morale of the Marine Corps.'" Ironically, The First Marine Division will be the first performance Marilyn puts on when she tours the Korean front in 1954.

Louella Parsons revealed on July 18th, "Monroe Gets Role In *Cold Shoulder*...Marilyn Monroe, who packs the same punch Lana Turner did in her early days gets her first starring role in *Cold Shoulder* with Vic Mature and Richard Conte. Marilyn, who hasn't a relative in the world and who was brought up in an orphanage, is one of the nicest girls in this town and everybody is plugging for her to succeed. She must be proud that she is clicking big in 20th, the studio which once let her go. Marilyn did not have a big role in *Asphalt Jungle*, but what she did was so punchy that 20th brought her back home at many times what she had received before. I'm told she is excellent in *All About Eve*, which is whispered to be a honey. The *Cold Shoulder* epic has a gangster theme. George Jessel will produce." Also, on the 18th, Thomas Brady mentions Marilyn joining the cast of, "*Cold Shoulder*, a gangster comedy."

In the screen test with Richard Conte she again wears her own sweater dress. Some believe this was a sound screen test for her contract with Fox, but according to legal documents from 20th Century-Fox, she was placed under contract on May 11, 1950. Darryl Zanuck decided not to make this movie after all and the plans were shelved, despite all the early publicity. It seems that George Jessel was still in her corner.

On July 27th Marilyn and Johnny Hyde attended a candlelight ball given by Betty Hutton for actor Louis Sobol and his fiancée' Peggy Strohl at the Beverly Hills Crystal Room. Mr. Sobol and Miss Strohl were married the next day. Hedda Hopper described the event as the "party of the year." Others in attendance were Frank Freeman, head of Paramount Studio, Charles Brackett, George Jessel, Bob Hope, Danny Kaye, Dinah Shore, Milton Berle, and of course, Hedda Hopper.

August was stacking up to be even busier than July. *Right Cross* finally started production at MGM. Marilyn was loaned out to MGM and played a short scene as Dusky Ledue, a femme fatale that Rick Garvey, played by Dick Powell, meets at dinner. Helen Rose designed the ensemble that Marilyn wore in the film. Sydney Guilaroff designed her hairstyle. June Allyson, who was married to Dick Powell at the time, remembers this about Marilyn. '"…You are not going to believe this but she was the sweetest, most delightful person I ever met. I remember when Richard was doing a film with her, and nobody knew who Marilyn Monroe was, and everybody was waiting for the new girl to come on the set, and finally after about an hour, the big stage door opened and this beautiful blonde girl came in. And she walked across the sound stage very slowly to where she was supposed to go. You could hear a pin drop on that stage. Every person just stopped and watched her walk. When she sat down, everybody sort of breathed.' Asked if Dick liked her, Miss Allyson responded, 'Very much. He thought she had a lot of talent and someday somebody would find it." Asked if she was jealous of Marilyn, 'You couldn't be. If you knew Marilyn you couldn't be jealous of her, she was so sweet. Such a good person. You know, if you said to Marilyn, 'I love that blouse you are wearing,'' she would give it to you. She was that kind of person.'"

Back at MGM, Marilyn was cared for by hairdresser Sydney Guilaroff. He was helping to transform her into Marilyn Monroe.

Marilyn was featured in the *Chicago Tribune* newspaper on August 6, 1950. Her color portrait was carried in the Picture Section, followed by a small article titled, "Star of the Week," by Frieda Zylstra. The most interesting part of the small article is the reference to Marilyn being in military films. These have yet to surface, but they may be out there somewhere. "Four years ago Marilyn Monroe was posing and acting in army air force films, but today she is playing big roles in Hollywood pictures…After her career in army films she given a screen test in Hollywood."

On August 8th photographer Ed Clark takes Marilyn on location in Griffith Park outside of Los Angeles for a photo shoot for *LIFE* magazine. Clark remembers that Marilyn read poetry to him. She wears a monogrammed blouse and also a bandana patterned sun-top with shorts and saddle-shoes. The results show a luminous young Marilyn in a natural setting. She is still refining her look and the photos represent her during her "Lana Turner" phase. She has yet to perfect the sensual, open-mouthed pose for which she will become famous. Nevertheless, she is enchanting. Her innate sexuality is evident and there is the ever present air of fragility which surrounds her expressions. In these shots Marilyn takes on the persona of a woodland nymph whose amorous freedom is celebrated, and like these nymphs, she will never see old age and will be frozen in time within the framework of these bucolic images. The photos were never printed by *LIFE* and lay undiscovered for over 60 years.

In mid-August Johnny Hyde escorts Marilyn to a party at Danny Kaye's home. It was given to welcome Vivien Leigh when she came from England to star in *A Streetcar Named Desire*. Sir Laurence Olivier was also in attendance. In six years he and Marilyn would make a landmark pairing when they starred together in *The Prince and the Showgirl*, with Marilyn reprising the role Miss Leigh had made famous on the stage. Elia Kazan saw her there and remembered being introduced to her by his agent Abe Lastfogel, who was also one of the four agents assigned to Marilyn at the William Morris Agency.

In an interview in *Photoplay* magazine, May 1956, Earl Wilson asked her if she had met Olivier before her press conference in February of 1956. Marilyn replied, "'Years ago. Before I was anybody. That was really years ago. Gosh! They wouldn't remember.' She got that far-away look in her eyes people get when thinking back across the years. 'I met them through Johnny Hyde.'"

On August 13th Marilyn has an important article come out in *Parade* magazine, "Another Lana?" by Kay Sullivan. "They're calling Marilyn Monroe a new Lana Turner. Like Lana, Marilyn is blonde, curvy and can play a sultry role so ardently that the film almost melts. She sidled through *Asphalt Jungle* as the baby-faced friend of a middle-aged, married man. She didn't have much to say but that was no matter: audiences were too busy gaping to listen. Ever since, Metro-Goldwyn-Mayer has been busy answering letters about 'that terrific blonde with the shape.' They recall that the same thing happened when Lana Turner made her debut in an *Andy Hardy* film...Marilyn's future looks star-like, too. Already she's been tagged the 'Mmmm Girl!' 'She just lights up whenever a camera turns on her,' says one photographer. 'She's sweet—with spice!'" The article mentions a few interesting things. One is the film *Cold Shoulder* that never got made. The other is three captioned photos taken during her *Love Happy* tour in New York City. They were taken on 42$^{nd}$ St., and at a stadium. Also featured was a photo by Andre de Dienes of Marilyn on Jones Beach, also from her trip to New York in 1949.

Bob Thomas quoted Lana Turner on Marilyn, February 22, 1954. "Marilyn Monroe may be beleaguered by her studio and badgered by rival actresses, but she has one firm fan— Lana Turner. 'Marilyn is one girl I'd like to meet. I've followed her career and I think she's got a lot of spunk. She must be a very interesting person. Now that she's on top, she'll be hit from all sides. I know just how it is. I've been taking it for 17 years in this business.'"

Marilyn registered her car with the State of California Department of Motor Vehicles on August 16th. She listed her address as 1301 N. Harper Ave. She registered a 1950 Pontiac. It listed the date of sale as July 1950. Her license number was 19B2992. She paid $24.00 in total fees.

Jack Lait, Jr., reported on the 19<sup>th</sup> that, "Luscious starlet Marilyn Monroe is taking body conditioning treatments. Marilyn needs body conditioning treatments like Einstein needs lessons in the multiplication table.

*The Chicago Daily Tribune* featured Marilyn on August 20<sup>th</sup>, in a 2 photo spread titled, "Portrait of Marilyn." Hollywood photographer Earl Leaf showcased Marilyn in photos taken on May 17th at Johnny Hyde's home. Marilyn is shown in Hyde's kitchen and with his cook, Herta. The women are stirring a pot on the stove. Marilyn is also featured in her bathing suit lying on a lounge chair reading. There is a one with director Joseph Mankiewicz, where she is lighting his pipe. The article also mentions that Marilyn got her start in Army training films.

Philip K. Scheuer devoted his entire column to Marilyn on August 27th. It is a very important one for her career. "Wolves Howl For 'Niece' Just Like Marilyn Monroe....Just about the time the late, great Prof. Lamberti, xylophonist extraordinary, used to go into the climax of his act, a comely strip-teaser would appear on the stage behind him and go into HERS. Launching 'The Stars and Stripes Forever,' or some such rousing air, the professor would whip himself into more and more frenzied paroxysms as the applause grew to thunderous proportions, unable to contain his glee at the mounting ovation. The cheers were all for the stripper, of course, but Prof. Lamberti never let on that he knew until the very last. Then he would turn and wrathfully empty the contents of a seltzer bottle upon the gal who had stolen his show.  Marilyn Monroe has yet to do a strip-tease and nobody has squirted even soda pop at her--but her mere entrance into a couple of movie scenes has had much the same devastating effect on audiences. When Marilyn fled Groucho Marx in *Love Happy*, every wolf in the house joined in howling pursuit. And when Marilyn called crooked Lawyer Louis Calhern 'Uncle' in *The Asphalt Jungle*, there wasn't a male within miles who didn't find himself hankering for a nice 'niece' like her. You see, Calhern wasn't really her uncle at all. Marilyn herself grew up in Los Angeles, only a wolf call away from hundreds of unsuspecting readers of this page, under the name of Norma Jeane Dougherty. The early death of her father and the prolonged illness of her mother made her practically an orphan. She was adopted by family friends, the E. S. Goddards, and she also lived with an aunt, Mrs. Anna Lower. She always wanted to be an actress--and now, at 22, she is. A regular 20th Century-Fox contract actress.  Marilyn, or Norma, was under contract to 20th before, but it didn't take. After completing her schooling at Emerson Junior High School and Van Nuys High, she started modeling 'to keep eating.' There was one month when her photographs made four or five magazine covers. 'Howard Hughes saw them,' she relates, 'and so did 20th Century-Fox. Hughes was in the hospital following his airplane accident, and the photos were shown to him there. But 20th tested me first--in color--and signed me for a year. I worked in one picture, *Scooda Hoo, Scudda Hay*--a little part, but they cut me out. After that they dropped me. Columbia signed me, put me in a nine-day musical--*Ladies of the Chorus*, in which I ended up as Queen of Burlesque--and dropped me after six months. By then I had really begun to take it seriously, wanting to act. But I realized I hadn't learned how, and I was pretty miserable. I had finished school at 16, married at 17 and been divorced at 18--never mind whose mistake it was and he has since remarried. Now it seemed it was my fate to be hired and tossed out by one studio after another. Things were tough. I got myself a good coach, Natasha Lytess, took a room at the Studio Club, limited myself to two meals a day--breakfast and dinner--and went back to modeling. I went without new clothes, everything, earning just enough to pay the rent and take my lessons.  One day an agent, not my own, stopped me and told me Lester Cowan, producing *Love Happy*, was looking for someone 'just your type' for added scenes. I rushed over and was hired on the spot, Groucho Marx directed the scene himself--and this time I not only got on the screen, but stayed there one full minute. I could hardly believe it.' Cowan made the most of that minute. He persuaded Marilyn to go on tour, plugging the picture, on the ground it would be good experience. It was. Marilyn plugged *Love Happy* in New York, Detroit, Chicago and other cities--meeting the press, taking hours for charity, appearing on TV. The day after she returned, 20th sent for her. She was asked if she could dance, and when she answered 'a little,' she was given a part as one of Mme. Adelaide's four girls in *Ticket to Tomahawk*.' The day she got back from THAT movie, filmed in Colorado, Marilyn received a call from MGM Producer Arthur Hornblow and Director John Huston to read for the role of Angela in *Asphalt Jungle*. Both approved, and Marilyn heard herself calling Louis Calhern, Uncle Lom. Houston, she reports, was 'very inspiring and very encouraging.' and Calhern advised her, 'You stick with it, kid.' Marilyn did. In no time at all 20th's Joseph Mankiewicz had looked at *Asphalt Jungle* and picked her to play Miss Caswell in *All About Eve* (Sardonic George Sanders introduces her as 'Miss Caswell, a graduate of the Copacabana School of Arts'-- a would-be actress who, unlike Miss Monroe, doesn't quite make the grade.) 'It was only a small part, but I was thrilled to be working with Sanders, Bette Davis and Anne Baxter--to say nothing of going from one Academy Award director to another!' When Darryl Zanuck saw the rushes he sent for Marilyn's agents and signed her up for keeps. She has since tested for the lead opposite Richard Conte in *Cold Shoulder*, which is now undergoing a rewrite job. She even met Zanuck, finally--and he told her he has plans for her future. Anyone, with half an eye would. Blue-eyed, blonde, 5-foot 5 1/2-inch Marilyn is a slick chick off screen as well as on. She also has the kind of poise that should protect her in the clinches. I mention this, to be sure, merely in the spirit of a kindly uncle."

September saw Marilyn's star growing brighter. She is becoming a regular in Louella Parsons column. She also appeared in a couple of Movie magazines. *Movie Play* magazine featured an article, "Promised and Hoped For Stardom;" and *Photoplay*, featured her in a new series. "How A Star Is Born...Beginning a New Series...*Photoplay* has selected certain Hollywood newcomers, at present unknown to motion picture audiences, who, in the opinion of the magazine, are destined to be the great stars of tomorrow. The first of these is Marilyn Monroe...The Sexiest Girl In Town," by Hedda Hopper.

John Engstead took the photograph that appeared with this article. "Another star who came to me before she had learned how to project her image was Marilyn Monroe. When, half of my work was photographing fashions, all the girls who had come to town for a stab at pictures would drop into my studio to see if they could pick up a few bucks modeling while waiting for their break. They were all beautiful, but usually they were a little too cute and a little too fat to fit the model outfits I received from manufacturers, and Marilyn was one pretty blonde I turned down. A couple of years later *Photoplay* magazine sent me a sketch for a two-page layout to be photographed with an unknown actress. There would be velvet draperies in the background and the starlet would stand in an elaborate gown with her hands outstretched with an isn't-it-wonderful expression. The caption was to be 'How a Star is Born.' The magazine selected Marilyn--at that time under contract to Twentieth Century-Fox--to pose for the photograph. The studio set up the background in their photo studio and the head designer, Charles LeMaire, took the top of one strapless evening gown and the big skirt of another to concoct the outfit. Marilyn came in exactly on time, hardly said a word, put up her arms, smiled, and that was that. Her pretty face was all that impressed me and I still wonder what transformed this sweet young thing into the superstar and sex symbol of a generation."

Although he is silent on the subject, Engstead also took some publicity stills of Marilyn for *All About Eve*, and will also photograph Marilyn in his studio on August 25, 1961 for *Look* magazine.

Dorothy Manners, who was subbing for vacationing Louella Parsons reported the first linking of Marilyn with *Gentlemen Prefer Blondes*, on September 2$^{nd}$, 1950, "If *Gentlemen Prefer Blondes* goes to 20th, how about Marilyn Monroe for the diamond crazy flapper? Betty Grable, doll of the box office, is supposed to be elected for the movie. But beautiful Betty is very hep, with such a vibrant personality it would be hard to hide it behind Lorelei's dumb facade. No reflection on Marilyn's I.Q.--but she gave a nifty account of herself playing a none-too-bright blonde in *Asphalt Jungle*--very similar to Anita Loos lady-like gold-digger."

On September 22nd a wire photo shows Marilyn wearing a Fez and posed with George Jessel to publicize the Shriners 76th Annual Convention held at the Los Angeles Memorial Coliseum.

October started with Marilyn giving money to Grace. She wrote a check for $10.00 on October 1st. *The Fireball*, was released on October 7th.

Marilyn had the first of her sessions with *Modern Screen* staff photographer, Bob Beerman, on October 10, 1950. He took some remarkable shots of her at Paradise Cove in Malibu. She posed for what he considered his best pin-up shot in her yellow bikini she had worn earlier for Anthony Beauchamp. "'I nearly fell into the swimming pool,' recalls Bob Beerman of *Modern Screen*, who took this picture of Marilyn Monroe, 'when she appeared wearing that suit!' Bob, a long-time veteran of the movie-star-plus (or, in some cases, minus) bathing-suit routine, tells the story this way: 'My editor told me to go out and shoot some bathing suit pix of Marilyn. Now, this is not exactly a thrill for me. I've taken pictures of starlets in bathing suits for years, and it never gets me excited. When Marilyn said she had a suit that 'might make me a pretty good picture,' I sat around waiting next to the pool, till she changed into it. A few minutes later, she came ambling out in it--and that's when I nearly fell in!' But, as Bob and the other photographers who've been shooting Marilyn around Hollywood all agree, she's a girl who doesn't flaunt her rather obvious charms. Instead, she acts as though she's wearing a Mother Hubbard. The perfect model, she falls into an alluring, sexy pose just as naturally and normally as she breathes. 'I can't take any credit for this remarkable pin-up,' Bob admits. 'It's all Marilyn's--er, fault.'" The photo of Marilyn in her yellow string bikini was selected by *Screen Album* for their Summer Issue 1952 as the best Pin-Up photo.

Beerman also captured her in another bikini and wearing a brown turtle neck and white shorts cavorting on some poolside furniture. She also posed on a cliff overlooking the Paradise Cove beach and the famous Paradise Beach Cafe. You can see the Paradise Cove Pier in the distance. These will be some of the most frequently used photographs of Marilyn.

Marilyn purchased gym equipment on October 11th from Marcy Gym for the amount of $64.03. Marilyn had always taken pride in her appearance and had been lifting weights since she lived in Catalina. Her work-out routine was good fodder for the fan magazines and she will be photographed inside her apartment pumping iron by Philippe Halsman and Mel Traxel.

Sheliah Graham reported in her syndicated column on October 12th that Marilyn and Peter Lawford were sighted cavorting on the beach.

Other sightings confirm that Lawford and Marilyn participated in the early surfing community at Malibu. "In 1950, Malibu was just a local teen hangout; as a surf spot, it was still largely undiscovered. 'You could count the number of people surfing there on two hands,' Robin recalls. North of the crescent-shaped beach was the Malibu Colony, home to many film actors, including Lawford. He adored the surfing crowd and often stuck around for the barbecues thrown by Quigg and his surfing buddy Matt Kivlin. They'd boil lobsters and break out cases of beer. Now and then Lawford brought one girl who just sat on the sand. 'So one time we said, 'God, Peter, who's that gal?' Vicki remembers. 'She's so white!' It was Marilyn Monroe."

On October 18th Marilyn wrote a check to Sparkletts Drinking Water in the amount of $8.65. She was ahead of her time being concerned with her drinking water.

Hedda Hopper refers to Marilyn, on November 2$^{nd}$, as, "…our new sex bomb, who's the nearest thing to Jean Harlow we've had in many a year."

Louella Parson observed in her column on November 7th. "Johnny Hyde is in Cedars of Lebanon Hospital trying to lick the flu. His girlfriend, Marilyn Monroe, will have two escorts to the opening of *All About Eve*. Johnny doesn't mind because he believes there is safety in numbers."

According to Jimmie Fidler's column on November 25, Marilyn did not attend the premier of *All About Eve*. "There's no particularly, to this little sidelight on Hollywood life, but because it's so typical of the nerve strain entailed in a youngster's bid for screen fame. I think it's worth telling. It concerns Marilyn Monroe, a 20th Century-Fox starlet who has her first real break in *All About Eve*. She's getting a chicken-feed salary, as Hollywood wages go, and having no other resources, has about as many personal wardrobe problems as the average working girl. With *All About Eve* getting the most deluxe premiere staged in years, 'good-business' reasoning dictated that she should be on hand. So she had made for the occasion a most expensive formal gown, and, furthermore, rented an ermine evening wrap. About an hour before she was to have taken off for the premier, she received a call from the studio. One of the company's biggest femme stars would not be able to play a scheduled role; she, Marilyn Monroe, was to test for the part early the next morning. Marilyn did some frantic thinking. It was important to be seen at the premiere, but the test was even more important and she should have a full night's sleep in order to be fresh for it. Regretfully, she laid aside the evening gown, donned pajamas, and went to bed. And there she lay, worrying about that all-important test as the clock chimed off the hours. It was four am before she managed to get to sleep."

Fox came up with a hokey publicity stunt for Marilyn as a little Pilgrim Cutie who is having no luck finding a turkey for Thanksgiving, despite the lurking presence of a large Turkey in the photo. It ran in various newspapers starting mid-November. Curly Twilford was the animal wrangler for "Tom" the turkey, who was three years old and demanded a fee of $35 for posing with Marilyn.

November 15th, Marilyn wrote a check to Helen Hunt for the amount of $100.30. It was noted on the check, "beauty salon." Miss Hunt was a hair stylist who had worked with Marilyn when she made *Ladies of the Chorus* at Columbia. Marilyn also wrote checks on the 15th to Dr. Seligman, MD, Louis Motchan, MD, and William D. Wallace, DDS.

On November 19th she appeared in an article in the *Omaha World Herald* newspaper supplement, "Provocative Blonde; Marilyn Monroe's Sex Appeal Hid Her Acting Ability." The article detailed her early life and the few movies she had been in before her big break in *Asphalt Jungle*. It had John Huston declaring after her screen test, "Why Marilyn,' she says he exclaimed, 'you're an actress!'"

Harrison Carroll reported, November 20th, "Marilyn Monroe fell and had to have eight stitches taken under her chin. To make her feel worse, her agent boyfriend, Johnny Hyde, is in the Cedars of Lebanon hospital. I understand he had another heart attack."

Dr. Michael Gurdin and his partner, Dr. John Pangman inserted bovine cartilage under her chin to strengthen her profile. It was not a silicone implant as some authors have asserted, as silicone implants had not yet been invented. They also performed a rhinoplasty on the tip of her nose, refining it by removing some cartilage on her nasal tip, and narrowing the bridge of her nose. It was financed by Johnny Hyde and bolstered her fragile self-esteem. She is ready to take on Hollywood and has Johnny Hyde to thank for it. In the summer of 1958, during the production of *Some Like it Hot*, she will again need the services of Dr. Gurdin when he finds that the prosthetic in her chin has become absorbed by her body.

Louella Parsons writes this in her column on November 24th, "Marilyn Monroe is an everyday visitor to the Cedars of Lebanon Hospital to see Johnny Hyde. She's been devotion itself to her agent and best beau."

In late December 1950 *Home Town Story* was filming at MGM. This was actually an industrial film with financial backing by *General Motors*. The slant of the film was pro Big Business. Marilyn played Iris Martin, a secretary. She again wears her own sweater dress in this film.

On December 2nd Marilyn participated in a publicity photo with *Pan American Airways*, captioned, "Christening Compania Mexicana de Aviacion's 'El Internacional' schedule with Douglas superpowered DC-6s, actress Marilyn Monroe wields an artist's brush and palette, painting huge map on nose of airliner to indicate route of new five-hour nonstop direct run from Los Angeles to Mexico City. Others mentioned are Consul General of Mexico, Salvador Duhard; CMA Captain, Roberto Pini, who commanded the flight; Woodruff de Silva, L.A. International Airport Manager; and W. O. Willy, General Manager for CMA."

On December 5th Marilyn signs a client/agent agreement, Screen Actors Guild with William Morris Agency.

Marilyn answers the growing habit of the press comparing her to Lana Turner in Frank Morris' column on December 6th, 'I don't think I'm another Lana Turner,' says bashful Marilyn, 'I think I have a personality all of my own.'...She can say that again."

Marilyn writes a check to Renna, on December 9th, for the amount of $55.00. Renna was a French cosmetologist who had developed a technique of giving facials using electrical impulses. Her husband, physician G.W. Campbell, administered the facials at their establishment, Renna's Salon in Beverly Hills. Marilyn remained a loyal customer until her death in 1962. Despite the electrical invention of her husband, Mme Renna will go on to say this about her as a customer, "We don't use instruments. We just lift up the muscles of the face to the natural position with the hands. We have taken care of her face muscles and neck. It's a beautiful piece of work."

Johnny Hyde's final act of devotion for her was to renegotiate her six month contract with 20th Century-Fox. It would be renewed again on May 11, 1951 and would then be a seven year contract. He had guided her career and advised her on what roles to take and groomed her for stardom. Only time will tell if she had learned her lessons well.

Wardrobe tests for *As Young as You Feel* were conducted on December 14th. Marilyn was outfitted by costume designer, Renie (Renie Conley). Renie will also design Marilyn's wardrobe in *Love Nest* and *Let's Make It Legal*.

It is during the making of this movie that Constance Bennett makes a famous witty remark about Marilyn. "…Marilyn Monroe once had a scene in which she walked past a camera with that Monroe hip wiggle. Constance Bennett watched and said, 'There's a broad with a future behind her.'"

A newspaper article on December 15th tells that Marilyn's white mink cape she wore in *All About Eve* will be auctioned off for charity at the Goldberg Gallery.

Johnny Hyde dies of a massive heart attack on December 18, 1950. The closest accounts to Marilyn's own memory of Hyde's fatal heart attack have her following the ambulance to the hospital, where she kept vigil in the hallway. His death impacts her greatly. She had lost her protector and her champion and must face Hollywood's pretense of moral outrage by herself.

In a *Redbook* article in June of 1952, Jim Henaghan quotes Marilyn herself about the incident. "He used to tell me that if he ever got really sick and I heard of it, I should go to him and hold him in my arms, and I'd bring him back to life. I tried it, but it didn't work. I was in the hospital corridor that last night, and he was in an oxygen tent in a room with his family. After a while a doctor came out and told me that Johnny was dead. I ran into the room and took him in my arms. His sons and relatives were there, but I didn't care. I held him in my arms and after about twenty minutes, his face grew cold as ice. Then I let him go. It was too late."

It is this incident that gets mistaken for an uncontrolled mourning at the gravesite and throwing herself on Johnny's coffin, screaming his name. Marilyn did not make a scene during his graveside service.

Marilyn writes a check to I. Magnin & Co. on December 19th, for the amount of $146.61, for a dress to wear to Johnny Hyde's funeral.

On the day of Johnny Hyde's funeral, his ex-wife barred Marilyn from attending the services. Marilyn and Natasha quietly attend the grave-side services at Forest Lawn Cemetery, disguised in black veils. After the crowds leave the grave-side ceremony, Marilyn lingers quietly at Johnny's coffin until the sun had started to set. When she arrives back at the mansion she has been sharing with Hyde she finds that his wife has ordered her things thrown out into the street.

Marilyn moves into the guest cottage at the Joseph Schenck estate. She will stay here shortly before moving in with Natasha Lytess, abandoning her small apartment at 1309 N Harper. Marilyn attempts suicide while living with Natasha. Needless to say, she is extremely upset over the death of Johnny Hyde.

Marilyn had this to say of the influence that Johnny Hyde had on her. "I don't live in fear anymore. That's the essence of how I changed as a result of my mistakes. I was afraid to talk about what I wanted because I'd been laughed at and scored when I seemed ambitious. You can't develop necessary self-confidence unless you express yourself, and even after I got to Hollywood, I was afraid that if I did so, I'd be conspicuous. Then I was terribly lucky in meeting a man who not only became my agent, but my dearest friend. When I first mentioned my acting hopes to Johnny Hyde, he didn't smile. He listened raptly and said, 'Of course you can become an actress!' He was the first person who took my ambitions seriously and my gratitude for this alone is endless. Most men I'd known thought all I cared about was clothes and parties. The truth is I've never been much of a party-goer because I was so shy in a group I'd barely open my mouth. 'Say what you believe,' Johnny told me. 'You are an individual, just like anyone else. You have a right to your opinion. If you don't know something, say so!' It was Johnny, too, who started me reading. Now I have to restrain myself from buying out Pickwick's Book Store on Hollywood Boulevard. There's a beautiful set of Michelangelo's paintings reproduced in book form I'd like to own as soon as I can. Johnny not only gave me self-confidence but he showed me how to make

the most of my time. I'd been used to dilly-dallying when I had no work call. Maybe I'd sleep a little longer. Maybe I'd have a long breakfast. Or I'd make lengthy phone calls to kill time. Johnny kept advising me to use every available moment to better myself. 'Think each situation through. Study!' he said. Suddenly, it no longer seemed an effort to wake up and plunge headlong into work. I found I was less misunderstood when I spoke up and explained myself, instead of avoiding a meeting of minds. 'There is nothing to be afraid of,' Johnny repeated. He also taught me punctuality. I was unconscious of timeliness. Circumstances always used to come up to make me late--now I arrange things to they don't, and it's fun to be dependable and known as a person who always keeps her word."
"Nobody understood, but Johnny was the kindest person I'd ever met. He was the only man I'd ever known who was completely kind to me. He talked to me and gave me the affection I'd always wanted but never seemed to attract. He loved me--and I guess I loved him."

In October of 1952 she told Florabel Muir, "I admired and respected Mr. Hyde too much to cheat him with false affection. He was the best friend I ever had, and I couldn't do anything but be level with him. When he died I felt as if I were all alone in the world again." And, "'Marilyn,' Johnny said to me one day, 'many times when you say so little, people think you are dumb. Sometimes for a whole evening you never say anything.' 'I guess there are several reasons I feel more comfortable not saying anything,' I explained, 'because I feel they'll only misunderstand me. When I feel a lack of contact with a person, I can't talk with him and still be completely myself.' Johnny said, 'Well promise me one thing—you'll never try to be the life of the party.' I think I understand what he meant."

Finally Marilyn would recall of the desperation that grasped her when Hyde was no longer around and the almost unbearable loss of her friend and mentor. "My great friend was buried. I was without his importance to fight for me, without his love to guide me. I cried for night after night. Sometimes I felt wrong in not marrying him and giving him what he wanted. But I also knew it would be wrong to marry a man you really didn't love. I didn't regret the million dollars I had turned down. I never stopped regretting the loss of Johnny Hyde."

Despite her personal drama, Marilyn's career is gaining momentum. She can't afford to waste time grieving over Johnny Hyde and he would not have wanted her to. She has to keep up the furious pace Johnny had set for her, for to become a star will be the best tribute she could give him.

On the 27th, *The Toledo Blade* has this interesting item about a photo of Marilyn popping up in a movie, *For Heaven's Sake*, staring Clifton Webb, "Adroit directorial touches abound in this feature. One of them is to have the camera pan back for a second look at the picture of the lush Marilyn Monroe, who happens to be a 20th Century-Fox starlet, as it sweeps through Webb's swank hotel room to denote his newly found interest in sex."

The December 27th edition of the *San Antonio Express* newspaper "Stars in Your Eyes," featured a four picture photo essay of Marilyn by Bob Beerman taken on October 10th. This popular series will be featured in magazines throughout the rest of her life, as they represent her as the classic California girl. "The deluxe equipment on view here may go places if Marilyn Monroe, a 20th Century-Fox newcomer, can maintain her early pace. A hit as a Lana Turnerish-looking blonde in *The Asphalt Jungle*, she has a good new bit as a chorine friend of George Sanders in *All About Eve*. She's shown here on an outing at Paradise Cove."

Finally, 1950 wraps up with a story about Marilyn's growing support from the men in Korea. Marilyn was the unanimous choice of occupation forces for the title of Miss Cheesecake of 1951. *Stars and Stripes* described her as a 'lovesome blonde.' Marilyn will ride this Cheesecake wave of publicity all the way to stardom. She is the first Atomic Age pin-up, and with the advent of the Korean War, she was, without a doubt, the most popular.

*Stars and Stripes* devoted a half page to Marilyn on December 31, 1950, and reveals that she was the lucky 7th Miss Cheesecake the publication had chosen. "Miss Cheesecake 1950...Marilyn Monroe, blonde, shapely 20th Century-Fox star, is the unanimous choice of editors of *The Stars and Stripes* as Miss Cheesecake of 1950. She is seventh in a line of beauties traditionally chosen at the close of each year on the basis of their appeal in photographs which pass over editors' desk. Miss Monroe is one of the stars of *All About Eve*, the story of an actress' ruthless climb to success, soon to be released in the EC. She was chosen by members of the 1st Marine Div. as 'Miss Morale of the Marine Corps' just before that division sailed for Korea."

Accompanying the article was a photo of Marilyn from *Ladies of the Chorus*, and two photos from *All About Eve*, captioned, "Lovely Marilyn Monroe in two poses from her latest film, *All About Eve*, which may indicate the reason for her popularity as a pinup girl."

# Chapter Ten
# Stalled On the Launching Pad

"When you have only a single dream it is more than likely to come true--because you keep working towards it without getting mixed up. I worked hard and all day long. I worked inside the studio and outside it."
Marilyn Monroe

Without Johnny Hyde to protect her interest at 20th Century-Fox, the powers-that-be allowed Marilyn to languish. None of her other three agents pursued her professional agenda at William Morris. Grudges were held and she bore the brunt of animosity for her affair with Johnny Hyde. The men of Korea and the 4th Estate clamored for more pictures and more stories. It wasn't until early March that 20th Century-Fox really understood the impact she was having with the men of America. Until then, Marilyn skillfully used the resources at the studio to make sure she was still a hot press item.

The popular comic strip *Beetle Bailey* was first published in mid-1950. It wasn't until 1951 and the Korean War that it took off and became a hit. Creator Mort Walker based the sexy character of Miss Buxley on Marilyn.

January 1st saw the release of a *LIFE* magazine article "Apprentice Goddesses...Hollywood Hopes Some of These Dozen Damsels Will Be Big Stars." Marilyn appears in a stunning photograph by Ed Clark, captioned, "Busty Bernhardt... Marilyn Monroe at 22 seems to have her future assured. It has been discovered that just by standing still and breathing she can bring men running from all directions. And after small but pungent roles in *Asphalt Jungle* and *All About Eve*, her studio, 20th Century-Fox, is convinced she will be a fine dramatic actress too." She was actually 24, but who's counting.

On January 5th, Bob Thomas devotes his column to Marilyn. In the article Marilyn comments on publicity. "GI's Pinup Gal, Is Real 'Book Worm....the first new pin-up queen of the war would frankly prefer to curl up with a good book than pose for cheesecake on the beach. Marilyn Monroe is the girl with the body beautiful that is threatening such pin-up stalwarts as Jane Russell and Betty Grable. This week she received work that she was named 'Miss Cheesecake' by the GI editors of Stars and Stripes in Germany. After a hasty appraisal, I could see that Miss Monroe is well qualified for the honor. She is busty, blonde and beautiful with a creamy complexion and a slinky movement that recalls Jean Harlow. It was therefore unusual to lean that she is more concerned with philosophy books than bathing suits. 'Oh, I don't mind cheesecake,' she told me. 'I realize it is a necessary thing in the movie business and it comes natural to me. I did a lot of posing for posters and calendars before I got into the movies. Also, I'm happy if the boys in the service like my pictures. I have received a lot of mail from Korea and that is very gratifying. I have tried to answer it all personally.' Aside from the physical aspects, Marilyn doesn't fit the usual starlet pattern at all. She doesn't drink or smoke and she doesn't like night clubs. She'd rather read a book. 'I have only one charge account,' she remarked proudly, 'and that's at a Beverly Hills book store.' Right now she is plowing through the life of Albert Schweitzer, the renowned philosopher/missionary. She is also reading all the works of Antoine de Saint Exupery, a French novelist and pilot who died in a plane crash during the war. 'I read a little bit of everything,' she explained, 'but mostly nonfiction.'...Her ambition? 'To be a really good actress,' she answered."

Erskine Johnson reported on January 13th, "Maybe Fox should change the title of

*Will You Love Me In December* to *Will You Love Me in a Sweater*. Busty Marilyn Monroe's complete wardrobe for the film consists of five different sweaters." This was in reference to *As Young as You Feel*.

Arthur Miller and Elia Kazan arrive in Hollywood, from New York, aboard the Santa Fe Super Chief on January 16th. Arthur was writing an original screenplay for Kazan to direct called, *The Hook*. They stayed at the home of producer and agent Charles Feldman. It is during the production of *As Young as You Feel* in late January 1951, that Marilyn meets Arthur Miller. Kazan, spurred on by Feldman, sought out Marilyn at the studio and Miller went with him. Kazan remembered meeting her last year at a party at Danny Kaye's house. She and Cameron Mitchell were on their way to the Fox Commissary and ran into the pair. Mitchell knew Miller, as he had appeared in the Broadway production of *Death of a Salesman* in 1949. He introduced the men to Marilyn. Miller has memories of Marilyn when they first met still grieving over the death of Johnny Hyde, and even remembers finding her crying over him on the set. Marilyn, Kazan and Miller spent considerable time together during Miller's short stay in Hollywood and the trio form a close bond. She begins to realize that the men from back east are different from the usual Hollywood types she has been around. She appreciates their intelligence and the respect they give to her. They seem to see her as a person, not just a sexy starlet. They talk to her and take her seriously, and she is hooked. A seed has been planted in her brain that she must go east if she is to be taken seriously as an actress. This is the first influence of New York that swayed her resolve about Hollywood. They represent the legitimate stage, plays and ultimately, acting. It would take her four years to culminate her plan, but she will end up in New York living her version of a dream.

Cameron Mitchell has unique memories of Marilyn in the early days of her stardom. "I'd seen her around, talked to her a couple of times. At first, till you know her a little, you figure her for the standard platinum blonde, no brains, just out for money, looking for a sugar daddy to give her the minks and the diamonds. Then as you know her, you find out she's no gold-plated birdbrain. She's a serious dame. At the time I first met her, she was on a big psychiatry kick. She was studying Freud, Menninger, that kind of thing."

After Miller went back to New York, Kazan and Marilyn would have an affair that would last throughout the summer. He wrote a superb and poetic analysis of his friend and lover, the young Marilyn. "Relieve your mind now of the images you have of this person. When I met her, she was a simple, eager young woman who rode a bike to the classes she was taking, a decent-hearted kid whom Hollywood brought down, legs parted. She had a thin skin and a soul that hungered for acceptance by people she might look up to. Like many girls out of that kind of experience, she sought her self-respect through the men she was able to attract."

Wardrobe tests for *As Young as You Feel* were held on January 22nd. Marilyn played Harriet, a secretary. Marilyn once again acts with Thelma Ritter. Jean Peters will make her first screen appearance in a film with Marilyn. She will follow up by taking a backseat to Marilyn in *Niagara*.

David Wayne recalls Marilyn on the set of this movie, "We've been in four pictures, but in the first, *As Young as You Feel*, she just did a bit, yet, I'll never forget it. This was a very expensive day at 20th Century-Fox. There were 300 or 400 extras, for we were to shoot an audience shot. A girl was supposed to come down the aisle and sit down right behind me. She wasn't supposed to say one line. We say there and sat there waiting for this girl. I finally said, 'For gosh sake, are they holding up this whole crew for an extra?' 'They're waiting for Marilyn Monroe,' somebody said, and I said, 'Who's she?' 'She's over there being made up,' they told me. About two hours afterward this girl finally slithered down the aisle with her hairdresser and costumer. I was kind of sore. I turned around to her and said, 'Well, I'm very happy you finally made it.' And she said, 'Well, that's the way I always do it. It wouldn't be right if I was not pretty.' She knew what she was doing. She would say, 'No one can look pretty before 11 o'clock.'" Yet, Wayne will pay her homage to her beauty, "Pity the poor actor who thinks anyone will be looking his way when Marilyn Monroe is in the same frame of film. I took an anatomy course in college, but, brother, it never included anything like this."

*As Young as You Feel* was based on an original story by Paddy Chayefsky. In later years Marilyn and Paddy Chayefsky would have a disagreement and he would pen an unflattering screenplay which mirrored the events in her life, called *The Goddess*. It was made into a movie starring Kim Stanley in 1958.

James Padgitt quotes Marilyn about her increasingly popular walk, in his column on January 24th. "You have to walk so that it makes you tingle,' advises Marilyn, 'which means that you have to put enough into it so that you exercise most of the muscles of the body.' When Marilyn gets down to serious walking, she discards her shoes because they get in the way and throw the body out of proper alignment, and restrain all natural tendencies toward flexing the muscles and bringing the torso into action." This is interesting because it is before her exposure to *The Thinking Body* by Mabel Elsworth Todd, or body movement teacher, Lottie Gosler's influence.

Charles Feldman gives a party in honor of Arthur Miller on January 26th. Elia Kazan is unable to attend, due to the fact that he had another date. Miller fills in and escorts Marilyn to the party. Marilyn is astonished when Miller insists upon picking her up at her home in person instead of meeting her at the party. She wasn't used to that kind of treatment from the men she normally dated in Hollywood.

Kazan finally showed up at the party, only to find Miller and Marilyn dancing. He remembers, "I watched them dance. Art was a good dancer. And how happy she was in his arms!"

The happy couple spent the evening in close conversation and, according to Marilyn he cautiously reached out and grasped her toe which expressed itself like a bolt of electricity shooting through her. They left the party early and Miller drove her home. After she returned home, she confided to Natasha, "I met a man. It was Bam! You see my toe? This toe? He sat and held my toe. I mean I sat on the davenport, and he sat on it too, and he held my toe. It was like running into a tree! You know, like a cool drink when you've got a fever." To Marilyn this was an erotic act of restraint on his part and somehow this small act coupled with his courtly manners revealed his respect for her. It is this night that Marilyn begins to fall in love with him. But this infatuation will have to hibernate within her heart until the time is right.

The next day Marilyn accompanied Kazan to take Miller to the airport to catch his plane. She and Miller had developed strong feelings for each other. They never acted on the desire they felt, but nonetheless, Miller would feel the guilt of his longing for Marilyn, and this would eventually be one of the factors that destroyed his marriage to his wife Mary.

Miller will write a letter to Marilyn within days of leaving Hollywood suggesting that she would do well to turn her admirations toward Abraham Lincoln. Who knows if he was aware of her love of Mr. Lincoln, but she was dazzled by the coincidence.

Shortly after Miller's visit, Kazan writes Marilyn a letter. In retrospect it is a very revealing letter about the emotional life of young Marilyn. "You said that I made you feel that you must never settle for a second best again. You've been crippled a little by being with men who keep knocking you down. Jim had no real use for you except to make him fall asleep fast. You were completely alone with him. Fred said you were only good for one thing, and generally got pleasure out of demeaning you. And Johnny--by far the best of the three--made you his when you really didn't love him--which is a terrible thing to do to anyone. You took shelter under his roof like a little hurt animal. And behind so many of the things you used to say to me--especially for the first couple of weeks there is a terrible sense of worthlessness. Why, for instance shouldn't Art M. come and get you in his car--why should you be 'used' to going to parties in a Taxi. Not because you're my sweetheart, but for christsake, you're so much better than the people who throw the parties! If you're good enough for me, just bear in mind, you're too good for almost anyone else! You deserve the best! And you'll get it. I don't want you to moan over me or Art either…I want you when you're ready, when you really meet the right guy to get married again and sleep every night with a fellow you love and have your own family and your own children and your own home. You can have all these things. You deserve them. Expect them!!! The whole first step is to build yourself up."
By 1/work. Make yourself into a professional actress. You're a kid with personality and looks now. Plus native talent, plus a good screen face! Learn everything!
 2/Get your own place. Live alone. Organize your life. Read a couple of hours a day. You piss away too much time on the telephone with idiots, being photographed by idiots, etc., riding around, christ knows doing what. All you've got is TIME...keep at least six hours of EVERY F_ _KING SINGLE GODDAMN day for yourself. Doing what you want to do, not what other people want you to do.
3/Get off that solo business with Natasha. Take my word for it she is DEADLY as your only friend. In more ways than I can possibly explain to you. I know much more than you do about these types. I even like her. REALLY I DO. But she is poison for you as a roommate. Fight for what you want. Take Clara with you. You will be happy! Do it now, soon. Never let her on the sound stage again. See her as an occasional interesting neurotic

friend. Enjoy her, but don't rely on her!!!!!!!!
4/Don't go out with Pat deC. etc. you'll never find anyone there except people you despise. Go out with young writers, directors...and...if you can't help yourself--actors and producers. In your heart which is both HONEST AND PERCEPTIVE you despise those jerks. It's insulting to yourself, and in a way to them, to go out with them at all.
5/Be proud of yourself. Rely on yourself. Read Ralph Waldo Emerson on Self Reliance. Invest in yourself. Take all lessons. Really go to college. Do it next week. Not next year! If you don't start right now. I'll think you never will. I'm being tough with you on purpose, but I mean it.
6/Don't let them lighten your hair too much. Don't let them put too floozie dresses on you. Speak up. Your taste is naturally excellent. Don't take any shit from anyone. But listen to everyone's point of view.
7/Do what I tell you.
8/ now.
Why do I end up lecturing you? I won't anymore. But report progress or I will! That is a threat! No night will ever be the same."

Taking Kazan's advice, in the early part of 1951 Marilyn moves in with Shelley Winters, 8573 Holloway Dr, Hollywood. She only stays a short time before moving into a home at 3539 Kelton Way in West Los Angeles. While living with Shelley, the women entertained Welsh poet Dylan Thomas. Shelley fixed the supper and Marilyn was in charge of drinks. She made gin martinis in a milk bottle, as they didn't own a pitcher. Mr. Thomas showed a great measure of respect toward Marilyn. He had made a pass the previous day to Shelley, but he made no cheap passes at Marilyn during the evening. He seemed to pick up on her unspoken need to be taken seriously and her tender vulnerability. Columnist Sidney Skolsky was also at the dinner and afterward Marilyn drove him home. She declined the invitation to continue the party with Shelley and Mr. Thomas at Charlie Chaplin's home.

February 1951 *Modern Screen* magazine article, "I Was an Orphan...But don't feel sorry for Marilyn--unless you're the type who weeps over Cleopatra, and pities a girl who has so much glamour, it hurts."

Twentieth Century-Fox issues a new press biography by Harry Brand on February 7th.

Louella Parsons reported on February 8th, "And there's more news about the new film. [*A Wac In His Life*] Marilyn Monroe, who has been almost in retirement since the death of her agent and friend, Johnny Hyde, joins Jeanne Craine in the glamour line-up for the Jules Buck production."

And again on the 10th, Miss Parsons gave out this information, "At Ciro's--and at the same table--were Jane Wyman with Greg Bautzer, Ronald Reagan with Nancy Davis, Joseph Schenck with Marilyn Monroe and Arnold Grant. Joe could have won a prize as the best rumba dancer, too."

Louella Parsons wrote again of the event on March 8th. "Greg Bautzer was dating Jane Wyman at Palm Springs and created a sensation recently when he and Jane came into Ciro's with Marilyn Monroe and Joseph Schenck. But that was nothing compared to the way eyes popped when the party was joined by Nancy Davis and Jane's ex-husband, Ronald Reagan. Everybody seemed very gay."

On February 11th Marilyn appeared in a Fox publicity photo as a cowgirl with a bow and arrow and a giant heart in the background, ready to ring in Valentine's Day. As implausible as it sounds, it worked. Marilyn's natural photogenic abilities lent themselves perfectly to the campy quality of cheesecake.

On February 12th Lou Goldberg from the William Morris Agency, Inc. prepared an analysis of her loan account and all transactions handled in 1950. Her total debt came to $7,142.80.

Also on February 12$^{th}$ enrollment begins in the Spring Semester class at the University of California at Los Angeles adult extension classes. The classes won't begin until April 5$^{th}$. Bolstered by the encouragement from Elia Kazan, Marilyn enrolls. She takes Background in Literature, taught by Claire Seay, and an Art Appreciation class. An interesting note is that Nancy Sinatra was also in Marilyn's Literature class. Her classes were held at the UCLA Extension campus on Hill Street in Los Angeles, room 616. The class was held every Thursday evening from 7pm until 9pm. Marilyn had to drop the class in mid-April as shooting began on *Love Nest*. Marilyn later said that she always made a point to sit next to a young black man in class. She thought him very intelligent. Whenever she heard a word she didn't know, she would reach across the aisle and poke him and he would tell her the meaning of the word. Of this time Marilyn said, "Then came the time I began to be known, and nobody could imagine what I did when I wasn't shooting, because they didn't see me at previews or premieres or parties. It's simple. I was going to school. I never finished high school, so I started going to UCLA at night, because during the day I had small parts in pictures. I took courses in history of literature and the history of this country, and I started to read stories by wonderful writers. The professor, Mrs. Seay, didn't know who I was and found it odd that the boys from other classes often looked through the window during our class and whispered to one another. One day she asked about me and they said, 'She's a movie actress.' And she said, 'Well, I'm very surprised, I thought she was a young girl just out of a convent.' That was one of the nicest compliments I ever got."

Of her Art Appreciation class Zolotow had this to say, "Her art teacher's lectures on the Renaissance made it 'sound ten time more important than the studio's biggest epic.' She learned about the works of Michelangelo, Raphael, Titian, Tintoretto and the other masters. 'There was a new genius to hear about every day. At night I lay in bed wishing I could have lived in the Renaissance. Of course, if I had lived in the Renaissance I would be dead now.'"

Marilyn will take more classes as her free time allowed during fall 1951.

*UP Wire Service* released a story on February 24th, "Marines Salute Sweater Girl...Sweater Girl Marilyn Monroe, who was just chosen 'Miss Cheesecake' by the armed forces magazine *Stars and Stripes*, got a congratulatory note from 25 Marines today. "We who are pinned down salute you who are pinned up."

On February 28th Marilyn attended the 8th Annual Hollywood Foreign Correspondent

Annual Awards Dinner. It was held at Ciro's. Marilyn was in the enviable position of having been in two of the movies vying for awards that evening, *Asphalt Jungle* and *All About Eve*. Both directors of the films, John Huston and Joseph L. Mankiewicz, were nominated for best director. *Asphalt Jungle* was nominated for two awards and *All About Eve* was nominated for a total of five awards. *All About Eve* won for Best Screenplay.

If February 1951 was any indication, the craving for all things Marilyn was reaching critical mass. 20th Century-Fox was uncharacteristically slow in using Marilyn to her full potential. Everyone seemed to realize she had legitimate star power, everyone but Fox. Marilyn herself, in order to create a buzz around her scored a big publicity coup when she decided to walk the six blocks from the wardrobe department to the photography studio in a sheer negligee' on the Twentieth Century-Fox lot. A studio executive remembers, "It was like the Lindbergh home-coming. People were leaning out of every window. And there was Marilyn, naive and completely unperturbed, smiling and waving up at everybody she knew, didn't know or hoped to know."

In another version "She was in an Angora sweater out to there. While we were shooting her in photography, the word got around and the boys rushed across the hall to get an eyeful. Next we did some layouts with her for picture magazines. We put her in a negligee, and she liked it so much that she wouldn't take it off. She walked all over the lot in it, yelling, 'Yoo hoo' at strangers as far away as the third floor of the administration building. Pretty soon the whole third floor was looking down at her. The first and second floors looked too. It's a bright, sunny day; the wind is blowing and she has Nature working for her. It has taken Nature quite a while to bring her to the ripe-peach perfection she reaches on that day, but it finally makes it. The wind does the rest. She walks all over the lot, has a ball for herself, and so does everybody else."

It is stunts like this that enrage Darryl Zanuck and he has little regard for Marilyn. Soon she would tip things in her favor by going over Zanuck's head. This was a risky move and later she would pay for it by engendering animosity from him, but the gamble would jump start her stalled career. Marilyn was to say that she learned the trick of making an entrance at a party. "This was to arrive around two hours late at a party. You not only made a special entrance, which was good advertising, but nearly everybody was likely to be drunk by that time. Important people are much more interesting when they are drunk." Marilyn creates a rousing entrance at an exhibitors luncheon, held at the Cafe' de Paris (the commissary at Fox Studio.) She followed her own advice and was late to the party. Spyros Skouras, the big money man at Twentieth Century-Fox, attended and sat at the head table with Darryl Zanuck. Marilyn had not made much headway with Zanuck, and she thought that if she could attract Skouras' attention, he could help to bring big roles her way. When he saw the entrance she made in Billy Travilla's chiffon and satin gown, and the clamor that the exhibitors made over her, he quizzed Zanuck about the upcoming pictures she was in. When Zanuck told him she wasn't in any, he flipped his lid and demanded she be put into any picture that required a sexy blonde. Skouras then went and retrieved her from her table and sat her between himself and Zanuck. Marilyn made this astute observation about the big wigs that ran the studios, "Studio bosses are jealous of their power. They are like political bosses. They want to pick out their own candidates for public office. They don't want the public rising up and dumping a girl they consider 'unphotogenic' in their laps and saying, 'Make her a star because we want you to make her a star.'"

Marilyn made the comment to Maurice Zolotow that she was aware of how Zanuck felt about her. "I just wasn't on any producer's casting list, and I didn't get a call, and I feel the reason was Darryl Zanuck didn't like me and everybody on the lot had the word he didn't like me for a good part in a picture, and they didn't want to offend Mr. Zanuck. Mr. Zanuck had never seen me as an actress with 'star quality.' He thought I was some kind of freak. I'm not making this up. He told somebody in the front office who told me later on that I was just a freak, and he didn't want to waste time on me."

The truth was this was a perilous time for Marilyn's career. She was almost 25 years old and she was still being labeled a "starlet," which was a young woman who was not yet an established star. Marilyn realized that her starlet days were fast coming to an end and if Zanuck continued to thwart her appearance in movies it could kill any chance she had of being an actress. It would be up to her to use everything in her power to gain the attention of the public. She was smart enough to realize that her career was in the hands of the ticket buying public and men in general. She started waging a campaign of sexploits that endeared her to the men in Korea in particular, and made her hard to ignore. She accepted an invitation to visit a military hospital. Actress Jane Greer recalls, 'I recently visited a veteran's hospital where Marilyn Monroe had been the day before. One of the nurses there was telling me about her visit. 'Honestly, Miss Greer, I admit that Miss Monroe is attractive, of course. But you should have seen the pandemonium that broke loose. I can't understand it—because she hardly said a word to them!' Miss Greer, herself, says, 'Wow!'" By September of 1951 Darryl Zanuck would have to concede that, "Marilyn Monroe is the most exciting new personality in Hollywood in a long time."

Of Marilyn's relationship with the public, she said this, "I guess I had known it all the time. I knew what I had known when I was 13 and walked along the sea edge in a bathing suit for the first time. I knew I belonged to the public and to the world, not because I was talented or even beautiful, but because I had never belonged to anyone else. The public was the only family, the only Prince Charming and the only home I had ever dreamed about."

Johnny Hyde was to tell Marilyn that he sensed something in her that the masses would like. And once again he was spot-on.

In 1953 Russell Birdwell, a public relations expert, had this to say on Marilyn's marketing to the public and why she was a success. "Marilyn Monroe is a package. She is a great package. Furthermore, she will be a great star, one of the greatest. Why? Because she has warmth. People seek more than mere entertainment. People want warmth. They want to feel friendly toward the entertainer, and they want the entertainer to feel friendly toward them. Marilyn Monroe, in addition to being a great talent, has great warmth. Harry Brand is one of the deep thinkers in the film industry. As director of publicity at Fox, he has successfully guided the careers of as many stars as anyone in the business. More important, he has never wasted his talent on undeserving people. Marilyn Monroe was a nonentity, but she had the talent and the ability and the warm personality. Harry Brand took it from there."

*The Toledo* Blade ran an interesting article which reflected the current state of affairs regarding Marilyn's popularity and how blind the studio was to it. "Much to the amazement of 20th Century-Fox which had printed more than half-a-million of those famous art 'studies' of Betty Grable in scanty white bathing suit looking coyly over her shoulder, the pin-up craving GI's are now presenting almost a solid front for revealing images of 22 year old Marilyn Monroe, who has appeared only in *Asphalt Jungle* and *All About Eve*. In each of these, however, she had startling characterizations that caused fans all over the land to herald her as the closest approach to a 'new Jean Harlow' yet uncovered. Seems the studio hasn't been making an adequate estimate of Marilyn's box-office potentialities, but now that the servicemen have elected her as their queen bee, 20th Fox brass is ordering immediate concentration on roles that will show off her curvaceous pulchritude to the best advantage."

Under Harry Brand's direction the publicity team at 20th Century-Fox kicked into high gear. "We took her to the beach with a lot of wardrobe changes, but the basic idea was that this is a beautiful girl with a great body, and that idea was always the same, although we did have different approaches to it. We had color shots, we had black-and-white shots, we had mountain shots, we had field shots, faked water-skiing shots--every type of approach we could think of. Picnicking, walking--anything a person does, we let her do it. When we began to see what she did best, then we concentrated on it.... Once we got rolling, it was like a tidal wave. We began to release some photographs of her, and as soon as they appeared in print, we had request for more from all over the world. We had the newspapers begging for art; then the photo syndicates wanted her; then the magazines began to drool. For a while we were servicing three or four photos to key newspapers all over the world once a week....Once this building up process started other people became interested in her. We called up the top cameramen around town who had their own outlets, and we told them what we had, and we asked them If they'd like to photograph her. They said, 'Ho, boy, yes.' We told them what the deal was. We said, 'We think this girl has got a great future, she's beautiful, her chassis is great, and are you interested. Each guy had his own idea of what he wanted and he let his imagination play upon her. This is the way such things get done. They're not created by one person. They're the creation of all of the press representatives who cover Hollywood for all the publications in the world, which means about 350 people. Everybody in the studio publicity department worked on her. The picture division, the magazine division, the fan-magazine division, the planters who plant the columnists, the radio planters, and so forth. Then, when you make a motion picture, a 'unit man' or 'unit woman' is assigned to cover it's shooting and he or she handles publicity for that film alone. In addition, the whole department works on the same picture. Our department is highly specialized, but each specialist in each department makes his contribution to the personality we're erecting in the public's mind. But the unit man is not always the same for a certain star's picture. Sonia Wilson's been unit woman on Monroe pictures, and Frankie

Neal's been a unit man on her pictures, but Roy Craft has been her unit man more than anyone else. Roy likes her. He gets along with her fine. We took her to all of the cocktail parties we thought were important."

In an interview with Bill Tusher Roy Craft remembers this time in Marilyn's career. "Photographically, Marilyn caught on like a prairie fire long before the revelations of her calendar art fanned the conflagration. 'We took 40 shots in various changes of bathing suits, both at the gallery and at Paradise Cove at the beach, with Gene Kornman on the camera,' Craft told me. 'Ordinarily, you shoot 40 shots of any pretty girl, and if ten of them come out nice, it's a good day. Well, with Marilyn every one of those 40 poses came out good. It was the all-time great sitting in pinup art, I think.' Monroe pictures, from the very inception of her tenure at $20^{th}$, kept disappearing from the files, negatives and all."

Grady Johnson, Fox publicist, shared his thoughts on Marilyn's publicity. "She falls into her role so enthusiastically that photographers accustomed to coaxing skirts up and blouses down have to use reverse English on her. 'Killed' photographs of her have become collectors' items. Having become a star by public demand, she will not, she says, permit the dignity of her new station to let her forget what folks want. She will continue posing for cheesecake—not coyly cover up as many another leg artist has done upon achieving stardom. There's a charming selfishness in the decision. Photographs of herself hold a childish fascination for Marilyn. After a sitting with photographers, she will consult half a dozen men for advice on which look best. If they like a shot which she doesn't, she will argue for hours, insisting that some be retouched, that others be discarded."

The one professional relationship Marilyn had coveted since her modeling days was friendship with the photographers who worked with her. She senses that they hold the secret she needs to finally burst into stardom. She is savvy about courting them. She convinces each on that she has such trust in their ability to bring out the magic in her printed image. "A group of photographers sat at the same table at lunch recently and somebody mentioned that he'd shot a layout of Monroe the day before and that she'd confessed to him that she liked him very much—that she wanted very much for them to be good friends. The fellows began comparing notes and discovered that each of them had had practically the same experience. 'How do you like that line,' one of them muttered. 'When she told it to me I believed it!'

Robert Cahn commented on Marilyn's growing appeal. "Today, spurred by Marilyn's impact on audiences, Fox press agents are in the midst of the biggest publicity build-up since the Jane Russell campaign. During the past 12 months, the studio's press department has sent out more than 3,000 pictures of Marilyn to newspapers alone. In Germany the editors of *Stars and Stripes* have selected her 'Miss Cheesecake of 1951,' and in Korea her pin-ups swiftly were rated as the choicest wallpaper obtainable. Like a famous predecessor, Jean Harlow, Marilyn's name is rapidly becoming the current Hollywood definition of sex appeal. After reading a Soviet attack on poems which have romantic ardor without social significance, on Hollywood columnist, Jim Henaghan, boldly suggested, 'Let's drop a handful of picture of Marilyn Monroe on them and see what happens.'…Her greatest handicap, odd as it seems, is her face and figure, which automatically have typed her as the brainless sort. A few persons who have looked a little closer have seen, behind the panchromatic make-up and the studied, protective starlet mannerisms, a face on which 23 years of living have written several anguished chapters. Sometimes, behind the false eyelashes, comes the look of a lost child.'

Marilyn appears in the March issue of *Photoplay* in a dress that will stir up extreme controversy in the coming year. It was a costume of Gene Tierney's in *Where the Sidewalk Ends*. Miss Tierney hated the gown and claimed she couldn't walk six steps in it. It was designed by Oleg Cassini. The gown not only had a fitted skirt which flared out into a mermaid flounce, but it also had a basket-weave bodice that almost didn't cover the bosoms, depending on which way she might move. One magazine called it, "the most risqué gown of the year....very décolleté, the bosom quite exposed and sustained by a clever manipulation of spaghetti straps." The movie was a Fox production so it wouldn't have been hard for Marilyn to have obtained the dress. Some biographers state that Marilyn bought the gown from a sale at Cassini's private salon, and if so, he retained ownership of the garment and not Fox. Cassini would later refer to Marilyn as, "the world's most marvelous marshmallow."

*The Los Angeles Times* ran a captioned photo of Marilyn, on March 8th, walking with some baseball players. Marilyn was the mascot for Major League All-Stars, a Kiwanis baseball game at Gilmore Field held on March 11th. She is shown with three Chicago White Sox players, Hank Majeski, Gus Zernail and Joe Dobson. She had met Zernail in 1949 while stumping for *Love Happy* in Chicago. This photo was used again in 1952 to advertise the Kiwanis Club charity baseball game, in which Joe DiMaggio would also participate. Roy Craft arranged for her to participate in Spring Training for the Chicago White Sox in Pasadena. Stars for five Major League Ball Clubs training in Southern California form the roster which opposed Fred Haney's Stars. The proceeds benefited crippled Children.

Marilyn will exchange letters with Arthur Miller. During his first letter to her he admonished her, "Bewitch them with this image they ask for, but I hope and almost pray you won't be hurt in this game, nor ever change...."

Marilyn writes to Arthur Miller on March 9th. Miller recalls receiving letters from Marilyn, "Occasionally I got a note from Marilyn that warmed my heart. In strangely meandering slanted handwriting that often curled down margins and up again on the other side of the paper, using two or three different pens with a pencil thrown in, she talked about hoping we could meet again when she came east on business, and offered to come without any excuse if I gave her some encouragement."

Arthur Miller responds to Marilyn's letter on March 13th. According to Miller he wrote back, "a muddy, formal note saying that I wasn't the man who could make her life happen as I knew she imagined it might, and that I wished her well. Still, there were parched evenings when I was on the verge of turning my steering wheel west and jamming the pedal to the floor. But I wasn't the man who was able to do that either."

At the 23rd Annual Academy Awards, March 29th, 1951, Marilyn presents the Oscar for Best Sound Recording to Thomas Moulton for *All About Eve*. Marilyn begins a dislike for bouffant skirts when she accidentally closes a door on the back of her skirt and rips yards of material off. She is comforted by Debra Paget, Jane Greer and Gloria DeHaven. Seamstresses were able to repair her skirt before she went onstage to present the award, but Marilyn's confidence in bouffant skirts could not be repaired. She walked onstage to the accompaniment of *Oh, You Beautiful Doll*. The event was held at the RKO Pantages Theatre in Hollywood with Fred Astaire hosting. *All About Eve* was nominated for 11 Oscars, and won 6. Bill Tusher interviewed Marilyn for his radio show after the awards. Marilyn was photographed that night by Fox master lensman, John Florea. She will covet relationships with people who are the best in their fields and she is savvy enough to realize that the closest way to the public's heart is through a camera lens. She and Florea become quite close and he even takes her into his family circle.

On March 30th James Padgitt devoted his entire column, "Around Hollywood," to Marilyn and her moles. "Honey-tressed Marilyn Monroe hailed as the new Jean Harlow, gives full credit to her assorted blemishes--a couple of moles--for her screen success. 'Time was, 'says the blonde charmer, 'when I felt the moles made me the original version of the ugly duckling. Now I realize what a distinct asset they are.' The screen newcomer, regarded as one of the most provocative creatures on the Hollywood scene, is currently adding her bewitching allure--mole and all--to 20th Century-Fox's *Will You Love Me in December?*, in which she plays a sirenish secretary. The one-time photographer's model, recently acclaimed by the discerning editors of *Stars and Stripes* as 'Miss Cheesecake of 1951,' points out that Hollywood boasts more beautiful girls than any other city in the world. 'It has reached the point where beauty alone is not enough,' elucidates Marilyn. 'A girl has to have something more, a certain charm, a distinctive character.' In her own case the pulchritudinous starlet says her moles have helped set her apart from the run-of-the-mill actress trying to get a footing on Hollywood's slippery ladder to success. One of the 'beauty spots' is prominently displayed on Miss Monroe's left cheek, just above the lip. Make-up men at times have set about to cover it over with pancake cosmetics, but the actress raises such a fuss that they quickly mend their ways. The other mole is located roughly four inches south of the starlet's right clavicle, and it won't been seen in her current picture because wardrobe gives her extremely high neck lines. 'It's no wonder,' says Miss Monroe, 'that women sometimes daub on beauty spots. They add the finishing touch.' She recommends such focal points of interest both for ravishing beauties and plainer women. Explaining that the spots help divert attention from various other features which might not be quite as perfect as desired. Miss Monroe credits her moles with an assist in winning her the *Will You Love Me in December?* role, pointing out that Director Harmon Jones interviewed dozens of stunning girls before being brought up short by Marilyn and her moles. 'And just to think,' she recalls with alarm, 'I almost cut off my career at the start when for a time, I was actually thinking of having the moles removed.' Marilyn entered the Hollywood scene as Louis Calhern's girlfriend in *Asphalt Jungle*. She scored again as George Sanders girlfriend in *All About Eve*."

That Spring Marilyn dated Peter Lawford occasionally, although, in November of 1952 she would deny that she had ever dated him. "Since I became known, I have been connected romantically with a few male stars, via press agents for restaurants. I have been reported as being seen here and there with Peter Lawford. As a matter of fact I never have had a date with Peter. We were at the same table at a night club (one of my few appearances at a nightclub, I don't care for them) and I may have danced with him. But that hardly constitutes a date, and certainly not a romance." But they did spend time together at Malibu beach in 1950.

By all accounts Marilyn pampered her little dog Josefa, and even fed it calf's liver she had prepared. Yet, Natasha Lytess would threaten to turn Marilyn into the ASPCA because of her lack of care for the animal. But the dog, which was given to Marilyn by Joseph Schenck for her 24th birthday, would prove too much for Marilyn to take care of. She gave her to a Miss Smithe to care for. In 1953 Miss Smithe sent three pictures of herself and Josefa to show Marilyn how happy her little dog was.

On April 1$^{st}$ Louella Parsons devoted her column exclusively to Marilyn. This was publicity that you couldn't buy. Louella's stamp of approval was life or death to a starlet. "Marilyn Monroe, the blonde menace in *Asphalt Jungle* and the chorus girl with mink, money and jewelry ambition in *All About Eve*, has her life all mapped out. Marilyn wants to be a great actress, and as she says this her eyes shine and she unconsciously puts on the air of a great star. But that's only when she is seeing visions. The real Marilyn is a very down-to-earth, frank, unassuming young lady. Marilyn doesn't try to hide the fact that she was brought up in a Los Angeles orphanage and that her early days were spent being farmed out from family to family. We were talking religion and when she told me her real name is Norma Jean Dougherty, I said, 'Irish, isn't it? Do you go to the church to which your name belongs?' 'No. I don't,' she replied. 'When I was little, you see, I went to the Sunday school and church that the family with whom I lived belonged. If they were Methodists, I was a Methodist, and if they were Baptists, I was a Baptist. I had no choice in the matter. Marilyn father died before she was born, and her mother, a hopeless invalid, had no visible means of support, so the baby became a ward of the county. Marilyn's first job was in the Los Angeles Orphans Home where she helped in the pantry, set tables, and took care of the younger children. She can scarcely believe that this same little hard working Norma Jean is now the motion picture actress Marilyn Monroe, who is certainly going places. 'I am naturally shy,' she told me, 'and I was so frightened when I first started to act that the words would not come out of my mouth. I was so impossible that after I finished school on the 20$^{th}$ lot I was fired. I had never met Darryl Zanuck, so when I came back to 20$^{th}$ he sent for me. He said, 'So you were fired? I didn't even know you were here.' Do you know what I said to Mr. Zanuck?' 'No,' I said, expecting she would say he didn't give her a chance. What Marilyn actually said was, 'I told Mr. Zanuck I should have been fired. I was no good. I was scared. I couldn't do a thing. But now I have studied voice and I have worked very hard. I was also fired from Columbia after six months. You know,' she went on, looking at me with those big eyes, 'I think maybe if other girls know how bad I was when I started they will be encouraged. I finally made up my mind I wanted to be an actress and I was not going to let lack of confidence ruin my chance.' 'How did you get *Asphalt Jungle*?' I asked her. 'I got it through Lucille Ryman, who is a good friend of mine,' she told me. 'She is in the casting department at MGM. Lucille telephoned my agent, Johnny Hyde, and asked him to bring me to Metro-Goldwyn-Mayer. Johnny got me a script and I really worked hard before I tested for the director, John Huston. When I got the job, everything changed.' Marilyn's young face grows sad at the mention of John Hyde's name. He was terribly in love with her, and when he died a few months ago it was the greatest heartbreak of her life. Little Johnny, who had such confidence in this girl, and who brought Rita Hayworth and other ambitious young actresses along the way, lived long enough to see his faith in Marilyn justified. She cannot talk about him without her eyes filling with tears. 'Some people thought I should have married Johnny,' she said, 'but I didn't love him and he understood that. It wouldn't have been right.' This is an insight into this girl's character. John was vice president of the William Morris agency, and as a man of means could have done much for her career. But Marilyn is going places on her own, and for that I admire her. 'When did you first know that you wanted to be an actress?' I asked her. 'Well, when I was through school I became a model. I had to earn my living as quickly as possible. My photograph was in a magazine and the casting department at $20^{th}$ sent for me. I was put in school on the lot, and then sent to the actor's lab before I was dropped. They certainly gave me every chance. But now I'm back at $20^{th}$ and very happy. In my next picture I play a WAC.' 'Are you a good girl in this one?' I asked. 'No. I'm not,' she answered. 'I steal William Lundigan from his wife, and I believe Jeanne Crain is going to play that wife.'"

  Wardrobe Test for *Love Nest* began on April 5th. Marilyn was dressed for this movie by costume designer, Renie. Marilyn always realized the importance of the people behind-the-camera to her career. She often courted their favor with small presents or photographs which she used to express her gratitude for the use of their talents in making her look good on film. In the spirit of such gestures, she inscribed two wardrobe test photos for Renie. One was a head-shot for makeup and hairstyle showing Marilyn wearing a hat from the film. She signed, "To Renie, Love and Best Wishes, Marilyn." The other is a costume show showing Marilyn wearing the dress that she wears in the party scene at the end of the picture. She signed, "To Renie--Same me 'with feeling.' I'm more grateful than words can express. Love and thanks, Marilyn"

  On April 11th Marilyn began to renegotiate her contact with Twentieth Century-Fox. The William Morris Agency intervened and succeeded in getting her a seven year contract and raising her salary to $500 a week for the first year, and increasing exponentially each year thereafter. The contract would become valid on May 11th. This was the only fiduciary act William Morris did for her after Johnny Hyde's death.

  There was another wardrobe Test for *Love Nest* on the 12th. A couple days later on April 15th Marilyn accompanied Elia Kazan to Santa Barbara for a preview of the upcoming film he directed, *Streetcar Named Desire*. The next day, the 16th, Marilyn went as Kazan's date to a party at Charlie Feldman's home. Afterwards, they went over to see Joseph Schenck.

Marilyn's final wardrobe Test for *Love Nest* was on the 18$^{th}$; also the day shooting began on *Love Nest*. Marilyn played Roberta Stevens, an ex-WAC who provides the sexual tension for the movie by renting a room from an old army buddy and his wife, who is none-to-pleased with the situation.

June Haver, who had worked with Marilyn in *Asphalt Jungle*, remembers her co-star in the January 1966 issue of *Coronet* magazine, "She was so young and pretty, so shy and nervous on that picture, but I remember the scene where she was supposed to be sunning in the back yard of the apartment house we all lived in. When Marilyn walked on the set in her bathing suit and walked to the beach chair, the whole crew gasped, gaped and seemed to turn to stone. They just stopped work and stared; Marilyn had that electric something-- and mind you, movie crews are quite used to seeing us in brief costumes. They've worked on so many musicals and beach sequences. But they just gasped and gaped at Marilyn as though they were stunned. In all my years at the studio, I'd never seen that happen before. Sure, the crew gives you the kidding wolf-whistle routine, but this was sheer shock. Anyway, Marilyn was aware of it and she just loved it. In her shy way, she smiled. But the crew's reaction gave her confidence because she was always nervous, always had trouble getting into a dialogue scene. But the warmth of the crew's reaction to her relaxed her. She suddenly seemed to be another person. She lost her shyness. I think it's the only time she felt confident-when she was in that bathing suit. Suddenly, she seemed to shine like the sun."

When Jack Parr was asked by Hy Gardner about his movie career, he remembered working with Marilyn. "Then I went to 20th Century-Fox and made a picture with Marilyn Monroe called *Love Nest* in which I played her boyfriend. It was a big bore. I was glad when the shooting was over. But I had to come back for stills. We had a date for 1 o'clock, and I hung around until Marilyn swings in around 2, bills and coos with characters over the phone, and finally gets ready at 4. We sat down and the photographer says, 'Grab her and kiss her.' But I'm disgusted and can't. So he grabs me and says, 'Paar, you're supposed to be an actor. I can see you can't stand this dame, but how about acting like you enjoy hugging and kissing her?'" When Gardner asked him if he thought at the time that "Marilyn Monroe would become the most popular and sexiest movie star of her time?' Jack shrugged, 'From the guys she knew, I figured she would."

After filming ended, Marilyn was still having an affair with Elia Kazan and would show up on the Fox ranch at the Brownsville set of *Viva Zapata!* Kazan's family unexpectedly showed up and Marlon Brando was enlisted to keep Marilyn "occupied." As it turned out, Marlon was interested in Jean Peters.

Anthony Quinn, who co-starred in the film, gives this unflattering account of Marilyn. "Gadge was visited on the Brownsville set by one of his Actors Studio disciples--an empty headed blonde with a fat rear end who would soon reign as the leading sex symbol of her time. Marilyn Monroe had surfaced in a handful of pictures, but had yet to make her mark and she arrived on the scene to soak up the director's insights on acting. Oh, Monroe was pretty enough to look at, but there were hundreds of better looking actresses poking around Hollywood. Even after she hit the big time, with *Gentlemen Prefer Blondes*, I could never see what all the fuss was about, but what the hell did I know? All I knew was that she walked around our dusty Texas set in a slinky dress that showed the crack of her ass, apparently unaware that her clothes could not hold her. All I knew was that there seemed to be precious little going on beneath her glorious blonde mane. At first, Monroe seemed to have a tremendous crush on Gadge, and she threw herself at him at every opportunity. Gadge in turn, threw her right back at Brando."

It was on location for *Viva Zapata* that she meets photographer Sam Shaw who was taking stills for the film. Marilyn ended up driving him to and from the location and in doing so gained a devoted ally. He became a lifelong friend and Marilyn gave him liberal access to her after she became a major Hollywood star. In return, Shaw's photographs memorialize her legendary beauty, starting with The *Seven Year Itch* and he chronicled her romance with Arthur Miller and her love of New York. He also captured some of the loveliest images of Marilyn on the beach at Amagansett, and in the bucolic setting of their Roxbury farm. Shaw will go on to say this when asked what Marilyn was like, "To all of them I say, 'she was like you. A young woman in a tough man's world—no tears, always witty and fun, an actress in every sense of the word; dedicated to her craft, searching for the truth in worldly characters she portrayed, searching the depth of truthfulness rather than make believe plots. As complex and chaotic life was (and is) she was simple, and always searching for knowledge and truth, always with depth and humor, like a teenager'—and she never lost that teenage quality—that is what I think the young women fans see and feel in her—knowingly or rather instinctively."

When they all got back to Hollywood, Marilyn, Kazan and Shaw used to hang out together. Of Marilyn during this time, Shaw recalls with tender insight. "All during production Marilyn had a big romance with Kazan, and because she was idle much of that spring, she and I and Kazan often drove out to the Fox ranch, where he was directing the picture. Usually we stopped off at some roadhouse or other on the return trip in the evening, had a beer, played the jukebox and danced. Everybody knows about her insecurities, but not everyone knows what fun she was, that she never complained about the ordinary things of life, that she never had a bad word to say about anyone, and that she had a wonderful, spontaneous sense of humor."

On May 2nd Jimmie Fidler mentions this about Marilyn in his syndicated column, "A few weeks ago, Marilyn Monroe rented an apartment about a mile from 20th Century-Fox and having viewed herself in the mirror and weighed herself on the scales, decided to whittle away a few pounds by walking to and from work. I asked her how the 'road work' was progressing and was informed that 'it had been discontinued,' so many men stopped their cars to offer her a ride that it became embarrassing. It's probably just as well. It seems to me that the offers of rides also proved that Miss Monroe will be able to get by quite well at her present weight."

Columnist Bob Thomas picks 10 young starlets destined for stardom. He actually gives a very good history lesson on the development of Cheesecake in Hollywood. "Hollywood Working Overtime Turning Out Cinderella's…The film factories are working overtime to turn out a new line of Cinderella's. This has long been one of Hollywood's most popular commodities—the beauteous young girls with graceful forms and stars in their eyes. Legs and pretty faces have always sold well, but there were two main periods of Hollywood history when such products reached peaks. The first came when a group of film press agents started naming the Wampas Baby Stars in 1922. The Wampas (Western Association Motion Picture Advertisers) continued this practice for a decade until it broke up, largely because of studio politics. Dozens of the Wampas baby stars first won recognition by being chosen for the honor and became big stars. Among them: Clara Bow, Joan Crawford, Joan Blondell, Janet Gaynor, Anita Louise and Loretta Young. Then next great period of youthful sex appeal in Hollywood came during the war years 1941-45. This grew out of the need for entertainment films and for GI pin-up pictures. Among the stars developed during those years were Betty Grable, Rita Hayworth and Jane Russell. The industry seemed to retreat from cheesecake during the postwar years. Pin-ups were considered 'undignified' by some spokesmen, and producers were intent on films attacking the worlds' problems. Also, the Hollywood depression cut down contract lists, eliminating most of the young girls whose legs might bring them stardom. The cheesecake output has increased recently, and there are signs of a full-scale revival. The reason for this new upsurge: The need for pin-up girls for a new army. The return to entertainment pictures in an effort to cure an ailing box office. The demands by theater men for new personalities. These three elements have brought renewed activity to the movie mills. Talent scouts are scouting for fresh teen-age talent. Press agents are pressing for new stunts to publicize the newcomers. With the aid of some Hollywood news and magazine photographers (who are perhaps the best judges), I have picked some of the most promising. They were selected for their physical attributes and their chances for stardom." Marilyn bio goes thus, "Marilyn Monroe, graduate of the school of hard knocks. Orphaned shortly after her birth in Los Angeles, she spent her youth in a number of homes and orphanages. She held a variety of jobs, from making five cents a week in an orphan home to a stock contract at a studio. Nothing much happened until John Huston cast her as the sexy moll in *Asphalt Jungle*. Her blonde beauty clicked and the roles got better. Named Miss Cheesecake of 1951, by *Stars and Stripes*, service paper." A picture of her in a bathing suit posing among piers and taken by Polowny accompanies the article.

One of the starlets featured in the Thomas article with Marilyn is Jody Lawrence, one of Doc Goddard's daughters. Thomas calls her, "Hollywood's most successful 'unknown' actress." Marilyn knew her as "Nona." She signed with Columbia in 1949, the year after Marilyn was there. In the coming year Marilyn will outpace the rest of the pack. Jody Lawrence herself had a modest career but will only be remembered because of her relationship to her famous foster sister.

Lawrence had this to say about Marilyn in an interview with Ezra Goodman in 1961,

"The first time I met Marilyn I was about eleven. I remember she was a shy, introverted little girl. Marilyn and I were neurotic children. That's why we have taken this business as a way of life. Instead of accepting things as they were, we sort of clammed up. We were very sensitive toward our surroundings. I've been in two dozen foster homes myself. But once you've been in a couple, you've had it. You become cagey, cynical and you know how to get the most out of people...Marilyn is not in this business for money or fame or glory. It's a release for her. It's as necessary as becoming an alcoholic or dope addict. She's looking for a father, a mother, a family all rolled up into one."

On May 7th Marilyn accompanied Elia Kazan to another party at Charles Feldman's home. The next day, May 8th, Marilyn agrees to pay for dental work for Natasha Lytess. The dentist, a Dr. George Hollenbeck, 15372 Dickens Street in Sherman Oaks, is threatening to sue Natasha for non-payment for $1800 worth of dental work. Marilyn will pay $200 per week out of her own salary. Natasha will in turn pay Marilyn $25.00 a week out of her salary. The agreement was made through the William Morris Agency on Marilyn's behalf. She confirmed her approval by signing the contract Natasha wrote.

On May 11th Marilyn's 7-year contract with Twentieth Century-Fox Studio finally goes into effect. She is guaranteed 40 weeks of income in each 52 week period. The first year she gets $500.00 per week, the second year she gets $750.00 per week, the third year she gets $1000.00 per week, the fourth year she gets $1500.00 per week, the fifth year she gets $2000.00 per week, the sixth year she gets $2500.00 per week, and by the seventh year she will make $3500.00 per week. Aside from the low pay, there were many other issues that concerned the control that the studio had over her career. Marilyn could be loaned out, whenever, to other studios who would pay handsomely for her appearance in one of their movies. She, of course would not benefit from these transactions, other than her weekly salary, unless Fox agreed. The Studio, on the other hand, would make lots of money in the deal. She had no say on what movies Fox wanted her to act in. Her paid appearances, such as for the theatre, T.V. or radio were prohibited unless Fox approved them, and if they did, she would get no compensation for her appearance. She was also prohibited from making any recordings, other that soundtracks for her film with Fox. Twentieth Century-Fox could capriciously choose to fire her at the end of each year, and she would have nothing to say about it. Without Johnny Hyde in her corner Marilyn did not have the leverage herself or from the agents at William Morris to make the contract equitable for her. She would even the score in a little over three years.

Hedda Hopper announced on May 13th, "Marilyn Monroe and Robert Wagner join the cast of *Don't Call Me Mother*, with Claudette Colbert. For the part of a young siren, Marilyn has gone so blonde that her hair looks silvery blue." The name of the movie will be changed to *Let's Make it Legal*.

On May 13th Phil Moore, who had worked with Marilyn on and off since 1948, reveals his six ladies he picked as the sexiest singers of the day, Lena Horne, Marlene Dietrich, Julie Wilson, Jane Russell, Marilyn Monroe and Ava Gardner. Moore laments, "They really put over a love song and put you into a mood. The rest of the girls sing nicely, but they just make pretty music. The other six make you lean back and dream dreamy thoughts." On Marilyn, Moore had this to say, "Marilyn Monroe, a newcomer to the Hollywood canaries, gets on Moore's high-powered list because, 'she has a husky insinuating voice and she knows just how much to insinuate with it.'"

Marilyn is featured in the June 10th edition of *Parade* magazine. This is a big deal for her as it is a widely read Sunday newspaper insert. "The Truth About Cheesecake: Marilyn Is Two Girls!...Ten to one, you know Hollywood's Marilyn Monroe as 'Miss Atomic Bomb', or as 'Miss Cheesecake.' Or as 'The Shape,' or even 'Miss Flamethrower,' because she's been that, too. You'd recognize her anywhere because she has one of the most photographed figures in the curve-conscious film world. She has personality appeal, too-- the kind that keep men movie-goers glued to their seats to see *The Asphalt Jungle* a second time. And Marilyn has had only a bit part in it! But: there's another Marilyn! Behind the cheesecake, the girl with the smile and the figure is a scholar and a student. Here's proof: She's enrolled for a literature course at the University of California at Los Angeles. She has only two charge accounts--both at book stores. 'You'll usually find her in the poetry department,' said a clerk recently. She writes verse herself. 'My poems are kind of sad,' she says, 'but then so is life.' She likes to talk about such cultural big-wigs as Thomas Wolfe and Walt Whitman, musicians Mozart, Beethoven. But she's also strong for jazzmen Lois Armstrong and Jelly Roll Morton. That's Marilyn the scholar, who's really a bright girl searching (as so many people are) for some meaning to life. Has it made her highbrow? Stuffy? 'Not a bit,' says Marilyn. 'If the boys like me and want my pin-ups. I'm ever so happy. The cheesecake and sexy pictures are parts I enjoy--as long as I can do them honestly. Right now, Marilyn's busier than ever. Her salary's just been raised to $750 a week, and her newest picture (*As Young As You Feel*, 20th Century-Fox) is just coming out. And the future? 'Acting--real acting,' she says. 'Not just posing. There are things inside of me that I don't know how to say except through acting.'"

This was an important article in that it emphasized to a larger audience the duality of Marilyn's personality. She would suffer much ridicule for her "highbrow" pursuits. Some people just couldn't understand why being sexy wasn't enough for her.

On June 15$^{th}$, Marilyn was also chosen by the 31$^{st}$ Polar Bear Regiment as "the girl we should most like to get a bear hug from." Also on that day Marilyn is photographed with several sailors celebrating the return of the USS Manchester to Long Beach from Korea, which caused a little stir amongst rival branches of the military in the June 30th edition of *Stars and Stripes*.

June 15th is the release date of *As Young as You Feel.*

On the 29$^{th}$ Jimmie Fidler makes this astute observation about Marilyn's career in his column. "In reporting that Marilyn Monroe, 20$^{th}$ Century's blonde Lorelei, is to be given the top role in a forthcoming musical, a trade paper columnist took time out to chide studio bosses for being so slow in lifting her to stardom. In my opinion they should be commended, rather than criticized. The Hollywood records prove most conclusively, that the player who serves a lengthy apprenticeship before being elevated to stardom is much more apt to have a solid success than the actor or actress who skyrockets, almost overnight, to topflight position. Check back into the professional histories of Gary Cooper, Joan Crawford, Clark Gable, Claudette Colbert, Betty Grable, Cary Grant, Rosalind Russell, Robert Taylor, Spencer Tracy, Barbara Stanwyck—in short, almost any of the stars who have remained on top for a phenomenally long time—and you will find that they were 'slow starters.' They played a long succession of supporting roles before they were accorded stardom, and in doing so they had time and opportunity to acquire both craftsmanship and a sane perspective. The 'overnighters,' on the other hand, have for the most part gone down the professional skids almost as rapidly as they soared to fame. Offhand, I can think of only four or five who, having won comparatively effortless stardom, have been able to hold it for more than five years. I'll agree with anyone who contends that Miss Monroe, by now an experienced actress as well as an exciting eyeful, is ripe for top roles, but I think her chances of STAYING on top are tremendously enhanced by the tardiness of her bosses in promoting her." The reference to the upcoming musical he was referring to was *Gentlemen Prefer Blondes*.

June comes to an end with the Pacific *Stars and Stripes* newspaper documenting the rivalry between the competing branches of the Armed Forces and Marilyn's affection on June 30th, "Miss Monroe Still 31st's Girl...Beauty Judges of the 31st 'Polar Bear' Regiment are beginning to doubt their choice of feminine pulchritude. They selected beautiful Marilyn Monroe as the 'girl we should most like to get a bear hug from.' she outpointed curvaceous Corinne Calvet and Mitzi Gaynor for the title. The day after the selection, a GI in the regiment received a photograph from a Los Angeles paper covering the return of the USS Manchester from Korean waters. Smack in the middle of the picture was Marilyn Monroe--with three sailors. The trio and Marilyn were engaged in--a bear hug. The beautiful screen star is still number one 'Polar Bear,' but the boys hope she confines her hugging in the future to the regiment and lets the Navy find their own pin-ups."

Lydia Lane features a pin-up picture of Marilyn with her column on July 3rd. "Too Much Sun Gives Skin Leathery Look." The picture is captioned, "Your tan must be kept smooth and feminine with extra lubrication after exposure, says lovely Marilyn Monroe, soon to be seen in 20th Century-Fox's *As Young as You Feel*." This marks the start of a professional friendship that will continue for much of Marilyn's career. It won't be long before Miss Lane will devote entire columns to Marilyn.

This little gem also appeared in newspapers on the 3rd, "Small talk: There are times when a director may be excused for over-looking realism in favor of logic. For instance, one day recently when Marilyn Monroe, clad in the briefest of playsuits, essayed a golfing sequence for *Let's Make it Legal*. 'I'm afraid my swing is so bad it makes me look unbelievable as a golfer,' she apologized. 'Honey,' countered Director Richard Sale, 'if anyone can look at you in that playsuit and still analyze your swing, the picture's a flop anyway.'"

Dorothy Manners reported on July 9th that Marilyn was sick. "Marilyn Monroe can't talk--a fate that should befall no woman. Her vocal cords are badly infected."

Dorothy Kilgallen reported on the 14th that, "Murray Korman, the glamour photog, is on the verge of another waltz up the aisle—this time with Marilyn Monroe." Korman was a renowned glamour photographer from New York. He photographed Broadway stars and debutantes.

On July 15th Marilyn is quoted about her desire to become a good actress, "'A girl can get along for a while just because her contours are in the right pattern,'" observed Miss Monroe. 'It isn't enough, though, for a long term program, especially if you want to pick up a thing or two about emoting.'"

Release date of *Home Town Story* is July 18th.

Jimmy Fiddler devotes his syndicated column to Marilyn on July 19th. "I hesitate to admit it for fear that you kiddies may generate in your disrespectful little minds an idea that I'm in my dotage, but the fact is that I'm even more impressed by Marilyn Monroe's intelligence than I am by her curves. And having made a confession that startling, I'd better lose no time in explaining it. This Monroe chick seems to be one of the very few Hollywood beauties with sufficient I. Q. to realize that 'being glamorous' is part and parcel of being a screen star, and that it imposes an around-the-clock job, just as demanding off-screen as it is on-screen. Keep an eye on her (a mighty pleasant occupation, by the way) and you'll note that she never appears in public, no matter how informal the occasion, without being thoroughly 'prettied up' from the crown of her blonde head to the tip of her carefully decorated toes. Under any set of circumstances that procedure would be good business for a gal who's in the business for a gal who's in the business of selling glamour, but here in Hollywood, with the majority of her rivals vying for the title of 'Miss Sloppy of 1951,' it becomes even better business. It gives her the chance to prove that only one half of a comparison need be odious, to wit, that 'half' which makes it a practice of arrive at the studio, or go shopping at the neighborhood store, in a tee shirt, a pair of none-too-immaculate jeans, and a frowsy, uncombed hair-do. Once I heard a press agent fume because, being assigned the task (?) of escorting Marilyn Monroe to an affair where she was to make a personal appearance, she insisted on stopping, just before reaching their destination, and spending 15 minutes or so in repairing her make-up. Instead of complaining, that press agent should have been busy praising Allah that there still are a few 'glamour girls' smart enough to be glamorous. They're the best sales gals this industry has ever had."

Hedda Hopper reported on the 19th that, "Marilyn Monroe is testing for the dame opposite David Wayne in *Wait Till the Sun Shines Nellie*, which George Jessel will produce. The boys at 20th call her 'Miss Flame Thrower of 1951.'"

Dorothy Kilgallen reports on July 20th, "Eric Von Stroheim's son Joe, a member of the Army's Signal Corps in Astoria, spends his weekend passes with Marilyn Monroe." Eric Von Stroheim was a director in Hollywood's early years and now had won acclaim as an actor. He was nominated for a best supporting actor award for his role as Max von Mayerling in Billy Wilder's *Sunset Boulevard*. Marilyn will work with Josef's brother Eric Von Stroheim, Jr. in *We're Not Married*, where he served as one of the assistant directors.

Armand Archerd reported on August 3rd, "Marines in Korea who have been drooling over pin-ups of Marilyn Monroe wrote to tell her, she's 'the girl we'd most like to wrap our arm-istice around.' Peace, fellas, peace."

On August 4th, Marilyn participated in a Cheesecake celebration that came out of the fertile mind of a publicity agent. As Miss Cheesecake of 1951, Marilyn was selected to cut a slice of cheesecake to celebrate Michael Gaszynski, a former Polish diplomat, who was had passed his final American citizenship examination. James Coop would report that Marilyn sliced the millionth cheesecake served at Michael's Cheesecake Stand at the famed Farmers Market. He also gave this glimpse of Marilyn, "At mid-way point the host introduced the Cheesecake Queen for 1952 (Marilyn Monroe) and there were oh's and ah's and a bit of standing-on-tiptoes as Miss Monroe stepped forward, with a sword, to slice Michael's millionth cheesecake." Also present that day at Michael's Cheesecake Stand in the Los Angeles Farmers Market were actor Edward G. Robinson and future *Time* magazine Hollywood reporter, Ezra Goodman.

Lydia Lane declared in her August 5th column, "All Women Have Beauty Potentialities Declares Movie Director Henry King...I have just been making tests of a little actress named Marilyn Monroe,' he replied, 'now she definitely does not have an old-fashioned figure--she is streamlined...she is slender. BUT...' Mr. King didn't have to state the obvious for at the moment Marilyn Monroe is considered the pin-up sensation of Hollywood...The following question has been asked of the four stars Mr. King named in this interview: 'What is the most valuable beauty secret or glamour trick Hollywood has taught you?' Marilyn replied, 'Hollywood made me voice conscious. When I made my first test I was amazed when I heard myself speak. I felt like running to the nearest voice coach. I started work immediately and have been grateful ever since.'"

Columnist Shelia Graham takes notice of Marilyn. They will develop a friendship and Miss Graham will be one of her greatest allies in her rise to stardom. "Marilyn Monroe, one of the prettiest blonde actresses in Hollywood, lost out to Jean Peters for the Nellie role in *Wait Till the Sun Shines Nellie* with David Wayne, was crowned Miss Cheesecake of 1951 by Count Michael Gaszynski, the Cheesecake king."

Wardrobe test for *Let's Make It Legal* were on August 8th. For the last time, Marilyn was dressed by costume designer, Renie. In this movie, Marilyn plays Joyce Mannering, the gold-digging girlfriend of Hugh, played by MacDonald Carey. The legendary Claudette Colbert and Texan, Zachary Scott also share screen time with Marilyn. Marilyn was reunited with Barbara Bates on this movie. They had first appeared together in *All About Eve*.

MacDonald Carey remembers the young Marilyn on the set. "She has just a few lines and she's late being made up on this particular day. I remember because we're shooting at Hillcrest Country Club, across the street from Twentieth Century-Fox, and I go back to my dressing room at ten o'clock to get something and stop by makeup for a touch-up. A beat-up Jeep is driving me over and back. Well, there is Marilyn being made up and a uniformed chauffeur comes in and says, 'Your car is waiting, Miss Monroe.' He walks out with her and takes her in the limo across the street to Hillcrest; I get in my beat-up Jeep and go back."

Carey also remembered that Marilyn was an hour and a-half late for the Ball Room scene. When she finally showed up, the director Richard Sale, who had previously directed her in *Ticket to Tomahawk*, confronts Marilyn and proceeds to reprimand her. She threatens to make a call to someone and have him fired. He told her that it was fine with him if she wanted to call someone, but first she would apologize to the company for causing delays. She did apologize, and she never made the threatened call. This was out of character for Marilyn. Rarely was she as publicly confrontational as she was remembered to have been in this situation. *Look* magazine photographer Earl Theisen commented to biographer Maurice Zolotow that Marilyn didn't like to be scolded, and being scolded in public was possibly more than she could stand. But after apologizing to the company all was forgiven and she completed the film without further incident.

Yet, Carey will give a quote to a fan magazine about Marilyn that is flattering. "Marilyn Monroe is the sexiest bundle ever to hit the screen. But perhaps the best word to describe her is 'intense.' She not only works hard, but tends to overdo to achieve her purpose. This interest, I think, is commendable, since it is a quality so many of our young players lack. It seems strange to me that many people don't realize how long Marilyn has been struggling for recognition. She's been in this business for five years and has a couple of dropped options to prove it. This is a gal who didn't get by with just her good looks. She has worked hard at becoming a good actress."

Dorothy Manners reported on August 11th, "Marilyn Monroe takes her classy chassis across town from Twentieth to RKO for one of her best and sexiest roles in *Clash by Night*."

Sydney Skolsky takes credit for introducing Jerry Wald to Marilyn. Before meeting her Wald wasn't impressed with her career so far and suspect of why no big studio had picked her up. He changed his tune upon meeting her. "Marilyn wore a pair of checked pedal-pushers that made you wonder how she had squeezed into them; a white blouse with a red rose tucked in where the cleavage begins; a pair of loafers and no stockings. The Monroe had dressed for the role she wanted. She walked across the room with her yet-to-be-famous walk. I introduced her to Wald and left. Later that day Wald phoned me and raved about Marilyn. The part is his picture was hers—if he could borrow her from Twentieth Century-Fox. Marilyn's home studio didn't have a movie for her and was pleased to loan her out for a price. They were frankly puzzled as to why anyone would want to borrow her."

The *Syracuse Herald-Journal* ran this article on the 14th, "Blondes a 'Must' in Hollywood…A sensational blonde is as much a part of every Hollywood studio's equipment as cameras, lights, directors and actors and actresses. There were Carole Lombard and Jean Harlow, who were replaced by Betty Grable, Lana Turner and Corinne Calvet. Now a long shot comes in and threatens to pay off big. She is Marilyn Monroe, a 22 year old beauty who can bring a wolf whistle to the lips of a tailor's dummy. This newest entry has, like Jane Russell, done most of her starring via the still camera." This is an example of the publicity that permeated small town America via local newspapers. It really didn't matter that the article got her biography wrong, what mattered was that the public bought into the fact of Marilyn being America's newest ambassadress of sex. It will become harder and harder for Marilyn to distance herself from her potent sexuality in the coming years, and it becomes the impetus for her deserting Hollywood in 1955. But hindsight is always 20/20 and now she is just glad to be realizing the fruit of all her hard work, so the seeds she will sew with this fruit have no meaning for her now. But she will pay in the future for her complicity in becoming a sexual star, rather than an actress, when the harvest she will reap will not be pleasant for her.

In mid-August 1951 Marilyn served as Hostess, representing the *Los Angeles Daily News*, aboard the U.S.S. Benham destroyer. The movie, *The Frogmen*, starring Richard Widmark, Dana Andrews, Gary Merrill and Jeffrey Hunter, was screened for the men. The USS Benham was docked at Long Beach, CA, before it was reactivated for duty on March 24, 1952. Afterwards, Marilyn sent the men an autographed cheesecake photo taken by the RKO studio publicity photographer Phil Burchman, showing her new short hairdo and posing in a Rose Marie Reid "Cut Diamond Magic" swimsuit. It was signed, "To the men of the USS Benham, Love and Luck--and come see me, Marilyn Monroe."

A newspaper clipping survives of the event from the *Los Angeles Daily News*, no date. "She Plays Hostess For the Ship…Gorgeous Marilyn Monroe will help honor the adopted ship of the *Daily News* tonight aboard the Navy destroyer, the U.S.S. Benham, during the first public showing in the Los Angeles area of *The Frogmen*. The Twentieth Century-Fox film depicts the exploits of the Navy's underwater demolition teams during the recent war and start Richard Widmark."

Roy Craft remembers getting Marilyn to the event, "Once Marilyn was to greet the sailors aboard a cruiser in Long Beach Harbor. For maybe the first time, Craft believed, she'd get there on time. Just before she got there, she asked the driver to stop at a filling station to take a quick look at her makeup. 'She was in the powder room 45 minutes,' said Craft, 'and even the station manager's wife couldn't get her out.'"

In another interview Craft recalled, "Craft told her she was to be there at 2pm, although actually it was for two hours later. She was chronically late for all appointments. 'We had her within 30 minutes of making it, but unhappily for us, the hairdresser and wardrobe women we usually took weren't along. We stopped at a service station so she could check her makeup. An hour passed, and she still was in the ladies room. We were helpless. Finally the service-station operator got his wife to go in. Marilyn was just looking into the mirror. It was like she was hypnotized, just staring at herself in the mirror. It was like time stood still for her.' It didn't matter. Marilyn Monroe had the ability to enchant the men around her. 'When we showed up on that cruise ship, the officers were hopping mad. Two minutes later she had them in her pocket."

On the 15th of August, Edwin Schallert reported that the part of the young romantic interests in *Clash by Night*, Marilyn, had been submitted to Fox for approval. Charlton Heston was first considered for the part that will eventually go to Keith Andes.

Sheilah Graham, on the 18th, reported that it didn't take Fox long to agree to loan Marilyn out, "Marilyn Monroe, the blonde beauty at 20th Fox, plays the ingénue in *Clash by Night* at RKO. Marilyn's career is now in high gear." Graham would say of the young Monroe, "I regarded her as a nice girl, caught in the Hollywood jungle. I must confess I didn't think she had much chance of breaking out of the overgrown forest into the bright sunlight of stardom."

Marilyn made a trip to New York in August to see *Gentlemen Prefer Blondes*. It was in the final week of its 4 week run at the Ziegfeld Theater. Betty Grable, who had been on suspension since May, was Fox's top choice for the role of Lorelei Lee in *Blondes*. This was Twentieth Century-Fox's way of trying to provoke her into coming back. Fox would employ these same tactics with Sheree North, when Marilyn was on suspension from *Pink Tights* in 1954 and throughout her self-imposed exile in 1955. It didn't work with Betty Grable and it wouldn't work with Marilyn.

Dorothy Manners reported on August 20th, "If Twentieth isn't hot in the bidding for *Gentlemen Prefer Blondes*--how come luscious blonde Marilyn Monroe is being sent to New York to see the way Carol Channing plays the dauntless dumbbell? Yes, before Marilyn reports to RKO for *Clash by Night* she makes a special trip to the big town to see the Anita Loos/Joe Fields hit in action. Physically, Marilyn fills the bill--but whether she is experienced enough to take on a top comedy performance remains to be seen."

The trip most likely occurred from shortly before or on the 20th and lasted several days, possibly until the 25th. Marilyn mentions meeting Marlon Brando at the Actors Studio and how it was raining. The only rain during these days occurred on the afternoon of August 21st. And Marilyn is reported in the gossip columns on the 26th as having been at the El Morroco nightclub.

A *NANA* Wire Service story on January 13, 1952 referenced Marilyn's trip to New York. "An undercover tussle is going on between Betty Grable and Marilyn Monroe--for the starring role in *Gentlemen Prefer Blondes*. Marilyn was promised the part, and sent to New York recently to see the play, but Betty wants it."

In his syndicated column on September 10, 1952, Leonard Lyons also mentions this trip to New York. "Marilyn Monroe was unable to see Joe DiMaggio at the Stadium last week because of her commitment to be in Atlantic City for the Pageant. Only a year ago, when Miss Monroe came to New York, she was so little known that the only publicity photos anyone wanted of her were taken at a beach club in the Bronx."

And finally, Earl Wilson reported on this photo session taken during her trip to New York in August of 1951 in his column on May 20, 1953, "Three years ago, Marilyn, not yet famous, posed for color pictures in the Bronx. One, in pink, almost flesh-colored, was sensational--but Bill White of the *N.Y. Daily News* killed it--'cause she looked almost nude."

Marilyn became attached to the Shorehaven Beach Club in the Bronx, and press agent Spencer Hare in particular, during her 1949 visit to New York.

This is the last time Marilyn will be in New York and enjoy some anonymity. The next time she is in New York in 1952 she is a full-fledged movie star and her popularity will make it near to impossible for her to walk the streets of New York, especially since she will be romantically attached to famed New Yorker Joe DiMaggio. After she moves there in 1955 she starts to don disguises in order to not be recognized.

There is a photo of Marilyn, taken during this time standing in front of the Sherry Netherland Hotel in Manhattan. She stayed in this same hotel during her *Love Happy* tour in 1949. While staying at the Sherry Netherland Marilyn became acquainted with pianist Dilson Petrey who played at the cafe bar in the Hotel. When he came to Hollywood in 1954 Marilyn went to hear him play.

During her trip Marilyn reunites with photographer Sam Shaw who escorts her around town. Shaw takes her to the Actors Studio and she meets its new director, Lee Strasberg. Marilyn had to be excited to have met one of the movers and shakers of the New York acting world. They had a mutual friend in Elia Kazan, who was also there that day, so she must have been familiar with Strasberg and his work at the Actors Studio. Elia Kazan re-introduces her to Marlon Brando. When Marilyn met Brando on the set of *Desiree* in October of 1954, he reminded her of this meeting. She replied, "I could never forget. It was raining so hard." While they had met on the set of *Viva Zapata*, they obviously didn't click. Now it was different, without the distractions of chasing their respective paramours, they became aware of the other. Along with her secret love for Arthur Miller, meeting Strasberg gave Marilyn another reason to set her sights on returning to New York. She would tell Strasberg's wife and daughter, when she met them on the set of *There's No Business Like Show Business* in 1954, that she was coming back east to study with him. Much to everyone's surprise, the next year she did just that.

Shaw, knowing her love of poetry, took her to Brooklyn and showed her where poet Walt Whitman lived and the places he frequented. At the same time thoughts of Arthur Miller must have raced through her mind when she toured Brooklyn, as this was his home. The very idea of seeing for herself places where he was a familiar figure made the idea of someday reuniting with him a sweeter dream and more of a reality.

During her trip to New York she also met with Joe DiMaggio, according to his attorney Morris Engelberg. "This is the one that DiMaggio told me, Joe Nachio, and his own son, at different times. It's the one I have regarded as the true one, because I never knew DiMaggio to lie to me in all our years together. Joe said he was at Roosevelt Raceway, a harness-racing track on Long Island, with Edward Bennett Williams, the Washington attorney and close friend. Joe must have been out only for an evening of dinner and conversation, because he never bet on a harness race (He was the most suspicious man I ever knew and harness racing was constantly under suspicion.) Not interested in the trotters and pacers pulling men in the sulkies, DiMaggio scanned the crowd in the dining room and his gaze stopped at, in his words, 'this beautiful blonde with big eyes and big bosoms.' He wondered who she was, and Williams told him. DiMaggio remembered seeing her in the photo with Zernail, and she looked even better in person. Williams introduced them, at DiMaggio's request, and he invited Marilyn to join him and Joe for dinner at Toots Shor's the following evening. The setting, where Joe felt most at home, was important, as was Williams' presence, because DiMaggio was often ill at ease in a one-on-one dinner conversation with someone he did not know—even at that stage of his life, as a mature, retired baseball star. The first date went well, because there were others…" The version by Joe himself is curious because in it there are reference's to Marilyn's trip to New York in the fall of 1951, and Marilyn's appearance in a photo with Gus Zernail in March of 1951.

Lilla Anderson wrote about Marilyn's trip to New York which included a comment about Marilyn meeting with DiMaggio while in New York. "Learning, in 1951, that *Gentlemen Prefer Blondes*, was to be made into a picture, she set her heart on the lead and gambled more than she could afford to go to New York to study the stage play. The trip was far from a red-carpet tour. Although, she had already appeared in a string of pictures as long as your arm, she passed unnoticed on the streets. Noon asked for her autograph, she ate in a cafeteria and, as she recently confessed, she was a long time paying her hotel bill…The private life importance of that New York trip before she was cast in *Gentlemen Prefer Blondes* centered around Joe DiMaggio. Marilyn had met the Yankee Clipper in Hollywood and, since business had taken him to Manhattan, they met again and Marilyn went home feeling sure he was the most fascinating man she had ever known."

On the August the 26th, columnist Jack Lait reports in Walter Winchell's column that he saw Marilyn at the El Morocco in Manhattan. The El Morocco was a Manhattan nightclub. A photo survives of this evening showing Marilyn with Pat Di Cicco sitting in the El Morocco's famous zebra striped booth. Another photo taken that night shows Marilyn with Joseph Schenck at the El Morocco. Schenck and Di Cicco were old cronies. One can imagine the amount of bile Marilyn had to choke down at having to "play nice" to these men. But her time was coming. It would not be long before the fates smiled down on her and she herself would be a name to be reckoned with.

# Chapter Eleven
## Heavenly Body

"The publicity department was already on the ball. The magazines seemed to be celebrating a perpetual Marilyn Monroe week. My picture was on nearly all their covers. People began to treat me differently. I was no longer a freak, a sort of stray ornament, like some stray cat, to invite in and forget about."
Marilyn Monroe

In his syndicated column, August 21, 1951, Jimmie Fidler reports on Marilyn's growing fame and reduces her growing popularity to cosmetic changes in two of her features. "If you're a regular reader of the many publications which devote space to Hollywood's stars, you must be aware of a gal named Marilyn Monroe, who in the past year--six months would be more accurate--has suddenly skyrocketed to fame as the most sexational young beauty of the day. Having seen Miss Monroe both off-screen and on-screen, I'm certainly not going to argue about the rating. She's got 'IT,' to use an expression dear to the late Elinor Glynn, and the 'IT' is in capital letters. The thing that would make her 'IT' even more impressive to the average woman would be a comparison between photographs of her, shot when she was just another would-be glamour star, and the photographs taken of her today. The features are the same, but the total effect is amazingly different, thanks to just two details--changes in her hairline and in the shape of her eyebrows. Those two changes made a new person of Marilyn Monroe, and may be principally responsible for her sudden success."

Philip K. Scheuer, reported on August 22nd that Wald and Krasna, of RKO, brokered a deal with Darryl Zanuck to borrow Marilyn for Clifford Odets, *Clash by Night*. This was to be her first dramatic role and the second feminine lead after Barbara Stanwyck.

Marilyn will be loaned-out to RKO for a term of ten weeks for a compensation of $1,000 per week. This is twice her usual salary. She is to have co-star billing, which was very unusual given her current ranking as a starlet, and would henceforth establish her as a major star in her own right. The starting date was September 24, 1951. Marilyn has finally made good the promise to herself concerning RKO while in the orphanage, "someday I'll be a star there."

Dorothy Kilgallen reported on August 29th, "Pat de Cicco is all thrilled about Marilyn Monroe, the starlet. Gents who've seen her full page, full color picture in the current issue of a men's magazine will know what he means."

In the fall of 1951 fellow actor Jack Palance introduced Marilyn to acting teacher Michael Chekhov and she begins to study with him. Michael Chekhov and his wife Xenia had actually seen Marilyn perform when on their anniversary in 1948 they saw *Ladies of the Chorus*.

Marilyn had benefited from the acting lessons that she had taken at the Actors Laboratory with Morris Carnovsky and his wife Phoebe Brand, and those with Natasha Lytess. With Carnovsky and Brand, Marilyn had the technique through "the Method," but no teacher with whom she could attach herself or who saw any potential in her. With Lytess, Marilyn certainly had become the focus of her teacher, but Max Reinhardt's broad philosophy of total artwork was a poor substitute for Stanislavski's focus on the actor. Marilyn was still seeking someone who would again connect her with "the Method." In Chekhov she found a perfect mixture of teacher and technique that she could give her devotion to. He brought with him the history and tradition of the Russian theater, by way of his Uncle, dramatist Anton Chekhov, and the Moscow Art Theater, and she became his most devoted disciple.  Marilyn said of him, "I learned more than acting. I learned psychology, history and the good manners of art--taste."

In 1953 she would tell Sheilah Graham this about Mr. Chekhov, "Chekhov is a great artist, a wonderful director and the nephew of the great Anton Chekhov. He's also a great human being, warm and sincere. He's interesting and fascinating to talk to. I've known him for a year and attended some of his classes. He's most concerned with the young generation of actors. He's written a book, *To The Actor*. He gives the impression he's lived through everything." Marilyn was deeply devoted to the idea of being an actress. Sidney Skolsky tells that she often quoted this line from *All About Eve*. "Once in a while somebody writes an article saying that actors and actresses are just like other people. We're not. It's because we're not that we're actors and actresses.'" Even though Marilyn wasn't in this scene, she identified with the idea that she belonged to this peculiar group of men and women who devoted themselves to the art of acting.

Michael Chekov published *On the Technique of Acting* in 1942. In 1953 he would publish an abridged version and title it, *To the Actor*. Yul Brynner wrote the preface to the book. Each book gave a detailed description of his acting technique. He would go on to record an audio version of *To the Actor* as well.

Marilyn would go to the Chekhov's Reseda, Calif., bungalow for acting lessons where he turned his bay window, in the east wall of his living room, into a makeshift stage by building a riser into the space and adding curtains he could open and close.  There his students would perform their scenes and receive critique from him. Marilyn was a frequent house guest as her fame grew. She studied with Chekhov until she moved to New York in December of 1954. After Chekhov's death in September of 1955 Marilyn remained close to his wife, Xenia, until her death in 1962, even naming her as a beneficiary in her will.

 Joan Caulfield, also a student of Chekhov's remembers some of his instruction. "Chekhov would say, 'Don't act a street.' This meant that the actor should give the audience credit for finding its own way in the development of a plot. He termed this "directed invitation." The actor should only indicate. He should feel 100%, but show only 10%. If he does this well enough, the spectator will do the rest. Chekhov is a sort of actor's psychologist. There isn't a problem, even remotely concerned with acting that he doesn't have an explanation for and a solution to."

Roy Craft, in an interview with Bill Tusher, recalls Marilyn's skill in discussing the philosophy of Stanislavski. "A typical example of how well the unpredictable Monroe handles herself was when Craft set up an ad lib tape recording with a radio commentator in the office of her drama coach, Natasha Lytess. It was a no-holds-barred interview, and the first thing the radio man did was hit her with a question about the famed Russian acting authority, Stanislavski, whom many regard as a deity in the field of drama. If the interviewer expected to stump Marilyn, he was caught with his encyclopedias down. She held forth for about 12 minutes running on the subject of the Stanislavski acting theories and told convincingly why she agreed or disagreed with him in various instances. Several friends were visiting Craft at his home two days later when the interview was put on the air. One of them yawned, 'Oh that dumb blonde! What press agent wrote that for her?' Roy's retort was a classic, if unduly rough on his own profession. 'Who ever heard of a press agent who even heard of Stanislavski?'"

Craft would go on to say in a later interview on Marilyn capabilities when confronted by the press, "She was smart, very smart, not the dumb blonde some of these New York intellectuals thought she was."

Michael Chekhov taught his own brand of Stanislavski, but with a slightly spiritual spin, due to the influences of Rudolf Steiner. Steiner originated a new spiritual tradition called Anthroposophy. He taught that, "Anthroposophy is a path of knowledge, to guide the spiritual in the human being to the spiritual in the universe. It arises in people as a need of the heart and feeling life. Anthroposophy can be justified only to the degree that it satisfies this inner need. It may be acknowledged only by those who find within it what they themselves feel the need to seek. Therefore, Anthroposophist's are those who experience, as an essential need of life, certain questions on the nature of the human being and the universe, just as one experiences hunger and thirst."

Marilyn fell head-over-heels for Steiner's philosophy and she would indulge in reading Steiner's works for the rest of her life. Chekhov blended anthroposophicaly and the dramatic arts when he talked of "opening and closing the self," "commanding the space," "imaginative flexibility," and "the psychological gesture." Marilyn learned exercises to use her body as a tool to fully reveal the character in a scene.

She was to inhabit the space by techniques such as "psychological gestures" which would reveal the essence of her character by even the smallest of mannerisms. If it is the measure of a good actor to fill the space in a scene, then she was truly improving. Between *Clash by Night* and *Niagara*, Marilyn had learned this lesson well. Every film she made from then on was under the domination of her luminous image. She will inhabit a frame of film like few actors ever have. Most actors would be satisfied with this ability, but Marilyn wanted more than to just fill up the frame, she wanted to continue to reveal her characters more thoroughly through her skills as an actress.

Recommended readings by Michael Chekhov were the works of Rudolf Steiner and Mabel Elsworth Todd's book, *The Thinking Body*. Miss Todd developed her theory of Ideokinesis during the early 1900's when physical exercise and dance had become very popular. Her ideas gained a widespread following during the 1930s among dancers and health enthusiast. After injuring her back in a fall, she regained strength and improved her ability to walk using specific aspects of anatomy and kinesiology. Miss Todd urged the combination of body alignment coupled with mechanical principles that she felt were the basis for physical as well as spiritual health. She touted Ideokinesis as a mixture of the physical mechanics of body movement and the subsequent psychological effects, tapping into the subtly influence of conscious intention and attention. She insisted that you could retrain your body using not only physical movement, but using your senses and your mind you could unconsciously alter your body as well. Miss Todd relocated to California in the early 1950's and lived her until her death in 1953. One likes to imagine a meeting of teacher and pupil taking place, but no evidence exist to suggest that it happened. Marilyn studied this abstruse volume for the rest of her life. She also credits her unique walk to applying the esoteric philosophy of this book. Miss Todd compared the pelvis to a short cantilever bridge and in one of her famous illustrations termed it, "the walking bridge." Marilyn learned that the psoas muscles control the pelvic girdle and in turn, walking. The pendulum motion of the psoas muscle gives the free leg its swing. Marilyn discovered that walking is composed of a falling and catching motion that eventually matures into an asymmetrical pendulum rhythm. The pendulum motion of the psoas must move separately from the pelvis, and only when the leg is articulated at the ball and socket is it free to move separately from the pelvis. This is vital to hip socket mobility and freedom of stride. Miss Todd declared that the thigh joints are the "hub of the universe" when it comes to walking. Marilyn practiced freeing her body so that she might emulate the pendulum action that natural, unrestricted walking should have. Miss Todd quoted a mechanical engineer about the technical aspects of walking. The terms he used to describe the mechanics of walking seem to fit Marilyn's famous walk. He said that walking was, "a combination of undulatory motions in three dimensions, the result of which described a spiral like that followed by a point on the helix of a screw-conveyor." Miss Todd commented that, "this resultant spiral movement is brought about by the tipping and tilting of the pelvis from side to side and from back to front as it rotates alternately on each femoral head." She tried out her new walk on Charlie Chaplin, Jr., and he declared it titillating. By the time she made *Niagara*, the whole world would find her walk titillating.

Miss Todd's book declared that the body was organic, in that it should be in balance with its environment. Human physiology and human psychology complement each other. Marilyn was photographed reading Miss Todd's book during this period of her life. She will go on to use the phrase, "organic," when describing why she doesn't like to wear underwear, as it leaves lines in her clothing that she feels are not "organic." Marilyn starts to take dance lessons at the Dance Center in order to further learn to free her body.

Chekhov would be the first to actually draw a conclusion to Marilyn's trouble being taken seriously at the studio. Zolotow writes of this moment, "Once they were doing a scene from *The Cherry Orchard*. When they finished, he asked her if she had been deliberately projecting sexuality. She said no because she knew sex was not called for in the scene. Chekhov laughed uproariously, slapped his thigh, pounded on the floor. He suddenly understood her problem. No matter how she tried to play a scene she could not help emanating powerful animal vibrations. Just now, the air had been filled with them. 'The whole world is already responding to your vibrations, Marilyn,' he said. 'What do the owners of the studio care if you're an actress or if you're not an actress? With your vibrations, you only have to stand in front of the camera and you're vibrating, and for them you make a million dollars.' 'I don't want that,' she said grimly. 'I want to be an artist, not a freak.'

In a later interview Marilyn aptly expressed her desire to become an accomplished actress, "I want to be an artist, not an erotic freak. I don't want to be sold to the public as a celluloid aphrodisiac. It was all right for the first few years. But now it's different."

Jean Negulesco, who directed her in *How to Marry a Millionaire*, also commented on her unconscious sexual vibrations. "I say to her that no matter what you do in a picture, if you pick up a glass of water and drink it, right away it's censorable. You cannot help being the essence of sex. To the whole world you stand for sex. So you don't have to sell this goddamn sex all the time."

Photographer Bob Willoughby commented on Marilyn when he photographed her in 1952. "Marilyn had some sort of energy field that it would seem she could switch on and off when she posed, which I don't think I will ever see again. Hollywood's publicity departments called it sex appeal and thought it was achieved by showing cleavage, but they missed the point. This attractive energy is something you are born with. It is there to see at any age. Some people have more, some less…"

Ralph Roberts, her friend and masseur remembers that the first time he met Marilyn, in the kitchen of the Strasberg's New York apartment in 1955; she radiated a "blue-whiteness" that permeated every inch of their kitchen. Her white hair, coupled with her pale skin and violet-blue eyes combined to make her radiantly beautiful, yet his experience went deeper than just the physical. Marilyn's aura of energy was, in the true sense of the word, spell binding.

Writer Saul Bellow said of Marilyn, "She was connected with a very powerful current but she couldn't disconnect herself from it. She had a kind of curious incandescence under the skin."

Yul Brenner discussed with Arlene Dahl the special quality that Marilyn had. "There is an 'aura' about some women, he contended, which is more spiritual than physical. These women have a way of lighting up a room as they walk into it."

In the tradition of Kundalini Yoga the seven Chakras of the body are vortexes of energy. The Kundalini is presented as a small white snake coiled around a phallus at the base of the spine. The coiled snake is a feminine symbol and she controls the male. It is only when she uncoils herself that the energy is released. It is believed that it is possible that the sexual energies can be directed up to the crown Chakra as the Kundalini energy is activated during sexual arousal. It seems that Marilyn was a rare person who had perfected the activation of her libido in such a way that it sent out waves of arousal to those around her. It wasn't a deliberate action on her part, but something that had been brought about as a result of those long silent days of her girlhood. She had a rich inner landscape, even by her own admission, as a girl. She told about dreaming in colors, which works in perfectly with the idea of Kundalini Yoga. It took a small leap of consciousness to release her reservoirs of energy, and since she used her sexuality to pry open the gates of the studios, that is the energy that was emanating from her. She was like the beautiful Lotus that grows from muddy roots. This is but one explanation to try and clarify the power of her enchantment.

September 1951 marks the start of Marilyn's domination of the magazine trade. If she is learning to fill a frame of moving film, she has already mastered filling the lens of the camera. She appears in two magazines in the fall and eleven in September of 1951, including three covers.

*Modern Screen*, September 1951, "Who'd Marry Me?" by Marilyn. In the article she gives a rare insight into her early modeling career, and how her nervousness sometimes created trouble for her. "I remember modeling once at Bullocks big store. My job was to pull down little roller signs. Painted on them were illustrations of the wardrobe accessories a designer was discussing for some buyers. 'Now here is a very versatile scarf that can be made to do for almost any occasion,' the designer would say, and I would pull down an illustration of a leather belt!"

There is another article in this issue of *Modern Screen* featuring Marilyn and three companions, Craig Hill, Nick Savano and Mala Powers, called "We Swam Our Way to Ciro's." It also featured the owner of Ciro's, Herman Hover. Nick Savano, who was Frank Sinatra's on-again, off-again manager, recalled the day, "The young lady was in her bathing suit, but she was all coiffed. Herman said, 'Grab her and pull her into the pool.' The photographer got a shot of me pulling. Oh, she got dunked! She looked great, wet, by the way.'" Her getting wet was not featured in the magazine, but what both articles featured was Marilyn in a gorgeous strapless Rose Marie Reed swimsuit made of 24 karat gold elasticisedone-piece shirred jersey swimsuit over-printed with a black Chantilly lace pattern. The suit has a boned separate nylon inner bra. This swimsuit is often mistaken for the one she wore in *Let's Make it Legal* by Renie.

*People Today* magazine centerfold, "Another Big Answer to TV" The photo is captioned, "Straining every muscle to match TV's big guns in the battle of the cleavages. Hollywood thrust a new salient into the front by bringing up a fresh secret weapon -- Marilyn Monroe, 20th Century Fox starlet. Marilyn joined the fray when she was crowned "Cheesecake Queen" at a big filmdom shindig. Between Denise Darcel and Marilyn, TV must watch, lest its forward position be flanked."

Sheilah Graham sent out a blurb in her column on September 4th than was intended to lure the straying Miss Grable back into the studio. "Marilyn Monroe will star in *Gentlemen Prefer Blondes* when her studio, Twentieth Century-Fox makes the picture. The famous Anita Loos classic of the twenties gets a complete rewrite for Marilyn, the most beautiful blonde to hit pictures since Madeline Carroll." *The Los Angeles Times* will also state that Marilyn should be cast in *Gentlemen Prefer Blondes* on the 9th.

On September 8th, Marilyn had an important appearance in an article in *Colliers,* "Hollywood's 1951 Model Blonde," by Robert Cahn. "She's filmdom's Marilyn Monroe, Miss Cheesecake to GIs, whistlebait in the studios--and an actress on her way up...Marilyn Monroe is not a girl anyone quickly forgets." A beautiful photograph by John Florea accompanies the article. It was taken on March 29th of this year, while Marilyn participated in the 23rd Academy Awards. This was Marilyn's first feature article by a prominent national magazine. Harry Brand, head of Fox Publicity, said that that time, "She is the biggest thing we've had at the studio since Shirley Temple and Betty Grable."

Mr. Cahn mentions a few gems hidden in the text. One being, Marilyn had been introduced to William Saroyan, Irving Berlin and California Governor Earl Warren. When Marilyn is making *The Misfits* in 1960, now Chief Justice Warren will go out of his way to stop by the set in Reno while he is on a hunting trip, to see Marilyn. Chief Justice Warren will take a front row seat at the investigation of the assassination of Pres. John Kennedy as head of the committee investigating his death. It would be known as the Warren Commission. In a less infamous vein, Cahn gives a list of some of the books on her bookshelves, Albert Schweitzer, Leo Tolstoy, Ralph Waldo Emerson, Walt Whitman, Arthur Miller, Ranier Maria Rilke, John Milton and Lincoln Steffens.

Roy Craft tells of Marilyn landing the story in *Collier's*. "Having learned of her background, it took no genius to recognize the perfect Cinderella, or Ugly Duckling, story—the unattractive, unwanted child blossoming into spectacular womanhood. When I told her that *Collier's* magazine wanted to do a full-scale text piece on her, a probing story of her life, she was distressed. 'What would you do,' she asked, 'if your mother was crazy and you never knew who your father was?' I assured her that neither mental illness or illegitimacy would reflect on her and that the press people would treat the matter with compassion and delicacy. Most of them did. The *Collier's* article ran and 'fan' magazines began to take an interest in her. Finally the columnists recognized her presence on the Hollywood scene. I like to think her buildup was the reverse of the norm—first the big magazine stories, then the movie books and finally the columnists, instead of the other way around."

In another interview Craft recalls the *Collier's* experience, "For quite some time, Roy Craft managed to have details of Marilyn Monroe's past glossed over in stories about her. There was her first 'in-depth' interview, with the now defunct *Collier's* magazine. 'She asked me, 'What would you tell them, if your mother was crazy and you never knew who your father was?' I said, 'We'll have to tell them the truth and ask them not to make a big deal of it, just to say that your mother is an invalid and your father died before you were born, that sort of thing.' And that's the way the story was used.' It wasn't a cover-up, Craft says. Times were different then. The reporters liked Marilyn. 'You could talk to them,' he says. 'They didn't find it necessary to point all that out.' It wasn't until much later that the truth about her background finally was printed."

Marilyn may have been the biggest thing that 20th-Century Fox had at the studio, but Marilyn's troubled financial standing is revealed in this series of checks. She wrote a check to the Beverly Carlton Hotel Company on September 10th for the amount of $317.08. She listed her actual address, 9414 W. Olympia Blvd., and her phone number as Cr55221. The next day she visited Schwab's Drugstore where she made a purchase for the amount of $30.00. Her address was given as 611 Crescent Drive in Beverly Hills. On September 15th Marilyn was charged $2.00 for two unpaid returned checks. The amount of the checks was $30.00 and $25.00. Marilyn wrote a check to Thrifty Mart on September 17th for the amount of $10.00. Marilyn wrote a check to J. J. Haggarty Stores, Inc., on September 18th, for the amount of $15.00, 611 N. Cresent Dr., and her phone number as Cr55221. Marilyn's bank statement from The Bank of America on September 22nd reveals a starting balance of

$305.52 on August 25, and an ending balance of $9.58 on September 22nd. It would take more time for her financial success to catch up with her growing fame. Marilyn seemed unconcerned about her lack of funds in her checking account. She was charged $2.00 for two unpaid returned checks on September 26th, each in the amount of $100.00. She also wrote a check to the Satyr Bookshop on September 28th for the amount of $1.30. She noted her address as 1309 N. Harper Ave.

*Clash By Night* goes into production on September 24th, and will be shot on location in Monterey, California.

Marilyn has her hair cropped before filming in a "Poodle Cut". The style frames her face in an ethereal halo of curls like a Botticelli angel. Thanks to Johnny Hyde she is, as Norman Mailer stressed, "without any fundamental flaw of feature." The studio estheticians have worked their peculiar brand of magic highlighting and shading the planes of her face. Her look is so unique that it will never appear again on any other woman without reference to her. She is "the Blonde," and all others will pay homage to her. Marilyn's palette of blonde hair, alabaster skin, dreamy blue eyes and red lips begin and end with her. She has become the reference point to which all blonde beauty will be matched. Marilyn Monroe is about to enter the public conscious as the most exciting personality Hollywood had ever produced and she will retain her hold as the Blonde of American myth 50 years after her death.

Louella Parsons daughter Harriet was producing *Clash by Night*. She had arranged to borrow Marilyn from Fox. She will tell her mother this about Marilyn, "She's bringing thick philosophy books on the stage with her and spends all her spare time reading them. I thought it was a pose until I talked with her. I'm not sure how much she's getting out of those books, but she takes them deathly seriously. And I thought she was just another sexy blonde."

Marilyn played Peggy, a sexy cannery worker who's in love with Joe Doyle, played by Keith Andes. Marilyn gives one of the most natural performances of her career. Her look in the film was a cooperative effort between costume designer Michael Woulfe, make-up artist Mel Barnes and hair stylist Larry Germaine.

Jane Russell recalls meeting Marilyn for the first time during filming, although, they had both actually participated in the Celebrity Baseball World Series in Chicago in 1949. Jane was driving on the RKO lot and Costume Designer Michael Woulfe was with Marilyn. Jane gave them a lift. Jane says when Marilyn "got into the car I realized she wasn't fifteen, she just looked it…I was aware of a natural curiosity in the way she looked at me. She has a soft little voice that sounds kind of shy." Before this, Jane remembers seeing Marilyn at a Hollywood party dancing with Nick Ray, but she had never actually met her until now.

Marilyn will immerse herself in the culture of the fishing village, so much so that columnist Bob Thomas will report on October 15th, "Marilyn is constantly amazing her employers. *Clash by Night* has a fishing village background. In order to absorb the realism, Marilyn rode all night on a bus to Monterey, some 300 miles from Hollywood. She spent a day talking to boat owners and cannery workers and returned home that night. She also amazed her co-workers when she virtually adopted a soldier when the company went to Monterey for location shots. 'I was walking down the street when this soldier looked at me and gasped,' she explained. 'I could tell he was lonely, so I invited him to come and watch us work. He showed up every day and we had long talks about his home town. Some were worried that the soldier might try something, but I could tell by the look in his eye that he just wanted somebody to talk to.' I suggested that she must be fairly accustomed to the gaze of men. 'Men,' she replied in the understatement of the week, 'are friendly.' Marilyn doesn't place her career above marriage, but she hinted that it would be a long time before she married again. (She was wed briefly as a teen-ager.) She declared that she doesn't have much hope of finding a husband in Hollywood, since the pickings are slim here. 'That's one of the reasons I would like to travel,' she added."

The soldier was Pfc. Emmet King. He was to write to Marilyn begging her to confirm his visit with her, and it would be published on June 22, 1952 in the *Baltimore Sun*. "The boys in my outfit simply won't believe it. You can make a hero or a bum out of me." Marilyn confirmed that she took him on a personally conducted tour of the movie location, thereby making him a hero to his fellow GIs.

Marilyn writes in a journal of her trip from Monterey to Salinas on the bus. She first rode with a bus full of Greek fisherman. She was enchanted with them. The bus became crowded with people and she slept in a seat next to a Filipino boy. She commented how sad the sailors on the bus looked.

Marilyn tells Hedda Hopper of her bus trip. "It wasn't exactly luxurious and I had trouble getting any sleep—it was a night run—but it was a chance to get close to humanity, something no actress should ever miss. I didn't use any makeup and I wore a shabby old camel hair coat and tied a babushka around my head. Nobody recognized me. It was quiet a trip, people mostly stare straight ahead or go to sleep on a night trip."

Marilyn was using everything she had learned of the Stanislavsky method of acting to impart realism into her character. She would even use her past work on an assembly line at Radioplane to help her connect with the woman she was playing. "I never forget what it was like to be one of those women."

Marilyn was made "Honorary Shop Steward" by the Fish Cannery Workers Union for her role as a fish cutter. Despite her earnestness in crafting her character for the role, during the filming she was plagued by nerves which manifested themselves as stuttering, rashes and the inability to memorize her lines on cue. On her first day of filming with Barbara Stanwyck, Marilyn was 2 hours late. When she finally arrived, she blew her lines 26 times. By all accounts this kind of behavior drove director Fritz Lang almost to madness. Lang had these memories of working with Marilyn. "It was not easy to work with Marilyn Monroe. She was a very peculiar mixture of shyness and uncertainty and –I wouldn't say 'star allure'—but let me say, she knew exactly her impact on men…Now, just at that time, the famous calendar story came up. I don't mind—what a woman does with herself is nobody's business—but the thing was, because of her shyness, she was scared as hell to come in the studio—she was always late, I don't know why she couldn't remember her lines…but she was very responsive."

Another problem that occurred was the amount of publicity directed at Marilyn instead of the stars of the film, Barbara Stanwyck and Paul Douglas. Douglas became enraged, but Barbara Stanwyck took it in stride. While watching the photographers crowding around Marilyn, a member of the crew asked Miss Stanwyck, "What do you think of her as an actress, Queenie?" To which she replied, "With a figure like that, you don't have to act!"

Yet, Barbara Stanwyck remembers the young Marilyn, "She was awkward. She couldn't get out of her own way. She wasn't disciplined and she was often late, and she drove Bob Ryan, Paul Douglas and myself out of our minds…but she didn't do it viciously, and there was sort of a magic about her which we all recognized at once. Her phobias, or whatever they were, came later, she seemed just a carefree kid, and she owned the world."

According to columnist Jimmie Fidler, "During the production of *Clash By Night*, the producers decided that they'd like to give Miss Monroe co-star billing, they had to ask the approval of Barbara Stanwyck, Paul Douglas and Robert Ryan, who contracts stipulated that they--and only they--would be credited as the picture's stars. Miss Stanwyck's answer was a prompt 'okay;' moreover, she personally called Ryan and Douglas and obtained their consent. Had Barbara Stanwyck said 'no,' she could have delayed Marilyn Monroe's elevation to stardom by nearly a year."

Two events occurred to Marilyn while working on *Clash by Night* that changed the course of her career. The first is she would be given star billing for the first time, thus speeding up the process of her becoming a star. The next thing that happened involved the nude images she had posed for in May of 1949. John Baumgarth didn't know what a good thing he had until Marilyn starred in the film *Clash by Night*. Baumgarth had printed a few of the calendars in 1951 to dismal results and he had even forgotten the model's name. His secretary brought it to his attention when she shoved a calendar in his face and asked if he knew who the model was. She told him it was Marilyn Monroe. To which he replied, "You're crazy." When he came out of shock, he locked the original in a vault and promptly stepped up production. The picture, perhaps prophetically, was entitled 'Golden Dreams.'

James Bacon recalls, "I knew about the calendar about a year or more before the story broke. I never ran the story. All the men columnists protected Marilyn…I was glad I didn't do it, but the story got a big play."

Natalie Kelley gives the story on how the calendar burst upon the scene. "Marilyn came by one afternoon and asked to see the calendar. She's never seen the photos she posed for. When I showed it to her she wasn't shocked or anything. Just looked at it as though she were looking at a stranger. She studied it carefully. 'Very good,' she said. 'A very good pose.' She was proud of it. She was working in *Clash by Night* at the time and phoned us from the set the next day to ask if she could have 25 calendars. We got them for her through the lithograph company. All I know is that as soon as Marilyn received those 25 copies she blithely passed them to some friends on the set, including a few photographers and newsmen. Dumb? I should say not. That girl knew her stuff. After that, all hell broke loose! Some of the 'friends' showed the calendar around, the papers picked up the story and Marilyn became the most talked about girl in Hollywood." Close friend, Mary (Karger) Short, whom Marilyn nicknamed "Buddynuts," was one of the people Marilyn will autograph her nude calendar to. "To My Buddy Mary; Love and Affection; Marilyn Monroe." The calendar top was Western Lithograph's "A New Wrinkle." Marilyn also autographed a copy of her calendar for columnist Earl Wilson. She wrote, "How do you like my new hairdo?"

When filming was completed, Marilyn gave Barbara Stanwyck, Paul Douglas, Robert Ryan and Keith Andes each a box of chocolates. Robert Ryan remembers, "She was a confused little thing even then. I did something for her one day and she sent me a five-pound box of candy. What a little girl thing to do! She was not equipped for all the cross-currents of Hollywood…She just could not cope with all the pressures."

Marilyn appeared in an article in *Pic* magazine's October edition. She wears a Jantzen swimsuit she will wear in various publicity photos. It is a one piece, "black all-over lace shirred on a white foundation to give a daring effect. The cuffs are black velvet." This suit will be confused with the Rose Marie Reid swimsuit, the Renie swimsuit, and the velvet wing bust swimsuit by Catalina. All of the swimsuits are remarkably similar and the other thing they all have in common is that Marilyn looks stunning in each.

The competition for Lorelei Lee was heating up. Sheilah Graham reported on October 10th, "'If Betty Grable will come back to work, I'll buy *Gentlemen Prefer Blondes* for her.' Thus George Jessel relayed a message to the still on suspension Miss Grable. 'But I thought Twentieth Century-Fox was buying the play for Marilyn Monroe,' I said. 'Betty can have it--if she'll come back to work,' said George, who added, 'we're scrapping the play entirely. Just keeping the title.'"

On October 14th, Marilyn appears in newsprint being crowned "Miss Medical Center Aides of 1951." Bernard Selber, President of the City of Hope Auxiliary had the honor of crowning her. She was to attend the annual dinner at the Ambassador Hotel on November 4th.

While at the RKO studios, Marilyn had several portrait sittings with Ernest Bachrach, the head of the photographic department. He described his technique for getting a good portrait. "I like to wear my women out with unusual poses and different lighting. Some of 'em cooperate fine. Others just sit there like a can of lard." The resulting images of the newly shorn Marilyn were stunning, proving she was no "can of lard". She was refining her "look" and these images gave her a new aura of sophistication. *Clash by Night* wouldn't be released until June 16, 1952, and Marilyn continued to utilize her access to Ernest Bachrach. In the future, as her hair grew out, he took another series of photos of Marilyn in a black negligee which was equally as powerful when it comes to solidifying her image as a sex symbol. One of which was used on the cover of *Cosmopolitan* in May of 1953, touting her as "Hollywood's Most Valuable Property." And by the looks of things, she was.

On October 16, 1951 Harrison Carroll reported, "Joanne Dru figures the Hays office insulted her, even though they approved some bathing suit pictures of her from *Return of the Texan*. They returned them with the following note: 'These are okay because we feel that Miss Dru is not the obvious sexy type. She has a very 'well-bred quality." When Marilyn Monroe posed in the same swim suit, the pictures were nixed by the same office."

Sheilah Graham gave this compliment to Marilyn on the 21st, "Then there are lots and lots of newcomers who will be the sensations of the next few months. I think a girl named Marilyn Monroe has brought sex back to Hollywood. What I really mean is glamour. The public wants back its dream world of youth, good looks and beauty—also some slit skirts and manly figures."

*Look* magazine partial cover and article on October 23rd, "Marilyn Monroe: A Serious Blonde Who Can Act," by Rupert Allan, and photographed by Earl Theisen. "At lunchtime, an awed hush cancels the noise of guzzle and gossip in Twentieth Century-Fox's studio commissary. Every eye in the place follows with varying degrees of calculation as a neatly delineated blonde makes her way, like a cat picking its way across a muddy path, to a far table. Oblivious to all, starlet Marilyn Monroe (23 years old; unmarried; 5'5 1/2"; 118 pounds; 34" hips; 23" waist; 36 1/2" bust) sits down to her lunch, calmly opens a book on anatomy. For others, the chatter and staring continue. Monroe is busy studying to be a serious actress....Marilyn is the mistress of the slow, calculated walk in the tradition of West, Harlow and Turner....Composer-voice coach Phil Moore says Marilyn has one of the sexiest voices on the screen. 'She always sounds as if she's just waking up. You'd be surprised what kind of effect that has on male listeners.'....Soaking up art and literature, Marilyn spends free evenings reading scripts and books--recent favorites: Tolstoy's *Anna Karenina* and Rilke's *Letters to a Young Poet*. The faded photograph is of the actress Eleonora Duse, Marilyn's inspiration....Marilyn has other assets at least as important as her impressive dimensions. Her bag of tricks includes a tri-dimensional walk, a sultry voice with a proximity fuse, and a smile of diversified insinuations."

Allan commented on how he saw Marilyn at the time. "I found another person entirely and I wrote the piece the way I saw it, which the New York editors wanted to change to be more in keeping with her screen image. There was never any change in Marilyn. When I first met her she was reading Dostoyevsky and she had pictures on her wall which she had got from a fine art magazine and had put up with Scotch tape…she hadn't enough money to put frames on them all…She had catholic tastes…was highly intelligent and self-educated. She had two photographs—one was a cutting which she framed of Duse (above her bed). The other was a small photograph of three men, and when I asked who they were she told me, Arthur Miller, Elia Kazan and I forget the third."

Marilyn will tell Erskine Johnson of her heady pursuits. "'I'm a bookworm and proud of it!' Marilyn adores Tolstoy and Dostoyevsky, totes around a worn copy of Rainer Maria Rilke's *Letters to a Young Poet* and admitted, "Sure, I'm a book girl. But I'm not an intellectual and I'm not interested in being one. I read because I want to expand as much as I can. I don't think men prefer dumb girls. But they're not looking for intellectuals, either.'"

Photographer Gene Kornman, studio photographer for 20th Century Fox, takes a stunning photo of Marilyn for the cover of *Look* wearing an ivory and gold lame' gown against a red background.

Photographer Earl Theisen recalls the circumstances with Marilyn during the shoot for *Look*. As usual she was a couple of hours late. "When she drove up to the studio beach set for the picture, she was wearing a fur coat. When she took it off, she was wearing a bikini. I scolded her and said it was no good; this was for a family type magazine. I told her to get into a dress or something. She didn't like to be scolded or corrected like that."

Theisen takes some unique pictures of Marilyn working out, jogging, visiting her old High School and with vocal coach Phil Moore. He did take pictures of her arriving in her yellow string bikini, wearing a checked cloth coat and posing on Fox's back lot beach, but these didn't make it into the magazine. She would pose in a more conservative one piece bathing suit by Rose Marie Reid, but she still looked like quite a piece of eye candy. Also included in the article is a sexy photo of Marilyn dressed in a potato sack. The photo goes largely unnoticed. Marilyn had yet to cut her hair when posing for the photographs in the article and the photos will lack the intense glamour she will gain by cropping her hair into a halo of curls. Gene Kornman, Fox studio photographer, will try the potato sack gag again in February of next year to spectacular results.

Earl Theisen would remember photographing Marilyn, "Everything she does for a camera has been studied carefully. She knows exactly what she's doing. You can watch her, as you're focusing your camera on her, getting ready to turn it on. She knows exactly how far she wants to open her mouth, how much to raise her upper lip."

Annie Lebowitz, a modern photographic genius and splendid portraitist said this of Marilyn, "I realized when I studied pictures of Marilyn Monroe that it almost didn't matter who the photographer was. She took charge. It seemed like she was taking the picture." Marilyn herself will say, "When the photographers come, it's like looking in a mirror. They think they arrange me to suit themselves, but I use them to put over myself. It's necessary in the movie business, but I often hate it. I never show it, though. It could ruin me. I need their goodwill. I'm not stupid."

Later master lensman Phillip Halsman will rhapsodize over her talent in understanding what makes a good photograph and taking over the creation of her image. "I know few actresses who have this incredible talent for communicating with the camera lens. She would try to seduce a camera as if it were a human being. So it is strange to see that the greatest flaw in her character, this inferiority complex which eventually destroyed her, was the main factor responsible for her career and the spectacular success. She knew that the camera lens was not just a glass eye, but a symbol for the eyes of millions of men; so the camera stimulated her strongly. Because she had a great talent for directing the entire impact of her personality at the lens and she was a remarkably gifted exciting model." Asked if Marilyn was afraid of him, Halsman responded, "Only in the beginning, but then she would come up very close, almost pressing herself against you, while looking like a frightened child that adored you already. She would look into your eyes, and you would have the feeling she was offering herself. Eventually, you were helpless; you desired her. Then she would feel safe and be at ease. That she was offering herself came through in all her pictures and made her the sex goddess that she was—a universal goddess, because it was so simple to desire this girl. Every man, intelligent or dumb, sure of himself or insecure, rich of poor, could imagine himself being with this girl who was always there available, offering herself. It is much more difficult for the average man to imagine himself alone with an artificial creature like Marlene Dietrich. What could he say to her? What could he do? But with Marilyn Monroe he wasn't expected to say or do anything in particular. She would accept anything.  This was the universal and incredible quality of the girl. She was extremely easy to photograph, because she so completely subordinated herself to you, becoming remarkable putty in your hands. There she was, adoring you, absolutely smitten; and, oddly enough, every man in the room got the same feeling. This all came from her feeling of inferiority. This same feeling pushed her away from the man she married, poisoned her relationship with all people. Though it made her a star, it also made her feel inside that she was not the great actress people expected her to be. In fact, to live up to the image she had created became more and more difficult and frightening to her; she could barely force herself to go every morning to the movie sets, where she knew she could not live up to expectations."

On October 24th, Jimmie Fidler dedicates his entire column to Marilyn. He makes this shrewd observation, "...Beautiful? There's no doubt about that. Marilyn Monroe is an absolute knockout! I've seldom seen a finer complexion, better features, more gorgeous hair or a better figure. But--and here's my point--Marilyn Monroe, the focal point of all this attention today, is certainly no more beautiful than she was a few yesterday's ago when she could walk into any studio cafe in town without getting a second glance. The difference is publicity; she was an unknown then whereas, today, she's being sold with all the salesmanship at Hollywood's command. Filmville's beauticians and coaches undoubtedly play a big part in the development of glamour, but they're unimportant in my opinion by comparison with the publicist. Once he's started people THINKING that a girl is glamorous, her battle is won."

Marilyn wrote a check to the Regents of the University of California for a total of $9.00. She listed her address as 611 N. Crescent Ave, and her phone number as CR 19111. There is also a penciled in number on the check, 31301. It seems a college education was much cheaper in 1951 than it is now.

Marilyn wrote a check to Dr. Abraham Gottesman on October 26th for the amount of $200.00. Dr. Gottesman was a renowned Beverly Hills psychoanalyst who treated Marilyn from 1951 through 1954. He eventually retired to Santa Ynez, California, where he practiced until his death in 2005. He graduated from New York Medical College and specialized in ego therapy and also worked with children. He was a member of LAPSI, the Los Angeles Psychoanalytic Society Institute.

Just as later on Lee Strasberg urged Marilyn to find a therapist in New York, Michael Chekhov may have suggested that psychotherapy would help her examine and free herself to apply the techniques he was teaching her. From this time on until her death, Marilyn would be under the care of a Freudian psychoanalyst. Freudian psychoanalysis was a very popular method of psychiatry at the time due to the influx of European's fleeing war torn Europe. Many people trained in Europe in the method of Freudian psychoanalysis eventually set up practice here in the United States.

Although, Freudian therapy was popular, in hindsight it was possibly not the best choice for Marilyn. Her therapy seemed to bind her to the past instead of freeing her from it. It appears that she was in an endless cycle of returning to her childhood in order to make sense of her current problems. She never managed to detangle herself from her tragic early years because of the constant rumination over them. She was forever chained to her victimization and Freudian analysis was unable to free her. But it might also have been that the methodology was sound, but the practitioners were at fault, especially Dr. Mariane Kris and Dr. Ralph Greenson, whom she will encounter after she moves to New York.

In 1955 Maurice Zolotow will reveal this about Marilyn's engaging in psychoanalysis. "People who know her say that the three years of psychoanalysis which Miss Monroe experienced, beginning in 1951, have helped her feel more secure socially and that now she opens up more at parties and gatherings."

Robert Young, interviewed by Sheilah Graham, picks Marilyn as one of his "10 top fillies to wear tomorrow's glamour garlands." This is what he had to say about Marilyn, "Bob was a top Metro star at the time when Jean Harlow was the most provocative blonde in the world. He remembered her as 'a whole lot of woman,' and named as her closest competitor, Marilyn Monroe. 'On and off the screen, Marilyn is like a champagne cork, with the tinfoil removed, and ready to pop.'" Mr. Young will gain a new measure of fame in the 70s hit television show, *Marcus Welby, MD*.

*Let's Make It Legal* was released on October 31, 1951. On the same day Louella Parsons announces in her column, "Marilyn Monroe, at this writing, is the hottest young property in town. There isn't a magazine that doesn't want a picture of her, and as for newspapers, she's good copy."

On November 6th Marilyn received a skin treatment from Renna. She listed her address as The Beverly Carlton Hotel and her phone number as Cr55221. Marilyn again visited her Beverly Hills psychoanalyst, Dr. Abraham Gottesman on November 7th and 9th, and was charged $150.00 for each session.

Lee Anderson, the desk clerk at the Beverly Carlton Hotel had this to say of Marilyn and her habits. "Miss Monroe is very quiet and demands little service. The person here at the hotel who deals with her mostly is the switchboard operator. I guess she must make about 100 calls a day…and receives as many. Every day she comes in in late afternoon and goes directly to her apartment. The only time she ever uses the pool is when magazine photographers come for pictures. Oh yes, when she was first here she took a sun bath at the pool. But everyone really stared and there was quite a commotion. Have you seen her in a bathing suit?!"

On November 7th Sheilah Graham devoted her entire column to Marilyn. "She'll Merely Play a Dumb Blonde; Marilyn's Really a Smart Girl…You'd think that a girl as beautiful as Marilyn Monroe would have the easiest time in the world getting to be a movie star, but from the moment she was born Marilyn, who is regarded as the most beautiful blonde in Hollywood, has had to fight every foot of the way to reach the point where 20$^{th}$ Century-Fox is going to star her in *Gentlemen Prefer Blondes*, when they buy the new film version from Anita Loos. Marilyn never knew her father and mother. She was raised in Los Angeles orphanages and later farmed out to poor, private families. At lunch with her at 20$^{th}$ Century-Fox we got acquainted because this pale-faced blue-eyed miss is one of our future big stars. 'I was born here in Hollywood,' Marilyn said. 'I bet you don't remember the first time I saw you.' I had to confess I didn't. It was the last day of *Scudda Hoo, Scudda Hay*,' she reminded me. 'You asked how it felt to be in my first picture!' That was when Marilyn was 18, under contract to 20$^{th}$ Century-Fox. 'They had an economy wave, and I hadn't done anything after *Scudda Hoo*, and I was dropped. I went to Columbia for six months, and had only a little part in an eight-day musical. I was chubby, baby fat, weighed 126 pounds. It was *Ladies of the Chorus*, and I played Adele Jergen's daughter.' Now Marilyn is a still-rounded 118 pounds, with a bust measurement of 37 inches, waist 23, hips 34. 'Then,' said Marilyn, 'I was in *Love Happy*, with the Marx Brothers. I had a very small part. In fact, it was an added scene after the picture was finished. It was embarrassing when I toured with the picture. People said, 'Were you in it? Oh, yes, you were the one in the tight evening dress.'' The next step was Metro—'where I read for John Huston. He didn't even test me; just said, 'You've got the part.' When Joe Mankiewicz saw the picture, he signed her for *All About Eve*. Do you remember her as George Sanders' dumb girl friend? 'Mr. Zanuck saw the early rushes, and signed me to a seven year contract,' she said. Her pictures ready for release are *Love Nest*, with June Haver and Bill Lundigan, and *Let's Make it Legal*—'I play the girl who tries to steal MacDonald Carey, Claudette Colbert's husband. In my next picture, I'm billed as a star for the first time, *Clash by Night*.' At 23, that's very good. 'I suppose all this makes you very happy.' I remarked. 'I'm happy,' Marilyn said, 'but I know I'll be happier, when I adjust a lot of things within myself.' 'Your beauty must be a great help,' this reporter observed. 'I guess everything helps,' she replied. 'Face, figure—but it's all in relation to success. When I started working, I was very tied up and tense. I used to try out for plays in high school and couldn't get on the stage. When I first started as a model I was painfully shy, but, little by little, you can hold your own better, but it's a painful process.' For a while, Marilyn lived with her drama coach, Natasha Lytess, but now the teacher has her own home. Marilyn lives in a one-bedroom bachelor apartment in Beverly Hills. 'How do you keep the wolves at bay?' I wanted to know. 'Basically, I like men,' she replied. 'When girls talk of trouble with men, I think it's exaggerated.' Marilyn was married once—'I was 16, in high school. I don't recommend it. The other girls whispered, 'Oh, she's married.' You feel very uncomfortable, like a strange animal.' There was a speedy divorce and the boy has remarried. Marilyn now thinks she'll wait. Even while hoping to star as the dumb blonde in *Gentlemen Prefer Blondes*, this beauty is nobody's dumb blonde. She is giving herself the education that she didn't get as a youngster. 'I go to the University of California, Los Angeles, nearly every evening. I'm taking literature and the background of social and political culture.' Instead of a guy on her arm, Marilyn usually has a book under it. I don't see how she can miss."

Marilyn told Michael Sheridan, "I don't mind if people think I'm a dumb blonde, but I dread the thought of being a dumb blonde." She shared with Sheilah Graham this about her intelligence when asked if being thought of as dumb bothered her, "It never has, Sheilah. You see, I've always known I wasn't. Things go on in my mind that no one knows about. I've always figured things out and done them according to plan. Oh no, I'm not calculating or tricky. But I know what I want."

Sheliah Graham, campaigning for Marilyn, writes in her column on November 14$^{th}$, "Then there is luscious Marilyn Monroe. Reared in a Los Angeles orphanage, Marilyn made her first impression on the movie moguls in *Asphalt Jungle*. This blue-eyed, sex-appealing Miss has reached the pinnacle where her studio is ready, willing and eager to star her in the movie version of *Gentlemen Prefer Blondes*."

*Love Nest* is released on November 14th

Harrison Carroll reports on November 15th, "I ran into Marilyn Monroe on the set of *Clash in the Night*. She told me she is studying body expressions under Lottie Goslar and taking a literature course at UCLA. 'But,' she added, dimpling, 'if I meet the right man, I'll forget about all these courses. Being a woman is more important to me than being an actress. In fact, being a woman is the most important thing that ever happened to me.' About a million guys will go along with her on that."

According to Ralph Roberts, Marilyn told him that Michael Chekhov had suggested that she take pantomime and dancing lessons from Los Angeles' famed Lotte Goslar. Xenia Chekhov even took her to see a production of one of Anton Chekhov's plays at the Turnabout Theater where Miss Goslar held court. Miss Goslar was a Viennese pantomimic danseuse who plied her trade at the Turnabout Theater. Miss Goslar was schooled in classic and modern dance techniques. She chose the music for her dances first because she had an understanding of its psychological significance and expressed it in her movements. In contrast to her classical mastery of dance, she was known as the dancing comic. Miss Goslar's pantomime dance routines at the Turnabout Theater were classics. Her philosophy of body movement combined perfectly with Todd's in *The Thinking Body*, and Marilyn used this information to fully grasp what she was learning in Goslar's classes. Marilyn benefited greatly as she studied with Miss Goslar and she was finally able to free herself and use her body as an instrument to interpret her characters.

Marilyn called Miss Goslar personally to have private lessons, but she thought it best that Marilyn take a group class. Miss Goslar was quoted in her autobiography about her famous student, "She turned out to be an outstanding student, full of imagination and very eager to accept my criticisms, especially when I warned her that any over-display of her natural sexy qualities could only lead to parody....Relaxed and without fears, barefoot, in jeans, with tousled hair and without any makeup, she looked her most beautiful. The natural bone structure of her face was exquisite, and her hands always made me think of medieval wood sculptures. Amazing and really touching was her modesty. Whenever I said something encouraging to her, tears would well up in her eyes....What do I remember most about Marilyn? The people who worked with her often told me that she was extremely generous; I found this generosity expressing itself in many different ways: in compassion, in concern, and in kindness. No matter where she or I were, she always called me on December 24--the German Christmas--and also on the anniversary of my husband's death; she never mentioned what had happened on that day, but simply let me know that there was a friend thinking of me. When one of the students in our class was drafted into the army, she took him out for lunch on his last day with us. All of this seems small, but to me it reveals a lot."

Marilyn's dancing technique was improved from attending Miss Goslar's lessons. She is more relaxed with her body and her movements have become more fluid. Her lessons will benefit her in the coming year when she is in production on *Gentlemen Prefer Blondes*. One has only to compare her dancing in that film with *Ladies of the Chorus* to see the consequence of Miss Goslar's influence. But Marilyn benefited the most from Miss Goslar in the development of her comedic skills. Starting with *Monkey Business* you get a glimpse of her charming comedic style. In *Gentlemen Prefer Blondes,* Marilyn shows a rare talent for comedy. Her timing, expressions and body movement have all been touched by the genius of Miss Goslar and will only improve with time. By the time Marilyn appears in *Seven Year Itch*, her skills are approaching perfection.

On July 10, 1952, Sheilah Graham will quote Marilyn on walking. "Marilyn Monroe, the beautiful butter blonde, has a theory for beautiful walking, 'Let everything go limp except for the coccyx, and you can move in any direction without too much trouble." A "*Reader's Digest*" version of Miss Todd's chapters on walking in *The Thinking Body*.

Marilyn will tell in an interview with Michael Sheridan that she is working to free herself. "Marilyn is also taking courses in body movement with Lotte Goslar, who is one of the world's finest dance mimes. And that's where Marilyn again speaks her mind. 'I like my body to be as free as my thoughts. If I can't express either, I might as well be a piece of marble in the Metropolitan Museum."

According to Ralph Roberts, Marilyn always had Miss Goslar on the set of her new movies. They will remain friends until Marilyn's death and Miss Goslar will be among the few invited by Joe DiMaggio to attend Marilyn's memorial.

*Quick* magazine features Marilyn on the cover and in an article on November 19th, "The New Jean Harlow....The most striking new property in Hollywood was the movie maker's accolade currently being lavished on 23 year old Marilyn Monroe, now hard at work on her first starring role in RKO's Clash by Night. Even rival studios agreed that Marilyn, a Twentieth Century-Fox starlet, looked like the long awaited Hollywood miracle--successor to the late Jean Harlow. But any attempt to characterize Marilyn Monroe as another Jean Harlow labors under one handicap: she does not have the worldly-wisdom beyond her years. 'But,' counters one director, 'Marilyn looks like she was born sultry.' Marilyn comments on her sexiness, 'At first, directors used to tell me, 'Act sultry.' That only made me nervous. Now they just say, 'Be yourself.' That does it."

This nervousness will never quite go away. Sir Laurence Olivier found that out when he directed Marilyn to, "Be sexy," in *The Prince and the Showgirl*, in 1956. Marilyn left the set, unable to just "Be sexy." Maybe he should have just said, "Be Yourself."

Virginia MacPherson reported on November 16th about Marilyn's natural sexiness, her dislike of nightclubs and her endearing naiveté. "Marilyn Monroe, the Combustible Cutie who doesn't go out on dates, said today she likes having the wolves hang around her anyway because 'they're men and I'm a woman...and it's all part of nature.' She can say that again. All Marilyn has to do is wiggle her way across a studio lot and nature starts acting up all over the place. Partly because this 23-year-old blonde has a fondness for skin-tight dresses--and partly because of her undulating walk. Not for nothing do they call her the 'hottest thing in town since Jean Harlow.' She could have her pick of practically any eligible wolf in town--and even a few who aren't so eligible. 'But, I have to care a lot for a man before I'll go out with him,' she sighed, tucking a fresh daisy in her plunging neckline. 'I don't go to night clubs. And I won't go out with a man just to be seen. I wait until I get a big crush. Then I'm with him all the time.' But she doesn't discourage the gents who stand around and drool in her direction. 'People keep asking me if I don't hate having the wolves pester me.' Marilyn dimpled. 'I don't. I like it. I like men. Lots better than women. And I like having them like me.' But she hardly ever does anything about it. The Monroe moniker is seldom seen in the list of 'woosome twosomes' huddling in the night clubs. 'I'm too busy learning to be a good actress,' Marilyn says. 'I have my first big part in RKO's *Clash by Night*. I don't want to spoil anything.' She poses for 'cheesecake.' 'I'll wear anything they want me to,' Marilyn says. 'That's how I got started on my career and I'm perfectly willing to keep at it. I like to do it. I'll pose any way they say--even upside down. And I've done it. I like anything that looks free and natural.' She's that way herself--and that's what keeps the studio big-wigs chewing their nails. The can convince her that a girl with a 37-inch bust, a 23-inch waist, and 34-inch hips shouldn't go around talking to every strange man she bumps into. 'But I have lots of interesting experiences that way,' Marilyn says happily. 'One night a boy walked up to me in the Union Station and asked me to marry him. I'd never seen him before but he thought I was stranded. Wasn't that touching?' And Marilyn STILL thinks he asked her because she looked lonely."

On November 18th the *Omaha World Herald Magazine* dedicated a page to Marilyn. "Hollywood Gag Stills, They're Part of Buildup for Young Actresses." The article featured 4 cheesecake photos of Marilyn. "The Pretty Pilgrim shown above in color is young Marilyn Monroe, the curvaceous blonde who has bomb shelled her way toward stardom out Hollywood way. It is very doubtful if Marilyn knows how to load and fire the old musket that is so handy, but even if she could it would probably be too late to wing the alert turkey perched in the tree. Nor does it follow that Marilyn knows how to shoot a bow and arrow just because she posed for the Valentine Day art, can best old man Bogey on the golf course, or keep her feet on skis (in the picture she's skiing on sand, anyway). 'Gag stills' such as Marilyn posed for on this page are just part and parcel of the Filmland buildup for any pretty young thing, and occupationally they don't mean a thing. Marilyn is an ex-baby sitter whose picture was on the cover of the *World Herald Magazine* long ago—on June 1,

1947. After toiling for many months for a model agency in Hollywood, she suddenly received calls within one week from four major studios for screen tests. She had a bit part in *Asphalt Jungle*, a bigger bit in *All About Eve*, and lately has been shoved into a succession of pictures, including *Clash by Night*. She is owned by Twentieth Century-Fox, but is sometimes loaned as are all Hollywood vassals."

Erskine Johnson quotes Marilyn for his column on the 18th. "Shapely Marilyn Monroe is biting into her fist dramatic role in *Clash by Night*, but she's not giving up the cheesecake that zoomed her into stardom. Even if *Madame* is next on the list for blonde Marilyn, she'll still pose in bathing suits. 'I don't mind cheesecake as long as it's honest,' she winked. 'There's honest cheesecake, if you know what I mean. I was doing honest cheesecake as a model long before I stepped on a sound stage. I kept yearning for the cover of the *Ladies Home Journal*, but I never got past the covers of men's magazines.

The *New York Times* reported on November 18th, that Marilyn and Richard Widmark were cast in *Night Without Sleep,* later to be renamed *Don't Bother to Knock*. The director was Roy Baker. He remembers Marilyn being upset about her nude calendar. "I couldn't understand what all the fuss was about. A photograph of a naked lady seemed perfectly harmless. But everyone was shocked to the core. The people in charge of the studios affected to take an extremely high moral tone. I think they were terrified that the Women's Association or the Mothers of the Revolution would get up on their hind legs and say, 'This is disgraceful and this must not go on.'"

Marilyn will tell Pete Martin of executives at Fox finding out about her calendar pose. "I asked Marilyn to tell me the story of that nude calendar herself, and she said, 'When the studio first heard about it, everybody there was in a frenzy. They telephoned me on the set where I was working in a quickie called *Don't Bother to Knock*. The person who called asked me, 'What's all this about a calendar of you in the nude? Did you do it?' 'Yes,' I said. 'Is there anything wrong with it? So they've found out it's me on the calendar. Well, what do you know!' 'Found out!' he almost screamed. 'There you are, all of you, in full color!' Then he must have gotten mixed up, for first her said, 'Just deny everything'; then he said, 'Don't say anything. I'll be right down.'" Continuing her story for Mr. Martin, "I was working on the Fox Western Avenue lot when this worried man from Fox came tearing in wringing his hands. He took me into my dressing room to talk about the horrible thing I'd done in posing for such a photograph. I could think of nothing else to say, so I said apologetically, 'I thought the lighting the photographer used would disguise me.' I thought that worried man would have a stroke when I told him that.'" Marilyn went on to say, "I'm saving a copy of that calendar for my grandchildren. But I've only autographed a few copies of it, mostly for sick people. On one I wrote, 'This may not be my best angle,' and on the other I wrote, 'Do you like me better with long hair?'"

Vocal coach, Phil Moore, remembers that during this time Marilyn came to his apartment upset about the nude photographs that she had posed for. She showed the photos to Moore, who thought them beautiful. He, in turn, showed them to mutual friend Dorothy Dandridge. "We couldn't imagine these shots impairing her career if they were published,' said Moore. 'They would certainly generate some scandal and notoriety, but we also thought the public as a whole, would not be offended.'

Bob Thomas gave Marilyn something to be thankful for, he dedicated his column to her on the 19th. Despite all the current cheesecake photos available, the article is illustrated in a 1947 photo of Marilyn in a Mabs of Hollywood "Hourglass" swim suit, taken during her early days at Fox. "It's time for a progress report on Marilyn Monroe, the atomic blonde. Miss Monroe has been chosen the sweetheart of various battalions, regiments and ships, as well as numerous individuals, and for very apparent reasons. She is presently the No 1 cheesecake gal of Hollywood, occupying the hallowed position held previously by Jane Russell, Rita Hayworth and Betty Grable. Aside from her obvious attributes, Marilyn is a serious gal who reads philosophy as well as movie magazines. She is quite intent on an acting career. I asked if being identified as a leg art queen interfered with her dramatic ambitions. 'Oh, I don't think so,' She answered in the sultry voice she has acquired. 'I think cheesecake helps call attention to you. Then you can follow through and prove yourself.' After a year of playing minor roles, she is coming into her own. Wald-Krasna borrowed her from 20th Century-Fox to play in *Clash by Night*, in which she will get star billing for the first time. Her name will appear along with Barbara Stanwyck, Paul Douglas and Robert Ryan. Then she returns to her home lot to play her first lead there. 'It's not a cheesecake role at all,' she emphasized. 'I play a very mixed-up girl with a lot of psychoses. It takes Richard Widmark to straighten me out.' Unlike some gals with dramatic leanings, Marilyn has no objection to cheesecake. In fact, she was disappointed when a national magazine ran a story about her and featured a photo of her in a high necked evening gown. 'They said they couldn't run cheesecake because it was a family magazine,' she said. 'Goodness, I don't think it would have hurt the homes to have had a little more exciting picture.'

On November 20th Marilyn ate Thanksgiving dinner at the home of Anne Karger which would become a tradition for her. Even though Marilyn was not dating Fred Karger, she continued to have a close bond with his mother Anne and his sister Mary.

The press loves to drum up boyfriends for Marilyn. On the 22nd Dorothy Kilgallen reported that, "Norman Krasna may be carrying a torch for Betty Hutton, as reported by the cinema sentimentalists, but it hasn't impaired his taste in pretty girls. He's dating Marilyn Monroe." Earl Wilson reported on December the 4th of Krasna and Marilyn being an item. On December the 11th, Miss Kilgallen again reported on the burgeoning romance and that Groucho was chaperoning. The reports of any romance between Krasna, who was one of the producers for *Clash by Night,* and Marilyn was squashed when it was reported in the press that he eloped with Al Jolson's widow and married in Vegas in December.

The press loved to run inane stories on Marilyn and the public ate it up. In his syndicated column on November 24th, Erskine Johnson writes, "Old Levi Strauss, who sewed up the first pair of blue jeans 100 years ago, would have been mighty happy. They put Marilyn Monroe into a pair for a scene in *Clash By Night*. She was supposed to look dowdy and unattractive as a cannery worker. They also gave her a dirty tee-shirt, mussed her blonde hair and took off all her makeup. Then the shapely Marilyn wiggled--there's no other word to describe her walk--on stage. The whistles sounded like Saturday night at a strip palace. 'It's no use,' groaned director Fritz Lang, 'let's go to work. What can you do about nature?'"

Harrison Carroll also reported on the 24th, "Marilyn Monroe and director Nick Ray, a luncheon twosome at Lucey's." Nick Ray and Marilyn will date on-and-off until she and Joe DiMaggio are a couple. Ray told Jane Russell about Marilyn, "She was a very sensitive, interested girl, but interested in all kinds of things that no one has any idea about—like Thomas Wolfe, philosophy, the classics, art and matters of intellectual taste."

On the 24th Bob Thomas reported on the ongoing search for Lorelei Lee. "Speaking of Grable, reminds me of the report that Marilyn Monroe, the atomic-age pin-up queen, will star in the recently purchased *Gentlemen Prefer Blondes*. Miss Monroe thinks she is going to get the role. Miss Grable hasn't been heard from, but you can expect fireworks."

The *San Antonio Express* runs a photo of Marilyn up at bat. She is wearing a kerchief in her hair, a dark long sleeved sweater and white shorts.

Hedda Hopper mentions this amusing story about Marilyn in her syndicated column on November 30th, "Looking at Hollywood...They're still chuckling at Marilyn Monroe at RKO. When an assistant director yelled, 'Marilyn, watch out for the equipment,' she promptly zipped up the neck line of her sweater..."

Earl Wilson, not wanting to miss out on predicting the star of *Gentlemen Prefer Blondes*, reports this on November 26th. "Marilyn Monroe, the 'new Jean Harlow,' hopes to get the Carol Channing role in the movie version of *Gentlemen Prefer Blondes*."

A captioned wire photo of Marilyn in a bathing suit ran on the 27th, "Actress Marilyn Monroe, described by a movie press agent as, 'the girl with the hour-glass figure and the sand distributed in the right places,' has been singled out by the Second Infantry division's 23rd regiment in Korea as the 'Girl We'd Most Like to Chogie Up a Hill With.' 'Chogie' is Korean slang for climb." These are some of the men who fought on Heartbreak Ridge.

December had Marilyn in four magazines with one cover. Her magazine appearances were leveling out, but the newspaper columnists were starting to run out of ink writing about her. *Focus* magazine December 1951, cover and article, "Marilyn Monroe: She Breathes Sex Appeal" featuring a centerfold captioned, "Hottest Since Harlow....When she sticks in her gut and stands on her dainty tiptoe, nobody would dare guess they once tried to cast her as a boy. Her name is Marilyn Monroe, and she's the hottest thing in town. Blonde, blue-eyed and busty (she measures somewhere between Lana Turner's 35 and Jane Russell's 37 1/2.) She bids fair to outstrip Betty Grable, June Haver and Rita Hayworth as the most sex-citing glamour girl on the 20th Century lot." While in Van Nuys High School, Norma Jeane tried out for a school play and was cast as a boy.

Wardrobe Tests for *Don't Bother To Knock* were held on December 3rd. Marilyn was dressed for the first time in a film by William (Billy) Travilla. He would go on to design many of the classic outfits that define the Monroe image and become a favored chum of Marilyn's.

The Brooklyn Eagle reported on July 20th, 1952, "Marilyn Monroe's Clothes a Problem to 20th Century...With the casting of Marilyn Monroe, Hollywood's newest glamour queen, as a beauty contest winner in *We're Not Married*, 20th Century-Fox's wardrobe department merely had to tighten a few swim suit seams in strategic places and pour in the curvy blonde. When it came to costuming Marilyn for her role as a small-town girl in the big city, in *Don't Bother to Knock*, however, studio designer Travilla found himself dealing with a new type of problem: What kind of bushel can you hide an incandescent light under? Several sequences of the drama call for the shapely star to wear a simple dress of inexpensive appearance, but the finished number, with La Monroe inside, looked like it was drawn up specifically to provoke wolf howls. After another session on the designer's drawing board, it took several days of alterations and special aging processes before the dress emerged looking like something just off the pipe racks. Only one thing remained wrong. Crew members still whistled when Marilyn walked on the set."

In Erskine Johnson reported on December 6th, "She's Just Herself...Marilyn Monroe is peeling off those labels that proclaim her as the new Lana Turner and Jean Harlow as fast as they are being slapped on her curvy chassis. It's yawn stuff to Marilyn, who says that, 'somebody's always another somebody in Hollywood, and I'm not like anybody else. Even in the roles I play. I have to play parts that are a little twisty. If they aren't a little twisty, I can't give them anything.'"

Additional wardrobe Tests for *Don't Bother To Knock* were held on December 6th. In *Don't Bother to Knock* Marilyn starred as Nell Forbes, a disturbed babysitter. She co-starred with Richard Widmark. This was rather a bizarre film. Marilyn never again played an emotionally disturbed character. This may have hit too close to home, given her family history of mental illness.

Richard Widmark remembers working with Marilyn, "I liked Marilyn, but she was God-awful to work with. Impossible, really. She would hide in her dressing room and refuse to come out. Then, when she finally would show up, she was a nervous wreck. It was all a result of fear. She was insecure about so many things and was obviously self-destructive. She was a wounded bird from the beginning." He would also say of her, "At first we thought she'd never get anything right, and we'd mutter, 'Oh, this is impossible—you can't print this!' But something happened between the lens and the film, and when we looked at the rushes she had the rest of us knocked off the screen!"

This is the first of two movies Marilyn will make with Lurene Tuttle. They will both appear together again in the movie that rocketed Marilyn to fame, *Niagara*. James Cagney's sister, Jeanne Cagney, played the phone operator.

Jim Backus, who was also in the film, remembers Marilyn. "Marilyn was always losing her car keys and I drove her to her apartment in the Beverly Carleton a couple of times. One night she asked me to come up to the apartment. I'll never forget how she said, 'Please, Jim, come up. There's something I've always wanted you to do for me.' I kept protesting that I was a happily married man but I finally asked what she wanted me to do. She said, 'Mr. Magoo.' At that anticlimax, I did Mr. Magoo in the car and waved goodbye to America's most famous sex symbol." Backus was the voice for the iconic cartoon *Mr. Magoo* which debuted in 1949.

The Studio's Publicity Department and Marilyn conspired to generate some publicity for the film by having Marilyn pose in a t-shirt that some sailors had sent her. The photos, taken by Ed Clark, went out over the *United Press Wire Service* with this caption, "The shirt off some sailor's back adorns the voluptuous figure of film star, Marilyn Monroe, chosen as 'Miss Torpedo' by 'The Torpedo Gang' of the Destroyer USS Henley 00-762. The choice of Miss Monroe, who is appearing in *Don't Bother to Knock* with Richard Widmark, backs up the reputation of the US Seamen as fine judges of explosive power."

"Marilyn Makes Heads Rotate," by Gene Handsaker, on December 9th,"Marilyn Monroe shot me a high-voltage jolt of sex appeal from the from the eyes and said: 'I think a woman always wants to be admired by the male sex--and it doesn't matter so much for what.' I'd ask if she wouldn't rather be admired for her acting than for her figure. For Marilyn has--and I don't expect this to arouse a storm of controversy among male movie goers--the sexiest chassis on the screen today. She's 23, a blue-eyed blonde with a vibrant, come-hither gleam. She's 5 feet 5 ½,118 pounds, has a 23-inch waist, 24-inch hips, and 37-

inch bust. 'Sometimes its 36 ½,' she admitted, 'depending on how I'm eating. The crew of a warship in Korean waters wrote to ask whether she accented these curves artificially. 'Half of us say yes, half of us no,' the Navy men explained. Marilyn's response--a photo of herself in a bikini bathing suit--settled all doubt. Maybe you saw her as George Sanders' girlfriend in *All About Eve*. Or as Louis Calhern's in *The Asphalt Jungle*. Right now she has her biggest part yet--sweetheart of Barbara Stanwyck's brother in *Clash by Night*. I watched her pose for some cheesecake art the other day in one of her costumes for the picture—a hip length nightie. Then we walked into the crowded studio restaurant for lunch. Marilyn had changed into a skirt and tight sweater. It was interesting to see scores of male heads rotate as if on ball-bearing swivels to follow her. Marilyn has an arresting hip-swish when she walks. She denies it is 'studied,' as one magazine claimed. Says 'it's completely natural.' Does she mind posing in bathing suit, negligees, and similarly scanty costumes? 'No. They're actually more comfortable.' But cheesecake, she thinks, should be 'honest,' that is a natural pose. 'Sometimes they only care about having your proportions showing.'"

On December 10th Darryl Zanuck writes Marilyn a letter reprimanding her for requesting that her dialog coach be on the set while she shot *Don't Bother To Knock*. He said that such a "Svengali dependence" would destroy her. Zanuck was referring to the presence of Natasha Lytess.

Marilyn gives out her beauty secrets to Arlene Dahl on December 21st, "....One of the most popular belles in Hollywood these days is Marilyn Monroe, who may soon win the late Jean Harlow's title as the screen's most spectacular blonde. I met Marilyn at a recent party and asked her some of her secrets as a siren. Her tricks can help any woman attain more allure for the magic minute when 1952 arrives. Marilyn's beautiful lips are a focal point of her charm. In applying her lipstick, she shades it for effect the way an artist does. First, she uses a light toned lipstick. After allowing it to set, she blots it and adds another darker shade of the same color. Then she wipes away the top coat slightly at the full, inner part of her lower lip. The result is a dewy shading of color far more tantalizing than one flat hue. Marilyn believes in making the best of figure assets. Since she is endowed with shapely shoulders and a beautiful bust line, most of her formal party gowns are strapless. By the same rule, she thinks a girl whose lovely back is her best feature should find a halter type neck line most flattering. If you are fortunate in having graceful, well-shaped feet, as Marilyn does, show them off in scant shoes. Her favorite are D'Orsay pumps and bare sandals. She further emphasizes the nude look with shell pink polish on her toenails as well as her fingernails. All that glitters is gala, in Marilyn's estimation. Her pet formal jewelry is a rhinestone bracelet and earrings...."

Miss Dahl relates this story illustrating Marilyn humor. "It happened at a party. Marilyn Monroe came over to a group—Cary Grant, Arthur Rubinstein, Joan Crawford and I were in it—that was discussing the poet Walt Whitman. Suddenly Marilyn broke in and said, 'Oh, I love him, and I love his chocolates, too!'"

Hedda Hopper reported on December 21st, "A capacity crowd is expected at the Academy Award Theater Sunday night for the unveiling of John Huston's picture *African*

*Queen*, starring Humphrey Bogart and Katherine Hepburn. Instead of giving his usual New Year's party, producer Sam Spiegel will throw a champagne party at Romanoff's following the preview." Marilyn attended the premier and the after party for *The African Queen* on December 23rd.

Gossip Columnist Edith Gwynn tells about the *African Queen* party, "Hollywood Party Line...There's one more party we must tell you about--because it was such fun and so gay. I'm referring to the night Sam Spiegel and Humphrey Bogart, who co-produced *The African Queen*, invited a hundred guests to a special showing, then wined and dined them later with a supper dance at Romanoff's. After that delightful movie, everyone was in a fun mood and when they got to Romanoff's they found hundreds of little toy monkeys strung from ribbons over the bar and their tables decorated with tiny mechanical elephants, lizards, etc., that really 'did their stuff' when wound up. Lauren Bacall, in a black and white cocktail dress, acted as hostess for such as Cary Grant and Betsy Drake, Marilyn Monroe with Nick Ray (being unwound from Gloria Graham,) Dan Dailey (stag,) the Ray Millands, Arlene Dahl with Lex Barker, Ann Miller (in white, trimmed with lots of white ostrich feathers) with Eddie Grainger, the James Masons (Mrs. M in a slinky black crepe gown), Eleanor Parker in flowing yellow chiffon."

On December 25th, Marilyn is found posing for a publicity photo that runs in newspapers. She is snuggled into a black stocking and posed teasingly against the fireplace mantle. She is the gift that all GIs, and men, would like to find in their stockings on Christmas morning.

Hedda Hopper made her yearly predictions on December 30th. "Hopper '52 Stardom Choices Spotlight Youth and Talent...Local Product--These good bit roles have paid off for Marilyn Monroe, Van Nuys High School graduate and former magazine model. She's featured in *Clash by Night*...Marilyn Monroe is a product of Los Angeles. But despite her proximity to Hollywood, it has been a struggle all the way. After graduating from Van Nuys High School, she worked in a defense plant owned by Reginald Denny, well-known silent star. To augment her pay, she became a model. One month her gorgeous figure graced the covers of four magazines. This naturally led to a screen test, and 20th was the lucky studio."

On December 31st Marilyn calls up James Bacon and asks to go to a New Year's Eve Party with him, he declines on the ground that his wife wouldn't understand. She finally found a date with Nick Ray. They went to a star-studded party given by Harriet Parsons, who had produced *Clash by Night*. Marilyn wore a revealing red evening gown, most likely her Oleg Cassini gown. Joan Crawford was there and referred to Marilyn as, "that cheap blonde." They didn't stay long at the party.

1952 would prove that 20th Century-Fox's 1950 gamble to re-hire Marilyn had paid off in spades. She generated so much interest that Fox scurried to handle all the publicity she generated. Not since the days of Jean Harlow had one woman been the focus of so much of the world's attention. Marilyn had one advantage that Miss Harlow lacked, technology. Marilyn was read about, seen and heard more often and in more places than the stars of previous generations, and with the advent of television she would be thrust into another orbit. Marilyn never had her own TV show, but even with her few appearances on the TV sets in the American homes, she was referred to and talked about in such frequency that the public was held in a constant state of fascination concerning the dramas playing out in her life. She was in the stratosphere of publicity, people were interested. Starting next year her movies, albeit her early ones, would be shown in homes across the country, giving the public a greater intimacy with her than ever before.

1952 will be the year of the "Calendar." On January 1952 Marilyn's nude calendar, the Western Lithograph "A New Wrinkle" version, makes its appearance on garage walls, back rooms and other such places. Although, the Baumgarth "Golden Dreams" version was actually released for the 1951 year to mediocre response, it wasn't generally known that it was Marilyn on the calendar until she was filming *Clash by Night* in September. It doesn't take long for people to start recognizing her. It is a dreadful situation for most young actresses, the news that you had posed in the nude could kill an otherwise promising career. Marilyn will not only survive the announcement, but will actually garner sympathy. Her career will kick into over-drive after it is officially announced in the press on March 13th that she is the nude on the calendar.

Marilyn starts the year off by being voted "Miss Radar of 1952" by the 502d Tactical Control Group in Korea. Her certificate stated, "We the men of the 502d Tactical Control Group in Korea are dazzled by Marilyn Monroe with her electrifying figure, high-voltage smile and beaming hair that we have elected her Miss Radar of 1952. The title honors her as 'The Girl With Whom We Would Prefer To Be Stranded on the Highest Radar Mountain.' We the men of the 502d Tactical Control Group in Korea can testify that she is beautiful on all types of screens, especially movie and radar." It is signed by Henry Rippa, Colonel USAF.

In January the *Pacific Stars and Stripes* ran this article on her appeal to the men, "Note to Marilyn Big Deal…With US 45th Div…The situation was strictly tactical in the operations and intelligence sections of the 179th Infantry Regiment's 2nd Battalion headquarters--even when the men are writing a shapely blonde movie star for her picture. Members of the two sections wrote to Marilyn Monroe asking for pinups to decorate the wall of their command post. For the operations section, Sgt. Ronald Kramer, Chicago, and M/Sgt. Joe D. Johnson, Lawton, Oklahoma, wrote, 'We make map overlays daily, but none have your contours' For the intelligence section the letter read, 'You have been selected the person we would most like to search and interrogate.' Two draftsmen decorated the letter with cartoons. They are PFC Richard D. Newman, St. Louis, Mo, and PFC Robert D. Colberg, Coeur d'Alene, Ida. One sketch showed a soldier standing in the snow, but keeping warm even in khakis by looking at Marilyn's picture."

*Movieland* magazine, January 1952, "What's Wrong With Sex Appeal?" by Leon Constantine. "'Sex is a part of life, a part of nature--and I'd rather go along with nature'-- says curvaceous Marilyn Monroe. 'I see nothing wrong in cheesecake--if it's sincere and in good taste. I hate cheesecake that looks like cheesecake.' 'Sex has nothing to do with what you wear or don't wear, with the shape of one's ankle or bosom---but with feeling.' 'There may be more sex appeal in the way you walk than there could be in any amount of clothes-shedding.' 'What's wrong with sex appeal? Doesn't every woman want it? It's nothing to be afraid of--or ashamed of!'"

The article also points out how important the GI's in Korea had been to Marilyn, and she, in turn, to them. "Marilyn's the No. 1 pin-up girl of the GI's--officially confirmed in her present position by *Stars and Stripes*, and other official publications. And she takes the responsibilities of her position seriously. 'I personally answer every letter from servicemen. It's quite a job in itself and a girlfriend helps me. I send pictures at my own expense. The studio pictures for fan mail are a little too small.' The servicemen must have their pin-ups. In every letter there is a request for them. They write to her when they see her in a picture or read a story about her. 'They like truthful, honest stories,' says this sweetheart of her GI's. 'They don't want anything phony or exaggerated. They want the real facts. Some advice me not to pay any attention to Hollywood wolves. Others want me to wait until they get back to the States, hoping I won't marry for some time. Most of them think I won't answer their letters because they aren't important. Actually, they are important to me. One boy in Korea was wounded while writing to me and his buddy had to finish the letter for him. When you get a letter like that, you can't read it without a lump in your throat.' They write to her from their fox holes. From training camps. From hospitals. From various American outposts in the far corners of the world. They say modestly they don't expect to marry her, for as a movie star they think she's beyond their reach, but she's a symbol of U.S. womanhood. She is an ideal to them--one of the things worth fighting for. Not all of them, Marilyn says, want to see her in a bathing suit or lying on some thick rug. Many prefer her in a skirt--just walking along. They've read she writes poetry, and they comment about it. Many enclose snapshots of themselves. To the question, would she marry a GI, Marilyn replies, 'I might. Why not? Who can tell? If I love him.'"

On January 2nd Sheilah Graham dropped this publicity grenade, which didn't explode until Aline Mosby pulled the pin out on March 13th, "Marilyn Monroe simply smiles when asked about those calendar sittings supposedly in her birthday suit--before she became a star. Anyway, her fan mail has increased."

Marilyn had a session with Dr. Abraham Gottesman and was charged $200 on January 4th.

Jet Fore, a Fox Studio publicist, remembers the reaction of Zanuck upon learning of Marilyn's nude calendar. "This will ruin the studio! We've got three of her pictures in the can." Fore remarked that her nude photograph was a shock "because in those days no famous actress had exposed her breasts." On January 5th, in an attempt to control the release of information that Marilyn had posed in the nude, Darryl Zanuck invited New York syndicated columnist and radio show host, Hy Gardner, to lunch. Harry Brand gave him a sanitized version of Marilyn's calendar scandal. Gardner wanted to see the calendar, but was told the studio had it locked in their vaults. For whatever reason, Gardner didn't use the story and didn't seem to take her seriously. Meanwhile, Marilyn was making her own plans for the leaking of her calendar romp.

Columnist Hy Gardner remembers meeting Marilyn around this time. "The first time I met Marilyn Monroe was when we had a luncheon date in the 20th Century-Fox commissary. She slank in carrying a volume of Keats under her arm. 'A Keats fan?' I asked. 'I don't know,' she shrugged, 'but the books the right weight to balance on my head to learn to walk right.' Sitting face-to-face (which makes you forget to even nibble on the food) I made some notes. When she talks seriously or thinks back to detours on the rocky road to fame, she massages her lips with her index finger. She likes to sport a plain black sweater, as if any sweater, any color, could look plain on her. She keeps her sweaters in shape by hanging them in a refrigerator. She walks--(or should I say wiggles) like jello in a frappe glass--or perhaps like she's wearing tight panties. She prefers gooey desserts, often doubles. She paints her toenails the same blushing shade as her fingernails. Also pencils her own eyebrows and frequently, for fun, adds a pair of horizontal asterisks speared with umlauts. If her handbag dropped and fell open on the sidewalk, passersby would be tickled at the contents that trickled out, including the usual girl treasures--cosmetics, lipstick, mascara, cigarettes, mad money, and keys, etc.--but also a tiny leather copy of the New Testament."

On January 5th Hedda Hopper reported, "It's hard to believe that Marilyn Monroe would lock herself in with Max Reinhardt's tome, 'Actors and Acting.' She's going to learn to act if it kills her--and it probably will."

On January 7th Aline Mosby devotes her column to Marilyn. "Sultry Marilyn Monroe Lived In Orphanage...Marilyn Monroe was busy being a gay, sultry, dizzy blonde at RKO today, but around the corner from the studio is a memory of heartbreak. She's co-starring in *Clash by Night* with Barbara Stanwyck, and she's hailed as the hottest thing since Harlow. But 13 years ago Marilyn lived in the Los Angeles Orphanage two blocks from the studio. She was a thin, freckle-faced orphan named Norma Jeane Baker. From the window of her tiny room she could see the sign on the studio water tower of RKO-Radio. She wanted to be an actress. She collected Barbara Stanwyck photos and hung them on the drab walls." Her father was killed in an automobile accident before she was born. Her mother was too ill to care for her, and died later. Marilyn had 11 sets of foster parents before she was 16. 'I had my first job at the orphanage for 5 cents a month,' she says, 'setting the table for 100 children three times a day.' Later she was shuttled from one set of foster parents to another, unloved and unwanted. 'They'd keep me for six months...or a year. Then they'd say, 'You make me nervous,' and the county or somebody would find another home for me. The families I lived with were all poor. I hardly ever went to movies. I didn't often have a dime for one.' Because of her insecurity, she was shy and she stuttered. 'To escape out of something,' she married a merchant seaman when she was 16 rather than move on to another family. The marriage didn't work, and she was divorced two years later. By then she had blossomed into a beauty. She worked as a cheesecake starlet at 20$^{th}$ Century-Fox studio, but was dropped. She was broke and hungry. Finally she got a break in *Asphalt Jungle*. Maybe it was her undulating walk or her baby stare, but a new star was born. Fox signed her again, and loaned her to RKO. She stars next in *Don't Bother to Knock*. 'To make up for the college she never knew, the 'dumb' blonde attends literature classes one night a week at UCLA. She reads the great classics because 'I get comfort from finding out that I'm not different...other people are alone inside, too, I'm trying to find myself now to be a good actress and a good person. Sometimes I feel strong inside, but I have to reach in and pull it up. You have to be strong inside, way deep inside of you. It isn't easy. Nothing's easy, as long as you go on living.' Marilyn doesn't like to talk about her past, 'Because it's an unpleasant experience I'm trying to forget.' She blinked her false eyelashes and said, 'I didn't have the nerve to tell Miss Stanwyck about those pictures.'"

On January 7th, Louella Parsons revealed that, "Vince Edwards, who used to have it bad for Shelley Winters, was with Marilyn Monroe at Jack's at the Beach--and that ain't bad." In November Marilyn would deny ever dating Vince and blame the publicity machine for making up boyfriends. On the press's infatuation with coupling her with another star, Marilyn had this to say, "About the only man whose name I haven't been linked with is the little French boy in Bing's new picture."

Marilyn's calendar had yet to reach the attention of the public, but it seemed to have a life of its own as an underground novelty. In addition to the columnist eager to break the story, on January 7th, *Terry & The Pirates*, a comic strip, mentioned Marilyn's calendar. Upon request for a large meeting room, one of the characters said, "It must be well insulated! The Marilyn Monroe Calendar Fan Club will meet there!"

Louella Parsons gave her advice for Marilyn's career on the 8th. "Don't tell Marilyn Monroe she's being groomed to be another Jean Harlow. She's a mild mannered gal, but those are fighting words. Even though she photographs like a million and has more sex appeal than almost any other girl in pictures today, she doesn't want to be compared to anyone. More and more she is getting better roles on the 20th lot. Cary Grant…has been switched *into Darling, I Am Growing Younger*, with Marilyn. All she needs is a couple of important pictures like this, with top stars like Cary to get into the front ranks herself."

The columnist vied for news about Marilyn on January 11th. Dorothy Kilgallen reported, "Marilyn Monroe and Nick Ray have become a Steady Thing." Erskine Johnson reported, "Marilyn Monroe on cheesecake photography: 'People ask me if it's distasteful to me. Far from it! Why, I get wonderful letters from the boys in Korea. They're so appreciative. One of them just wrote me. 'Don't bother with bathing suits and shorts. Just sit down wearing a sweater and skirt. But lift the skirt a little.'" And Hedda Hopper reported, "It sounds like a gag but Marilyn Monroe, who looks like a Varga girl in the flesh, attends U.C.L.A.'s extension division classes downtown at 9th and Hill Sts., one night a week. Her subject, 'An Appreciation of Literature.' The other pupils seem to be studying Marilyn Monroe."

Wardrobe test for *We're Not Married* were held on January 11th. Marilyn was dressed by designer Elois Jenssen. Marilyn stars as Annabel Norris, a beauty queen whose lust for a title is upsetting things at home with her husband Jeff, played by David Wayne. This was a movie with five interwoven stories. It was produced by Nunnally Johnson and based upon an original screenplay of his. Marilyn would go on to work with Johnson again in *How to*

*Marry a Millionaire*, which he also wrote the screenplay for. Christopher and Jonathan Milne, first twins born in Los Angeles after January 1, 1951, doubled for each other as Marilyn's baby in the film. They were the sons of Mr. and Mrs. Douglas Milne. Marilyn had worked with or will work again with many of the cast members including David Wayne, Victor Moore, Paul Douglas, Mitzi Gaynor, Louis Calhern, and Ginger Rogers. Noreen Nash was in the cast, but uncredited. She will go on to marry Dr. Lee Siegel, Fox's doctor to the stars.

If Hy Gardner had been slow on the up-take, Erskine Johnson wasn't and picked up on Marilyn's calendar escapade and revealed this on January 16th, "Fox high brass has decided to do nothing about those 'September Morn' calendar pictures that Marilyn Monroe posed for before her movie breaks."

Louella Parsons leaked her information on Marilyn calendar on January 21st. "There's divided reaction over a calendar for which Marilyn Monroe modeled sans clothes some time ago. Marilyn is crazy about the calendar portrait and has autographed copies for any number of people. Her bosses do not share her feeling, however and have asked her to restrain her enthusiasm. In fact one of her bosses was so concerned when he found out about it that an order was given to buy them up. Marilyn's argument is 'art for art's sake.'"

Even with all the columnist making statements in the press, the calendar did not reach social consciousness until Aline Mosby's column on March 13th, when Miss Mosby interviewed Marilyn about the calendar. Marilyn would reference Miss Parson's quote, "art for art's sake," and deny saying 'the silly quote.'

On January 26th Marilyn is awarded a Henrietta Award by the Foreign Press Association of Hollywood, for Most Promising Box Office Personality of 1951. The others selected for the award were Tony Curtis, John Derek, Mitzi Gaynor, Leslie Caron, and Patrice Wymore. They would all appear in a magazine article together, photographed by Ed Clark. The Award ceremony cost $10 per plate and was held at the Del Mar Club in Santa Monica. Marilyn appears at the awards ceremony in an extremely low-cut red velvet gown by designer Oleg Cassini she had bought in early 1951. She had worn the gown before, but never to such effect, and the women in Hollywood would make trouble for her, like never before. The press would have a field day generating publicity that the dress stirred up. If the old Hollywood axiom is true, that any publicity is good publicity, then Marilyn was in for a windfall. Marilyn adored the gown and she would also wear it to the Junior Prom at UCLA and also to entertain the troops at Camp Pendleton and the El Toro Air Base.

The Henrietta was a precursor to the Golden Globe Award which is given by the Hollywood Foreign Press. Thirty seven members of the Hollywood Foreign Press Association, representing 900 publications and radio broadcasting stations in 50 countries, took part in the selections. Always a favorite in foreign countries, Marilyn would go on to win three Golden Globe awards in 1954, 1960 and in 1962.

    Marilyn would give this comment on the gown in the July 1952 issue of *Modern Screen*. "My first expensive evening gown was the one I purchased for the Foreign Press Association's annual dinner, where I was presented with a Henrietta award, and named as one of Hollywood's most promising young players. I very gratefully accepted the award, and later, was told I looked nice doing it. But I also heard that some of the women present had thought my gown a trifle extreme for the occasion. I seriously considered these comments, but, in my opinion, they were not reason enough to a take the gown back to Oleg Cassini, who designed it. I've always admired his taste and imagination in women's clothes, and my gown is no exception. It is a red velvet creation which fits snugly down to the knees, in the Lillian Russell tradition. It plunges somewhat in the front, but not extremely. Frankly, I love the gown wish I had more occasions to wear it."

    German actress Hildegard Knef, who was also at the Henrietta Awards, witnessed the transformation of Marilyn from girlishly sweet to full blown siren. They met earlier in the day in a dressing room at Twentieth Century-Fox. "The sleepy looking girl, with the transparent plastic shower cap over her white-blonde hair and a thick layer of cream on her pale face sits down beside me. She digs around in a faded beach bag and takes out a sandwich, a pillbox, a book. She smiles at my reflection in the mirror. 'Hi, my name's Marilyn Monroe, what's yours!'" Without the benefit of makeup and gown, Knef thought she looked like "a child with short legs and a fat bottom, scuffing over to the makeup room in old sandals." In less than two hours Marilyn had been transformed and Knef would observe, "Only the eyes are still recognizable. She seems to have grown with the makeup, the legs seem longer, the body more willowy, the face glows as if lit by candles." Later, at the awards dinner Knef recalls, "Now she's wearing a red dress that's too tight for her; I've seen it before in the Fox wardrobe—although it's too tight, it looks like one of Mum's old ones dug out of the wardrobe. Eyes half-closed, mouth half-open, hands trembling a little. One glass too many, a child's first go at the punch. The photographers hold their cameras up high, flash into her cleavage. She leans and stretches, turns and smiles, is willing, offers herself to the lenses. Someone bends forward and whispers into her ear. 'No, please,' she says. 'I can't.' the trembling hand knocks over a glass. Finally she stands up, the people snigger, the tight skirt presses her knees together, she trips to the microphone. The walk is absurd and she's got miles to go; they stare at the dress, wait for it to burst and liberate the bosom, the belly, the bottom. The master of ceremonies roars, 'Marilyn Monroe!' She steadies herself on the mike stand, closes her eyes, leaves a long pause in which one hears her amplified breathing—short, panting, obscene. 'Hi,' she whispers, and starts the trip back."

Sheilah Graham reported on January 27th, "Marilyn Monroe came to an interview in the Twentieth Century-Fox cafe wearing a loose dressing gown over a black bra and black panties. That's all, brother." Marilyn will later say in her defense, "I suppose, however, because of my background as a model, I will always have to expect that a tinge of daring might seem to be associated with my attire. Not very long ago, I wore the bathing suit which I model in *We're Not Married* to lunch in the commissary at Twentieth. With a robe over it, of course. The next morning, I was surprised to read in a column that I was seen eating lunch in my bra and panties. I suppose that from across the room, the flesh-colored inset on my suit made me seem scantily attired. But I wasn't."

Marilyn is gathering a reputation as not only being a sexy girl, but also engendering bad press about the way she parades herself in racy clothing, making her seem more wanton and loose, than sensual. Marilyn will overplay her hand when it comes to her sexuality and will pay for it next year when a big backlash over her promiscuous demeanor will culminate in bad press and a revamping of her appeal to women. But until then, Marilyn continues on, unrestrained by studio, agent or friend, throwing her sexuality onto the world stage. It is an amateur mistake and she will learn the lesson the hard way that she doesn't need the salacious clothing and in your face lewdness to keep the public's attention.

Marilyn had a session with Dr. Abraham Gottesman and was charged $60 on January 28th.

In February David March, a business agent, had made friends with Marilyn for the aim of getting her business. He worked for the Leslie and Tyson firm and was trying to get Marilyn to let them handle her finances. During this time he paid her traffic tickets and ran errands in an attempt to convince her that she needs his help.

Marilyn is seeing plenty of press attention in February due in large part to her devotion to her cheesecake photos. Newspapers in early February started carrying a photo of

Marilyn sitting on a diving board, which is captioned, "No diva, film lassie Marilyn Monroe attains glamour in other lines. Like them?" The photos were taken by Phil Burchman. In the February issue of *Silver Screen* she is shown once again in these popular photos wearing Rose Marie Reid Swimsuits. "A suit with a magic length—elasticized nylon power net, designed to adjust in length to meet your needs. 'Cut Diamond Magic' suit is hand painted, comes in canyon gold and shades of blue. About $25. Other features: built-in bra, girdle control." The other suit is described as, "To mold, flatter and reveal a pretty figure—'Cut Diamond Magic' suit. Lace patterned and elasticized, this suit comes with removable straps. At about $25. In shades of gray, poinsettia, or glade green." These Rose Marie Reid suits flattered Marilyn's body due to the architectural design of the suit. According to designer Elgee Bove, Marilyn understood this aspect of clothing design and often collaborated with him on her gowns. Edith Head said that Marilyn understood fit and fabric. Not a bad compliment coming from the great costumer of Hollywood. Another photo, from the *Sunday Star Pictorial Magazine*, shows Marilyn as an ice skater. "Although no great shakes as an ice skater, starlet Marilyn Monroe glamorizes a novel bright-blue mouton costume. There's no ice, either, but it didn't faze the cameraman." This publicity stunt harkens back to the days when she dressed as an Indian maid and sat on a block of ice.

February 7th has Marilyn posing in the newspapers for Valentine's Day in the gorgeous bathing suit from *We're Not Married*, designed by Elois Jenssen. She was photographed by Art Adams.

On February 9th Harold Heffernan joined the growing list of Hollywood insiders that were chomping at the bit to tell of her calendar exploit. It seems, according to the article, Marilyn was sending her calendar picture to soldiers upon request. "Six years ago, in the midst of World War II, Betty Grable, Esther Williams and Lana Turner were tops in pin-up photos with Yank troops. Today the boys will trade a dozen of these for one of a saucy blonde newcomer named Marilyn Monroe. There's little doubt about Marilyn's photo status in Korea. A famous photographer just returned from that battle front reports that his chief claim to distinction was that he knew Marilyn personally and had photographed her. The armed forces newspaper in the Far East prints her picture at least once a week. When the paper can't dig up a new shot of her, it reprints an old one. All this attention is being lavished on a girl who made one startling appearance in *Asphalt Jungle* a couple of years ago and has two completed pictures, *Don't Bother to Knock* and *Clash by Night*, awaiting release. Soldiers who have written to Miss Monroe personally asking for art subjects based on her own curves know how cooperative she can be. In fact, her studio, 20th Century-Fox, has requested of Marilyn that she burn up the prints and negative of a certain pose which a Los Angeles photographer shot of her some months ago. And they are asking further, that she submit to them first any poses of herself with which she intends to reward the eager boys who write to her direct. The combined mailing activities of 20th-Fox and Miss Monroe have deluged American service camps throughout the world and much more prominent sister starlets making entertainment junkets to these camps have reported on the situation rather bitingly. This has only inspired the lovely blonde siren to set in motion some additional exploitation plans. The champ of the pinups should certainly visit the scenes of her latest triumphs: hence, Marilyn is asking 20$^{th}$-Fox to let her off for a while, say about eight weeks, so she can head a junket that would hit Europe, Japan, Korea, Newfoundland and Alaska."

*The California Eagle* reported on February 10$^{th}$, about evidence of Marilyn's charitable nature. "The Coffee Sip held at the Zenda Ballroom...The affair sponsored by the Postalettes, a group of Postal employees drew more than 500 people including many celebrities. Special guests and entertainers including...Marilyn Monroe 20th Century-Fox star...The St. Augustine-West View Hospital will be built at 53rd and Main Streets and will serve more than 300,000 people now living without any other adequate hospital facilities."

On February 11th Marilyn was invited to attend the *Photoplay* Gold Medal Awards Dinner by her old friend, Adele Whitely Fletcher, one of the editors for *Photoplay* magazine. The dinner was held at the Ambassador Hotel. Miss Fletcher remembers being surprised that Marilyn had arrived early for the dinner, "'Marilyn!' I said, 'you came!' The surprise in my voice must have been apparent to her. 'I told you I'd come. I'm awfully early!' I can still hear her soft breathlessness and her laughter at the idea of her, usually hours late, being early. 'I came straight from the studio so I wouldn't get held up anywhere. They did my hair, and dressed me.' Her hair was smooth and lovely. But I've never forgiven the wardrobe people for rigging her up in red satin and black silk fringe. Her dress looked like something out of an old movie about the gold rush days."

On February 18th, Sheilah Graham pointed out Marilyn's scandalous attire and antics at the *Photoplay* awards. "How could Marilyn Monroe sit down in the tight dress that hugged her body especially from the waist to the knee? While the *Photoplay* awards were being presented, Marilyn was posed by the photographers every which way on the far side of the Embassy room. She certainly stole the spotlight, if not the awards."

Marilyn's dress was designed by Christian Dior and was her own. It was a personal favorite of hers. This was just the kind of fashion faux pas that Amy Greene would have a strong hand in changing when Marilyn moved to New York in 1955. Marilyn seemed to think that if a sexy gown had a designer label it made it appropriate to wear. In the future she would learn how to refine her sexuality in a chic wardrobe from New York designers like Norman Norell, George Nardiello and John Moore.

In the July issue of *Modern Screen*, Marilyn describes the gown. "I have another evening gown which women criticize, but which has won me an appreciable number of comments from men. It is a strapless red silk taffeta, snug from the bodice down to the hips, which is covered in black French lace. At I. Magnin's, where I paid a still price for it, I was told that the dress was the only copy of an original purchased by a San Francisco social leader. I wonder if her dress has ever been criticized in her set the way mine was the night I wore it to one of the few formal Hollywood parties I have attended…it was the proof positive, they claimed, that I was utterly lacking in taste. I'm truly sorry, but I love that dress."

Three years later Marilyn will tell Elizabeth Toomey about her dress, in an interview for her column. "I've learned a lot from all this—the last few years. I mean. I remember saving up my money to buy a special dress for a party when I first started to be known. It cost a lot, and I thought it was beautiful; red silk and black lace. The next day they wrote about me and said it was a cheap and vulgar display. Those were the words they used. I couldn't understand it. The saleslady told me there was only one other dress like it and a big society woman bought that one. I was heartbroken."

More on the infamous gown…Sheilah Graham, February 15th, "Marilyn Monroe, wearing a strapless red and black lace gown for lunch at Twentieth Century Fox, indignantly repudiates George Jessel as her new boyfriend.' All he did was take me to the Louis B. Mayer party for the Henry Fords.' Marilyn tells me."

Dorothy Kilgallen reported on the 13th, "Claude Terrail, owner of the famed Paris restaurant Tour de' Argent, is Hollywood's current social lion. His two pet dates out are starlet Marilyn Monroe and dancer Gwen Verden (Jack Cole's partner.)" Miss Verden would later assist Jack Cole with Marilyn on her dance moves in *Gentlemen Prefer Blondes*.

On Valentine's Day Marilyn wrote a check for cash, $200, and noted on the bottom of the check, "N. Lytess."

Erskine Johnson was getting impatient to ignite the calendar scandal and again reported on February 20th, "Marilyn Monroe is completely unruffled about those September Morn calendar pictures she posed for b.s. (before stardom) and has even autographed a couple for studio pals." Fox would not be long in dealing with the growing problem of Marilyn's calendar.

*Toledo Blade* newspaper ran this blurb on February 22nd, "Marine Corp Alexander J. Stefka, Monroe, Mich., chatted with Marilyn Monroe, movie actress, after a recent USO show at the Marine Corps Air Station, El Toro, CA."

Marilyn performed for the Marines at El Toro and for the Marines of the 1st Division at Camp Pendleton, singing *Do It Again*. She wore one of her favorite gowns during this time, the revealing Oleg Cassini gown from the Henrietta awards. She drops this jewel of a line while talking to the men, "I don't know why you boys are always getting so excited about sweater girls. Take away their sweaters and what have they got?!" She would perform for them again in two years when she toured the Korean Front in February of 1954.

Bob Hope recalled his experience with Marilyn at Camp Pendleton. "...there were about 800 kids come down from Roosevelt's Raiders out of the mountains after the training. And she walked out, and said, hello. That's all. They went right to the ceiling, and I was with them."

Pete Rendina recalls seeing Marilyn perform at Camp Pendleton. "I saw Marilyn perform at Tent Camp 2 at Camp Pendleton at the Outdoor Theater right before I left for Korea in 1952. With me was a friend, Robert Jowder from PA. 50 years later we live across the road from each other. Anyway, Jowder and myself were stationed at Tent Camp 3 in the 3rd Brigade. Bob ran up on stage and kissed Marilyn before the MPs could drag him off.

We could not hear her singing--only her lips moving because the guys were yelling so loud. She was bent over singing to the guys in the front row and her bust was about to fall out and the guys went nuts. The guy that set the record for pole vaulting at 16 feet, Rev. Bob Richards, was there with Marilyn and pole vaulted across the stage."

Bob Richards, aka "The Vaulting Vicar," would go on in July to win the first of his back-to-back gold medals for pole vaulting in the Summer Olympics in Helsinki, Finland. Mr. Richards was the first athlete to appear on the cover of a box of *Wheaties* cereal.

The December 1952 issue of *Leatherneck* magazine has this to say about Marilyn's visit to Camp Pendleton. "We asked Marilyn what she thought about Marines. 'I like them better close up,' she whispered, then reflected a moment. 'And at a distance, too.' she added, probably thinking of the near riots her personal appearances at Camp Pendleton and El Toro have caused. Nine thousand Marines jammed the outdoor stage at Pendleton to see Marilyn. 'But I didn't get close to any of them,' she remarked regretfully. Probably just as well--and a lot safer. Pendleton and El Toro are the only bases she has visited so far."

One reason Marilyn agreed to perform for the men was an attempt on her part to convince the studio that she could sing and dance well enough for the part of Lorelei Lee in *Gentlemen Prefer Blondes*. Thank you Phil Moore.

The next day, February 23rd, James Bacon features Marilyn and her ever increasing attention by the men in the Armed Forces in his column. "Even Press Agents Love Marilyn Monroe, A Landslide Pinup...Marilyn Monroe is the kind of girl sailors dream about. Ever since she first made brief screen appearances in *The Asphalt Jungle* and *All About Eve*, this shapely lass has inspired pinup poets in Quonset huts throughout the globe. Her studio tells her she gets more GI fan mail than any other player on the lot. A USO entertainer just back from Korea reports in a trade magazine that the service papers run a Marilyn Monroe pinup daily--even if it means running the same picture two or three times in a row. Marilyn herself has a knack for getting herself voted something or other by the GIs. Here are some samples culled from the fan mail she stacks in her Beverly Hills house. 'The girl we would most like to go AWOL with,' from a student training squadron at Keesler Air Force Base, Miss. 'The girl we would most like to chogie up a hill with,' from a Marine battalion in Korea. Chogie, it seems, is Korean talk for climb. And the First Battalion, Seventh Marines in Korea voted her 'The girl with the eyes we would most like to pull the wool over.' C W Section 13$^{th}$ Communications Sq., APO 238, Okinawa, votes Marilyn, 'The girl who has more effect on the CW radio operators than high speed code.' The 323$^{rd}$ Marine Fighting Squadron, VMF323, calls Marilyn 'The girl we'd most like to have on a strike with us.' 'The woman most sailors dream about,' is the way the sailors on the USS Orion (AS-18) describe her. Then Battery C, 101$^{st}$ AAA Gun Battalion, Camp McCoy, Wis. labels her 'The girl we would most like to send a requisition in for.' Down at Lackland Air Force Base, San Antonio, Tex., the 3716 Training Squadron voted her 'The girl we'd most like to fly with.' Even the small fry get into the act. She was elected 'Miss Campus of Kiskiminetas Springs School.' The Saltsburg, Pa., prep school is better known as Kiski. It's no novelty for a shapely Hollywood starlet to become a campus or any other type of queen.

It's just one of the time-tested tricks of the press agents' trade. But when titles come in apparently without the benefit of press agentry, that's when the producers get interested. So what happens to this bundle of sex appeal? Producers Jerry Wald and Norman Krasna put her in *Clash by Night* with Barbara Stanwyck, Robert Ryan and Paul Douglas. Marilyn can't act like Stanwyck, but she's getting the same star billing. 'It's the voice of the people that makes Marilyn a star,' comments Jerry Wald. He also concedes that in this case most of the people are men. To which, Marilyn chimes in, 'I like men.'"

Of Marilyn, Wald had this to say, "Marilyn Monroe was born sexy. When she walks, when she stands up, she's like a snake uncoiling—slow and easy does it. It's natural with her. There's a 'babe' quality about her that makes minds dwell on romance. Maybe some men don't think of her in terms of long range planning, but here are very few men who don't think of her in terms of whistlebait. What she wears has nothing to do with it. A bathing suit doesn't add to her allure, although her figure is lush. Marilyn could wear perfume, jewels, ankle strap shoes—and that wouldn't be the definition of what she has. Marilyn, herself, is the answer. She doesn't have to make like a strip tease dancer and show acres of flesh to make men's heads turn like cranks when she walks by. She could be dressed in a Mother Hubbard and still 'get' you. For Marilyn has true sex appeal. It's in her face, the way she looks at you. It's in her walk and what she's thinking about when she's walking. More than anyone else in pictures today, she demonstrates the fact sex is an attitude, a mental rather than a physical thing."

Wald will tell Maurice Zolotow this about Marilyn's sexuality, "Her sex is just something that is there, like a bottle. It is not natural—I mean it doesn't come out of her nature. You might say she's almost a prim, puritanical person, a nice kid. The sex is acquired. She opens the bottle and uses some when she needs it for a purpose and then she puts the cork back in the bottle." It is almost as if her sexuality resides like a Genie in the bottle of her "magic friend," her body. This is a very revealing comment about how she uses her power. Zolotow will also say that her sexuality is the "lever with which she might move the world."

Wald will rhapsodize about Marilyn to Milton Shulman, "Stars are self-illuminating bodies. She has a tremendous radiance and projects it to her audience. If we knew what that chemical or quality was we'd feed it to our actors three times a day."

On February 25th Marilyn appeared in one of her most popular publicity stunts that had her thumbing her nose at the snobs in Hollywood and women in particular. One woman reporter said that she looked cheap and vulgar in her dress she wore to the Henrietta Awards on January 26th, and that she would have looked better in a potato sack. This comment prompted the Fox Publicity Department to take photographs of Marilyn looking glamorous and dripping with jewels, wearing a potato sack, giving life to the old adage, that she would look gorgeous even in a potato sack. William Travilla whipped up her glamorous costume. He said, "Marilyn has the most fantastically perfect figure in the world. No matter how you dress her, she looks sexy. You could even put her in a burlap bag. I know because I did it. She still looked great—although I doubt if she'd like it for a regular wardrobe." Gene Kornman's photographs of her in this outfit were published in over 400 newspapers starting in late February, proving once and for all that Marilyn looks wonderful in anything she wears. "Burlap Can't Her Hide Beauty...Studio publicity men had a quick comeback when Hollywood columnist criticized Marilyn Monroe's clothing, saying it lacked style and smartness. They thought she'd be a welcome eyeful in or out of any garment. That explains the potato sack she wears here."

Roy Craft recalls the Potato Sack stunt. "What happened is that one of the columnist had written that Marilyn would look great even in a potato sack. That gave us an idea and I went down to the market and got an Idaho potato sack. We got the hairdresser, the wardrobe mistress and assistants, the makeup man, the body-makeup woman. You know, by California state law we had to have a woman do the body makeup. We fringed the potato sack, and clipped it on her back and shot the picture. God, it went all over the world. She did look good in a sack."

But not everyone appreciated Marilyn's potato sack tour de force and she experienced a bit of a backlash when Dorothy Kilgallen reported, on March 8th, "The recent publicity pictures of Marilyn Monroe wearing a dress made of burlap left me cold and at the same time feeling a little sorry for the eager Miss Monroe. Case histories of the stars show that from Miss Barrymore to Miss Bankhead, few of the great ones ever resorted to such silly stunts."

Marilyn has a session with Dr. Abraham Gottesman and was charged $160 for her visit on February 26th.

The studio was trying to plot a strategy to reduce the expected injury the calendar would cause to Marilyn's career. In two weeks' time, Marilyn herself would orchestrate a way to "leak" it to the press without any harm to her. Her skill in handling this publicity crisis was superb.

*O'Henry's Full House* began filming around this time. Marilyn's costume was designed by Carey Cline. Marilyn played a prostitute in the vignette "The Cop and The Anthem." She co-starred with the great Charles Laughton. This movie was made up of five stories, with an all-star cast. Her part had a very short screen time and she was through with filming in a couple of days. In the future, Marilyn would avoid playing prostitutes, even going so far as to turn down the lead in *Irma La Douce*, which was directed by Billy Wilder. He eventually made the film in 1963 with Shirley MacLaine, and she was nominated for an Oscar for her performance. Marilyn had known Charles Laughton since mid-1950, when they were among the guest invited to a party at the honeymoon home of photographer Anthony Beauchamp and Sarah Churchill.

*Movie Life magazine*, March 1952 ran this article, "Watta Co-Ed!...When the boys at U.C.L.A. decided to toss a formal dance, they really do it up in style. Luscious Marilyn Monroe, invited to the Junior Prom, gets a red-carpet-type welcome, from Dane Lund and Jerry Perenchio, juniors' entertainment chairmen...She'd promised not only to appear in the floor show, but to dance with any of the lads who wanted a whirl, so Dane and Irving Goldring figured class's collective date rated orchid. Show featured songs by Joan Evans,

Kay Brown and Keith Andes...It pays to be a football hero, Paul Cameron finds, as Marilyn gives last season's star special award. [she gave him a kiss] She wasn't really an outsider; had been taking U.C.L.A. extension courses before starting RKO's *Clash by Night*."

The Prom was held at the Beverly Hills Hotel in February. Marilyn wore her infamous Oleg Cassini, red strapless gown. Keith Andes had invited Marilyn to come to this event. She agreed to go only if he would be her date. Marilyn appeared in the 1952 University of California at Los Angeles (UCLA) Yearbook, *Southern Campus*. The captioned photo showed her arriving at the Junior Prom. It was captioned, "All smiles, Dave Lund and Jerry Perrenchio welcomed evening's sensation, Marilyn Monroe."

On March 1st Dr. Elliot Corday diagnosed Marilyn with appendicitis. Dr. Corday would become a leading heart specialist in Los Angeles. Marilyn was admitted to the Cedars of Lebanon Hospital and released with an insulated icepack to wear in the hopes of warding off another attack. She delays surgery until April 28 in order to complete filming on *Monkey Business*. Her strenuous scenes of roller-skating, swimming and the car stunt will be postponed until after her surgery.

Sheilah Graham gives another salacious view of Marilyn in this report on March 4th, "Marilyn Monroe, in a dress that barely contained her at the recent *Look* party, said that she is going east as soon as *Darling I Am Growing Older* is completed. New York will get as complete a view of Marilyn as she will get of New York."

Hedda Hopper reported on April 4th about Marilyn attending the *Look* party and the attention she got. "At the party *Look* magazine tossed at Romanoff's for managing editor William Lowe and his wife and Sports Editor Tim Cohane, Marilyn Monroe proved to be the main attraction. We had to elbow our way through a circle of men to get a word with her, but we heard several catty remarks by women on the revealing gown she wore."

Once again, it seems to be her beloved Oleg Cassini gown that is proving to be too much, even for Hollywood. Marilyn will attend another *Look* party for Sports editor Tim Cohane in November.

Marilyn doesn't spend her time worrying about what others, especially women think about her, as illustrated in this quote from *Photoplay* in April 1952. "I see no reason for worrying about what other people think or say about me as long as I can face myself. I owe no apologies to anyone and have no intention of going around making explanations."

Impossible to separate from the image of Marilyn Monroe is Joe DiMaggio. When they began dating there was a shift in Hollywood's axis and suddenly Marilyn became a legitimate movie star. She not only had a successful Hollywood career, but she was transported into the rarified air of celebrity when she was wooed by the elegant, courtly icon that was Joe DiMaggio. Roy Craft remembers when Marilyn and Joe DiMaggio met. "I recall the morning after her first 'blind date' with Joe DiMaggio when, in her dressing room, she told our little group—her hairdresser, her makeup man, her wardrobe mistress and myself—how she had met an interesting man and made us guess his identity. She was like a little girl playing '20 questions' and from her sparkle I knew it was the real thing. It was at times like this she was completely different from the sultry, breathless Monroe the public came to know."

Harrison Carroll reported on March 8th, "Marilyn Monroe and Joe DiMaggio have discovered each other in a big way. Their favorite spot is the dimly lit Villa Nova restaurant."

And Dorothy Kilgallen followed up on March 10th, "Joe DiMaggio is burning up the long distance phone wires to Marilyn Monroe, the zowie young starlet."

There are a few versions and dates of Marilyn and Joe's first meeting. The most published version is the story of David March, who was contacted by Joe DiMaggio to set up a date with Marilyn. Joe was in town for a charity game between some retired players and the A's. Joe had seen a publicity photo of Marilyn posing with Philadelphia Athletics outfielder, Gus Zernial. He mentioned the pretty blonde to Zernial, who gave him the name of David March. Joe contacted him to set up a date with Marilyn. She was hesitant to go on the date, not knowing exactly who Joe DiMaggio was. Finally, March was able to set up a double date at the Villa Nova Restaurant. Joe, March and his date Peggy Rabe, waited for an hour for Marilyn to show up. March finally called Marilyn, who was still making up her mind about attending the date. She finally showed up. It wasn't until Mickey Rooney came to the table that she finally grasped Joe DiMaggio's fame. Men were coming over to their table, not to see her, but to see DiMaggio. At 11:00 Marilyn announced that she needed to go home. She was going to drive Joe back to his room at the Knickerbocker Hotel, but he wanted to just drive around instead. After driving for 3 hours, they ended up at Marilyn's apartment.

A second, similar version starts with David March and Vince Edwards setting Joe up with Marilyn. Joe looked lonely, and the guys thought Marilyn would be a good date for him. The rest of the story proceeds the same way.

Marilyn herself said the meeting took place in February of 1952 in an interview she did with Liza Wilson. Marilyn's version to Miss Wilson was that it was a blind date set up by a friend. She also told Aline Mosby the same story of a blind date in her column on November 26, 1952. "He arrived alone…I arrived alone…we left together."

Marilyn told a slightly different version to columnist Louella Parsons about their meeting. "I'll tell you how it happened. I was having dinner with some friends who knew Joe DiMaggio. He sent word over to our table that he would like to meet me. I wasn't interested in baseball and he meant nothing to me. We were introduced and I thought he was very nice."

Another version of the first meeting between Joe and Marilyn, which is similar to the one she told to Louella Parsons, comes from Johnny Hyde's nephew, Norman Brokaw, who was chairman of the William Morris Agency. He took Marilyn to the *Lights, Camera, Action* television show in Los Angeles. Afterward, they went to the Brown Derby for lunch. Joe DiMaggio and William Frawley were also eating lunch at the restaurant. Joe sent him over to Norman's table with a request to meet the young lady. Norman brought Marilyn over as they were leaving. The next day, Joe called for a date. She was, according to Brokaw, still living with Johnny Hyde at the time, at 718 North Palm Drive. This would have made it 1950. The version by Norman Brokaw seems to fit Marilyn's account of the events that she told to Louella Parsons except that it's a little too early. And Marilyn was famously faithful to Johnny Hyde. Not to mention if Marilyn and Joe DiMaggio had started dating in 1950, something would have been published about it.

Another tweak to this version is from Bill Frawley, who told Lee Ferrero in an article on January 7, 1954, that they met on a blind date, but he didn't remember the particulars, and that he was there and he even quoted Marilyn and Joe from the night.

The last version is from Joe DiMaggio himself. He recalls meeting Marilyn during her trip to New York in August of 1951 and having dinner with her at Toot's Shor.

But, however it happened, Marilyn and Joe DiMaggio were a couple. The fascination they stirred up in the public's imagination was all encompassing. Each was a publicity dream by themselves, but together they created a maelstrom of attention in the press. Gable and Lombard, Bogart and Bacall, whose names evoked legendary Hollywood love stories, were soon eclipsed by Monroe and DiMaggio. Long before the days of Bradgelina, one of the first super-couples staked their claim in the pantheon of publicity and set the bar at an all-time high.

# Chapter Twelve
## Riding the Publicity Rocket

"Even in fertile California where the natives grow everything jumbo size, Marilyn Monroe is this year's prize in a bumper crop of Hollywood starlets. Acclaimed by talent scouts as the 'hottest thing since Harlow,' and selected by service men on *Stars and Stripes* as Miss Cheesecake of 1951, Marilyn's one of the tastiest dishes to be served up to the curve-hungry public in many a moon."
*Eye*, March 1952

**M**arilyn uses Aline Mosby to break the story to the media that she is the girl on the nude calendar. Marilyn and two studio publicity agents, Sonia Wolfson and Johnny Campbell, join Miss Mosby for lunch. In the course of the meal, Marilyn invites Miss Mosby to join her in the ladies room. Unbeknownst to the publicity agents, Marilyn reveals the details of the calendar story to her.

In her syndicated column, Aline Mosby reported on Marilyn's calendar caper on March 13th. Marilyn maintains her honesty and escapes unscathed from a publicity drama that could have ended her career. "Marilyn Monroe Admits She's Nude Blonde of Calendar...A photograph of a beautiful nude blonde on a 1952 calendar is hanging in garages and barbershops all over the nation today. Marilyn Monroe admitted today that the beauty is she. She posed, stretched out on rumpled red velvet, for the artistic photo three years ago because, 'I was broke and needed the money. Oh, the calendar's hanging in garages all over town,' said Marilyn. 'Why deny it? You can get one anyplace. Besides, I'm not ashamed of it. I've done nothing wrong.'....A photographer, Tom Kelley, had asked me before to pose but I'd never do it. This time I called him and said I would as soon as possible, just to get it over with. His wife was there. They're both very nice. We did two poses, one standing up with my head turned profile, and another lying on some red velvet.' Marilyn speaks in a breathless, soft voice, and she's always very serious about every word she says. "Tom didn't think anyone would recognize me," she said. 'My hair was long then. But when the picture came out, everybody knew me. I'd never have done it if I'd known things in Hollywood would happen so fast for me.' Marilyn's bosses at plushy Fox Studio reached for the ulcer tablets when the calendar blossomed in January. 'I was told to deny I'd posed... but I'd rather be honest about it. I've gotten a lot of fan letters on it. The men like the picture and want copies. The women, well...One gossip columnist said I autographed them and handed them out and said, 'Art for Art's sake.' I've never said that. Why, I only gave two away,' said Marilyn, and blinked those big, blue eyes."

An unexpected fall-out from her calendar was a strain in the relationship with Sam and Enid Kneblecamp. They disapproved of Marilyn having posed in the nude and didn't hide their displeasure, but they eventually got over it.

John Huston said of Marilyn's nude, "it's done more for the movie industry than all the new processes of film making. It's the kind of thing the public expected of Hollywood in the golden era. There's nothing vulgar about it and this town was never meant to be a prim place."

Billy Wilder will say of her calendar, "When you come right down to it that calendar is not repulsive. It's quite lovely. Marilyn's name was already quite big when the calendar story broke. If it hadn't been, nobody would have cared one way or the other. But when it became known that she had posed for it, I think that, if anything, it helped her popularity. It appealed to people who like to read about millionaires who started life selling newspapers on the corner of Forty-second and Fifth Avenue, then worked their way up. It was as if

Marilyn had been working her way through college, for that pose took hours. Here was a girl who needed dough, and she made it by honest toil."

William Bruce interviewed Marilyn shortly after the calendar broke and gives this interesting look at Marilyn. "When she finally arrived and I looked her over, my first thought was: What's all the shouting about? I saw before me a nondescript blonde, carelessly dressed, wearing no stockings. Her eyes were sleepy and her hair tousled. She spoke with a slow drawl that was not particularly sexy. She reminded me of a girl who had just gotten out of bed; and, unlike eager Terry Moore, she was completely relaxed. I thought of a comfortable rousing cat. I can now see how all these elements brought to polish make the Monroe of to-day; I could not envision it. She became immediately as friendly as a next-door neighbor; and her seeming naiveté was most disarming. When I mentioned something about a picture, she exclaimed, 'Oh, you mean that calendar!' I said I didn't wish to discuss that, but trying for a new angle, I added that I had heard that she was a fan of the writer Thomas Wolfe. At that Marilyn woke up. Taking over the interview, she began to ply me with questions about Wolfe's works, even his obscure ones. I could see that the girl knew what she was talking about and that she was hungry for more knowledge."

Hedda Hopper offered this blurb on Joe and Marilyn, on the 14th, "Our little Marilyn Monroe, the town's newest glamour girl, is being seen more and more often with Joe DiMaggio, former center field star with the Yankees. They were recently dining at Jack's at the Beach. Marilyn snagged more magazine space last month than any other actress. Her face and her figure are more money in the bank, and Joe seems fascinated with her. He is strong on the looks, too, and his popularity, both as a person and as a baseball idol, is great."

Sheilah Graham weighed in on the calendar, "…even though she is one of the few people who does not own a copy. 'If I had one,' she told me with a grin, 'I'd save it for my grandchildren.' She meant it seriously and I knew what she meant. It's the most beautiful body ever exposed to the not-so-casual scrutiny of the world, including Manet's Olympia, Goya's duchess of Alba, all of Renoir's nudes put together. And Venus de Milo. 'You mean that when you're an old woman you'd like your grandchildren to know what you looked like once upon a time, and they'd be proud of such a body.' She flashed me a thoughtful look and said, 'You really do understand don't you?' Understand! All I know is I'd give my eye teeth to have a figure like the Monroe's."

Roy Craft remembers that when the calendar story broke, reporters asked him for a copy of Marilyn's nude calendar. "The publicity department didn't have any. Finally I heard about a guy on the lot, a movie extra, small-time actor, and he had a connection through whom he was able to get a supply of these calendars for nothing, and he was selling them for $1 each. I bought calendars from him for distribution and gave them out to the press."

Joe DiMaggio and Marilyn went together to the Hollywood Stars vs Major League All Stars Benefit Baseball Game for the Kiwanis Club, at Gilmore Field on March 17th. Joe played centerfield and Marilyn served as the hostess. According to some, this was

Marilyn's first time at a baseball game, although she had attended a game while in Chicago for the *Love Happy* Tour in July of 1949, and another Kiwanis Benefit game in March of 1951. But it was her first time to see her legendary boyfriend play baseball. Joe got two hits from four times at bat, resulting in a single and a home run. He showed Marilyn his skill at the game of baseball by having an errorless night. A news article from the time features a photo of Marilyn and three baseball players, captioned, "Home Was Never Like This...Why does any kid want to by president when he can play ball, bask in the sunshine of California, and meet a gal like Marilyn? The three gents with the broad grins are White Soxers Hank Majeski, Gus Zernial and Joe Dobson. The beauty with the beautiful eyes is Twentieth Century-Fox Starlet, Marilyn Monroe, who acted as hostess for the annual Kiwanis Club Hollywood Stars vs. Major League All Stars Benefit Baseball Game." Gus Zernial now played for the Philadelphia Athletics. This photo actually ran in newspapers on March 8, 1951 promoting the 1951 Kiwanis Major League All Stars Benefit Baseball Game in which Marilyn acted as mascot.

After a date with Joe on March 19th, Marilyn went over to the Bel Air Hotel to be with Elia Kazan. He remembers her telling him that she knew the man she wanted to marry. He was surprised when she told him it was Joe DiMaggio. Kazan had expected her to say Arthur Miller. The next day, March 20th, Marilyn accompanied Elia Kazan to a post Academy Awards party at Charles Feldman's home. Kazan was disappointed that he had not won an Oscar for *Streetcar Named Desire*. It won four Academy Awards but lost the Best Picture Award to *The African Queen*.

Hedda Hopper reported on March 22nd, "Marilyn Monroe is becoming noted around town for her off-hand remarks. She's been seeing quite a lot of Joe DiMaggio. Somebody asked her if she were particularly interested in baseball. 'Don't know,' replied Marilyn. 'Joe and I haven't gotten around to discussing it yet.'"

Louella Parsons had this little tid-bit about a new man in Marilyn's romantic life. "There are those who said it was only a question of time before Marilyn Monroe and Dan Dailey would discover each other. Well, they dined together at the Gourmet-Beverly."

On March 24th Hedda Hopper reported, "Marilyn Monroe tells us that when she was a small girl and people asked what she wanted to be after growing up, she always said, 'An actress.' but the other kids heckled her so over the preposterous idea that she quit talking about it. She can start talking again, because 20th is giving her a really dramatic role in *Niagara,* as well as star billing along with Joseph Cotten and Anne Baxter. Her part is that of a two-timing wife of a war veteran who's trying to come out of a nervous collapse. She and her lover plot to murder the husband; but he gets wise to the scheme and after a long suspense chase sequence, kills the wife. The picture, which Charles Brackett will produce and Henry Hathaway will direct, is to be shot on location at Niagara Falls this June. It'll be the second time Marilyn has had star billing. After seeing her work in *Clash by Night*, Barbara Stanwyck, Robert Ryan and Paul Douglas, who headlined the cast, decided that Marilyn should have billing along with them above the picture title, meaning star status."

Harrison Carroll reported about the tiff between Marilyn and Billie Holiday, on March

25th. "That calendar cropped up in Marilyn Monroe's life again. She and an escort went to the Tiffany club. They heard the manager had a copy of the calendar hanging in his office. Marilyn's escort asked to see it. An entertainer, who happened to be in the office, tore the calendar off the wall and thrust it at him. But, in a few minutes, the manager appeared and demanded his calendar back. Situation was tense but nobody got hit."

Marilyn and Billy Travilla had a short lived affair when his wife is out of town, and so was Joe DiMaggio. One evening they went on a night out on the town at the Tiffany Club where Billy Holiday was holding court. Travilla remembers Marilyn wearing a white turtleneck sweater, a black fitted flared skirt, red high heels and handbag. When he passed the manager's office on the way to the men's room he noticed Marilyn's calendar on the wall. When he came back to the table he mentioned it to Marilyn, who wanted to see it. They went back to the office and found Billy Holiday using the office as a dressing room. They apologized and told her they came to see the calendar. Upon hearing that they had come to see the calendar and not her, Miss Holiday proceeded to rip the calendar off the wall and threw it at Marilyn, along with some other expletives, saying, "Here, look at it good, honey." Marilyn and Billy went back to their table and gathered their things. The manager tried to talk them out of leaving, but they were too shaken by Miss Holiday's behavior to stay.

They left the Tiffany Club and went to the 5-4 Ballroom in the Watts section of Los Angeles and finished the evening dancing. Billy remembers that Marilyn took off her high heels to dance with him so she wouldn't be taller than him. The duo had the misfortune to be photographed at a table with a black man, possibly legendary jazz pianist Hank Jones. Neither Marilyn, nor Travilla thought much about the evening until the studio got wind of it. They considered that Travilla cavalierly put their biggest asset in jeopardy by taking her to such a place in "that part of town," and then having the audacity to submit to a photograph of the event. Posing nude on a calendar was one thing, but crossing the racial divide could stop her career in its tracks, cold, and permanently. She might never recover from the stigma of associating with black men. Fox had been grooming her for the part of Lorelei in *Gentlemen Prefer Blondes* for the better part of a year, and now it was peril because of this reckless night out on the town. Fox came down hard on Travilla and rattled their sabers and threatened to fire him. Marilyn defended her friend, going on to say, "if he goes, I go." Fox was able to keep the story out of the press and *Gentlemen Prefer Blondes* continued as scheduled. Travilla stayed on the film and at Fox.

Marilyn was ahead of her time as far as crossing racial lines went. She had befriended Dorothy Dandridge early in her career. She would work with Phil Moore and Gerald Wiggins on her voice. She loved jazz and would go hear Eartha Kitt and Ella Fitzgerald sing. She would befriend Sammy Davis, Jr. in late 1954. Although, she got into hot water with the studio for her associations with African Americans, she maintained an attitude towards them that would be reminiscent of future stars during the Civil Rights Movement of the late 1960s.

March 26th was the release date of *Okinawa*, a film which uses a clip of Marilyn from

*Ladies of the Chorus*, in which she dances onstage with other chorus girls.

Syndicated columnist Ida Jean Kain writes about Marilyn's weight lifting exercise routine on March 28th. Marilyn is an early practitioner of strengthening your core. She has learned her lessons well from Mabel Todd and Lotte Goslar. "I think it's important for a woman to stay firm and keep in shape. Exercising with weights helps fight gravity....She believes all limbering exercises should be for the purpose of helping the body to move freely. She disagrees with the old rigid rules of shoulders back...that prevents free movement. 'Release the shoulders, but keep control at the base of the spine. Have a long spine...long in the back, and pull up firmly with the girdle muscles. This control keeps the body in balance....She eats for strength, too--vegetables, meat, fruit and milk. She loves sweets, but never eats them. 'I could be the round type,' was her amazing comment."

Marilyn visited her psychoanalyst in Beverly Hills, Dr. Abraham Gottesman, on March 31st, and paid $200 for the session. From the way her life was going she needed him more than ever.

Wardrobe test for *Monkey Business* were held on April 1st. Marilyn was again dressed in this film by her buddy Billy Travilla. He considered the pleated dress as his "first memorable dress for her." She hated the dress with the pleated skirt, thinking it didn't show her bottom off to full advantage. She wore it her way, by parting her butt cheeks and catching a couple of pleats. You can even see this in the film if you watch closely.

Another interesting fact about Marilyn's time on the *Monkey Business* set is that Natasha Lytess had also made a movie starring Cary Grant and Ginger Rogers, *Once Upon a Honeymoon* in 1942. Natasha even made it into print when photos of she and Ginger Rogers swapping costumes made in into newspapers. "Part of the excitement in Leo McCarey's *Once Upon a Honeymoon* comes when Ginger Rogers trades identities with a hotel maid (Natasha Lytess) to save the latter's life from Nazi storm troopers. The switch in personalities enables Ginger to play a hilarious scene with co-star Cary Grant, in which they throw the razz right into 'der fuehrer's face.'" It is never mentioned whether Lytess brought up to Ginger Rogers and Cary Grant that they had made the movie together. No reporter picked up on it, not did Marilyn ever mention it.

It is also evident that Marilyn is letting her hair grow out again. She had cut it short in the fall of 1951 and had kept in that way until recently. Gladys McCallister, whom Marilyn called "Gladness," styled her hair for this film. She would be a member of Marilyn's close inner circle of skilled artisans who helped perfect the Monroe image. Miss McCallister had this to say about Marilyn's hair, "There are several problems in doing Marilyn's hair. Her hair is very fine and therefore hard to manage. It gets very oily if it isn't shampooed every day. And her hair is so curly naturally that to build a coiffure for her, I have to first give her a straight permanent. She doesn't prefer any one style of coiffure. She can wear anything--a pony tail, a poodle cut, Italian style, elegant pompadour, shoulder length. When she has an important date, I will do her hair for this. She never likes to wear her hair the same way twice. The way we get her shade of platinum is with my own secret blend of sparkling silver bleach plus twenty-volume peroxide and a secret formula of silver platinum to take the yellow out. I have to do her hair every three, four days, when she's working in a picture."

Andre de Dienes would photograph Miss McCallister styling Marilyn's hair during this time. It is fair to say that Marilyn's level of physical beauty during the making of *Monkey Business* was extraordinary.

Helping to create her beauteous look was another of Marilyn's inner circle, make-up man Whitey Snyder. He confided that, "Marilyn has make-up tricks nobody knows. Some of them she won't even tell me. She has discovered them herself. She has certain ways of lining and shadowing her eyes that no other actress can do. She puts on a special kind of lipstick; it's a secret blend of three different shades. I get that moist look on her lips for when she's going to do a sexy scene by first putting on the lipstick and then putting a gloss over the lipstick. The gloss is a secret formula of Vaseline and wax. You see, when I have the lipstick on, which may take almost an hour, then I'll say, 'Kiss me, honey,' and when she puckers up her lips I put on the gloss. Interesting thing about Marilyn is she's one of the few gals you can photograph full face and she'll look good, the most of them you take it three quarters or side view. Her left profile is great and she's great in three quarters. Her right profile is bad, for some reason. She's got a bad jaw line on that side. If she has to work a scene with her right profile to the screen, we have to do a lot of work on the right jaw line."

Marilyn played Lois Laurel, a secretary who had other, more obvious skills, than the ones needed to run an office. As her boss, played by Charles Coburn declares in classic comedic style, "Anyone can type." She held her own in slapstick bits with greats Charles Coburn, Carey Grant and Ginger Rogers. She would also play with Charles Coburn in *Gentlemen Prefer Blondes* as his romantic dalliance. Cary Grant said of Marilyn, "The publicity about her is far in excess of her talents, but not in excess of her sexual impact."

It is important to remember that as lively and seductive as Marilyn looked in this film she was suffering from appendicitis and would require surgery to resolve the condition. George "Foghorn" Winslow portrayed a Little Indian in this film. He would go on to act in *Gentlemen Prefer Blondes* with Marilyn, playing the precocious Henry Spofford III. While filming the swimming scene Marilyn was photographed giving boxer "Gentleman" Joey Barnum an autograph. He would later be hired to be her bodyguard on *Gentlemen Prefer Blondes*.

Vic "Chic" Masi was a friend of Joe DiMaggio's and a professional roller skating referee who gave Marilyn skating lessons for her role in this film. He acted a bit and he also cooked on sets. He had owned a restaurant and, for a year, was the head of Frank Sinatra's "Puccini" trattoria in Beverly Hills. Marilyn would grow close to Chic and his family, wife Marie and daughter Dolores. Joe and Marilyn would spend much time hiding out from the ever curious eyes of the press at the Masi's San Fernando Valley home on Saloma Ave. in Sherman Oaks.

According to Marilyn, she was already quite an accomplished roller skater. "'One time I had to prove that I wasn't just 'a nobody,' as someone in a fit of anger had said. They were having a skating contest at school. I had a pair of old skates, and I began secretly practicing, and I won the block skating championship. It was the first time anyone approved of anything I did. I can never forget that.' Recently when Marilyn was making *Monkey Business* she went to a large skating rink for a sequence. Marilyn, who hadn't put on skates since grade school, was soon skating all over the floor like a professional."

It is while on the set of *Monkey Business* that she gets interested in a young actor, fresh from Greece, Nico Minardos. They begin to have an affair, which will last for approximately the next 6 months. He will eventually be edged out by a jealous Joe DiMaggio and Marilyn's growing fame.

Marilyn was lunching at the Brown Derby when *LIFE* writer, Stanley Flink, presented her with an advanced copy of April 7th *LIFE* issue with her cover portrait and accompanying article. Marilyn burst into tears of joy upon seeing it. Although, after reading the article more carefully and seeing that it included a picture of her nude calendar, she was inconsolable. Marilyn was horrified that her nude calendar photo had been included in what was a family magazine. Even though she was not ashamed of the calendar, in and of itself, she was trying to move past it, especially with this publicity coup of a *LIFE* magazine cover and article. Her ability to generate publicity for herself was a double-edged sword. The public's ability to take her seriously as an actress seemed to always be compromised by her pin-up antics. The calendar that was published in the magazine was the "New Wrinkle" by the Western Lithograph Co.

Marilyn was upset and called close friend, Sidney Skolsky who was in Little Rock, Arkansas, on April 2nd. After the phone call he was unable to sleep and wrote her a 4-page letter at 11:30pm, trying to console her. He addressed her as "Dearest Sunshine." He goes on to say in his letter, "….I can't go to sleep anymore after talking to you, for two reasons. First there's a 250 piece orchestra playing lovely music on my heart—that's your voice; talking to you, that did it. I close my eyes and try to see you in your room…and I melt away into softness. And then, I can't sleep because you sounded so low, so upset. And me chattering away like a magpie. I must have sounded so foolish, trying to give you not only comfort, but strength—trying to pass along to you my heartbeat that kept on saying, 'Marilyn it is something I can help on—if the intensity & fierceness of love could transmit itself across the [illegible] then perhaps it would help. What else can I say, Sweet Sunshine. How can I tell you how sure I am, of you, for you? A beautiful thing cannot be destroyed. And you are an infinitely beautiful being. Pain and heartbreak and tragedy are a crucible—not that we go looking for such things but when they do come we must let them fall by the wayside, not us. Otherwise—in my own case for example—I would have been dead 5 ½ years ago. Otherwise now—when I love you so much—and with all the 'complications'—I would jump off a bridge or something. Bur I am for life—as you are and must be [illegible] the important thing. Not that I'm in any way trying to equate my problems with yours, Sweet Sunshine. It's rough enough though, when other people, other things, create heartaches for us. But we can't ever allow ourselves to stick the daggers into ourselves. For what? What does it solve? How docs it help being the 'baseball?' I don't know what the other problem is—but that putrid Stan Flink article—so what? Can you undo it by torturing yourself? Can you alter what is irrevocable—your family?—by feeling like what the morbid & inhuman Catholicism says about 'the sins of the father' being 'visited on the children?' You are Marilyn Monroe, a person, a human being on your own, born 24 years ago this coming June 1<sup>st</sup>, and a wonderful thing for the world is it, too! For all the [muckraking] 'ace reporting' I'll take the opinion of that cab driver who took me to your hotel that Wednesday night, just 3 weeks ago today—why, he glowed when he talked about you! Have you had rough knocks? Have you perhaps done some things you oughtn't? Or whatever. That's <u>past</u>, Sunshine! Let the 'ace reporter' wallow in his filth. He has covered himself with it—not you. And actually what has he 'found out?' Does it mean that <u>you</u> are less of a warm, wonderful, beautiful human being? Of course not. Are you going to tear yourself apart because of that? Perhaps this you think may hurt your career? What does a career mean, Marilyn? Is it 'success?' Is it recognition? You want to 'prove' that you are <u>Somebody</u>? Or should it be rather that in whatever you do, you don't aim for the Milky Way—but rather [illegible] there is this steadfast knowledge that in your life, with your life, that it weren't 'Enough'—is this failure? <u>Of</u> <u>course</u> <u>not</u>!! Even the greatest of actors & actresses (speaking of this particular field although it is true in everything) never, never reach the pinnacle they themselves want. I think that that is part of the beautiful wonder of life—that makes us all keep on going. Even happiness—no one is ever 'satisfied' nor should they ever be. That's what makes the human being so wonderful, the continual search for answers, for the best. And I don't mean being [grasping] or discontented. Rather, like the lover, continually seeing new ways, new things, new expressions to show his love to the [illegible] Maybe this sounds mixed up—I hope you know what I mean. Heartaches and problems are terrible weights to carry around—it's like walking in chains. Sometimes the fetters can't be burst [illegible] mighty blow—Sometimes they must be broken link by link. But—they <u>must</u> be broken! Oh, here I am just groping [illegible] over what must be causing you so much misery. [illegible] last year you told me a few lines of a poem you had written.

'…Oh, time be kind
Help this weary being to forget
What is sad to remember.
Easy my mind
While you eat my flesh.'
And I say, for you that must no longer be. Strike out the first line entirely—and for you it shall be:
'This weary being casts aside weariness
What is sad to remember passes away.
My mind is eased, but more—
My eyes are lifted.
My heart sees beauty and seeks beauty
Ugliness cannot harm me for I,

Will not be eaten away.
But instead I will eat and drink the beauty of life…'
As a poet, I am as they say in Brooklyn, strictly from hunger. But the feeling is there. This is the tender yet brightly burning flame I want you to keep lighted in your heart—forever. I'm not going to let you be the baseball—but I need your help, darling. Because you are really Sunshine. It wasn't just a 'cute' name I tossed about. I could see it right from the first time I met you. You're not going to make a fibber out of me, are you? Tch, tch! As they [illegible] in the old novels—heaven forfend!! I'll call you Friday night, too….Goodnight Sweet Sunshine. So beautiful in such [illegible] slip off to sweet dreams, with a sweet smile on your [sweet face]…wipe away the 'bad' things—because you could never do anything bad…ever. And I want to try to help bad things never happen to you…Love, Sid….P.S. If you'll get some more records, well, don't be surprised. With a one-note, cigarette-cough flattened tenor I wouldn't dare try to serenade you. So I'll let good artists do it!!"

The tone of the letter suggest a greater intimacy between the two than has been suggested in other biographies. Not to say that they were lovers, but they had a very close relationship indeed. Marilyn would be 26 on her birthday in June, not 24.

Roy Craft was actually the one that had her nude calendar published along with the story. He justified it this way, "*LIFE* magazine was preparing a cover story on her when it happened. A stroke of genius hit him: He had a print of the picture flown to *LIFE's* offices and it appeared with the story. 'That gave the picture prestige, took it out of the category of a dirty French postcard--because it really wasn't dirty--just barbershop calendar nude.'"

He recalled in a later interview, "She was three hours late for posing for her *LIFE* magazine cover, something Roy Craft had worked hard to sell. She was a starlet then and needed the publicity. 'That guy must have packed his bags three times,' Craft says. Like all the rest, he, too, was mesmerized within minutes. 'You could put 50 men in a room, and 49 of them would be around her.' It was *LIFE* magazine that also diluted the sensational impact of the news that Marilyn earlier had posed nude for a calendar sold to barbershops. 'They had closed a color cover on her. The inside layout was ready to go to press in 12 hours. When the calendar story broke, we figured it was murder. Everybody would think it was obscene. It wasn't. The calendar actually had flopped in the barbershop market. So we called the calendar company and they knocked out a special poster in half an hour and put it on the plane to New York City. *LIFE* ran it in miniature saying that she had posed for it when she was broke. That took it away from being dirty. Everyone could see it was a decent nude. It was the best thing that could have happened to Marilyn."

The day before the *LIFE* was on the stands, April 6th, Marilyn signed autographs at the Owl Rexall Drug Store, 8490 Beverly Blvd, which had an early supply of the magazines. She stated that she would only sign the outside of the magazine, thus avoiding the scandalous calendar picture that had caused her such notoriety.

Syndicated columnist Gerry Fitzgerald writes in his column, "Will Nude Art Hurt? Marilyn Monroe Asks….Actress Marilyn Monroe was putting up a brave front as readers throughout the country scanned a national picture magazine's reproduction of her famous nude calendar pose. But despite trepidations the newest Hollywood heat wave could not resist the tumultuous popular demand for personal appearances. So she accepted a date at a Hollywood drugstore to autograph copies of the magazine. The blonde was quick to point out, 'But I will only sign covers.' Miss Monroe would not admit she had autographed copies of calendars for friends. She asked, making with her baby blues, 'Do you think this will hurt me?' If anything, the busty blonde bombshell probably has just struck a gold mine. She is the favorite movie actress of practically every garage mechanic and barber in Hollywood, and there is a big trading market for a 'genu-wine' Monroe calendar. But Marilyn says she is worried and nervous. And when Marilyn says she needs reassurance, every man in Hollywood is ready to give it. She's had five columns of consolation from one reporter alone. Marilyn said she only drew a $50 fee when she modeled in the nude three years ago, but her studio has realized untold thousands of dollars' worth of free publicity. Miss Monroe receives 5,000 fan letters a week. Miss Monroe said she is going to autograph covers of the magazine for her fans, but she is fretting about a possible ban in the Bible Belt.' She pleaded, 'But when I posed for the calendar I didn't do anything wrong. I never would have posed if I didn't need the money.' The very idea of Marilyn needing anything leaves most men shocked. All this cutie needs to do is walk and she stops traffic. No one knows better than the traffic cops. They arranged an extra detail to handle the crowds at the drug store."

Gene Handsaker reported on April 7th, "Marilyn Monroe in Switch, Plays New Role All Covered Up...Well, here's a switch, Marilyn Monroe's doing her movie-acting these days all covered up. 'Clear up to my neck,' the blonde knockout mused, smiling. 'Higher than my neck, really.' She fingered a pinned-on little scarf that muffled her right up to the chin. 'It feels,' she confessed, 'kinda different.' Different indeed. Miss Monroe has been showcased heretofore in shorts, bathing suits, tight skirts, plunging necklines, and off-the-shoulder gowns. Anything that would tend not to minimize her sexy curves and walk. But there were squawks. From her public? 'Oh goodness, no,' Miss Monroe cooed. 'The people who write in say, 'Wear anything you want.' The complaints were from columnist. Lady columnists. The men columnists never have complained,' Marilyn said. That figured. A woman writer said the dress Marilyn wore to a party was 'horrifying' and 'ill-fitting.' It was 'too tight in all the wrong places' and made her look 'cheap and vulgar.' Another claimed Marilyn still didn't know how to dress properly. And so her present costume was designed with such complaints in mind. It's of champagne-beige wool jersey, and has a long, full, pleated skirt. Marilyn twirled to show me the effect of a pleated skirt. 'There's a scene from the back, which is very effective,' she guaranteed. My guide said there's another scene where Marilyn goes roller-skating with Cary Grant. 'Can you imagine that skirt flaring up?' the guide asked. Yes. I could. Marilyn said she hasn't permanently abandoned more revealing duds on the screen. 'It all depends on the character I'm playing.'"

Isabel Moore illustrates how Marilyn's publicity was getting out of hand. "But the calendar story and Marilyn's well known approval of her own beautiful body has caused the studio to be wary about her publicity. When one interviewer asked, 'What kind of bed do you sleep in, Marilyn? Twin or double?' and Marilyn said innocently, 'Why a twin bed, but a wide twin bed,' the publicity representative leaped forward to whisper, 'Don't say that, Marilyn. It will make people think things.'…The fact that she is fascinated by her own form and face, there is no doubt. She can spend solid hours in front of a mirror, just plucking out an eyebrow, smoothing a line of lipstick—but mostly being entranced by the lovely reflection she finds staring back at her. But all this is not the work of a monster ego. It's something a lot simpler than that. It's a childish delight at discovering, all over again, that the skinny little ugly duckling of the Los Angeles Orphanage days is really this beautiful young woman…So now Marilyn's mirror, and the eyes of admiring men, and even her success reassure her. She is pretty; she is an actress; she does have a gorgeous figure. And so the skirts get tighter, the necklines lower and the female protests over this 'vulgar' display louder."

    *LIFE* Magazine hit the newsstands on April 7th, with a cover and photographs by Philippe Halsman and accompanying article by Stanley Flink.

    Halsman reflects on photographing Marilyn. "I found her living in the outskirts of Los Angeles in a cheap one-room apartment and driving a beat-up second-hand Pontiac. She was much less self-conscious than before. When I came into her apartment, I saw dumbbells on the floor and learned that she was exercising her belly to keep her figure in trim. In the living room, which was also her bedroom, she hid a photograph from me. The *LIFE* researcher who was with me told me later that he had got a glimpse of it. It was of Arthur Miller, whom she then had apparently worshipped from afar. Another picture, left unturned, was of the great actress Duse. Thinking it was just an affectation; I asked her about Duse and learned to my surprise that she knew everything about her. In the corner was a bookcase filled with books I certainly didn't expect to find in her apartment. I remember a few of the titles: The Story of Fabian Socialism, The Negro in American Literature, books by the great Russians, and other extremely intellectual works. I realized that here was a girl not satisfied with what nature or education had given her and who worked all the time trying to improve herself. I photographed her in all kinds of situations. At this time, she was at the height of her sex appeal, and everything she did, every motion, was a mixture of conscious and unconscious sex appeal and challenge to the desire of men. The way she giggled, the way she stood in the corner flirting with the camera, and especially the way she walked, for with every step her derriere seemed to wink at the onlooker. I tried to capture this wink with a camera, which with a still picture is not so easy. It is incredible that $20^{th}$ Century-Fox had had her under contract for many years and had never thought of photographing her from behind."

    Upon meeting Marilyn again after photographing her three years earlier, Halsman reflected that her dumb blonde image was undeserved. "I was astonished when I first went to photograph her, to find that the girl owned almost no clothes—at least for someone in her position. Instead, she had books and records. She has no chitchat and no veneer. When you ask her a question, no matter how light, she answers you seriously, although sometimes with a pixie sense of humor. She may by ingenuous, but she is certainly not a dumb blonde." "I found Marilyn anything but stupid, with an amazing frankness and a good sense of humor, and her company stimulating even in a spiritual way. The trait which struck me most was a general benevolence, an absolute absence of envy and jealousy, which in an actress was astonishing." "She had changed all right, in the three years since I had seen her; it was remarkable to note how much. She no longer tried to be sexy--she was sexy. She had become a warm, sensuous, if still timid, woman, who was intensely, almost pitifully anxious to please, to give out everything she had--with her whole personality--to the camera or any male who faced her...I had to show in my pictures that Monroe's sexiness was not only her weapon, but her very essence, that it permeated everything she did--talking, sitting, eating, lying down."

Halsman had decided to show in his photographs that Marilyn was the ultimate sex goddess and that it could be seen in anything she did. His opening picture, the cover, would establish the general theme. The rest of his photographs of her would prove his point.

He decided to shoot the cover photo in her apartment. Halsman selected an evening gown from Marilyn's small selection in her closet. He chose a white slinky one by Ceil Chapman. The only problem with it was that it had a bow on the left hip. He convinced Marilyn to cut the bow off, explaining that simple lines are more elegant. She took her scissors and discarded the offending bow. She put on the gown and posed barefoot, framing herself between the closet door and wall. John Baird, Halsman's assistant was present that day, along with the legendary comedian, Harold Lloyd, and *LIFE* writer Stanley Flink.

Harold Lloyd was President of the *Hollywood Stereo Club*. This was a club whose interest was taking 3-D photographs. Other stars who belonged to this club were Joan Crawford, Art Linkletter, Ronald Coleman and Dick Powell. Lloyd took 3-D photographs of Marilyn on that day and had several more sessions with her in the following year. A book was eventually published in 1992 which showcased 7 of his photographs of Marilyn, along with other movie stars. However, his huge collection of 3-D nudes and semi-nudes didn't make it into the book.

While photographing Marilyn, Halsman tries to engage her in some risqué' conversation. He asked her how old she was when she first had sex. She answers, 'I was six.' Flabbergasted, Halsman asked how old the man was. Marilyn coyly replied, 'younger.' Harold Lloyd who had been sitting in a camp chair with his equipment, somersaulted backward into the hallway, through the open door upon hearing her reply.

Halsman and Lloyd also photographed Marilyn in a couple of different negligees. Halsman photographed her working out with a set of weights in her apartment, dressed in a terry cloth bikini top and jeans. He asked her what she did with the weights. Marilyn replied, "Phillipe, I'm fighting gravity." She inhaled deeply to prove her point. Halsman also photographed her in the situation of applying for a job, capturing her in the act of seducing a man.

"The next day on our way to lunch, I photographed Marilyn's remarkable walk, trying to catch it's amazing turbinate undulation. But I felt that I kept missing something. With a motion picture camera it would have been child's play, but to seize the essence of the walk in one shot, if it were possible at all, demanded the utmost concentration. After lunch, we went to a drive-in restaurant--to show that Marilyn looks sexy even when eating...Marilyn was now history's most phenomenal love goddess. Why? Most people think that the main reason is self-evident, especially when Marilyn wears a snug evening gown...Paradoxically, the main reason with Marilyn is inside. Her very weakness is her main strength: Her inferiority complex, her pathetic, almost childlike lack of security are the very things that make her appeal irresistible. One evening I saw Marilyn enter a cocktail party at the Beverly Hills hotel. I remember sensing the fear and trembling tension inside her face every time she came face to face with a man she did not know. She was deathly afraid of not being liked or approved. For an instant, she would stand there just looking at him timidly and submissively. It seemed that it was she who implored, who wooed, who offered herself. As for the man before her, how could he not like and desire a girl so beautiful, who seemed to find him irresistible? And by the light in the man's eye, Marilyn would know, and one could feel her sort of relax and breathe normally again, sunning herself in the warmth of the new admiration. Being wanted would make her happy and secure."

His last pictures of Marilyn showed her at the top of the stairs by her apartment door. She was casually dressed in a skirt and clinging knit top that she wore in previous photos, on the landing of her apartment. Halsman had succeeded in showing what he felt was the true essence of Marilyn, that her sensuality penetrated everything she did.

Halsman will later say of Marilyn, "She could overcome her sense of inferiority only be feeling desired. When she was placed before a camera, she would try to seduce the lens. As pathetic as it was, her effort to excite a desire for her always made a wonderful picture."

Jack Lait dangled this bit of information on April 8th, "Maybe Marilyn Monroe is serious with Joe DiMaggio, but she's said to be dating Vince Edwards on the Coast."

Aline Mosby devoted her column to Marilyn on April 10th, "'Teach Marilyn Monroe How to Dress' Columnists Chorus…Marilyn Monroe sighed today she's being criticized more for wearing clothes than taking them off. Marilyn recently confessed to the United Press that she posed nude for an arty calendar three years ago because she was broke and needed the $50. The reaction was a tolerant sympathy, and thousands of requests for the calendar. But now the gossip columnists are needling the blonde beauty that her clothes are 'atrocious and vulgar' and 'Fox Studios ought to send her to a charm school so she'd learn how to dress.' 'Women are so critical,' pouted Marilyn. 'But men appreciate what I wear. I dress to please them. I like clothes with feeling. They're more interesting. Most women look at *Harper's* and *Vogue*. But that long and lean look is not my type. I'm the round type. It all,' she explained, 'has to do with nature. I don't like full skirts. They're quite inorganic. Clothes should follow the body line.' The frantic fuss over her fashions started when she appeared at various parties in two organic evening gowns, not at the same time. Both are red and Lillian Russell style. They are less than strapless and cling to every Monroe bodyline except for a flounce at the bottom. 'These gowns aren't cheap,' she said indignantly. 'The velvet dress was designed by Oleg Cassini and the lace by Christian Dior.' Another Monroe trademark is a fresh flower that she sticks into her plunging neckline. This raises an eyebrow here and there, too. 'It's feminine,' said Marilyn in that soft, breathless voice. 'Sometimes I wear a plain black tailored suit with one button. Instead of wearing a blouse I stick a full blown rose in the neckline. Then I wear a red beret. You see all black and skin and red,' she beamed. She said, 'See? I wear simple clothes. What are they complaining about? Sometimes I wear a man-tailored blouse.' She went on. 'It's thin, you can see through it. To make it feminine I pin on a cameo brooch of two figures in each other's arms.' The newshens also have the claws out for the interesting way Miss Monroe puts one foot ahead of the other. 'They criticize the way I walk,' she said. 'I don't walk like anything. I just walk. Just because it's not conventional…' Marilyn who says she stays home to read weighty books about mind and things, said slowly. 'I want freedom in my actions. It's a quality to do with the growth and development of a human being.' Furthermore, she added, the dress she had on today she will wear in *Darling I Am Growing Younger*, and it is 'simple and high-necked.' It is jersey. It clings, every stich of it."

Jimmie Fidler reported on the 11th, "If Marilyn Monroe, the new rage at Hollywood, has been holding on to financial worries, despite her sudden climb to stardom, she can banish them now, for it seems that her role in *Clash by Night* has opened up other means of livelihood for her. In that picture, she plays a blue-jean clad worker in a fish cannery. The cannery owners in Monterey, California, where most of the picture was shot, are a live bunch of boys and they've been making her offers. One has bid high, wide and handsome for the privilege of using her picture on his can of sardines, another has offered her a fat fee to make a personal appearance at a forthcoming picnic he's staging for his workers. And the manufacturer of the blue jeans she wore wants to pay her a handsome stipend if she'll model for his ads."

Harold Heffernan illustrated on of Marilyn's growing problems in his column on April 12th, she was alienating women. "Disliked instinctively by most of the girls on her home lot, stars and secretaries alike, and by many who have yet to meet her. Marilyn is fast becoming a 'man's girl.' When asked recently what quality she disliked most in the opposite sex. Marilyn answered, 'I like everything about them—I guess I just like men!'"

On April 13th, Edith Kermit Roosevelt interviewed Ben Bard who was an acting coach in Hollywood. He had this to say about Marilyn. "The dramatic school teacher warned no coach or system can give a person talent who doesn't have it. Occasionally, he said, someone who cannot act at all is cast into the right role for them and becomes famous overnight. But if they wish to stay in the public eye, they must learn to act. 'Marilyn Monroe is one beautiful piece of cheesecake who is wisely trying very hard to learn to act as well as to look alluring.'" Miss Roosevelt was the daughter of President Theodore Roosevelt.

Leonard Lyons remarked on Marilyn's calendar, "Twentieth Century-Fox tried in vain to suppress the calendar which displayed the nude photo of MM. The studio now is trying to stop Miss Monroe from autographing the picture, which shows her lying nude, on her left side." Cameraman Lucien Ballard sent Marilyn his calendar to be autographed. Marilyn wrote, "This is not my best side."

April 14th seemed a popular day to comment on Marilyn. Columnist Fairfax Nesbit had this to say about Marilyn's *LIFE* appearance. "They say that the April 7 issue of *LIFE* magazine, the one with Movie Cutie Marilyn Monroe on the cover and uncovered inside in the reproduction of the famous calendar for which she posed, jumps the mag's sale for that issue to astronomical figures." Newspapers report that, "Five extra people have been employed by the Western Lithograph Company to take care of the orders for the Marilyn Monroe calendar."

On April 23rd Marilyn's step-father, John Stewart Eley, died of heart disease. Gladys had married the electrician in April of 1949. Marilyn never knew him. Although, Gladys thought Mr. Eley was still married to a woman when he wed her, she kept the last name for the rest of her life, being known as Gladys Pearl Eley. His obituary states only two survivors, his sister and Gladys. No other records support another wife. Gladys and Mr. Eley had made their home in Santa Monica, living on the fringes of family and relations.

Jimmie Fidler reported on April 24th, "For years the Hollywood Ball Club has sold billboard space on its outfield fence, and for years the firms using that ad space have awarded prizes to any batter who hits their respective ads. This week the batters have a new target to shoot at--a big billboard advertising the RKO picture, *Clash By Night*, and featuring a rather sexsational picture of Marilyn Monroe. 'If Howard Hughes can just arrange a date with Marilyn for any batter who hits that poster,' one of the Hollywood players remarked to me the other day, 'I think you're going to see our boys smack out a record-breaking number of off-the-fence doubles in the next few weeks.' Speaking of pictures of Marilyn Monroe, and who isn't in Hollywood these days, after seeing page 84 in the current issue of *Popular Photography* Magazine?--and her studio bosses are becoming a bit worried. They've asked the luscious Miss M. to try and stop the publication of any more pictures like the one referred to above or the completely undraped shot which is now decorating American's most talked about calendar. She'd like to stop them to, but she's powerless in the matter. When she worked as a photographer's model, she signed a release every time she posed. The photographers who took the pictures have every legal right to sell them and pictures of Marilyn Monroe have suddenly become valuable property."

Louella Parsons reported that same day, "Snapshots of Hollywood collected at random: If you don't think Marilyn Monroe is hot--the fans broke out cheering when she flashed on the screen at the preview of *Clash by Night*."

Marilyn writes a check to The Cedars of Lebanon Hospital on April 26th for $303.86. She listed her address as the Beverly Carleton Hotel.

Louella Parsons devoted her entire column to Marilyn on April 27th. "Joe DiMaggio Just a Good Friend Marilyn Monroe Says of Romance." In the article Marilyn reveals her status with Joe DiMaggio and her dramatic aspirations. 'Tell me about Joe DiMaggio,' I shot at her. 'Oh, Joe is nice,' said Marilyn. 'I like him. He has been a wonderfully good friend, but I have no plans for marriage.' 'Perhaps he is too old for you,' I suggested. 'Age doesn't count where love is concerned, ' said Marilyn. 'I don't care what age a man is if you love him. I don't have much time for social activities and I want an escort to whom I can talk. I made five pictures in a row and have classes every night so you see I'm working hard.' 'What are you studying?' I asked her. 'Oh, I am studying pantomime, body freedom and dramatic acting,' she answered with all the seriousness in the world." Marilyn had this to say about her nude calendar, "'Marilyn,' I said, 'tell me the truth about the story that you posed in the nude.' 'The truth is that I was not only one month behind in my rent but four months,' she said. 'I expected to be thrown out in the street. I didn't have enough money to even to eat, and when Tom Kelley asked me to pose I was glad to accept. Mrs. Kelley was in the room with me all the time. I don't suppose anything would have come of the whole thing if someone hadn't suddenly discovered there was such a calendar. I am not ashamed of it and I wouldn't do it today because I don't have to, but if I had to do it over, and it was a question of being tossed in the street, I'd do it again.' I like that quality in Marilyn Monroe. The quality of telling the truth. So few people have it. One of her friends, and one of the people who believed in Marilyn from the beginning told me: 'Can't you suggest to the Monroe child that she stop acting like Duse? She dramatizes everything. Let her be just a simple young girl.' Well I never got around to telling Marilyn because I don't think it's important whether she dramatizes herself or doesn't The important thing is that she is trying hard to be a good actress, and if in trying to achieve that aim she has been a bit too dramatic at times, I can only say she's young and she'll outgrow it. I have said from time to time that I wished someone would take her in hand about her clothes. She goes into the studio wardrobe department and, left to her own devices, picks out anything that catches her eye. I wanted to say, 'Oh, Marilyn, please take someone with you to advise you on what to buy.' But I suppose Marilyn's clothes really do not matter when today she has had more publicity than any young actress in Hollywood. She has been on more magazine covers than any actress at RKO. When she made *Clash by Night* and was surrounded by a group of big stars it was she the reporters sought out for stories. The one thing Marilyn wants most in the whole world is to play in a drama. 'And Mr. Zanuck,' she said, 'is going to allow me to do that in *Don't Bother to Knock*, in which I'll have a big dramatic role after I finish *Darling, I Am Growing Younger*.' Are you pleased about playing the life of Jean Harlow, I asked. 'Yes. Indeed,' she said, 'because so many people say I look like Jean Harlow, and I'd love to do her life story.' Well dear readers, all I can say is: Keep your eye on Marilyn Monroe. Nothing is going to keep that girl from getting to the tip top and staying there."

Marilyn will tell Michael Sheridan her views on romance and a career. "I don't think at this stage of my career romance has a place. I would only neglect the boy who loved me for something I love better than love…a job, and doing it well…I have been hurt too many times to pretend. Once love let me down, and several times my movie career let me down—until I came back to earth with a bang. Now I'd rather stay on the ground with a little firmness until I can afford—through experience and security—to walk in the clouds."

Marilyn finally has her appendix removed on April 28th by Dr. Marcus Rabwin. Marilyn wrote a note to the doctor in pencil and taped it to her stomach. It read, "Most important to Read Before operation. Dear Doctor, Cut as little as possible. I know it seems vain but that doesn't really enter into it--the fact that I'm a woman is important and means much to me. You have children and you must know what it means--please Doctor--I know somehow you will!  thank you--thank you--for God's sake Dear Doctor No ovaries removed--please again do whatever you can to prevent large scars. Thanking you with all my heart. Marilyn Monroe."

Natasha tells of a gift she gave Marilyn during the operation. "I had a talisman to bless me and my daughter, a very old silver medal with a figure of the Christ child on it. When Marilyn had to be operated on several years ago for her appendicitis, the doctors feared her fallopian tubes would have to be removed. When Marilyn was so distressed at the thought that she might never be able to have a child, and on the day she was to be operated on, I gave the talisman to her. During the operation, Marilyn clutched it in her hand. When she left the operating table, she was still able to bear children. The fear that her fallopian tubes might be infected proved to be unfounded. She wore the talisman for a long time after that. On a silver chain around her neck."  If you look carefully in photographs taken after this time, Marilyn is wearing the medal. It appears in candid photos from filming *Niagara* and also photographs when she was recording her radio program.

The medal was an "our lady of Mt. Carmel" or "the Virgin of Carmel", and it pictured the Madonna holding the Christ child. It was meant to give aid in times of need and inspire the wearer to pray.

Wire Services ran over each other in their haste to publish a photo of Marilyn in her hospital bed reading get well cards. Before leaving, Marilyn had to submit to a hairstylist and make-up artist dolling her up for her photo session.

Marilyn's first visitor was her stand-in, Irene Crosby. Joe DiMaggio sent her two dozen red roses. Dan Dailey sent her a tree of tulips with tiny canaries in the branches that actually sang. Marilyn would later tell Jock Carroll, a Canadian newsman, that while she was in the hospital, "the nurses kept popping in and saying, 'Why, she looks like a kid of sixteen.' I remember one big, stout nurse came striding in and she growled, 'Hell--what's so menacing about you?!'"

It is while attending to Marilyn in the hospital that she extracts a promise from Whitey Snyder that he will do her makeup for her funeral. It is also while in the hospital that the studio learns that her mother is indeed alive. Syndicated columnist Erskine Johnson has learned the truth and is about to reveal the news to the world. They demand an answer from her during the time of her hospitalization. She owns up to her end of the deceit, and Johnson's article hits the papers on May 3rd.

Hedda Hopper revealed this on April 30th, "Will the X-rays of Marilyn Monroe's appendix sell as well as the picture on that famous calendar? The Blowtorch Blonde is so hot that college boys from all over the country have been inviting her to be queen of their June proms. Just before she took off for the hospital for her appendectomy, she had calls from Tuscaloosa, Ala., and Ithaca, N.Y., but the studio wouldn't let her take them on the set because production would be held up. Long distance calls intrigue Marilyn because she was always too poor to make 'em. The other day a man named Monroe, who works in a Beverly Hills mortuary, called up claiming to be her father. What he did not know was that Marilyn's father died soon after her birth. Her real name is Norma Jean Dougherty."

On May 1st, Producer Jerry Wald sent Marilyn a note. "Dear Marilyn: I know this is going to be the first of a long shelf of hits! It will always make me happy to know that your first Star Billing role was for me. Warmest personal regards, Sincerely, (signed) Jerry Wald." It was addressed to "Miss Marilyn Monroe; Beverly Carleton; 944 West Olympic; Beverly Hills, Calif." Jerry Wald was the producer of *Clash by Night*.

Jimmie Fidler reported on May 2nd, "Considerable excitement in press circles the other day, boss, when Marilyn Monroe bought a plane ticket to Niagara Falls, but it was short lived. She's going to be doing a screen role there next month, and bought her own ticket because she wanted to precede the rest of the troupe by a few weeks and pick up extra change doing personal appearances. By the way, Cary Grant, who's been working with the Monroe chick in *Monkey Business*, calls her 'Miss Income Tax' because she's such an impressive figure."

Another publicity bombshell hit the press on May 3rd when Erskine Johnson revealed that Marilyn's mother was very much alive, "Hollywood's confessing glamour doll who made recent headlines with the admission that she was a nude calendar cutie--confessed again today. Highly publicized by Hollywood press agents as an orphan waif who never knew her parents, Marilyn admitted that she's the daughter of a one-time RKO studio film cutter, Gladys Baker, and that 'I am helping her and want to continue helping her when she needs me.' Recovering from an appendectomy in a Los Angeles hospital, Marilyn gave me an exclusive statement through the Twentieth Century-Fox studio following the appearance at the studio of five women claiming Marilyn as their 'long-lost daughter.' Said Hollywood's new glamour queen: 'My close friends know that my mother is alive. Unbeknown to me as a child, my mother spent many years as an invalid in a state hospital. I was raised in a series of foster homes arranged by a guardian through the County of Los Angeles and I spent more than a year in the Los Angeles Orphans Home. I haven't known my mother intimately, but since I have become grown and able to help her I have contacted her. I am helping her and want to continue helping her when she needs me.' Hollywood friends of her mother supplied the rest of the story: 'When Marilyn was a small child, her father was killed in an automobile accident and her mother subsequently suffered a nervous breakdown. A friend of her mother was appointed her legal guardian. Marilyn's mother recovered from her illness in 1945 and lived with her daughter for a short time in 1946. In the same year her mother remarried and became a widow for the second time last week when her husband died following a short illness. The news that Marilyn's mother is alive in Hollywood came as an eyebrow-lifting surprise because of the extensive studio publicity that Marilyn had never known her mother or her father. But the new star's confession that her twice-widowed mother is in Hollywood and that 'I am helping her' came as a relief to the Twentieth Century-Fox legal department, which has been confronted with wild claims by women insisting that Marilyn is their 'daughter.'"

Erskine Johnson will write about discovering Gladys in an article in the September 1952 *Motion Picture* magazine, "Marilyn Monroe's Mystery Mother."

A glimpse of just how vulnerable Marilyn actually was during this time appeared in an *American Weekly* magazine article on June 8th, "No Next of Kin" by Isabel Moore. It is articles like this that really started to create the image of a vulnerable, fragile young woman in the mind of the public. It tells of Marilyn's stay in the hospital. "Marilyn Monroe is Hollywood's newest star--but she can't shake that 'all alone' feeling. Up until then, the routine hospital questions had received routine replies. Age: 22. Address: Beverly Carleton Hotel, Beverly Hills, California. Occupation: Actress. 'And who is your next of kin to be notified in case of an emergency?' The very blonde and very beautiful young girl lying beneath the white coverlet in the high, narrow bed of a private room in Hollywood's Cedars of Lebanon Hospital looked startled, then bewildered. 'The who?' The admissions clerk repeated it. It didn't seem possible that the question didn't have an answer, that in the space provided on the hospital admitting card, the clerk would have to write in the lonely word, 'None.' The girl wasn't some out-of-work, out-of-luck actress. She was Marilyn Monroe, newest star to appear in Hollywood...The little girl who'd climbed out of bed in the Los Angeles County Orphanage--her name was Norma Jean Baker then--to kneel at a window and look across the street to where the neon- lighted sign of one of the greatest studios in the world burned through the night, and to whisper, 'Someday I'll be an actress. A star, even. I'll have lots of pretty clothes and I'll be pretty, too, by then, and everybody will like me and I'll never be alone anymore--' had realized her most dazzling dream. Except for one thing. With Hollywood at her feet and success in her hip pocket, Marilyn Monroe finds herself as much alone as ever. She was alone in that hospital room and put in a call, finally, to a young man she knew only casually, in a business way. A business manager. [David March] With the same childlike ingenuousness and over simplicity (which Hollywood characterizes as 'dumbness'), Marilyn had decided that since she was possibly going to place her business account with his firm, it would be alright to ask him to go do this favor for her: To come down to the hospital, to bring her script to her from the studio, to pay a forgotten parking fine, to buy a jar of hand cream, a box of talcum. 'It was so funny,' she said to me when I went to see her for the purpose of this interview. 'So queer and--and awful--to realize I just didn't have anyone. But then,' she said, 'I've always been alone, and I suppose I always will be--'...After she told me her no-next-of-kin story in the hospital, she sprang a surprise. It was a surprise not only to me, but to everybody in Hollywood, including her bosses and even her press agents: She suddenly blurted out that she knows who her mother is and that the woman is alive. She admitted that she didn't know her mother when she was a little girl but found out about her after feeling alone and unwanted in a series of foster homes. I know that, in her heart, she still feels she has no next of kin."

On May 4th Hedda Hopper devoted her entire column to Marilyn and attached a new moniker she had come up with in her column on April 30$^{th}$, "The Blowtorch Blonde." It is an important and lengthy article and it helps to ratchet up Marilyn's career another notch. "Blowtorch Blondes are Hollywood's specialty, and Marilyn Monroe, who has zoomed to stardom after a three-year stretch as a cheesecake queen is easily the most delectable dish of the day. Males from Korea to Kokomo have developed an appetite for Monroe pin-ups far beyond the studio's ability to keep them supplied. *Stars and Stripes* features a Monroe on its front page every day—often has to run repeat shots while waiting for a fresh batch to come in. Her fan mail is handled in bulk, like department store stuff, arriving at the studio in packing cases at the rate of 3,000 letters a week. Art calendars of Marilyn au naturel, against a background of red velvet, have swept the nation like a virus epidemic. She is fast supplanting Sam Goldwyn as a source of anecdotes and every producer at $20^{th}$ is bidding for her as box-office insurance…" Hedda goes on to give a biography of Marilyn and her rise to fame in Hollywood.

On the $4^{th}$ Marilyn is featured reading the new, revised, *American Weekly*. It was recently revamped by William Randolph Hearst, Jr. Marilyn's photo appears alongside Ava Gardner, Rita Hayworth, Debbie Reynolds and Dana Andrews. Marilyn comments on whether or not she will still continue posing for cheesecake stills. "I think cheesecake pictures are just as important as formal portraits, perhaps more so. Each serves a purpose and each in equally important in its field. People ask me if I am going on making cheesecake pictures now that I'm a star. My answer is that as long as there is a boy in Korea who wants a pin-up of me, I'll go on posing for them."

Yet, Marilyn will give this thoughtful response to the transition from cheesecake to acting. "All women have sex appeal, and many women are much better equipped than I to make men drool. I like to think that I can act, too—and that behind the shadow of the cheesecake there is the substance of something a little more worthwhile."

On May 6th Marilyn leaves the hospital following her appendectomy. She returns to her Beverly Carleton residence to recuperate. Shortly after this, Marilyn moves into the Bel Air Hotel, 701 Stone Canyon Road, in Beverly Hills. She rented bungalows 133 and 135. Her phone number was GRnalt 2-1211.

*Pacific Stars the Stripes* newspaper article, May 7th, "Men Pick Marilyn for Mountain Top…Who is the girl with whom you would most prefer to be stranded upon a mountain top? According to officers and airmen of the 502d Tactical Control Group in Korea, she is Marilyn Monroe of 20th Century-Fox studios. In a recent popularity poll, men of the 502d Group selected Miss Monroe for the distinction from among some 25 movie stars. Hollywood studios had furnished appropriate photographs to aid the men in their choice. The exact question on the ballot was, 'With whom would you prefer to be stranded on the highest radar mountain?' After the votes were counted an attractive scroll, signed by Col. Henry Riera, group commander, was forwarded to Miss Monroe designating her 'Miss Radar of 1952.'"

Louella Parsons reported this insightful incident on May 11th, "Provocative, exciting and strangely naive Marilyn Monroe and the 25,000 letters she has received from boys in Korea. When asked if she could afford the $500 worth of pictures she ordered to send there (her salary is not yet in the big league), she said, 'No, but I never want to think I didn't send a picture to a boy who might not come back.'"

Marilyn appears in a *Parade* magazine article on the 11th. "Does a Model Have to Look Hungry?" The article was a follow up on Grace Palmer, a model who was normal size, but couldn't find work because she wasn't thin enough. Various stars commented. Marilyn had this to say, "I don't think Grace is too fat. I do think a few exercises would tighten her up in the middle; she needs a better waistline. The rest of her is just fine. The 'high-fashion' type of girl is too thin in my book. If I were a man, I'd choose a girl like Grace anytime. She has a real feminine figure. After all, men don't like girls with boyish figures, do they?"

It is also on this day that Marilyn started to receive $750 a week on her Fox contract.

Hedda Hopper reported on May 16th, "Marilyn Monroe, who's recuperating from her appendectomy by sun bathing in the nude daily on her private patio at the Bel Air Hotel, says Joe DiMaggio is just a friend, although she sees him daily. She has one added scene to make at 20th next Monday, then will take off for Niagara Falls to do the picture *Niagara*, which begins June 2. The Blowtorch Blonde will have a 10-day stopover in New York, her first trip to the big city since she became a success. I can imagine the reception she'll get there. It has been reported by everyone that Marilyn is an orphan; actually her mother is still living. The mother used to be a cutter at Columbia Studio."

Harrison Carroll reported on May 19th, "Marilyn Eases Worries of her 'Calendar Fans'…That question on the mind of every calendar fan has been answered: Marilyn Monroe says, 'The appendectomy scar is so low that I can even wear bikini bathing suits. As a matter of fact, pretty soon, you will not be able to see the scar at all--not with the naked eye.' Marilyn is recuperating at the Bel Air Hotel where she has a lovely room 'with a sun porch where I can sun-bathe in the nude.' She will remain there for another two weeks before she heads east for the location scenes of *Niagara*. Before that, she will do the beach scenes in *Monkey Business*, no swimming sequences, just shots in a bathing suit. Boyfriend Joe DiMaggio is in town but she doubts they will fly back to New York together."

When Marilyn releases these titillating habits to the press, that she sun bathes nude, for instance, it generates massive publicity and begins to solidify her wild reputation in the press. Couple that with her increasing public displays and she walks the fine line between sexy and slutty. By the end of the year she will realize that she has overdone the sex angle, but for now, she is too busy breaking the sound barrier to notice the storm clouds on the horizon.

Marilyn related this poignant story of how easily her feelings could be hurt. "It was at a party one night recently, after I'd finished work on the picture *Monkey Business*. As I started into the powder room I heard my name under discussion. It was just like that old crack about eavesdroppers. I stopped cold. I certainly didn't hear anything good said about me. One girl was knocking my clothes. Another was hammering my manners and other things. I stood there dying, just outside the half-opened door, not knowing whether I should burst into the powder room or run out of the party. Then I heard a third voice, serene and lovely. 'But do you know Marilyn?' asked the voice. 'Have you really met her? The moment you do, you'll know that most of the things said about her are false.' I walked in then to see who was speaking. Eleanor Parker's eyes met mine, and she smiled like one best friend greeting another. 'Hello, Marilyn,' she said. 'How nice you look tonight.' I gulped. 'Thank you,' I said. The other two cats left hurriedly. And as the door closed on them, I could feel the tears stinging against my eyelids. The truth was that Eleanor Parker and I had never exchanged a word before that moment, except 'How-do-you-do' as we had been introduced to one another earlier that same evening. Now I fumbled for words. I'm not much of a word girl anyway, because the best way to talk to men, of course, is to listen. Finally, I said, 'I honestly don't know how to thank you.' 'Let's be friends,' Eleanor said. 'That's payment enough for me.'"

The "panty raid" phenomenon has swept over eastern college campuses. Marilyn was quoted in a May 21st *INS* article on the subject. "No stretch of the imagination could bring the nationwide 'panty raid' craze to California, bosomy Marilyn Monroe insisted as the analyzed the current collegiate fetish. Marilyn blinked her big blue eyes and solemnly said: 'It's not just a prank, it's a revolt. It's a revolt against saddle shoes and blue jeans. Men yearn for the feminine touch. If the only lace they can find it is tucked away in dormitory bureau drawers—that's where they'll go. In California schools, where the girls dress their feminine best and there is beauty everywhere—on campus, the beach and the tennis court—there hasn't been a whisper of such goings-on.'" This will prove ironic commentary from a woman who was to insist to Earl Wilson on August 26th that she does not wear any underwear at all, of any kind, whatsoever.

Wardrobe test for *Niagara* began on May 21st. Marilyn was dressed in this film by Dorothy Jeakins. The red dress alone is worth the price of admission. Miss Jeakins will design costumes for another Marilyn film, *Let's Make Love*. Her designs didn't fare as well for that film, partly because Marilyn had gained weight and didn't project the same sparkling aura from the screen that she was known for. Miss Jeakins was hired for *The Misfits*. On that occasion, however, she will fail to please Marilyn and will stand-down.

Sydney Guilaroff designed a hairstyle for Marilyn to wear in *Niagara* that consisted of looser curls. It was a more unkempt style, keeping with the wanton nature of the woman she played.

Location filming for *Niagara* begins on May 26th. Marilyn stars as Rose Loomis, an unfaithful wife who tries to murder her husband, George, played by Joseph Cotten, only to be murdered herself. Marilyn would not actually arrive on location until June 5th.

On May 29th, Joe DiMaggio's former wife, Dorothy Arnold, was seeking a modification of the DiMaggio 1944 divorce decree. Miss Arnold was going to court on June 2nd to stop Joe, Sr., from taking their son, Joe, Jr., on his dates with Marilyn. Miss Arnold reported that the boy came home using the words "beautiful legs" and "doll" after DiMaggio took the boy along on a date with Marilyn. She will not keep Joe from seeing the boy, but was concerned with the language he had picked up and wanted him kept away from Joe's girlfriends in general and Marilyn in particular.

Marilyn appeared in the June issue of *Redbook* magazine, "So Far to Go Alone" by Jim Henaghan. "Strange, even for Hollywood, is the story of Marilyn Monroe--the lonely orphan who finds no solace in wealth or fame....Marilyn Monroe is Mother Nature's answer to Hollywood's eternal prayer. She is, according to the industry, what Hollywood spends a million dollars a year searching for and finds once in ten years—a youngster who could stop a stampede of stevedores with a smile, lure a lovesick grocery clerk's last dollar out of his watch pocket in front of a movie house....David Hepner, a 20th Century-Fox producer, who stated, 'She wears the expression of a racy woman who has just been hit on the head by a sash weight.'...Marilyn Monroe is all these things and she is also the greatest Cinderella story in Hollywood history....'It doesn't make any difference where a kid like Marilyn comes from,' Wald said. 'The shortest distance to stardom is from the screen to the seats in the front row of a movie theater. She's traveled it—and her background doesn't make any difference. She has inner illumination, temper, but not temperament, everything it takes, including a native talent to be big box office.'"

This is an important article because the story in *Redbook* also concluded that her father was dead and the death of her mother followed shortly. This story will go on to haunt her and she will be compelled to write Wade Nichols, the editor of *Redbook*, a letter of apology. Nichols held no grudge and once again the pathos of her childhood and her honesty gains her another powerful supporter.

On June 17th Erskine Johnson writes a follow up to her letter. "Magazine Gets Bum Steer And Marilyn Monroe Apologizes. Marilyn Monroe's exclusive confession to me a month ago that her mother is alive, and that she's helping with her support, left the publishers of *Redbook* magazine red-faced over a big 'orphan's life story about her in their June issue. Now it can be told that Marilyn sent her 'deepest apology' to editor Wade Nichols in a letter which read in part: 'I frankly did not feel wrong in withholding from you the fact my mother is still alive...since we have never known each other intimately and have never enjoyed the normal relationship of mother and daughter.'"

In light of the press discovering the whereabouts of her mother, Marilyn gives Grace Goddard permission to have Gladys flown to Florida to live with Berniece. Nobody realized how fragile Gladys' mental state was at this time. The stress of Marilyn's publicity concerning the nude calendar and her coronation as a sex-goddess must surely have upset Gladys. Doc and Grace had moved back to the Los Angeles area in late 1951 and had helped Marilyn out with her day to day issues and provided some banking services as well. She needed people around her she could trust, especially with her mother.

According to other biographers of Marilyn, on June 1, 1952, her 26th birthday, she finds out she has the lead role of Lorelei Lee in *Gentlemen Prefer Blondes*. The press will not be aware of that decision for some time after that, possibly the studio was trying to drum up press and publicity for the film. She dines alone that night in her room at the Bel Air Hotel and talks to Joe DiMaggio on the telephone.

On June 1st the *INS Wire Service* runs this article, "Grable Given Blondes Role, Marilyn Monroe Picked As Girlfriend...You can stop wondering who is going to play in *Gentlemen*

*Prefer Blondes*. Sol Siegel, in charge of all Twentieth Century-Fox musicals, says that both Betty Grable and Marilyn Monroe will be in the Anita Loos play. Lorelei goes to Betty. The role of her wise-cracking girlfriend goes, Dorothy, will be played by Marilyn. That means that Marilyn's blonde tresses will have to be dyed. Richard Sale is the director, and Mary Anita Loos has collaborated with him in adapting her aunt's play." Marilyn had worked with Richard Sale and his, wife Mary Loos, on *Ticket to Tomahawk*, which they co-wrote and he directed. Mary Loos was the niece of playwright Anita Loos who wrote *Gentlemen Prefer Blondes*.

Then next day, June 2$^{nd}$, Hedda Hopper wrote, "Sol Siegel's getting nasty letter from the fans complaining about making Marilyn Monroe a brunette in *Gentlemen Prefer Blondes*. Monroe fans like her as she is. If she's in the picture Sol will have to make up his mind whether to have Anita Loos or the public hate him. He's too smart not to see the light. Siegel has put in a bid for Josephine Baker to do the French sequence in the picture."

Also on June 2nd, Hedda Hopper published a note sent to her by a Corporal in Korea, who wrote: "Marilyn Monroe's calendar picture is being copied over here in Pusan by the 162nd Engineers Topographical Co. and distributing as tokens of friendship for favors rendered. Amazing for the interest created by a piece of map reproduction paper put to the use of a morale builder. Rather reminds us what we are over here for. Please express my appreciation to the young lady."

Joe DiMaggio goes to court to contend with his former wife's suit against him. His lawyer is Lloyd Wright, Jr. They appear before Hon. Judge Elmer Doyle. Joe wins his case against his ex-wife, Dorothy Arnold, who was suing him over increased spousal support and visitation limitations for their son, Joe, Jr. The Judge denied her petition and Joe was to have visitation rights every other week and there would be no increase in the spousal support. Judge Doyle was obviously a Yankees Fan and impressed with Joe. In the future Joe will not fare so well with Judge Doyle, who grants Marilyn her final divorce decree from him on October 31, 1955. Joe's lawyer Lloyd Wright, Jr. will defend Marilyn upon her return to Los Angeles in February of 1956 for a driving violation that went unheeded and turned into a bench warrant.

Gerry Fitzgerald devotes his entire column to Marilyn and her view of older men. "Marilyn Monroe said today that men are like wine—they improve with age. But she hastily added that she had nothing against young men. Marilyn mulled over the question of the effect of advancing years last Sunday when she celebrated her 24$^{th}$ birthday over long distance telephone with baseball player Joe DiMaggio. Joe, who has already scored 37 years, presented Marilyn with an expensive bauble, which she is not ready to talk about—yet. But Hollywood's most shapely blonde was full of thought on advancing age. "Older men are mellower, fuller and richer. Look at Cary Grant, there's a lot of life in him.' The bosomy blonde sighed over Clark Gable wished she could work with him. She breathed, 'You know, he's got something.'…But Marilyn does not want to neglect the younger men. She lauded Marlon Brando, 'He is a young man with great maturity. You feel that he has seen and done a great deal.' Marilyn said experience does a lot for a man. She added,

'Experience rounds a man out and makes him more desirable.' But young or old, Marilyn is not ready to let the world know if she is ready to decide on marriage now. She would only admit, 'I want to love and be loved more than anything else in the world.'"

On June 5th Marilyn arrives at Niagara Falls, Ontario and checks in to the General Brock Hotel, to shoot her scenes on location for *Niagara.* Actual location work for the movie began on May 26, 1952. Photographer Jock Carroll takes Marilyn to lunch at the Rainbow Room of the General Brock Hotel. While on location, he will take some stunning photographs of Marilyn for an article in *Weekend Magazine,* a Canadian publication. Marilyn also took a room in the Park Hotel in Ontario during the filming, possibly for clandestine meetings with Joe DiMaggio.

Whitey Snyder, her beloved make-up man and friend, will take candid photos of her that show that she can make even an amateur photographer into a pro if she poses for him. The camera loves her face and that is just the simple truth. Marilyn is blessed with a special brand of ethereal geometry that produces a perfect concoction of beauty when the light plays off the planes and angles of her face.

Sheilah Graham keep ups the interest in the casting of *Blondes* on June 6th, "If Betty Grable and Marilyn Monroe do *Gentlemen Prefer Blondes,* a lot of people here think Grable should play Dorothy, with Marilyn as the preferred fair-haired girl."

Marilyn films her first scene in *Niagara* on June 6th. While filming some of the location shots, Marilyn uses the office of Captain Lawrence McGuinn as a dressing room. Captain McGuinn is the manager of the Maid of the Mist Steamboat Company whose boats take tourist to see the falls. Marilyn thrilled the employees by talking with them and posing for photographs. While on location in Niagara Falls, nine different men volunteered to go over the Falls for director Henry Hathaway if Marilyn would be their reward. The offers were ignored. The press and the local residents took over 2500 photos of Marilyn during her first week there.

Marilyn had to learn to smoke for the role of Rose Loomis. When she couldn't inhale, she said, "I don't want to acquire any bad habits." She finally mastered the task, but not without burning her fingers, singing her eyelashes, and ruining two of her skirts when sparks landed on them. Photographer Jock Carroll would capture Marilyn as she learned the art of smoking a cigarette. She will smoke off and on for the rest of her life.

During one of her first evenings on location she attended the nightly cocktail party hosted by Joseph Cotten in his room. Marilyn arrived the first night wearing white terry cloth slippers and a white terry cloth robe with "Sherry Netherland Hotel, New York" stitched across the back in red thread. Someone commented about her robe and she said, "Oh, that. I thought I had stolen this robe, until I paid my bill." This was in reference to her 1951 trip to New York when she was ensconced at the Sherry Netherland. Asked in a 1952 interview by Charles Lyons, what was Cotten's idea of a sexy girl. "Not all girls who meet the standards of beauty are sexy. Deciding whether a girl is sexy is an instinctive reaction. I need no yardstick,' he smiled. He readily conceded that la Monroe was indeed sexy. 'I could tell that as soon as I saw her photograph when we were casting for *Niagara.*'" Joseph

Cotten had sweet memories of Marilyn. "A rather lost little girl I found her to be...She was a pretty clown, beguiling and theatrically disarming."

Marilyn heads for the Drake Hotel in New York between her shooting schedules. Joe DiMaggio has reserved two rooms for them. While in New York she will attend the ball games at Yankee Stadium where Joe is broadcasting his televised sports show. She tries to help Joe by giving him some advice on improving his skills as a sportscaster, but the advice goes unheeded and unappreciated. While he is broadcasting the show from the studio underneath the stands, Marilyn stays in the press box, where she is kept company by one of Joe's friends. On one such occasion Lenny Lewin was asked to sit with Marilyn. Of the experience he said, "All I remember is how pretty and charming she was, and how everyone in the stadium seemed to be looking at us."

Norman Rockett, prop man on *Niagara* tells this interesting story about working with Marilyn. "Director Henry Hathaway had thrown everyone off the set except for five people: his assistant, the cameraman and his helper and Marilyn Monroe and Norman Rockett. Hathaway's selection baffled Rockett. Why would the director keep him--a mere property man--on the set? As Rockett puzzled over the situation, Hathaway turned to him and declared, 'The reason I want you to stay, Norman, is because you're going in the shower with her.' And that, Norman Rockett said, is how he ended up in the shower with Marilyn Monroe. The following year, 1953, anyone with the price of a ticket could see Monroe showering behind a filmy plastic curtain while Joseph Cotten searched for his cigarettes in an adjacent room. The scene lasted about five seconds in the movie *Niagara*. Hathaway didn't want any problems with 'the water pressure, the water heat, or anything else,' Rockett said. 'So I got some swimming trunks from the wardrobe guy and crouched down out of sight in the shower. Marilyn was supposed to be nude, of course. But she really wore a body stocking.'"

During the filming of *Niagara*, Hy Gardner wanted Marilyn to appear on his nationally broadcasted show. Frank Neill, Marilyn's publicity man, was busy arranging the details with Gardner on the telephone. Marilyn told Neill she would agree to do the show provided she wasn't asked any questions about Joe DiMaggio. She finally got on the phone with Hy Gardner himself to try to iron out the details. He asked her if he could ask her about baseball. She said sure. Then he asked if he could ask one question about Joe DiMaggio? She again refused. He asked her if he could at least ask her about "Butchie," Joe's young son. Marilyn said, "Absolutely not!" She refused to go on his show because it would have violated her relationship with those she was close to.

On June 12th the Pacific Telephone and Telegraph Co. sued Marilyn for $168.00 in unpaid telephone bills for October 1951 through June 1952 on phone line GRstvw 4-4280, while living, on and off, with Natasha Lytess at 611 N. Crescent Dr.

Walter Winchell reported on Marilyn's obvious attributes on the 15th, "Marilyn Monroe wiggles through *Clash by Night* in a rumpled pair of old blue jeans--looking so gee-whizzy that you are reminded of the two chaps looking at a nude and one sez: 'Wait'l you see her with clothes on.' Marilyn has a pash for good reading. Her pet authors are Freud and

Proust. One assumes a good book enjoys cuddling up with her."

On June 18th Aline Mosby interviewed an old photographer friend of Marilyn's, Lazlo Willinger, "Photographer Says Most Film Queens Could Never Pose for Nude Pictures...A top Hollywood photographer said today most movie queens could never pose for nude calendars like Marilyn Monroe did, because they have exotic faces or unshapely figures. Laurence Willinger shoots more magazine covers and other commercial photos--using models clothed or otherwise--than any other lensman in the Cinema City. But finding a female who's adaptable all over for nude photos is 'very, very difficult.' Only a handful of movie stars could sell a calendar in their birthday suits, he said. 'A nude model has to have a sexy body but an unsexy face,' he explained. 'She has to look corn-fed and completely blank. You can't sell a face that looks exotic.'....Miss Monroe was a model for Willinger with her clothes on. He sold 82 photographs of her for magazine covers, ads and bill boards. 'She's not a raving beauty, and she has short legs, but she's the best model I ever had,' he said. 'She had that innocent face. But now her studio make-up department seems to have changed that.' The fuss over the famed Monroe calendar, he went on, was 'infantile.' He knows three other top actresses who posed for nude calendars in their modeling days. Furthermore, he said, there isn't much demand from calendar companies for nude photos, anyway. 'That's only about five per cent of my work,' he said. 'There's much more demand for babies, puppies, and landscapes.' But he's still anxious to find models who can pose nude at his swank Sunset Strip salon. 'Nude models needn't worry about the photographer,' he grinned. 'When I spot a girl who looks boring, I know she'll make a good model. But it's strictly business. They're opposite the type I like personally.'"

While in Niagara Falls, Marilyn participates in a Father's Day contest. The *Niagara Falls Gazette* revealed on April 15, 1953, "A father's day promotion similar to last year's event, which saw Marilyn Monroe select prize winning fathers will be staged again this year, the Chamber of Commerce men's wear group decided yesterday."

Another article in the *Niagara Falls Gazette* appeared on April 25, 1953, and revealed, "Down in the Chamber of Commerce offices there is a picture of Marilyn Monroe presiding at last year's Father's Day contest, sponsored by the Chamber's men's wear group. This photo shows Miss Monroe rearing back with a surprised look. She got that way because (we are told) she is given to rolling her tongue around as she converses. One of the contest officials was fascinated by this tongue-wagging. Finally, when he could stand it no longer, he blurted, 'You stick out that tongue at me once more and I'm going to bite it right off!' So, shocked, she reared back on her haunches. At least, that's the story."

Marilyn leaves Niagara Falls and boards a train to New York on June 18th where she will spend three days visiting Joe DiMaggio, before returning to Hollywood to finish principle filming on *Niagara*.

Jess Stearn writes an article for the *Omaha World Herald Magazine* on the 22$^{nd}$. "Jolting Joe and Miss Monroe." It is an article about Joe DiMaggio's ex-wife, Dorothy Arnold's, suit against Joe in order to stop their son from being around Marilyn. Mr. Stearn starts out with nice things to say about Marilyn and ends the article with a short bio of DiMaggio and

Arnold's relationship. "There is really nothing for the ex-Mrs. DiMaggio to worry about if anything, actress Marilyn Monroe should be an exemplary influence on the life of her 10-year old son, Joseph Paul DiMaggio, Jr., son of the former Yankee Clipper of the same name. It is a cinch that if the ex-Mrs. Di, who is the former Dorothy Arnold of stage, screen and radio, would only read what Miss Monroe's press agents say about her, she would forget all about that suit she's started to keep Joe, Sr., from taking Joe, Jr., on his dates with the blonde actress with the free-wheeling motion."

Earl Wilson reported on Joe and Marilyn in New York on June 25th, "The Marilyn Monroe-Joe DiMaggio romance is on again--right here in New York. The blonde beauty sneaked in and they dined at Le Pavilion and walked on Fifth Ave., occasionally with an arm around each other while her skirts blew beautifully in the breeze. Fifth Avenuers gasped at her glamorous gams and bare shoulders. Marilyn Monroe returned to Hollywood after a 3-day visit here with Joe DiMaggio. Incidentally, there's a rumor that Marilyn's gowns are padded upstairs. We don't believe it."

On November 5th, Wilson added more detail about their time in New York, "The lure of 5th avenue grips non-New Yorkers, too, you see. One night I saw it work its effect on Joe DiMaggio and Marilyn Monroe. They'd take a car from near 55th and 5th, ridden maybe two blocks then decided to walk on 5th. They arm-and-armed along. Marilyn's skirts swirling in the breeze to 59th, where they considered taking a handsome cab through the park. And though they spooned along, this much-headlined couple wasn't recognized. I think, by anybody but this working newspaperman. For the other arm-in-arm couples weren't interested in anybody but each other...and their taste in books, and pastries, and liqueurs, and travel, as they paused to window-shop."

In his syndicated column, Erskine Johnson also reported on Marilyn's New York trip on July 3rd, "Now it can be told that Marilyn Monroe and Franchot Tone had a big date in Buffalo while she was working in *Niagara*, at Niagara Falls. But an hour after the picture completed, she hopped a train for New York to spend three days with Joe DiMaggio. A big lace nightgown that Marilyn wears in the film finally was approved by the censors--on one condition. She could be photographed in bed, but not standing up."

On July 20th, Earl Wilson reported that Marilyn went to hear Al Martino when he was singing in Buffalo, New York, when she was filming *Niagara*. This is most likely when she had her "date" with Franchot Tone.

On June 20th, M. Oakley Stafford gives a good appraisal of the marketing of Marilyn. "Hollywood is smart...Barbara Stanwyck is for the older generation. Marilyn Monroe is for the younger. Her photo is the ones GIs are clamoring for...They say she has what the late Jean Harlow had. She has the 1952's addition to it. The ready come back. The blow-for-blow. The carefree abandon of the man, which girls of today are trying to believe, is natural for them. She has everything Hollywood needs for a star build-up. And they were so wise to start her off in dungarees not glamour clothes, to show that it is she herself not her clothes, which will pull in box office patrons."

On June 23rd, Hedda Hopper broke the news about final casting decisions for

*Gentlemen Prefer Blondes.* "Now it can be told. The girls chosen to costar in *Gentlemen Prefer Blondes* are Marilyn Monroe and Jane Russell. Betty Grable, announced for *Blondes*, tells me she never asked to play the part. The only part she asked Darryl Zanuck to buy for her was *Annie Get Your Gun*."

When Carol Channing, who had originated the role on Broadway, found out that Marilyn had been cast in *Gentlemen Prefer Blondes*, she sent a 200 word collect telegram to 20$^{th}$ Century-Fox studio.

The *Dallas Morning News* pratted, "Well, Marilyn Monroe may be a gal of her word after all, the current legal hassle notwithstanding. Months ago when 20$^{th}$ Century-Fox bought rights to *Gentlemen Prefer Blondes*, the good Marilyn announced she would get the Lorelei Lee lead. And she's got it."

Back in March police were trying to catch a band of men who were peddling pornographic photographs. On April, 27th they arrested two men, Jerry Karpman and Morrie Kaplin. They were carrying 20 envelopes at the time that contained photographs and stamped on the envelopes was "Marilyn Monroe." Accompanying the photographs was a purported letter from Marilyn. Marilyn was served with a subpoena at the 20th Century-Fox lot on June 25th. Dep. City Atty. Adolph Alexander and prosecutor, William Still issued the subpoena in her legal name of Mrs. Norma Jeane Dougherty in order to save her from bad publicity. She agreed to appear in court to testify as a witness for the prosecution against two men who claimed to have her permission to distribute nude photos of her. Marilyn was quoted as saying, "'If the District Attorney wants me to testify, I will,' she declared. 'That's the least I can do for the cops in a case like this. These men are really low…'"

The next day Marilyn testified against two men, Jerry Karpman, a photographer, and Morrie Kaplan, a salesman, in the courtroom of Municipal Judge Kenneth Holaday. The case involved nine counts of mail order selling without a license, violating the State Business and Professional Code, by sending letters 'known to defendants to be untrue and misleading,' and of unlawfully using the name of Marilyn Monroe 'for the purpose of selling nude and indecent pictures represented to have been posed by Marilyn Monroe.' The come-on letters used by the defendants were purportedly signed by Miss Monroe, Marilyn Miller, Marilyn Martin and Marilyn Marach. They read in part, "Hello there, my name is Marilyn Monroe…I am out of a job and I have to raise some money quickly. Therefore I have had to do something I would never have done under ordinary conditions. A short time ago, two friends of mine and myself got together and took some pictures in almost every pose imaginable. They got a lot more enjoyment out of it that I did, but of course that is only natural. Due to the nature of these pictures it is very important that you keep this matter very confidential as I am not too happy about the whole thing. I feel that these pictures, which are not easily obtained, are worth more than the price I have found ordinary pictures are selling for. I will send you eight pictures (absolutely unretouched) for $4 or all 16 that we took plus two very unusual shots given by a friend for just $7."

"Two studio agents ran interference for her when she appeared in court, fetchingly attired in a robin's-egg blue skirt and jacket, and open-toed shoes. She listened attentively to police testimony that 1,500 'letters' and two truckloads of film were impounded in the raid…Her evidence sent Karpman and Kaplan to jail, with Judge Kenneth L. Holaday denouncing the crime as a 'vicious scheme to profit by using the names of well-known actresses for filthy purposes.'"

Marilyn's name was cleared of any connection with the two men and their illegal racket. Later that same day Morrie Kaplan and Jerry Karpman were convicted on five of nine misdemeanor counts, including mail order selling without a license and for using Marilyn's name for the purpose of nude and indecent pictures represented to have been posed by Marilyn Monroe.

Photographer George Silk was on hand to capture the whole proceedings for *LIFE* magazine, though many of the images never made it into print. Despite the courtroom drama playing out, Marilyn still manages to shoot the "Kiss" scenes for *Niagara* at the studio on the 25th and 26th.

It seems the pornographic drama was still playing out. A trunk full of pornographic photographs was taken into custody in August. A policeman took an envelope containing pictures of who he thought to be Marilyn engaged in sexual activity with a man. In September he tried to blackmail Marilyn with these photos. After stalling him for a while, she was backed into a corner and finally ended up going to the executives at Fox, and then to the District Attorney's office. They then ran an internal investigation on the policeman. It was handled internally and instead of their being charges filed against him, he was fired. Marilyn was exonerated after they found a birthmark on the woman that she didn't have. Marilyn commented on her courage during this situation. "One crooked individual even tried to blackmail me with the truth, which was something of a laugh. When he got tough, I turned him over to the police. I can get tough, too"

Marilyn indulges the nation's pressmen and posed for publicity photos and interviews at the 20th Century Fox Studio, against a backdrop of the Niagara Falls. Fred Woodress, entertainment editor for the *Birmingham Post-Herald* was one of many newsmen from around the country that photographed and interviewed Marilyn for *Niagara*.

It was reported in the press that Carol Channing agreed to come to Hollywood to make a test for *Gentlemen Prefer Blondes*, but changed her mind. She gave the reason as being that she had to be in London to open in *"Blondes"* there. The studio offered her a test as a gesture only. It had already made up its mind to star Marilyn. Another reason Fox decided against Miss Channing could be that Marilyn gets $475 a week and Miss Channing would have cost them a great deal more.

June 30th, Bob Thomas, quoted Marilyn about the bikini, which had been getting bad press lately. "But now the bikini acquires a champion in Marilyn. Of course, it's possible that she is merely anti-clothes. She's the girl who posted for those calendars in nothing more than a smile. 'I like the bikini,' she insisted. 'They're very comfortable. And they're very practical for sunbathing. I love sunbathing. I think you should expose as much area to the sun as possible. As a matter of fact, I think nude sunbathing is the best of all. The doctor advised me to get a lot of rest and nude sun baths after the operation for my appendix. Luckily, I have an enclosed porch at the Bel Air Hotel, so I can do that.' I asked her if she had any trouble from helicopters while sunbathing. 'No, not from helicopters,' she remarked cryptically. 'I don't know why you can't swim in bikinis,' she commented in reply to Esther Williams. 'If the suit is fastened properly before you go in the water nothing should go wrong. At least, I've never had any trouble with mine.'"

Marilyn appeared in an article in *Modern Screen*, July, "Am I Too Daring?" Marilyn appears in a lovely gold sculpturized swimsuit, called "The Sea Scallop," by Rose Marie Reid.

M. Oakely Stafford published this poetic thought on Marilyn in her July 3rd column. "I think so often of the parents of Marilyn Monroe, who must have disappeared from her life since she spent most of her time in orphanages and working homes. Today how proud they would be. Maybe they didn't know about the swamp lily. So beautiful and it grows in swamps."

On July 5th, Sheilah Graham reported on the continuing casting dilemma of *Blondes*, "Dick Sale may pull out as writer on *Gentlemen Prefer Blondes* because of a disagreement over how it should be done. But he'll stay as director. And David Wayne is the only one really set--as Henry Spofford. Of course, the ideal casting would be Marilyn Monroe as Lorelei and Debby Reynolds for Dorothy--would give it the young flavor of the Anita Loos book."

Marilyn had one great love in her past, Freddy Karger, whom she had met while on contract at Columbia. He abruptly ended their romance in late 1948 and Marilyn was broken hearted. He seems to have resurfaced in late July according to the gossip columnist. On the 21st, Bob Farrell reported, "Marilyn Monroe and Freddie Karger, an old flame, can't extinguish the blaze." Then next day Dorothy Kilgallen reported, "Bad news for Joe DiMaggio: Marilyn Monroe is very quietly reviving an old romance with Freddie Karger, a bandleader."

On July 25th Marilyn paid her rent at the Bel Air Hotel. She was charged $1000. She listed her address as 20th Century-Fox and her phone number as CR62211.

Joe DiMaggio is undeterred by her reported dalliance with Freddie Karger and Marilyn accompanies him to San Francisco on July 26th. While in San Francisco Marilyn attends a press conference at the Hotel St. Francis. She was interviewed by reporter Bill Walsh for the *San Francisco News*. The *San Francisco Examiner* also covered the event and several pictures of Marilyn survive. She was accompanied by her press agent Roy Croft. She was wearing the same dress as she would wear for her radio debut on August 24.

The next day the press reported her trip to San Francisco as an opportunity to meet the DiMaggio family. Fox even got in the act by denying there was any significance to the meeting and that they know of no wedding plans involving Joe and Marilyn.

Earl Wilson reported on July 30th, "Cary Grant and this sneaky interviewer got into a fiery conversation recently in New York about Marilyn Monroe's right to pose in the nude for a calendar. 'I think,' I told him, 'that my mother-in-law, who is a righteous lady, would not think that Marilyn did wrong. Mr. Grant thought it was a funny interview--me doing all the talking, but he leaned back in his dressing gown there at the Sherry Netherland, sipped some coffee, and said: 'I know that when Marilyn was on our set, there was a great craning of necks and they weren't craning in my direction. She reminds me somewhat of Mae West. I was in pictures with her. I went to a London dinner party about that time, and afterward, when the women had gone to powder their noses, these very important men said, 'Well tell us now about Mae West!' I said, 'Well she doesn't drink and doesn't smoke'--I don't think Marilyn does either. But when Mae walked down the street, you couldn't keep your eyes off of that dame!' 'You think it was alright morally for Marilyn to pose in the nude?' I asked. 'I see no reason a girl shouldn't,' he said. 'But they didn't think it was alright for Hedy Lamarr to be nude in *Ecstasy*.' 'They say Dali uses his wife as his model,' Grant answered. 'Renoir used his niece. Listen, this is really a profound question you've asked me and who wants to be profound in this weather?' 'I like the question,' I said, and I did, for Grant, being in this picture *Monkey Business* with her, was slightly on the spot. 'There are a lot of models who pose in the art studios for hours. Nobody thinks wrong of that!' Grant said. 'But there not movie stars, models for the younger generation.' 'Let's forget about Monroe,' groaned Grant. 'Let's don't,' I said. 'Well there wouldn't be any great art if the girls hadn't posed in the nude,' Grant said suddenly. 'Think of those great Titians. I don't think those girls were even paid.' 'But is it a calendar?' I asked. Grant grinned. 'So you've come out for nude calendars?' I heckled. 'Now, look, you buzzard. I'm not for nude calendars!' he said with a laugh. 'But after all, what the hell is wrong with looking at a beautiful body if it really is beautiful?.' And so Grant, if not for nude calendars, at least was out for Marilyn Monroe. 'When we made the picture,' he said, 'I had to sit in a little car with her, and MG--quite a lot.' 'You HAD to? You couldn't get out of it anyway?" 'I found her a very shy and rather smart girl. A real person. A very dear person. She reads every book that comes out. The publicity about her is far in excess of her talents, but not in excess of her sexual impact. She tries hard to apply herself and all the crew's going. "Wwww---. 'Grant gave an impression of a stagehand whistling. 'They're all telling her to wear something revealing, and the child wants to be in blue jeans and an old flannel shirt.' 'It's nice to know,' Grant added, 'that I'm happily married,' Grant hopes Marilyn will save her money and her sex appeal like Mae West did. He recalled the story of how the great Hollywood producers Jerry Wald and Norman Krasna, envisaged a terrific movie titled, *Mother Knows Best*, with Jane Russell and Marilyn Monroe as the daughters and Mae West as the mother. Everybody thought it was sensational. They sold the idea to everybody and finally went to get Mae West's assent. She heard the boys through to the end. 'I'm sorry boys,' she said, with a wiggle and waggle, no doubt, 'but I don't play mothers.' Miss Monroe must never play mothers either he feels, until she's a great grandmother."

   In August of 1952 Natasha Lytess needs a throat operation and Marilyn felt obligated to help with the cost. Marilyn sold her mink coat, given to her by Johnny Hyde, and gave the money to Natasha to pay for the operation. Natasha made a remarkable recovery, which led

Marilyn to speculate to friends, and Joe DiMaggio in particular, that Natasha might have exploited the bond between them, thus crossing a boundary with Marilyn that she would find hard to overlook. This incident laid the foundation in Marilyn's mind that Natasha wasn't to be trusted. But until she could find a replacement coach on the set of her movies, she had to retain Natasha. She would be swiftly replaced in March of 1956 when Marilyn filmed *Bus Stop* and Paula Strasberg started as her on-set coach.

Marilyn gave these words of wisdom about a career vs marriage in an interview with Harrison Carroll on August 1st, "Marilyn put marriage above her career and doesn't think a mate will spoil her film popularity.' A career comes out of your life,' she said, 'not your life out of a career.'"

On August 1, 1952, Hollis Albert sent a memo to Jack Cole regarding the dance numbers in *Gentlemen Prefer Blondes*. The memo was titled, "Bumps and Grinds." He advised Cole that Bumps could only go backward, not forward. And that Grinds could only move side-to-side, not around. If you notice in the finished film, Cole choreographed the dance numbers with this restriction in mind.

On August 3rd, Marilyn was quoted in an article about Dior's fashion prediction for the fall. "It isn't what a woman wears,' said curvaceous Marilyn Monroe. 'It's how she is and how she wears it. New or old look, it all amounts to the same thing--how much looking can you attract'"

1952 was filled with legendary publicity stunts that Marilyn gamely participated in. One of the most flamboyant stunts put on by the studio was on August 3rd at a party given in her honor at the home of Bandleader Ray Anthony. Before her big event Marilyn spent time with her friends Dorothy Dandridge and singing coach Phil Moore. Marilyn prepared at Dandridge's home on Hilldale, which was a duplex that she shared with Moore.

Helicopter Pilot, Lt. Jimmy Mann of the U.S. Navy flew Marilyn to Ray Anthony's home in Sherman Oaks for a party in her honor. She was flown in by helicopter, taking a cue from the new song, written in her honor, that she was an "angel in lace." Ervin Drake and Jimmy Shirl had written a song for her titled simply, *Marilyn*. Ray Anthony recorded it for Capitol Records. This was an opportunity not only to publicize the new song, but Fox used it to advertise Marilyn's current movie, *Don't Bother to Knock*. Over 400 guests were invited to attend the festivities. They included film stars, musicians, disk jockeys from the Los Angeles area, models like Gloria Pall, entertainers like Tennessee Ernie Ford, Frank DuVall, Mickey Katz and even Lassie attended. Marilyn joined Ray Anthony and Mickey Rooney onstage for a version of the song and Rooney gave her a lesson in how to hold a drum stick. She spent the rest of the time meeting the press and greeting her famous fans, and signing autographs. This was a big publicity coup for Marilyn. Columnist Barney Glazer labeled her, 'The Rear Admirable,' after following her around at the party. She had no dress to wear, so Henry Hathaway, director of *Niagara*, suggested that she wear the red dress from the film, and also the shoes. Earl Theisen from *Look*, Lani Carlson, Phil Stern and Bob Willoughby were among the photographers who captured Marilyn during the event. Lee Gilette filmed the event with his 8mm camera.

Mr. Willoughby recalls shooting Marilyn, "Marilyn headed up the stairs directly toward me. For one magic moment I had her all to myself, and as I peered down into the viewfinder of my Rolleiflex, I could feel the hairs on the back of my neck rising. Marilyn was looking right at me, right through me! Wow! My fingers clicked off several shots, and then she was gone, pushed by the thundering horde. But I had my photos, and I realized for the first time what all of the shouting was all about...Marilyn had some sort of energy field that it would seem she could switch on and off when she posed, which I don't think I will ever see again. Hollywood's publicity departments called it sex appeal and thought it was achieved by showing cleavage, but they missed the point. This attractive energy is something you are born with. It is there to see at any age. Some people have more, some less, and I prefer to call it gender."

After the dust settled from Ray Anthony's party, Marilyn's career went into overdrive. Marilyn's witty remarks are becoming fodder for the columnist. She is a gift from the gods that pumps up readership every time her name is mentioned in an article; hence, entire columns are devoted to her.

Erskine Johnson reported on August 8th, "Marilyn Monroe Inherits Harlow's Mantle....Hollywood took fourteen years, three-score screen tests and a couple of million dollars to find a successor to Jean Harlow, who melted movie celluloid from 1927 to 1938. Several movie dolls claimed the late platinum blonde's Hollywood 'Sex Queen' title from time to time. But moviegoers, and Hollywood itself was not so sure. Then zippy, blonde Marilyn Monroe came along to the lifted eyebrows and the wolf whistles. The verdict came fast and the vote was unanimous. Hollywood's 14-year search was over. Like Jean Harlow, Marilyn is blonde, young (24), and saucy. When asked what she thought about sex she flipped, 'I've never given it a second thought.' Even Jane Russell came out second best to Marilyn at a Hollywood party for the editor of a national magazine. 'All the studios brought their top glamour girls,' a press agent remembers. 'I brought Marilyn and paraded her around like a horse in front of a grandstand. Jane Russell was ignored. Marilyn was the hit of the evening.' Like Jean Harlow, Marilyn is hot newspaper and fan magazine copy and is the most talked about personality since Mary Astor burned her diary and Ingrid Bergman went to Stromboli. In the spicy reading department so far this year were: Her confession that she posed in the nude for a calendar when she needed money. Her 'I Don't Remember Mama' story about being an orphan—debunked when I revealed that her mother is alive and living in Hollywood. Her indignant role in a Los Angeles courtroom as the state's star witness against two men charged with using her name on letters hawking nude photographs of her 'in every pose imaginable.' And her romance with Joe DiMaggio. Also like Jean Harlow, Marilyn is happiest when she's wearing as few clothes as the law will allow—a sort of 'best undresses' star complex. The story is told that one day Marilyn walked into the 20th Century-Fox studio cafe wearing only a skirt and a red sweater--that's all. A studio official took a good look and admonished her about the undress of her attire. Marilyn gave him that sexy smile and cooed: 'What's the matter--don't you like red?' Jean Harlow never was accused of being a great actress and neither has Marilyn. It took bit roles in five films—and that nude calendar—before she became a star. But Hollywood had the right idea about her from the very beginning. She was wolf whistle bait. Asked just the other day if she had anything on for the calendar photograph, Marilyn quipped, 'Sure. I had the radio on.'....Marilyn, born and raised in California, the land of the sun tan, has skin as white as snow. Asked why she doesn't like to tan. Marilyn explained, 'I like to feel blonde all over.' Hollywood's next 'Sex Queen' may not say all the Mae Westish things movie press agents claim she says. But intimate comments from her, like the reason she doesn't tan, and 'What do I wear when I go to bed? I wear Chanel No. 5.' have helped make her the most talked about girl in Hollywood."

Pete Martin asked a Roy Craft about her "radio" quote. "As you know, in this business you can be destroyed by one bad story—although it's not as true as it used to be—and when the story broke that Marilyn had posed in the nude for a calendar and the studio decided that the best thing to do was to announce the facts immediately instead of trying to pretend they didn't exist, we said that Marilyn was broke at the time and that she'd posed to pay her room rent, which was true. Then, to give it the light touch, when she was asked, 'Didn't' you have anything on at all when you were posing for that picture?' we were supposed to have told her to say, 'I had the radio on.'" 'I'm sorry to disagree with the majority,' he said firmly, 'but she makes up those cracks herself. Certainly that 'Chanel Number Five' was her own.' When I told Marilyn about this, she smiled happily. 'He's right. It was my own. The other one—the calendar crack—I made up when I was up in Canada. A woman came up to me and asked, 'You mean to say you didn't have anything on when you had that calendar picture taken?' I drew myself up and told her, 'I did, too, have something on. I had the radio on.'"

In a 1956 interview with Milton Shulman, Marilyn gave the origin of this, her most quotable quote. "'It was a large press conference,' said Marilyn, 'and some very fierce woman journalist—I think she was Canadian—stood up and said: 'do you mean to tell us you didn't have anything on when you posed for that nude picture?' Suddenly an old night-club joke popped into my head. 'Oh, no,' I said. 'I had the radio on.' I just changed the words around a bit, but I thought everybody knew it.'"

Roy Craft, in an interview with Bill Tusher, gave the origin of the "blonde all over" quote. "Then there was the time when a magazine writer quoted Marilyn as saying she didn't like to sunbathe because a heavy tan confused her wardrobe and made it difficult to choose colors. When Craft showed her the copy, Marilyn balked. 'But I didn't say that,' she protested to Roy. 'Suntan has nothing in the world to do with your wardrobe.' 'Well, you've got to say something,' Roy remarked. Marilyn thought a minute, picked up a pencil, crossed out the part about the wardrobe, and penciled in her own substitution, 'I do not suntan,' she wrote, 'because I like to feel blonde all over.' And that, hatched in her very own fertile brain, was how another widely quoted Marilyn Monroe bon mot was born." In another interview Craft commented that "She changed a rather stuffy passage into a vivid and sensual image, a remark that has become a minor classic." He also commented that he "never made up any of the clever sayings attributed to her, and I don't know anyone who has,' he said. 'She can turn a neat phrase along with a neat ankle.'"

Alice Craig Greene tells more of the "blonde all over" story. "Tom Carlyle had a rush story to do for *Colliers*. In it he mentioned Marilyn's not liking to go out in the sun because she thought blondes didn't look their best in a suntan. A Fox publicist, tongue in cheek, phoned Tom who was teetering on a deadline. 'Sorry, Tom,' he said, 'but our little girl has insisted on some revisions.' Tom let out a moan envisioning an entire rewrite. Whereupon the publicist chuckled, 'I don't think you'll mind this change. Just change it to read, 'Marilyn doesn't go out in the sun because she likes to feel blonde all over!' What a wonderful line! And Marilyn's own idea, not the publicity department."

The magazine was actually *Pageant's* September 1952 issue, photographed by Andre de Dienes, not *Colliers*. One section was titled "How to Feel Blonde All Over," and has Marilyn making the quote, "I'm personally opposed to a deep tan because I like to feel blonde all over."

Martin Shulman recalled, "Marilyn herself is not sure just how seriously she wants these remarks to be taken when she makes them. 'There is always a stupid sincerity about them, even when they sound ridiculous.'"

David March, Marilyn's would-be business manager, introduced her to real estate agent Franklin Archer, through whom she rented a frame house at 1211 Hilldale Ave in West Hollywood. Marilyn liked the privacy and was eager to live near her friends Dorothy Dandridge and Phil Moore. Earl Wilson visited Marilyn at her home with a photographer and comments in his column on August 26th, "I was at the window of the house she then had on Hilldale, looking out over the sloping neighborhood, 'Marilyn has a nice view from here, 'I said. 'Marilyn,' retorted the photographer, has a nice view from anywhere.'"

On August 8th, John Rosenfeld dedicates his syndicated column to Marilyn. He includes several quotes from her which are interesting. "Otherwise she has cultivated a kind of dumb blonde mystique that makes fine press copy and confuses everybody. You can't figure out whether she is a total fool or completely smart....She moons for reporters, 'I'm alone. I haven't any friends. I have to fight my shyness all the time.' Or, 'People don't understand me. They think I'm a dumb, sexy blonde. I'm not. I'm not a stereotype. I'm a complex human being. I have my dreams, my desires, my disappointments.' 'I want to be a great actress. That's the most important thing in my life. Someday I'd like to have a baby. But for right now my career comes first. Not for the prestige or money, but because that's the way I can express myself best.' Miss Monroe can be pinned down on matrimony as follows, 'I'm looking for a man who is all soul, who is manly yet sensitive. Until I find him (sigh) I'm just going to keep on walking. That's my favorite sport. I sometimes walk for three or four hours at a time, alone just thinking.'....To another interviewer she explained her acting technique as 'relaxed tension.' To illustrate, she leaned back on a sofa, dropped her cheek on the cushion and shot sparks from her eyes. The reporter suddenly felt he had to leave. He was a man...As for Miss Monroe's histrionic genius, her director, Henry Hathaway, has the final say, 'She can make any movement, any gesture insufferably suggestive.' This is alchemy of personality, not derelictions of conduct. It is merely Miss Monroe acting the unwritten screenplay with singular eloquence while her less gifted self plays badly a drama not half so well written." After her death Hathaway will say of her, "Marilyn's heartache was that after she became a star, she was never permitted to play any other role than the dumb blonde. Yet she was one of the most intelligent girls I've ever known, and her longing for knowledge and a change to prove she could act was the tragedy of her life."

Dorothy Manners mentions Marilyn's bright clothing on the 10$^{th}$. "Marilyn Monroe's wardrobe of culottes, all shades—candy-stripes, Kelly green, orange, yellow—and the bright strands of painted beads she wears with sweaters…"

*World Wide Photo*, August 10th, "Beauty At Bat--Film actress Marilyn Monroe oozes a lot of appeal as she takes her stand at the plate while two Hollywood studio employees act as umpire and catcher. She could dazzle any picture into helplessness. Marilyn has become quite a baseball enthusiast. She sponsored her own team, composed of studio workers, and it hasn't lost a game yet in the 20th Century-Fox studio League." This picture showed Marilyn wearing her own brand of baseball uniform, high heels, short shorts, a tight fitting sweater and a head scarf.

An article by James Bacon accompanied the photo, "Sexy Marilyn, Joltin' Joe Still Only 'Good Friends…'Marilyn Monroe, who thought the Yankee Clipper was a New England barber until she met Joe DiMaggio, now sponsors her own baseball team. 'I offered to buy their uniforms and bats,' she smiles, 'but being young, virile men, all they want is a kiss from me if they win in their league.' Needless to say, the team, composed of studio workers, hasn't lost a game yet in the 20th Century-Fox studio league…. Hollywood at first thought the romance was cooked-up for publicity purposes. The tenor of thinking on the DiMaggio affair has changed in recent months. In fact, some of the high brass at 20th Century-Fox are pretty worried about Joe and Marilyn. The bigwigs worry because they feel marriage might deglamorize one of the industry's most glamorous packages. Marilyn has made nine pictures in 18 months and most of them are yet unreleased. Although she gets more publicity than any other actress in town, her studio feels she needs to be seen in a few more to make her a topflight star."

Hy Gardner names the "New Faces of 1952…Marilyn Monroe, who hardly won her notoriety as a 'New Face,' was getting the Jean Harlow build-up by Twentieth Century-Fox when a columnist on the *New York Herald Tribune* found out about her art study calendar and didn't keep it a secret. This 12-month piece of literature made her the most talked about new box office attraction of the year. Her romance with Joe DiMaggio didn't hurt either."

On August 10th Jack Geyer reported, "Football fans attending the eighth annual *Times* charity game betwixt the Los Angeles Rams and the Washington Redskins at the Coliseum Aug. 21 will be given an opportunity to see two of the most highly publicized performers in two of the nation's most popular industries--professional football and motion pictures. They'll see Choo Choo and Woo Woo. Choo Choo, of course, is the legendary Redskin half-back from North Carolina, Charley Justice, while Woo Woo would be none other than Marilyn Monroe, the beautiful actress who is one of the most delectable dishes in

Hollywood, the city of delectable dishes. The Blowtorch Blonde, whose pin-ups grace walls from Seoul to Savannah, will be one of the headliners at the terrific halftime show which is an annual feature of the charity contest. Marilyn, the girl who said, 'I've never given it a second thought,' when someone asked her opinion of sex, will be introduced by Ken Murray, whose 'Blackouts' flourished for years and years in Hollywood and became as much a part of the Cinema City scene as Hollywood and Vine."

*Time* magazine ran a review of *Don't Bother to Knock* on August 11th and devoted nearly the whole piece about Marilyn. "Something For the Boys...What lifts the film above the common place is it's star, Marilyn Monroe, who is an inexpert actress, but a talented woman. She is a saucy, hip-swinging 5 ft. 5 1/2 in. personality who has brought back to the movies the kind of unbridled sex appeal that has missing since the days of Clara Bow and Jean Harlow. The trademark of Marilyn's blonde allure (bust 37 in., hips 37 in., waist 24 in.) are her moist, half-closed eyes and moist, half-opened mouth. She is a movie press agent's dream. Says Director Henry Hathaway, 'She can make any move, any gesture, almost insufferably suggestive.' She currently gets more than 5,000 letters a week for smitten admirers. Soldiers in the Aleutians voted her 'the girl most likely to thaw out Alaska.' A whole U.S. battalion in Korea recently volunteered to marry her. Students of the 7th Division Medical Corps unanimously elected her the girl they would most like to examine.... A loud sustained wolf-whistle has risen from the nation's barbershops and garages because of Marilyn's now historic calendar pose, in which she lies nude on a strip of red velvet. Uneasy studio executives begged her last January to deny the story. But Marilyn believes in doing what comes naturally. She admitted she posed for the picture back in 1949 to pay her overdue rent. Soon she was wading in more fan letters than ever. Asked if she really had nothing on in the photograph, Marilyn, her blue eyes wide, purred, 'I had the radio on.'"

In a letter to Louella Parsons, Clara Bow said this about Marilyn, 'Not to Elizabeth Taylor, not to Brigitte Bardot, but to Monroe did I mentally bestow the 'It Girl' tag some time ago. She and Jean Harlow are the only women I've ever seen who possessed the flesh impact that people said I had on the screen."

On August 13th, Marilyn signs an agreement with Saalfield Publishing Co. of Ohio. She gives them permission to manufacture and sell play sets, puzzles, books, reproduced photographs and likenesses of Marilyn for two years. Marilyn will receive an $1,000 advance and a 4% royalty on the wholesale price of each item. She will have the right to final approval of all merchandise. In April of 1953 the Saalfield Publishing Co. released a book of *Marilyn Monroe Paper Dolls*.

Sheilah Graham revealed on August 14th that Marilyn had a new home. "Marilyn Monroe quit the Bel Air Hotel for a house in Westwood. It ain't much, but it's her first real home."

Harrison Carroll reported on August 15th, "Joe DiMag Keeps Love B.A. Secret...Baseball's bashful beau, Joe DiMaggio, is keeping his batting average with Marilyn Monroe a secret. However, things must be going along smoothly because the couple flew up to his home town, San Francisco, for a visit. 'I don't like to talk about my personal affairs,' the very shy baseball great said. 'I'm just a guy going along with life. If there's anything you want to know about the Yankees, I'll be glad to tell you.'"

Dorothy Kilgallen revealed on August 16th, "A dark horse in the Marilyn Monroe romance derby is Bob Slatzer, former Columbus, Ohio, literary critic. He's been wooing her by phone and mail, and improving her mind with gifts of the world's greatest books."

This is the first appearance of writer Robert Slatzer in print. He will turn their short-lived friendship into much more than it ever was, even going so far as selling books and granting interviews, and becoming an aficionado on Marilyn's death. By his own admission he and Marilyn had met in 1947 when she was a bit player at Fox. When they both lost their jobs they also lost touch with each other. In an interview with Florabel Muir Marilyn gave this description of a man she used to know, which sounds much like Robert Slatzer. It is an unflattering remembrance and she gave him the boot after discovering that he was actually married. "The men Marilyn met in the early days were crude amateurs, she recalls, when compared with the ones she met after her name began to appear in movie columns and fan magazine. 'For instance,' says Marilyn, 'there was the screen writer whose approach was strictly on the intellectual level at first. He talked to me about my career and gave me books to read. He warned me not to be seen in the night clubs too often and not ever to go out with playboys. Brother, that from him! He was like a brother to me and that's how I felt about him until I discovered he was a long range operator. That brother act is a quite a routine when an intelligent man plays it. I soon found out, however, that there isn't any such thing as brotherly interest. One night my big self-styled brother called me and said he had some fine steaks and would like to come over and cook dinner. I asked him if he was going to bring his wife and he laughed heartily and told me I was some little joker. I told him another big brother had asked me to dine at Romanoff's and I thought it was safer than his proposition. He lost interest in me from then on.'" It seems that Slatzer had a wife back in Columbus.

Slatzer showed up on the Canadian location shoot of *Niagara* and accidentally ran into Marilyn. He claims that he had no idea that Norma Jeane had turned into Marilyn Monroe. He took advantage of the situation and had several pictures taken with Marilyn. The meeting is memorialized by Arthur Everett Scott in 1954, although, he doesn't mention Slatzer by name. "A loyal friend, Marilyn hasn't forgotten those she left behind as she soared to fame. Recently in Buffalo to shoot a film on location, she recognized an old newspaper-reporter buddy in the watching crowd. Leaving the set, she went for a long walk with him, talking about the good old days and assuring him a good time whenever he could get to Hollywood. He commented later, 'Every time you take a look at Marilyn, you have trouble breathing. But in five minutes you feel like her big brother, and you're ready to slug any guy who even makes a pass at her with his eyes." After her death he embellished their relationship and claimed they never lost touch with each other after 1947. He claimed to have been there during her calendar shoot and behind the scenes guiding her career and as an on again off again lover. He even boasted that they were married in Mexico in October of 1952. This is his most outrageous claim. He asserts that the studio made them undo the marriage, and lucky for him, there is no record of it. What evidence there is though is a check Marilyn had written to the Jax Store in Beverly Hills on October 4th, the day Slatzer claims they were married, disproving the marriage story. That he actually knew Marilyn is attested by Dorothy Kilgallen and Whitey Snyder, but he has made far more of it than what it in reality was.

Harrison Carroll reported on August 19th, "Marilyn Monroe denies the rumor that she has a chauffeur/bodyguard. Says the only threatening letter she knows about came before she left for the east to do *Niagara*. 'It was obscene and unsigned,' she explains. 'I'm not sure what the studio did about it. I think they showed it to the police.' Marilyn now has that house of her own--a small place above Sunset Strip. Says she doesn't expect to see Joe DiMaggio for a month and is not dating anybody else--seriously, that is."

On the evening of August 21st Marilyn made an appearance during a half-time event at the 8th Annual *Los Angeles Times* charity football game between the Los Angeles Rams and the Washington Redskins, at the Los Angeles Memorial Coliseum. Dennis Day was the star soloist at the event. "With Day to carry the ball and ballads, Master of Ceremonies Ken Murray to pass the quips and block puns, Glamour Gal Marilyn Monroe replacing the single-wing with the double-wow and Spike Jones and his City Slickers on hand to throw everyone off-tackle, off-tune and off-ten, the annual *Times* charity between-halves talent line-up is the greatest 20 minutes in football history."

Jack Benny also led the crowd in the "world's largest community-sing." Also, there that night were John Boudreau's 60-piece Rams Band and Musical Organization, the 60-piece Camp Pendleton Marine Band and the L.A. Motorcycle squadron with 25 sirens, which prompted the *Los Angeles Times* to quip, "while 20th Century-Fox gets in the act with just one siren--That's Marilyn Monroe. Need we say mo'?"

Ken Murray recalls inviting Marilyn to attend, "I had contacted Marilyn Monroe to ask if she would appear with me at the *Times* charity football game between the Los Angeles Rams and the Washington Redskins. She readily agreed and also made her first television appearance on my show later. There were a lot of fancy runs in the football game at the Los Angeles Coliseum that hot August night in 1951, [actually 1952] but none was more thrilling than the fifty-yard dash luscious Marilyn made from the sidelines to the center of the field when I introduced her. Ten huge spotlights aimed at her flaming red dress that appeared to be sprayed on, the one and only Marilyn Monroe bounced across the field with a run that charged more batteries than the generator at Hoover Dam. I felt called upon to comment that she 'had better be careful or the referee will penalize her five yards--for backfield in motion.' During half time I asked the crowd, 'All those in favor of seeing Marilyn put a motion before the house say ,'aye!'" That big concrete and steel bowl simply rocked." Bob Martin took some lovely photos of Marilyn at the game.

Harrison Carroll reported on August 21st, "The only catch Marilyn Monroe made on her trip to San Francisco with Joe DiMaggio was three salmon. He took her fishing and she's sporting a sunburned nose from the experience. Marilyn's driving Joe's big Cadillac these days, but he'll put it in storage before he returns to N.Y."

When asked what she thought of leap year, Marilyn "yawned that leap year is an old fashioned idea anyhow. 'I'm a moon cultist,' the shapely blonde announced. 'I believe in romance and the urge to marry are at their height with the appearance of the full moon. It's more fun than leap year, 'cuz it comes more often.'"

Marilyn recorded her role on NBC's, *Bakers Theatre of Stars* on August 24th. The episode was titled, *Statement in Full*, and was recorded at the KNBC Station's WWJ studio. Marilyn played the role of a murderess. Carleton Young was one of her co-stars in the production. Wendell Niles was the host for the program. Afterwards, Marilyn was given a party honoring the event, complete with a specially decorated cake. This was a repeat and recast program which had originally aired on January 15, 1951. The then named NBC Hollywood Playhouse, first aired *Statement in Full* with Joan Crawford. The show changed its name after its third network change to NBC in 1952. The show was sponsored by The American Bakers, hence the name, *Bakers Theatre of Stars*. The program aired August 31, 1952.

*The Morning Advocate Magazine* reported what role Marilyn would play on the Radio Show, "Marilyn Monroe will portray June Cordell, who in a moment of fury kills her boyfriend when she discovers he never intended to marry her. She then blames another man for her crime and is haunted, not only by the eyes of the innocent man, but also by the anguished cries of the grey-haired woman who claims to be the accused man's mother."

The Press announced on August 25th that the officials of the Miss America Beauty Pageant shattered an 82-year-precedent today by naming Marilyn as the grand marshal of the 1952 Miss America Beauty Pageant.

Marilyn arrives at La Guardia Airport in New York City on August 25th to promote *Monkey Business*. She agreed to this trip back east only because the studio promised her some time in New York to be with Joe DiMaggio. But before going on to Atlantic City on September 1st, Marilyn will visit a children's hospital and will be busy rehearsing for the premiere of *Monkey Business* at the Roxy on August 28. She ended up not having as much free time with Joe as she had anticipated. The day after her arrival in New York City, Mel Torme', who is playing at the Roxy Theatre, agrees to include Marilyn at the end of his first show on Thursday evening. Between his afternoon shows Mel went over to the Sherry-Netherland Hotel where Marilyn was staying. Marilyn's performance was tied to a sneak preview of *Monkey Business* after Mel's 7 o'clock show. Mel came up with a duet between Marilyn and himself of "Do It Again." He also wrote the dialogue for the short sketch they would perform. They begin their rehearsals today.

Roy Craft remembers Marilyn's hectic time in New York. "I recall one time in New York when studio brass had set up a schedule of personal appearances and interviews that would have taxed the energies of a longshoreman. Because she was late for an appointment, one executive phoned and, over my protests, personally berated her for her tardiness. Getting me back on the phone, he told me to get her to the appointed place, and right now, that she wasn't sick and the whole think was just a stall. I told him she might not be sick, but she was in the bathroom throwing up at the moment, and if he wanted her there on time he'd better come after her himself. As for me, I respected a lady's privacy when she was vomiting. I called a doctor and she was given some sedatives and soon a floral offering arrived from the executive with a note of apology. It would have been a conversation piece at Legs Diamond's funeral. Marilyn revived, as things turned out, made her appointments late, 'killed the people' as usual and during the balance of the day was the breathless Marilyn, sweeping everything before her."

On the 26th Earl Wilson shook things up when he revealed that Marilyn shuns undies. "Sexsational Marilyn Monroe revealed the secret of her success today--she confessed to me that under her dresses she wears nothing, but nothing, at all. Panties, slips, girdles and bras are never worn by the MMMMmmm Girl, who refuses all undergarments. 'I like to feel unhampered,' she explained, as we sat in her new home. 'All those lines and ridges in undergarments, girdles and brassieres are unnatural, and they distort a girl so! So I never wear them. Except,' she added, 'I will wear a brassiere when I have on something very sheer...' Some years ago Clark Gable got the textile industry in a rage by saying he wore no undershirt. But here was Marilyn saying fearlessly that she wore neither underskirt nor undershorts nor underanything. 'At first,' Marilyn said, sipping a Dubonnet, 'one of the fitters here refused to fit me because I wore no undergarments.' Marilyn wouldn't give in. 'I don't see why it matters whether you wear underwear,' she argued. 'Nobody sees it!' So, she won. In this baring-all interview, Marilyn was unconventional which is not surprising. Some of the lady Hollywood columnists recently blasted her for the way she dresses and she replied: 'I dress for men, anyway.' She was candid about her romance with Joltin' Joe DiMaggio. 'Joe and I are friendly, and you can put friendly in quotation marks,' she giggled. Joe'll be 38 this year and that isn't too much older, she made clear.' A girl wants a man to have a lot of strength and fortitude so she can lean on him,' she said. 'I'm not going out with anybody else...tonight...last night...or tomorrow night.' Miss Monroe was kind enough to remember that I interviewed her three years ago, the first of the Broadway mob to do so. She was then in *Love Happy*. In *Niagara* and *Gentlemen Prefer Blondes*, which'll be coming along from 20th Century-Fox, she should be bigger than Jean Harlow was. Near Marilyn's new house there's a city street sign that says: 'Put Out Your Cigarets. Fire Zone.' The neighbors have had fun about that since she moved in. As I looked out the window down the hill from her house, I said, 'Marilyn has a nice view from here,' the photographer flung back: 'Marilyn has a nice view from anywhere!'"

Marilyn told Dorothy Kilgallen this about her underpinnings, "By the way, it's untrue that I wear no underclothing. It's just stockings I hate—and girdles, too. Remember, my dear, that men seldom jump hurdles for girls who wear girdles!'"

One of the most ironically inane interviews was reported by Phillis Battelle on August 28th, when Marilyn was given an intelligence test by the press during her visit to New York. "Miss Marilyn Monroe--a well-rounded girl in a number of ways--was asked today to prove that she has an I.Q. along with her S.A. She's no PhD, see. But neither is she a B.D.B. (beautiful dumb blonde). Marilyn was thrown a few curves, encyclopedia type, in a question-and-answer interview set up for the express purpose of discovering whether Hollywood's latest glamour girl has a brain along with her other attributes. She had just come out of the shower and was wrapped in fascination and a towel when the questions began. She did not look particularly ready for an intelligence test but it's hard to tell about a girl in a towel. 'I'm a little wet behind the ears,' she said with literal honesty. 'But I'm game--shoot.' The first question went like this: What is heat? Marilyn grimaced. 'Gee,' she said. 'It's something you generate--I mean it's something that is generated. Gotta be careful with those differentials.' Question 2: What is the principle of the atom bomb? Answer: 'Between you and me, I'd like to know. They've called me one so many times.' Question 3: How many stomachs has a cow? Answer: 'Either two or four, but I think it's a camel that has four.' Question 4: Why do our faces keep warm without clothes? Answer: 'Now, really. I don't think they do keep particularly warm. But if they do it's 'cause there's not so much tissue to get cold.' Question 5: How long can a whale stay under water? Answer: 'Well, I've never been terribly interested in whales, but I'd say that a whale is a mammal so it probably can't stay as long as--but then a seal is a mammal and it does--ah, I don't know.' Question 6: Is a woman's brain smaller than a man's? Answer: (enigmatically) 'Some.' Question 7: What is the largest diamond ever known? Answer: 'Now there's a subject I'm more interested in than whales. I guess the Hope diamond, but I'm no authority.' Question 8: The U.N. Technical Assistance Board has announced that contributions have been received from 26 countries and total $9,949,793 or 53 per cent of the $18,800,000 pledged by 64 countries at the Paris conference. How do you feel about it? Answer: 'What?' Question 9: Why does starch stiffen clothes? Answer: 'Oh, it's made with sort of a chemical that forms a sort of gravy with water. It's one of those things you don't question. You accept.' Question 10: How many stars in the Milky Way? Answer: 'I think it's unknown. But who really cares?' Question 11: What were the 12 labors of Hercules? Miss Monroe, glamour girl, and star of 20th Century-Fox's *Monkey Business*, stood up the length of a bath towel, a pretty head and two long legs...'I'm sure the Greeks were interested, but I don't care in the least!'"

Marilyn will say of her intellect, "Because I have had so very little education, I know my limitations. While I want to be neither a quiz kid nor a pseudo-intellectual, I would like to know what makes things tick."

On August 28th Marilyn and Mel Torme' have their last rehearsal this afternoon. When she shows up at the Roxy later that evening, at a quarter to seven, Mel senses that something is wrong. Marilyn is followed by a group of people, all talking at the same time, and even a hairdresser who is curling her hair as she walks around. He has everyone but Marilyn to leave his dressing room. Marilyn, who has been drinking wine, confesses to Mel how frightened she is to go on stage. She feels that the women in the audience already hate her and have just come to make fun of her. Somehow, Mel is able to convince Marilyn to go on with the show. He begins the show at 7 o'clock. Marilyn appears on cue at the end. They are a hit. The theatre is packed with people, all of whom respond with great enthusiasm to Marilyn. She doesn't stay for the sneak preview of *Monkey Business*; instead she leaves to meet Joe DiMaggio at Toot Shor's club for dinner. But she spends the next fifteen minutes in Mel's dressing room. Marilyn is so pleased with how their routine went. She asked Mel if he would like to meet Joe DiMaggio and invites him to join them for dinner, but Mel has to refuse because he has another show that evening and is afraid he would be late for it. It would be another two years before Marilyn and Mel would see each other again.

On August 29th, Aline Mosby ran a story that gives voice to 20th Century Fox's inability to understand Marilyn's potential and how best to handle her current status as a movie star. Aline Mosby reported, "Marilyn Monroe's Buildup As Sexy Glamour Girl Accidental...Marilyn Monroe has zoomed to stardom as one of the sexiest glamour girls since Jean Harlow--but actually it's an accidental build-up that even her own studio frowns upon....Her studio had little to say about it. Marilyn Monroe drifted around movietown, broke and unnoticed for years. She even was under contract to Fox studio years ago, but she looked like the girl-next-door type then. With experience and age, Marilyn acquired a different charm. She won a part as a sexy mistress in *Asphalt Jungle*. The press clamored for pictures and interviews with Marilyn, and then Fox hastily hired her back. As one Fox publicist says, 'we never did any particular sex build up on Marilyn because we didn't have the right picture or part for her. In fact, we still don't.'....Once she needed $50 for rent, she posed nude for a respectable calendar photographer. When the calendar was issued two years later, Marilyn proudly handed autographed copies around her movie set. The gossip columns began to buzz about a blonde who had posed in her birthday suit. And word got around it was Marilyn. Her bosses sternly lectured her never to admit to the press she had posed for the calendar. But one day I was interviewing Marilyn on the subject, and decided to check on those calendar items. Marilyn told all in an exclusive interview. 'When that story hit the front pages I bought every newspaper copy in the studio,' a studio publicity man confessed today. 'But somehow I missed a copy and it got around. We publicist thought there'd be hell to pay. But Darryl Zanuck (the studio head) wasn't upset, so it was alright.' Later Marilyn told me, 'when I first read the story I was horrified. I never dreamed you'd print it. But then I read it again and it was in good taste so I decided it was the best thing for me. It disproved the rumor, anyway, that there was something bad about the picture.' The publicist says, 'most of her publicity is what she's done herself. It's her own idea to wear a rose stuck in her plunging neckline, and wear sexy clothes.' Fox publicists even have hopefully asked the press to forget about the calendar, but nobody does. Somehow I think Marilyn's glad they don't. Since her calendar became public property, Marilyn says, she has received thousands of requests for a copy, but not one complaint."

Marilyn has this to say to Helen Hover Weller about dressing for the opposite sex. "Accent your womanliness. If you have a good figure do it by wearing contour hugging clothes. Even when you wear a tailored suit it can add sex appeal if you try tucking a real or a good artificial rose in the neckline instead of wearing a blouse or a gilet. Of course, the rose should go in the lowest part of the V.

Jean Peters, Marilyn's co-star in *Niagara* had this to say about Marilyn, "Marilyn

Monroe, her 'good friend,' also a co-star in the picture 'is always late--at that infuriates me,' Jean said. But then she said, 'Marilyn's a very kind girl. She's tender and cries easily.'"

The same day Earl Wilson revealed this bit of risqué news, "Natural Girl Marilyn Monroe had trouble buying shoes a couple of years back. 'Cause she wore no stockings while trying 'em on. Ditto dresses, 'cause she wore no undies. Now salespeople say the shoes and dresses feel honored to touch 'Her Nudeness.' She favors Ceil Chapman."

Marilyn's press is heating up. Another story appeared on the 29th, Bob Ruark devoted his entire syndicated column to Marilyn. "It's A Wonderful Life...I don't know what the poor folks were doing the other day, but I was having a cocktail with Marilyn Monroe. She drank a Dubonnet. During this time she was not asked whether she wore pants, which has been asked of her. She was not asked about the status of her romance with Joe DiMaggio, or whether she once posed nude for a calendar, or what she slept in. Marilyn Monroe is quite a lass to look at. She is equipped with more than the average appurtenances, and she peers at you deceptively with a large set of eyes. She listens. She has a name for being an enfant terrible which has made undeserved reputations for quite a few press agents. She stutters, too-you know--a tiny little stammer that comes up mostly when she is really startled and hasn't prepared her script to cope with the surprise. I know a lot about Monroe, and truly she stutters. I will tell you about a lady who spent a lot of time being handed around from this asylum to that when she was a kid, with a hard parental problem to lick and the wonderful kind of uniforms they give little girls to wear in places where tax-payers pick up the tab. They say you stammer from insecurity and this girl has had enough to put Joe F-f-risco out of b-b-business. She is a hot girl in the movies today, and I think that her next one is called *Monkey Business*, which gets that out of the way. She is also in love with a nice gentleman, name of Guiseppe DiMaggio. Somebody on a news service asked her about Joe once and she answered simply, 'We haven't talked about baseball yet.' A much better writer than most people you meet these days, Somerset Maugham, once wrote a piece about a dame named Jane. This one, while not overendowed with anything, made a great reputation in the more sophisticated circles of London by an odd device. She spoke the truth, with a straight face. Marilyn Monroe, who has been billed for the shape of her body and the shape of her wisecracks, is much like this Jane of Mr. Maugham's. She looks you smack in the eye and she gives you the honest answer, and it sounds so funny coming out of a Hollywood operation that she makes a great name as a wit. And she's not the smartest. She is just the honestest. Like the question that they, not I asked her about the big nude calendar pose. 'Did you really have anything on while you were posing?' they asked. 'Sure,' Marilyn said cheerfully. 'I had the radio on.' Somebody asked her once time why she didn't sun-bathe. 'I want to be a blonde all over,' she said. Remembering the ancient days of the lamented Jean Harlow, I asked her if she weren't real weary of being on the opposite end of a wolf whistle. Monroe is the nearest thing to Harlow we've seen in 20 years. 'Any woman who says she's bored with being grabbed at is a liar,' says Miss Monroe cheerfully. Here is a woman being featured by the movies and exploited by the press agents and being shoved around in the personal appearances. Here is one that had it tough all the way up and now she has it good and is grateful for having it that way and is willing to play it straight and not go grande dame. Here is one of the few honest ones I have ever met in the movie business, outside of Annie Sheridan, who had a lot of advantages to start with. Here, despite her build-up, is a real nice woman named Monroe, in a racket that easily ruins nice honest people. If they louse this one up they got trouble out of buster, here and in my time I have made some Trouble, I mean."

Leonard Lyons reported on Ruark's cocky display at meeting with Marilyn. "One late afternoon at Toots Shor's Robert Ruark twirled his mustache, bared his teeth and leered just as if he were William Powell. Then he casually mentioned that he was about to have cocktails with Marilyn Monroe. The drools soon swamped the earshot corner of the restaurant. I alone showed restraint. I gave it the Ronald Coleman, arched my neck and gently replied that I, ahem, was about to have cocktails with Marlene Dietrich. Ruark's William Powell suddenly became Mickey Rooney. 'Hey, let's swap,' he eagerly proposed."

Marilyn had a hectic schedule on her trip to the Big Apple. On August 30th while in New York Marilyn planned to see Joe play in an Old Timers Game at Yankee Stadium, but she spent so much time visiting the Betty Bacharach Home for Crippled Children in Longsport, NJ, that she nearly missed the game. She stayed until she had visited with each child, despite the best efforts of the studio publicity man to get her to leave. There is fleeting newsreel images of her visit with the children. Joe DiMaggio had never seen any of Marilyn's films. While she was in New York a private screening was arranged at the Long

Island home of 20th Century President, Spyros Skouras.

Alan Frazer reported on Marilyn at the Old Timers Game. "Marilyn Monroe, whose figure is currently the most publicized in the movies, might marry Joe DiMaggio, as everybody knows and as her Hollywood bosses fear, since they want her to remain in circulation until they plant her firmly on the heights…There is considerable difference in age of course. Marilyn is so young that she saw her first baseball game. It was in Yankee Stadium, but Joe, who climbed the heights of stardom in that pasture was playing with the Old Timers…A young Old Timer, but an Old Timer, nevertheless. One of the other Old Timers taking part in the anniversary game was Jumpin' Joe Dugan, a former Yankee hero, but in retirement, a Bostonian…Dugan took his son, Joe, Jr., along and the 15 year old lad worked out in uniform with the former stars and with a son of Wally Pipp…After a while, Dugan, Sr., beckoned to Jr., and said, 'Here, I want you to meet Joe DiMaggio."…The boy walking up for the introduction exclaimed, 'I don't want to meet Joe DiMaggio, I want to see Marilyn Monroe!' DiMaggio is a quiet serious man, according to Dugan, but upon hearing the crack, he started laughing and after shaking hands with the young Joe, he said, 'If you really want to see her, she's in mezzanine box 22—right up there.' Young Dugan, unabashed, after the manner of young America, walked over to the grandstand, picked out Marilyn with his gaze and coolly appraised her. Then he returned to his dad and the other Joe and, puckered his lips, whistled 'Whew!' The incident escaped the attention of the filled stands but DiMaggio and Dugan enjoyed it immensely."

*The American Weekly*, August 31$^{st}$, carries an article, "Those Young Ones," by Betty Betz. Marilyn, strangely has no photo in the article, but is referred to in one sentence. "Marilyn Monroe was hired when an agent was told to find a voluptuous blonde to be chased by Groucho Marx."

On August 31st, the newspapers heated up again with, "Curves Still Paying Off," by Hal Boyle. "Girls, our success formula for today is simple: 'Stay in there and keep pitching those curves.' The symbol of this vibrant maxim is Marilyn Monroe, who has proved an ambitious girl doesn't have to come to the big city to get ahead. She can do it in her own home town.... In Hollywood, where she is rated as one of the most sultry discoveries since the late Jean Harlow, this naturally is considered peonage. 'They keep saying that one of these days they'll tear up my contract and write me a better one,' she said. 'And one of these days I wish they would.' She arrived for our luncheon appointment in good time--well before dusk. 'They keep me so busy,' she complained, 'sorry I'm late.' She turned her wide blue eyes on me, and I had an uneasy feeling they would melt and drip on the table. Then she sat down beside me--real close--and I had an uneasy feeling that maybe I'd melt. 'I was having my hair fixed in my hotel room, and all I had on was a towel,' she said, and added carefully--'a small towel. Some reporters were on the other side of the door asking me questions. And such questions! They wanted to know how many stomachs a cow had, and they seemed real surprised when I gave them the right answer--four. Then they asked me if I know what heat was?' I told them sure--Heat is something that is generated. Isn't that right?' At the moment, she is rather amazed by the public interest in her disclosure that she never wears brassieres, girdles or any other form of underclothing, and sleeps raw except for a nightly dab of perfume. 'It's more comfortable not to wear underclothing, and I don't like to feel wrinkles,' she said. 'What's so unusual about that? You must know a lot of girls who do the same thing--and who put on perfume before going to sleep.' (Editor's note: If Boyle does, he never mentioned it before)...Miss Monroe feels most American women should follow her example and emancipate themselves from bras, corsets and girdles. 'But, first, some of them ought to exercise,' she said, 'in order to be…to be…you know…firm. I exercise with weights myself. I lie on my back with my arms overhead and lift the weights 15 times. It is a kind of pull against gravity, I guess. I used to walk a lot, too. Walking up a steep hill is the best things for a woman's legs.' But what about the subject on the minds of 10,000,000 girls this leap year—how to catch a husband? Marilyn, whose own marriage at 16 didn't last, gave two simple rules: '1. A girl should follow her instincts. 2. That will about take care of things, as instincts are important.' As for sex (a current events topic most movie stars and baseball players usually have opinions on), Miss Monroe said: 'Truthfully, I've never given it a second thought.' And she was gone before I thought of asking her what her first thought was."

Marilyn bust her acting chops in her radio debut. *Statement in Full*, aired on the radio from 5:30 p.m. to 6:00 p.m. on August 31st.

Marilyn gave an interview which ran in the September issue of *Pageant* magazine, "How I Stay in Shape…Frankly I've never considered my own figure so exceptional; until quite recently, I seldom gave it a second thought at all. My biggest single concern used to be getting enough to eat. Now I have to worry about eating too much. I never used to bother with exercises. Now I spend at least 10 minutes each morning working out with small weights. I have evolved my own exercises, for the muscles I wish to keep firm, and I know they are right for me because I can feel them putting the proper muscles into play as I exercise. Each morning, after I brush my teeth, wash my face and shake off the first deep layer of sleep, I lie down on the floor beside my bed and begin my first exercise. It is a simple bust-firming routine which consists of lifting five-pound weights from a spread-eagle arm position to a point directly above my head. I do this 15 time, slowly. I repeat the exercise another 15 times from a position with my arms above my head. Then, with my arms at a 45-degree angle from the floor, I move my weights in circles until I'm tired. I don't count rhythmically like the exercise people on the radio; I couldn't stand exercise if I had to feel regimented about it…A Set Bizarre Eating Habits: Breakfast. I've been told that my eating habits are absolutely bizarre, but I don't think so. Before I take my morning shower, I start warming a cup of milk on the hot plate I keep in my hotel room. When it's hot, I break two raw eggs into the milk, whip them up with a fork, and drink them while I'm dressing. I supplement this with a multi-vitamin pill, and I doubt if any doctor could recommend a more nourishing breakfast for a working girl in a hurry. Dinner. My dinners at home are startlingly simple. Every night I stop at the market near my hotel and pick up a steak, lamb chops or some liver, which I broil in the electric oven in my room. I usually eat four or five raw carrots with my meal, and that is all. I must be part rabbit; I never get bored with raw carrots. PS. It's a good thing, I suppose, that I eat simply during the day, for in recent months I have developed the habit of stopping off at Wil Wright's ice cream parlor for a hot fudge sundae on my way home from my evening drama classes. I'm sure that I couldn't allow myself this indulgence where it not that my normal diet is composed almost totally of protein foods." Accompanying the article are photographs by Andre de Dienes. They were taken in early March of 1952. Marilyn is at her tip-top shape and resembles a country girl raised on sunshine and clean air. De Dienes will recall that the sitting ended abruptly when Marilyn received a call from the studio about her nude calendar. Earl Holliman, of *Police Woman* fame, was a struggling actor in the early 1950s and worked at Wil Wright's. He remembers that Marilyn would come in every night and order an ice cream sundae, then she would sit and read a book of poetry while eating her ice cream. According to Holliman she jogged down to the shop and jogged home.

It is in September that Gladys, having somehow made her way back from Berniece's home in Florida, lands on Doc and Grace Goddard's doorstep. She is ranting and raving and creating a scene. The Goddards call the police, who end up taking Gladys to Norwalk State Mental Hospital. Grace is savvy enough to know that Marilyn has to come up with another solution concerning care for Gladys other than a state run facility, especially since she is a movie star and the public will perceive that she is rich enough to take care of her mother. Once Gladys is stabilized she is moved into the Hawthorne home of Wayne and Ida Bolender, Marilyn's first foster family. While Gladys was at the Bolender's Marilyn had called Ida to check on her mother. Ida remembers the phone call to Ezra Goodman, "I've never seen a picture of Norma Jeane's. I talked to Norma Jeane on the phone about two years ago when her mother was staying with me between time in hospitals. On the phone I said, 'Norma Jeane, why don't you come to see me?' She said, 'I always thought because I'm in the movies you might not like me anymore.' 'Because you're in the movies don't make any difference,' I said. 'You come see me.' But she didn't."

The newspapers carry this tid-bit on September 1st, "One of the most popular men on the set of the *Abbott and Costello Go to Mars* set is Vic Massey. Reason: he's Marilyn Monroe's secretary, and everybody wants to know what she's really like. Vic has been in 10 Abbot and Costello pictures and does his secretarial work at night."

Earl Wilson also reported that her date at The Embers was Jack Nichols.

On September 1st Marilyn, accompanied by Twentieth Century-Fox's studio publicity man in New York, Bob Fleisher, almost missed the Parade in Atlantic City to promote her film *Monkey Business*. Her cab was caught in traffic, so they missed the 9am train at Penn Station. The studio chartered a 46-seat Eastern Airlines Falcon at La Guardia for $800.00.

Roy Craft remembers when Marilyn missed the train and he had to get her to Atlantic City. "The only thing available was a 45-passenger Eastern Air Lines plane, which we chartered. Marilyn slept. The hostess had nobody to serve coffee to but me."

They were met at the airport by a Sheriff's car and Marilyn arrived via motorcycle escort, 3 minutes after the train pulled into the station at Atlantic City. She was met at the station by the Mayor, who presented her with a beautiful bouquet of roses and a multitude of fans. Marilyn then rode to the Claridge Hotel on the back of a convertible, wearing a two-piece white dress and dark gloves. The car bore a banner on either side promoting the premier of *Monkey Business* that evening. She was preceded in the parade by a marching band. One member of the press remembers, "She sat up there like Lindbergh riding down Broadway on his return from Paris. The people and the cops and the beauty-carnival press agents followed behind like slaves tied to her chariot wheels. That is, she managed to move a little every once in a while when the crowd could be persuaded to back away. Then Marilyn would pitch a rose at the crowd and it would set them off again, and there'd be another riot. This sort of thing went on--with variations--for several days. It was frantic."

When she arrived at the Claridge Hotel, she kept the kept the local press waiting for an hour at a cocktail party in her honor while she showered in her room. Photographer Sid Ross remembers, "When she walked into the room you could hear the jaws drop. The blasé, cynical gentlemen and ladies of the fourth estate acted as if they had been chloroformed." Marilyn was wearing the red dress from *Niagara*. Ben Ross took some stunning candid photos of her at the cocktail party in the infamous dress.

Newsman Michael Sean O'Shea remembers meeting Marilyn at Atlantic City. "She had finally made it as a star. She had 'arrived' as a sexpot and there wasn't anywhere for her to go but up. She bubbled over with energy and was more exciting to see than any of the beauty pageant contestants. She was all female and as All-American as any girl could be."

Marilyn arrived that night at the premiere of *Monkey Business*, hosted by the Stanley Theatre, in another banner covered car with a blaring motorcycle escort. Inexplicably there was a local marching band and the rousing rhythms of "My Country Tis of Thee," to greet her. The two showings of *Monkey Business* were at 8pm and 10pm.

Photographer Ben Ross remembers the premier. "The most interesting pictures were not of Marilyn, but of the audience. Row upon row, 2,000 jaws hung agape at the vision before them. Nobody stirred. Nobody laughed at the corny routines. It was mass paralysis.

*Keystone Wire Service* photo, September 1st, "Warm Reception For Marilyn: Marilyn Monroe, Hollywood's No. 1 box office attraction, is received at Atlantic City by a youthful committee headed by David and Charles Washington. Sultry actress was in town to help premiere her latest movie, *Monkey Business*." This photo also ran in *the Atlanta Daily World*, an African-American newspaper on September 7th.

Marilyn had her photo made with the contestants during registration, many of which ended up in hometown newspapers. Some of the ladies who posed with Marilyn were Miss South Dakota, Sandra Kay Hart, who remembered Marilyn to be "a lot thinner than I expected. She was very sweet to me. She even remembered my name among all the people she met today." Others were, Miss Alabama, Gwen Harmon; Miss Colorado, Chardelle Hayward; Miss Michigan, Karol Ann Dragomir; Miss Nevada, Bonnie Wilson; Miss Montana, Karen A Whittet; Miss Iowa, Carolyn E. Hill; Miss Idaho, Zoe Ann Warberg; Miss Ohio, Carol Jean Koontz, who thought Miss Monroe was "very striking,"; and Miss Indiana, Ann Garnier, who sketched a portrait of Marilyn and was also photographed drinking tea with her.

It wasn't until she participated in a photo intended to promote the branches of the Women's Armed Forces that she found herself in the middle of an unforeseen predicament. While surrounded by four women from the various branches of the armed forces, the photographer stood on a chair to get a better angle of the group. In the resulting photograph, Marilyn is dumping a bushel full of cleavage into the middle of the photo. About 3 hours after the picture had been transmitted to various newspapers the Military Brass tried in vain to squelch the photo because of Marilyn's low décolletage. This only spurred on the publication of the photo by the nation's press. Marilyn was asked about it and her response was, "It doesn't bother me, but I just don't understand it. That was a Ceil Chapman original and certainly should have been all right."

Marilyn's press agent Roy Craft remembers, "Those who were with her told me afterward that it had been a murderous day, as any day is when you're with Marilyn on a junket. The demands on her and on those with her are simply unbelievable. But finally she hit the sack about midnight because she had to get up the next day for activities. The rest of her crowd had turned in too, when they got a call from the *U.P.* in New York, asking them for a statement from Marilyn about 'that picture.' 'What picture?' our publicist-guardian asked, and it was then that they got the story. They hated to do it, but they roused Marilyn out of bed. She thought it over for a while; then issued a statement apologizing for any possible reflection on the service girls, and making it plain that she hadn't meant it that way. She ended with a genuine Monroeism. 'I wasn't aware of any objectionable décolletage on my part. I'd noticed people looking at me all day, but I thought they were looking at my grand marshals badge.' This was widely quoted, and it had the effect of giving the whole thing a lighter touch." In a 1956 interview with Milton Shulman both Craft and Marilyn say that Craft came up with the quote. "Roy Craft, who looked after her publicity for six years at Twentieth Century-Fox, is often credited with the authorship of many of these bon mots. He vehemently denies responsibility and can describe in detail the accidental circumstances under which most of them were made. 'It's nice having a reputation for being such a bright boy, but it just isn't true,' said Craft. 'I have only made up one wise-crack for Marilyn in my life. It was when she went to Atlantic City for a Miss America beauty contest. They had made her a grand marshal of the city and given her a big badge to wear. While we were there an Army major arrived with four representatives of the women's armed services—and Army, Marine, Navy and Air Force girl. They thought it might help the recruiting drive if Marilyn was photographed with these girls. But before he left the Pentagon the major had been warned that there was to be no cheesecake photographs and that they were to be taken with the greatest dignity. Unfortunately, one of the photographers stood on a chair to get his shot. When the major saw this particular picture he was appalled. For much more of Marilyn was revealed than was needed for a recruiting drive. He issued a War Department communique addressed to all the editors asking that this picture be killed. So instead of the picture ending up in most editor's wastebaskets as just another Monroe publicity stunt, it made the front pages as the picture the War Department wanted to ban. And, of course, every press agency in the country was phoning me asking for a comment from Marilyn. But it was after midnight and the girl had had a tough day and was in bed. I decided not to wake her and when I was asked: 'What did Marilyn think everybody was looking at when the picture was being taken?' I replied that Marilyn thought they were looking at her grand marshals badge. And now it's become a classic Monroe-ism.' When I asked Marilyn to comment on Craft's story, she said: 'Yes. That's the only joke Roy ever made up for me, and I didn't like it.'"

Marilyn's shrewdness in handling her own publicity was remarked upon by her Roy Craft, "They just happened to her. She was a literate, perceptive gal, and didn't need anyone to dream up stunts." Milton Shulman commented, "The studio press agents soon learned that the best way to get Marilyn into the papers was to stand aside and let her be herself. She was constantly baffling and delighting journalists with such pointedly witty comments that it was assumed they were manufactured for her by some sharp publicity man."

"Major Frank W. McWalters, of Washington D.C., project officer for joint Army-Air Force recruiting, explained he had asked only that the pictures be withdrawn voluntarily. Major McWalters pointed out that the armed services have no jurisdiction over private photographs, and said he just wanted to substitute some other pictures of Marilyn and the four servicewomen, taken from another angle. The Major blamed the angle for the whole episode. The picture set up at the request of Miss Monroe's press agent, Hal Marshall, shows the four servicewomen in uniform and Marilyn in a low-cut dress, leaning over. Maj. McWalters explained the photo as arranged was to be shot from the front all right, but just as photographers snapped the pose, Marilyn leaned way over."

Concerning the banned picture, Craft remembers, "It wasn't a startling picture, and probably was thrown in the wastebasket by picture editors all over the country that night. But a Major got frightened when he saw the shot was made from above--and Marilyn was wearing a dress designed to be shot from eye level.' The major ordered the picture killed. When the kill-order went out, picture editors fished the discarded shot from their wastebaskets. Many metropolitan papers played it full page." Craft recalls that, "Marilyn issued a statement that she had meant no disservice to the service and the next day we extracted an apology from the Pentagon for reflecting on Marilyn."

The next day, Marilyn acted as Grand Marshall of the Miss America Pageant in Atlantic City, New Jersey, becoming the first woman to fulfill this role. She participated in the Miss America Pageant parade down the Boardwalk. She changed into a dress which will forever be associated with her image. It was a navy blue dress with a white collar which plunged to her waist. No one but Marilyn could have gotten away with such an outrageous outfit. An image from this parade was used on the first cover of Playboy magazine in 1953, officially deifying her as the goddess of sex.

Miss Texas, Connie Wray Hopping, was delayed by bad weather and did not get a chance to meet with Marilyn at the registration. During Miss Hopping's ride in the parade, her driver gave her some "inside" information on Marilyn that she found very surprising. It seems he told her that "'Marilyn doesn't wear any underclothing but lets her figure seek its own level under no other confine than a thin dress, especially when she is meeting her public…." (It seems he had read Earl Wilson's column.) "Marilyn wore that kind of dress Tuesday in the parade in which she was grand marshal. It was a navy blue gown with a neckline that cut to her waistline. When the screen star's auto stopped at the reviewing stand in front of convention hall, her car was guarded by a daisy chain of policemen and movie agents. They said they wanted to keep away autograph hunters and thrill seekers who might have colds. A sneeze, it seems, could have blown off her dress…" Connie, said her only regret was not seeing the golden haired actress. 'I'd just love to cast my peepers on her.'"

Roy Craft, remembers the day, "She murdered those poor little Miss America's. All the photographers walked backward, shooting only Marilyn in her auto at the head of the parade. Her dress was kind of low-cut, and she carried a bouquet of roses. The cops would beat back the crowds, and they would stay back for a minute--then Marilyn would throw another rose. And they would crash the lines wildly again. Marilyn loved it. Traveling with her was like traveling with a buzz saw."

According to Walter Winchell, "Marilyn Monroe (just before planing West) devouring a mountain of Café Victor spaghetti and telling the waiter: 'Scads of garlic!'"

The next day, September 3rd, amid rampant rumors about her risqué dress, Marilyn flew home to Los Angeles from Atlantic City on *American Airlines.* Upon landing in Los Angeles, the *Herald-Examiner* gives Marilyn a copy of their newspaper and photographs her reading the headlines. "Actress reads the *Herald-Express* account of her row with the Army over her ultra-revealing dress."

Marilyn was reported to have been uncharacteristically cold and remote to the reporters and photographers gathered at the airport. Marilyn curtly replied when asked about the revealing photo, "'So the photographer stood on a chair to shoot it.' A photographer reminded her, 'You don't get paid to have a temper.' The ripely curved actress commented, 'I get paid.'"

Herald Heffernan came to the support of Marilyn. "…No question about Marilyn Monroe having hit the heights of movie fame. All her old films are being revived—and she—not the old-timers such as Barbara Stanwyck, Bette Davis, Anne Baxter and Ginger Rogers—gets the very top marquee billing. Marilyn is the greatest shot in the arm injected into the business since Jean Harlow walked nearly naked into *Hell's Angels* 22 years ago, and today it needs the tonic more than ever."

Dorothy Kilgallen had this bit of news on September 4th, "Marilyn Monroe didn't spend all her New York time with Joe DiMaggio, her most-publicized romance. She also had Very Big Eyes for Jay Kantor, the youthful MCA executive."

Jay Kantor would be instrumental in helping guide Marilyn in 1955 when she established Marilyn Monroe Productions, Inc. He will also serve as her escort for the *East of Eden* Premier on March 9, 1955.

Jay Breen interviewed Marilyn on the 5$^{th}$ about her thoughts on dating and marriage. "After months of dating Joe DiMaggio, tawny Marilyn Monroe said today they still haven't gotten around to baseball. Miss Monroe said she didn't have much faith in advisers on romance who say a girl should discover a man's interest and get him to talk about them. 'When I go out on dates, it's pretty obvious what interests the man. I don't work at it, just let things drift around to the topic of me.' The curvaceous blonde film star insisted that she and Mr. Baseball had set no date for marriage, but she had some illuminating comments on the wedded state in general. For one thing, she definitely wants a man who won't 'expect her to wear Mother Hubbard's after I marry him.' She said she had noted this tendency in other men who married well-endowed girls, and she considered it unfair. 'A girl realizes that she's made a choice for life when she gets married, but she still wants to be admired once in a while,' Miss Monroe explained. She said she was gratified to note no inclination on DiMaggio's part to cover her up. On the other hand, a little male jealousy never hurt a pretty wife and Marilyn frankly admitted she would like to see some green dragon showing every once in a while. 'It would be pretty dull without that, occasionally,' she said, 'but it's like salt on a steak. All you need is a little bit.' Miss Monroe philosophized briefly on the tricks of fate which brought her to the east coast to reign as grand marshal of the Atlantic City beauty pageant. It just so happened that in her next-to-last movie she played the role of a contestant for the crown of Miss America. 'With all respect to those little girls at Atlantic City, I think I rather win the Mrs. America title in real life. I think a happy marriage sort of ripens a pretty girl, if you know what I mean.'"

On September 5th, Earl Wilson gave this report of Marilyn in New York City, "Marilyn Monroe became ill here and was attended by Dr. Jack Weinstock, co-author of 'Tom Corbett, Space Cadet.' She recovered sufficiently later to munch smoked salmon with Joe DiMaggio at El Morocco."

Leonard Lyons reported, "Marilyn Monroe went to El Morocco with Joe DiMaggio. They were chaperoned by Georgie Solotaire, the ticket broker who is the subject of an article in the current *Park East*. Solotarie and DiMaggio share living quarters at an East Side Hotel. The trio went to the candle lit Champagne Room of the night club, where little was spoken except by Solotarie. Miss Monroe and DiMaggio mooned at each other. The few words Joe spoke were to me: 'And she can cook, too!' At frequent intervals, chaperone Solotaire--who sat facing them--would shut his eyes. 'I do that,' he explained, 'because I figure they'd like to be alone for a while.'"

Dorothy Kilgallen commented on the 7th, "Hollywood is talking about…The chummy way Marilyn Monroe and Jane Russell are hitting it off in advance of *Gentlemen Prefer Blondes*, and the fond hope the good humor continues when the cameras start turning."

Jane Russell reveals the origin of her nickname for Marilyn, "the round one." "I'd joke with her all the time and she really didn't know whether I meant it or not. One day they were trying to pose her for a picture standing on one leg with the other knew up and she couldn't keep her balance. I called to the photographer, 'That girl can't stand up on one let; it's impossible, she's round—round all over!"

On September 7th, "Dusting the Desk," by Bud Magnin, *Chester Times*, PA, devoted a big chunk of the column to Marilyn. "Never was quite sure what the Monroe Doctrine was all about except that it's something you usually hear of when the nation is in grave danger. Last week we found out that it was undoubtedly named for a girl named Marilyn, who has plunged the country into its gravest danger since the British burned up Washington. Ever since Miss Monroe posed for a certain calendar and thereby pulled off the most successful bit of press agentry in many a year, most of the adult male population of the U.S. has been in mortal danger of becoming drooling imbeciles, incapable of little except gawking at pictures of this girl and uttering incomprehensible sounds. Monroemania has affected even newspapermen, who are supposed to be more or less immune to such blandishments. Let a new Monroe photograph come into the *Times* newsroom via mail or telephoto and the guys almost come to blows over who gets to see it next. She's dangerous, this Marilyn, and for the good of the country we think they ought to exile her from Hollywood forever, slam the celluloid door in her face, bar her from ever making another movie. Yea, Hollywood, get rid of Marilyn at once. Send her to Chester!"

Earl Wilson reported on the 8th, "Marilyn Monroe and Joe DiMaggio planed out to Hollywood Tuesday night, Marilyn by American Airlines, the Jolter by United a few minutes later. But first said she to me: 'Hello! How about the Army picking on that Ceil Chapman original! It's the one I had on when I posed with you. You liked it! Did I have anything on under it? Well, you know me. If it hadn't been for that one bright photographer standing on a chair, shooting down. Married to Joe? That's not true. If I were I wouldn't have any reason to deny it. Sure I missed the train to Atlantic City last week. They chartered a plane. How much? Twelve hundred dollars. Gee, I'm expensive.' Marilyn then said g'bye. She's always late. The least late she was for an NY appointment was 50 minutes. They say she's always late because she finds it necessary to stop and look at herself. When other people'd be so willing to do it for her!"

Also on the 8th, Louella Parsons wrote in her column about Joe's "cousin," Chic. This was actually Vic "Chic" Masi, a good friend of Joe's. "Chit-chat and vice versa: Joe DiMaggio's cousin, Chic DiMaggio, stands interference for the baseball star at the Hollywood Knickerbocker hotel and no one can get Joe without first talking to cousin. Chic cannot be as uninformed as he sounds--no one could! 'Are Joe and Marilyn Monroe going to San Francisco,' I asked. 'I don't know,' he replied. 'Are they getting married?' 'I don't know.' 'Where is Joe?' 'I don't know.' After five 'I don't knows' he wore me down and that's not easy to do."

An interesting article on Marilyn appeared on September 9th in the *Brooklyn Eagle*. "Marilyn Monroe: 'But a Red Rose Against Pink Skin...' Three years ago Marilyn Monroe was a scared young blonde trying to earn a living in films. Today she is a front-rank celebrity. She is the most quoted, photographed and interviewed star in Hollywood. Recently, when she went on location for *Niagara* at the famous falls, 480 press and magazine writers gathered to shake hands, interview or merely gaze at her from afar according to how much freedom her working schedule permitted. While she was shooting *Don't Bother to Knock*, *We're Not Married* and *Monkey Business*--the latter is now at the Roxy--producers found it almost impossible to keep the time schedule allotted because of the demand for Monroe art and interviews. The Blowtorch Blonde, as she has come to be known is tops in the feminine field today largely because of her candid approach to sex. A child of nature, Marilyn bowls the boys and girls over by her direct answers, lack of 'side' and refusal to gild any situation with untruths or apologetic flummery. Marilyn was fast gaining a public when she was given the role of a secretary with Cary Grant in *Monkey Business*. About this time, word ran through news grapevines that some color calendars of Marilyn posed in the nude had put in an appearance in some of our classier barber shops. Studio bigwigs advised Marilyn to refuse comment. Marilyn, however, simply said: 'Yes. I posed for them. I was hungry and three weeks behind in my room rent. I did nothing wrong and the photographer's wife was present. Why should I deny it?' She developed a flair for interviews, her random remarks being quoted again and again. One writer observed that when other girls wore flowers they merely looked overdressed, whereas Marilyn became very exciting. 'It's how the flower is placed,' murmured Marilyn. 'A bunch of sweet peas on the shoulder of the dress is nothing but a red rose against pink skin...well, that's another story. Marilyn believes a wise girl puts some cool witch hazel packs on the eyes and lies down to think things over instead of flying off the handle. When a femme correspondent was taking a daily fling at little Marilyn in her column, everyone stood back to watch the fur fly when Monroe finally came face to face with her at a big party. They were disappointed because Marilyn was very sweet and gracious. 'How come?' asked a friend. 'I thought you would skin her alive.' 'It was more cruel to leave her skin as it is,' said Marilyn, 'and when I looked at that sad drooping figure I just felt sorry for her.' Her succinct answer to an interviewer who asked: 'What do you wear to bed?' was 'Chanel No. 5.' To a query as to whether or not she intended to marry Joe DiMaggio, she said, 'Just say we're friendly...and you might put that friendly in quotes.' To the correspondent who asked: 'Why don't other girls have the same effect on men that you do?' Marilyn confided that most girls don't know how to walk: 'It's the little bounce and jiggle of a body without a girdle that makes a girl irresistible.' And her reply to the query: 'Why aren't you sun-tanned like other Hollywood beauties?' got the $64 answer: 'Oh, I just love to think of myself as blonde all over.'"

*Look* magazine, September 9th, features Marilyn on the cover as a Georgia Tech Cheerleader, in a photo by Bob Sandberg. This photo was taken while she was on location filming *Niagara*. He also took various shots of Marilyn with the crew, having her makeup applied, and a special series of Marilyn demonstrating how to walk.

The *Augusta Chronicle* predicted that the issue should be "filed away in the hope chests of Tech old grads. A picture feature on the Tech team appears inside and Marilyn Monroe fills out a White and Gold sweater on the cover. The Techsters had better enjoy life while they can."

Ned West, sports information director at Georgia Tech, utilized a copy of her cover photo for their football press guide this year. The Georgia Tech football team went undefeated this season and were the National Champions. Eddie Barker remembers trying to coax Marilyn into attending a Georgia Tech football game. "My most interesting newspaper assignment,' I was saying, 'was interviewing Marilyn Monroe in a shower bath.' Until that time I had caused little stir at the party, but now there I was, center stage. 'That's right,' I said answering the question again. 'I interviewed Marilyn Monroe in a shower bath.' Before anyone could claim me all wet I assured them that it was Miss Monroe's idea, not mine, although I will be the last to admit that it didn't add a lot to the interview. 'You mean to say,' said the host, 'that you talked to her while she was bathing.' 'And while she soaped and rinsed off, too,' I informed the crowd, which was now pressing closer. 'What did you talk about?' asked one girl who seemed the only one interested in whether we talked at all. 'Mostly about how she looked in a sweater.' I said. One listener showed utter disgust. 'While you're interviewing Marilyn Monroe in a shower,' he said, 'you talk about how she looked in a sweater?' 'That's right. You see Georgia Tech wanted her to come down and be a sponsor for a football game after she appeared on the cover of *Look* magazine in a Yellow Jacket sweater. We were talking about that mostly.' 'Well,' said one eager beaver, 'what did you decide?' 'She decided,' I replied, 'against it. Said she didn't know how to play. Football wasn't her game.' 'But passes, man, passes,' said another. 'Didn't you think of that?' 'No, no I didn't. You see we quit talking football and got on baseball. At the time she was stuck on an ex-player named Joe DiMaggio.' 'Never mind all that,' said a man with a more direct mind. 'Tell us how she looked.' 'You mean in the Tech sweater?' 'No!' he screamed. 'I mean in the shower.' It was a cruel thing to do, but I saw the time had come to tell them that all the electricity between Miss Monroe and myself wasn't all he-and-she reaction. More than 1,000 miles of it was telephone line. She was in Atlantic City, New Jersey and I was in the sports department of *The Atlanta Journal*. I had called and the screen queen decided to take the call while she showered. 'Are you really taking a shower?' I remembered asking her. 'If you don't believe me, honey,' she cooed, 'just listen to the water running.' I could hardly hear it over a heavy heart beat."

Sharp cookie, Dorothy Kilgallen reported on September 9th, "Reporters who interviewed Marilyn Monroe while she was in Gotham got the distinct impression that she was pretty casual in her feeling about Joe DiMaggio--or else she's a better actress than she seems to be on the screen."

In his syndicated column on September 11th, Leonard Lyons reported, "One of Marilyn Monroe's friends who heard Joe DiMaggio boast that Marilyn is a good cook, sampled the cooking of the dazzling blonde, who served the dishes herself. 'If you're a man, and not blindfolded, Marilyn is a good cook,' was the report. 'But if you're blindfolded, or a woman--she can't.'"

*The New York Amsterdam*, an African-American newspaper, ran this item from Betty Granger's column on the 11th, "Arthur Prysock's opening night at the same nitery [Birdland] found movie star Marilyn Monroe ring-siding with guests to catch the groovy-o-reenies of Slim Gaillard."

On September 14th Marilyn participated in the "I Am an American Day" at a huge rally at the Hollywood Bowl. It honored 2500 new citizens of the United States. An array of personalities from stage, screen, radio and television were there, including Danny Thomas and Jack Carson, serving as masters of ceremonies. The entertainment included Marilyn Monroe, Jimmy Durante, Constance Moore, Lee Scott Dancers, Peggy Lee, Tony Martin, Audrey Trotter, Jimmy Wakely, Mickey Rooney, Marta Toren and the Will Mastin Trio. Surviving photographs of this even show Marilyn with Danny Thomas and Jack Carson at the Hollywood Bowl. There is also one of Marilyn and Sammy Davis, Jr., posed by a car.

Finding her Hilldale home too isolated, Marilyn signs a six months lease for another home on September 15th. It was located in the Outpost Estates development, in the Hollywood Hills. She wrote a check to real estate agent, Franklin Archer, for the first and last month's rent on 2393 Castillean Dr., in the amount of $450.00. She and Joe DiMaggio would use this address as a hide-away retreat. She leased the home from writer Charles Grayson.

On September 22nd, Harrison Carroll reported about her move to the Outpost Estates, "Marilyn Monroe pleaded so movingly that she needed a place to live that Charles Grayson couldn't resist, so he moved out of his house and into the Garden of Allah, giving Marilyn a place to hang her hat."

An editorial by Mel Heimer, on September 24th, revealed an odd interview with Marilyn while she was in New York. "That was one of the items that got me a little miffed about women--the cold, calculating mien of a female tennis player. The other was the behavior of a Hollywood performer named Marilyn Monroe. Miss Monroe came to town the other day to plump for *Monkey Business*, a new film she is in and I made a date to breakfast with her at Reuben's. That was for 10. Well, first the date was switched to 11 and the scene switched to her hotel room--and after that I waited around for a half hour, or until 11:30, for Miss Monroe to show. I could have spent the time picking horses. She never did show. The harassed press agent finally told me she was in the next room having her hair done and why didn't I interview her through the bedroom door, hah hah. I went along with the gag and I interviewed her through the bedroom door, which was slightly ajar, but she didn't say anything breathtaking, and try as I might I couldn't even get an angle look at her in the bedroom mirror, which was visible. Behavior like that was entirely indefensible, even if Miss Monroe had apologized, which she did not. I left her suite finally, thinking to myself that men actors are pretty hopeless people but they usually have the grace to apologize when they have been on the boorish side. Well--there they are, just a couple of incidents in a New York camp, as Browning would say. But for a while now they have had me a little sour on women. Nothing that a good night's sleep and a smile from a beautiful blonde don't fix. Sure wish I could have gotten a little look at that Monroe in the mirror, though. Even if she does have no manners."

On October 13th, Mel Heimer will run an interview with Ava Gardner who came to some very thoughtful remarks of her own about Marilyn in response to his article on the 24th. 'Miss Gardner had been reading my dark remarks about Miss Monroe, wherein I suspected that Marilyn had been reading her press clippings and fancied herself a person of some importance. 'Listen,' Mrs. Sinatra said, 'I'm not really defending Marilyn, because in the first place I don't know her. However, just stop and think. Did you ever really know any business in the world like the movies for giving you a big head? This is the business where everybody in the country knows you and some of them think you the greatest thing since I don't know what. It's the easiest thing imaginable to figure that it's the only business in the world and that you're the big wheels in it.'"

On September 28th Sheilah Graham also reported on the move, "Joe DiMaggio and Marilyn Monroe have found an eight room house on Cloud No. 8 in the Outpost district." The only party she gave in this house was for the 20th Century Fox's film cutters. Marilyn had sponsored them in a softball team the past August, and they had won the championship. She gave this party for them and their wives. The team was in no way connected with a professional baseball team as has been stated in several auction sites.

Beauty columnist Lydia Lane devotes her entire column to Marilyn on the 28th. A picture accompanies the article showing Marilyn and Miss Lane. Marilyn is wearing the same outfit, down to the kerchief in her hair, as she wore when she performed the radio drama, *Statement in Full* on August 24th. "Marilyn Monroe was just another blonde trying to crash Hollywood until she was cast as Louis Calhern's sexy girlfriend in *Asphalt Jungle*. After that picture she was a star. 'Congratulations on the nice notices you received from the New York critics for your part in *Don't Bother to Knock*,' I told Marilyn as we lunched at the 20th Century Fox commissary. 'Only some of them liked me,' Marilyn said. I knew that here was a girl who would not stop until all the critics accepted her as an actress. It was logical that my first question should be, 'How does a girl make herself attractive to men?' 'Try to be beautiful, but don't underestimate your frame of mind,' Marilyn answered seriously. 'You must feel attractive and desirable to make others feel it. You can't be mentally fighting a battle of the sexes. This sometimes happens unknowingly—a carry-over from childhood when you wished you were a boy because they had more freedom. The basis of being attractive to men is your enjoyment of being a woman.' 'Do you dress to please men or women?' I wanted to know. 'If you can't trust your own instinct to find an answer to that question, then never ask a woman for advice.' Marilyn answered, confiding that she always knew what was right in the magazines until you find somebody that is your type and try to dress like them. But once you're with a boy, forget all about how much time you spent fixing yourself up,' she added. 'When you're on a date relax and don't be nervous about your appearance or anything else.' 'That's good advice,' I had to agree. 'When a girl puts on an act—pretends to be something she thinks will impress the boy she is with—she ends up being cramped inside with a feeling of insecurity.' Marilyn continued. 'Be what you really are, and you will find men are interested in you. They admire frankness.' 'Do you think men dislike makeup?' I asked. 'A man doesn't like to look at a woman and be conscious of her makeup,' Marilyn answered. 'But when you put it on carefully you can use everything there is without his being aware of it.' I asked Marilyn to tell me her favorite make-up tricks. She told me that every girl should study her face carefully and decide where she is to focus attention. 'It's not what comes from the mouth that you can trust,' Marilyn confided, 'but what the eyes tell is always a true story. European women know this and make up their eyes so you look there first. I agree with this idea. It makes you more desirable to have a sheen on your eyelids,' she added. 'Just a dot of oil over your powder will make your eyelids glisten invitingly. How do you feel about perfume?' I asked. Marilyn agreed that being fragrant was an important part of being attractive. 'I have a favorite scent, but I also like to change,' Marilyn said. 'I rarely use it on my clothes, but when I start to dress I spray it on my ankles, the back of my knees and all the way up to my eyebrows so that the fragrance really belongs to me.' I asked Marilyn if she did any exercise to make her body more beautiful. 'Yes. I have three favorites,' she said, frankly confessing that she had improved her figure with a carefully worked-out routine. 'I have a wonderful exercise for giving legs and ankles a better shape and another which strengthens the chest so that an uplift bra will never be necessary. Women have a tendency to be flabby under their upper arms, so my third exercise gives these muscles a workout.' 'What about the most obvious places—your waist and hips?' I inquired. 'I have a naturally small waist and I'm not in favor of a flat backside,' Marilyn said frankly. 'You shouldn't get out of proportion, but if you notice artist models and even calendar nudes have curves,' she added with a twinkle. 'An important thing to remember is to carry your body well,' Marilyn concluded. 'When you walk, think up in front and down in back. But what really puts you over is how you feel inside. So remember: Relax, don't be nervous, and always be yourself.'"

On September 15th the Hollywood Jr. Chamber of Commerce hosts the Sixth Annual *Out of This World Series* celebrity baseball game at Gilmore Ball Park. Marilyn, who served as one of the *Bat Girls* for *The Curtis Jets*, and she also threw out the opening pitch. 7,000 fans watched the antics on the diamond. It was reminiscent of the Charity Baseball game she participated in at Chicago in 1949. Of course Marilyn can't seem to do anything without upsetting women. In an *INS* article from November 14$^{th}$ Marilyn is taken to task for a photograph taken during the ballgame. "There are in Hollywood a highly vocal group of young female stars who were highly peeved at the acclaim Marilyn Monroe received for a 'going away' picture. It was at the 'Out of This World Series' baseball game, where starlets clad cutely in shorts and sweaters appeared for the charity affair. Not Marilyn, no sir-ree. The 'blow torch blonde' took her turn in the pitcher's box clad in a skin-tight skirt. The photographers had a field day from the second-base view, and Miss Monroe's fan mail at Twentieth Century-Fox jumped 1,000 letters a week."

*Long Beach Press Telegram* newspaper reported on September 16th, "Marilyn Monroe in Extra Role...Marilyn Monroe worked as an extra in a movie scene and without getting paid for her dramatic stint. Richard Widmark, Joanne Dru and Audrey Totter were making a scene for 20th Century-Fox's *My Pal Gus* outside the Beverly Carleton Hotel, which happened to be Miss Monroe's place of residence. Hearing early morning activity in the hotel courtyard, the shapely blonde went to the window of her apartment to investigate. Seeing that a movie was being made, she quickly ducked out of sight. Director Robert Parrish decided to keep Miss Monroe's ad-libbed acting in the picture--but without giving her screen credit, of course."

James Bacon reported some tantalizing tid-bits on Marilyn and her undies on the 16th. "Marilyn and I watched rushes of her latest picture *Niagara*. In one scene she wears a clinging, black satin dress that forms a new Monroe Doctrine. 'I don't have a stitch on underneath,' she explained. That was shocking but not surprising because Marilyn is on record as anti-lingerie…Said Peter G. Rosenfeld, president of the Beverly Vogue Company, and also president of the California Fashion Creators, 'Miss Monroe no doubt will soon learn that the power of suggestion is more effective than bald fact and obvious much less desirable than the implied. Fifty million American women can't be wrong…It must be because women everywhere are intelligent enough to add to their charms by wearing this very necessary garment.'"

Robert Slatzer writes about educating Marilyn in Dorothy Kilgallen's syndicated column on September 18th, "The Voice of Broadway... (Dorothy Kilgallen is on vacation. Pinch-hitting for her today is Robert F. Slatzer, literary critic of Columbus, Ohio) I am a man with an enviable task--that of telling the facts of literary life to Marilyn Monroe. If anyone now offers to give Marilyn a book, she needn't reply with that hackneyed chorus gal gag of: 'No, thanks. I have one!' Marilyn has dozens of them--many of them from my library. Marilyn and I daily have an adventure together, even when we are 3,000 miles apart. But it is strictly of mind. I got into the education of Marilyn in 1947, when she was Norma Jean Baker, a bit player at 20th Century-Fox. I was working for the same studio and the nervous girl of 19 and I became friends. We both lost our jobs at the same time. I didn't see her again until last June in Niagara Falls where I had gone to have a dinner date with another motion picture star. I didn't know that Norma Jean was Marilyn. When I discovered it, I forgot all about my other date. Men will understand this amnesia of mine, but the other star didn't. I nearly swallowed my olive when Marilyn insisted on talking about books because she was interested in my job of reviewing them. When I asked her why she was so interested, the Bishop of Durham would have been proud to know that she was able to quote the answer he gave in 1473: 'Books,' said Marilyn, in effect, 'are masters who instruct us without whips or hard words. If you approach them, they are awake. If you question them, they conceal nothing. If you mistake them, they do not grumble. If you are ignorant, they cannot laugh at you...And don't you laugh at me,' Marilyn continued. 'My favorite activity is reading!' I didn't, even when she told me she preferred classical literature. I even quoted back to her the rule, 'Some books are to be tasted, others swallowed, and a few chewed and digested.' 'Send me some for the main course when you get back to Columbus,' said Marilyn. I don't remember getting back to Columbus from Niagara Falls, but I apparently did--so, after much thought (for who would want to go wrong on the education of Marilyn Monroe), I selected the following to send her, Thomas Wolfe first. I picked *You Can't Go Home Again*, and *Look Homeward Angel*. I thought Marilyn would 'dig him the mostest!' She had his zest for life. Her living in dozens of foster homes as a child gave her the background that would enable her to appreciate what Wolfe was trying to say. Next, in Hollywood, went *Greek Gods and Goddesses in Art and Legend*. Marilyn, I realized, had become a symbol for many things. She might have been a simple, troubled girl to herself, but she had become a symbol of many things she didn't even suspect to the millions who saw her and read about her. I thought this would enable her to have some understanding and appreciation of how mankind needed heroines and how others had been selected. *The Rubaiyat of Omar Khayam* was selected on the grounds that while books could not teach us to enjoy life, they could at least help us to endure it. Marilyn, by this time, was sending me books. One she picked was *The Prophet*, by Kahlil Gibran. She was so much under his spell she didn't like my kidding question, 'Do you think it will make a picture?' I asked her why she wanted me to read *The Prophet*. She said, 'It is very inspiring. It is more or less a pattern for everyday living.' I decided that Marilyn's imagination would be stirred by *The Works of Poe* and *Tales from the Arabian Nights*. She was so intrigued with Poe that she read some of the short stories two or three times. As a guy who reads books partly for pay, I began to envy Marilyn the joy with which she devoured these. If it is true that the university of these days is a collection of books, Marilyn was up to her B.A. and at the rate she was going would soon get her M.A. and even Ph. D. Can you picture calling her Dr. Monroe? The last book I shipped her was *The Disenchanted* by Budd Schulberg. I thought reading this would prepare her for any of the cruel slings of fate or professional heartbreaks that might lie ahead for her in Hollywood. One of her suitors, apparently jealous of the competition he was setting from the printed page, dug up the words of Disraeli, 'Books are fatal. The greatest misfortune that ever befell man was the invention of printing. They are the curse of the human race. Nine-tenths of the existing books are nonsense.' Marilyn looked at him pityingly and was able to find her way to Alexander Smith's quote to reply, 'Books are a finer world within a world.' My only regret is that I have but one library to give to Marilyn Monroe."

Marilyn was to tell Dorothy Kilgallen, "If you want your ear talked off, mention Novelist Thomas Wolfe to me. I just guess I've practically memorized his books."

On September 28th Marilyn received another dubious award from the GIs, she was elected "Miss Hospital Trains of 1952," because she was just what the doctor ordered.

*The Boston Pictorial Review* ran a full page article, "Fabulous Marilyn." It is a rehashing of her biography and features a page length photo of Marilyn at bat. The author's name is not given. "At first glance it is at once apparent that Marilyn Monroe has everything—and everything she has looks good. What she has is a matter of understandably warm interest to every man-jack in the nation—perhaps to every boy-jack, too. For the fact is that even the gallant youths of Kiskiminetas Spring School in a place called Saltsburg, PA, named her 'Miss Campus Queen'—and, to their credit be it noted, before her celebrated photo against a background of red velvet appeared in almost every garage and barber shop from blue-nosed Boston to green-eyed Hollywood. Not since the lusty, busty days of the late Jean Harlow—a woman of some blondness and some beauty, too—has a movie star of such desirable proportions so swiftly captured and so securely held the imagination of the public. Marilyn is making *Gentlemen Prefer Blondes* now, a statement that could stand without challenge even if small letters were substituted for the capitals."

On October 4th Marilyn wrote a check to the department story, Jax, for the amount of $313.13. She indicated that her address was 2393 Castilian Drive, Outpost Estates and her telephone number as He.1755. She went shopping with Natasha Lytess on this day. This information contradicts Robert Slatzer's allegation that he and Marilyn eloped to Mexico on this date.

It was announced in the press that at a Famous Republicans' auction in Falls City, Neb., to raise cash for the GOP campaign fund, one of Marilyn Monroe's sweaters sold for $11.

Hedda Hopper tells the *Omaha World-Herald's* Better Living Forum on the 7th, how she feels about Marilyn. "I love Marilyn Monroe; she's an exhibitionist. She's over worked and she's friendly and she doesn't have to act. If you can pose in the nude, you don't have to. But Marilyn has one bad fault; She's never on time for appointments." A little catty, but for Hedda, not too bad.

The *Chicago Tribune* ran an exclusive story about Marilyn in the *Grafic Magazine* of the Sunday's edition on October 12th, "Marvelous Marilyn Monroe," by Florabel Muir.

*Parade* magazine article, October 12th, by Sid Ross. "How Marilyn Monroe Sees Herself...In an exclusive interview, America's most envied girl tells how brilliant success can still be perplexing...Relaxed in a hotel easy chair, Marilyn Monroe tells why a girl with 100,000,000 cheering fans has often found herself lonely and 'left out,'" by Sid Ross. "'People expect to find me one of two things. Either a tart or a dumb blonde. I'm neither.

The fact is that I'm lonely—in spite of the fastest ride to popularity that any girl ever had. Too much publicity makes you lonely. Suddenly you see people speaking to you and being nice to you. But they never did before, and you feel it's happening only because you're now a personality. And with me, I know, it would have meant a lot more to have had a few words of encouragement before—when I really needed them. As it is, publicity dominates my life. All this publicity makes me a little shy and afraid. I'm afraid that people will expect too much of me, right now when I've only really started acting. I'm beginning to feel like a piece of statuary that people are inspecting with a magnifying glass, looking for imperfections—taking apart my dress, my voice, my figure, my acting—everything about me. When you're an obscure bit player or starlet, nobody cares whether you can act. But when your name is up in lights, it's different. I do a picture like *Don't Bother to Knock* and some people say, 'Leave the dramatics to Bette Davis and Olivia de Havilland. Keep Marilyn Monroe in a tight dress and let her drip sex.' It kind of gets me. Some days I think most critics have ulcers. But then along comes one who is a human being and who says I'm not setting the world on fire, but that I have promise. Comments like these are few and far between. I want more of them.'" On the press inventing stories about her, Marilyn had this to say, "'This sort of thing happens all the time. It upsets me. I can't get used to it, and I wouldn't be telling the truth if I said I just shrugged it off. It's 'good publicity,' I'm told. Is it really?' 'What do you want, Marilyn? Where are you really going?' 'My career—it's not the end, and I know it. That's one big thing I've learned in the last year. I don't think I'm different when I say that I want things that concern only me and my happiness. In the movie business your career comes first. But I want to start with my life first—and then pick and choose what else I want. For me, marriage and career won't mix permanently. I think a man and a woman should be interested in each other basically, with no outside force coming in between. Often, in Hollywood, men, women—even married couples compete with each other. That's no good. I want something more than this sort of success—something more real, more tangible. Any woman wants another kind of life with a man, marriage, a home, children…I'm not exception. Maybe it's corny to say, but I don't want to be just a woman alone…I want to belong…'"

    There is one large photo of Marilyn in the chair and a panel of small candid expression stills by Ben Ross. In December of 1954 Ross will also photograph Marilyn for *Parade* in a series of expressions. Marilyn is also shown in a photograph arriving for the *Monkey Business* Premiere. The interview took place in her room at the Claridge Hotel. Sid Ross was a freelance writer. He worked with his brother, photographer Ben Ross. An article in the May 1953 issue of *U.S. Camera* also contained photos and an interview with Marilyn during the same time period by Ben Ross.

    On October 13th Twentieth Century-Fox gave Marilyn permission to appear on two episodes of the *Edgar Bergen Radio Program* for the purpose of promoting *Monkey Business.*

    Hedda Hopper on October 18th reported Darryl Zanuck's comments on Marilyn. "Whom do you consider the most promising young star on your lot?' I asked. 'Marilyn

Monroe is the biggest potential we have as a box-office attraction,' he said, then laughed. 'You know I once had her under contract here, but let her go. Then I saw her do a small part in *Asphalt Jungle* and got her back again for *All About Eve*. Her glamour seems to have captured the interest of the whole American public. We have to fight to keep publicity down on her.'"

Sheilah Graham explains why Marilyn chooses not to go to the studio as often as they would like, on the 18th. "They want me to say things they want, I want to say things I want."

Louella Parsons reported on why she chose Marilyn as Hollywood's Most Exciting Woman, October 19th, "Most Exciting Woman...No One Wins Eyes and Polls as Easily as Marilyn, the 'Blowtorch Blonde [funny that Louella uses a phrase that her nemesis Hedda Hopper had coined]....To be exciting, a star doesn't necessarily have to be beautiful. But she does have to have the electric something that spells sex appeal and which fires interest. She has to have a personality that attracts the eye of the public and keeps it focused. I've chosen Marilyn Monroe to head my list. She had to be the winner. Why, you may ask, when there are so many more beautiful girls than Marilyn, and certainly more talented ones as actresses? True enough. And yet it is Marilyn who is Number One on all the G.I. polls of Hollywood favorites and Number One on exhibitors' polls of box office favorites. She is the Number One cover girl of the year and certainly Number One in public interest. I was at a party a few weeks ago, when Marilyn walked into the room. It was a gay social event and the room was filled with famous beauties and stars. Yet the moment Marilyn entered the scene, all conversation stopped and the eyes of everyone, men and women alike, were riveted upon her. She wore a dress that fitted her skin-tight, and I might add, it was obvious she wore nothing but her skin under it. In some girls that would have been extremely vulgar; In Marilyn's case, strangely enough, it was entirely inoffensive, except perhaps, to a few of the other girls who were plain green-eyed with envy at the attention she received from the men. What is the appeal? It is difficult for me to pin point it. Her lavishly endowed figure, of course has a lot to do with it; when the tape measure says bust 37, waist 24, and hips 36, it spells female in very plain letters. Her pretty face, particularly her provocative and half-opened, sexy mouth is another asset. So is her naïve manner and witty honesty in evaluating herself and her place in the public eye. But most of all and beyond any doubt, it is that same sizzling something which Jean Harlow had—and no other Hollywood girl has possessed in the same measure since the advent and sad death of Jean. I can't put a name on it, nor tell any woman how to acquire the Marilyn Monroe popularity, but this I do know: It is an ingredient as rare as it is priceless in the creation of exciting appeal. How little that description fitted the Marilyn I first met at a small dinner party. She walked into the room, full of well-groomed and beautifully dressed women, frightfully overdressed in a slinky red satin gown, obviously borrowed from the wardrobe department of 20th Century-Fox studios, where she was under contract. It showed off her voluptuous figure, but it was in atrocious taste. I was incensed that someone had not taken this girl in hand and guided her to a better selection of a gown in which to make a social appearance that was so important to her. 'Don't worry about that little girl,' my escort answered. 'Let her wear anything she wants, bad as her taste may be. But you wait and see; in a short time, I promise, no one in Hollywood will be able to catch up with her success, on the screen or off! No man will care what she wears.' How right this prediction was! So far no one has. I will never forget the day Marilyn telephoned and asked if she could come and see me in my home. 'I have to talk to you, Miss Parsons,' she said, and there were tears in her voice. It was about a week after the death of Johnny Hyde, the agent who had loved Marilyn Monroe so desperately—little Johnny, who had gone with me to Rita Hayworth's wedding, and who was more responsible than anyone else for Rita's tremendous success. Marilyn knew I knew Johnny, who had guided her career as her agent and as the man who loved her. His faith in her had worked miracles. Lovable little Johnny had been desperately in love with Marilyn—desperately and hopelessly, and there was a hurt in her heart that she couldn't return that love. 'Do you think I was wrong not to marry Johnny when I didn't love him?' she asked me. 'You know I was genuinely fond of him. I shall always be truly grateful for all he did for me and I might never have gone so far nor had that chance in *Asphalt Jungle* if it hadn't been for Johnny, but I didn't love him and he knew it. Wouldn't it have been wrong, then, to have married him? Wouldn't I have hurt him more if, not loving him, I had married him?' That honesty and willingness to face reality, is as characteristic of Marilyn today as it was then. I've often wondered what Johnny would have done if he had lived to see the famous calendar in which Marilyn posed in the altogether, and the Atlantic City episode when the photographer shot down and her low necked gown was so revealing. One reporter suggested that she shows a bit too much cleavage in the neckline of a gown. Marilyn came right back with, 'what's wrong with a good healthy body?' Often she pops up with an answer that really stops her interviewers. And, I might add, makes for snappy headlines. During a press conference in San Francisco, for instance, one newspaperman asked, 'Are those really your own long eyelashes?' Marilyn batted her big blue eyes at him. 'Oh yes,' she said softly, 'everything belongs to me.' The man she loves and is loved by in return is the baseball idol, Joe DiMaggio. Some insist they already are secretly married, and it wouldn't surprise me if this were true. Certainly they are devoted to each other. Naturally the quips about her fly thick and fast. My favorite is her classic statement made after she served as grand marshal of the 1952 Miss America pageant in Atlantic City. She led the parade perched high in an open car, and her low-cut gown, more revealing than ever, stirred up a first class furor. Said Miss Monroe, 'Can you imagine that? And here I thought all those people were just admiring my grand marshals badge!' Yes. Marilyn has what it takes."

    Louella reported that Marilyn contacted her about his article. "Marilyn Monroe telephoned twice before she could catchup with me, and I was very pleased to have her tell me that she liked my story about her very much. I elected her one of the 10 most exciting women in Hollywood. In fact, she was first on my list. 'You have always been good to me,' said Marilyn. 'Even before anyone knew who I was, you wrote a story about me, the first story ever written about me in Hollywood.' In this town where success makes the best of them forget, it was very heartwarming to receive this telephone call."

The *Coshocton Tribune* carries a quote on Marilyn about sex, "I think everything counts. Curves are all right, but I think there should be something underneath the curves, too—a lot comes from the inside as well as the outside."

October 26th was Marilyn's first scheduled appearance on *The Edgar Bergen and Charlie McCarthy Show*. Many think this was a one-time event, but there were actually three separate shows, October 26th, November 2nd and November 6th, and Marilyn appeared on the first and third ones. Tonight she had her first date with Charlie McCarthy. This date led Charlie to propose to Marilyn. Surprise! Surprise! She said yes! In his syndicated column, "Just Listening," King Charles reported, "Charlie McCarthy is likely to break out with a rash of splinters today as he dates calendar girl Marilyn Monroe on the *Edgar Bergen-Charlie McCarthy* show. Report is that Charlie has been practicing wolf calls and romantic sweet-nothings for the past week to make an impression upon the inimitable Miss Monroe."

Marilyn was chosen one of the 5 sexiest movie queens by famed sculptor Yucca Salamunich. He said of Marilyn, "Miss Monroe projects sex in a more flamboyant manner.

Grace Goddard wrote to Marilyn on October 28th, suggesting that Gladys needs to go into a sanitarium instead of staying with the Bolenders. Grace found Rockhaven Sanitarium in Verdugo City, but it wouldn't be until February 8, 1953 that they could move Gladys.

Erskine Johnson lets the cat out of the bag on the 29th, about Marilyn's diamond bikini for *Blondes*. "Marilyn Monroe's due for a big boost in salary—from $750 a week to $2500. Marilyn will sing *Diamonds Are a Girl's Best Friend* in *Gentlemen Prefer Blondes*, but methinks the men will be saying, 'Gentlemen Prefer Marilyn.' Her costume: A bikini affair made entirely of diamonds."

Marilyn was slammed by Actor Mel Ferrer, "Miss Monroe is the epitome of nothing more than a certain kind of very obvious high school physical appeal." Marilyn countered with a letter she received from the Navy Department, from "'a ship full of men facing death for our country in Korea.' She quoted the letter, "We the officers and crew of the USS Kanthal nominate you, Marilyn Monroe, 'Miss Explosive.' Despite the fact that our ship has been out here longer than any other non-rotating ship, the morale of the crew has been high because of you. You have given us so much pleasure in everything you do.' Urbane Clifton Webb scoffed at Ferrer's criticism. 'Mature charm is a quality invented by the mature to console themselves for the loss of powers of immaturity.' Victor Mature called Marilyn, 'The People's Choice.' She was discovered and exalted by the American people. It is difficult for anyone in show business to criticize the public's tastes.'"

Sheilah Graham reported on October 31st, "Dell Publications President George Delacorte, at the jam-packed *Modern Screen* party, declared that, all the way across the country people gave him messages for Marilyn Monroe....As for the blonde doctrine, she kept trying to get away from the party because--'I have to cook dinner for a man who used to play baseball.' When I asked Marilyn, 'How does it feel to be famous so suddenly?' she replied, 'I always keep in mind that the bubble can break.'"

Marilyn attended the *Modern Screen* arriving at the party alone. She wore the black version of the cocktail dress that she will wear in Korea. Marilyn was one of eight recipients of the Most Promising Star of 1952. She was awarded a miniature loving cup by George Delacorte and was interviewed on the air by Jim McCulla as she received her award. "She matched him quip for quip as she accepted her award. 'Do gentlemen prefer blondes?' Marilyn staggered the commentator with her famous look and replied lazily, 'Gosh, Jim. I hope so!'"

Marilyn crashes the wedding reception of Fred Karger and Jane and Jane Wyman, on November 1st. It was held at Chasen's. Marilyn had an affair with Fred Karger in 1948. According to Sidney Skolsky, this was the "one bitchy thing" he ever witnessed Marilyn do. However, the story is disputed by Louella Parsons in the May 1953 edition of *Modern Screen*, who erroneously remembered the occasion as a birthday party. Nevertheless, she absolves Marilyn of any "bitchery." "What's all this about Marilyn Monroe 'crashing' the birthday party Jane Wyman gave for Freddie Karger at Chasens and 'everybody being SOOOOOO embarrassed because Freddy used to date Marilyn before he married Jane!' Oh, now--Please! In the first place, a guest at Jane's party in the new private room at Chasen's ran into Marilyn (dining in the cafe' proper,) and insisted that the Monroe join the party for a cocktail. Marilyn didn't even know whose party it was until she dropped in for a hot five minutes. As for Janie and Freddie being embarrassed--that's a whole lot of mush. That Wyman girl whom I love so much is far too good a scout for such nonsense. She asked Marilyn to remain for dinner--but the gal had a couple of escorts waiting for her in the cafe'. Poor Marilyn. No matter what she does, she usually gets a blast from some quarter."

King Charles reported in his syndicated column on November 2nd, "Charlie McCarthy goes forward with plans to marry Marilyn Monroe. Tony Martin guests to throw a bachelor dinner for the lucky suitor."

On November 4th John Crosby devotes his entire column to his interview with Marilyn, whom he dubs, The Nation's #1 Sex Thrill. "Marilyn Monroe Hot Topic of Hollywood Conversation...She is, at the moment, the nation's number one sex thrill. Next to Adlai and Ike, she's the hottest topic of conversation in Hollywood. And she's a very likable--is that the word I want exactly?--girl. One thing that rather astonished me about Marilyn Monroe is that the wives--those, at least, who have met the girl--like her just as much as their husbands, though in a somewhat different way. 'Everyone loves Marilyn,' said Dinah Shore. 'How can you help it. She's so honest.' But Marilyn doesn't think so. 'I've had friends tell me: 'I had to defend you last night against the women.' So I say: 'What did the men say?' Then my friends tell me: 'The men just sit there, grinning a little.' That makes up for it--a little.' And she smiled. When Marilyn smiles, she smiles all over. Her lips part, her eyes narrow, her eyebrows shoot up, and the whole vastly publicized body moves around a little bit. I suppose that would be the definition of a lot of other smiles, but Marilyn does it more expertly than anyone else. Watching her I remember what Joseph Cotten told me just after he'd finished a picture with her: 'Everything that girl does is sexy. She can't even light a cigarette without being sexy. A lot of people--the ones who haven't met Marilyn--will tell you it all just publicity. That's malarkey. They've tried to give the same publicity build up to a hundred girls out here. None of them took. This girl's really got it.' I thought I'd better test Mr. Cotten's cigarette theory and I offered her one. She's only recently learned to smoke, having been required to do it in *Don't Bother to Knock*. She does it as if she had been at it for years and after watching her for a while, I decided the Cotten theory was sound, very sound. 'I haven't heard anything but the kindest things about you since I've been here,' I said. 'Oh, you are very nice to say so. But I know what they say, the women. I get letters from the women. 'What are you trying to do' they say, 'put the country in a worse state than its in.' Now it's my fault--the state the country's in. They accuse me of starting all the rapes. Rapes went on long before I came.' This girl, I thought, is a very interesting bundle of neuroses. 'Crank letters,' I said. 'Everyone gets them. What the hell do you care what a few cranks say? You're the hottest thing in pictures. You've got the country at your feet. Why worry about a few cranks?' But she does worry. Some of the Hollywood hatchet girls--and the place abounds in them--have given her the full treatment at parties. This has cut deep. And the critics, who have had a field day with her acting, have wounded her to the marrow. 'They are so cruel, the critics. Sometimes I think they just take out their frustrations on other people.' She speaks in a low throaty murmur, the sound coming from far back in her throat. Both her inflections and the structure of her sentences are more European than American, which is odd because Marilyn has lived in Los Angeles all her life. 'My wardrobe mistress says that, too. She is a Hungarian and she is my closest friend. She says I am more like a European girl because I enjoy being a woman.' She thought a moment, the lips moving a little. The face is never quite still. 'I don't know where I picked it up. I was born on the wrong side of the tracks, you know, and I used to play with a lot of little Mexican boys. Perhaps there.' 'When did it start, the sex appeal?' I was beginning to use the same sentence structure, the delayed object. I think I was about 12 when things changed--radically. The boys didn't have cars. They had bicycles. They'd come by the house and whistle or they'd honk their little horns. Some of them had paper routes. I'd always get a free paper.' Marilyn's childhood is shrouded in contradictions. She says she was moved from household to household, that she saw her mother but rarely. This has been disputed, and it's hard to know what is true. But it wasn't a happy childhood. 'Ever since I can remember I've wanted to be a movie star. I loved the movies. When I was a little girl, it seemed like the only time I was alive was when I was at the movies. The movies were much more real to me than my life.' Well, she'd got there all right. How was it being a star? 'Well--it's exciting. The first time I saw my name in lights I just stopped the car and stared at it for 20 minutes. I thought this is some kind of ultimate. But, of course, you never quite get everything, do you? I want to be a great stage actress. No, honestly, I do.' But there were the unkind critics. One critic, in particular, said all she could do was 'wiggle my fanny,' the unkindest cut of all. 'I know what I'm doing,' she said fiercely. 'I know I can act. I can play Gretchen in *Faust* or Therese in *Cradle Song*. I know I can.' She probably can, too, and will. She's come a long way. Somehow, I never bothered her to ask what, if anything, she wore under her dress."

On November 4th the first hint that the Monroe/DiMaggio relationship wasn't going well hit the press when Marilyn admitted that her romance with Joe DiMaggio had cooled. She said she hadn't been seeing much of Joe, but felt that things would work out okay.

Sheilah Graham reported this interesting bit of information on November 5th, "Camp Roberts SOS'd Juel Park last week for the red nightie she designed for Marilyn Monroe on the cover of *Movie Life*. They wanted it for their Halloween ghost show." Marilyn wore the negligee in a photograph taken by David Preston.

Hair and Makeup Test for *Gentlemen Prefer Blondes* were held on November 8th.

Sidney Skolsky gives this intimate view into Marilyn's mindset as *Blondes* started production. "When Russell, under contract to the Howard Hughes Tool Company, came over to Twentieth Century-Fox Studios to make *Gentlemen Prefer Blondes*, she arrived with all the fanfare and justified importance of a visiting celebrity. Hughes was shrewdly protecting the most glamorous product of his tool company. He had clauses in the contract which provided for Jane to bring her own cameraman, Harry Wilde; her own make-up man, Lane 'Shotgun' Britton; her own hair-dresser, Stephanie Garland; and her own wardrobe girl, Mary Tate. Well, this is like Rocky Marciano going into a fight with lead in his gloves. It would be absurd to say that Marilyn wasn't disturbed and worried by this. In plain words, Marilyn didn't like it. For the first few days on the picture Marilyn and Jane merely greeted each other cordially and stayed with their respective friends. This situation existed because neither knew how to break the ice. The ice was finally broken when, while rehearsing a scene, Jane and Marilyn offered each other suggestions. This led to their speaking about their mutual interest in ball players. 'Only they play different kinds of ball, don't they?' asked Marilyn. Bob Waterfield came on the set several times and met Marilyn, but DiMaggio never visited. Ultimately Jane and Marilyn became very friendly and Marilyn even attended two of Jane's religious group meetings." A candid of Jane, Marilyn and Bob Waterfield survives and was auctioned at Heritage Auctions.

Marilyn appears on the *Edgar Bergen/Charlie McCarthy Radio Show*, November 9th, during which, Charlie McCarthy and Marilyn attempt unsuccessfully to get married. The show was sponsored by Hudnut Hair Products.

On November 10th Earl Theisen has a photo session with Marilyn for an upcoming edition of *Look* magazine, which will come out on December 30th. Marilyn is supposed to be writing out her defense of American men and will rebuttal Zsa Zsa Gabor. Miss Gabor will be photographed in elegant clothing and Marilyn will be photographed in quite casual clothing, with a kerchief in her hair, and more natural poses sitting on her sofa. Theisen will capture Marilyn thoughtfully, pencil in hand, contemplating the virtues of the American man. She has posed herself in various ways, stretched out, sitting with her legs pulled under her, half reclining with one knee up and a hand resting on it, and even standing up, all the while doing her best to consider the comments Miss Gabor has made against Marilyn's most ardent supporters. It is a silly assignment at best, but what comes through is the relaxed relationship between photographer and model. With Marilyn having confessed to her mother's whereabouts did Gladys' old acquaintance ask about her? One might wish to think that he was glad that Marilyn's secret was out in the open and that his friend had one less weight pulling her down.

Wardrobe tests begin for *Gentlemen Prefer Blondes* on November 12th. It isn't overstating to point out Billy Travilla's contribution to the Monroe myth. In this one movie alone he created the iconic pink dress Marilyn wore in the "Diamonds" number, the red sequined gown from the "Little Rock" number, the orange gown from the dining room sequence, and the little gold gown she did the Rumba in that would cause a stir at the *Photoplay* Award's Dinner in February of 1953. Although Billy Travilla created the costumes for Marilyn in this movie, her French beret was designed by John Frederick under his label, "Mr. John."

Marilyn was among nine persons honored on November 14th by the Parents League of America as 'Youngsters of the Year.' Dr. Robert M. Maimes, league president, cited the film actress for achieving "the fondest ambition of every talented young girl, becoming a top ranking star."

On November 13th Marilyn attended a "Welcome" party for *Look* magazine's sports writer, Tim Cohane, at the Brown Derby. *Long Beach Press-Telegram* newspaper column, November 21st, "In the Sportlight," by Fred Delano, reports about Marilyn at the *Look* party. "This is how engrossed I am between the upcoming battle 'twixt USC and UCLA. Thursday night, [13th] when an obviously beautiful woman leaned against the fireplace at the Hollywood Brown Derby and languidly inquired how I was betting, I got all the way to the third point before I realized I was talking to Marilyn Monroe...at which point I started seeing double. Everything started coming in twos about then...touchdowns, fumbles, interceptions, the drinks, coaches and even Marilyn. In fact, if Red Sanders hadn't offered me a slide rule I might not even have made it home...come to think of it, I'm not sure I did....The occasion was a welcome for *Look* Magazine's affable sports writer, Tim Cohane, and somehow a few of the ink-stained wretches of the fourth estate were allowed to mingle with a typical Hollywood outpouring, a word which I used advisedly after calculating the ratio between the décolleté of Miss Monroe, Esther Williams, and the ounce-and-a-half which every waiter supplied when he began to feel your eyes boring into behind. Quite a bunch of lads were there, such as John Wayne, Pat O'Brian and Joe E. Brown, but I had eyes only for that threesome of Monroe, Sanders and Hill...What a secret weapon she would be Saturday! ...And I do mean, 'secret!'....Oh, yea, Arlene Dahl was there, too, and she'd fit reasonably well into a backfield with La Belles Monroe and Williams, though there might not be room for a fourth, try as I may to fit her in. Fun, huh?"

*Time* magazine features a fabulous full-page color portrait of Marilyn by Nickolas Murray. It is captioned, "Marilyn Monroe...A full-blown 26-year-old answer to the prayers of Hollywood for a sexy showpiece, she worked as a model before landing bit parts in pictures, hit the publicity jackpot with 1) nude calendar art, 2) a warm friendship with ex-Yankee Centerfielder, Joe DiMaggio. Her acting talents, if any, run a needless second to her moist "come-on" look, which will next be seen in *Niagara* and *Gentlemen Prefer Blondes*."

Nicholas Murray had earlier photographed Frieda Kahlo in Mexico and had an affair with the artist. His posing of Monroe is reminiscent of the influence Miss Kahlo had on him while south of the Border. He poses Marilyn with a bowl of fruit, which to Miss Kahlo represented sexuality, such as her *Still Life With Parrot and Fruit*, 1951.

Starting on November 16th the American Weekly ran a two part article on Marilyn by Liza Wilson, "The Truth About Me." It is written "by Marilyn Monroe," and edited by Miss Wilson. In the first installment Marilyn tries to set the record straight. "Some surprising—even vicious—untruths have been printed since I became a star, it is high time that I come out and tell the truth,' Marilyn lamented. "Miss Monroe settled the controversy over her true name (she was born Norma Jeane Baker and later re-named Marilyn Monroe by a movie executive). Until she was grown up and established contact with her mother and sister, she considered herself an orphan, and spent her childhood in a series of foster homes as a county ward. During her early years she was a shy, skinny, confused and lonely child. An attempt to settle down, via marriage to James Dougherty when she was 15, ended in divorce. She had always dreamed of becoming a famous movie star someday, but neither her few friends, nor her husband took her seriously."

Sheilah Graham reported on the lull in the Monroe/DiMaggio coupling on November 17th, "Marilyn Monroe is vacating the house she rented from Charlie Grayson, because Joe's pals don't seem to know there's been a breakup. But Joe's Cadillac is still parked in the garage."

Marilyn will move into the Beverly Hills Hotel, 9641 W Sunset Blvd. On Beverly Hills Hotel stationary Marilyn wrote these notes to herself, possibly from one of her classes with Michael Chekhov. "stretch; expansion; open; free; Keep the rule to begin with a ray tension; Keep the balloon and dare not to worry dare to let go--so loose Then you pick up Stretch into your tone; Sense of humor Keeping a giggle inside; Let go of my eyes--so relaxed only let my thought come through them without doing anything to them."

Filming began on November 17th for *Gentlemen Prefer Blondes*. Marilyn starred as Lorelei Lee, a gold-digging blonde. She co-starred with Jane Russell, who adored Marilyn and dubbed her, "the round one." This was one of her greatest movies, and contained perhaps the most closely associated musical number to her legend, *Diamonds Are a Girl's Best Friend.* Lionel Newman was the musical director on the film. Jule Styne and Les Robin penned, *Two Girls From Little Rock, Bye Bye Baby,* and *Diamonds Are A Girl's Best Friend.* Before production began, Hal Schaeffer worked with Marilyn on her vocals. Still, much of the credit for her singing style goes to Phil Moore who had worked with Marilyn since mid-1951 to get her ready for this role. An interesting bit of trivia is that Marnie Nixon was recruited to sing the high notes in the "Diamonds" number. Hogie Carmichael and Harold Adamson penned, *When Love Goes Wrong*. Marilyn proved once and for all what a capable songstress she was. Given great songs by the best song writers of the day, she proved she was more than equal to the task.

Marilyn had been asked what she thought of the philosophy behind *Diamonds Are a Girl's Best Friend*. She replied, "Do I belicve diamonds are a girls' best friend? I can't answer that. I don't own a diamond. But loaded with gems as I am in the picture, I can understand how a girl would feel a sense of security in them."

Marilyn will work with renowned director Howard Hawks. Hawks said this of Marilyn in a 1970 interview, "I have a theory that the camera is kind to some people and unkind to others. By being kind, it registers what some people think. Others can think but it won't register. Among the men, Duke, Gary and Cary Grant are the greatest examples. For women, I'd choose Marilyn Monroe. She had absolutely no sex appeal sitting around a set, but put a camera on her and it was a different story. She was utterly unreal and she belonged to unreal pictures.'"

Howard Hawks will tell Harry Evans his feelings about Marilyn while making *Gentlemen Prefer Blondes*. "But the silly comparisons. Dozens of reporters have compared her to Jean Harlow. Isn't that ridiculous? Jean was bright and sharp—she exuded authority, self-confidence. She led a life of her own, made her own rules, and everybody loved her. No Marilyn is nothing like Jean. She's the perfect paradox—the shy sorceress, sexy and self-conscious. The reluctant tease. Cold facts, these. Marilyn has been established as the screen's femme fatale. That's her handicap. That's why she occasionally overplays—just trying too hard…And when her nervousness tends to mount, we can relieve it by breaking up long scenes by simplifying business and rephrasing dialogue…She's a girl with limited dramatic experience who's expected to carry more than her share of the load in a picture. And at this stage of her development she needs material patterned to her ability. Photographically she's blessed beyond human understanding. The motion-picture camera makes love to some women. Some it tolerates. Some it actively dislikes. It adores Marilyn, but she has to help."

Marilyn will also share screen time with young George "Foghorn" Winslow who plays Henry Spofford III. He had also acted in *Monkey Business*. The studio hired boxer "Gentlemen" Joey Barnum, whom she had also met on the set of *Monkey Business*, to be her bodyguard during the filming. He remembers her as being very nice and that she even went to some of his fights.

Jane Russell had this to say of Marilyn, "Here was a girl who had the same kind of buildup that I had had, except that she as blonde awhile I was brunette. I wondered how that buildup had affected her, what it had done to her life, both professional and private. After I met her I couldn't see that her publicity had gone to her head in any way. I thought she was far more beautiful, too, than I had expected to find her. Her sincerity is impressive and her willingness to listen to and take advice is one of her outstanding qualities. Marilyn is wonderfully sincere in her work. She is always trying to improve and wants to do her best in every scene, yet she makes no effort to steal a scene or upstage anyone ever. I know what Marilyn is going through because I had the same kind of provocative excitement as an impetus to my career. For one thing, she's a generous person with her time—as I was. So I'd like to help her realize she can't allow people to take up all of her time. She has to learn how to say 'No' to things. However, I've found that Marilyn is capable of taking care of herself in most matters and far more so than most people give her credit for. Everybody assumes because she's got a famous figure that she hasn't any sense or sensitivity. But this girl has, and she's a good actress with it."

Jane also does a pretty good job of explaining the real Marilyn. "She used to study all through lunch. Once I got her lunch in a paper bag and took it back to her on the set. She was reading Kahlil Gibran and asked me what I thought of his philosophy in, 'Give your hearts, but not into each other's keeping. For only the hand of Life can contain your hearts. And stand together yet not too near together. For the pillars of the temple stand apart, and the oak tree and the cypress grow not in each other's shadow.' She is intensely serious and studies longer and harder about everything. Vincent Price once gave me a book on true culture. And in it was explained that true culture is simply people doing the most natural thing in the world for them to do and liking something truly individual rather than what some big shot said they should like or what society at the moment said they should do. Out of that you gather that true culturists have kind of a native instinct for why they do what they do…This, to me, explains what Marilyn really is. She doesn't bother about why she likes it—it's pretty, or the shape is pleasing—it's like a child wanting an ice cream soda…She has to take things a little easier so far as the mental strain goes. In fact, she already is taking things a little easier. She must learn to concentrate on the most important things in life and learn to laugh at the rest. Stand way off, Marilyn, and look at it—and it's pretty funny! You'll be a happier girl."

Marilyn was gracious enough to entertain a visitor from England on the set of *Gentlemen Prefer Blondes*, Jean Snow. Miss Snow was visiting her aunt and uncle. Doc Goddard was a friend of Miss Snow's uncle and he arranged a visit for her to the Twentieth Century-Fox studio lot and to watch filming on *Gentlemen Prefer Blondes*. Miss Snow got to see Marilyn and Joe having lunch in the studio commissary. She watched Marilyn and Jane Russell perform *Two Girls From Little Rock*. Marilyn talked freely with Miss Snow and seemed curious about her family back in England. She then pulled two red sequins off her dress and gave them to her and signed a publicity photo for her, "To Jean, Warmest Wishes Always, Marilyn Monroe." Miss Snow remembers Marilyn as "stunning" and "so friendly."

Columnist Bob Thomas reported on November 19th, about veteran glamour photographer Gene Kornman on photographing Marilyn and Jane Russell. Of Marilyn, Kornman had this to say, "Don't underestimate Marilyn's intelligence. She's a smart gal when it comes to posing, and she's easy to get along with too...Marilyn Monroe is better when she closes her eyes just before the picture is snapped,' he said. 'She takes her time to get ready. Then when I give her the signal, she opens her eyes and blossoms like a rose coming out of the bud... For pure beauty, it's best to get them when they're fresh,' he replied. 'That means in the morning or early afternoon. But sexiness is a different matter. I found I get my sexiest shots of Monroe when she is a little bit tired. Her eyelids begin to droop and her whole face looks languid."

On November 19th Marilyn demands that Charles Feldman get Natasha Lytess an increase in salary.

On November 20th Joe waits two hours for Marilyn at the Brown Derby Restaurant to eat Thanksgiving dinner. He wanted to get there early so that they might have a quiet meal. Bernie Kamber, one of Joe's pals was in town and joined them. Even though it is Thanksgiving Day, Marilyn had to attend to some business at the studio. When she finally comes to the Restaurant Joe is livid with her and refuses to talk to her. She, in turn, refuses to talk to him, so they eat their Thanksgiving dinner in silence, each of them only talking to Bernie. Marilyn had also showed up at the home of Anne Karger to have Thanksgiving dinner. She brought Nico Minardos, a Greek actor she had met on the set of *Monkey Business*. They had an on-and-off affair which ended shortly after this. One reason that Nico has given is as Marilyn's fame grew, he was uncomfortable with being Miss Monroe's boyfriend, and also, Joe's famous jealousy was an incentive to step out gracefully. This might have been the "studio business" which delayed her eating with Joe.

The *American Weekly* carries the 2$^{nd}$ installment of Marilyn's autobiography, "The Truth About Me." It is a rehashing of her biography.

On November 22nd Sheilah Graham reported on the status of Marilyn and Joe DiMaggio. "It's time for a change on the love-front in Hollywood. Marilyn Monroe has given the old heave-ho to Joe DiMaggio. The rift started a few weeks ago when she kept DiMag waiting for a home-cooked dinner until way past 10 pm while she dined at the Beverly Hills Hotel in a large party with the John Russell's, John Wayne and yours truly." This was in reference to the Dell publications party for *Modern Screen* that Miss Graham had reported about on October 31$^{st}$.

Inez Wallace of the *Cleveland Plain Dealer* was in town and had a chance to interview Marilyn. It was published on November 22nd. She also scooped the studio and other big name columnist in town by finding the answer to the question, "Are Marilyn and Joe Through." "Marilyn was through with DiMaggio, said the papers. Her studio had stopped the romance, said the radio commentators. Her career had ruined the affair because she career came before love....I had a long talk with Marilyn on the rehearsal stage where she is learning to dance for her new picture....Her voice has a breathless quality as though she is about to tell you some great secret and she fears that something will happen before she can speak. When I asked her if it's true (since her pin-up portraits have saturated every country this side of the iron curtain) she has received more than 2,000 letters each week and in six months nearly 600 proposals of marriage. She said, 'Yes--I wonder why. I'm not really a glamour girl. I live in a small three-room flat near the studio here. I don't smoke and only take an occasional cocktail when everybody else drinks. I never had any 'folks.' My dad died before I was born and mother, a helpless invalid, was always 'away' and never with me. She is still alive, so I'm not an orphan. Still, because of conditions, I spent my childhood in a series of orphanages and private homes where I was placed as ward of the County of Los Angeles. I can remember only about six or seven ok these—just as well. I was 15 when I went to work in an airplane factory and did modeling on the side for extra money. My picture appeared on the cover of four magazines in one month and brought offers from the film studios. You'll get an idea of my success when I tell you I was dropped by three of them—the first being 10$^{th}$ Century-Fox, where I'm now given this star build-up. My first small part in a movie here left me lying on the cutting room floor and I was dropped fast. Columbia then signed me as a burlesque queen and dropped me after that. I moved into the Studio Club, posed for artists, eating only two meals a day. I also engaged a dramatic coach. MGM called me for *Asphalt Jungle*. The role was small but it got audience reaction and again 20$^{th}$ cast me in *All About Eve*. I was the girl George Sanders took to the party. This was the fourth time 20$^{th}$ had used my services and, as soon as Mr. Zanuck saw that picture, he signed me to a long-term contract—and here I am. Believe it or not, every big story written about me calls me 'a discovery.'" 'What about the calendar for which you posed in the nude?' 'Yes. I did that too. I've admitted it, and still see nothing wrong with it. My rent was due. I needed the money and the artist paid me $50. Art galleries feature the Venus de Milo with no cloths and that is art. What's wrong if I do the same thing? It can't be art today and something to blush at tomorrow. I've had a hard life. I've had to fight and work for every nickel I ever made. Right now I want to be an actress, not Exhibit A on some magazine cover. Why won't they let me graduate and go on to other things?'...She looked at me and said suddenly, 'Do you believe that a studio has the right to dictate about my personal life? Is it not true that I must live my own life that I must be me as an individual first and an actress secondly? In other words, can a career be everything?' 'You've asked the $64 million dollar question,' I replied. 'The answer is that you are right. Fame and glory are alright--but they become a hollow thing compared to one's actual everyday existence. You do have the right to live with yourself, and if, in your present problem with this ballplayer, you feel that you are right, don't let anybody tell you differently. They may fill you lap with gold, give you Cadillac's and pearls, but, when you are old, they can't give you the love or companionship of a good man.' 'I knew I was right,' she replied emphatically. 'Thank you. I will not give up on him--ever.' I was half way home before I realized that inadvertently (and due to no special effort on my part) I had found out the one thing which even her studio does not know. They must have sensed that she had told me something, though, because when they queried me about our 'whispered conversation,' I said, 'Yes, she talked—but if you want to know what she said, you must read it in the *Cleveland Plain Dealer*.' And that's just what they'll have to do."

Hedda Hopper reported on November 24th, "The back of my hand to Tony Beauchamp, Winston Churchill's son-in-law. Two or three years ago when he was living at Bebe Daniels Santa Monica beach house, Tony took numerous pictures of Marilyn Monroe, many in bad taste. He must have had a hunch she'd be a star, because he held the negatives back and is now selling them to magazines who have the price to pay. Twentieth's trying to buy up the negatives and take them out of circulation." It seems that the pictures of Marilyn in her teeny-weeny yellow bikini have finally been released.

Also on the 24th, Aline Mosby dedicated a three-part series to Marilyn. "Marilyn Monroe—wearing diamond-studded transparent panties and bra—started her first starring role in a big movie today—but she figures she'll wind up as a tragic actress. You may think of the full blown blonde as the girl you'd like to be stranded in a furniture factory with, but both Miss Monroe and her voice coach, Natasha Lytess, think she is destined to win Oscars as a dramatic tear-jerker—because hers is the most tragic life story to be spun in movietown. "The diamonds are placed in strategic places,' smiles Marilyn, and goes back to playing the sawdust-brain Lorelei in *Gentlemen Prefer Blondes* at $20^{th}$ Century-Fox studio. Today is mostly a rehashing of her biography, but she had this to say about Marilyn and her books, "To make up for the college she never knew, she attended literature classes at UCLA last spring. She reads the classics because 'I get comfort from finding out I'm not different...other people are alone inside, too. I'm trying to find myself now, to be a good actress and good person,' she said. 'Sometimes I feel strong inside, but I have to reach in a pull it up. You have to be strong inside, way deep inside of you. It isn't easy. Nothing's easy, as long as you go on living.'

Miss Mosby's second installment on the 25th dealt with Marilyn's voice. She recruited Natasha Lytess to fill in the blanks. "Marilyn Monroe Learned to Talk In 'Bedroom Voice' After Movie Flops...This is the second of a three-part series on the life and loves of Marilyn Monroe. Today her voice coach tells how the star developed the 'bedroom voice.'....But when Natasha Lytess discovered her, she was just a squeaky-voiced, awkward blonde. 'When she came to me she was in a shell,' the voice coach said. 'She couldn't speak up. She was very inhibited. I had to ask her not to talk at all. Her voice got on my nerves. She'd say 'all right, thank you. G'bye.'" shrilled Natasha in the style of Judy Holliday's *Born Yesterday*. 'I taught her to let go--to be relaxed, to have authority and power and to speak naturally, from below the diaphragm. To speak like Marilyn, you must have a free voice in a free body, with free emotion. Marilyn had been under contract at Fox Studio but they dropped her 'because they didn't think she could walk or talk.' A producer at Columbia Studio sent the actress to Miss Lytess, then voice coach at Columbia, 'to find out if this girl had anything. I liked her,' the coach said. 'She had a wonderful intensity, a child-like openness. After I worked with her, Columbia put her under contract, but in six months they dropped her. She was heartbroken, frantic and broke. She came to my home and cried her eyes out.'.... Then she got a chance for a role in *The Asphalt Jungle*. Miss Lytess worked with the bosomy beauty 'until all hours of the night.' Marilyn won the role-- and it made her a star. 'Fox called her back and when she walked in and said 'Hello,' Mr. Zanuck, the studio boss, didn't believe it was the same girl. Zanuck asked where she'd gotten the voice and walk, so she hired me to be Fox's dramatic coach. I've worked with Marilyn ever since.' Every day Miss Lytess and Marilyn spend their lunch hours going over her lines. 'She's not all bust and fanny,' the coach added. 'I think tragic roles are her forte. There's a strangeness about her...an unreal quality.'"

Marilyn had wardrobe test for *Gentlemen Prefer Blondes* on November 25th.

On November 26th Aline Mosby published the third in a series of articles about Marilyn. "Marilyn Fond of Joe--But She's Not Ready to Marry...This is the last in a series on the latest phenomenon in tinsel town, Marilyn Monroe...Marilyn Monroe confessed today she's still 'stuck' on Joe DiMaggio, but 'I'm not ready to jump into marriage at this time.'....We have the same interests. But not necessarily dancing and books. We don't discuss baseball, either.' Marilyn claims she is just a budding housewife who thinks 'it would be wonderful to have children. My career would have to work into that life, or I'd do without the career,' she said. 'My life comes first. A career is wonderful. But you can't curl up with a career on a cold night.'"

Jimmy Fidler comments on Marilyn's publicity on November 26th. "I have many times remarked on the wrong slanting of studio publicity, and how such publicity has often injured, instead of helping a personality reach stardom, or stay there after attaining the goal. I wish to quote this item from a well-known columnist. She says, 'I resent the way many people who had nothing but praise for Marilyn Monroe have turned against her and are now saying, 'She's just another flash—and just another blonde. Hollywood is filled with them.' To me Monroe has what she always had, and is just starting to come into her own. The studio ought to take special precautions and try to regulate Marilyn's publicity which has gotten out of control.'"

Harrison Carroll reported this mystery on the 29th that "a woman who knew Marilyn Monroe as a bride is selling early-day pictures of the star to magazines."

In an interview with Hedda Hopper, Marilyn discusses this sticky subject. "Did you know that your ex-sister-in-law is trying to sell all sorts of stories about you around Hollywood?' Marilyn nodded, 'Yes. I know. I read about it. That's the way I learn most things about me, true or untrue—by reading the newspapers. So I investigated and found out that one publication had bought a story from her, but that another magazine had turned down another story she wanted to sell them, because they didn't want to print anything about me that wasn't firsthand. You see, my sister-in-law hardly knew me at all. And I knew her very little when I was married to Jim Dougherty. She was married at the time, and had three children. And we were all busy, so we had little or no contact. She is married to another man now (I didn't know her name was Nelson until you told me), and I understand that he is a writer of sorts. They need money pretty badly, probably, and I guess she thinks this is a good way to get some.'" Elyda Nelson published an article in *Modern Screen's* December issue. "For the first time! The true life story of Marilyn Monroe by Elyda Nelson, Marilyn's ex sister-in-law." Included in the article were several rare family photos of Marilyn with the Dougherty family. Marilyn was actually closer than she let on with her sister-in-law. She participated in various family events while married to Jim and she watched her son Larry while Elyda was pregnant, then helped with the baby.

Sheilah Graham wrapped up November with this revelation on the 30th, "Marilyn emitted a startling statement recently--'a happy marriage is the only satisfactory climax to all my good fortune.' Paging Joe DiMaggio. You can buy the ring."

*Parade* magazine carries an article by photographer Andre de Dienes on November 30th, "They Charm You….This town of beauty and talent abounds with '10 best' lists. But here's a new one. It's my selection—for the coming year—of Hollywood's 10 'most interesting' women. I've spent a dozen years photographing Hollywood beauties, and I've never seen more charm than there is in Hollywood right now." You might think he would have chosen Marilyn for the cover and the largest photo in the article, not to mention in the text that he would say she is his current favorite. But, no. He chooses Ursula Thiess instead. His comment for Marilyn was saved for a small photo of her taken in early 1952, and she has a towel wrapped around her head. He captioned it, "Marilyn Monroe is young, exuberant. Her moods change from gay to sad—a nature very suitable for an actress. She uses sex appeal as a front to draw attention." He mentions nothing about her beauty or expertise as a model. For all his other subjects in the article he commented on their beauty and charm, how much he liked this portrait of them or how far their talent will take them. His silence on Marilyn is deafening. Charmed, I'm sure.

Dorothy Kilgallen devoted her entire column in support of Marilyn on December 1st. "I hope all lovers of the clean cut American girl type will get ready to participate, at a moment's notice, in a mail-telegram-telephone campaign to keep Marilyn Monroe status quo. Recently there have been disquieting indications that Marilyn's studio has acquired ultra-refined notions about how she should behave, that she is about to be forbidden to pose for cheesecake pictures, and that the tycoons who own her contract want her to curb her impulsive quotes when she is talking for publication. They'd obviously like to give her an Emily Post veneer now that she's an important star. This is, of course, a form of professional homicide. Marilyn is the most refreshing young star to hit Hollywood since Jean Harlow--frankly gaudy, deliberately alluring, unabashedly interested in her effect on the male population--and if she lets the nervous Nellies of the industry to push her into a more dignified mold, she's a dope. The mold nature gave her is good enough for any girl, and a lot of girls who were born dignified would love to trade with her. If she's smart, she'll stick with her own brand of TNT. Refinement is very nice, and so is culture, but those boys in Korea aren't pasting Emily Post's picture in their foot-lockers."

Zanuck will also comment on Marilyn and her publicity, "Sometimes publicity can be more damaging than helpful. I mean it can grow and grow and get out of hand. Then you have to fight to control it. That's what happened with Marilyn Monroe. We gave her the publicity buildup at the beginning. But now it has gone too far. We have to stop it before the public gets sick of her. As for the girl herself, well, she's temperamental. She's not very fit, either. Wave a script in front of her face and she comes down with a cold."

Marilyn bid on and won a collection of Max Reinhardt's production notebooks on December 3rd at an auction held at the Goldenberg Gallery in Beverly Hills. She bid $1335.00 for the rare set. Marilyn phoned before the auction and asked if they could delay the start for 15 minutes until they could get there. Long after others had dropped out, Marilyn and the University of Southern California's representative, Jake Zeitlin, a rare book dealer, kept bidding. The collection was made up of 178 items and consisted of Reinhardt's original working scripts of such classics as *Faust*, *Oedipus Rex*, *Midsummer Night's Dream*, and *The Miracle*. All were annotated in Reinhardt's own handwriting, in German.

Roy Craft, Marilyn's press agent, was awakened one night by a phone call from a reporter. "'What's this about Marilyn Monroe buying the complete collection of Max Reinhardt manuscripts?' Craft answered, 'you must have the wrong number, and if you haven't the wrong number, who's Max Reinhardt?' Max Reinhardt, he was told, was the famous German theatrical producer who had died in California some years before, and Monroe had just paid $1,335 at an auction for 178 of his annotated scripts. 'It's a good publicity stunt, but what's the angle?' But Roy Craft was not just playing coy. He was as baffled as everyone else. The story made all the papers and I was asked to take a bow for a great publicity coup. In fact, I built quite a reputation in Hollywood just be being around this dame. But you didn't have to invent publicity for Marilyn. It just happened naturally….Suddenly all America was bleeding for Max Reinhardt. No one would have looked at these scripts before and now everybody wanted them. Harvard, Stanford, California put in bids. And who could read them anyway? They were in German. In the end it became too hot a potato for Marilyn to handle.'"

Milton Shulman declared, "The decision to buy Reinhardt papers was directly stimulated by Lytess, who, as a former pupil of the German producer, was horrified at the prospect of his scripts being broken up by auction. 'I told her what a wonderful thing it would be for America if these books were given to some university. We drove together to the auction rooms and she bought them. I know it was idiotic of me, but it never occurred to me that anyone would think it a publicity stunt.'"

On December 7$^{th}$, Edith head commented on Marilyn's clothes. "Designer Edith Head claims that certain actresses are terrific in definite kinds of clothes and should never wear any others." For Marilyn, "Edith conceded that the current sweater girl of them all is luscious Marilyn Monroe. 'Who else?' she queried."

The Weekly Theater Review in Austin, MN, printed this interesting article about Marilyn's various hair colors on December 6$^{th}$. "'Some girls prefer to change hats. I just prefer to change my hair color,' says Marilyn Monroe. Most gentlemen who prefer blondes prefer Marilyn Monroe, and probably never notice from one picture to the next that the exact color of her blondeness is never the same twice. Nor do they seem to care if they do notice. When one writer carpingly referred to Marilyn as the 'chameleon blonde,' Marilyn felt it necessary to come to her own defense. 'The changes give me a lift, and certainly we owe it to the fans to give them a change,' she states. 'We can't very well switch faces, but actresses can and should avid monotony by changing the personality of their coiffeurs and clothes. It gives me a transformed feeling.' Marilyn started out an ash blonde in *The Asphalt Jungle*, switched to golden blonde for her showgirl role in *All About Eve*, was silver blonde in *As Young As You Feel*, amber blonde in *Let's Make it Legal*, and smoky blonde in *Love Nest*."

Edwin Schallert reports on the 9$^{th}$ that Jane Russell has passed a virus on to Marilyn. Miss Russell was sick for four days, and Marilyn will get just as ill. Howard Hawks will have to figure out how to shoot around Marilyn.

Harrison Carroll reported, December 15th, "Marilyn Monroe is bedded with the virus."

Erskine Johnson hands out these quotes about Marilyn on December 15th. "Movie fashion designer Elois Jenssen, about Marilyn Monroe: 'Every time I design a gown for her, the censors raise the neckline about three inches.' Louis Calhern, on the subject of

Marilyn Monroe: 'She's certainly gone places. We all thought she was dumb when she made *Asphalt Jungle*. And when I saw her while making *We're Not Married*, her façade was one of utter stupidity. But I sensed that she was no jerk. Nobody was putting anything over on her.'"

In an attempt to control her exploding publicity, Marilyn tries to pursue legal means to stop her calendar picture from being marketed on ashtrays, high ball glasses, cocktail trays and the like. She has ridden the calendar rocket to fame and would now like to get off. That is easier said than done. In an *INS* story on December 18th, Marilyn protest the marketing of her calendar pose. "Marilyn is not 'ashamed' of the photos, but she admitted: 'I had hoped I would never be identified as the girl in these pictures. Now, when I see them I feel like I'm dressing in a room without window shades! I don't know exactly what rights I have, but it seems to me I should have some say in the way my own picture is used.' The photos, showing Marilyn in various languorous poses, were taken by Hollywood ad lenser Tom Kelley who says all he is getting out of the deal is a 'reputation for being a nude photographer.' Kelley revealed he is about to use the U.S. Postal Service without defraud because an established artist decided the nudes have 'dynamic symmetry' and 'artistic merit.' Said Kelley, 'That puts the calendars in a class with Toulouse-Lautrec!' Kelley admitted he would 'like to make some money' from the photos, but said he would not want to do anything to hurt the reputation of the blowtorch blonde. Kelley charged that Marilyn was 'personally responsible' for the notoriety she has received 'because she autographed a whole batch of the calendars and gave them away to friends.'"

In another news story on December 19th, more details of Marilyn's growing concern for her image appear. "Marilyn Monroe isn't anxious to have folks look at her nude photo as they quaff a holiday drink. She has asked 20th Century-Fox lawyers to see if anything can be done about stopping use of the celebrated picture on trays and drinking glasses. Their offhand opinion was that nothing could. But they said they'd dig deeper in legal tomes. A spokesman said he and Marilyn had seen the picture on cocktail trays. They'd hear of its use on glasses. He didn't think she'd make a real legal fight of it unless the practice got to be 'a national institution.' The shape of things to come in calendars was indicated, meanwhile, by Western Lithograph Company, one of two companies which own calendar rights to Monroe poses in the altogether. Both poses were made at the same sitting. First brought out in 1951, the calendar was reprinted for '52 and '53 and in January will be available for '54 said Roy Johnson, sales manager for advertising specialties. He said his and a Chicago firm, which issues the other pose, have sold 'several hundred thousand' copies. A Post office rule forbids nude calendars in the mail. They have to go by railway express or freight, Johnson said, but—'We do not consider this a lewd picture. We consider it art—definitely art.'"

On the 19th it was announced in newspapers, "'Legal representatives of 20th Century-Fox studio are making preparations to institute legal action against companies and individuals engaged in unauthorized commercial exploitation of the Marilyn Monroe calendar photographs. The contemplated court action will be based on the contention that reproductions of the photographs are being used for commercial purposes in an unethical and indiscriminate manner.' The manufacturer said he wanted to remain anonymous behind his firm name—M&M Sales. He said the initials stood for Moskovitch & Murphy, partners of his, and were only coincidentally the same as Marilyn's. He had an agreement with the photographer who took the Monroe pictures—and a release signed by her when she posed in 1949. He quoted it: 'I consent to the use of my name, portraits and pictures…for advertising and trade purposes…' A Fox spokesman said the studio's attorneys are studying to determine if 'some imperfections' might be found in the agreement."

On the 21st, Juanita Merrill compared three starlets in her article for the *Pictorial Review*, "Sexy Sirens: Can They Top Jean Harlow?" The candidates were Marilyn, Rita Gam and Elaine Stewart. Of the three Miss Merrill says, "It will be interesting to see which, if any, of these three promising bombshells really does emerge as Jean Harlow's successor. Probably no one ever will, for Jean died only seven years after *Hell's Angels*, her incandescence undimmed by the years." Little did she know that Marilyn's *Candle in the Wind* will shine brighter and longer, surpassing Jean Harlow's glow.

Erskine Johnson reported on December 24th, "'Soulful' Marilyn Wants To Bid For Dramatic-Actress Award…Marilyn Monroe, Hollywood's 'Movies Are Hotter Than Ever' kid, and 20th Century-Fox Studio are going 'round and 'round about her future career blueprints. The studio wants sexy Marilyn to alternate between low-brow comedies and high-kicking musicals, but she has dreams of someday competing in the Oscar race for the best dramatic actress award. 'This girl's soul doesn't belong in that body,' her dramatic coach, Natasha Lytess, is saying. 'She has emotional depths that should be developed.' Natasha, by the way, was with Marilyn when she rushed to an auction and wrote a $1335 check for 178 Max Reinhardt dramatic manuscripts, written in German. But there will be no evidence of Marilyn gone "Reinhardt-ish" in the studio's ad campaign for her next film, *Niagara*. The billboards will show a filmy-gowned Marilyn superimposed over all of Niagara Falls and the eye-popping words: 'So lusty that nature herself couldn't tame her.'"

Continuing the saga of the Max Reinhardt books, Victor O Jones gets his say about the matter on the 25th. "Abelard and Heloise, Romeo and Juliet, Caesar and/or Anthony and Cleopatra, George Bernard Shaw and Mrs. Pat Campbell, Dante and Beatrice, Hero and Leander, Elizabeth and Essex, Nelson and Lady Hamilton, George Sand and Chopin—the list of celebrated romances is long. To it should be added a multiple one involving on one side Marilyn Monroe and, on the other, a swarm of suitors composed of the librarians of Stanford, UCLA, Harvard, USC, and Kansas. Librarians, even college librarians, are generally not considered as prime examples of romantic ardor, and it is possible that even the obviously desirable Miss Monroe is not what motivates their courtship. Men have wooed before this for profit rather than deep-seated personal attraction. And in the present case of Miss Monroe has something librarians want. Of course she has a lot of other things that even non-librarians set considerable store by. (Never end a sentence with a preposition, even when you are writing about somebody propositioning Miss Monroe.) In any case, it wasn't until Marilyn acquired 178 prompt books annotated by the famous producer, Max

Reinhardt, that the college librarians started writing love letters to her. The object of these particular billets doux wasn't marriage, though it can't be said that the intentions weren't at least faintly honorable. What the librarians wanted was those prompt books. Miss Monroe had outbid the University of Southern California at the auction and now the librarians suggested that maybe she'd like to give them the books and manuscripts to them. This was natural enough. Any woman as beautiful as Miss Monroe hardly needs Max Reinhardt's annotations to advance her career—certainly not in Hollywood, where acting is scarcely at a premium. None of the colleges has offered to buy these manuscripts, but at least one, the University of Southern California, has taken an undue advantage over its rivals. Of course, everything is fair in love and war, but any idealist must view with antipathy USC Librarian Dr. Lewis F. Steig's inviting Miss Monroe to attend the Rose Bowl game as his guest. He even offered seats on the 50-yard line. This clearly was taking advantage of the rival librarians, whose football teams weren't playing in any bowl and it is to Miss Monroe's credit that she saw through to the sordid motive. 'I think he's only interested in my books,' she told friends. 'I regret that I cannot accept your invitation,' she wrote Dr. Steig coldly. Harvard has written, too, though not, naturally, inviting Miss Monroe to any football games. They have, as yet received no reply. Harvard's theatre collection is as famous now as its football teams used to be. It is housed in a gem of a building, the new Houghton Library, where the temperature never varies and where the humidity is always exactly 50 percent. Maybe in the end, this will do the trick. Miss Monroe certainly wouldn't want her manuscripts to be exposed to the rigors of sitting on the 50-yard line, even in Southern California. And if the books do come to Harvard, the students can be counted upon to insist that a picture of Miss Monroe, in Technicolor, be hung in the room housing her Reinhardtdia."

Marilyn will be photographed giving a rose to University of Southern California halfback, Al Carmichael. She also presented him with roses for his team mates in the upcoming New Year's Day football game, The Rose Bowl. The University of Southern California faced Wisconsin. Even though she refused the invitation sit on the 50 yard line, she makes this gesture to the guys on the team. No hard feelings, but she was nobody's fool.

Joe DiMaggio makes a surprise visit to Marilyn on Christmas Eve and brings her a Christmas tree, which she claims is the first one anybody ever gave her.

Edith Kermit Roosevelt, daughter of President Theodore Roosevelt, again interviews Marilyn and it is published on December 28th. "Marilyn Monroe said today her ambition is to become not only Hollywood's glamour girl, but a competent actress. 'I plan out every gesture and every movement I make,' said Miss Monroe in that breathless manner of talking that she uses. 'When I go home at night I study vice and dramatics with my coach. I also do exercises every day.' Since Miss Monroe is through work at 6pm, this doesn't leave her much time for fun. She admitted she had little social life these days. 'I never see anybody much unless I'm stuck on them,' she said. 'Then I see them all the time.' (Her current date is ex-baseball player, Joe DiMaggio). 'I read most every chance I get. I like the classics. I also write poetry--the sad kind. I listen to the rain hitting my roof. Then I write about death, destruction and the broken heart.' 'Marilyn is essentially a tragedian,' a co-worker once said of the star, now appearing in *Gentlemen Prefer Blondes.* Concerning her future, Miss Monroe said she hopes to get married someday and have at least one child. She said she regrets that when she does marry she won't be able to wear white. Miss Monroe is a divorcee. 'Of course, I might still wear white just the same. But I don't know if it's one of my best colors.' As she sat in her dressing room adjusting the left side of her page-boy hairdo, she complained she had been criticized for wearing sexy dresses. 'I only wear the studio wardrobe out,' she said. 'I have few clothes of my own.' Matter of fact, Miss Monroe said, she doesn't much care about clothes or possessions. When she moves out of a place, she said, she sells everything but her books. Right now she is staying at the Beverly Hills Hotel. 'But I keep most of my things at the studio,' she said."

*Look* magazine article December 30th, "American Men? Inside Tips About The Men and How to Get and Hold One!" by Marilyn Monroe and Zsa Zsa Gabor. Earl Theisen photographs an unusually casual Marilyn for this article. Marilyn will later say of this article, "Zsa Zsa Gabor was supposed to write an article for a magazine on the subject: What's Wrong With American Men, and I did marginal notes for it. The editor cut out my best lines. I wrote, 'If there's anything wrong with the way American men look at sex it's not their fault. After all, they're descended from the Puritans, who got off the boat on the wrong foot—or was it the Pilgrims?—and there's still a lot of that puritanical stuff around.' The editor didn't use that one.'"

Costume Test for *Gentlemen Prefer Blondes* on December 31st. The costume is for the "Diamonds" number. She is photographed from the front. Travilla remembers, "I did a '$4000 dress, necklace, and hip girdle made of real jewels. The costume consisted mostly of fishnet hose tights, headdress of extravagant real aigrettes, and the minimum of bandeau-bra bodice, with a brief skirt which divided. It was brief and revealing, a sensuous costume, but it was in good taste."

The 20th Century-Fox in-house magazine *Action!* featured a captioned photo of Marilyn and a GI. "M-M-M-M-M-M BOY!—When Airman John Loeffler, son of film editor Louis Loeffler, asked Marilyn Monroe to send an autographed picture to him in Korea, she did. She added that they would have lunch together next time he came home. Her promise materialized into a luncheon and day on the set for young Loeffler during his recent leave. He heads back to Korea soon, loaded with prints of the above pic. 'I'll be mobbed,' he opined."

Marilyn had more wardrobe test for *Gentlemen Prefer Blondes* on January 2nd. She is once again tested in the rhinestone encrusted bikini for the "Diamonds" number. This time she is photographed from the rear. It doesn't take long for word to come down from the Fox offices..."Cover her up!" This was in reaction to her calendar photo which was still a big deal. In desperation Billy Travilla designs her classic pink strapless gown for the *Diamonds Are a Girl's Best Friend* number.

Travilla remembers, "The studio felt she had to be presented in a more ladylike way. My orders were to cover her, that she was beautiful and exciting enough. I was told to do the costume so as not to be so aware of her body. So I designed a strapless candy-pink evening gown in the heaviest, stiffest, Italian pure silk satin. Before I draped the dress I lined this stiff fabric with another layer of the same heavy silk. I wrapped the fabric round her body and overlapped it at the back to form a huge butterfly bow. The only part of the garment that was actually closed was the 5in.-wide tailored satin belt. Yet on the screen, even with this double layer of heavy fabric draped round her, Marilyn's undulations showed up. I might as well have made the dress of clinging silk jersey."

On January 5th Marilyn finally decided who was going to get her collection of 178 script books of the late impresario Max Reinhardt. In a press statement released by her studio she declared, "I feel that placement of the books should be the decision of Mr. Reinhardt's son, Mr. Gottfried Reinhardt. He insists on reimbursing me for the auction price.'"

Marilyn hated the bad press she had gotten by purchasing the Reinhardt collection. Max Reinhardt's widow had just returned from a trip and was surprised that the manuscripts sold for so little. She had her son Gottfried contact Marilyn and make arrangements to purchase the manuscripts. Mr. Reinhardt said, "I was astonished when told that Miss Monroe had purchased the scripts. I couldn't imagine what she would do with them. In the first place all my friends stayed away from the auction because they didn't want to bid against my wife, Silvia, who represented me at the bidding. Only two other people bid, a representative of the University of Southern California and Miss Monroe. By the time I was notified that the young lady had bought them, it was too late to put in a higher bid. I got the material back into the family through Miss Monroe's drama coach, Natasha Lytess. She once was a student at the Max Reinhardt School here in Hollywood. She knew my father and understood how much the scripts meant to me. Miss Monroe was a perfect lady throughout my dealings with her. She is utterly charming, and was delighted to return the scripts to me. I will always have a soft spot in my heart for Marilyn Monroe." Marilyn generously let the family have them for what she had won them for. Marilyn never followed through with the actual payment, so Gottfried Reinhardt bought the collection from the Goldenberg Gallery itself. In 1965 Reinhardt's brothers Gottfried and Wolfgang donated the collection to Israel's Chaim Weizmann Institute. It was then valued at $50,000.

According to Ralph Roberts, Marilyn felt betrayed by Natasha Lytess over the whole Reinhardt auction. She felt that Natasha has "played politics." Natasha would never have the same hold over Marilyn as she had enjoyed in the past. By 1956 Natasha was permanently out of the picture.

On January 5th Dorothy Kilgallen gives evidence for some sort of relationship between Marilyn and Robert Slatzer. "Marilyn gives the boys trouble even when she's not around. The other night when she was attending a press party, two of her most ardent suitors--Joe DiMag, of course, and Bob Slatzer--would up cooling their heels at her house. The dialogue that ensued was frosty, but they both left at the same time." By April Kilgallen would describe Slatzer as "a young denizen of Hollywood who has very big eyes for her but has not progressed past the Good Pals or 'Gosh I'd like your advice!' stage in her attentions."

Earl Wilson reported on January 10th that legendary exotic dancer Sally Rand made these comments about Marilyn. "'What do you think of the Marilyn Monroe craze?' I asked Sally. 'About the calendars,' she answered, 'I can't imagine in this enlightened day and age anybody taking a dim view of calendar art....'But I'm not sure the people looking at calendars are interested in art,' I mentioned. 'The calendar art I've seen is innocuous.' 'Anyway, Marilyn Monroe said she needed the money...and I guess you did, too.' 'It never occurred to me that posing in the nude was any great sacrifice to modesty or dignity or anything else.'"

Marilyn had more wardrobe test for *Gentlemen Prefer Blondes* on January 13th. The next day David Conover, the photographer who discovered Norma Jeane working at Radioplane in 1945, pays a visit to Marilyn on the set of *Gentlemen Prefer Blondes.* He has his photo taken with Marilyn next to his panel-job, complete with advertising for his resort in Canada that he ran with his wife Jeanne. The sign on his car read, "Wallace Island, Canada's Most Unique Resort." He also has a couple of photos taken with Marilyn backstage.

"In Hollywood," by Gene Handsacker, substituting for Bob Thomas, ran this on January 19th. "Predictions of fireworks when Jane Russell and Marilyn Monroe squared off to act in the same picture have fizzled. Jane even has become Marilyn's sisterly adviser in matters of love. Marilyn didn't seek Jane's counsel; Miss Russell says she volunteered to Miss Monroe the view that it's a good idea for an actress to marry a man in another field, like sports. Jane is married to retired football star Bob Waterfield. Marilyn says she and retired baseball star Joe DiMaggio are 'good friends.' Jane's reasoning goes like this: 'It's great to have somebody like that to go home to. If you have blown-up ideas about yourself he talks you out of them in a hurry. If you sound unhappy with your job he tells you to quit. Joe and Robert'--Jane calls her husband Robert--'are sensible moneywise. Marilyn isn't and I've never been. That's another opposite quality, which is great. Then you have a whole.' Jane said she and her husband 'have a healthy disregard for each other's profession. When we do something in common, that's when the beefs start. This way everybody minds his own business.' The forecasts of jealous rivalry between glamour champs Monroe and Russell were perhaps reasonable. Scene stealing and all that. A Paramount producer told Jane when she set out for 20th Century-Fox and *Gentlemen Prefer Blondes,* 'Shake hands with Marilyn, flip a coin to see who'll make the first catty crack, then let the fur fly.' Jane says some gossip--lovers have urged her, 'Please, couldn't you and Marilyn have just a small beef? And let me be the first to hear about it!' But after two months work on the picture, Jane calls Marilyn, 'a real nice, sweet kid. She works a lot harder than I do.' As for scene-stealing: 'In all the years I've been in pictures, I have not run into that.' Marilyn expresses equal esteem for Jane and calls her 'a good actress in the kind of thing she likes to do.' Miss Monroe prefers more serious vehicles for herself. Others on the set confirmed that there have been no temperamental outbursts. One is Mrs. Bunny Gardel, body make-up woman, one of whose tasks is to paint out the mole that is like a beauty mark on Marilyn's left side and leave in the one on the right. Otherwise too much of a good thing. She compares the girls this way: Jane is 'more tom-boyish' and Marilyn is 'more feminine.' Cameraman Harry Wild says his only problem is making the lighting suitable for both Marilyn's taffy hair and Jane's coffee tresses. Director Howard Hawks says, 'They get along beautifully.' He's advocating a Russell-Monroe series like the Crosby-Hope pictures. Scraps between stars make good copy, of course. As I left the set, a press-agent muttered unhappily, 'I wish they'd fight.'"

*Hollywood Today*, reported on June 27, 1958, an inside look at Gwen Verdon at work on the set of *Gentlemen Prefer Blondes*. "You never heard about the time Gwen Verdon the assistant Hollywood dance director now starring in the film version of *Damn Yankees*, advised two of Hollywood's sexiest dolls about sex appeal? Well Gwen handled it like John Foster Dulles. One of the dolls was Marilyn Monroe and the other was Jane Russell and it could have been as disastrous as Nixon telling Ike his gold grip is all wrong. Gwen had to tell Marilyn she was acting too sexy and tell Jane she wasn't sexy enough. Gwen was coaching Marilyn and Jane's song-and-dance numbers in *Gentlemen Prefer Blondes* and she thought Marilyn was wriggling it up a little too much. Instead of coming right out and saying it she put on the soft velvet gloves and told Marilyn, 'Honey when you're that active it's hard for the cameraman to focus on you.' Marilyn, no fool, let the man have his focus. Jane's problem was in two other directions. Gwen thought she was being too flamboyant about it all and that it detracted from her sex appeal. But she didn't tell busty Jane in so many words. 'I just told her,' Gwen told me, 'that maybe smaller movements would be better for her. I'll never forget Jane's answer. She told me, "Gwen, I'm not one of the LITTLE people!" What Jane Meant by 'little', you know, of course, and by now you know how Gwen, one of Hollywood's little people danced her way to fame on Broadway in *Can, Can, Damn Yankees* and *New Girl in Town*. It all came after red-haired, green-eyed Gwen had been buried in Hollywood teaching stars like Lana Turner, Betty Grable, Marilyn and Jane how to dance. She was dance director Jack Cole's assistant unknown to the public."

Jane later recalls working with Cole and Verden in *Gentlemen Prefer Blondes*. "Marilyn and I had never danced before; we were a pair of klutzes. Jack was horrible to his own dancers, but with us, the two broads, he had the patience of Job. He would show us and show us and then turn us over to Gwen."

# Chapter Thirteen
## Sex Bomb

"Everything that girl does is sexy. A lot of people--the ones who haven't met Marilyn yet--will tell you it's all just publicity. That is malarkey. They've tried to give the same publicity build-up to a hundred girls out there. None of them took. This girl's really got it."
Joseph Cotten

On January 21, 1953 *Niagara* is released. Marilyn sizzles her way through the movie and into legend. Everything previously written about her finally erupts on the screen in a Technicolor sex bomb. Who is ready for the erotic wave of energy she focuses onto the world. There is no one like her who can flaunt her shameless sexuality in your face yet still project a mystique of innocence. This is her gift and this is the reason it has taken Hollywood so much time in trying to understanding her. She was like the mythic Chimera, a feminine archetypal image who combined opposing traits into one being. This would also be the seed of her undoing, trying to integrate these different selves into one person.

This will also be the year that Marilyn starts to court the fairer sex. Until now she had played only to the men. Her publicity and interviews had been geared toward making her the ultimate sex star. But philosophers have always known that "the hand that rocks the cradle, rocks the world," and writes letters to the studio, and refrains from buying tickets.

Women were making their displeasure over Marilyn's marketing known. It is a miscalculation on her part that she will rectify largely on the basis of her relationship with Joe DiMaggio. She will garner a lot of press on the trials of being in a relationship, a problem common to all women, and for being famously loyal to him. Marilyn will also soothe ruffled feathers with her role in *How to Marry a Millionaire*. She will start to display, as her character does, a measure of modesty about her own appearance that charms the public. She will be less raunchy in her public displays and less offending in her interviews. 1953 will be the pivotal year that Marilyn enchants the world, women as well as men, to fall hopelessly in love with her.

Harrison Carroll reported on January 28th, "Wind Ends in Injury to Marilyn Monroe…Strong winds recently may have blown somebody some good luck but not Marilyn Monroe. Marilyn got up around 2:30 a.m. to close a shutter, tripped in the dark and fractured the fourth toe on her right foot. It's now in a splint and her work on *Gentlemen Prefer Blondes* may be delayed. And that's not the worst of it. There are only a few plot scenes left in the picture. These she can do. But the musical numbers are yet to come. And doctors say Marilyn will have to postpone dance rehearsals for two weeks. This in turn means an additional delay in the start of her next movie, *How to Marry a Millionaire*. By the time they eventually make the picture, Lauren Bacall, who'll play one of the leads, probably could have gone to Europe with Humphrey Bogart and remained with him for most of his stay."

Marilyn meets with the renowned English poet, Dame Edith Sitwell in February of 1953. Dame Edith, who was in town writing the screenplay for her book, *Fanfare for Elizabeth* at Columbia, entertains Marilyn in her apartment at the Sunset Towers. Dame Edith recalls meeting Marilyn, "Immediately on my arrival in Hollywood, a certain American magazine with a huge circulation asked me to write for them a description of the place. But still more important to them was that Miss Monroe and I should be brought face to face, since it was obvious that we were born to hate each other, would do so at first sight, and that our subsequent insults to each other would cause a commotion when repeated. They never made a greater mistake." Dame Edith described Marilyn, who arrived wearing "a green dress, and with her yellow hair, as looking like a daffodil…In repose her face was at moments strangely, prophetically tragic, like the face of a beautiful ghost--a little Spring-ghost, an innocent fertility-daemon, the vegetation spirit that was Ophelia. We talked mainly, as far as I remember, about Rudolf Steiner, whose works she had just been reading." Marilyn had been introduced to the works of Rudolf Steiner by her acting teacher Michael Chekhov. She became interested in Steiner's philosophy of Anthroposophy, that spiritual development should be humanities foremost concern. The two book lovers talked about Rudolf Steiner, and spent the brief time laughing over Helen Rootham's "unfortunate Steiner phase." Helen Rootham was Dame Edith's former governess and later became her companion. The interview was to be published in a later magazine article, but it never made it to print. She continued with a touching assessment of Marilyn, "In private life she was not in the least what her calumniators would have wished her to be. She was very quiet, and had great natural dignity (I cannot imagine anyone who knew her trying to take a liberty with her) and was extremely intelligent. She was also exceedingly sensitive. What will power she must have needed in order to remain the human being she was, after the cruelty with which, in the past, she was treated! That is over now, and she is accepted as the fine artist that she was. But that cruelty was completely odious. It arose partly, I think, from the envy of people who are devoid of beauty, and partly from the heartless stupidity of those who have never known a great and terrifying poverty. There are people, also, who cannot believe that beauty and gaiety are a part of goodness. When we think of cruelty, we must try to remember the stupidity, the envy, the frustration from which it has arisen."

Dame Edith suggested that Marilyn should meet L.L. Whyte, a physicist and philosopher. He had a profound effect on psychology icon Carl Rogers and the development of his theory of congruence. Dr. Whyte was interested in the mind/body connection, much like Rudolf Steiner. Marilyn would have no problem coming up with questions to discuss with him. *Motion Picture* magazine, September 1955, carried this about the meeting. "Dr. L.L. Whyte was touring this country, engaging in many conferences with men of science, collating knowledge for a new book. When he met Marilyn, there were only a few people present, but apparently what happened there took their breath away. For fully two hours, little Marilyn, the dumb blonde, engaged in active conversation with the famed physicist, plying him with questions and comments about scientific origins, nuclear patterns, the meaning of life. They were two minds working, one eager for knowledge, the other challenged by intelligent questioning. And when they parted, Dr. Whyte shook Marilyn's hand and thanked her for a stimulating time. 'It's simply amazing,' he said to her, 'the difference between the public figure of Marilyn Monroe--the one we read about--and the real person I've met today.' When Marilyn heard that, she almost cried for joy.

Dorothy Kilgallen reported on the pair in her column on October 5th, 1953, "A national magazine, which succeeded in bringing together Edith Sitwell and Marilyn Monroe for a two-hour interview, has decided to junk the history-making dialogue 'because it would be over the heads of the public.' Sidelight: Just before the meeting, Marilyn dashed out to buy nylons. She explained breathlessly, 'I just couldn't let Miss Sitwell see me without stockings!"

Reuters reported in an April 26th, 1954 article, "Edith Sees No Evil in Hollywood," Dame Sitwell's opinion of Marilyn, "She did not throw her figure about, she was entirely natural, sensible and intelligent."

Bennett Cerf reported on the odd pair in his column on August 24th, 1954, "A meeting in Hollywood recently was arranged between two girls seldom bracketed in the public imagination: Miss Edith Sitwell and Miss Marilyn Monroe. What's more, Miss Sitwell, famed for her poetry and her beautiful hands, and Miss Monroe, who boasts charms a trifle more obvious, were soon lost in most friendly and animated conversation. An eavesdropper avers that the subject under discussion concerned astrology in general and the constellation Sagittarius in particular. 'I had no idea that you believed in astrology,' exclaimed Miss Sitwell. Miss Monroe's ingratiating reply was, 'I believe in everything--a little.' Later Miss Sitwell confessed that two of her best friends were panting to meet the glamorous movie star. 'Goody,' said Marilyn. 'Who are they?' Miss Sitwell told her, 'Aldous Huxley and Igor Stravinsky.'"

On March 14, 1955, Leonard Lyons reported on Dame Edith's reaction to meeting Marilyn, "A party in London where Dame Edith Sitwell plans to present the most interesting woman she'd met in all Hollywood--Marilyn Monroe. Not Katherine Hepburn, who's coming here to join the Old Vic in a tour of Australia, but Marilyn Monroe. Even the oldest Punch-reading club member was stirred by this fortune. Marilyn Monroe, indeed, by jove. I ssssay there, ol' boy, must be quite a dish. Quite."

Miss Sitwell has this to say of Marilyn in an article in *Australian Women's Weekly*, April 6, 1955, "'Miss Monroe is a very nice girl--simple and serious. It's true she is stupendously proportioned, but is that a crime? I was impressed by her dignity and bearing. But what really surprised me was her interest in the Austrian philosopher Rudolf Steiner. She was the first person I'd met in this part of the world in years who talked about him. Miss Monroe is to be commended. Hollywood was a slave's life. In fact, some slaves enjoyed life far more.' Dr. Edith Sitwell has in mind a diet of improving reading for Marilyn. 'Schopenhauer,' she mused, 'should suit her.'"

Dame Edith finds that an acquaintance with Marilyn can bring unwanted attention. She carped to the press on June 30, 1955 that if she hears Marilyn's name again she will shriek. She claimed she wasn't feuding with Marilyn, but was just so weary of being asked about her friendship with Marilyn. She remembered her short meeting with Marilyn as pleasant and that Marilyn was a nice, quiet girl. She extended an invitation to Marilyn that if she ever found herself in London they should meet for tea. Since then, the press has made her life, "an absolute hell." It seems Dame Edith didn't quite grasp the implications of having tea with Marilyn.

Leonard Lyons reported on Marilyn's plan to visit Dame Edith in England in his column on May 22, 1956, "All the current magazine stories about Miss Monroe mention the reunion she is scheduled to have with Dame Edith Sitwell in London. The British poetess was intrigued by Marilyn at their meeting in Hollywood. She asked the star how much she earned, about her work hours, makeup, etc. Miss Monroe answered all the questions and said that for makeup purposes she had to be at the studio at 5:30am. Dame Edith was appalled. She said, 'No artist ever should be required to get up so early for such money.'"

Back across the pond to Hollywood, Hedda Hopper reported on February 3rd, "When Marilyn Monroe sings *Diamonds Are a Girl's Best Friend*, she'll be against a background of red velvet and on a red floor. She does the old burlesque bumps and grinds in *Gentlemen Prefer Blondes*. Marilyn visited a burlesque show and when she came out, she said, 'Just imagine. Some of those girls didn't have a stitch on!'....Marilyn Monroe's the only dame I know who could give Niagara Falls its come-uppance. People who've seen the picture, *Niagara*, are surprised the water didn't stop running. It's a smash hit."

Jack Cole choreographed Marilyn's dance routines in *Gentlemen Prefer Blondes*. His assistant was future Broadway star Gwen Verdon, who had the job to teach Jane Russell how to seem more sexy, and to teach Marilyn how to tone down her sexuality. Miss Verdon would go on to marry Broadway choreographer and dance legend Bob Fosse. In a note of interest, one of the dancers on the *Diamonds Are a Girl's Best Friend* number was 19 year old George Chakiris would go on to win a Best Supporting Actor Oscar for his role as Bernardo in *West Side Story*. According to Chakiris, "Marilyn was great to work with. She acted like a professional all during the grueling three day rehearsal for the "Diamonds" number."

Hal Schaefer, a musical director at Fox, remembers that Marilyn had fluidity as a dancer. Her lessons from Lotte Goslar had paid off. What Jack Cole was to develop in her was strength and he cleaned up her lines. Jack, according to Schaefer was brilliant in telling her what to do and he was one of the few people she would actually listen to. Schaefer gives an example of their working relationship, "He wanted her to make a move, and she put her arm out. It just kind of drifted. Jack said, 'No, wait. Sharp, I want it sharp!' 'But Jack, I'm supposed to be a sex queen,' she said. And he answered, 'That's not sexy. That's like a limp fish. Put that arm out there, strong! That's sexy! That's life, that's alive, that's energy!' And he was right."

Writer Debra Levine points out that Jack Cole's role in *Gentlemen Prefer Blondes* was more important than he has been given credit for. "Much more than a choreographer, he actually directed film sequences, famously the three major song-and-dance numbers in Howard Hawk's *Gentlemen Prefer Blondes*." Miss Levine goes on to comment about Cole's influence on the screen, "He enhanced features and figures, camouflaged defects, and zoomed in the camera for glamour shots of pouty lips, limpid eyes, and velvety skin. After coaching his charges in practice studios, he mirrored their moves to them as the cameras rolled. Cole was indeed a performance coach, habitually advising on line readings and songs, significantly with Monroe, but also with others."

Music arranger Peter Matz makes this statement about Cole's influence on Marilyn.

"The persona Marilyn showed in her film musicals was Jack Cole. He grabbed on to something in her. She followed everything he gave her. Phrasing! The gestures, the walk. All of it!"

In fact, the *Diamonds* number was directed by Cole. Hawks gracefully bowed out to a higher authority when it came to the musical numbers. Jane Russell remembers that Howard Hawks didn't even come to the filming. Gwen Verdon reveals, "Jack decided where the camera should be, setup by setup, in consultation with Harry Wild. He also synced camera angles with Hugh Fowler. Hawks stood by and let Jack do what he wanted."

Hal Schaefer insists that Cole rewrote the number from the linear stage version to one more suited to film. "Cole redid it in a sensual way for Marilyn. He told me, 'I want to make it swing. I want to get it loose.' The part where she bumps and grinds, sensually naming famous jewelers, Tiffany's, Cartier, Black Starr -- that's not in the original. That's Jack's material. He wrote it. Then he taught Marilyn how to move on it."

Jack Cole said of Marilyn during this time, "There is a terrible positive directness to Baby-Dolls doing everything sideways. Maybe she will take the curved way to get there, but she'll get there. She is like a dog with a bone; she is going to get there!"

Jack Cole is known as "the Father of Theatrical Jazz." Cole studied dance with the experimental Denishawn Dance Company in New York, led by Ruth St. Denis and Ted Shawn, and with modernists Doris Humphrey and Charles Weidman. He also studied Indian dance with Bharata Natyam. His Jack Cole Dancers performed in nightclubs in the 1930s. Cole finally settled in Hollywood and became a top choreographer in the 1940s and '50s. The best glimpse of him can be seen in the film, *Designing Woman*, which starred Lauren Bacall and Gregory Peck. It is a rare chance to hear him and see him dance. Debra Levine aptly said, "in general, a Jack Cole routine is hip, hard and cool."

Erskine Johnson reports on February 4th about Marilyn's aspirations to be a good actress. "Marilyn Monroe, the calendar girl, is all tuned up and 'ready' for a chance to shift her zippy gears and join Olivia, Claudette and Bette in the high-emoter league. That's the flash from her dramatic coach, Natasha Lytess, who has The Doll rehearsing scenes from *Wuthering Heights* and *Cradle Song* when she isn't wiggling her derriere as baby-talking Lorelei in *Gentlemen Prefer Blondes*. And it was Marilyn herself telling me, 'Really, I'm serious about acting. I don't want it to be *Gentlemen Prefer Blondes* for the next ten years.' But the box-office bells are ringing, the studio stockholders are beaming and Marilyn's leap into high dramatics, it's said, is about as remote as Mickey Rooney playing *Camille*."

On February 4th columnist Vernon Scott quotes photographer Frank Powolny as saying, "Marilyn Monroe has Hollywood's best figure rear view, and Jane Russell has the best full length profile. The graceful curves of Monroe's back, shoulders and thighs are the loveliest I've photographed." Powolny will also say of Marilyn, "She's a pleasure to photograph because she's so natural—and the next morning, when I see the proofs, it's another pleasure to see what registered on film. She has the kind of glamour that explodes right into the lens of a camera."

Marilyn wrote a check to Grace Goddard for the amount of $250.00 on February 4th.

Grace was handling the care of Marilyn's mother Gladys who was going into the Rockhaven Sanitarium in a few days.

On February 5th Marilyn selected a sailor to be "Mister Taconic." Troops of the USS Taconic sent Marilyn their pictures, asking her to select "Mister Taconic." She picked Robert L. Provost, of Northfield, Vt. Her criteria for choosing "Mister Taconic" was, who would she most like to be cast adrift with. Her choice was announced at a ship's dance. Marilyn sent Provost a photo of herself, inscribed, 'when do we get together?' She chose him because of his 'shyness and intelligence.' She sent regrets that she could only choose one man.

On February 6th Emily Belser carried a quote from Mamie Van Doren, a blonde bombshell in her own right, who was never quite able to wiggle out of Marilyn's shadow. "Rival Studios Priming Beauties To Compete With Marilyn Monroe....The only one of the contenders to comment on Marilyn was Mamie Van Doren. She had this to say, "Blonde, bombastic, and busty, Mamie has a word for Marilyn: 'Nothing! She has just nothing,' said Mamie in no uncertain terms. 'I will challenge her to a singing, dancing, wiggling, and what-have-you-contest any time she'll go for it and I'll win!'"

*The Toronto Star* newspaper article about the Hollywood Christian Group, February 6th, "Sirens On The Screen, Glamour Girls Quietly Religious After Work Hours...Marilyn Monroe, shapely siren, was recently introduced to the group. Miss Russell always arrives covered from head to toe in slacks and sweaters. At the last meeting she introduced Marilyn Monroe, her co-star in *Gentlemen Prefer Blondes* to the group." Others who attend the group are Terry Moore, June Haver, Roy Rogers and Dale Evans, Marie Wilson, Connie Haines and Colleen Townsend. Yet, to Jane's dismay, Marilyn didn't attend any more meetings after this first one. On July 20th, 1953 *Time* magazine featured this quote from Marilyn about the Bible Study. 'Jane, who is deeply religious, tried to convert me to her religion (she is actually nondenominational), and I tried to introduce her to Freud. Neither of us won.'"

Harrison Carroll reveals in his column the disappointing tensions between Betty Grable and Marilyn, as everyone is expecting fireworks between the two Fox beauties. "Hollywood has tried to stir up a battle for power between Betty and Marilyn to determine who will be queen of the Twentieth Century-Fox lot. I get Betty off to one side and do a little probing. 'Are you kidding?' she laughs. 'If I had been worried about somebody taking my place, would I have laid off pictures for practically a year? The whole thing is silly anyway. Why does there have to be a queen of the lot? When I came on the set the first day, nobody would introduce me to Marilyn so I came up and said hello. I think Marilyn handles herself wonderfully well.'"

On February 8th Marilyn makes arrangements to move her mother into Rockhaven Sanitarium in Verdugo City, CA. Gladys had been out of an institution for several years and having to have her mother recommitted weighed heavily on Marilyn. Grace Goddard once again came to the rescue. She would take on the responsibility to care for her friend and see to it that Gladys wanted for nothing. Marilyn never visited Gladys in Rockhaven and only called her one time. It was not from lack of concern, but a fear of the institution and an overwhelming fear for her own mental health. Marilyn would see that Gladys had everything she needed by her financial support during her lifetime and after she was dead.

Marilyn did not have the luxury to brood about her mother. She had to get glammed up and attend the *Photoplay* Gold Medal Awards Dinner the next night, February 9th, where she was awarded the Fastest Rising Star of 1952. The awards were held in the Crystal Room at the Beverly Hills Hotel. Perhaps it was a certain freedom she felt now that Gladys was safely tucked away in Rockhaven, or an acting out inspired by familiar feelings from the past when her mother was institutionalized the first time. Whatever had gotten into Marilyn, she would make this a night to remember, even by Hollywood standards. If they wanted a sex-queen, she would give them their due. No longer Norma Jeane, the orphan girl that nobody wanted. Tonight she was Marilyn Monroe, the most desired woman in the world.

Marilyn wore a gold lame' gown from the wardrobe of *Gentlemen Prefer Blondes* to the award dinner and lit the fuse to a legendary Hollywood feud. She was supposed to wear it in a song and dance number with Charles Coburn called, "Down Boy," but the number was cut from the film. A short clip survives in the movie of her in the gold gown dancing with Mr. Coburn. Shot from the back and doing the Rhumba, the gown gave the intended effect in that short viewing. Marilyn had to be sewn into the dress, as she wanted it to fit like a second skin, both for the movie and for the award dinner. The difference in how she wore the gown in publicity photos and how she wore it to the *Photoplay* Awards was in the daring décolleté. In the publicity photos, the bodice is open to her waist line. At the Awards show, the bodice was sewn up to her bust line. After looking at Marilyn in her gown, Joe DiMaggio refused to go with her dressed "like that," so Sidney Skolsky escorted her to the award dinner. Marilyn is photographed sitting next to producer William Goetz.

Billy Travilla recalls to Erskine Johnson about Marilyn and the gown she wore to the award dinner. "It was a Travilla gold lame gown into which Marilyn was sewn for her most provocative still photos and most memorable screen appearance. 'The gown', he said, 'was designed for a quick scene to accent Marilyn's hip wiggling. When she decided to wear the dress to a Hollywood banquet. I said to her, 'You're a little idiot. That dress can't be worn anywhere except in front of a camera. I won't allow it out of the studio. It was all part of her plan, however. She went over my head and got studio permission. We sewed her into the dress--there was no zipper--and well--when she walked around the tables into the banquet the roof practically caved in.'"

Travilla gives us a short history of dressing Monroe, and skintight is the phrase. "I argued with her about it many times, but she never gave in. When she wore them, she had a certain innocence that kept her from seeming vulgar. Many of those dresses were so tight she had to be sewn into them every morning. If she gained a pound or two, we couldn't sew her into them. There was a sunburst-pleated gold-lame gown that I had designed for *Gentlemen Prefer Blondes*. Since the material was not too solid, Marilyn had worn a flesh-colored slip under the dress in the film. Some months later, she decided to attend the

*Photoplay* Awards in that dress, but without the slip. Since she had put on a little weight, she had to have a high colonic before she could get into it. When she arrived that night, undulating her posterior, it was really a scandal."

Travilla will later recall Marilyn's reaction to the night's events, "So I told her, 'If you insist on wearing it, for heaven's sake, don't wear any jewelry with it. The dress is elaborate and glittering enough. Have your hair done as simply as Joan of Arc's. And, above all, watch the way you walk.' I reminded her that this dress had no zipper in it. She promised. And she did have a simple coiffure and she wore it without jewels. I was sure if she subdued her walk, if she were careful, everything might be alright. The next day she called me to come over to her dressing-room. She was crying hysterically. She said, 'I had my hair done the way you said. I didn't wear jewelry. But, Billy, when I had to step up to the stage with my back to the audience, there was a table in the way and I had to go around it. In squeezing round the corner of that table with my back to the audience, I had to sort of lean forward and rise on my toes, so my derriere stuck out in full view of everyone.' She sobbed that if she had just walked up, it would have been alright. But having to navigate the table undid all her dignity. Everyone saw the famous Monroe derriere trying to wriggle round that table. Marilyn was mortified."

Charles LeMaire has his own version of the story. "Marilyn's sexy publicity had brought on some blasts from women's clubs and her latest picture, as a result, was not doing well. The studio was worried. Then came this dinner. Darryl Zanuck, head of the studio, ordered me to dress Marilyn for the dinner. Even Joe DiMaggio, then her boyfriend, called me to make sure there would be no slip-ups. I designed a dress that was chic and in good taste. It looked sexy on her. That couldn't be helped because we once proved that even a burlap bag looked sexy on Marilyn's form. We ordered a special foundation garment that gave her nice lines. Then a mink stole was added. I coached her how to walk. I told her that when her name was called, she should keep the stole on until she reached the podium. There she could remove it and make a stunning appearance in receiving the award. She promised to follow my orders. When her name was called, she suddenly came through a door at the back of the hall, immediately threw off the mink stole and started that hip-shaking walk. It looked like two puppies fighting under a silk bedspread. Marilyn had shed the foundation garment. The next day she called me, 'Charlie, I'm sorry, but that foundation felt uncomfortable. I just couldn't wear it.'"

On February 12th, Marilyn replied to the trade paper *Variety* report yesterday that complaints from women and women's organizations were 'pouring in' to the studio, deploring the effect of the Monroe character in the film *Niagara* on children, husbands and sweethearts. "Marilyn Monroe has an answer to criticism of her realistic movie role as a brazen babe: 'I just did the best I could. The part called for a tramp. I couldn't play it like an ingénue.' Her studio, 20th Century-Fox said there have been complaints, 'but not any unusual number and absolutely none from organizations.' Miss Monroe recalled criticism for another role in which she played a psychopathic baby-sitter. 'People said then I couldn't act--that I was really crazy,' she said. 'I know myself. I'm not crazy and I'm not a tramp.'"

Marilyn also told the *INS*, "I never intentionally have offended the public taste, and I haven't seen or read any letters criticizing my performance in *Niagara*. I was playing a role in this picture. It seems to me the only legitimate comment must be confined to how well or how badly I played it."

Armand Archerd reported on February 13th, "The Power Behind Marilyn Monroe...Today I'm going to let you in on a secret. Marilyn Monroe has a dramatic coach! 'Who needs it?' you ask. Apparently her studio and Marilyn agree she does. After all, they claim, how much pure unadulterated sex can you sell without backing it up with ability? And they know Marilyn has a tremendous box office potential if she can act just a wee bit. Just as Marilyn had gone all out, so has the studio in getting her the best professional advice. Marilyn's mentor is Natasha Lytess, a prematurely gray, 34-year-old actress, director and coach. Natasha, a slight, but tremendously dynamic Russian-born, German-educated woman, now the power behind the throne is everything that Marilyn does in front of the cameras. She is strict, persistent and patient with her young pupil. Lytess, who worked with the Max Reinhardt group for many years, is no newcomer to teaching beautiful girls how to say 'yes,' 'no,' and other more difficult lines....Marilyn and she are inseparable. They study every free moment between scenes and at night, too. 'They call me a Svengali,' Miss L. frankly told us, 'but I don't care. I want to do the best job I can, and Marilyn is very loyal and anxious to do a good job, too.' We asked if Marilyn had any acting ability. And then she took off. 'She is not a natural actress,' said Natasha. 'She has to learn to have a free voice and a free body to act. She must learn to act with her eyes. If her eyes don't say the words then her body and voice will say nothing, too.' (I interrupt to point out this is all a system of 'Natural Acting' which Miss Lytess was explaining). 'Marilyn could go on by herself without any help, but she wants to learn, which is good. Every young actor needs direction and guidance. She needs to build confidence. A great actor understands life. She is, of course, very young to understand it yet. Her life has not been happy up to now, anyhow. And don't tell me that her experience will help make a good actress out of her. The more pictures Marilyn does doesn't mean the experience will be good,' Miss L. continued. 'Experience in films can be fatal to an actor. They can stagnate in the habitual ways they keep in picture after picture. They have to become natural instead of habitual.' (I interrupt to point out again this is all a system of 'Natural Acting' which Miss Lytess is explaining). 'A young actor has ropes around him which must be untied so he (or she) can learn how to act. When they finally give a performance with their mouths completely covered, then they are great actors. When you hear someone say, 'they were great, they weren't acting at all, they were natural'--that's a lot of poppy-cock. A good actor has learned to act so well that everything he does and says sounds 'natural.' Luckily Marilyn has a wonderful instinct for the right timing. I think she will eventually be a good actress.' Yeah, she looks like a natural to me."

Andre de Dienes has an article in *Parade* magazine on February 15th, "I Like These Best...For two decades Hollywood's Andre de Dienes has shot pictures of beautiful women. The result is more than 50,000 photographs, and many happy memories. Which pictures are best? At *Parade's* request, Dienes recently searched his files, found these winners. Which do you like best?" A photo of Marilyn from 1946 accompanied the article. She has her brown curly hair, wears a pinafore and is holding a lamb. "Who is she? You'll be lucky to guess this is film star Marilyn Monroe taken in 1946. He helped 'discover' her." Once again de Dienes slights Marilyn by choosing this early photo of her as one of his all-time favorites instead of one of the many beauty shots he had taken of her. He is making a point to her and is using *Parade* magazine to do it. It is quite possible that he had wanted another sitting with her since she had exploded onto the scene and she ignored him. They would never have that or any other sitting. Richard C. Miller, Gene Lester and to a lesser extent, Bruno Bernard would be the only ones of her early modeling photographers that would work with her again as she became famous. Lester was on the set of *No Business Like Show Business* and in 1956 photographed her for the *Saturday Evening Post*. Bernard photographed her at the Five Disc Jockey Charity Show for St. Jude's in July of 1953. Miller was on the set of *Some Like it Hot* and *Let's Make Love* as a stills photographer. Even with them she kept her distance. Marilyn was not one for looking back. From now on she would primarily work with up and coming, hot photographers, such as Milton H. Greene and Richard Avedon. Bernard and especially Andre de Dienes felt the sting of being dismissed by her. Bernard would participate in an interview about her in 1961 that was bitter and acerbic. And de Dienes will try for that sitting with her well into 1962. He will try and court her favors with notes and telephone calls, but to no avail. He will eventually write her a bitter letter and air his grievances to her. Her silence was deafening.

After her death he will be interviewed about his relationship with Marilyn. He will state, "I put her face on magazine covers. I made her famous. I loved her. I was going to marry her. And she never mentioned me—not in 15 years. It was the only fact of her life that she didn't throw out to the press. And I've never mentioned it to anyone before. But I have ego, too. That's why I'm willing to talk my heart out now." De Dienes goes on, "Don't think she didn't like to be talked about. She had an ego like crazy. She used to come here and cook breakfast, wash dishes, just like a little housewife. But never in her interviews with the press has she every mentioned me. She used to say, 'Andre I wonder what my life would have been like if I hadn't met you?' Was she in love with me? Of course she was in love with me. I loved her. When you're young you're idealistic. But I should have seen that a girl who wants to be a model is out, as a wife."

Yet, one can only imagine the beautiful photos he would have produced of the mature Marilyn. In July of 1953 he tries to recreate the magic of his early sittings with Marilyn with another girl. He takes the model to the beach, poses her with sheep in a bucolic setting and finally takes her to the San Juan Capistrano Mission, all places her had photographed Marilyn. But without his muse the photos are nothing special and carry none of the magic of his photographs of his beloved Marilyn. If he was trying to make her jealous, he failed miserably. In November he will try another tactic when he pens an article in *Modern Man* magazine about discovering the young beauty. Still silence from her. He will content himself with creating montages of her early photos and will become so angry at her that he buries the negatives in his backyard. Oh, l'amour is a double edged sword.

Emily Belser reported on February 16th, "Marilyn Monroe, confined to her bed with a fourth attack of flu in six weeks, lashed out feebly today in defense of her portrayal of a 'lewd' woman in the film *Niagara*. Protests against the actress' interpretation of the role had been pouring in to the star's studio--20th Century-Fox from throughout the nation. 'I never intentionally have offended the public taste,' insisted Marilyn, 'and I haven't seen or read any letters criticizing my performance in *Niagara*. I was playing a role in this picture and it seems to me the only legitimate comment must be confined to how well or how badly I played it...'"

Marilyn wrote a check to Mrs. Mertz in the amount of $400.00 on February 18th. Mrs. Mertz was the landlady at Marilyn's apartment on Doheny Drive, Apt. 3, 882 N. Doheny Drive, Los Angeles--H6--California. Her phone number was listed as CR6-2211, ext. 234.

In an inter-office memo to the staff on February 20th, Charles Feldman, head of the Famous Artists Agency, declares that Marilyn Monroe has to have Natasha Lytess present on her pictures. Natasha will go on to say in her peculiar brand of hyperbole that, "Marilyn needs her like a dead man needs a coffin."

*Look* magazine announced the winners of its 12th Annual Motion Picture Achievement Awards on February 22nd. Gold plaques are to be presented to the winners by *Look* editor Gardner Cowles. The awards will be later in the week. Marilyn was selected as the Most Promising Newcomer, along with Fernando Lamas from MGM.

Marilyn wrote a check to the Embassy for $98.54, listing her phone as CR 62211.

On February 24th Marilyn makes an appearance on the *Martin and Lewis Radio Show*. She participates in a skit and receives her *Redbook* Silver Cup award from editor, Wade Nichols. Nichols, who forgave Marilyn for saying that her mother was dead in *Redbook's* June 1952 article by Jim Henaghan, has become one of her biggest supporters. Marilyn was awarded a two handled sterling silver loving cup. This also begins a lifelong friendship with Dean Martin and Jerry Lewis.

Sidney Skolsky tells of the evening of the radio show. "I recall a Martin and Lewis radio program on which Marilyn was the guest star. She was extremely nervous before the show. Jerry Lewis visited her dressing-room and said, 'I know you're scared. Don't be. I was awfully nervous when I went on the radio for the first time, with Bob Hope.' He pressed her hand. 'You'll be great,' he said, and left the room.' This brief talk and vote of confidence from Lewis helped Marilyn considerably. She has loved Jerry Lewis ever since. Marilyn was great on the program. After it, Jerry said to me, 'She's got nothing to worry about. She knows more about sex than I do about comedy.' Which is about the highest compliment a comedian could bestow on an actress who is selling glamour."

A few days later a party was held for the *Redbook* Awards. Jim Henaghan tells of Marilyn at this party. "A small stage was set up at one end of the room and a well-known comedian made a short speech, telling to whom the awards had been given. Dean Martin and Jerry Lewis were mentioned and immediately bounded to the stage. The next name mentioned was Marilyn Monroe. The lads called for her to join them, but no one could see her in the room. Finally, she appeared at the edge of the stage and swaggered into the spotlight as easily as Ethel Barrymore taking a curtain call. She didn't say much, but she was an impressive sight, and as poised as a traffic cop. Now let's go back to the time her name was first mentioned. She was seated in a corner of the room with a table of friends. As soon as she heard her name, she flew into a panic. She turned pale. 'They didn't tell me I would have to get up,' she gasped. 'I can't do it.' A tug-of-war began, with a couple of her friends and a 20$^{th}$ Century-Fox publicity man trying to drag her out of her chair. The trio finally got her on her feet. They then got behind her and began to push—literally—and with Marilyn holding on to everything in sight they shoved her through the darkened room to the edge of the stage. She knew then she was whipped, so she assumed the position of Marilyn Monroe, movie star, and carried it off like it was a pleasure. The moment she left the stage, however, Marilyn dashed for the door and ran almost in tears to her car and went home."

Sheilah Graham reported on the *Redbook* Awards party and Marilyn's behavior. "Why, she practically fainted at a banquet when she was called to the platform to receive an award. The studio man with her had—literally—to pinch her in the side to get her up on her feet. Her swaying wriggle came perilously close to a stumble before she managed to stagger to the microphone."

When Marilyn finally made it up to the microphone at the *Redbook* Awards party, she relied on Martin and Lewis to get her through. "'But I can't do anything,' she sighed. He leered at her, 'Just breathe, honey,' he begged. 'Breathe good and heavy.'"

Photographs taken of Marilyn at the *Redbook* Awards party show her looking elegant in an all-black ensemble, including a fur stole, gloves and a scoop-neck dress with draped bodice and a satin poof on one side of her skirt. Marilyn is shown dancing the rhumba with Judge Harlan G. Palmer, publisher of the *Citizen News*, Hollywood.

On February 28th the Harvard University's humor magazine, *The Lampoon*, selected Marilyn as the Worst Actress of the Year. She replied, "I'm so glad those boys see my pictures. I'm happy indeed to share this honor with talented Jerry Lewis and so many famous predecessors like Elizabeth Taylor and Shirley Temple."

*Photoplay*, March 1953, carried a lengthy article by James Dougherty, "Marilyn Monroe Was My Wife." It seems Adele Whitley-Fletcher was no longer an editor at the magazine. Had she been there, and considering her relationship with Marilyn, this article might never have been run. Marilyn had always refused to say much about her marriage to Jim Dougherty to the press. She didn't want his current family to be harmed. Between his sister's article which came out in December of 1952 and now Jim's account being released, it seems Marilyn's loyalty was not reciprocated.

*Photoplay* magazine, March 1953, British edition, article, "Please Try To Understand Me!" by Hedda Hopper. Marilyn responds to Hedda's questions about her early life and the break that landed her an acting career.

Hedda: There's been a lot of tales about your name. Why did you call yourself Norma Jeane Baker?

Marilyn: When I was a tiny tot, I was told that was my name. I did not choose it. So far as I knew, I was Norma Jeane Baker, and I never heard anything to the contrary until I was in my teens. You see, my mother was married to a Mr. Baker, but he was not my father.
Hedda: What about your own father?
Marilyn: All I know is that he was killed in a motorcycle accident before I was born. My mother has not told me anything else about him.
Hedda: You've been accused, I believe, of telling untruths about your mother. Some of the stories say that you gave out information that she was dead.
Marilyn: People jumped to conclusions. I told them I became a charge of the State of California and the County of Los Angeles because my mother was incurably ill and could no longer take care of me. They assumed when I said 'incurable' that she had subsequently died. But they did not ask me, 'Is she dead?'
Hedda: Is it true that your ex-husband, James Dougherty is now a police officer in Los Angeles and that he discusses you and his marriage to you very little?
Marilyn: Yes that is true. He seldom discusses me, because his wife prefers that he shouldn't. He has children now, and perhaps they would like the children to think he hasn't been married before--it could be something of that sort.
Hedda: The story that's told, Marilyn, is that you married without love. Is that so?
Marilyn: It's so hard to define reasons for something as emotional as marriage--especially if you're as young as I was. But I suppose you could say that having a home of my own had something to do with it. But there were other considerations--just being in love with love, or sex, or whatever you want to call it. We both realized soon that it wasn't going to be a success.
Hedda: It is true that you lived near Culver City when you were married?
Marilyn: I never lived near Culver City, though the story's been printed again and again. I lived in Van Nuys, California. And it was there that I worked for the defense plant.
Hedda: Did you have a movie career in mind at that time? Were you studying drama?
Marilyn: I never thought about a career when I was working in the plant. In fact, I never did anything about it at all until after my divorce. In some article recently, it said that I started studying with Phil Moore during the defense plant days. But that's not so. I first started to take lessons from him about a year and a half ago.
Hedda: But you had some sort of movie break hadn't you, when you were in the defense plant?
Marilyn: Some Army public relations man used me in films of a defense plant in action, and those films were the basis for my getting started with the studio. It was these films and nothing else.
Marilyn tells Hedda of her philosophy of handling rude interviewers:
Marilyn: One woman asked me how long I thought a whale could remain submerged before it would die. Since I hadn't the faintest idea, and any guess I might make would look ridiculous in print, I asked her why she wanted me to answer such a strange question. 'It's a kind of intelligence test,' she said. I wondered whose intelligence was at stake--hers

or mine. But I learned long ago that you have to take the good with the bad. And it doesn't pay to lose your temper when untruths are printed. Sooner or later, the truth always comes out.

On March 2nd Bob Thomas starts one of the most infamous feuds in Hollywood. "Marilyn Monroe Too Sexy Joan Crawford Declares,...Joan Crawford today aimed this curt message to Marilyn Monroe: stop believing your publicity. The curvaceous blonde has been the subject of hot controversy during the past fortnight. Women's clubs have protested about the nature of her publicity and the advertising photos for her pictures. When I addressed the Women's Club of Hollywood a week ago, the members were eager to know what the producers were doing to curb Miss Monroe. Adding fuel to the fire were reports that her latest picture, the first with which she could demonstrate public box office pull, was doing disappointing business. Then there was her much-publicized appearance at the *Photoplay* awards dinner. Miss Monroe showed up in a zipperless metallic gown into which she had to be sewn. When she stepped up to get her award as the outstanding new personality on the screen, she put on a hip-swinging display that brought the house down. 'It was like a burlesque show,' said the horrified Miss Crawford, who was present at the affair. 'The audience yelled and shouted, and Jerry Lewis got up on the table and whistled. But those of us in the industry just shuddered. Certainly her picture isn't doing business, and I'll tell you why. Sex plays a tremendously important part in every person's life. People are interested with it, intrigued with it. But they don't like to see it flaunted in their faces. Kids don't like her. Sex plays a growingly important part in their lives, too, and they don't like to see it exploited. And don't forget the women. They're the ones who pick out the movie entertainment for the family. They won't pick anything that won't be suitable for their husbands and children.' The durable Miss Crawford, who has lasted longer than any film star in history, said the Monroe buildup was clever and well planned. It was the work of master exploiters, she remarked, but it got out of hand. 'The publicity has gone too far,' she said. 'And apparently Miss Monroe is making the mistake of believing her publicity. Someone should make her see the light. She should be told that the public likes provocative feminine personalities; but it also likes to know that underneath it all the actresses are ladies.' Discussing other glamour buildups, she remarked that Jane Russell had managed herself well. 'Howard Hughes tried to make her out a sexy dish at first,' she said, 'but Jane managed to keep her feet on the ground. Then there was Jean Harlow, who was first painted as a platinum blond vamp. When the novelty wore off, she turned redhead and become a successful comedienne. Apparently 20th-Fox has the same thing in mind for Monroe. Although she wants to be a dramatic actress, the studio is grooming her for comedies like *Gentlemen Prefer Blondes*.' Miss Crawford, who is up for her second Oscar with *Sudden Fear* added, 'I think she'd better become a comedienne--or something.' I think Miss Monroe also believes it's time for a change. Her performance at last week's *Redbook* dinner was far different from the *Photoplay* event. Again chosen as the outstanding young personality, she showed up in a conservative (for her) black cocktail dress. When Martin and Lewis urged her to come up to the microphone, she declined until three of her advisors urged her to do so. Then she walked quietly up and expressed her thanks in a small, frightened voice."

Marilyn attends the Premiere of *Call Me Madame* at the Fox Ritz Theater on March 4th. She wore a white version of the "Diamonds" gown from *Gentlemen Prefer Blondes*, also created by Billy Travilla. *Call Me Madame* was written by Irving Berlin, and starring Ethel Merman, Donald O'Conner and Mitzi Gayner. Irving Berlin based the musical on the life of Perle Mesta. She was a famous socialite, a fund raiser for the Democratic party, a renowned hostess known as "the hostess with the mostest," and President Truman appointed her as Minister to Luxemburg. Perle took Marilyn under her wing during her "New York" period. Together they helped raise money for the benefit performance of *Baby Doll* for the Actors Studio, December 18, 1956. Many people confuse photos of Marilyn at the premiere of *Call Me Madam* with the premiere of *There's No Business Like Show Business*, on December 9, 1954, which Marilyn did not attend. The main reason for this is that Marilyn is photographed with Donald O'Conner, who appeared in both movies. Newsreel footage shows Marilyn being interviewed by Ken Murray. This was considered her television debut.

On March 5th Marilyn attends a reception for columnist Sheilah Graham and her new husband, Wojciechowcz S. Wojtkiewicz at their home in Beverly Hills. Sheilah Graham wrote in her column on March 28, 1953 about the event, "...Marilyn Monroe wore the same black, fairly covered-up dress in which she accepted the *Redbook* Award. Don't know where Joe DiMaggio was, but her escort was columnist, Sid Skolsky, who went to the studio where Marilyn was finishing *Diamonds Are a Girl's Best Friend* number in *Gents Prefer Blondes*, and waited patiently for an hour for the girl who is always late, only this time she really couldn't help it. The day before, Joan Crawford had given an interview panning Marilyn for her over display of sex. Joan, in a bright red dress, was with her new director, Nick Ray, and a collision with Monroe might have been awkward--if Marilyn had got there earlier. Fortunately, Joan had a dinner date, and left before Marilyn arrived." Marilyn had dated director Nick Ray the year before.

Jimmie Fidler reports on the 5th, "Marilyn Monroe's friends are advising her to consult a neurosurgeon to determine the cause of recurring migraine headaches. Production on Miss Monroe's new picture has been held up three different times because of the headaches. Even when she has been able to work the pain has been severe."

In interesting article appears on March 8th by Harold Heffernan. "Ear Makeup for Film Stars Includes Interior Paint Job....Miss Bunny Gardel, one of several technicians handling 'body' makeup at Twentieth Century-Fox, has become an important person around the lot. Bunny has the job of seeing that Marilyn Monroe—from the ears down, that is—looks photogenic in her many scantily-clad scenes. She knows secrets, Bunny does. She is authority for the information that Miss Monroe has matching beauty moles on either side of her thorax. 'They are so strategically placed as to be diverting,' she says. 'So we paint out the one on the left.' The actress bruises easily, too. 'Her skin is milky and thin,' Bunny said. An actor grabbing her by the arms in a scene can leave blue marks. Recently she was black and blue all around her waist after hanging in a ship's porthole all day for scenes in the picture. She's ticklish in the ears, too. I use water pancake on a small brush to paint inside the ears and very few actresses like it. We do the ears and everything from the Adam's apple down.' For 12 years Bunny has gilded some of Hollywood's most gorgeous lilies, including Betty Grable, Susan Hayward, Jeanne Crain, June Haver, Jean Peters, Gene Tierney and Lauren Bacall." Miss Gardel would work for Marilyn for the rest of her film career. She became one of Marilyn's inner-circle of people that she could not do a film without.

On March 12th Marilyn is officially represented by Famous Artists. Charles Feldman was the head and her career is now being managed by Hugh French. Marilyn had been represented by the William Morris Agency since December 5, 1950. It was through the William Morris Agency that Johnny Hyde had been able to negotiate a 6 month contract on behalf of Marilyn with Twentieth Century-Fox in May of 1950. After his death the William Morris Agency renegotiated a standard 7 year contract with Twentieth Century-Fox. Her contract would have five more years to go. She tried in vain to persuade the William Morris Agency to get her out of this contract with Twentieth Century-Fox. Her dissatisfaction with her studio contract wasn't just over money, she wanted more control of her career. The William Morris Agency said simply, "it couldn't be done." Marilyn left the William Morris Agency and was without representation for a short time. She was wined and dined by several other agencies before deciding to sign with the Famous Artists Agency. Although, Famous Artists had no more luck that the William Morris Agency in getting Twentieth to release her from her contract, they did a better job of representing her, so she was satisfied with them. At least until September, when photographer Milton Greene began whispering notions of freedom and New York in her ear.

Walter Winchell writes a rebuttal to Joan Crawford on March 13th, "Showfolks flabbergasted over Joan Crawford's blast at Marilyn Monroe for being 'too sexy'...Ohjoannowlookahere! Don't you remember only 20 years ago when you shook your torso even moreso when you were Marilyn's age?"

In his column on March 14th, in the African American newspaper, *The Chicago Defender*, poet and writer Langston Hughes list, "Some Wonderful Women I Would Like to Know Better Include--." The last woman on his extensive list is Marilyn.

On March 16th by Aline Mosby has Betty Grable defending Marilyn in her column, "Betty Grable Rips 'Jealous' Critics of Marilyn Monroe...Everybody's picking on Marilyn Monroe, an indignant, Betty Grable complained today, and she thinks they're 'just jealous.' Miss Monroe, who bounced to movie fame via her publicity on her undressed calendar, has been the target for today in a local sniping campaign. Actress Penny Edwards sniffed that Marilyn wore falsies; the *Harvard Lampoon* said she can't act; and a London beauty expert said she'll wind up fat. The final blow was flipped by Joan Crawford, publicized as a hot number in the 30's, who suddenly decided Marilyn's publicity was too sexy. 'Everybody wants to help you on the way up, but the minute you get to the top, they hammer away at you,' bristled Miss Grable, the defender. 'Why, Marilyn's the biggest thing that's happened to Hollywood in years. The movies were just sort of going along, and all of a sudden, zowie, there was Marilyn. She's a shot in the arm for Hollywood.' The two famous blondes had not met until they wound up starring in the same picture, *How to Marry a Millionaire*, along with Lauren Bacall. Miss Grable, as observers of the success ladder in Hollywood know, is the queen bee of the 20th Century-Fox lot while Miss Monroe, it could be said, is a lady-in-waiting. But blue-eyed Betty isn't perturbed by the vision of a possible successor to her throne. She has the poise and assurance of a long-time ruler who'd just as soon go to the races as act, anyway. 'I'm not envious of Marilyn,' smiled La Grable. 'There's room for us all. I'd never met her before. Everybody figures actresses all know each other, so we'd never been introduced. I went over to her on the set today to say hello. She seemed surprised I'd do that. I like Marilyn. She's a nice girl. It's not fair the way people criticize her. It's like fans at the race track booing a winning horse owner.' Marilyn and Betty are now the best of friends and next thing you know they'll be sharing the same eyeshadow pot..."

Emily Belser keeps the fire burning of Marilyn's feud with Joan Crawford on March 18th, "Marilyn Monroe Sulks As Publicity Buildup Backfires...But from gorgeous Miss Crawford came the unkindest scratch of all. After viewing the blowtorch blonde's hip-swinging display at the *Photoplay* Awards Dinner, Miss Crawford commented, 'The audience yelled and shouted, and Jerry Lewis got up on a table and shouted. But those of us in the industry just shuddered. It reminded me of a burlesque show.' There were a few persons, Miss Monroe not among them, who were quick to point out that Miss Crawford started up the Hollywood ladder on hip-swinging Charleston and black-bottom renditions. But there is no getting around the fact that $20^{th}$ Century-Fox, Marilyn's home studio, is not too happy over the lukewarm reception of the new Monroe film *Niagara*. A studio spokesman said that the picture 'is carrying its weight' but is 'not breaking any records.' Perhaps the cruelest blow of all to Marilyn in a week of rather cruel blows was that tossed at her by British beauty expert, Joseph Bloom, who made unflattering comments about her figure. Said he, 'Miss Monroe is a lovely girl, I'm sure, but her body makes me shudder--especially those heavy knees.'"

Sheilah Graham has come to like Marilyn and plants this positive tid bit in her column, "Marilyn Monroe carries around a thick black book titled, *Prayer Changes Things*." This book by Dana Gatlin was one of the many books in Marilyn's personal library that was sold in 1999 at the famous Christie's Auction of Marilyn's personal property.

On March 23rd Hedda Hopper reported on Marilyn's reaction to columnist Bob Thomas, "The reporter who wrote the story in which Joan Crawford did in Marilyn Monroe, called to ask Marilyn to ask what she had to say about the yarn, 'No comment,' said the Monroe girl. Later the reporter met Marilyn at 20th and said, 'I had to write that story, but I still want to talk to you.' 'Fine,' replied Marilyn. 'All I've got to say is: No Comment.' Then she blithely disappeared from the scene."

In an attempt to counteract the damage done to her image by Joan Crawford, Marilyn wrote a letter to columnist Dorothy Kilgallen, which was run on March 26th, in which she tried to explain that the different roles she had done were acting and it didn't reflect her true self. In her explanations you can see how she has developed as an actress and in her ability to view the different roles she plays in context of their place in the movie. She has gained great knowledge from the professional acting coaches she has surrounded herself with and Michael Chekhov in particular. "Dot Doesn't Mind Now How Marilyn Walks...By far the most interesting communiqué aimed in the direction of this desk during the past few days was a letter from the Bernhardt of the pin-ups, Miss Marilyn Monroe. I can't think of anything short of a personal note from Malenkov that I would have been more delighted to receive from the standpoint of newsworthiness; and getting around to the matter of sheer fun, I think Marilyn has it all over Georgi, plus the fact that with her, no translation is required! I value Marilyn's epistle--handwritten in pale blue ink on white bond paper--chiefly because it is so soul-searching. It is a rare example of a motion picture star's evaluation of herself as an actress, and a lucid explanation of her approach to her art. Besides, it proves she can spell a lot of words Joe DiMaggio doesn't even know how to pronounce. Marilyn opens her letter by referring to a recent column in which I printed--and answered--the criticism aimed at the Monroe performance in *Niagara* by a lady named M.A. Clark of Corona, L.I. Marilyn writes, 'This letter especially interest me because it is from an honest and literate person whose opinion is worthwhile. I have much to learn as an actress and it is certain that a screen portrayal is only as good as the acceptance by the people who pay to see it. I should like to discuss briefly the *Niagara* portrayal as distinguished from characterizations I have given in other pictures. In particular, I should like to refer to the 'silly walk' which has been the subject of some controversy. In *Asphalt Jungle* I played a vacuous rich man's darling attempting to carry herself in a sophisticated manner in keeping with her plush surroundings. I saw her as walking with a self-conscious slither and played it accordingly. In *Don't Bother to Knock*, I was an emotionally unstable, unfortunate girl driven to attempted homicide by fear. I believe those who saw the picture will agree that whatever the merits of my performance dramatically, there wasn't a hip-wiggle in evidence. In *All About Eve* I was an untalented show girl walking with deliberate exactness. In *Monkey Business*, a light comedy, I played a slightly dumb secretary who couldn't type. Again the portrayal--and the hips--were played down except for one scene that figured in the dialogue. Now as to *Niagara.* The girl I played in that was an amoral type whose plot to kill her husband was attempted with no apparent cost to her conscience. She had been picked out of a beer parlor, she entirely lacked the social graces and she was over-dressed, over made-up and completely wanton. The uninhibited deportment in the motel room and the walk seemed normal facets of such a character's portrayal. I honestly believe such a girl would behave in that manner. In *Gentlemen Prefer Blondes*, my current film, I play the Lorelei Lee role. Her preoccupation with diamonds is a harmless enough interest, in the sense comparable with the murderous cunning of the *Niagara* girl. Consequently, I am playing it from an entirely different point of view than *Niagara*. I am well aware of the audience response to *Niagara* and I'm afraid since people associate the girl on the screen with myself as a person. Please believe that I try to deport myself with reasonable decorum in private life, that I am not given to murdering people off screen, and that when I work on a sound stage I am trying my best to play the role assigned me in a manner called for by the script and the director. Besides, I'd like to see any woman--playing a murderous floozy--walk a block in spiked heels on a cobblestone road with the camera trained on her derriere, and not look wobbly to at least part of the audience. Thanks Miss Kilgallen for giving me the benefit of the doubt. Sincerely yours, Marilyn Monroe.' I invite all students of etymology as it applies to the calendar girl to study the above carefully. Regard, if you will, the phraseology. Note the apt usage of such words as 'vacuous,' 'amoral,' 'uninhibited,' and 'facets.' Dig the way she tosses around 'preoccupation' and 'decorum.' There is even a French word in the letter, and nobody has a better right to use it than Marilyn. Personally, I'm with her and I'm convinced. And if at any time in the future she wiggles, wriggles, slithers, slides or slinks across my neighborhood movie screen, I am prepared to regard it as sheer, unadulterated, undiluted Art. Anybody who thinks otherwise is just picking on her."

On March 27th columnist Bob Thomas writes about the hot water he got himself into when he wrote about Joan Crawford's diatribe on Marilyn. "Marilyn, Adhering Too Closely To Publicity, Resents Criticism...The Joan Crawford-Marilyn Monroe controversy still rages. Going on eight years, I have been working the Hollywood vineyards. No story I have ever written has evoked as much fuss as the one in which Crawford lambasted Monroe for allegedly believing her sexy publicity. So perhaps we'd better review how it all happened and what has happened since. The story was no press agent's plant. Crawford's press agent would probably have shushed her up if he had gotten the opportunity. I was lunching with Miss Crawford, and we were discussing her new TV venture, Academy Awards and other topics. Nothing exciting had evolved, so I tossed Monroe at her. That did it. The Monroe thing had been brewing for a couple of weeks. Her picture had failed to do the business expected of it, and women's clubs were beginning to protest about her sexy advertising and publicity. The climax came at the *Photoplay* dinner. Monroe showed up in one of her traffic-stopping movie gowns. When she went up to get her award, she put on a hip-waving exhibition that brought the house down. Many of the onlookers were amused; Crawford wasn't. Hence the blast. Since the *AP* always gives the opportunity for both sides of a controversy to be heard, Monroe had a chance to answer Crawford's statements before they appeared in print. She declined. When the story appeared, things started popping. Some columnists came to Monroe's defense. Most of the commentators pointed out that Crawford had a pretty racy buildup when she was a starlet in the flapper days. (But isn't that all the more reason why she should be qualified to comment?) At least two columnists recorded a breathless moment--when Crawford and Monroe almost met at a party. This week Mike Connolly of *Hollywood Reporter* said, 'somebody' important at 20th-Fox wrote Crawford: 'Don't apologize to Marilyn. Your advice was good for her.' That seems to be the consensus. Her bosses at 20th-Fox were concerned about overdoing the sexy buildup and tried to persuade Monroe to tone it down. She couldn't see it that way, since the routine had made a star out of her. But now she has become much more conservative. Monroe got a lot of sympathy from the story and a new outlook on her publicity. Crawford got plenty of news space with no damage to her reputation. The only one who may have suffered was me; I'm not sure how I stand with the two girls. I met Crawford at the Academy Awards. Or rather she hailed me out of the crowd. 'Lord, the trouble you got me into,' she exclaimed. She said she had received tremendous mail, not all of it complimentary. But she admitted the story could have been worse. Then she dashed off. Monroe was equally vague. When I saw her on a movie set, I asked her how she felt about the whole business. 'No comment,' she replied. I said I hoped she wasn't mad at me. 'No comment,' she added with a Mona Lisa-like smile. So here I am, possibly on the outs with a couple of glamour gals. Oh well, it was fun while it lasted. And Marjorie Main still loves me."

*Look* magazine article, March 30th, on the *Look* Annual Movie Awards, featuring a full page of Marilyn, who was named Newcomer of the Year.

Marilyn had this to say of her appearance in theaters via her old movies. "When Columbia pictures reissued *Ladies of the Chorus*, a small budget quickie made in 1949 with Marilyn third from the left, she was in the mood to picket the theater that played it. The No. 1 Body snapped, 'I think it's terribly unfair. It was the first time I ever was in anything. That picture was shot in nine days. Why don't they be fair and add a line to the opening credits, 'This girl was dropped FLAT by this studio just after she made this picture!'"

On April 4th Marilyn participated in an Easter Parade Fashion Show at the annual Easter brunch at the Beverly-Wilshire Hotel. Marilyn described her outfit as, "I am a symphony in silver gray'...She selected a silver-gray silk faille slim dress with an Ascot of silver blue mink. The dress was topped by a full-length matching coat with push-up sleeves. The coat was collarless so the mink on the dress would show." Barbara Stanwyck, Loretta Young, Mitzi Gaynor and Jeanne Crain were some of the other celebrity participants.

Also on the 4th, Alvin Chuck Webbt in his column, Footlights and Sidelights, for the African American newspaper *The New York Amsterdam*, give Marilyn this compliment. "For Males Only—Sexiest screen siren to hit the celluloids in years is Marilyn Monroe…some critics, mostly women, claim that M.M. is not actress, that she's got only a beautiful body 'going for her'…but who cares if she can't act, all the has to do is WALK!"

Marilyn went with Nico Minardes to observe an Easter Service at a Greek Orthodox church on April 5th. She was infatuated with the goings on and insisted on staying for the full service.

Harrison Carroll reported on April 9th that "a kiddies cut out book of Marilyn Monroe will soon be on the market." *The Marilyn Monroe Paper Doll* book was soon published by Saalfield Publishing Co., Akron, Ohio. It contained two paper dolls of Marilyn, each printed on heavy cardboard. The book came with six pages of clothing for Marilyn to wear.

Wardrobe Tests for *How to Marry a Millionaire* were made on April 9th. The screenplay was written by producer Nunnally Johnson and was based on the play by Zoe Akins, *The Greeks Had a Word For It*. Johnson had this to say of Marilyn in *Millionaire*, "I believe that the first time anybody genuinely liked Marilyn for herself was in *How to Marry a Millionaire*. She herself diagnosed the reason for that very shrewdly, I think. She said that this was the only picture she'd been in in which she had a measure of modesty. Not physical modesty, but modesty about her own attractiveness. In *Millionaire* she was nearsighted; she didn't think men would look twice, because she wore glasses; she blundered into walls and stumbled into things and she was most disarming. In the course of the plot she married an astigmatic; so there they were, a couple of astigmatic lovers. In her other pictures they've cast her as a somewhat arrogant sex trap, but when *Millionaire* was released, I heard people say, 'Why, I really liked her!' in surprised tones.'" As for working with Marilyn, Johnson had this to say, "When I talked to her when she first came on the lot, I felt as if I were talking to a girl under water. I couldn't tell whether I was getting through to her or not. She lived behind a fuzz curtain." He would later make this bitter remark to Maurice Zolotow, "I cannot stand this woman and she'll never be in another picture I produce. She cannot learn her lines. She either fluffs or freezes on the first four takes. You can't get an idea across to her. Talking to her is like talking to somebody underwater. You stick a pin in a sloth's belly and eight days later he will say, 'Ouch!' She lives behind a fuzz curtain. You can have her….I used to by sympathetic with actresses and their problems. Marilyn made me lose all sympathy for actresses…I don't think she can act her way out of a paper script. She's got no charm, delicacy or taste. Nobody will ever call her America's Sweetheart. She's just an arrogant little tailswitcher. She's learned how to throw sex in your face…No matter how many times you've been introduced or how often you've been with her, you're never sure she knows who you are. She walks right by you with those glassy eyes, like she's in some hypnotic trance…Marilyn's a phenomenon of nature, like Niagara Falls or the Grand Canyon. You can't talk to it. It can't talk to you. All you can do is stand back and be awed by it."

    The years seem to have softened Johnson and he will write in the fly leaf of Edwin Hoyt's biography of Marilyn, "I knew one Marilyn who was a blinding headache. I knew another who was an angel child."

    Again Travilla created the look for Marilyn in this film. In most of her costumes she looks trussed up like a Christmas Goose. Her dresses appear to almost be molded to her body. The red diamond studded bathing suit not only made it into the film, but into many of Marilyn's cheesecake photos of the time. A set of 3-D photos showing Marilyn lounging around a pool were taken during this time by Harold Lloyd at his Greenacres estate. A short film clip of Marilyn taken that day at Greenacres survives in an Air Force documentary, *Security is Common Sense*. Military personnel and government workers in the documentary are admonished to keep information on Atomic testing secure. "Don't be careless," is the last advice the announcer gives. Marilyn is then shown poolside, reclining on a chaise lounge. She looks into the camera and says, "I hate careless men," after which she give a lingering look into the camera. Her bathing suit has been covered up by a terrycloth towel.

    Marilyn starred as Pola Debevoise, and along with Lauren Bacall and Betty Grable, formed a trio of gold-digging models determined to marry a millionaire. Marilyn gave one of her most self-effacing performances as a near-sighted blonde bombshell who is worried that her glasses will spoil her looks and chances of snagging a husband. She had Lotte Goslar to think for her superb comedic style.

During the filming of this movie Richard Burton comes on the set and is photographed with Marilyn, Lauren Bacall and Betty Grable, by Jean Howard. He was on a break from working at another soundstage on *The Robe*, for Fox. Incidentally, Jean Howard was the wife of Marilyn's agent Charles Feldman. Miss Howard first met Marilyn back in 1950 when she had accompanied Elia Kazan to her home to meet with her husband, Charles Feldman.

William Powell, who also starred in the movie, was once the love of Jean Harlow and told this to Marilyn, "You remind me of a girl I loved very much. You don't look like Jean, but you have the same warmth and inner radiance that made Jean such a loveable person." Marilyn will later say, "I think that is the sweetest compliment I ever had."

Cameron Mitchell, who had introduced Marilyn to Arthur Miller on the set of *As Young As You Feel* in January of 1950, appeared in the film as the love interest of Lauren Bacall. This was also the fourth film that Marilyn worked in with David Wayne, who played her love interest. They had shared billing in *As Young as You Feel*, *We're Not Married*, and *O'Henry's Full House,* although they didn't actually appear together in that film. Marilyn would visit backstage with David in the 1954 Broadway production of *Teahouse of the August Moon*, when she was in town to film *Seven Year Itch*.

Wayne remembers filming the airplane shot with Marilyn, "We shot that scene all day long in the hottest, most enclosed situation and she had trouble doing the scene because of her fears. When she'd get a little perspiry, she'd stop, go fix her hair, change her makeup, and come back as though nothing happened. It got worse as the day went on, from exasperation. She had no fear of using other people's time or money in order to learn how to act. Eventually it was worth it to the studio and to the picture. But how many Marilyn Monroe's can we afford? Still you couldn't help but say, 'What a nice girl she is,' because she was."

David Wayne would tell Nancy Anderson of working with Marilyn. "'What was the greatest number of takes you ever did for a single scene?' he was asked. 'That was with Marilyn in *How to Marry a Millionaire*,' Wayne answered without having to stop and think about it for a minute. 'We went 28 takes. This was the first picture ever completed in CinemaScope. I think *The Robe* was first released, but this was the first completed, so they were still experimenting a lot with the lenses. And, because of the lens, in the plane scene that I did with Marilyn, they couldn't break away. They had to keep everyone in place. All the extras, everybody. And it became incredibly hot because of the Technicolor lights. Marilyn blew take after take. But eventually we got her on the 28$^{th}$ take. I'll never forget that, because it was just heartbreaking—so rough—so rough on everybody…However, there was something about her which had nothing to do with talent that made the public like her, something in her face. Not intelligence, but a vulnerability. It's hard for me to judge her potential, because Marilyn was very inexperienced when we worked together.'"

Earl Wilson reported an interview with David Wayne on April 9, 1953, "...Even then she was carrying around books by Kafka. I don't know whether she knew what she was reading, but she was making a hell of a try. She was out to get somewhere.' 'Did you see her possibilities then?' 'Frankly, I didn't,' admitted Wayne. 'I did not believe she had the talent to make it the big way. But she has made it the big way already. And she's going to stay there, too, because of her will and her need.' 'How about the stage?' 'I don't think she'll ever be a stage star. The motion picture business is dominated by personalities. It is not an acting medium, it is a personality medium. Marilyn's one of the most phenomenal personalities of our time. One of the studio heads called her in. She'd turned down a picture. He roared at her, 'I've been in this business a long time and I know what's good for you.' She said, 'I've been in this business a very short time and I know better what's good for me than you do.' Out of this pretty face and from this almost vacuous exterior pops something that I would call instinctive wisdom. You can't believe that it comes from her. Never get her wrong, though. Once a wealthy man offered her the most beautiful fur coat in the world to go home with him. She knocked him tail over tea-kettle. I hope,' David Wayne added, 'that nothing I've said will be considered censure of her. I adore her.'" Another fan magazine carried this quote from Wayne about the private Marilyn. "She was difficult to get to know and always seemed anxious to get off by herself. Ate lunch alone in her dressing room or sat off in a corner alone. I guess she was shy, but she's a wonderful person."

A photograph of Marilyn and two visitors on the set standing in front of the airplane was taken by Bert Fink. "Stunned is the only way to describe Ray Blocker, Western region director of special promotions, touring the 20th Century Fox lot at Hollywood with Marilyn Monroe during the filming of *How to Marry a Millionaire*. Jim DeLong, TWA director of advertising, seems to be bearing up under the strain. Several scenes in the picture, starring Marilyn, Betty Grable and Lauren Bacall, were filmed in TWA's mock-up 1049 Constellation designed for use by motion picture and TV studios."

Marilyn would also work with Rory Calhoun again. She had previously appeared in *Ticket to Tomahawk* with him and would appear in the upcoming film, *River of No Return*. In this film, he played the love interest of Betty Grable.

The press tried to stir up trouble between Betty Grable and Marilyn. Ever since Marilyn had been awarded the chance to play Lorelei Lee in *Gentlemen Prefer Blondes*, rumors have been circulating that Betty Grable was upset at her for being overlooked for the role. If Miss Grable was unhappy with Marilyn, she hid it well. On the set of *How to Marry a Millionaire*, Miss Grable acted like a true lady in her comments to the press about Marilyn, and in her conduct with her. Miss Grable has always maintained that she truly like Marilyn.

Betty Grable, who Marilyn surpassed as the reigning musical star at Fox, adored her. She told Aline Mosby, "That's the way it's always been at the studio. Alice Faye was there, and then they brought me in, and she left. While I was at Fox they tried building up new stars, June Haver and Mitzi Gaynor didn't make it, but Marilyn Monroe did. I like working with Marilyn better than the other two. She's nice and I like her love life. She sticks to one fellow and doesn't go out to nightclubs with different men." Miss Grable will say of Marilyn, "Marilyn Monroe, who just fascinates me to no end. Everyone tried to start a feud between us when we worked together in *How to Marry a Millionaire*, but her friendship meant more to me than the picture."

Marilyn will say of Betty, "Betty is the most real girl I've ever met." Marilyn and Betty had actually never met until they were cast in *How to Marry a Millionaire*. Betty had been the golden girl at Fox and now Marilyn was replacing her, but she was nothing but gracious to her young rival. Betty told Marilyn, "I've had it. Go get yours. It's your turn now!" Sidney Skolsky gives insight into their working relationship. "Throughout the filming of *How to Marry a Millionaire*, Marilyn was simultaneously trying to get Betty to like her and trying to reassure herself that Betty did like her. Driving me from the studio one evening, Marilyn said excitedly, 'Betty told me today that I'm the first actress who never tried, even subconsciously, to upstage her. I guess this means she likes me. I hope so.' Another time I was on the set when Marilyn was playing a scene in which she had to nudge Grable. She did and Betty fell on her fanny! Marilyn was all apologies. 'I'm so sorry!' she said. 'I didn't think I had pushed you so hard!' 'It wasn't your fault,' Betty replied lightly. 'I was standing on one foot.' Marilyn was so distressed by this accident that later, doing another scene, she carelessly stepped on Betty's shoe. 'I know this was my fault, and I'm terribly sorry!' she apologized. 'It's nothing,' Betty said. 'But I dirtied your shoe!' persisted Marilyn. 'Forget it, will you kid?' said Grable. 'The shoe doesn't show in the shot—and besides, it belongs to wardrobe.'"

Lauren Bacall had this to say about Marilyn, "She's a hard girl to get to know. But you have the feeling that she wants to be liked. That seems important to her. Her instincts are those of a nice gal, not a phony. She's wary of people and probably with good reason; she's been stung by many of them."

While filming *How to Marry a Millionaire*, Marilyn was photographed by photographer Frank Worth. The images of her taken by Worth document her beauty during this period. She was a dreamy dish. During this time she wrote him a note which said simply, "Dear Frank, It was nice having you in me, Love Marilyn." Frank had first photographed Marilyn during her starlet days. According to him, they had a secret affair.

Another photographer on the set was Allan Grant. In 1962 he would take the pictures to illustrate Marilyn's last interview which appeared in the August 3, 1962 issue of *LIFE* magazine.

A future TV icon was introduced to Marilyn while she was filming *How to Marry a Millionaire*, it was Ed McMahon, Johnny Carson's sidekick. Captain McMahon was stationed at El Toro Marine Air Base in California. Cpt. McMahon was on the 20th Century lot visiting an acquaintance who was the assistant musical director at Fox. He asked Ed if he would like to meet Marilyn Monroe. After Marilyn had finished filming a scene they brought her to meet Cpt. McMahon. Marilyn invited him into her trailer for a short visit. She was wearing slacks and a blouse. Ed remembers her as being very sweet. He told her he was headed for Korea. She said that she was going there to entertain the troops. He asked if he could take a picture of her to take with him. She suggested that someone take a picture of them together instead. She went to her dressing room to fix her hair. When she returned she was wearing a mink coat. While being photographed Marilyn whispered to Ed that she had nothing on under her coat. He recalled later that her breathless disclosure was the reason for his broad smile in the photograph.

Frank Morris reported on April 10th, "So maybe you'd like to hear about Marilyn Monroe, and the gentlemen will please wipe those leers off their faces. All that happened was that Marilyn said 'hello' to me. I said 'hello' to Marilyn, and she said, 'It's a nice day and I hear Winnipeg is a nice town.' The point is, however, that la Monroe, who has become famous (or infamous if you want to put it that way) for posing for calendars clad in nothing but a coat of tan, can make even the most innocent remark sound like a veiled invitation in indecorous behavior. When I first met Miss Monroe a couple of years ago I was heard to remark that I'd met more high-powered sirens in my days. Since then, however, Miss Monroe has become more inflammable, or else I'm more susceptible in my foolish forties. At any rate, in the two minutes conversation I had with Marilyn in private she had me percolating like a pressure cooker. When a cameraman moved in to record the event, Miss Monroe sidled in even closer. Mother told me there'd be afternoons like this. I earned the lasting hatred of a two-star general and a flock of other high military brass with enough spaghetti on them to stock the entire Pentagon in Washington. Miss Monroe is appearing out at 20th Century-Fox in *How to Marry a Millionaire*. Her co-stars are Misses Grable and Bacall. They were not in the scene I saw, but they were watching it, along with the military mucky-mucks. Miss Grable looks very fetching, too, and she doubtless watches Miss Monroe ascendancy with a fair amount of calm. Betty has had her day. She has set a popularity mark that even la Monroe has to top....I don't know how to describe what Miss Monroe was wearing, but it was bright red satin that clung like Scotch tape wherever it should cling and billowed out where it should billow out. The bodice (I think that's what you could laughingly call it) was cut as low as the law allows it to be cut on such occasions, and it was held up by a single strap. The set was an elaborate night club and Miss Monroe made her entrance on the arm of a gentleman who was wearing a black patch over one eye. The wide screen of Cinerama allowed the whole scene to play with Miss Monroe walking the whole length of the audience going in the wrong direction, bumping into a man and finally managing to take a seat. For plot purposes, Miss Monroe is supposed to be very short sighted and this angle is being played for comedy. Miss Monroe's walk, I might record, is rather on the order of a beautifully functioning, expensive wrist watch...a veritable 21-jeweled movement. It took a good many shots to get the scene made, but the two-star general and his companions were not complaining. They stood in an admiring know watching her. Between 'takes' she wandered over to consult her dramatic coach. Miss Monroe will never rival Duse, Bernhardt or Garbo, but she is courting the muse of Thespis ardently and spends all her spare time studying the right inflection of a line. Well, when she wandered over in our direction I couldn't resist tapping the two-star general on the shoulder an asking: 'How's your blood pressure, sir?' 'It's all right, mister,' he said, 'but the captain is in a bad way. He's just at the susceptible stage.' The captain, who was outranked by his companions, blushed furiously. When Marilyn wafted off in the direction of her dressing room, I was herded over to meet her and I heard the general say: 'What's that guy got that we haven't got?' Only a paper with a big circulation." *The Winnipeg Free Press* also ran a photograph of Marilyn and Mr. Morris.

On April 11th Marilyn is hospitalized at Cedars of Lebanon for bronchial pneumonia on instruction by her physician, Dr. Elliot Corday. Joe DiMaggio sends Marilyn a dozen red roses from Halchester's Flowers in Hollywood.

Hedda Hopper also reported on Marilyn's hospital stay on April 25th, "When Marilyn Monroe went to the hospital with virus last week, she had to send out and have herself a pair of bedroom slippers bought. Seems La Monroe never wears the things; but the good doc forbade her to walk around in her room in her bare tootsies."

The day after Marilyn got out of the hospital she went to Louella Parsons home dressed in a discreet suit and discussed the Joan Crawford incident with her. The conversation will be recorded in the July issue of *Modern Screen*. Miss Parsons commented about Marilyn, "Then I realized what a shy, ill-at-ease girl she really was, despite all her lush, sexy beauty. Her sudden, dizzying success had given her confidence--but not much." Marilyn said of the hurtful article, "I think the thing that hit me the hardest about Miss Crawford's story is that it came from her. I've always admired her for being such a wonderful mother—for taking four children and giving them a fine home. Who, better than I, knows what it means to homeless little ones. Although, I don't know Miss Crawford very well—I met her once at a dinner party, she was a symbol to me of kindness and understanding to those who need help. At first, all I could think of was, 'Why should she select me to blast?' She's a great star. I'm just starting. And then, when the first hurt began to die down, I told myself she must have spoken to Mr. Thomas impulsively, without thinking. In view of many things that have happened since the article appeared, I'm beginning to look on it as a blessing in disguise. If it had never been printed I might never have realized how many friends I have, even ones I've never met. Lots of GIs wrote me letters saying, 'We like you the way your are.' Miss Parsons, that meant a lot to me. It's one thing that made me decide to go to Korea if I never do another thing in my life. I couldn't get over the fact that so many kids, who were having it so bad themselves didn't want me to have my feelings hurt. That's not all. People in our business were so unexpectedly kind. As you know, I don't know many stars outside of the few I've worked with. Think of it, Betty Grable, the biggest star on the 20$^{th}$ lot asked me to lunch with her and she said, 'Marilyn, don't let this get you down. I've taken plenty of criticism and so have other actresses. Just keep plugging. The important things are your career—and trying to improve yourself.' I love Betty, she's such a good person. Maybe this seems silly, but we were doing a scene for *How to Marry a Millionaire* and Betty noticed I had no polish on my toes as I had worn in a previous day's work. She ran and got that polish and put it on herself. There were no press agents or newspapermen around, so she didn't do it as a grand gesture....the part of Joan's article which hit her hardest was the reference to her vulgar walk in *Niagara*. She said, 'You see, the character I played was a tramp. The role called for me to wear very tight dresses and high heels. The combination of a dress I could scarcely move in and the high heels caused me to 'wobble' when I walked. With all the publicity I've had and everything, I suppose it will be hard for many people to believe that I never deliberately throw my sex around, thinking, 'If I do this, it's sexy—or if I look a certain way, it's sexy." Miss Parsons finishes the article with this acute observation, "Sex has been the stepping stone to her career—and she's not knocking it! But the lowcut dresses and the dreamy-eyed photographs have served their purpose, and she's eager to go forward as a performer and as a person."

On April 16th Marilyn receives a Testimonial of Appreciation, *A Halo for a Saintly Sinner*, presented by the Saints and Sinners of Los Angeles.

Dorothy Kilgallen reported on April 16th, "The controversial blonde Marilyn Monroe continues to star in fascinating vignettes, off screen as well as on, and today this department is happy to present one as reported by a young denizen of Hollywood who has very big eyes for her but has not progressed past the Good Pals or 'Gosh I'd like your advice!' stage in her attentions. He deposes: 'A couple of nights ago I stopped in and much to my surprise Joe DiMaggio answered the door and said 'Marilyn isn't here.' Just as it was closing in my face, a feminine hand caught the door and said, 'Oh, but Marilyn IS here!' And there she stood, inviting me in for a nightcap. The look J.D. gave me would discourage a bull moose in mating season. Then a while later she said, 'I think you fellows ought to be going. I'm sleepy.' Chalk this up as the latest incident. Nobody won!" The man in the story was Robert Slatzer and it is interesting that according to Kilgallen, Marilyn had no romantic interest in him. This is the last we will hear of Robert Slatzer until his ridiculous claims after her death.

On the 19th beauty columnist Lydia Lane devoted her entire column to Marilyn. It was actually a repeat on an article published in September of 1952. Perhaps the studio pressured Lane to print it again in hopes of giving Marilyn some much needed good publicity.

Erskine Johnson reported on April 22nd, "Hollywood and Grapevine: Fox is worried about Marilyn Monroe's migraine headaches and air of depression. Insiders blame it on Joan Crawford's newsprint tongue-lashing and sniping at Marilyn from other directions..."

Marilyn wrote a check out to Dr. Elliot Corday on April 22nd for the amount of $130.00. Dr. Corday was her doctor for her recent bout of bronchitis

Louella Parsons one-upped Miss Hopper on April 26th, "Marilyn to Star In *The Egyptian*...Still so choked with a cold she could scarcely breath, Marilyn Monroe came to see me the day she checked out of the hospital. She wheezed out the news that she's going to be the girl in *The Egyptian*, Mike Waltari's bestselling novel. Her blonde hair will be concealed under a Cleopatra-type red wig. Although Marilyn told me she couldn't possibly do all the pictures 20th has set for her, I hated to tell her that she starts in June in *River of No Return*, a western to be made in the Salmon river country. Before that Marilyn goes to Korea. She said, 'so many GIs have written to me, saying that they'd like to see me, and this is the thing I most want to do. I'll take a guitar player and some pretty clothes and a comedian because I think the boys want laughs as well as glamour.' All they'll need is

Marilyn, according to the many letters I've had."

Earl Wilson reported on April 27th, "Joan Crawford tried to reach Marilyn Monroe in L.A. to 'explain' her attack on Marilyn. But Mmmm was out of town. When you see Mmmm in 'CinemaScope,' you may not be able to figure what holds up her blouse. But being extra sharp, I've figured out what holds it up...Mmmarilyn does."

Marilyn attended the premiere of *This Is Cinerama* on April 29th, it was held at the Warner's Hollywood Theater on Hollywood Boulevard. Afterwards she attended a *Cinerama* Premier Party at the Coconut Grove nightclub. Among other stars in attendance were Donald O'Conner, songwriter Cole Porter and gossip columnist, Louella Parsons. *Cinerama* was a process akin to *CinemaScope*, and 3-D. There are surviving photographs of Joe DiMaggio picking Marilyn up from the party, as was his habit; he refused to attend with her.

The May issue of *Cosmopolitan* magazine features a fantastic image of Marilyn on the cover, by Ernest Bachrach, and an article, "Marilyn Monroe Hollywood's Most Valuable Property" by Robert L. Heilbroner. "Marilyn Monroe, a blonde in a bananaskin dress, with a walk that threatens to unpeel it, is the closest thing we've go to a national institution to come out of Hollywood in fifteen years. In this world of changing values, she has been guided by the basic principle that sex, after all, is here to stay...The Monroe magnetism depends on a staggering set of measurements: 37, 23, 34. But statistics are only part of the story. For behind such rather obvious matters lies one of the heaviest and most skillful publicity barrages in years...In Marilyn the boys saw a chance to fill the nation's empty theatre seats with a new dose of that old magic. They flooded the mail with pictures of her. They dreamed up tags for her: the Woo Woo Girl, the Girl with the Horizontal Walk, the AC-DC Girl. When a woman columnist accused her of appearing in 'organic' clothes, they rushed to her defense with a statement that she'd look as good in a burlap bag—and proved it with a picture that hit 427 newspapers."

Walter Winchell had this to say about the cover, "*Cosmopolitan's* cover is decorative. A sexhibibt of Marilyn Monroe. Peekabootiful."

*Eye* magazine proclaimed, "Gentlemen Prefer Marilyn Monroe...whether she's sunning on the sand, bubbling in the surf, brightening America's billboards, or emoting for films, it's clear gentlemen prefer Marilyn."

*Movie Stars Parade* featured a photo essay of Marilyn on the campus of UCLA, shot by Mel Traxel back on February 12, 1952. "Marilyn Monroe Off Guard...Never judge a book by its cover—especially when the girl inside it is a dish like Marilyn Monroe."

In May 1953 The Greater Los Angeles Press Club was honoring Walter Winchell with a testimonial. The dinner was held at their headquarters in the Hotel Ambassador. The President of the Los Angeles Press Club, Bill Kennedy, suggested that Walter bring Marilyn to receive their honorary "8 Ball Award." On the dais, Marilyn whispered, "Walter, I can't make a speech. I never have. What'll I say if they ask me?" To which Walter replied, "When they give you the award, just give them that great big 'ohmygoodness' of a smile, and say two words--like Thank You--blow a kiss at them and sit down." "Oh Walter,"

Marilyn gasped, "tell me again, I know I won't do it right." Photos that survive of that event show a Marilyn who was simply ravishing, even by her own standards. Marilyn was chosen as their first "8 Ball" girl back in 1947 when the Greater Los Angeles Press Club was first started.

On May 2$^{nd}$ columnist Jimmie Fidler reported, "Marilyn Monroe, looking very serious, lunching with Joe DiMaggio, the man of her heart, at the Brown Derby."

Theda Bara, a great sex symbol of her generation, was interviewed by Emily Belser in an article that appeared on May 3rd. Miss Bara said of Marilyn, "Theda has never seen Marilyn on the screen but her photos inspired her to say, 'I think, like everyone else, that she is sexy. But I don't believe she likes it much, does she? She probably will have the same trouble I have had. She will never be able to live down her reputation." Marilyn will portray Theda Bara in a *LIFE* magazine photo essay in 1958 photographed by Richard Avedon.

Birthday Party for Walter Winchell was held at Ciro's nightclub in Hollywood on May 3rd. Although the party was for Walter's birthday, he also honored columnist Louella Parsons that night. Miss Parsons was escorted by Jimmy McHugh. Marilyn, who was running late, walked into the party with Betty Grable, who was also running late because her daughter was sick. This event benefited the Damon Runyon Cancer Fund.

Betty Grable remembered how Marilyn felt on the night of this party. "We're both scared of big gatherings. I remember the time Marilyn and I were going to the party Walter Winchell was giving at Ciro's. She was shaking like a leaf because she wanted to make a good impression on Mr. Winchell. She told me she was scared to death, and I had to admit that I was, too."

Jimmie Fidler wrote some of the most insightful articles on Marilyn career and the balance between her public image and her desire to be taken seriously as an actress. On May 21$^{st}$ Fidler wrote about Marilyn's Plans to "Do More Real Acting, Less Cheesecake…Marilyn Monroe has reached another milepost in her career. And this one should definitely be a vital marker along her road to success which, until now, has been meteoric. The executives at 20$^{th}$ Century-Fox are fully aware of Marilyn's scanty bathing attire attractions, of her extremely pleasing personality. And these will not be placed under a bushel. They will be exploited—but not as heretofore in purely sexy fashion. Marilyn Monroe will be given roles calling for a degree of dramatic ability. The girl can sing, in spite of rumors to the contrary. Some have said that Marilyn wants to be known as a screen siren, the explosive third point in the eternal triangle in love plots—and all that, Marilyn, I know, seeks full movie success, and will play cheerfully the roles that will insure that success, but she also wants to register in pictures as a woman of culture and a serious outlook on life. Until now Marilyn's publicity has run the limit in sex and the display of limbs, hips, busts and her celebrated wiggle. Some of that will remain, but n a more refined presentation. From now on out, Marilyn will do more real acting, and occasionally she'll sing a song. Much of her sexy publicity I'll admit, has come from interviews and stories by columnists and outside writers, over which the studio had no control except to keep

Marilyn in seclusion. Movie stars are not the product of seclusion. They are developed in the broad light of publicity and the advantageous presentation in screen roles, therefore the studio bigwigs do not drive off interviewers, outside writers and photographers. Marilyn has been a choice morsel in the sexy stuff, and some mediums have gone the limit in exploiting that phase of her. If Miss Monroe hereafter will be smart and do what her studio thinks is wise, her popularity and place in the screen world will grow upon a solid foundation—to endure through the years, What about it, Marilyn?"

Walter Winchell reported about the party on May 23rd, "The Ciro's management agreed that the party for Louella Parsons (attended by scads of stars) had the 'best press coverage' in a long, long time. Every cameraman covered it...Joseph M. Schenck sat on this side of the honored guest and her Best Friend, James McHugh, on the other...When Jane Kean (the Kean Gals) went into her hilarious take-off on Lolly, she rocked with laughter, too...The devastating satire of La Monroe was the one the crowd waited for--knowing Marilyn hadn't seen it, but had heard about it... The frightened girl was a good sport about it, however, and said, 'they are very clever girls. I thought I got off easy'...It was Marilyn who stole the show...They kept taking her picture from 9:30pm until almost 2 a.m....At the party were: Esther Williams and groom Ben Gage, Jane Russell and husband Bob Waterfield, Merle Oberon, Dr. Rex Ross, Cole Porter, Nancy Sinatra, Mrs. Harry Brand, the Zanucks, the Michael St. Angles, Lucy and Desi, Betty Grable (on the left and Monroe on our right, yet!) And we danced with both gals...'First time I've danced in over a year.' said Monroe. 'Joe doesn't like dancing.' ...When we told that to Grable, she said, 'Same here. Did you ever hear of a band leader dancing? My Harry (James) hasn't done a two-step in 10 years!'...Grable, who had been a big star many years, adored the talented Kean sisters act."

Sheilah Graham reported on the 4th that, "Joe DiMaggio's first date with Marilyn Monroe when he arrived back in Hollywood was to take her to a ball game…Next morning Marilyn took off for a rest in Ojai."

Frank Morris, who had interviewed Marilyn on the set of *How to Marry a Millionaire*, and reported glowingly about her sex appeal, now reviewed *Niagara* on May 8th, and raked Marilyn across the coals. "The movie at the Capitol Theater this week might safely be descried as a documentary because it gives complete, and on the spot, pictures of two wonders of nature…Niagara Falls and Miss Marilyn Monroe. The Falls are caught by the Technicolor camera in various stages of splendor. Miss Monroe is glimpsed in rear view shots as she walks down the street in skin-tight skirts, and whenever she comes through a door it is not her head that appears first. *Niagara*, truth to tell, however, is an unadulterated bit of corn and in trying to make a siren out of Miss Monroe they have turned her into a burlesque of every two-timing hotsy-totsy who ever lived."

Marilyn signs a contract with Deeco, Inc. on May 19th. She was photographed by Mischa Pelz, who worked for Miller Photography, Inc., for the ad campaign on Deeco's aluminum outdoor furniture. The images are some of the most powerful images of Marilyn's legendary sex appeal. She was posed sitting, standing and cavorting on the outdoor furniture in a white two-piece. Although the ads appeared in black and white, there were also color images of Marilyn taken that day. She looks scrumptious posed in her white Catalina two-piece against the orange cushions. The release was tied in with her appearance in 20th Century-Fox's *Gentlemen Prefer Blondes*. Deeco produced, in addition to its print brochures, a free booklet, illustrating New 1954 Deeco series, called Hollywood Film Stars At Home. Some of the photos were sold to the "SunMaster" Garden Umbrella of the California Umbrella Company, and appeared on their advertising booklet back cover. Jayne Mansfield made the front cover. Marilyn is shown in black and white, demonstrating the new release system for lowering your umbrella without pinching your fingers or straining your back.

Louella Parsons reported on May 19th, "Here's a scoop for the listeners to my radio show: Tomorrow night Marilyn Monroe, our popular glamour girl and the No. 1 pin-up favorite of the GIs is my guest."

On May 20th Marilyn attended the opening of Jimmy McHugh and His Singing Stars at the Coconut Grove nightclub in the Ambassador Hotel. McHugh was Louella Parsons boyfriend. Louella spoke of that night, "As a star, there were certain functions she had to perform, certain places where she had to go. She found that she had to do these unescorted. I recall one night when my friend Jimmy McHugh opened at the Ambassador Hotel and a group of Hollywood's most important stars were there to catch him in his new act and be introduced. Marilyn was one of this group, but she came alone. Late in the evening a waiter came to our table with a message for her. Joe was outside in the car waiting for her. He wouldn't even come in long enough to exchange greetings."

Grace Goddard stayed with Marilyn for a few weeks in mid-May. She deserved a rest after caring non-stop for Gladys for so many months.

Hedda Hopper reported on May 22nd, "Jean Negulesco, who directed Marilyn Monroe, Betty Grable and Lauren Bacall in *How to Marry a Millionaire*, tells me that Marilyn is one of the most receptive actresses he's ever worked with."

Marilyn and Negulesco will develop an odd relationship while filming unlike any she will have with her other directors. They will have clandestine dinners and meetings where art and literature is the topic of discussion. She will watch him paint her portrait, which will later hang in her apartment. He explains the technique he is using and it spurs a conversation between them about the post-impressionist painters such as "Matisse, Chagall, Derain, Pascin, Braque, Gauguin, Picasso and Buffet." He observed that, "her questions were sensible. Once she sighed and said, "'I can't seem to understand these modern paintings.' Negulesco said, 'Art is like sex. Art is not to be understood but to feel.'" He seems to understand her yearning to be educated. He will remark, "This girl has a hunger for knowledge. She's slow to absorb, but she absorbs. It is difficult to come close to her. She becomes vague. She puts up a curtain between herself and people." He spoke to her literature and even lent her *Old Man and the Sea*, by Ernest Hemmingway, *Green Mansions* by W.H. Hudson, and *Lust for Life*, by Irving Stone. After she finished reading them they would discuss the books.

Negulesco will go on to say about Marilyn, "She is stupid like a fox. I have sat for hours with her, talking about art or literature, and the wisdom of this child is fantastic. She has the gift of absolute concentration that may make it hard for you when she's in a movie. She may seemingly ignore you, but it will be because Marilyn concentrates to the point of being ridiculous. You can tell her a joke, and it will go right over her head, because she is thinking so hard about a scene. This ability to block out everything and concentrate pays off. It might not look too impressive from scene to scene. But when you see the finished picture, you realize that she has sustained the performance from A to Z. Marilyn is the best actress on the Fox lot today. If I were directing *Johnny Belinda* again tomorrow, I wouldn't hesitate to put her in it." *Johnny Belinda* was a 1948 drama that starred Jane Wyman and her performance garnered her an Academy Award. This would have actually been a wonderful role for Marilyn.

Negulesco made this insightful remark about the burden of Marilyn's image. "She represents to man something we all want in our unfulfilled dreams. She's the girl you'd like to double-cross your wife with. A man, he's got to be dead not to be excited by her. You have to understand this woman. She is a fine, sensitive, sweet person. But she has a terrible problem. How can a human being do a simple everyday act like, oh, like eating mashed potatoes, if they know 50,000,000 men want to make love to them? It is a terrible strain for this woman."

Whitey Snyder comments on Marilyn's concentration while working. "She's seldom relaxed. She's always studying what she had to do. Some actresses can exchange small talk between scenes—but not Marilyn. She's too busy concentrating on every little movement. But, in all the time I've worked with her, she has never once given any evidence of having temperament. Even when she's immersed in thought, she's polite and cooperative."

On May 22nd, in his syndicated column, Al Bennett, editor of the *Atchison Globe* devoted the entire space to Marilyn. "We have decided to write to Marilyn Monroe, the film star, and see if she has an answer to the baffling situation encountered in Atchison. It's best to go directly to the person involved. Will she reply? Maybe, or maybe not. Anyway, here goes:
Marilyn Monroe
20th Century-Fox Studio
Hollywood, Calif.
Dear Marilyn:
Recently in Atchison, Kansas, where we have a Fox theater, we have just seen your picture, *Niagara*. Also we are getting ready to see you in a 3-D film. The screen is being prepared right now for 3-D pictures. We have been sounding out popular opinion concerning you in our city and we're glad to report you are plenty popular. The 'box office' has been good, according to Jack Maes, local theater manager. But here's what's troubling us...Some of the opinions we've gathered together indicate you are MORE popular with the men, and LESS popular with the women. The former say you are the hottest thing this side of the A-bomb, and maybe on the other side too. That is, most of them. The latter admit you have a good figure but they won't go much further than. The men's answer to all this is to be expected,

that he women are simply jealous. In this column we have tried to compare you with Marlene Dietrich, Jean Harlow, and some of the other 'greats' in the so-called 'sexy' field. Bill Stanton, who operates a funeral home here, tells us he doesn't believe you quite measure up. Nels Greenlund, who is in the real estate business here, is emphatic on the other side--even brought in photo-magazine pictures of you to prove his point. But in the main, in Atchison, Kansas, the men are wild about you and the women, well, they'd just as soon have vanilla. Now what we want to know, Marilyn is this: In this male-and-female difference of opinion in Atchison typical of that in other cities across the nation? If so, it isn't a good thing for you, is it? What we mean is that so often it is the girl or the woman on a date or a night out, who decides which movie to see. If the girls and women really want to, they can divert their men to other movies. Can't they? We'd appreciate it if you would:

1. Tell us in your own words if, during your lifetime, you have noticed any animosity on the part of other girls and women, jealousy symptoms, etc., or on the other hand if you have had close, personal friendships with girls and women which would indicate they really like you as much as the men do. Back in high school did girls elect you to office, or give you parties, or in other ways demonstrate real affection and friendship?

2. Send us some photos of yourself (the more the better) which in your opinion (a) appeal to men and (b) appeal to girls and women. Perhaps it is too much to expect that the same photo will appeal to both.

3. Tell us, in your own words, if you think your film career in the future should cater to the men with glamour-siren-sexy roles or if you think the feminine audience could be captured, as well, with a few clean-cut American-girl-in-gingham pictures. Marilyn, we're interested. And you should be also. Maybe you are too busy to bother with us, but if you'll drop us a letter and send along some photos to prove the point, we'll sure use 'em. Many thanks."

After waiting a month, Al Bennett, editor of the *Atchison Globe*, in Atchison, Kansas, again devoted his syndicated column to Marilyn on June 23rd. "Today we sent a telegram to Marilyn Monroe, the shapely movie star, reminding her we haven't had an answer from her in regard to our question: 'Why are you quite popular with the men, but not so popular with women movie-goers?' We told her lots of us were awaiting her reply. And we sent another copy of our May 23 column in case she or her press agent misplaced the first one. Now maybe we will hear from her. Maybe we won't. In support of our statement that Marilyn leaves male patrons panting, but leaves feminine patrons slightly cold.

On June 28th, Al Bennett, editor of the *Atchison Globe*, Atchison, Kansas, was still waiting for a reply from Marilyn. "Well, here's a note from Marilyn Monroe's press agent or business manager, 'Miss Monroe is out of the city at present and therefore has not received your wire. I will, however, do my best to expedite matters for you.' His name is Harry Brand. And we feel now that some progress is being made."

In a follow-up column on June 30th, Al Bennett of the *Atchinson Globe* takes columnist Irene Kuhn of the *Topeka State Journal* to task for her dislike of Marilyn. [Mr. Bennett goes on to print most of Miss Kuhn's column, which appeared on June 16th.] "Well, when you read the above, and consider it was written by a woman columnist, you begin to see what we mean about the feminine reaction to Marilyn. There's a definite difference between the viewpoints of men and women concerning Miss Monroe. In almost every line of Miss Kuhn's newspaper article you can hear the 'meow' and feel the scratch of a kitten's paw. Miss Kuhn recognizes that most people hate to be laughed at more than anything. So she writes a piece about how lots of folks are laughing at Marilyn Monroe. We're not going to dispute Miss Kuhn's newspaper article. She may be right. But that part about the Folies Bergere in Paris...we'd like to register a mild protest. As one pop-eyed tourist who saw one performance we'd like to go on record--it was the prettiest thing we've seen! Unfortunately, we weren't in the front row so we missed the goose-pimples. But from the cheap seats the performance seemed to us to bear out, once again that 50 million Frenchmen can't be wrong! In an earlier column we asked Miss Monroe if animosity on the part of other girls and women has been apparent throughout her life. Did she have close girl friends or was she lonely? Did other girls seek her out and elect her to office in their high school clubs? Or were they jealous and indifferent toward her? Also we asked Marilyn for some photos of herself, some which in her opinion appeal to men and some which appeal to women. We've received nothing, absolutely nothing, and all we're worried about is Marilyn's career. We're afraid this growing dislike on the part of women may hurt Marilyn's box-office. Well, maybe the telegram reminder will bring a reply."

Marilyn finally responds on July 16th to Al Bennett, Editor of *The Atchison Globe*, Globe, Atchison, Kansas. *The Globe* had asked her several questions to which she replied in her letter: "Your column of Sunday, May 23, reached me upon my return to the studio following a vacation. Naturally, I have found it fascinating. Since it is an 'open letter' and since it was read by your thousands of readers before it reached me, I found its intimate contents quite an experience, something like having an appendectomy at the corner of Hollywood and Vine. However your questions are more than welcome since my career means a lot to me and maybe I can get some answers by talking it over this way, woman to man. First of all, I agree with Bill Stanton, the mortician, that I am not Marlene Dietrich or Jean Harlow. I have great admiration for both but, as I've been told, they could happen once in a generation. On the other hand, I love Nels Greenlund, the realtor, for being on my team and thinking I'm wonderful. Let's please not talk him out of it. Now as to this business of women not liking me. In my work as an actress (and I want to be known as a serious actress and am working toward that end) I need the support of both sexes. According to letters I receive, a lot of women are on my side but others seem to resent the roles I've played and the type of publicity I've had. I will defend my screen roles on the grounds that they were patterned after various types of real people and I tried to play the part according to the script. Specifically, take my role in *Niagara*. The girl I played in that was completely wanton and the plot was built around her attempt to kill her husband so that she could go away with another man. She had been picked out of a beer parlor, she was entirely lacking in the social graces, and she was over-dressed and over-made-up. I walked the way I did because that was the way I 'saw' her walking. I do not walk that way in every picture. In *Gentlemen Prefer Blondes*, the Technicolor musical, I play the Lorelei Lee role (the girl who believes that diamonds are a girl's best friend) and this calls for an entirely different interpretation. I'm afraid some people (mostly women) confuse me with the parts I play. Actually, I do not go around murdering people as in *Niagara*, nor am I as crazy for diamonds as the girl in *Blondes*. You ask if I have found jealousy in the women of my acquaintances. I have been criticized in print by some newspaper women but I usually attribute this to the fact that it makes a good story. I have had many wonderful friendships with women, although I admit that men are sometimes more approachable. In high school I had a few good friends, but during that stage of my life I was poor, I had few presentable clothes, and I shied away from parties and gatherings that would have been at the time embarrassing to me. I was never elected to office or anything of that sort as I wasn't much of a mixer. I have since been told that my stammering was a result of this shyness. I must admit the boy's didn't seem to mind if I stuttered, but the girls made fun of it. I would like to play more sympathetic roles in the future and I have just such a part coming up in *River of No Return*, which will be shot in CinemaScope and Technicolor in Canada. Robert Mitchum and Rory Calhoun will be the co-stars. In this I play a sort of rough girl but--this is very important--with a heart of gold. As for shifting to gingham dresses and buttons-and-bows, I don't care for this sort of costume. I feel my transposition from the role I've played should be both gradual and convincing. In *River* I will be wearing blue jeans most of the time, anyway, and I do not think anybody would want me to go around in baggy overalls. I would like to say here and now that I believe if I turn in a good performance, women will come to like me even though the wardrobe department insists on closely tailored clothes. I am well aware the pin-up pictures have helped me get started, thanks in great part to the wonderful letters sent in to the studio from the men in Korea, Germany and other outposts, but I hope eventually to be remembered for something besides pin-up pictures. I am forgetting the rough years when just eating was a problem and am looking ahead to the pleasure of being really established. Right now I'm working at being an actress and I think women will come to like me as well as men. Please tell Jack Maes of the Fox theatre that I'm glad business was good with *Niagara* and I hope he plays *Blondes*, *How to Marry a Millionaire* and the others to good business. To you and your readers, thanks a million. Sincerely, Marilyn Monroe."

Marilyn sent several photographs which she thought appealed to men, to women and one to both sexes. It is important to note that she points out that her goal is to be a good actress. She is aware of her buildup and the animosity it has generated with members of the opposite sex. That she wants to resolve this problem with women says a lot about her.

Harrison Carroll reported on May 26th, "Marilyn Monroe apparently went to Palm Springs to get over her bronchial condition. Anyway, she and Joe DiMaggio showed up down there at the Doll House." The Doll House was a legendary night-club in Palm Springs.

On May 28th Marilyn goes on a short trip to Ensenada with Joe DiMaggio. On Memorial Day, Joe's brother Mike was found dead, his body floating in Bodega Bay.

Marilyn and Joe were in Ensenada when they were told of the accident. Marilyn didn't join Joe when he left her to go to San Francisco and join his family. She later told Sidney Skolsky that it was during this tragedy that her heart was opened to Joe.

Louella Parsons also reported on the death of Joe's brother, "Marilyn Monroe spent her birthday Monday all by herself. She and Joe DiMaggio, who had two days in Ensenada, were informed there of the death of Joe's brother, Mike, by drowning. They hurried back and Joe went on to San Francisco. Marilyn didn't go with him, and she told me that all those rumors that she is married to Joe are untrue. 'But we will marry someday,' she said, 'because we love each other.' She said she was spending her birthday all alone because she didn't want to go anywhere while Joe feels so badly about his brother."

Louella Parson dedicates her column to Marilyn and her thoughts about Joe DiMaggio. "Marilyn Monroe, who sometimes stops by my house for a little talk after she has finished at the 20th Century-Fox Studio (which is not too far from where I live) told me in a rare burst of confidence that someday she wants to marry Joe DiMaggio. 'I'm sure I'm in love with him. I know I like him better than any man I've ever met. But right now my career is very important to me. When I marry I want to have children. I think I could be a very good mother because I know how lonely a child can be without real love. I am ambitious to be a fine actress and before I marry I want to do a play on the stage and have a really big dramatic role on the screen.'" Louella noted that Marilyn look gaunt after a bout with the flu. "'Where did you meet Joe?' I asked Marilyn after we had had a cup of tea and a sandwich. She looked so thin I felt she should eat something. She had taken off 15 pounds and can no longer be classified as plump." It is an interesting response Marilyn gives on how she met Joe. It doesn't go along with the blind date story. 'I'll tell you how it happened,' Marilyn said. 'I was having dinner with some friends who knew Joe DiMaggio. He sent word over to our table that he would like to meet me. I wasn't interested in baseball and he meant nothing to me. We were introduced and I thought he was very nice.' Louella also give insight into meeting the young Marilyn. 'She has improved so much since the first time I interviewed her. Then she was frightened, although I met her at dinner at Joseph Schenck's on several occasions. I feel she trusts and likes me when she asks my opinion. She is a sensitive little thing and eager to be liked and respected." Louella finishes the article with a popular quote by Marilyn on sex. "'Sex is something you're born with,' has been in most of the magazine interviews with her. She added to it when she told me: 'You shouldn't add to natural sex because that's what attracts the men.' I had to laugh at that, because Marilyn, who was married at 16 to have a home and who is not a night club girl, does not go around with men, other than Joe."

*Why* magazine runs an interesting article about Marilyn, June 1953, cover and article, "Sex Symbolism and Marilyn Monroe," by Ellis Whitfield. "Marilyn has been publicized in the press and in the magazines as 'the walking blowtorch,' the 'two-look girl,' the ' MMmmmmmm girl,' and 'the girl with the horizontal walk.' She has become almost overnight, the greatest single box-office draw in motion pictures. Unscrupulous exhibitors now bill her as the star of old movies in which she had only the tiniest of bit parts. As many women have bitterly observed, Miss Monroe has no more tangible assets than any other 26-year-old female, although they are somewhat better arranged than most. She has a seductive, if rather full-blown figure, and when she wears anything she wears low-cut blouses and too-tight skirts. She undulates when she walks, and she keeps her eyes half-closed and her mouth half-open under a carefully disheveled shock of blonde hair. While it is easy to catalog her charms, it is hard to characterize the overall effect. The newsmagazine *Time*, has settled for the word 'moist.' A more accurate, if less refined observer, has said, 'She looks bed damp.' Everything Miss Monroe says and does is calculated to heighten this humid impression...How did Miss Monroe get this way, when so many other girls tried so hard and failed? The only answer is partly to be found in Marilyn's own heredity and environment, and partly in the attitudes of the society which idolizes her. The real question is not how Miss Monroe got this way, but how America did. For Marilyn is more than just the nation's sex thrill--she is the end product of symbolist and voyeurist trends in the U.S. that have their roots in the Victorian age, and their high-flung branches in the advertising and entertainment techniques of 1953...The danger today, which Miss Monroe tends to symbolize, is that we will come to put a higher value on these symbolic and voyeurist satisfactions than on real-life relationships. It is easy to fall into this trap because sex symbolized and sex observed imposes no responsibilities. By implication our society supports the Victorian theme that sex in marriage is a dull business. Like Walter Mitty, the average husband is constantly invited into an extra-marital dream world in which conquest is an end in itself, without physical or emotional aftermaths. Let us again quote Havelock Ellis, 'From a primitive point of view a sexually desirable woman is one whose sexual characters are either naturally prominent or artificially rendered so; that is to say, she is the woman obviously best fitted to bear children and to suckle them.' It is doubtful that any of Miss Monroe's admirers have ever given a second, or even a first, thought to her qualifications for child-bearing. The drama is in Act I, and in the modern dream world nobody stays for Acts II and III. Few of us are entirely immune to this emphasis on form rather than content. Miss Monroe herself is not. Her own emotional life has suffered to some degree from her preoccupation with how she looks, rather than what she is. She was adored for some time by a Hollywood agent named Johnnie Hyde, but found herself unable to return his love. The romance with Joe DiMaggio appears to be flickering out with no lasting relationship established. At this point no one can say whether Miss Monroe will be able to solve the problems that have followed her out of her childhood. For the rest of us, the problem is simpler. It lies in the recognition that lasting attachments need not be dull, and that one sound real-life relationship is worth a century of voyeuristic daydreams. If we remember that 'the walking blowtorch' represents only part of the normal sexual cycle, we can enjoy her beauty and appeal and need not worry about symbolism."

    Marilyn has this to say about being sexy. "If you are born with what the world calls sex appeal, you can either let it wreck you or use it to your advantage in the tough show business struggle."

Marilyn has a photo session with renowned photographer Alfred Eisenstaedt in June of 1953. He photographs Marilyn on her patio, in her home writing in a journal and getting in to her car. She is dressed in a dark turtle neck top and white peddle pusher pants. He is so excited to take her picture that he loads the wrong film into the camera. Nevertheless, he takes some of the most beautiful images of Marilyn ever photographed. He will say of Marilyn, "She was so frail. She was much thinner than I thought." She writes him a note, "Alfred, You made a palace out of my patio--But next time let's take more time. Love, Marilyn Monroe, June 1953."

On her birthday, June 1st, Joe DiMaggio had gifted Marilyn with an expensive set of golf clubs in hopes this would inspire her to take up the sport that he dearly loved. She gamely gave it a try on several occasions, but it was just not the game for her. Marilyn had this to say about the golf clubs, "They are so beautiful that bystanders stare at me when I try to play. It's embarrassing."

Marilyn and Joe would pal around with Vic "Chic" and Marie Masi, who lived in Sherman Oaks, in the San Fernando Valley. There exists footage from a home movie camera of Marilyn, Joe DiMaggio and Marie Masi at a golf range. Marilyn was hitting balls on the driving range with Joe and Marie trying to improve her skills. Marilyn appeared so lovely. She literally looks like the fabled girl-next-door. Sweet and wholesome are words that come to mind as she practices her golf swing and laughs at her mistakes. She mugs for the camera and only then can you see any glimpse of the sex queen lurking beneath surface of this beautiful young woman. This sweet girl is the foundation of all of Marilyn's lasting friendships. It is not hard to see why some people were hopelessly devoted to her. Even after her divorce from Joe, Marilyn was a visitor at the Masi home. It wasn't until her self-imposed exile from Hollywood and her marriage to Arthur Miller that Marilyn lost touch with the Masi family.

Sports writer Russell Voigt reported about Marilyn on the links on September 20th, "Marilyn Monroe, filmdom's No. 1 glamour girl, is still drawing raves--but this time on the golf links. Boyfriend Joe DiMaggio bought her a set of clubs. Marilyn supplies her own form. She plays regularly, according to an *Associated Press* story from Hollywood, but is puzzled about the status of her progress. 'All the men gather 'round the tee to watch me. All of them say I have a beautiful swing, yet I seldom hit the ball.'"

James Coop reported on June 5th, "Spotted Joe DiMaggio and Marilyn Monroe at Oblath's Beverly."

On July 7th a special article to the *Boston Sunday Advertiser* appeared in the newspaper. "Marilyn Goes Patriotic…Proves Bombshell in Swimming Suit," by Jackson Jones. Five pictures of Marilyn in various swim suits accompany the article. The one chosen for this Fourth of July is the jeweled suit from *How to Marry a Millionaire*. These will go on to be unforgettable images for Marilyn's fans. "She achieves special effect while posing for studio lensman…Marilyn Monroe lighted a firecracker in honor of Independence Day, of course, and how else to do it but in a swim suit. For it seems, it would be a shame to waste her luscious talents otherwise, even if it is for Fourth of July publicity. Out Hollywood way, there's a sense of fitness about these things. And when it comes to fitness, Marilyn goes all the way. The firecrackers for her stunt came from the prop department. They are nice big red firecrackers, which look like they would make a noise when Marilyn sets them off. Marilyn's swim suit came from the wardrobe department, and it had to be just the right suit to get the Independence Day effect. The candid camera got a glimpse of Marilyn being helped into one of these outfits by a helpful wardrobe mistress. Marilyn looked at the result in a mirror, and she was satisfied with what she saw. A technician assigned to the job by the 20th Century-Fox studio, however, overruled her. So Marilyn tried on a couple other swim suits. Finally, she had the technician's approval. This suit is a pert little number, with a costume-jewel spangle on the hem. Apparently, this is supposed to be something like the shower of sparks with which a fireworks bomb lights up the Fourth of July night. Now it was time for rehearsal. Behind the scenes, Marilyn practiced the poses for the pictures. There was a certain sincerity in her work that becomes readily apparent in the final shots. There's one dainty setting in which Marilyn gingerly approaches the giant firecracker. There's another in which she waves a patriotic scarf. And there's the last scene, in which the sparklers light her up in a blaze of glory. All of these pictures are good to look at. But, frankly, when you look at them, what you really see is Marilyn. Her fans have been very vocal in acclaiming what they see in Marilyn. So, probably, it's all for the best. Hurrah for Marilyn and the Fourth of July."

Marilyn gamely posed for publicity photos for the Jr. Chamber of Commerce Convention to be held in Minneapolis, Minnesota. Marilyn stood in front of a banner for the Hollywood, California branch of the Jaycees. She was holding a sign which read, "Visit the California Jaycees...Minneapolis...June 9-12...Marilyn Monroe."

Costume test were underway for *River of No Return*. Once again Travilla designed the wardrobe for Marilyn's character. Charles LeMaire will have this rather unflattering account of Marilyn showing up to the studio with Vaseline all over her face, which was her habit these days. "She was marvelous on the screen, but very difficult to work with. When she first came to Fox, she was in the department one day when Loretta Young came in to fit her nun's habit for *Come to the Stable*, 1949. Loretta always had specific ideas of what she wanted, but nobody minded because she was so charming about it. She was always so lovely and well-groomed that all my staff would be delighted to see her. Marilyn noticed this. She told me that when she got to be a big star, she was going to be just like Young. A few years later, Marilyn was a big star. Bill Travilla was designing her clothes, and I was having a hell of a time getting them made. The fitters told me they'd rather quit than go near her. Marilyn would sometimes stay up all night and then come in for a fitting without having bathed—her hair coated with petroleum jelly. I finally gave her a bar of soap and told her to take a shower. Behind the scenes, Marilyn was a most unremarkable girl. At the peak of her fame, Travilla would take her to lunch and nobody would recognize her...Marilyn could turn on the star quality like a switch. And when she turned it on, there was nothing like it. I could show you 100 actresses who were more beautiful, had better figures and always arrived on time, but none had a trace of what Marilyn had."

On location for *River of No Return* columnist James Bacon interviewed Marilyn and she appeared with her face slathered with "cream." "Her hair was in tangles. She had cold cream all over her face, and her eyebrows were smeared. She was the same old Marilyn in spirit, but on the outside she was Dracula's daughter. I couldn't get out of there fast enough." Whitey Snyder also remembers Marilyn and her greasy mask. "...even on trips into the nearest town. Whitey Snyder, the trusty makeup man, finally told her, 'Get that crap off your face. You scare people.'"

Her sloppy way of presenting herself was also present when she came to rehearsals for recording. Stanley Rubin commented, "Rubin recalled how she'd come to rehearsals wearing a ragged T-shirt, from which the shoulders had been cut, and Capri pants, with lanolin smeared all over her face and hair. 'I asked her one day, 'Marilyn, what have you got on your face?' 'Sex hormones,' she quipped.'" The studio went so far as to issue a memo to her requesting that she wear proper attire when recording with an orchestra of musicians.

*The Brooklyn Eagle* carries an article about boy designer Elgee Bove on June 8th. He talks about fitting Marilyn for a gown. "Elgee dropped the information that he didn't believe in fitting his famous clients over their garments. He molded his creations to the woman herself. Did That mean what I thought it meant? It did. Did that mean Marilyn Monroe? 'It was true,' he said, 'that he fitted his shapely clients as they stood unencumbered by anything other than his draping material,' but I had gotten the wrong idea. The cloth was first placed on the client by feminine fitters. Elgee only put in the artistic tucks and folds. Oh, well, it still was Marilyn Monroe." Elgee would design the iconic purple cocktail dress that Marilyn wore to Korea.

Marilyn wrote a check to J. Russell on June 9th, for the amount of $23.00. On the top of the check it was noted with this social security number, "563-32-0764."

Sheilah Graham's boss, John Wheeler, took over her column for the day and wrote this interesting piece about Marilyn on the 11th. Miss Graham and her husband picked Mr. Wheeler up at the airport and invited him to dinner the following night. When asked who he would like invited to the dinner, he replied, "How about Marilyn Monroe?" To his surprise Marilyn showed up, escorted by Roy Craft. Mr. Wheeler had met Marilyn earlier in her career and predicted then that she would go far, but no one could have predicted the amount of ground she had covered in such a short time. He records part of their conversation:

"The blonde star seemed to be a very pleasant young lady whom I had met before she had made the headlines. We got to discussing her professional career. Her ambition is to become a star on the legitimate stage, a sort of Sarah Bernhardt. In the next breath she admitted that she would like to get married and have several children, although it didn't seem to this aging observer that the two patterns would fit very well.
'Do you get a lot of mash notes?'
'Yes. Especially from soldiers.'
'What do they write you about?'
She blushed a little. 'Lot of them want to know whether I wear anything underneath my dresses. Some ask me to send them an old bra or a pair of panties. The poor guys are so lonely. I had a letter from a poor fellow in Korea the other day that went something as follows:' 'Please write me and say we went to High School together in Van Nuys, Calif. I have been boasting to my buddies that I know you.'
'What did you do about it?'
'I replied that I remembered him, although I don't know whether he came from Van Nuys or not. Maybe it made him happy.'
'We asked her about her sexy walk in the picture *Niagara*. She got up and demonstrated it...here are the directions straight from the star's mouth. Bring your shoulders forward and drop them. Then pretty well let loose from the waist down. However, you must look a little like Miss Monroe to make the desired impression.'"

On June 17th Marilyn attends a Masquers Roast and Rib Dinner for Charles Coburn's birthday at the Beverly Hills Hotel. Also in attendance were Jane Russell and Ronald Reagan and his wife Nancy. After the party was over, Marilyn met columnist Earl Wilson for an interview in the Polo Lounge. In his syndicated column on December 24, 1953, Earl describes the nights events, "Marilyn Poses for the Cam-Ham...I'm camera-crazy...guess you could call me a 'cam-ham'--and I recently realized the dream of every amateur. I photographed Marilyn Monroe. This fateful event in American camera history occurred about 11:30 on a Friday night in the Beverly Hills Hotel in Los Angeles up in room 258. My B. W.-- The Beautiful Wife was there. You see, I'd make an interview date with her for Saturday forenoon. But I had a message that she wanted to fly to San Francisco next day to be with Joe DiMaggio. So how about a night interview? 'She's gone to a party for Charles Coburn...and she's all beautified up...and will look better than she would tomorrow,' the man said. And so there she was...standing radiantly in the lobby...giving off heat waves...keeping her date with me. 'Oh, hul-lo,' she said babyishly, 'I just left your friend, Jane Russell.' Many Hollywood gals stick out their kissers to be smooched. Marilyn doesn't--or didn't. I seized her by the hand and led her straight to a back booth in the darkness of the Polo Lounge...away from the wolves. Gently, I removed the white fox stole from her famous low-cut shoulders...Delicately, I asked if she'd mind the picture idea--my wife would be there. Marilyn smiled that she wouldn't. 'There's a press room upstairs,' I mentioned. Marilyn bounced up--and off we went. After fixing up for three minutes, she wiggled out and greeted me with: 'Oh, a Rolleiflex! I have one. Joe gave it to me.' I gave her orders to do all sorts of poses. Reclining on a couch, leaning across it, sitting on the floor, leaning across the floor...it was mostly leaning, I'm afraid. 'I'm not allowed to lean too far since Atlantic City,' she apologized, referring to that censure of her by the Wacs and Waves. 'I have no stockings on,' she added. 'That's not the area we're working on anyway,' I said. I kept on shooting. 'Do you have a flash outfit?' I asked, indicating my flash outfit. 'I only take pictures in the day time. I have other things to do at night,' she said. She was leaning across a chair now for a closeup and I was putting a handkerchief across the flash. 'You take longer to focus than I do!' she said. She posed with her shoes dangling, and we mentioned the calendar pictures--for which she got $50--and the recent tendency to deemphasize sex as regards Marilyn Monroe. Now Marilyn posed with a couple fellows there who would become big men with these pictures...and next she said to me, 'I think I should take your picture.' She had me recline on the couch and directed me. 'I don't like you hand that way,' she said. 'Turn it this way.' You'll be surprised--as my B. W. was--that the pictures all turned out good. Of course, if they hadn't, I'd have given up photography. I should have mentioned that when the interview was over, Marilyn drove home...alone...'in Joe's little old Cadillac.' 'You mean she actually went home alone?' one of the men said. 'Somehow it seems such a waste of automobile seat.'"

Marilyn plays golf with her new set of golf clubs at Reages Fairways on June 20th. Also on that day Joe DiMaggio takes his son, Joe Jr., on a vacation to Hawaii.

The Leathbridge Herald, a Canadian newspaper, was anticipating Marilyn coming to Canada. "The buzz around town to the effect that Marilyn Monroe will be flying through Lethbridge on a Western Airlines plane within the week had the boys at the fair wondering whether they couldn't hold over for a few days…There's not much truth to the report, by the way. Miss Monroe (how's that for being formal?) plans to fly by a Western DC6 up the

West Coast to Vancouver and then by North Star to Calgary…she's making a picture in Banff."

Florence Cadrez, in her column on the 22$^{nd}$, in the African American newspaper, *The Los Angeles Sentinel*, encourages readers to see *Gentlemen Prefer Blondes*. "When you see Fox Studios' *Gentlemen Prefer Blondes* you'll hear the beat of George Jenkins' fine drumming—he's reeeeal happy to be working on the pic that features popular star, Marilyn Monroe."

Henry McLemore writes in his column on June 24th, "Film Actress Mighty Pretty and Real Sweet...This column is about Joe, Marilyn, and Fred. Joe is Joe DiMaggio. Marilyn is Marilyn Monroe...and Fred is Bill Frawley of the *I Love Lucy* show. I ran into them last night and what do you think we talked about? Baseball. I am probably the only living columnist who knows the name of the best pitcher of all time--according to Miss Monroe. Not Walter Johnson, not Pete Alexander, not Three-Finger Mordecai Brown, not Bob Grove--but Mel Harder, late of the Cleveland Indians. 'Why do you rate Mr. Harder as the best pitcher?' I asked Miss Monroe. 'Joe could never hit him,' Miss Monroe answered. I asked Joe if that was true. He said it was. 'I couldn't get a scratch off Mel,' Joe went on. 'Everybody hit him but me. He had me whipped and kept me that way.' Frawley spoke up at this point. The real nice thing for Frawley to have done was to keep quiet. The same goes for myself. When he started talking. I did, too. He asked me to name the best catcher I ever saw. I said Bill Dickey. 'Cochrane was better,' Frawley said. I asked Joe about it, figuring he knew more baseball than Frawley and McLemore put together. 'You're both right,' Joe said. 'How could you lose if you had either one of them?' While Joe and Bill talked baseball, I talked to Miss Monroe. This is my impression of her. She is mighty pretty. In fact, the prettiest girl I ever saw. And she is a nice girl. What you see of Miss Monroe on the screen isn't the real Miss Monroe. You can take my word for it, or not take my word, but she is quiet, gentle, gracious and the sort of girl you'd like to bring home and say, 'Mama, this is Marilyn.' Miss Monroe is real sweet. This isn't the testimony of a 46-year-old man trying to get in solid with Miss Monroe. I think she likes Joe and Joe likes her, but I'll bet that thousands of Americans think Marilyn and Joe are putting on an act for the sake of publicity. That's not so. She's famous and he's even more so. Maybe it won't work out. I hope it does, because nothing could be nicer than two champions running side by side. Let me repeat: Miss Monroe is a lady from way back. She's quality goods."

On June 26th Marilyn and Jane Russell are honored at Grauman's Chinese Theatre and both stars leave hand prints and footprints in the cement. Marilyn had suggested that Jane leave an imprint of her breasts and she could leave an imprint of her buttocks, but that request was turned down. Marilyn requested that the "i" in her first name be dotted with a rhinestone, and flakes of gold be sprinkled on her patch of cement. Her "i" was dotted with the asked for sparkle, but was soon stolen by a fan. Marilyn's hairstyle had been created by Sydney Guilaroff, who was inspired by the coiffures of the 1930's. Danny Thomas acted as Master of Ceremonies. Afterward, Sidney Skolsky treated Marilyn and Jane to a steak dinner at Chasen's. They were joined by Joe DiMaggio and Jane's husband, Bob

Waterfield.

Sidney Skolsky escorted Marilyn to a preview of *Gentlemen Prefer Blondes*. "Before the picture flashed on the screen, Marilyn whispered to me in that low, sexy voice that is natural with her, 'Hold a good thought for me.' She always says that when embarking on a venture. She feels much better when you tell her you will. Marilyn didn't like the way she looked on the screen, especially the hair. She didn't think she had done the scenes and many of the numbers as well as she could have. She liked herself, especially her hair, in the *Diamonds Are a Girl's Best Friend* number. She genuinely enjoyed Jane Russell and actually laughed aloud at a few of Jane's remarks." Skolsky also remember this funny incident after the preview. "She got ready to race out of the theatre before the end of the picture so as not to have to discuss it with certain people. But she couldn't make her fast getaway because one of her shoes was missing. She finally located it in a row in front of where we were seated, but by then the picture was over and the people were waiting for her."

Sydney Guilaroff had designed her hairstyle in the *Diamonds Are a Girl's Best Friend* number. It was a loose pageboy style, designed to spring and move during her dance routine, and yet fall effortlessly back into place. He colored her hair a restrained platinum that further enhanced the diamond-like effect of her makeup.

Ed Wynn told a funny joke that was making the rounds of Hollywood. "It seems two Indians horsebacked into Beverly Hills from their nearby Palm Springs reservation hoping to meet Marilyn. When they were proudly shown her footprints in the cement at Grauman's Chinese Theater (as near as they could get to her), one Indian turned to the other and said, 'We never catch her today. Mud has been dry long time.'"

The next day Louella spotted Marilyn and Skolsky eating at Fairchild's.

Louella Parsons devoted her whole column to Marilyn and Betty Grable on the 28th. "Glamour Queens Marilyn and Betty Upset Predictions of Cat Fight….In this town when you hear that two glamour girls in the same picture profess great friendship, immediately you are suspicious. But I can tell you that there's nothing fishy about the real friendship between Betty Grable and Marilyn Monroe, both of whom are in *How to Marry a Millionaire*. Marilyn, who I see often, had told me of Betty's great kindness to her and how she went out of her way to help. Marilyn isn't one who expresses herself on any subject that she doesn't mean, and then later I had a long talk with Betty Grable, who was very frank about Marilyn. 'Let's face it,' said Betty, whose honesty has always delighted my soul. 'Marilyn is younger, she's been widely advertised as my successor at 20th. You'd expect me to be jealous. That would be natural, wouldn't it? Well, I never had a jealous moment with this little girl. I feel somehow protective toward her and when you tell me that she says she likes me, that makes me very happy.' At Walter Winchell's party, given for me, the two glamour queens of the 20th lot, Betty and Marilyn, walked in arm in arm….Betty was late in getting to Walter's party because that very day her eight-year-old Jessica had fallen out of a swing and was threatened with a concussion." Given Marilyn's habit of arriving late, that is probably the real reason they walked in together. According to Betty, Marilyn is the only member of the cast to have called her home to ask about her daughter, and this gesture endeared Marilyn to the former Pin-Up Queen of Twentieth Century-Fox, and helped make passing the torch easier.

On the 28th of June Sheilah Graham captured an interesting interview with Darryl Zanuck, head of Fox. He gives some rare insight on how her feels about Marilyn and blames her for her sex build-up getting out of hand. Zanuck never fully understood Marilyn during her time at Fox and this interview provides a window into his perception of her inability to play by the rules, the "Twentieth Century-Fox rules. "From now on, when Marilyn Monroe bats her long, lustrous eyelashes, they may get lost in the crowd because according to Darryl F. Zanuck, 'there will be 65% less close-ups in CinemaScope…You won't miss the closeup. There are wonderful love scenes in *The Robe* and *How to Marry a Millionaire*, but we don't fill the screen with two heads. Marilyn Monroe's sex campaign is off until we see what happens after *Gentlemen Prefer Blondes*. It will be ready to be shown in July. She over-did it, and the campaign got out of hand, especially when she went east for the army. They got a bad photo of her, the camera pointing down at her cleavage. The public sent considerable mail saying we over-emphasized the sex angle. The same thing happened with Jean Harlow. But it has never happened to Betty Grable. That's because she is in musical comedies, and you expect abbreviated costumes. But in *Blondes*, Marilyn is sexy without trying to be—and very funny. So what sex she has, you forgive. She justifies it, for the flirting is not accidental."

*Modern Screen* magazine, July 1953, featured this blurb, "Listen to this: psychiatrists have diagnosed Marilyn Monroe's frequent colds and asthmatic attacks as "psychosomatic" (meaning an illness brought on by frustration.) 'She needs to feel that she is loved and wanted,' say the mental-medics, 'She suffers physically from a sub-conscious yearning for affection!' Wait 'til the Army, Navy and Marines hear this!"

In early July, Manny Lippett of Santa Monica, representing the Jewelry Academy, is photographed showing Marilyn the famed "Moon of Baroda" diamond, as she is named, "The Best Friend a Diamond Ever Had" for her portrayal of the diamond hungry Lorelei Lee in *Gentlemen Prefer Blondes*. Marilyn was given an engraved makeup compact. The "Moon of Baroda" was a 20.9.5 carat, pear-shaped canary diamond which supposedly had a history of bestowing bad luck to anyone who wore it.

Hy Gardner writes an article for *Parade* magazine on July 5th titled, "Does it help—or hurt?...Stars have queer ways of treating colds...I asked Marilyn Monroe how she treats a cold and she said, 'I treat it miserably—just like it treats me.' As a matter of fact, Marilyn wasn't telling the entire truth. As she walked away from me, I detected the remedy she uses so successfully: like everything else, Marilyn just plain shakes off a cold!"

On July 10th Marilyn performs at the Five Disc Jockey Charity Show, held at the Hollywood Bowl, to raise money for the St. Jude's Children's Hospital in Memphis, Tennessee. The event began at 8:30 p.m. Teaming up with Danny Thomas as Master of Ceremonies for the event were Disc Jockeys from KLAC, Alex Cooper, Dick Haynes, Gene Norman, Bob McLaughlin and Peter Potter. The program featured many stars, including Robert Mitchum, who told some jokes, Jane Russell who sang *Diamonds Are a Girl's Best Friend,* and dedicated it to Marilyn. Marilyn did a comedy bit with Danny Thomas. Other celebrities on the program that night were Red Buttons, Danny Kaye, Toni Arden, Kay Starr, Tony Martin, Tennessee Ernie Ford, Gloria Wood, Tex Williams, the Ames Brothers, Mae Williams, Rusty Draper, John Payne, Josephine Premice, Harman McCoy's Swing Choir, and the Sonny Burke's Orchestra. The event wasn't broadcast or televised, but the public was encouraged to turnout to see all the stars. The benefit raised $75,000.00 for St. Jude's. Marilyn had a run in, literally with 22 year-old college student George Forrester. He was working as an attendant for the entrance for the stage show. While coming back from getting a coke, he bumped into Marilyn and spilled his coke on her dress. A guard was ready to remove Forrester from his duties. Marilyn intervened and the two talked for a while. When she found out he was majoring in theater and minoring in pre-dental, she told him to stick to pre-dental.

Bruno Bernard, Frank Worth and Janice Sargeant, took some classic images of Marilyn that night. Janice Sargeant, was not a professional photographer, but a legal secretary whose hobby was photographing the stars. Miss Sargeant will take photos of Marilyn on one other occasion, when she caught Marilyn and her then husband Arthur Miller strolling down a New York street in 1958.

Dorothy Kilgallen printed a notarized letter from Darryl Zanuck on July 10th, regarding Marilyn's singing in *Gentlemen Prefer Blondes*. "Letter From a Hollywood Tycoon, Dear Dorothy: I am sending you herewith a little affidavit about Marilyn Monroe's singing, as you asked me to tell the truth. If I just wrote you a note there might be reason for a lingering doubt. The affidavit is my solemn oath, so you can be sure, I'm not kidding. Marilyn's voice was a surprise to me, and even more of a surprise to the MGM record company and the musicians and technicians who took part in the recording. Best personal regards, Sincerely, Darryl F. Zanuck."

Miss Kilgallen replies, "Dear Darryl: Of course, I DO take your word for it, notarized or otherwise, but you can understand my skepticism can't you? It just floors me that a girl who can sing as well as Marilyn does on the *Gentlemen Prefer Blondes* soundtrack (okay, it's not Dinah Shore, but it's a competent, professional job) just happened to pick up the talent recently. I would have thought that a girl who looked like Marilyn and could sing like that--or even considerably worse--would have bought herself an $18 black satin evening dress with a low-cut V neckline and snagged a job as a singer in a grade B nightclub when things got tough for her. I listen to a great many singers in all kinds of cafes in the course of a year, and I guarantee you most of them warble a lot worse than Marilyn and don't come anywhere near to her in the appearance department. My question is, if she could sing that well, why did she have to pose nude for calendar pictures to get eating money?..."

Dorothy Kilgallen published this dish about Joe and Marilyn on the 10th. "Marilyn Monroe admits to her best chums that although she's been seeing a lot of Joe DiMaggio for two years, she just fell 'really in love' with him recently. And that's when she started deciding on the wedding details. (The pals insist this is the funny part of the romance: although she may soon be Mrs. Di, she still thinks Joe used to be a pitcher!)"

An Australian newspaper, *The Barrier Miner*, gave Marilyn three columns. "Hollywood's Fall Girl…London: 'The two most electrifying sights in the world—Niagara Falls and Marilyn Monroe!' On the vast poster which stretches across a bomb-site in Bond Street she lies at full length across the top of the falls—one dimpled elbow a spray-fall from Fort Weller, Canada; two dainty feet, demurely crossed, in the suburbs of Buffalo, USA. Over her hips stream the raging waters before taking their downward plunge. 'In this film,' wrote American columnist Hedda Hopper, 'Niagara plays a strictly supporting role.' The gush of Hollywood ballyhoo which has carried Miss Monroe along on its ever quickening skelter would make Niagara look like a dripping tap. On the face of it, she is just another Hollywood blonde, with butter-colored hair—styled or tousled, moist lips parted and sweetened by Technicolor, and a walk that suggests that her hips work on ball-bearings. The US Infantry in the Aleutians voted her 'the girl most likely to thaw Alaska.' Doctor Edith Sitwell found her just 'a nice, quiet girl.' When US Assistant Defense Secretary Mrs. Anna Rosenberg toured Korea to discover what comforts were desired by the fighting forces, the answer was 'Marilyn Monroe.' The greatly publicized 'Kiss song,' claimed as one of the highlights of *Niagara* ('she sings of love just as she lives for love), has brought torrents of protest from American housewives' groups and scores of individuals, who say it will have 'a bad effect on husbands and children, and sweethearts.' This has caused Miss Monroe some distress, and she has been cutting up rough with her publicists. In fact, she merely appeared to me to be having trouble with a raspberry pip embedded between her back teeth. Marilyn, whose age is given as between 22 and 26, was born Norma Jean Mortenson. Orphaned at a very early age, she became a ward of the country, and was dumped indiscriminately upon a succession of foster parents. This does not indicate that she particularly endeared herself to her guardians, and yet no sooner had she become America's number one Oomph girl than a number of women claimed to be her mother. At 15 she married a sailor called Dougherty—but this little episode lasted only two years, leaving Marilyn at 17 the bachelor girl she has remained ever since. Marilyn's first picture was called *Scudda Hoo, Scudda Hay*—but her part in it ended up in the tangle of celluloid on the cutting-room floor—because her curves stole the attention from the stars. Since a year ago, when Darryl Zanuck called her 'the biggest box-office potential we have,' and ignoring fancy phrases, *Look* magazine said she was 'the most promising female newcomer,' every honeyed word that has dropped from those moistly parted lips has been faithfully recorded. Her sayings place her almost equally in two categories. Dr. Edith Sitwell's and the American infantry's. In number 1 category, Miss Monroe is reported as saying, 'I hate all the ballyhoo about my life and glamour, but publicity does help pay for my meals and clothes.' Category 2, 'Any girl who says she is bored at being grabbed is a liar!' Category 1, 'I was born under Gemini. That goes for intellect. I've just discovered Tolstoy—he's wonderful!' Category 2, 'I prefer to be interviewed by men. Men and I have a mutual appreciation of being male and female.' Category 1, 'I prefer beer. It's really prettier than champagne, but I suppose it doesn't sound so glamorous.' Category 2, 'One good kiss deserves another.' Category 1, (on the subject of sex) 'I have never given it a second thought.' Dizzy? No. 'I'm blonde, but neither dumb nor dizzy—a serious actress, that's me!' she says. Her drama coach in the studios, Natasha Lytess has remarked somewhat cryptically, 'That girl's soul does not belong to her body.' And yet Marilyn showed that she had real potentialities as an actress in a witty portrayal of a dumb blonde in *All About Eve*. There is, however, one picture of herself which she has never disputed—that of a lonely girl, baffled and frightened, shunning the gay life, going for long, solitary nocturnal walks, and returning home to a lonely fireside to read Emerson."

Marilyn appears on the radio show, *Robert Q's Waxworks*, on *WABC* at 10pm on July 12$^{th}$.

On July 12th, Barbara Berch Jamison wrote in her column, "Body and Soul: A Portrait of Marilyn Monroe Showing Why Gentlemen Prefer That Blonde...The lady behind the latest expression of unbridled male admiration--an admiration so wide-spread and universal that it has transformed her from a sometime model and obscure bit player into one of Hollywood's most important properties in a scant three years--is a blue-eyed, high-color blonde, with dimples and a preposterous past including childhood as a ward of the Los Angeles Orphanage, marriage at 15, divorce at 17, nude calendar modeling, and a long-time romance with Joe DiMaggio. Plopped in a big chair in a musician's bungalow at Fox, dressed in an oversized shirt and creased slacks, wearing no lipstick or shoes, and fussing with unset hair that looked like something out of Marjorie Main, Miss Monroe last week discussed her life and times with this reporter. 'I'm thrilled, of course,' she admitted in a dialect she's developed for herself, which sounds like a cross between a British accent and baby-talk. 'Everything's so wonderful--people are so kind--but I feel as though it's all happening to someone right next to me. I'm close--I can feel it--I can hear it--but it isn't really me. Has she bought a big house then? A mink coat? Picked up any of the more tangible evidences of Hollywood success? 'No—nothing,' she says thoughtfully. 'Oh—I did move out of the furnished apartment I was living in into an unfurnished apartment. And I bought a new bed—sort of a sofa.' She grows more excited. 'It's covered in orange velvet—sounds horrible, but it's dreamy.' She pauses. 'Yes, actually, I do have this wider bed now.' She sighs. 'What I really notice about my success is that I have to watch my health. I've turned anemic since all this happened—have to drink raw liver juice and stir uncooked eggs into my milk.' She grins. 'And I eat steak for breakfast every morning. Never had to worry about my constitution before.' She's not too surprised that she's become the world's most desirable female. Her success with men dates back to adolescence and contains some pretty concrete proof of their warm approval. 'At 12 I was pretty thin—the boys used to call me 'string-bean,' she says wryly. 'Then I started to fill out—'she drops her eyes—'and they've never called me string-bean anymore.' She was queen of the campus at high school, queen of the plant at the airplane factory where she worked during the war, and winner of every beauty contest she ever entered. Now, with Hollywood stardom as her reward, she's the proclaimed sweetheart of three-quarters of the world's masculine population. Her mail comes to the studio in truck loads, her picture is run frequently in *Stars and Stripes*, the Army newspaper…I want to grow and develop and play serious dramatic parts—my dramatic coach, Natasha Lytess, tells everybody that I have a great soul—but so far nobody's interested in it. Someday, though—someday--.' Meantime, the studio is keeping her soul in reserve and starting her in multi-million-dollar musicals like *Gentlemen Prefer Blondes*, in which she competes with Jane Russell, an old-timer in the business of popping gentlemen's eyeballs, and *How to Marry a Millionaire*, in CinemaScope. Nights, before her health started to wane, she took courses at UCLA's extension school in downtown Los Angeles, in literature and philosophy, and after the first shock of her appearance in these classes wore off she went out for coffee with six or seven of her male classmates regularly. She does a lot of reading on the set even now, and during the shooting of *Gentlemen Prefer Blondes*,' she and Miss Russell became good friends. Thus, instead of spending their time painting their toe nails, 'Jane,' says Miss Monroe, 'who is deeply religious, tried to convert me to her religion and I tried to introduce her to Freud. Neither of us won.'"

Marilyn's Doheny apartment is described by columnist Kendis Rochlen. "Marilyn has a small, beautiful apartment on Doheny Drive, a few blocks below Sunset Boulevard. She and Joe often spent the evening there. Unlike a lot of stars, Marilyn hasn't gone overboard by buying a big, luxurious showplace of a house. Nor does she spend a lot of money on fancy duds. Her apartment is modern in theme, one of four in an eye-catching building of snow-white stone with a beautiful entrance leading into a little courtyard, with separate doors to each flat. The apartment has a living room with a fireplace, a bedroom and a little kitchen with a dinette. Marilyn did much of the decoration herself, with Jane Russell helping out with some ideas and elbow grease."

Marilyn's doctor, Elliot Corday, put her own a special diet for anemia. "He's giving me iron and vitamin shots but they don't seem to help. Of course, I try to do what he prescribes. Just listen to some of the awful things I have to eat and drink. For breakfast I have two raw eggs beaten in a glass of warmed milk. Before lunch I'm supposed to drink a glass of tomato juice with two tablespoons of raw ground liver in it. Even lime and Worcestershire sauce hardly mask the taste. At 5 I have a hard-boiled egg and gelatin in orange juice; rare steak and spinach for dinner."

Dorothy Kilgallen reported on July 14th that, "Without telling anyone, Marilyn Monroe slipped out of Hollywood and trekked to San Francisco to visit at Russian River with Tom and Lee DiMaggio, brothers of the Joltin' Joe. She wanted to do the spending-time-with the-family-of-the-prospective-mate but without fanfare." Lee (Louise) DiMaggio was actually Tom's wife.

On the 16th, Betty Scheibel, a columnist for the *San Antonio Light*, reported that locals, Eddie Gonshor and Norman Schaefer, recently took a trip to Hollywood and Las Vegas. "The brightest moment came when Marilyn Monroe walked into Groumet's in Beverly Hills and they walked over to talk to her. Beer goes for $1 a bottle at Groumet's, Gonshor says, but for Marilyn it was worth it."

Although, it is not known when their visit took place, on July 20th photos were developed showing Joe DiMaggio and Marilyn in Puerto Penasco, Sonora, Mexico. A group photo was taken with Carlos Alberto Gonzalez, umpire for the Mexican team. There were also candid photographs of Marilyn and Joe on the back of a boat and several candid's of Marilyn in front of a modern home.

On July 25th cast and crew arrives on location for the *River of No Return*. Marilyn flew in a United Airlines DC 6 from Los Angeles to Vancouver International Airport. There is a photograph of her sitting in front of the plane on some luggage, she has her hands up and looks radiant. While at the airport she was interviewed by Vancouver morning radio legend Monty McFarlane of C-FUN. From there, Marilyn and the cast and crew fly to Calgary, and from there take the Continental Limited train to Jasper.

*Winnipeg Free Press* newspaper, Canada, picture and article, July 27th, "Curves Monroe Attracts Town As Muscles Mitchum Ignored...Marilyn Monroe, the vivacious Hollywood screen star, attracted about 2,003 people at the Canadian National railways station here Sunday afternoon as she stepped off the Continental limited from Vancouver. The greeters-- practically the whole population of Jasper and several hundred guests from the Jasper Park lodge were well armed with cameras and the popular actress obliged by posing for many pictures. Off the same train, and almost unnoticed, were several other actors, directors and producers, who are taking part in the 20th Century-Fox production, *River of No Return*, which will be filmed in Jasper park starting Monday. These included actors Robert Mitchum and Rory Calhoun, Tim Wallace, Mr. Mitchum's stand-in, and Otto Preminger, the director. Robert Mitchum was accompanied by his wife and 16-month-old daughter, Petrine and Rory Calhoun by his wife."

The photo of Marilyn standing between two Mounties was captioned, "Marilyn Monroe, 20th Century-Fox screen star, needed help from two stalwart members of the Royal Canadian Mounted Police at Jasper Saturday as she stepped off the train from Vancouver. The help she needed and got was being escorted to a waiting car through a large crowd of people who were at the station to get a glimpse of the vivacious movie star. The lucky Mounties are Constable J.E. Snider and A.P. Dirk, both of Jasper."

Sheilah Graham pointed out that Marilyn "is usually teamed with unhandsome, nonromantic types, with the exception of Robert Mitchum in *River of No Return*. 'He was the first guy they let me get hold of,' she said."

Marilyn stayed in a cabin at Becker's Bungalows on the Athabasca River, located in Jasper National Park. According to Bob Sanford, historian with Canadian Pacific Hotels and Resorts, Marilyn didn't stay at the Jasper Park Lodge. Though she did try to dine at the Lodge's restaurant, but was turned away because she was wearing jeans, and didn't meet the dress code. This caused no small stir in Jasper.

After she was settled in, Charles Feldman called Marilyn to tell her that he had just screened *Gentlemen Prefer Blondes*, and she was wonderful! Marilyn is overjoyed with the news and starts this film with high hopes.

Marilyn stars as Kay Weston, a saloon singer with a heart of gold. She co-stars with old acquaintance Robert Mitchum. She has some effecting scenes with young Tommy Retting, who will go on to fame in the television series *Lassie*. Jack Cole choreographed her saloon numbers. Even though Cole was known for his modern dance with an Asian twist, Marilyn's saloon routines still managed to be sexy, despite the constraints of the era. One of the saloon girls was played by Barbara Nichols, who will go one to be a 'B-Movie Marilyn.' Helen Thurston played Marilyn's stunt double in the movie, although, Marilyn did do much of the difficult filming herself. On hand for Marilyn were hairdresser Gladys McCallister and Make-up man Whitey Snyder. Marilyn will say of this movie in 1956, "Only today a taxi driver said to me, 'Why did they ever put you in that little stinker, *River of No Return*?' I thought it was a good question. I'm with the taxi driver. He's my boy. Knowing what I know now, I wouldn't accept *River of No Return* today. I think that I deserve a better deal than a Z cowboy movie, in which the acting finishes third to the scenery and CinemaScope. The studio was CinemaScope-conscious then, and that meant that it pushed the scenery instead of actors and actresses."

While in Jasper, Marilyn befriended some of the town's younger residents. Alden Bradley, his brother Terry and a friend, Ray Knight, rode their bikes three miles in search of the Blonde Bombshell. Hoping to find her at her cabin, they were told she had gone for a walk. Undeterred, the young fans decided to chase after her. When they caught up with her, she seemed smaller and younger than they imagined that she would be. Marilyn asked Alden if she could ride his bike. His bike was made from spare parts and was not a really fitting ride for a movie star, but he agreed to let her ride it. After peddling for about a mile with the boys and Alden running alongside her, Marilyn returned the now prized bike. The boys recall her laughter that afternoon, and how she changed a boy's old bike in to a priceless possession and the envy of all his friends.

Another day, Marilyn's limousine stopped alongside two boys who were also on their way to see her. Jim Robinson and Robert Blewett not only got Marilyn's autograph, but an invitation to visit her on the set and she granted them permission to bring along their buddy, James Kulak. A few days later Marilyn invited the boys to meet her friend, a baseball player, who was coming into town.

Marilyn poses for a series of publicity pictures on the shores of Lake Louise. She also poses for local photographer Ray O'Neil. He posed her by a fence and with a horse. These are splendid and sweet images of Marilyn.

The logistics of filming in such a remote area came to be compromised by the large crowds of people that showed up for filming. Harold Heffernan commented on June 21, 1954 that, "Fans swarmed into the area in such numbers that the problem of supplying food and other living necessities for the cast and crew from hotels, restaurants and stores in the community became a serious problem."

Filming begins today, July 28th, on *River of No Return*. At 7:30am each morning a train which was specially commissioned by Canadian National Railways took the cast and crew to the filming location near Devona Flats. This was about 15 miles East of Jasper. The conductor, Bob Sansom, remembered the sleepy Marilyn curling up each morning in his sleeping bag, which was in the caboose. He said she was, "a rather endearing, but tired little girl."

On October 21st, Harrison Carroll writes of his time on the set of *River of No Return*. "It's the Northwest again on the *River of No Return* set at Twentieth Century-Fox. I go out to watch director Otto Preminger shoot a scene where Marilyn Monroe warbles a song in a smoky tent saloon. The place is full of rugged looking characters, drinking beer on upturned barrels, playing cards or making love to dancing girls. In a minute, Marilyn will step out on a platform with imitation egret feather and wearing a low-cut, spangled gown with a deep slit in the skirt revealing the shapely Monroe legs in black net hose. Marilyn is waiting on the sidelines now. The dress corsets in her normal 23-inch waist to the point where she looks as if one touch would break her in two. 'It's not so bad now,' she tells me. 'I've got it unlaced in the back. When I do the shot, though, my waist will be squeezed to 19 inches.' Producer Stanley Rubin nods approvingly. 'This is her introductory sequence' he explains. 'She must be very beautiful because in most of the picture, she wears blue-jeans and looks like a drowned rat.' A wardrobe woman comes over. Marilyn draws in her breath. The wardrobe woman pulls mightily at the laces. As her waist hits the required 19 inches, all Marilyn does is let out a little gasp."

On the 29th Bill Latham reports, "Marilyn Monroe visited old friend pianist Hal

Schaefer at the Saratoga, and joined in the community sing."

Sigmund Spaeth, music critic for the *Oakland Tribune*, sang the praises of *Blondes*, on the same day. "The musical film, *Gentlemen Prefer Blondes*, is infinitely superior to the stage version, in which the hapless Carol Channing was turned into a horrible caricature. Marilyn Monroe looks and acts like a girl on whom gentlemen might actually lavish gifts, and her brunette friend, played by Jane Russell, is even more attractive. Two new songs by Hoagy Carmichael also help."

*Stag* magazine article, August 1953, "Marilyn Monroe Answers 33 Intimate Questions...Editor's Note: Marilyn Monroe--weight: 118; Height: 5'5"; bust: 37; waist: 24--is the hottest thing to sizzle on a movie screen since platinum blonde Jean Harlow got 'into something comfortable' in *Hell's Angels* some 20 years ago. When Monroe moves her vastly publicized body the nation's wolves whistle; when she sighs, men quiver; when she talks, people listen--and look. Because most men are too distracted ever to hear what she says. *STAG* publishes on these pages 33 of Marilyn Monroe's most revealing public statements of her private life...

1. Are you bothered by wolves?
    Monroe: This would be a very uninteresting world if there weren't any wolves. But a girl has to learn to handle 'em.
2. What type of wolves have you come across?
    Monroe: Some are sinister. Others are just good-time Charlies trying to get something for nothing. Others make a game of it. The last type is most interesting.
3. How do you avoid trouble with wolves?
    Monroe: All you have to do is look stupid, and pretend you don't know what they're talking about.
4. Why did you pose for THAT nude calendar?
    Monroe: A photographer friend of mine, Tom Kelley, and his wife, Natalie, had been coaxing me for weeks to pose for a nude calendar they had an order to do. When I received an eviction notice from my apartment, I phoned Tom. I decided I'd be safer with him than with some rich old guy who might catch me in a weak moment when I was hungry and didn't have enough to buy a square meal. Kelley told me he'd camouflage my face. But it turned out everybody recognized me.
5. What did you have on when you posed for that nude calendar?
    Monroe: The radio.
6. What is your current attitude about that calendar?
    Monroe: When I see them now I feel like I'm dressing in a room without window shades.
7. What is your marital status?
    Monroe: I have no plans for a wedding in the near future! When

I'm ready, I'll get married. As for Joe DiMaggio, that's very private. We're friendly--put that friendly in quotes. When and if he asks me, I'll know. Right now we're not seeing each other. Maybe things can be worked out later. But I'll keep my eyes open, and won't ignore other men.

8. What about all those 'cleavage' photos taken of you?
    Monroe: What am I going to do? The photographers stand on a high platform, and shoot down. What kind of pictures can anyone expect will come out of that?
9. What do you wear to bed?
    Monroe: Chanel Number 5.
10. Do you like sun baths?
    Monroe: I don't like myself dark-hued. I like to feel my body blonde all over.
11. What is your favorite activity?
    Monroe: Reading. I prefer classical literature. If you're ignorant, books won't laugh at you.
12. Do the remarks that women make about you bother you?
    Monroe: It's a little dull when they don't make remarks, isn't it?
13. What's the best thing that ever happened to you.
    Monroe: They say it's a man's world; I don't mind being a woman in it.
14. Were you sore when the Army censored a picture taken of you with four members of the military services at the Atlantic City Miss America Parade?
    Monroe: I was surprised and hurt. People looked at me all day. I thought they were admiring my Grand Marshal's badge.
15. How does a girl make herself attractive to men?
    Monroe: Try to be beautiful. But don't underestimate your frame of mind. You must feel desirable and attractive, to make others feel it. You must enjoy being a woman.
16. Do you dress to please men or women?
    Monroe: If you can't trust you own instinct to find an answer to that question, then never ask a woman for advice.
17. Do you think men dislike makeup?
    Monroe: A man doesn't like to look at a woman and be conscious of her makeup. But when you put it on carefully, you can use everything there is without his being aware of it.
18. What about perfume?
    Monroe: I spray it on my ankles, back of my knees, and all the way up to my eyebrows, so the fragrance really belongs to me.

19. How should a woman walk?
    Monroe: When you walk, always think UP in front, and DOWN in back.
20. Are those really your own eyelashes?
    Monroe: Oh yes. Everything belongs to me.
21. What are some complaints that people have against you?
    Monroe: I've gotten crank letters from women. They say, 'What are you trying to do? Put the country in a worse state than it's in?' They accuse me of starting all the rapes. Rapes went on long before I came.
22. How do you feel about the critics?
    Monroe: They are so cruel, the critics. Sometimes I think they just take out their frustrations on other people. One said all I can do is just wiggle my fanny.
23. When did this 'sex appeal' stuff of yours start?
    Monroe: I think I was about 12 when things changed radically. The boys didn't have cars. They had bikes. They'd come by the house and whistle or honk their little horns. Some had paper routes. I'd always get a free paper.
24. What did you think of Anna Rosenburg's statement that GI's kept asking 'send us Marilyn Monroe?'
    Monroe: I think she must have been joking. But, like all American women, I have the boys in Korea very much in mind, and would do anything to contribute to their happiness.
25. How did you get your name of Marilyn Monroe?
    Monroe: My mother's maiden name was Monroe. I'm a direct descendent of President Monroe. Then a studio man told me I resembled Jean Harlow and Marilyn Miller. Marilyn sounds better with Monroe than Jean. So it became Marilyn Monroe.
26. How do you live now?
    Monroe: I have a horror of signing a lease. I live alone. I don't even have a servant, yet. I do my own cooking and dishwashing. Maybe I should see a psychiatrist!
27. Do you think underwear hampers a girl?
    Monroe: Women have sent me bras and girdles, with notes saying, 'You need these more than I do.' I want everybody to know I don't wear what I don't wear. All those lines and ridges in undergarments, girdles, and bras are unnatural. They distort a girl so, so I never wear them!
28. True or falsie?
    Monroe: Of course, that's silly! First, those who know me better,

know better. Second, it's just not true. It's a false statement.
29. Should women marry younger men?
Monroe: I understand women live longer than men. Then women will have to marry younger men to make things come out even--or else they'll have to spend the old age in a rocking chair.
30. What do you think about older men?
Monroe: Older men, of course, are mellower, fuller, richer. Look at Cary Grant. There's a lot of life in him. And Clark Gable. You know he's got something. Experience rounds out a man, and makes him more desirable.
31. When are you most at ease?
Monroe: I talk better lying down.
32. What do you like about men?
Monroe: They understand me.
33. Does anything ever give you trouble when you take sunbaths?
Monroe: Nothing--not even helicopters.

Ezra Goodman asked Robert Mitchum "if he believed Monroe really read the high-toned books she was so widely publicized as perusing, and Mitchum told him this relevant incident that took place during the making of *River of No Return*. 'Marilyn was reading a dictionary of Freudian terms. I asked her why she was reading it and she said, 'I feel one should know how to discuss oneself.' I said, 'What chapter are you up to now?' She said, 'Anal eroticism.' I said, 'That's charming and do you think that will come up in a discussion?' She went back to reading and looked up after a while and said, 'What's eroticism?' I explained. A minute or two later she looked up from the book again and said, 'What's anal?' My stand-in, Tim, who was working on a scratch sheet nearby, couldn't stand it any longer and butted in, 'That's the keester,' he said.'"

Marilyn wrote check to Mrs. E. S. Goddard on August $2^{nd}$, for the amount of $851.04. Marilyn noted on the check that the money was "For--G.P. Eley," who was also known as Gladys Pearl Baker, her mother.

On August 3rd, Marilyn takes over for Dorothy Kilgallen and writes a very revealing column about herself. "(Dorothy Kilgallen is on vacation. Pinch-hitting for her today is the screen's most talked-about blonde. Marilyn Monroe.) Marilyn Monroe writes: I'm going to pull a typical female stunt. I'm going to prop a mirror in front of the typewriter and try a Monroe story myself. Now, this isn't going to be one of those Don't-believe-what-you've-heard-This-is-what-I'm-really-like stories. But it will be an objective look at Marilyn Monroe by Marilyn Monroe. I think this is as good a time as any. I'm not aware that my career is approaching a peak. First, for the records: I consider myself a lucky girl. When 20th Century-Fox put me under contract three years ago, I was no better an actress than I was four years earlier when I couldn't find a job. I weighed then as I do now. 118 pounds. I was 5 feet 5 1/2 inches tall, had blonde hair and blue eyes. These statistics haven't changed.

I was trying to get a break in pictures and--I was scared of the very thing I sought. Today I'm still scared--I just hide it better. Seven years ago I was hungry and couldn't pay my room rent. Today I'm well paid and photographers stop me to take pictures. It has been said before that I'm trying to 'find myself.' I guess that's true. The usual goal is to achieve as much happiness as possible and for a woman, the worthwhile goal is marriage and children. I hope it happens to me. Because I've played sexy, dumb blondes, people laugh when it's suggested I read books. But if you want your arm talked off, mention Thomas Wolfe to me. I've practically memorized his books. I write poetry. Usually sentimental and philosophical. Not the best in the world, let's face it, but I get satisfaction from putting my thoughts on paper. I like to write on rainy nights. I like to take long walks on the beach alone. Someday, I want to have a house of my own with trees and grass and hedges all around, but never trim--just let them grow as they please. I like people but don't make many close friends. My drama coach, Natasha Lytess, calls me 'tragic.' She thinks my childhood in an orphanage has made me sad. But I think it's just my nature to be serious and to worry about little things. I have a sense of humor, although it's not spontaneous. Every now and then some reporter will ask me for a comment on something or other and I have to stall him until I can think of what I consider exactly the right thing to say and the right way to keep up my strength. This is where I straighten out a little legend about me that has been making the rounds, i.e. that I wear no underclothing. This story started when I had to try on a slinky dress for a picture and people insisted that I wasn't wearing underwear. I admit I hate stockings and I've never worn a girdle (men seldom jump hurdles for girls who wear girdles). But other than that I'm always well clothed in the undergarment department. I'm nearly always late for appointments. I've tried everything I can think of to cure myself--with no luck. Some wag suggested when we went on daylight saving time that I not be told about it. I have other sloppy habits. I don't put things away where they belong and often wear jeans because the dress I didn't hang up is wrinkled: I lose telephone numbers and forget to mail letters. I don't like makeup and don't use it except for work or dress, although my skin is too pale without it. I've been warned against saying what I think. Not that I'm tactless-it just doesn't occur to me to lie. No one can condemn you for being honest if you're honest in your honesty. Someday, I think, I should like to do a legit play. But I'm afraid I would stutter. When I'm nervous the words won't come. Once, in a school play, I became so frightened I ran off the stage without doing my part. Shoes bother me and I slip them off whenever possible. The greatest disappointment of my career is that some critics didn't think I did my own singing in *Gentlemen Prefer Blondes*. But the recording company which put me under contract later was satisfied no one was standing behind me doing the vocal. I like the titles GIs have given me, like "Blowtorch Blonde," "Miss Flamethrower of '53" or "The Girl We'd Most Like To Come Between Us and Our Wives." This is their version of a wolf whistle--and nowadays a girl doesn't call the police if a man whistles like a gentleman. I like to lie on the floor while talking on the telephone. It rings often, mainly because I give the number to newspapermen who ask for it. Movie stars aren't supposed to do this. I think it's impolite not to. Besides, I like men."

On August 11th, Jane Russell fills in for Dorothy Kilgallen while she is on vacation. "When I came on the 20th Century-Fox lot recently for the first time to co-star with Marilyn Monroe in *Gentlemen Prefer Blondes*, I was advised how to deal with her. 'Shake hands, make the first dirty crack and come out fighting,' a well-meaning friend said. This counsel was in the best space-grabbing tradition of Hollywood and Broadway. Any press agent worth his salt knows that the best way, short of scandal, to get a client's name in the newspapers is to have him feud with a rival. And naturally, it was assumed that Marilyn and I could not get along. Two girls sharing equal billing and equal responsibilities for a picture and having publicity building in common are expected to battle tooth and nail to outshine one another. According to the rules, you see glamour girls must feud with glamour girls, strip teasers with strip teasers, cowboys with cowboys and dancers with dancers. But Hollywood feuds are different. For one thing, no blood is shed. The only weapons are the quip, the insult, the slight and the behind-the-back remark routed forward. It's all supposed to be good clean antiseptic fun--bitterness without wounds. Sometimes, of course, the combatants get serious and pride is injured. But as a rule, nobody gets hurt except the press agent who started it. After examining Hollywood feuds--both sincere and synthetic--I was convinced that feuding was not for me. Who needs it? In the first place, I'm too lazy for hair pulling. In the second place, I never could have brought myself to say anything unkind about Marilyn Monroe."

In another article Jane reveals the private Marilyn that she loves. "This Marilyn is a kind girl…sensitive, shy, yes, but very philosophical with good sound evaluations. She's not to be underestimated in depth or spiritual character. As the kids around the Fox lot say, 'She'll never be high hat or a malicious dame. She'll always have due regard for the little guy and the big. She can't be bothered with prejudices.' Her mind is so full of studies and books and things ethereal that she's five worlds away—so people call her vague or dumb. But I don't know anybody else who has tackled so many things to learn and do at once, and she's dead serious and very sincere. Jack Cole heard someone remark, 'That dame's in a fog.' He said, 'There's a kind of terrible determination and direction to Baby Doll's elusive methods. She knows exactly what she wants and she usually gets it.' And I think it's wonderful that she has the desire for such good healthy things as work and friends. She desperately wants a family to belong to, children, and a husband she can depend on, who trusts her and knows that the outside pressures are not her choice. Marilyn once said to me, 'You can stand almost anything as long as at least one person understands—and has faith in you.'…She's already developed migraine headaches from the tension caused by trying to please everyone, and be the best actress in town. Now that her publicity agents have made her known to the public, I think it's the time the real Marilyn was introduced. She'll please even more people, men and women fans. Right now, Marilyn's going through a crisis. She's worked hard on the stylized, sexy Marilyn that Hollywood wanted but the thing got a little out of hand. She started getting private and public scoldings and she was bewildered. She's been deeply hurt by lots of wise guys, and people who suddenly changed their attitude toward her. Two bits of advice 'Doll.' First: develop your sense of humor! You really need it in this town. Second: I pass onto you a 'prayer for today' given me by a dear old gentleman, "Lord, help me to be truly myself—with due regard for the edification of others.'"

Joe DiMaggio arrives in Jasper to do a little fishing on August 11th with pal Georgie Solotaire. He tells reporters that his visit was, "strictly coincidental...I'm up here for the fishing." While in Jasper, Joe stays at the Tocara Lodge. Marilyn met him there each evening after filming was over.

"A pal," commented on Joe's visit. "'He planned to drive her around some of the beautiful Canadian countryside where they were shooting,' a pal said. 'But just about the time he got there she hurt her leg in a scene and he ended up more of a baby-sitter than as an escort around Canada.'"

Marilyn had invited Jim Robinson, Robert Blewett and James Kulak to greet her "friend" when he came into town. Their mothers took them to the small landing strip in Jasper, and before long a plane landed. Out stepped the baseball player Marilyn had told them about, Joe DiMaggio. He came over to the boys and greeted them, saying, "You must be Marilyn's friends." It is seeing him be so cordial to young fans like these boys that makes Marilyn's heart become close to him.

On August 13th the press reported that the 18-foot, 150 pound cutout of Marilyn from *Gentlemen Prefer Blondes* was stolen from the front of Grauman's Chinese Theater.

Marilyn injures her ankle on August 13th when she fell in the river while filming scenes for *River of No Return*. Although she has a stunt double in the film, Helen Thurston, Marilyn is used as much as possible. She tells Sidney Skolsky of calling for Joe. "When I was at Banff with the twisted ankle, I was so confused and frightened. Some doctors up there told me that if I walked before a month, I'd injure the ankle permanently. The studio was sending a doctor. Joe was vacationing with George (Solotaire). I know how Joe hates publicity and movie sets. But when he phoned and asked if he should come on, I said yes.' Marilyn continued about Joe and the ankle, and how he quietly took charge and conferred with the doctor flown up from Beverly Hills. She said that after Joe's arrival everything straightened out."

*Canadian Press Wire Service* story, August 14th, "Screen Star Nearly Drowns After Stumble...Screen star Marilyn Monroe was reported nearly drowned Thursday when she stumbled in swift waters here during a scene for the film *River of No Return*. The blonde star had donned chest-high rubber waders during rehearsals to protect her costume. She slipped on a rock, the waders filled with water and she was unable to rise. Actor Robert Mitchum and a dozen crewmen leaped in and pulled her to shore. Examination disclosed a seriously-sprained left ankle which may force her out of the film for several days." Marilyn returns to work the next day despite her "seriously-sprained" ankle.

*Canadian Press Wire Service* story on August 14th, "Added Attraction In Rockies...Screen actress Marilyn Monroe rides the caboose of the 'Million Dollar Special,' which daily carries her, along with actors Robert Mitchum and Rory Calhoun, to Devonia, Alta., from Jasper village, in the heart of the Canadian Rockies. Devona was selected for its breath-taking scenic beauty to be the site of a Technicolor film. The train was purchased by the movie company to help transport equipment and personnel daily over the rough terrain from Jasper to Devona."

On August 17th the cast and crew move to Banff to shoot more location footage. Marilyn stays in the Banff Springs Hotel, Room #816. Although, Joe DiMaggio stayed behind to fish at Lake Louise, he drove the 40 miles every day to lunch with Marilyn; he even taught Marilyn how to play golf on the Hotel's course. It was one of the most expensively designed golf courses of its day. A photo survives of Marilyn playing golf. It is captioned, "Marilyn Monroe pauses before a swing at the famous Banff Springs Hotel Golf Course during the shooting of *River of No Return*. Her ankle injury forced her to seek recuperation off the movie set."

Jon Vachon takes a lovely photo of Marilyn and Joe sitting by a window. The uncropped version of this image reveals Marilyn's cast. Marilyn also used her time off to pose for publicity stills. She mugged for the camera at the Hotel's pool, where she wore a two-piece swimsuit and stood on her crutches. In one shot she smiles invitingly at the hotel swimming instructor, Wolfgang Karbe. Marilyn also posed with some Canadian Mounties, the Banff sign, riding a ski lift, paddling a canoe, and with bears at a trading post. For Vachon's lens Marilyn emanates a tender beauty that gives the viewer pause.

Marilyn re-injured her ankle on August 19th in another accident while filming *River of No Return*. Dr. Robert Rosenfeld, a Beverly Hills orthopedic surgeon, was sent by the studio to treat Marilyn. Early reports indicated that she had torn several ligaments and tendons in her left leg.

Robert Mitchum tells Earl Wilson in a 1961 interview about his admiration of Marilyn while they worked together on *River of No Return*. "'Any girl with that much guts--why she tried to save my life once,' said the Hollywood hero celebrated for not letting stunt men take more risk than he will. 'We had a rough scene on a raft, headed for a big rock in the rapids. They wanted me to use a stunt guy, but I said, 'how could I, when Marilyn and the kid were out there in the river." Suddenly, when I saw we were shooting right at the rock, I said, 'I think we've bought it!' I said to Marilyn, 'I don't want to panic you, but it could be a matter of life and death. Lie down flat on your belly on the raft and stay down! Otherwise we're going to crash right down on 85 miles of rapids.' Pretty soon we saw the little rescue boat. There was only room in it for two. And it had a big hole in it. Marilyn said, 'No, I don't go unless he goes. He's sick and besides he wouldn't be here if it weren't for me having to do the scene over.' So I squeezed in the rescue boat and held my elbow in the hole to keep the water out. Any dame with that much guts--.'"

On August 21$^{st}$ and 22$^{nd}$ Marilyn's pastel mink coat, silverblue mink stole and stone marten scarf she wore in *How to Marry a Millionaire* were sold at a public auction in New Hampshire. They were part of a large collection designed by Al Tietlebaum of Hollywood to go on the auction block.

Before leaving for Hollywood, Marilyn attends the Alberta Theaters Association convention dinner held at the Banff Springs Hotel.

Location work is finished in Canada for *River of No Return* on September 1st. Marilyn flies back to Los Angeles. She is photographed, still on crutches, with Robert Mitchum on the ramp of the plane. Lyle Linblad, passenger agent for United States Airlines autographs Marilyn's partial cast while she waited clearance through U.S. Customs at Seattle. Poor Mr. Linblad was so nervous he misspelled his name and broke his pencil.

During the filming of interior scenes at the studio, Marilyn was reunited with an old neighbor from her childhood, Julian Arnold Smith. Young Norma Jeane used to play with his son, Julian Jack Smith, when she lived with the Bolenders. The older Julian is an actor and is playing an extra as one of the cowboys in the bar. His face is just to the right of Marilyn's right shoulder as the scene at the bar was filmed.

Back in the studio, Hal Schaffer helps Marilyn with her vocal numbers. Marilyn meets photographer Milton Greene on the set of *River of No Return*. They are introduced by Rupert Allen. The classic exchange takes place where Marilyn says, "He's just a boy," and Milton replies, "She's just a girl." Marilyn and Milton quickly develop a close friendship, and according to him, they have a sweet affair that lasts only a short time. He will never admit this to Amy, his wife. "Amy knew I was friends with Marilyn. She didn't know about the sex. She said, 'is that true?' And I said, 'believe what you want to believe, Amy.' Even if I was caught in bed by my wife, I'd say it's not true."

The next day he photographs Marilyn in the black sweater that is the first in a series of images that quickly supplant the way she will be photographed from now on. The tacky cheesecake settings will give way to a more sophisticated and elegant approach to photographing her. After Milton Greene's photographs of her are published, the other photographers who work with her follow suit and, for a while, her beauty is the sole focus of their lenses. But like Milton Greene, they will learn, her erotic essence is never far from the surface.

Greene takes some photographs of Marilyn on the set of *River of No Return*. She drives him to the airport and they part as a people whose relationship is a bit closer than friends. Milton will return to Hollywood in a few weeks with his new wife Amy, who is pregnant, and will photograph Marilyn for *Look* magazine. After the studio sessions are completed, Joe takes Marilyn back to San Francisco for a short rest.

Back in Los Angeles on September 10th, Marilyn attends rehearsals for her appearance on *The Jack Benny Show*. Writer, Milt Josefsberg remembers the thrill she created among the cast members during rehearsals, "One of the great pleasures that all the men on the set enjoyed was watching Miss Monroe walk, either toward them or away from them. She was rehearsing a scene where she was on the stage solo and had to walk away from the camera. All of us, including Jack sat in the front seats of the studio watching her. Our director, one of TV's best, a young man named Ralph Levy, made her repeat the walk several times. Each time she did so, there would be some whispered, off-color comments by those of us seated in the studio. Finally, Jack, in an attempt at humor, whispered, 'I don't know why everyone raves about Marilyn. I've got a pretty good ass myself.'"

Edwin Schallert reported on September 10th, "Marilyn Monroe has thrown her crutches away, although she is still limping. Amusing is the fact that the only thing stolen when her residence was burglarized was the TV script for Jack Benny's show. It is only her second appearance in that medium."

*The Jack Benny Show* gets off to a great start when they have Marilyn appear on the opening show of the 1953-1954 season on September 13th. Marilyn performed in a skit with Jack Benny, titled "The Honolulu Trip:" Due to contractual reasons with Twentieth Century-Fox, Marilyn receives a 1954 black, soft-top convertible Cadillac in lieu of payment. After she received her car she drove it over to show Uncle and Sam and Aunt Enid Kneblecamp her prized possession.

The show was held at the Shrine Auditorium in Los Angeles. Marilyn wore the same gown she would wear to the premier of *How to Marry a Millionaire* on November 4th. It was designed by Billy Travilla. The only difference was that the sash which ran across her bodice and down her left side was made of tulle netting for her appearance on *The Jack Benny Show*. Later it was changed to satin for the premier of *How to Marry a Millionaire*. Off-camera, Marilyn walked with the help of a cane, due to her injured ankle.

On working with Marilyn, writer Milt Josefsberg states, "...and regardless of the stories about her laxness and lateness later in her career, she was punctual and a pleasure to work with in those days." One of the reasons Fox allowed Marilyn to do the show was that she plugged upcoming CinemaScope productions, *The Robe* and *How to Marry a Millionaire*.

On September 21st columnist John Crosby writes, "The Last TV First...It's always a pleasure to welcome Jack Benny back. Naturally I was right there, waiting. I didn't know Marilyn Monroe was going to be on. Honest! I was just sitting there enjoying Mr. Benny and suddenly this blonde shows up. Quite a lot of blonde. It may easily have been the best kept secret of the year. Oh, there were a couple of press releases and maybe a quarter page ad here and there, but in general, they kept her under wraps. Then just before she marched out in front of the cameras, they removed the wraps--most of them anyhow. This was a television first of some dimension. I remember way back when they first linked New York and Philadelphia. Then Chicago swam into view. Finally came Los Angeles, throwing open the Far West to Milton Berle. Gads, historic moments on TV we've all shared--Kefauver, Virginia Hill, J. Fred Muggs, Queen Elizabeth II, the bonfire at the Democratic National Convention, Arthur Godfrey in four colors, Harry Truman playing Mozart. And now that we've seen Marilyn, live and in the flesh--as much flesh as the law allows--I don't know what we've got to look forward to. This may be the last of all television firsts. It's going to take an awful lot to surprise me from now on. It would have been interesting to have been in on the story conference when the Benny crowd found out they had Marilyn Monroe on their hands. After all these years, I think I know how the mind of a gagwriter works and it's my guess that at least one of them leaped in with the suggestion, 'We'll put the girl in a Mother Hubbard.' A gagwriter's mind runs strongly toward the old Switcheroo and veiling the Monroe shape would have been about the biggest switcheroo of all time. If such a suggestion was made, it was overruled, conceivably by Miss Monroe. She came aboard in a white dress so tight-fitting that it must have taken all four of Benny's gagwriters to hook her into it. From there on she was pure Marilyn Monroe, a girl who has made a very good thing out of sex and isn't going to be talked out of it by any gagwriters. She batted her sleepy eyelids at Benny, pawed him in a way that made me very nervous, spoke in that babyish, almost European whisper which she must have invented because it has no real reason for existing, and sang at him. In short, she behaved just exactly as you'd expect Marilyn Monroe to behave. You may think it odd for me to be so surprised about this, but I am. The trend is all the other way. The usual thing is to take Helen Traubel and make a clown of her. Or you take some big muscle man like Buddy Baer and make him mince around the stage with his hands on his hips. Or make Margaret Truman do bumps and grinds. Never, never do you allow them to be themselves. In that regard, Miss Monroe's appearance was a triumph. Or perhaps that's the only way she can act."

Elsie Lee revealed the real pay-off for Marilyn after having appeared on the *Jack Benny Show*. "Biggest boost of all to Marilyn's new place in the hearts of American women probably came from her television appearance with Jack Benny. For one thing, women who wouldn't have gone across the street to see Marilyn in a movie couldn't resist the free opportunity to take a look for themselves at this American phenomenon. They turned on their TV sets; they saw—and Marilyn conquered! 'I still don't know that she can act,' said one viewer, 'but she was real sweet! I was surprised...she has such a gentle voice and she seemed so quiet, and just—nice, somehow. You know, I think we've all misjudged her.'"

Louella Parsons, in her syndicated column, had this interesting bit of news on September 23rd, "A huge picture of Marilyn Monroe in the reception room of the New York offices of Twentieth Century-Fox, was stolen right off the wall while the secretary was at lunch."

In Mid-September Marilyn had her first formal sitting with Milton Greene for *Look* magazine in which he photographed her in the Twentieth Century-Fox portrait studio, dressed in a slip and holding a mink; with a sweater over her slip; then strumming a balalaika and smoking a cigarette. A close up of this last sitting of Marilyn made the cover of the *Look*, November 17, 1953. Marilyn arrived for the photo shoot with her ankle still bandaged from the injury she received while making *River of No Return*.

Greene also took Marilyn outdoors to Laurel Canyon, where he photographed her sitting in a tree, and nestled against a cliff. Milton took a cue from Alfred Cheney Johnston's portraits of Ziegfeld girls by incorporating props, layering various textures and posing her with a seductive lack of affect. This was a daring way to style her. These images were different in taste and substance from the normal poses she was asked to do. Most photographers relied on her cheesecake past to capture a marketable photo, but all Milton relied on was her trust in his talent. Milton brought to Marilyn a sense of class and sophistication, and in short, elegance. Through the suppression of the blatant sexuality, seen in most of her current images, Milton was able to let the woman behind the pin-up shine through. For once, she herself was the focus of the photograph, not her sexual allurement, and yet you never lost sight of her sensual nature, which was now displayed in the rarefied light of Milton's genius. This was the first in a series of sittings which would help to solidify her iconic status for future generations of fans.

Milton said of photographing Marilyn for the first time, "I felt I didn't have to show her practically nude. I felt she was a tremendous person. Something about this girl was very different. She was very honest and sincere and sensitive about her work."

During this shoot, Marilyn met Fleur Cowles, an important editor of women's fashion, and publisher of *Flair* magazine, which defined chic taste in fashion and home. Marilyn will spend some time at Miss Coweles home when she migrates to New York in the winter of 1954.

Marilyn attends a party at Gene Kelley's home. She arrived late and didn't participate in the on-going game of charades. Instead, she and Milton huddled in a corner and talked for the rest of the evening, making plans to reinvent her career in the far away kingdom of New York.

Grace Goddard commits suicide on September 28th. She will be buried at Westwood Village Memorial Cemetery, where Aunt Ana Lower is buried, and where Marilyn will be interred in the late summer of 1962. Marilyn, according to Bebe Goddard, did attend the funeral, and family members remember Marilyn at the reception held afterward at the Knebelcamp's home.

Evidence proves that Grace provided young Norma Jeane with her most stable relationship during her perilous childhood, and without her Norma Jeane would have been lost in the state foster care system. Grace was one of Norma Jeane's greatest supporters and her positive influence in the life of Marilyn Monroe cannot be disputed. Yet, having said all of that, as a child Grace was available to Norma Jeane only from a distance, shuffling her from home to home. Grace and Marilyn had a relationship marked by inconsistent starts and stops, and always under the shadowy influence of Gladys. As an adult, Marilyn seemed to have worked past those issues to a point where Doc and Grace helped her manage her growing career, assisting with her day to day issues and her finances, and finally caring for her mother, Gladys. Marilyn had also stayed in touch with Sam and Enid Kneblecamp and their extended family, attending family events and assisting in home repairs.

After Grace's death, Marilyn seemed to drift away from her old roots and the people she once knew. It was as if Grace was the rope that moored her boat to the pier. Without Grace, she drifted ever further out to sea, forever widening the chasm between Norma Jeane and Marilyn Monroe. She will give interviews in the future that will not even hint at the normalcy she had with any of her early families. These families will be done a great disservice by Marilyn in the way that she allowed the press to portray them. The Bolenders, the Goddards, the Martins, the Howells and the Knebelcamps deserve their due as having been positive influences in her life and relationships that she carried into her fame as Marilyn Monroe. Maybe Grace's suicide affected her more than anyone knew, but what can be known is the gulf that she created between her childhood and the present, a span that she would not allow any to cross.

Marilyn will choose Inez Melson as the successor to Grace's management of her private affairs and for the care of her mother on November 2nd.

On October 26th Erskine Johnson reported on Grace Goddard's obituary, "Marilyn Monroe's One-Time Guardian Got 4-Line Obit...Exclusively Yours: There were only four lines in the obit columns about it, but the Grace Goddard whose funeral was held recently was Marilyn Monroe's one-time legal guardian. She took over raising Marilyn when her real mother, Gladys Baker, went to a sanitarium. She was also the stepmother of film actress Jody Laurence."

This time will mark a period in her life where she will look elsewhere for support, and specifically toward Joe DiMaggio. Even though another influence has drifted into the picture, Milton Greene, he will have to wait his turn. First Joe DiMaggio takes center stage as the man who controls Marilyn, as the press will come to dub him. What no one seems to realize is that no one controls Marilyn Monroe, and as the year plays out and rolls through 1954, this will become evident.

Marilyn has more sittings with Milton Greene in early October. He photographed her at Joe Schenck's villa in bed surrounded by sheets and also posed her with an oriental statue of Schenck's. Milton captured more informal images of Marilyn in her beloved stripped pedal pushers holding a drink, on the phone, and sitting on a patio underneath an umbrella drinking a beverage. An image of Marilyn in bed made the cover of the May 1956 edition of *Look* magazine. Marilyn also made the cover of the July 1956 edition of *Elle* magazine posing with Schenck's statue.

Marilyn wrote a check to Beverly Hills psychoanalyst Dr. Abraham Gottesman on October 7th, for the amount of $275.00.

Sheilah Graham reported on the 11th, "Marilyn Monroe was telling at lunch of the strangest experience that happened to her recently. 'I was eating my lunch in the studio café and someone whispered to me: 'Quick, take off your coat and walk to the ladies' room.' When I asked why, I found out I'd pass the table where Winthrop Rockefeller was sitting. Huh! I love that 'quick-take-off-your-coat' routine!' Money has never meant too much to Marilyn, even having Joe DiMaggio as a beau."

Marilyn attends the premiere of *The 5,000 Fingers of Dr. T* with child actor Tommy Rettig on October 11th. Young Rettig starred in this classic live-action movie by Dr. Suess. Marilyn and Tommy had starred together in *River of No Return*. Tommy will later go on to appear in the TV series *Lassie* as Timmy.

*Stars and Stripes* published a captioned photo of Marilyn on October 17th. "M. Sgt. Floyd M. Underwood receives a congratulatory squeeze from film star Marilyn Monroe on being named Camp Roberts, Calif, 'Soldier of the Year.'" Marilyn was dressed in a costume from *River of No Return*.

On October 18th Sheliah Graham asked Marilyn to "name the 10 most fascinating men in the world, she cooed, 'I haven't met all of them.' Marilyn was wearing a white eyelet embroidered camisole and tight frontier pants. 'The Indians have just torn off my blouse for a scene in *River of No Return*. I hate to put Joe first because it's so obvious. So put him second—but he's really first.'…Now for the 10, and La Monroe's reasons. 'Chekhov is a great artist, a wonderful director and the nephew of the great Anton Chekhov. He's also a great human being, warm and sincere. He's interesting and fascinating to talk to. I've known him for a year and attended some of his classes. He's most concerned with the young generation of actors. He's written a book, *To the Actor*. He gives the impression he's lived through everything.  Please cut down a little on what I say about Joe DiMaggio. People think he is shy. He isn't, not when you know him better. Joe has a restraint about him that's very attractive, which is misunderstood for shyness. He doesn't care for parties—neither do I—except intimate parties, which we both like. He doesn't eat much. That's the first thing I noticed about him when we met on a blind date—he didn't eat. He's very sincere and very direct—as direct as a human being can be. There's a wonderful directness about him. And physically I think he's very attractive. He has a wonderful grace and beauty, like a Michelangelo painting. I enjoy being with him.' So we came to John Huston. 'Any woman who has ever worked in movies with Huston just can't help having a crush on him. He's gentle but he can be fierce at the same time—you know what I mean?' Marilyn met Arthur Miller several years ago. 'He wakes up people. I love the things that he writes. He's good for us. I've read all his books and plays. He's the real writer of our times—the writer for my generation. He's still young, and didn't he write *All My Sons* when he was only 32?' Now for Robert Mitchum. 'I admire him very much. He's one person who doesn't talk much about it, but he really lives from the middle of himself. He's the kind of a fellow who'd offer you his left hand to help you out. He's a complete individual. He doesn't cater to anything that's external. He pretends to care about nothing, but he cares about everything. He's wonderful.' Sidney Skolsky is the glamour gal's father confessor. 'He had faith in me when things were tough and I didn't have enough to eat.

'You're going to be a star,' he would tell me. I'd laugh. 'You don't believe me?' he'd say. 'No.' I would tell him, 'and right now I'm having trouble with my room rent.' Whatever I do, a movie or a TV appearance, I know Sidney will give me the worst and the best. We have a good friendship. If I'm late Sidney always understands.' Brando appeals, too. 'Marlon Brando is another individual like no one else. I admire him for his work. He doesn't settle for anything except the best that he can do. He has real talent. And I find him tremendously sensitive and yet he radiates masculinity without doing anything.' As to photographer Milt Greene: 'I enjoyed having him take my pictures; never felt I had to pose.' Regarding Nehru, she said, 'I've never seen him or met him, but I like what he stands for—nobility, I think I'd call it.' Now for No. 10, he is the comedian Jerry Lewis—and is he going to be surprised! 'I think that Jerry has a lot of sex appeal. It might have something to do with his vitality. I can't figure out what it is. He makes funny faces because he thinks people want him to make funny faces. But behind it all there's something serious and very sexy. I just think he's sexy.'"

 Edwin Schallert devoted his entire column to Marilyn on October 25th. "Marilyn's Responsibility Has Opened Her Eyes: Star States Own View of Calendar Picture... 'Responsibility' was the flabbergasting word which Marilyn Monroe shot across to me over the long-distance telephone last week from San Francisco. 'A star has a great responsibility,' she said. 'I have learned that through the letters I receive and through other contacts with the public. Most of all I have learned it through what servicemen have said and written to me. It has opened up a new world.' 'Responsibility' is something that just doesn't associate itself with the young star who recently made such an outstanding hit as Lorelei Lee in *Gentlemen Prefer Blondes*, and who afforded her studio, 20th Century-Fox, a tremendous amount of grief and tribulation locating her for this interview, for which this writer felt she was due in connection with her booming career. The emissaries of 20th spent the better part of a week trying to discover where she was in the Bay area, and even became exasperated. They finally located her at the sister of Joe DiMaggio, named Marie, and Marilyn was ready and willing to chat extensively over the phone, and also to proffer an explanation of why there were so many complications about reaching her. 'I have been working almost steadily for three years,' she said. 'I had only two days between *Gentlemen Prefer Blondes* and *How to Marry a Millionaire*, and even worked on one of those. So I really felt that I was entitled to a rest. I know if I didn't sort of hide out for the time being I simply wouldn't have any rest. So that's the main reason I didn't let anybody know where I was. All I've been doing is resting and fishing since I've been up here the past week or two, and I'll be back at the studio again soon. But I did need the rest.' During our half-hour chat over the phone the entire Monroe horizon, past and present, was scanned by the star and this writer, including even the issue of the famous calendar picture, concerning which we now for once have her version. She said simply, 'It is not true that Tom Kelley, who shot the photograph, took pity on me on account of my financial condition. It is true that he once lent me $5. But the arrangement about the photograph was strictly a business deal. He and his wife of that time, Natalie, had asked me whether I would pose, and he kept asking from time to time if I would. I was living at the Studio Club and had accumulated certain obligations which I wanted to discharge. I knew this money was available and finally one day I determined this was a solution to my economic problem. So I said I would do it, and 'please, let's get it over with as quickly as possible.' And that's all there was to it, but certainly it was definitely a business deal.' Marilyn put forth a clear-cut, simple explanation of the transaction. She also met the question about whether or not she will marry Joe DiMaggio with a straightforward, 'I have no plans.' She made it clear they are not wed and further that he was not available to talk on the telephone when I asked about that. The fishing expeditions, which I gathered were with DiMaggio, were on San Francisco Bay. 'What I really hope to do in the immediate future is take a trip to Korea, probably as near Christmas as possible,' she said. 'It is our hope to have a very big star, famous for his comedy, when a group of us go on the trip, but I cannot disclose his name.' Private investigations disclosed that this might be none other than Jack Benny. 'I am not sure just when *Pink Tights* will start filming, though that is pretty definitely scheduled as my next picture,' she continued. 'I think it might be after the first of the year. I have played in CinemaScope for *How to Marry a Millionaire*, and it strikes me that it is much more like the stage than the older system of film-making. I also worked in CinemaScope in *River of No Return*, but that was completely different because of being photographed out of doors. I count that one of my most strenuous experiences. My ankle was pretty badly injured, though it is much better now. It happened when I was crossing the stream on stones. I was wearing boots at the time. I didn't think too much of it at first, but it was terribly hard to get the boot off after the accident and that strained a tendon. It was really wonderful working with Robert Mitchum on that picture and though I don't count myself an outdoor girl by any manner of means. I think the experience was really beneficial. What I have really set my heart on is dramatic parts in pictures. Consequently I always look back on *The Asphalt Jungle* as having been one of my finest experiences and *Don't Bother to Knock* as another. I know, of course, that *Gentlemen Prefer Blondes* has meant a great deal for my career, and it was fun working with Jane Russell in that film. Also in *How to Marry a Millionaire* we had a wonderful group with Betty Grable and Lauren Bacall. Working with Jean Negulesco as the director was a great advantage. But I have set my heart on more dramatic parts as I go along. I also want to live up fully to what people really seem to feel about my work in pictures. I have had two instances which have brought me a great sense of responsibility. Once it was a Marine who came to the door of my home after having been in Korea. He told me how much pictures had meant to the men in service and while he talked he started to cry. I can't tell you how deeply I was touched. Then there was another case told to me in a letter by a soldier. He said he had clipped my picture out of *Esquire* magazine, and carried it with him. He had been at the fighting front in a foxhole, and found it necessary to move to another position under fire. He remembered he had left the pin-up picture in the foxhole, and though he had started to the new position went back for it. It was amazing. He said that returning for that picture had saved his life. Shots had been fired that would have hit him if he'd been in the other location. So he thanked me for saving his life.' Miss Monroe is today the top skyrocket star of the movies. Her ascendancy compares with any and all of the famous ones of the past like Barbara La Marr, Jean Harlow and other rare beauties whose fascination has also been linked with a certain fatality. People came from miles to Jasper National Park, where *River of No Return* locationed, just for a chance glimpse of her. She has caught the imagination of a multitude of people--not simply men in the service but a vast civilian population of both sexes. She is reckoned beautiful in a thoroughly modern-day sense and is simultaneously both charming and alluring in a peculiarly unobtrusive way. This was rather specially caught in *Gentlemen Prefer Blondes*, despite that this does not, perhaps, represent her highest ideal of a picture."

Harold Heffernan wrote in his column on October 27th about the growing problem of smog in the Los Angeles area. Marilyn commented, "I'm glad for Los Angeles's sake that the doctors have warned us of the health dangers. I've had colds and a sinus ailment now for months. They say I'm anemic. I'm sure the foul air is responsible."

Marilyn writes a check to Beverly Hills psychoanalyst Dr. Abraham Gottesman in the amount of $100.00 on October 31st.

Writer Lee Belser spent the evening of Halloween with Marilyn who handed out apples and cookies, brought back from San Francisco and baked by Joe's sister Marie, to the children who came by her Doheny Apartment. Belser found it amusing that as the evening got later, the trick-or-treaters got older and pretty soon he took over answering the door and turning away men in costumes.

Andre de Dienes try's another tactic to get Marilyn's attention and pens a flattering article for the November issue of *Modern Man*, "I Knew Her When…" He writes of meeting Norma Jeane and her sweet innocence. He ends the article giving praise to Marilyn. "Yet I want to give all credit to Marilyn. She grew up to be what she is. In rapid steps she became smarter and more beautiful. And in addition she exercised her tremendous talent for getting along with people. This is especially true in Hollywood where they are ready to tear you down for the slightest mistake. Marilyn had the willpower to go after her success and pursue it relentlessly. I flatter myself that while I worked with her I was able to give her many valuable pointers. They say that her studio has since been amazed by the way in which she makes every movement, every gesture, sexy. They talk about the habit she has of parting her lips slightly before her picture is taken. I feel that Marilyn's career as a pin-up model is in great part responsible for these tricks. She learned what the pin-up photographers want and she has never forgotten it."

On November 1st, Lydia Lane Quotes Jean Negulesco about Marilyn, "Film Director Admires Honesty More Than Any Other Trait…When I started working with Marilyn I realized she was one of the most atomic personalities ever to come out of Hollywood. But I was surprised to find out how hard she worked and how much she wanted to give a good performance.'...Mr. Negulesco predicted that with such singleness of purpose there will be no stopping her." Jean Negulesco was the director for *How to Marry a Millionaire*. This column will be repeated on January 24, 1954. Jean Negulesco directed Marilyn in *How to Marry a Millionaire*.

Marilyn sent a letter to Twentieth Century-Fox Film Corporation on November 2nd saying "Gentlemen, Please be advised that I have made arrangements with Mrs. Inez C. Melson whose address is 9128 Sunset Blvd., Los Angeles 46, to take over the management of my affairs. All salary due me will continue to be picked up by my agent. Please direct all statements, correspondence, etc. concerning my affairs to me in care of Mrs. Melson. Very truly yours," (signed) Marilyn Monroe. Mrs. Melson has taken the place of Grace Goddard in Marilyn's life. She will take over the care of Marilyn's mother Gladys, and will continue after Marilyn's death.

Marilyn was supposed to inaugurate the oil well being drilled on the lot of $20^{th}$ Century-Fox on November $3^{rd}$, but the oil rig workers wouldn't have it due to superstitions against women on drill rigs. Rory Calhoun did the honors instead.

Marilyn and Robert Mitchum make some very telling remarks to Clement Jones about working on movies. "'This is the toughest part of movie-making,' Robert Mitchum said, taking a long drink of water and mopping his brow. 'Compared to this, learning lines, doing scenes, fighting Indians is nothing. And even making love to the leading lady is easier.' Marilyn Monroe, long accustomed to the Mitchum humor, refused to rise to the bait. 'He's absolutely right,' she said, ignoring the last remark. 'I'd rather meet Bob in the boxing ring than do this.' The 'this' that had them both running for cover wan an intricate process known as dialogue re-recording, or dubbing. When a movie is made outdoors, as was $20^{th}$ Century-Fox's Cinema Scope-Technicolor *River of No Return*, in which they are starred, it sometimes is difficult to obtain clear recordings of the dialogue. The sounds made by planes, trains and cars, picked up by the sensitive microphones, would be out of place in a picture set in the Great Northwest about 1875. So the dialogue is later rerecorded in the dubbing room. As the picture is flashed on a screen, the actors repeat their lines from the scenes. They must try not only to re-capture exact inflections and intonations, as set down by the director, but must time the lines so they are in perfect synchronization with the lip movements on the screen. 'This really puts a performer to the test,' Marilyn said, 'because we dub only a few lines at a time, and you don't get the chance to feel a scene, to catch its mood and emotions. Unless you're very careful, you find you're merely parroting the lines, robbing them of any meaning.' 'Very true,' added Mitchum. 'But I'll tell you why I dislike this so much. I get to see the whole picture, and then there are no surprises left when I go to the preview.'"

And speaking of premiers…November 4th was the legendary Premier of *How to Marry a Millionaire* at the Fox-Wilshire Theatre. Marilyn started getting ready at one in the afternoon. She received flowers, telegrams and phone calls from well-wishers, including Joe DiMaggio who, much to Marilyn's chagrin, was in New York on business. The town of Monroe, New York notified her that they had changed the name of their town to Marilyn Monroe, New York for that day in her honor. An imposter was using her voice and calling around Hollywood attempting to book hotel suites and dinner parties, and the imposter even tried to book a flight to London, via TWA for herself and Joe DiMaggio.

After six hours and twenty minutes, Marilyn was finally ready. Gladys McCallister had given her a straight permanent, bleached and tinted her hair, setting it for shoulder length curls, and painted her fingernails and toenails. Ann Landers, her wardrobe mistress helped her put on her gown, jewelry and furs. According to Sheliah Graham, "The glittering picture was out shone by Marilyn's sparkling white gown. And Al Teitelbaum whipped her up, especially for the occasion, a single white fox boa—which didn't constrict Marilyn in anyway." The gown had been worn before during her appearance on *The Jack Benny Show*. For this evening, however, the sash which flowed over her bodice and trailed down her left side was changed from tulle netting to an elegant satin. Whitey Snyder then skillfully applied her makeup, creating "the Face."

"Great White Hope Attends Premiere." In three captioned panels Marilyn is photographed getting ready for the premiere. "1. Before leaving for the theater around 7pm, she gave a finishing touch to her eyebrows. What she saw in mirror was result of seven hours in studio beauty shop. White was to be theme. 2. Long, white satin gloves complete outfit. A strapless lace gown lined with nude-colored crepe was molded to her frame. Thousands of sequins on it glittered with every move. 3. As she talked with friend Kendis Rochlen before leaving for the premiere, she brought out her new fox stole. She posed in front of the mirror, practiced draping the stole this way and that.".... "Hollywood served up its magic mixture of stardom, excitement and glory the other night and Marilyn Monroe walked away with a king-sized helping. It was a rich and tasty dish and the blonde with the wondrous wiggle found it to her liking. There were all the ingredients--it was the world premiere of Marilyn's newest and biggest picture, *How to Marry a Millionaire*. Her day began shortly after noon when she drove onto the lot in Joe DiMaggio's sleek black Cadillac--he's now in New York, but left his car for his girlfriend to drive. The studio's great white hope bounced into her dressing room wearing a Hawaiian print shirt and beige slacks. Experts immediately took over. Her hair was bleached and set, platinum polish was applied to her fingernails and toenails and she was made up from her hairline to her neckline. Pictures above show finished product."

Kendis Rochlen, writer for the *Los Angeles Mirror-News*, was allowed to sit in on Marilyn's metamorphosis. She would later report of her experience in her column, *Candid Kendis*. Miss Rochlen drove Marilyn to a party in her honor and in honor of Lauren Bacall and Humphrey Bogart, given by producer Nunnally Johnson's wife, Doris at the home of director Jean Negulesco. Marilyn was photographed by Darlene Hammond, talking with Rock Hudson, Terry Moore and Robert Mitchum. After dinner and three stiff drinks, the party, including Humphrey Bogart, Lauren Bacall and Nunnally and Doris Johnson, got into their limousine and went to the premiere at the Fox-Wilshire Theatre.

Nunnally Johnson said of the night, "Then, as we we're about to get in the car, a hired limousine with a driver, she asked for her third drink, a really stiff one this time. Gentlemen to the last, Bogey and I drank with her on the way to the theater. By the time we made our entrance you couldn't have found three more amiable people in the whole state of California."

At the sight of Marilyn, pandemonium broke out. The crowd screamed her name, and legions of reporters vied for her attention. Newsreels show a radiantly beautiful Marilyn. She seems to float along the red carpet. She had arrived. This night was the culmination of all her desperate childhood dreams. She was a movie star, and this night she was "the" movie star. Her stunning presence eclipsed all others in her wake.

Quoting Nunnally Johnson again, "In short she was tight. She was tight when she had to go to the ladies' room as the picture began. Mrs. Johnson, not tight, accompanied her, for clearly she needed company. She was tight in the ladies' room, and in a tight dress, for she had to be sewn into it...It was a wild and exhausting business (my wife told me afterward) getting Marilyn in condition for the john and then properly dressed again to return to her seat. Women who have been sewn into their clothes should never drink to excess..."

Marilyn declined to attend any after-premier dinner parties. She was worn out by her evening of glamour. The studio limousine returned her to the studio, where she disrobed and put on her beige slacks, buttoned up her Hawaiian print blouse and slipped on her loafers. She was restless, and cruised the Pacific Coast Highway. There was no doubt that Marilyn was the brightest star in Hollywood that night and as hard as it might be to believe, she would be destined to become even more famous in the near future.

*Motion Picture and TV Digest* Magazine, November, cover and article by Jim Henaghan about the evening of the premier, "Marilyn Monroe-Loveable Fake." The article give a revealing portrait of Marilyn at the premiere of *How to Marry a Millionaire*, "If you saw the newsreel of the last big Hollywood premiere, you saw Marilyn Monroe make the coolest, fanciest entrance into a theatre lobby since Pola Negri made the same walk years ago leading a snarling leopard on a leash. Marilyn got out of a fancy studio limousine, dripping white mink, in a dress she had to be sewn into, and with that luscious wet lipped smile, pranced a hundred feet past screaming fans and frantic photographers to the waiting area of a studio publicist. Then, taking that arm, she tossed a last smile of genuine delight over her shoulder at her public and stepped into the theatre. That's what you saw in the newsreel. A movie star, confident as all get out, serene and elegant as a queen, taking her bows on the way to see a movie. But the newsreel cameraman should have been beyond the door that Marilyn entered. Inside, in the darkened foyer, Marilyn seemed to sag. She clutched slightly on the arm of the press agent and leaned against the wall. 'I've got to get out of here,' she said. She was pale and her forehead was moist, and she trembled a little. The publicity man led her down the side aisle of the theatre to an exit, opened it slowly and then slipped out into the cool night air. Marilyn took several deep breaths as the agent waited for her to compose herself. He was used to this. Then they walked to a side street and he opened the door to Marilyn's small car. She threw the fur into the back seat, whispered a thank you and drove off to be swallowed up in the heavy traffic. The man looked at her sadly, then shook his head and went back to the movie. Marilyn Monroe wasn't nervous that night, she wasn't scared, she was terrified. She had done this same thing, in one fashion or another in most of the big cities around the country--and she was terrified every time she had to go through it. Although, she is the most photographed girl in the world, the most sought after celebrity in Hollywood; every time Marilyn Monroe has to make an appearance in public she suffers torture. The smooth walk is something she learned to do, the warm greetings she gives are the result of hours of coaching, and the bright smile of enjoyment is a fake. Marilyn Monroe hates all of it."

Longtime supporter of Marilyn, Adele Whitley-Fletcher, sent her this note after seeing her in *Millionaire*. "Ever since I saw *How to Marry a Millionaire* I've wanted to tell you what a grand job you did in it. For my money it's your picture absolutely. Now, 2 weeks after seeing it, your nearsighted Pola is still so charmingly vivid in my memory that I had to write you. All the Best, Adele Fletcher"

After all the hustle and bustle of making three movies and non-stop publicity Marilyn needs a night on the town. Since Joe DiMaggio refuses to escort her to these events, she calls upon Sidney Skolsky. "I'll pick you up at Schwab's at ten-thirty,' Marilyn said. Joe DiMaggio was out of town and here I was again. Through no fault of my own I wasn't able to be at Schwab's at the appointed time. So I phoned to leave word I was on my way, never thinking Marilyn would be on time. Eileen, who answered the Schwab's phone, told me that Marilyn had been there and had left a note for me. It said she had gone on to Mocambo and I should join her there as soon as possible. 'You should have seen the store when she walked in,' Eileen said. 'The idiots acted like they had never seen a girl—even those with girls! Such excitement. The place went into shock!' I hurried to the Mocambo and didn't have to be directed to where Marilyn was seated. I merely went to where everyone was staring. The Mocambo was in shock, too…The lights dimmed and Eartha Kitt stepped out on the platform and began to sing. During her second number, Eartha hesitated and stared, as if she had just spotted Marilyn. Then the two leading exponents of singing sex smiled at each other. When the show was over Marilyn was approached for autographs. I couldn't help but realize how much success had helped The Monroe. She had poise. Yet, she hadn't lost that rare faculty of being part of the crowd as well as aloof at the same time. She disposed of the autograph seekers quickly, charmingly…Charlie Morrison came to the table and asked Marilyn if she would go backstage because Miss Kitt would like to meet her. 'I'd love to,' Marilyn answered. 'I wanted to meet her, but I didn't dare ask.' Backstage was downstairs under the club. 'I enjoyed you so much,' said The Monroe. 'I've liked you very much on the screen,' said Eartha Kitt. Some more small talk and Marilyn and I were on our way. 'Think we could catch Johnnie Ray at Ciro's?' Marilyn asked. 'I feel like doing the town.' 'We can try,' I said, and I called for Marilyn's car. As we drove away I heard the doorman say, 'He's got the prettiest chauffeur in town.' The car arrived at Ciro's. There was a twenty minute wait before Ray went on for his last show. Marilyn and I didn't have much chance to talk, though, for the parade of autograph seekers started. The place went into shock. Johnnie Ray came to the table. I introduced him to Marilyn. 'May I sit with you for a while?' he asked. 'I know this sounds cornball, but I'm a fan. I know you get it a lot, but I'm sincere.' The singer who has been mobbed and whose clothes have been torn by admirers summoned a photographer. 'Take a picture, please,' Johnny said. 'This I've got to show to my friends.' Later, as Ray got up from the table to make ready for his show, he said in an aside to me, 'Greatest chick I ever met.' Marilyn liked Ray's singing. She thought there was something basically sad about it that came from within."

Marilyn mentioned going to see Eartha Kitt and Johnnie Ray to Earl Wilson and he had this to say in his column, "I asked her what she'd been doing. 'I usually don't go to night clubs, but I went to see Johnnie Ray and Eartha Kitt with Sidney Skolsky and my agent, Hugh French. Oh, I told Joe first!' she hastened to add."

On November 13th Marilyn attended a luncheon hosted by the Motion Picture Association of Motion Picture Producers in honor of King Paul of Greece and his wife Queen Frederika. Even though it was the Royal Couple of Greece, Marilyn was still 20 minutes late. The royal couple was touring the United States, and was spending the next two days in Los Angeles. They had toured the RKO studio lot and the Twentieth Century-Fox studio lot. After Marilyn was introduced to the Monarchs, the press wondered if the Greeks had word for "It." This was a play on the original title of *How to Marry a Millionaire, The Greeks had a Word for It.* In photographs taken of Marilyn and the Grecian monarchs she is wearing a chocolate brown ermine trimmed suit on the steps of the new administration building. The conservative suit was designed by Charles LeMaire and fastened at the neckline with a rhinestone encrusted brooch. This is the exact suit she will wear to wed Joe DiMaggio in January of 1954

*Look* magazine cover and article, November 17th, "Marilyn Monroe Photographs," taken by Milton H. Greene. These carefully chosen images help to define a newly emerging Marilyn. The focus was on the woman behind the "sex-bomb" image. Marilyn has a new more mature and chic image. In her desire to be taken seriously, she now engages her most potent weapon, the camera. With Milton's help, she will soon wage a war against a seemingly unconquerable giant, Twentieth Century-Fox. When the dust settles, she will be the victor, a David against a Goliath. She assaulted the giant much like David, unprotected by any visible means of armor, and with a weapon which caused the enemy to laugh at the incredulous action of one who appeared so vulnerable and unprepared. But Marilyn's smooth stone she flung at Twentieth Century-Fox was Milton Greene. He was able to reinforce her image and capitalize on her powerful alliance with the public. He made it impossible for Twentieth Century-Fox to live without her.

Marilyn told Sheilah Graham this about Milton Greene, "I enjoyed him taking my pictures, never felt I had to pose. I have a lot of friends who are photographers. But Milt is a fascinating man. He gets the most out of you. He took a simple picture of me holding a coffee pot and it became a portrait."

The Muscular Dystrophy Telethon aired on television and radio on November 25th. According to Glenna M. Lowes, "Dean Martin, Jerry Lewis, Marilyn Monroe, Bing Crosby and Frank Sinatra have pledged their services to enlist the aid of West Coast televiewers in a campaign to help sufferers of muscular dystrophy." In another story about the MDA Telethon, "Not a telethon this time, it will provide real entertainment. Some of the biggest names in show business will appear, such as Martin and Lewis, Bing Crosby, Frank Sinatra and Marilyn (Wow) Monroe." The show aired on November 25th.

Earl Wilson reported on November 26th, "Marilyn Reads While Joe's Away...Marilyn Monroe has gone up to San Francisco to spend a week with Joe DiMaggio--who's there pheasant-hunting--and we learned that while daddy goes a-hunting, baby will curl up with a lot of good books. Marilyn spends Thanksgiving at the DiMaggio home on Beach St., in the Marina district of San Francisco. Joe's sister Marie cooks the holiday meal. Marie lives in the downstairs part of the 3 story, 10 bedroom house, with her daughter, Betty."

Vernon Scott devotes his column to Marilyn on November 26th in an attempt to get her take on men's reactions to her. "We gulped when the curvesome actress stood up to say hello. She was dressed in a tight black sweater and a tight black skirt--even her shoes looked tight. 'Sit down,' she said in that breathless voice she uses on the screen. We tried desperately to recall the subject of the interview. Marilyn looked a little bewildered when we finally explained we wanted to talk to her about how men react to meeting her for the first time. 'Gee,' she murmured, 'that's hard to say. Usually they act as if they expect me to be aloof or something--and you can't get to know a fellow when he feels like that. It's a real disadvantage for me. I think it's sorta immodest for me to talk about myself, don't you?' she asked with a dazzling smile. Generally when I meet a shy man, he get all the more shy. The bold ones seem to get bolder. Men just talk easier and are more brave in bunches, but when there's just one fellow, there's usually sort of a stutter. Some funny things have happened, too, but you couldn't possibly print them. It must have something to do with the subconscious--you know, Freudian impulses. I like meeting people,' Marilyn said happily, 'especially men. But honestly, I've never made a study of their reactions. I'm sure they interest me as much as I interest them.'"

Joe and Marilyn fly back to Los Angeles on November 29th. Joe offers moral support to Marilyn, who has been engaged in a battle with the studio since August over her reluctance to appear in the film, *The Girl in Pink Tights*. Even though she would have starred with Frank Sinatra, she considers it an inferior story and stands her ground with the studio.

Frank Morris reported on November 30th, "Shelley Winters always has an explanation for her public spats....Shelley and Marilyn Monroe stood screaming at each other at a recent Hollywood party...Shelley said they were arguing over whether Robert Mitchum should try for a change of acting pace instead of doing the same old roles over and over again."

*Los Angeles Herald-Examiner* article December 1953, "Marilyn Monroe joins the Marines in their campaign to give a toy to every unfortunate tot in the Los Angeles area on X-Mas.  Sgt. W.L. Callen and Cpl. Coyle accept her donation for the children." Marilyn is photographed with the two Marines for the Annual "Toys For Tots" Campaign held each year by the United States Marine Corps.

Marilyn writes a letter to the airmen at Thule Air Base Greenland in December 1953, "Mr. Secretary Talbot has done me the honor to say he would bring you my message.  I'm a lot more disappointed than you are that I can't be with you this New Years. But the fact is I'm sick and my doctor won't let me go, but as soon as I'm able I'll be there anytime you can persuade Secretary Talbot to give me a seat in a plane, to do a show for you, to meet you all and tell you I think you're the best men in the world. I love you all. Happy New Year. Marilyn Monroe." Marilyn would never perform for the men of Thule Air Base in Greenland.

*People Today* cover and article, December 2nd, "Marilyn: More'n More...MM"s Trade

Secrets...In the midst of a studio campaign to take the mmmm out of MMonroe (she wears eyeglasses in *How to Marry a Millionaire*), Marilyn poses radiantly for *People Today's* photographer, showing tricks of trade. To make her leggier, camera is aimed at navel. Chronically tardy (she can spend an hour facing a make-up mirror), MM 'more than makes up for it' when she finally arrives at a photo studio. She works fast, has her own ideas. 'It helps,' says Fox still Chief Frank Powolny. A typical MM notion: the umbrella shown on these pages. She thought it made her look 'sweet.' A studio photo session with MM sees photographer, assistant, hairdresser, make-up man, wardrobe woman all on duty. To improve figure (she does not always look 'that' way), she's shot off-angle. Posing open-mouthed was her idea; it's now standard for pin-up queens who want to look 'animated.' She's most appealing with her mouth ajar, eyes lidded and spine S-curved. Strong-minded MM suggested this red suit against turquoise background—'sensational.' Favorite color: gold; she patriotically seconds red, white and blue. She moistens lips for every shot, dons light make-up for color, street make-up for black & white. Powolny, who has lensed her most, likes a 'little shine to her face. It makes her more natural.' Easy study, she's good for fast 20 poses an hour." It is interesting to note that although, Frank Powolny is mentioned in the article, the accompanying photos and the cover shot were actually taken by Bert Reisfield.

In his syndicated column, Erskine Johnson quotes June Allyson about Marilyn on December 3rd, "She's wonderful for all of us in Hollywood. She makes people want to see other performers and more pictures. I can't understand why so many people say unkind things about her."

On December 3rd, The African American newspaper *The Los Angeles Sentinel* prints an article boasting of Phil Moore as "The Man Who Made Marilyn Sing." Moore and Marilyn had a six-page article in *BOLD* magazine. The newspaper said, "Though it was hush-hush at the time, 20th Century had picked Marilyn for the Lorelei Lee role in *Blondes*, but realized her voice was not up to the part. For 18 months, Moore worked with Marilyn."

*American Weekly* runs an article on December 6th, "Me and Joe," by Liza Wilson. This is a rehashing of the history of their romance, and is used to let the public know that they are not secretly married. A few choice nuggets by Marilyn are found in the text. "Neither Joe nor I care about nightclubs or parties. Joe likes best to have quiet dinners at my apartment. Sometimes he cooks. He's a fine cook. Sometimes I cook. I'm a fair cook. But most of the time we fix part of the meal. I'd like to learn to cook some fancy Italian dishes for Joe—all I know how to cook is spaghetti, and Joe has to make the sauce for that—but I simply don't have the time. There are so many things I want to do. I fly off in all directions—but Joe is a good balance for me. When we're together we never talk baseball or motion pictures. But lately I've caught him reading *Variety*. One night, recently, he whistled and said, 'Well look what *Gentlemen Prefer Blondes* grossed in Chicago! Socko!' I got a big kick out of that…I'm the only girl Joe ever has known, I guess, who runs around in blue jeans and without make-up. He never criticizes me, but I'm sure he likes a girl to dress conservatively…I love long white gloves and earrings that dangle down to my shoulders—but I can always wear them in pictures.'"

*Parade* magazine article on December 6th, "5 emotions by Marilyn Monroe...A Girl Who Wants To Be a Good Actress," by photographer Ben Ross. He will capture in this session an amazing array of poses by Marilyn. In these portraits she is nothing less than spectacular, dressed only in a turtleneck and her striped pedal pushers. Marilyn is in the full bloom of her womanhood and she beguiles the reader with her changing emotions. Extraordinarily beautiful, even by Monroe standards, Ben Ross's December images will be reproduced for years to come.

In the article Ross poses the question of whether Marilyn could act. He puts her through the paces of varying emotions. He asks the reader, "Her portrayals were impromptu--done after a hard day at work. What do you think? Can she act?"

When Ross gives her direction on which emotion he wants her to portray, she not only slips into the sentiment, but gives her own commentary about each, couching it in actors-speak. On being exuberant Marilyn said, "I don't do well with laughter or happy moods. I do the sad ones better." In a pensive mood Marilyn reflects, "Being an actress is a big responsibility, if you're sincere about it. Audiences deserve nothing less than the best. That's what I want to give them. I don't like to think about failure, but if I do fail, I know that I have tried to do the best I could." Ross asked her to portray being frightened, and of this she stated, "I don't do this often, Directors think all I have to do is wiggle a little, not act." Portraying reluctance, Marilyn said, "They throw me from one picture into another. I don't travel, see things, meet people and know them under normal circumstances. I want to know how people really are, so I can portray them better." Marilyn was spot on when she embodied joy. Of this she said, "I know what emotions like joy and love are, but the problem is freeing myself from them and projecting them to the audience."

Writer Leonora Goldberg, who knew Ben Ross and called him a "creative curmudgeon," stated that Marilyn showed up at Ross' Hotel Room at almost midnight. She appeared well rested and was ready to work. Marilyn suggested they start the shoot now and use his hotel room to have privacy and relax. Marilyn, according to Goldberg, "went through this whole gamut of emotions from fear; to laughter, and the difference between tickle laughter and gentle laughter and a big guffaw laughter; and sadness; she was like a rolling thunder, she just changed; sad and smiled, tilted, laid down on the carpet and she smoked; and he just kept shooting and shooting." When it was over Ross had amassed arguably one of the most beautiful collections of portraits ever done of Marilyn. It is sublime in its simplicity and she is astoundingly beautiful. It brings to mind a quote by Norman Mailer concerning Joe DiMaggio's adoration for her. "If it is necessary to speak of her varieties of beauty, then a thousand photographs are not worth a word. Doubtless she is, when alone with him, nothing less than the metamorphosis of a woman in one night, tough in one hour and sensitive in another (at the least!), but she has also the quality she will never lose, never altogether, a species of vulnerability that all who love her will try to describe, a stillness in the center of her mood, an animal's clam at the heart of shyness, as if her fate is trapped like a tethered deer." Ben Ross perfectly captured her toughness, sensitivity and her vulnerability.

Marilyn has come a long way since her emotional portraits taken by Philippe Halsman back in 1949 for *LIFE* magazine. Then, Halsman found only her sexy picture believable. Marilyn has come her way as an actress and all of Ross's images are valid representations of the emotions she was portraying.

On December 7th Marilyn did not show up for the rehearsals for *The Girl in Pink Tights*. On the 8th Darryl Zanuck himself sent for Marilyn to dub a scene from *River of No Return*. Marilyn thought the studio was trying to trick her to show up for *The Girl in Pink Tights*, so she refused to go. But Darryl Zanuck had sent a telegram to the studio on October 29th requesting that some of the scenes in *River of No Return* needed to be reshot.

On December 8th Marilyn attends a children's Christmas charity event at the Shrine Auditorium, sponsored by the *L.A. Examiner* newspaper. Also in attendance were Jack Benny, Bob Hope, Danny Thomas, Vess & Co., Shelley Winters, Vic Damone, The Rhythmairs, Joanne Gilbert, the Wiere Brothers, Phil Regan, Ann Blyth, Red Skelton, Gene Nelson and Constance Moore. Phil Stern was on hand to photograph the event. His photos have showed up as poster art in recent years. Marilyn wore the same dress she would wear to the 1954 *Photoplay* Awards.

The studio called on December 9th to say that she really did need to re-shoot three scenes from *River of No Return*. Marilyn hesitantly returned to the Twentieth Century-Fox studio on December 11th to re-shoot the scenes from *River of No Return*. On the 14th Zanuck arranged for Jean Negulesco to be there when Marilyn did the retakes. He knew that Marilyn was friendly with him and he got Negulesco to talk to Marilyn about settling her differences with Zanuck. The trick didn't work. Marilyn finished her scenes for *River of No Return*, then left without giving *Pink Tights* another thought.

The Baton Rouge *Advocate* ran a captioned photo of Marilyn on the 11th and reported sinister comments by a communist magazine. "She Drives Us Crazy, Too—Lovely Marilyn Monroe has been described as an agent of Communist-hunter Sen. Joe McCarthy by an East German weekly magazine. Describing the pretty screen star as a 'super-blonde offensive against culture,' the Communist weekly, apparently unhinged by the blonde bombshell's impact, alleges Marilyn is being employed to help Americans forget the tribulations of life in the U.S."

On December 15th Marilyn and Joe DiMaggio attend a party for Gen. William F. Dean, given by Bob and Dolores Hope. Gen. Dean was a Korean prisoner of war and a bonified war hero. He was a guest on Bob Hope's television show this night and after the show he was given a party at the Hope's home. Many sports stars attended the affair, Casey Stengel, Jack Dempsey, Johnny Weismuller, Joe DiMaggio, Frank Leahy, Tom Harmon, Bones Hamilton, Leo Durocher and a few others of athletic prominence. The general was quoted as saying about Marilyn, "She's a lovely lady."

Braven Dyer's syndicated column on December 18th, "Sports Parade," was devoted to the party honoring Gen. William F. Dean, December 15. Of Marilyn, he wrote, "The general got a big kick out of posing with Marilyn Monroe. Of course, old fogies like Stengel and I didn't pay too much attention to Joe DiMaggio's girlfriend, it says here. (Voice offstage: That's so much pablum, Dyer, and you know it.)"

On December 17th Marilyn invites Bebe Goddard and family over to her apartment to celebrate Bebe's birthday. She remembers that Marilyn served overcooked liver and baked potatoes, but despite the food, it was a fun evening. She also recalls that Marilyn drank wine and smoked, something she never used to do. All in all, it was a special evening.

Marilyn flies to San Francisco on December 23rd to spend the Christmas holidays with Joe DiMaggio and family. Marilyn used the name Norma Dougherty while purchasing her airline ticket in order to avoid any press attention. The press never took notice of her departure. Marilyn showed up at the Burbank Airport with 122 pounds of luggage. She was allowed 40 pounds of free baggage and was charged $9.29 for 82 pounds of extra baggage.

On Christmas day Joe gives Marilyn a luxurious Maximillian mink coat that she cherishes. On New Year's Eve after dining at Joe DiMaggio's restaurant, *DiMaggio's* on Fisherman's Wharf, Joe and Marilyn head back to the DiMaggio home on Beach St. After watching the New Year's Eve programs on TV, he proposes to Marilyn. She accepts saying, "Whenever and wherever you say, Joe."

On January 1, 1954 Marilyn receives the *Motion Picture Herald* Award of Achievement.

Marilyn didn't show up for the first day of shooting on January 4th for *The Girl in Pink Tights,* with Frank Sinatra. According to some sources he is not really angered by this. Other sources say he was indeed angry and this was the reason he participated in the later "Wrong Door Raid" with Joe DiMaggio on November 5, 1954. Frank eventually got over any anger with Marilyn and she became very dear to him, even contemplating marriage in 1962, much to DiMaggio's chagrin. But Joe got back at Frank by excluding him from Marilyn's funeral.

Marilyn will say of this time, "When a studio stumbles on a box office name in its midst, it means millions of dollars income. And every studio has learned to be very considerate financially towards the goose that lays their golden eggs. The trouble was about something deeper. I wanted to be treated as a human being who had earned a few rights since her orphanage days. When I had asked to see the script of a movie in which it was announced I was going to star, I was informed that the studio didn't consider it necessary for me to see the script in advance. I would be given my part to memorize at the proper time."

When Marilyn finally is given a copy of the script, she doesn't like it. She has good enough taste to realize that it is not a good story and will make a sub-par movie. She now resorts to playing hard ball. Encouraged by Joe DiMaggio, she makes a move that will succinctly reveal her opinion of the script and at the same time will only antagonize Zanuck. She sends him a telegram, "I finally receipted script. Am exceedingly sorry, but I do not like it. Sincerely, Marilyn Monroe."

Zanuck is livid and Marilyn is put on suspension. But she still has a few tricks up her pretty sleeve and 1954 will start out with a bang for Marilyn.

# Chapter Fourteen
## Mrs. DiMaggio and the Boys

It was a very cold afternoon, and it was snowing. All the soldiers sat in their winter uniforms. I appeared in a décolleté evening gown, bare back, bare arms. And I was so happy and so excited that I didn't know it was cold or snowing. In fact, the snow never fell on me. It melted away almost before it touched my skin. That was the happiest time—when the thousands of soldiers all yelled my name over and over."

**1**954 started out in a swirl of rumors that Marilyn, disgruntled with her studio, had run off and married Joe DiMaggio. One of her agents, Jack Gordean, vehemently denied this. The press couldn't find her in San Francisco, Reno or Las Vegas. Sightings of Marilyn and Rock Hudson in New Orleans were leaked by Delta Airline, which proved to be false. Tracking down leads and verifying rumors would take all of two weeks and would only be solved when Marilyn herself alerted the press that indeed, the Blonde Bombshell and the Yankee Clipper were tying the knot.

Marilyn and Joe are busy making wedding arrangements during the second week of January. Marilyn and Joe's sister Marie shop at Joseph Magnin's for a wedding outfit and honeymoon outfits, however she will decide to wear her own Charles LeMaire designed brown broadcloth suit trimmed in white ermine for the nuptials. She had worn this suit last November when greeting the King and Queen of Greece when they visited Twentieth Century-Fox Studios. Given Joe's conservative views, and this being her second marriage, it was the perfect choice. When Marilyn divorces Joe and moves to New York in late December of 1954, she gives the suit to Milton Greene's wife, Amy.

Marilyn is suspended by Twentieth Century-Fox on January 11th for refusing to show up for work on *The Girl in Pink Tights*.

On the 12th Joe's good friend, George Solotaire, arrives at the El Rancho in Las Vegas, to meet with El Rancho owner Belden Katelman. The press is in a furor, assuming that he came to Las Vegas to arrange the wedding for Joe and Marilyn. Abe Schiller, manager of the Flamingo, makes several calls to Reno Barsocchini, one of the managers of *DiMaggio's* and Joe's best friend, in vain trying to make arrangements for Joe and Marilyn to marry and stay at the Flamingo. He tells Reno that he knows for a fact that Joe and Marilyn are in Las Vegas. Reno replies, "I don't think so. Joe is in the restaurant right now eating." "Oh," was the reply on the other end of the phone.

Joe was making his own arrangements. Joe invited Judge Charles Perry, of the San Francisco Municipal Court, to lunch at *DiMaggio's*. While there, they discuss the best way to quietly handle the wedding ceremony. Judge Perry suggested Marilyn and Joe get their required blood test and tell no one. They shouldn't apply for a marriage license, wait until the ceremony and have it typed in his chambers. The best time would be between 12 noon and 2 p.m., because that is lunch time and court is in recess. Joe suggests that they do it tomorrow, but Judge Perry reminds him that tomorrow is the 13th, so they agree to wait another day.

Joe asks Reno Barsocchini to be his best man. Joe also asks his brother Tom and his wife Lee to stand in as witnesses. Reno, Tom and Joe's other brother Dom all manage *DiMaggio's*. Joe's brother Dom will stay behind to manage the restaurant. Marilyn later asks Reno's wife Betty to be her matron of honor. It is while attending the christening of the Barsocchini's daughter, Rena that Marilyn first mentions to Betty that if she ever got married to Joe, she would like her to be her matron of honor. Marilyn remembers her promise to Betty, who is thrilled to accept.

On the afternoon of January 14th Tom and Lee DiMaggio, along with Reno and Betty Barsocchini arrive at Joe's Beach St. home at 12:45. Joe and Marilyn follow them to the City Hall building and park on Larkin St. Marilyn, in lieu of an earlier promise to the studio, had made a call at 12:30 to let Harry Brand, the studio publicity boss, know that she and Joe are about to be married. The press is already there in full force. The wedding party and a battalion of reporters and photographers finally make its way to the chambers of Judge Charles S. Perry. After a chance to photograph the couple and ask them questions, Judge Perry cleared the chambers and shut the door. Reporters climb up to the transom and overhear the ceremony, marking the time. David Dunn, deputy clerk, brings the marriage license, but there is no typewriter. After a short delay, the typewriter arrives and Marilyn, then Joe, signs the document. At 1:46 in the afternoon, Judge Perry performs a 2 minute and 20 second ceremony to unite the famous couple. Best man and matron of honor, Reno and Betty Barsocchini, witnesses Tom and Lee DiMaggio, and Lefty O'Doul and his wife Jean form the wedding party that shares in the hectic celebration. The press is eager to get photographs of the newlyweds and is finally let into the chambers. A newsreel camera captures the couple shortly after the ceremony in the judge's chambers, and asks them for kiss. While Marilyn is used to such shenanigans, Joe is not and soon gets fed up with the demands of the photographer for "just one more kiss," and growls, "let's get out of here." The men of the wedding party form a wedge that quickly hustles out the bride and groom. They turn down the wrong hallway and end up in the Real Estate office. They then backtrack and make their way out of the basement exit, and Joe and Marilyn rush to Joe's waiting Cadillac. In all the mayhem, Judge Perry laments that he forgot to kiss the bride. A newspaper comments on Joe's demeanor, "'This is a fine thing--dodging your loyal fans like this, Joe,' said a member of the crowd who had wormed his way into the elevator. DiMaggio took umbrage and, after much this and that, shouted, 'Don't you tell me what to do!'"

As Mrs. DiMaggio, Marilyn will walk a fragile line in pleasing Joe and submitting to the request of the press. On this day Joe hustles her off, but she manages to find the cameras as they run and even while being whisked away by Joe.

Joe and Marilyn drive to Paso Robels, California. They dine at a little restaurant at the Hot Springs Hotel. The diners soon recognize them, so the manager, Ned Lutz, moves them and their steak dinners to a secluded corner table complete with candle light. They mention to Mr. Lutz that they are going back to Los Angeles. When they leave, they head toward Los Angeles, but back track and stay at the Clifton Motel in Paso Robels. E.B. Sharp, the manager of the motel, recognizes Joe DiMaggio at once. He keeps a promise to Joe to not divulge their whereabouts until they have left the next day. The press, meanwhile, is tearing Los Angeles apart looking for Joe and Marilyn. Art Ryan reported on the couple and their nuptial night in his syndicated column on the 20th, "For our money, of course, the quote of the week came from the manager of the Paso Robles motel where Joe and Marilyn spent their wedding night, 'I think,' he said, 'they stopped her because of our sign out front saying we have television.'"

After Joe and Marilyn leave the Clifton Motel on January 15th, manager E. B. Sharp informs radio station *KPRL* that Joe and Marilyn spent the night at his motel. Joe and Marilyn drive through Los Angeles, right under the nose of the waiting press, who had been staking out Marilyn's Doheny apartment and other locations where they thought the newlyweds might be. Bill Mastro, caretaker at the Clifton Motel finds a discarded stocking of Marilyn's in the trash as he was cleaning up their room. He sends it to his pal, Charlie Pringle, who treasures the memento.

The DiMaggio's drive through Palm Springs, up into the San Jacinto mountains, to the Idylwild Estate of Marilyn's lawyer, Lloyd Wright, Jr. There, in this snowy mountain retreat, they spend a secluded honeymoon. The caretaker of the Estate, Harry Gibbons, kept the secret of the famous honeymooners. Marilyn makes a call to Lloyd Wright, Jr. and finds out that she is no longer suspended by Twentieth Century-Fox, but they still require her to make the film, *The Girl in Pink Tights*. She and Joe spend ten days romping in the snow, playing pool and taking rides into the desert. After their secluded honeymoon, Joe flew to New York to conduct some business and Marilyn secretly returned to Hollywood on January 24th, talking only to her business manager, her agent, and close friends.

Starting on January 17th, Lee Ferrero of the *INS* tells the story of Joe DiMaggio and Marilyn Monroe in a series of three articles. The first was "Love Blossomed From Blind Date…Joltin' Joe DiMaggio, of baseball immortality, and blonde Marilyn Monroe, one of the most exciting women of modern times, married in San Francisco the other day—and culminated one of America's most publicized romances. In the first of a series of three, how the two met on a blind date and fell in love at first sight." Ferrero quotes William Frawley, who played Fred Mertz on *I Love Lucy*, as he was a good friend of Joe DiMaggios. According to Frawley he was also at the blind date. "'It was a blind date. I can't remember the particulars about how it came about, but Marilyn was so impressed with Joe as a fine fellow. She had never seen him play baseball, so it wasn't his big reputation that impressed her. They just sat and talked. There was no dancing. Just a dinner date at the Villa Nova restaurant. She kept saying to me, 'Isn't he wonderful, Bill.' After the date, the Yankee Clipper told him: 'Bill, there's one terrific girl. Do you think she's dumb or just beautiful—or both.' Frawley recalled that he told DiMaggio, 'She is the type of girl who takes a lot of knowing.' But for Marilyn, it was love at first sight."

The second part of Leo Ferrero's series came out on the 18th. "'Class' Won Fame And 'The Girl,' Too." Joe DiMaggio's history was recalled in this article. A couple of quotes by Marilyn ended this installment. "She said of her marriage to Joe, 'It is the real thing and it is for keeps. I couldn't be happier. I've always wanted a home of my own. I don't want anything pretentious—just something comfortable. Where I am now in Hollywood I can't move around very much. I want a place where I can stretch out. All my life I've wanted a green lawn.'"

In the third and final installment of Leo Ferrero's series on the 19$^{th}$, he finishes their storybook romance. "Marilyn and Joe Conquer Obscure Starts…They came out of the cloudy American environs of poverty and struggle. In best story-book style, they came out of low beginnings, lacked advanced education, suffered similar heart-breaking first marriages, moved into polished adulthood—and eventually into each other's arms as if it had been so ordained by destiny. Both of them were ugly ducklings. Joe was gangly, painfully bashful, shock-haired and possessed of a prominent proboscis and bobbing Adam's apple. Marilyn was the unkempt, scraggly-haired misfit she herself now describes as 'the blonde that nobody wanted.'…Joe's fabulous career as the Mr. Big of the national pastime was ending, strangely enough, when the bombshell blonde was forging to the front with each appearance on the screen. Marilyn became an international celebrity when she took a chance on a red velvet rug and the resultant furor over her nude calendar shot made her—as Louella Parsons, queen of film-land's columnists, said, 'The most exciting woman in Hollywood today.' An astute brass-hat at 20$^{th}$ Century-Fox studios, who asked his name be withheld, put it this way, "A good marriage never hurt a movie star. Just look at Betty Grable. And who is to beef when Miss America marries Mr. America? There are plenty of us who predict Marilyn will become even bigger than she is today, and the studio certainly will not trim the grandiose plans we have for her.'"

While Marilyn was on her honeymoon, the Golden Globe Award Show was held at the Club Del Mar in Santa Monica. Marilyn won the award for 1953's World Film Favorite, Female.

On January 25th Marilyn had a message delivered to the studio which stated that she read the script and does not care to do the picture. Marilyn is once again suspended for not showing up to film *The Girl in Pink Tights*.

Joe DiMaggio has plans to accompany "Lefty" O'Doul on a trip to Japan to promote baseball. The men plan to visit Tokyo, Osaka and Yokohama. They will lecture, appear on TV and Joe will coach at a training camp for Japan's Central League. They plan to include Marilyn and Lefty's wife Jean to come along for some sightseeing.

Marilyn quietly met Joe DiMaggio in San Francisco on January 28th. She was vaccinated for a trip to Japan by Dr. Clifton Bennett. The next day Marilyn received her passport (16918) just in time to depart for Japan. Marilyn signed her passport as Norma Jeane DiMaggio and underneath as Marilyn Monroe. She filled in her home address as "2150 Beach Street, San Francisco, California" She listed her contact to notify in case of accident or death as "Mr. Joseph Paul DiMaggio; 2150 Beach Street, San Francisco, California."

*Associated Press Wire Service,* January 29th, "Marilyn, Joe Off For Tokyo...America's most famous newlyweds, Marilyn Monroe and Joe DiMaggio, are shown strolling toward Federal building here, Friday, to pick up their passports for flight to Tokyo. Lefty O'Doul, great slugger's first baseball manager, accompanied them on hop to Japanese capital. Studio has suspended Monroe."

*Times County News Service* story, January 29th, "Joe, Marilyn Off to Tokyo...Screen actress Marilyn Monroe and her new husband, baseball great Joe DiMaggio, left here at 12:32 p.m. today aboard a Pan-American Clipper for a visit to Japan. The couple left Mills Field accompanied by DiMaggio's friend, baseball manager Lefty O'Doul. Pan-American had received the reservation late yesterday from O'Doul for himself and two 'no-name' passengers. However, at the air terminal, the couple was seen boarding the plane for the trip to Tokyo, where DiMaggio and O'Doul will make arrangements for another United States baseball tour. Marilyn and Joe arrived at San Francisco's International Airport only 30 minutes before take-off time because Marilyn broke her right thumb last night and had to have it bandaged and splintered this morning. 'I just bumped it against the door,' she explained. Miss Monroe, currently at odds with her studio, 20th Century-Fox, had not been expected to make the trip. Then, late yesterday, Pan-American offices at Mills Field reported that O'Doul had made reservations for three persons. The fact that Miss Monroe was to accompany her husband was confirmed shortly before the Clipper took off here."

According to Milton and Amy Greene, Joe broke Marilyn's thumb when he was engaged in a conversation with Lefty O'Doul and she came up behind Joe and hugged him. He flung her arms away, and in that powerful gesture, Joe's flaring temper combined with his unrestrained strength was enough to break her thumb. Another story has it that he slammed a suitcase shut, not knowing that her thumb was in the way.

The foursome has a layover in Honolulu, Hawaii. This is the first indication of the frenzy that the public will display toward Joe and Marilyn on their trip.

After arriving at the Honolulu Airport on January 29th nearly 2000 people were gathered to greet Marilyn and Joe. The Hawaiian Visitors Bureau arranged to have Hula dancers welcome them to Hawaii. Marilyn, Joe, Lefty and his wife Jean were draped in leis. Policemen escorted them safely to the Pan American passenger lounge where they were served Hawaiian pineapple juice. Marilyn was exclaiming to Joe that the crowd kept grabbing at her hair. There was a hint of real fear in her voice. They then met with reporters and photographers. Louis Benjamin, the owner of a bar called The Log Cabin, had been recruited to be their driver. Joe had met "Benny" during World War II. He drove them to the Royal Hawaiian Hotel in a powder blue convertible. The Royal Hawaiian Hotel, also known as the "Pink Palace," was on Waikiki beach. Marilyn and Joe checked in and were given the special honeymoon suite. Marilyn strolled along the beach in front of the hotel. Joe's friend then took them sight-seeing around Oahu. They visited Joe's old friends from when he was stationed in Hawaii during the service. One friend they saw was Theodore Searle of Honolulu Stadium. Lefty O'Doul told the press when asked about their plans on Hawaii, "they're going to spend time staying away from the mob, you know--lovebirds on a honeymoon."

*AP Wire Service* story, January 30th, "Marilyn and DiMaggio on Their Way To Japan...Couple Extend Honeymoon by Flying With Baseball Man Lefty O'Doul on Tour...Marilyn showed up with her thumb in a splint, hidden most of the time under her mink coat. 'I just bumped it,' she said. 'I have a witness, Joe was there. He heard it crack.' She declined to go into details about the injured thumb. Their trip to Japan, both asserted repeatedly, is 'an extended honeymoon.' Joe said Marilyn will make some appearances at GI hospitals in Japan and she added, 'Yes. I hope to do that.' When asked if she is going to make another movie soon, Mrs. DiMaggio said, 'I don't know. I'm under suspension.' 'We're not concerned about that now,' Joe said, 'we're on our honeymoon.' Their honeymoon had been interrupted for four days while DiMaggio flew to New York for a television commitment. He returned here last night, and Marilyn flew back from Hollywood. Marilyn was wearing a black tailored suit and a leopard skin choker. As she was boarding the plane she was given a Hawaiian lei by a Pan American employee who had just had it flown in for his girlfriend, not Marilyn."

On January 30th the newlyweds prepare to leave Hawaii in route for Japan. Marilyn, Joe, Lefty and Jean get the necessary visas to visit Japan. Early on the morning of January 31st Marilyn and Joe leave Honolulu on a Pan American jet, Flight #831, at 2:05 am (HST), in route for Tokyo. They were due to arrive in Tokyo on February 1$^{st}$ at 3:05pm, Tokyo time. Marilyn and Joe are given certificates titled "Domain of Phoebus Apollo" in honor of crossing the International Dateline when they fly to Tokyo.

*Algona Advance*, Iowa, reported on March 18th, "Of Things & Stuff," by Mrs. Walter Weisbrod. "...little 7-months-old Kathy, daughter of Lt. and Mrs. Paul Schenck would be of special interest to movie-goers and baseball fans. If what I hear is true, she would be the envy of quite a few of the men. Kathy's father went to Japan last August, where he is stationed with the Marine Corps. In February she and her mother flew to Japan to join him. On the same plane were Marilyn Monroe and her new husband Joe DiMaggio. Marilyn took little Kathy and held her up and called, 'Look, Joe, isn't she cute.' Just like any other ordinary girl who loves babies!"

A news story starts to hit papers about Marilyn returning to posing for Earl Moran. "Mrs. Joe DiMaggio, Marilyn Monroe to you, is the subject of a new calendar drawing by Earl Moran, who calls the famed shape 'one of the best' that ever posed for him. The new calendar brings the screen star back to the field in which she scored her initial success." Marilyn didn't actually pose for the new drawing. Mr. Moran just used the reference photographs he had taken of her when she was posing for him in the early 50s. Emmeline Snively remarks about these calendars, "…sometimes calendars take a long time to get published. Four Earl Moran photographs of Marilyn are appearing on the 1954 Brown and Bigelow calendars. These were shot years ago." What appeared were not photographs, but artwork from Moran.

A crowd of about 4,000 at Tokyo International Airport swept guards and official delegations aside at 3:40pm. The Stratocruiser was delayed for almost two and a half hours. Marilyn and Joe arrive in Tokyo at 5:45pm at the Haneda Airport. The crowd waited in near freezing weather to see the couple. The DiMaggios wait 20 minutes before facing the mob outside. In the glare of the Kleig lights and the threat of the surging fans, Joe and Marilyn endured only 5 minutes of madness before taking refuge back inside the airplane.

PFC Don Towles, for the *Stars and Stripes*, commented that, "The world's most beautiful blonde and her 'Yankee Clipper' husband came to Tokyo last night amid a freezing wind and 2,500 wild fans who almost turned Tokyo International Airport into a riot. Misty-eyed, moist-lipped Marilyn Monroe tired but still smiling after a day which saw their arrival delayed five hours, and Joe DiMaggio, former Yankee outfielder, arrived aboard a Pan American World Airways plane at 5:45pm." Columnist Keyes Beech reported that, "Marilyn wore a long mink coat, a slinky black dress and a liquid smile. Her blonde hair was tossed wildly by the stiff wind and she drew back in dismay when a Japanese radiocaster pushed a microphone into her face. Her husband looked rather glum."

They hoped for the best, but it was worse than the reception in Hawaii. Marilyn was showered with flowers and the cry "Monchan," a term of endearment meaning precious little girl. They are sufficiently frightened of the growing unruliness of the fans and after 5 minutes of madness, go back inside their airplane and wait for the mob to settle down. A reporter from the *UP* was allowed to ask a few questions. Joe DiMaggio's reply to the question, 'would Marilyn go to Korea to entertain the troops,' was classic Joe. "Let's face it,' DiMaggio said. 'Marilyn doesn't have an act. She will visit hospitals in Japan if she is asked. Remember, she's not here on her own. She's here with me and we're on our honeymoon. We paid our own way over here.'"

Kashio Aoki, the precious cargo manager for Pan American Airlines, was assigned to Joe and Marilyn. He waited with them on the plane until security had arranged for safe passage to their hotel. While waiting, Kashio asked for permission to take several candid photos of Joe and Marilyn. Joe grudgingly gave his consent. After taking two photos of the couple and one of Marilyn alone, Joe became annoyed with the photo-taking and announced that it was over.

Another 45 minutes went by before Joe, Marilyn and the O'Douls escaped through a baggage hatch on the other side of the plane into the waiting limousine. The Japanese, who had crowded the runway, now threw themselves on top of the limousine, threatening to collapse the roof. The party headed for the Imperial Hotel and a scheduled press conference. The originally scheduled route included a caravan of cars down the Ginza to the Imperial Hotel. Joe DiMaggio refused to have anything else to do with the unruly crowd and ordered the driver to take an alternate route. This left thousands of Japanese fans, who had been waiting hours to see the famous couple, standing in the cold.

Two hundred policemen tried to control the crowd of over a thousand at the Imperial Hotel when Joe and Marilyn arrived. They were surrounded by a throng of enthusiastic fans and literally ran a gauntlet into the hotel. Then bedlam broke loose. Plate glass windows broke, the revolving doors were stuck with people jamming themselves in for a look, and two sight-seers were knocked into the Koi pond. Marilyn, Joe, Lefty and Jean finally got to their adjoining suites. Marilyn commented on the frenzy that surrounded their arrival with, "These people, they're mad." O'Doul sent word that the Couple would be down in 10 minutes. The crowd surrounded the hotel calling Marilyn's name, and refused to leave until she came out on the balcony to wave and blow kisses at them. Marilyn appeared in a black dress and greeted the unruly gathering below. Two men tried unsuccessfully to climb up to where she was. Marilyn would later say she felt "like I was a dictator or something." Lost in the shuffle was the fact that DiMaggio and O'Doul, manager of the San Diego Padres, had come here to help coach Japanese Central League baseball teams for three weeks.

The next day Marilyn and Joe attended a press conference in the Treasure room, where Marilyn was given the seat of honor. Marilyn wore a red wool suit with a fox stole. In one of her wittiest remarks, she assures the reporters, when asked about her stole, that "it's fox, but not the Twentieth-Century kind." When asked about her lace slip under her suit and her habit of not wearing underwear, she remarked that she was going to buy a Kimono while in Japan. She is interviewed by eighty-five journalist. The questions they posed to her were rude by any standard. "Do you sleep naked? Do you wear underwear? How long have you been walking like that?" Joe positioned himself against a back wall and answered questions from four avid sports writers that had spotted him. Joe denied reports that his wife would entertain troops in Korea. 'Let's face it, Marilyn doesn't have an act. She will visit hospitals in Japan if asked. Remember she is not here on her own. She's here with me and we're on our honeymoon. I don't mind playing second fiddle to Marilyn. She's my wife and I'm glad for her.' Finally, Joe has had enough and literally drags Marilyn out of the room by her arm. She is turning all the while to answer questions and smile for photographers. News of their arrival in Japan and her interview streak across newspapers with headlines blaring, "Wolf-Whistling' Japanese Mob Marilyn Monroe, DiMag," "Marilyn Says She's Not a Baseball Fan," and "Marilyn Dominates Jap Press Parley."

*Stars and Stripes* newspaper, Pacific edition, February 3rd, features a photograph and article, headline, "Monroe Sidesteps Queries on Tour, Family, Lingerie...Beaming Beauty, vivacious Marilyn Monroe smiles as she poses for a battery of photographers at the Imperial Hotel yesterday afternoon. The blonde film star honeymooned here with husband, Joe DiMaggio, was wearing a skin tight flaming red dress. The Hollywood dream girl and the former Yankee baseball great were married about 2 weeks ago in San Francisco." PFC, Don Towles reported, "America's Princess of Pulchritude, Marilyn Monroe in a skin-tight, flaming red dress which had a habit of creeping up over her knees, turned on her 100-degree charm late yesterday at a press conference attended by more than 150 reporters and cameramen...Outfitted in the bright dress with black collar, black pumps, seamless stockings, carrying black gloves and a fox fur piece, and wearing a tiny pearl chocker, which she said O'Doul gave her, the shapely bride said she 'might have some news about that later' when asked if she would visit Korea. 'If I could get a piano player I might sing some songs in the hospitals there,' she replied. However, the question of a Korean trip was left undecided until the twosome has had a chance to complete plans here. As numerous questions were asked about the number of children she planned, Marilyn gave noncommittal answers until Joe turned with a broad smile and said, 'Why don't you ask me that question?' Miss Monroe pointed out that there were several Hollywood actors she enjoyed working with but then turned and put her arm around DiMaggio saying, 'But this is my favorite man.'" Asked if she thought home life and career would mix, Joe answered for her with, 'It's going on every day.'" When queried if she still followed her custom of not wearing lingerie, the only answer the famous actress would give was, 'I'm planning on getting a Japanese kimono.'"

The GIs want to get in on the act and the *INS* runs an article quoting some impatient GIs. "In winter-gripped Korea, PFC J.G. Ulleny, 21 of Chicago, IL, spoke the sentiments of many GIs when he said: 'To hell with those base troops in Japan. Get Marilyn over here where she's really appreciated. That gal would really melt some of the ice around these bunkers. Marilyn is our favorite pinup girl.' Cpl. Robert R. Woodbury, 21, of Flushing, NY, said: 'Joe's always been my idol. But after a guy has frozen in Korea for a while, sometimes he changes idols. Let's have Marilyn over here by all means. Turn Joe over to the women marines in Japan.' 'Just seeing that blonde would warm an entire regiment,' declared S-Sgt. Gilbert E. Postelle, 25 of Tallhina, OK, as he pulled his fur-lined parka close against a chill wind. PFC Walter Henry Steen, 20 of Brooklyn, NY, said: 'Marilyn's picture is on practically every locker box and bunker hall in Korea. She ought to come there and receive the homage of her fans.' PFC Johnny Jones, 21, of Tacoma, WA, said it was 'wonderful' just to know that a woman like Marilyn existed."

The Tokyo newspaper, *Yomiuri* on February 3rd sponsored an exclusive reception at the Imperial Hotel. The President of the *Yomiuri* Newspaper Company greets the DiMaggios. Bobby Brown, a friend of Joe's and a former Yankee Star, joined Marilyn, Joe and Lefty.

The press starts to carry the first definite plans for Marilyn to tour the Korean truce front.

On February 3rd Marilyn made thousands of GI's wishes come true when she announced that she would tour the Korean truce front for four days starting on February 16th. C. Roberts Jennings, a reporter for the *Stars and Stripes*, Pacific edition, said that "The announcement of her visit spread like wild grass fire across the tense neutral zone...Some GI's actually wept. Others froze in a sort of yearning silence." Marilyn was to tell Jennings of the importance of the Korean GI's to her career, "When I first started I had several little parts at Fox. Then the letters began pouring in from Korea and my studio was so impressed they began to give me wonderful parts. Thanks to Korea, my fan mail jumped from 50 letters to 5,000 letters a week." Walter A. Bouillet, Special Services Officer said she would sing a few numbers, but mostly just stand there.

A Boston newspaper reported, "The Army, in what passed as a masterpiece of understatement, said that the blonde actress 'will be most welcomed.' Marilyn will leave Japan in a few days and will include frontline units in her tour. 'I have wanted to go to Korea to see the boys for a long time now,' she said. 'Now, even though I am on my honeymoon, I have the chance to go—and I'm going for at least four days.' La Monroe said she was trying to 'round up a piano player' so she could sing a few songs for the troops. For the GIs that will be just frosting on the cake. They'll be satisfied just with looking at Marilyn and leave the talent for more artistic spirits. Still, they wanted to keep her happy, and as PFC Melvin Schramm of Brooklyn said: 'Guys are volunteering who haven't played a note since they were 10.' Cpl Phillip Oulmep of Orne St., Dorchester, Mass, was more specific. 'I'd climb Heartbreak Ridge with a piano on my back to hear her sing,' he declared. Pianos and players of same were considered just so much unnecessary trapping by PFC, Johnnie Boskul, of Pittsburgh, who said: 'Never mind a piano or piano player. They'd just be in the way. All we want is Marilyn standing in a good strong spotlight.'

In classic Marilyn fashion she took to her bed with an upset stomach and a mild case of nerves. She was a bit overwhelmed by all of the attention directed at her and needed to rest up for her upcoming publicity events and her tour of the Korean front. Marilyn's personal maid for her stay in Tokyo was Toshiko Takeya. Marilyn was given Shiatsu massages during her stay by T. Namikoshi, the director of the Nipon Shiatsu Institute in Tokyo.

On February 3rd Walter Winchell gave this sweet toast to the couple. "There is nothing more popular than love, or the love stories of popular people…There's the story of Marilyn Monroe and Joe DiMaggio. Theirs is really the oldest and most wonderful story of them all. The Cinderella story…Marilyn's glass slipper was the moving picture camera. Her pumpkin coach was make of celluloid…The Yankee Stadium was Prince Charming's castle…Marilyn and Joe are national idols because both personify national ideals: Love, beauty, sportsmanship and the pursuit of happiness…So here's a toast to the Queen of Hearts and the Ace of Diamonds. May they love happily ever after."

The next day General John E. Hull officially invites Marilyn to tour the troops in Korea. At first Marilyn was hesitant, insisting that she didn't have a pianist to accompany her. She was assured that a competent pianist would be found. The Army called on Pvt. Al

Guastafeste, who was excited, yet a bit concerned about Marilyn's ability to sing. He was given a copy of *Gentlemen Prefer Blondes* to watch. Afterwards, he arranged her performance around a couple of songs from the movie.

On the 4th, GIs weigh in on Marilyn's visit in an INS news story. "The first reaction of many GIs contacted in Korea by correspondent Robert Pennell was 'what will she wear?' 'Four glorious days,' chortled PFC Francis S. Soistman, 21 of Baltimore, MD. 'That will be enough time to defrost all of Korea. That gal would melt ice for miles around.' Another soldier, Sgt. John Yale, 21, of Midwest, WY, pounded his fist into his palm and cried, 'This is the greatest morale boost for the troops since rotation was invented.' PFC Frederick A. Gentile, 22, of Middletown, NY, said: 'My division, the 45th, is being pulled out of here just when Marilyn will be arriving. The boys would sure like a look at her. I never heard of anyone deserting to stay in Korea, but a situation like this calls for drastic action.' Pvt. Patrick R. Laux, 21 of Appleton, WI, reflected the general view when he said: 'The sooner she comes and the longer she stays the better we'll like it.'

On hearing of Marilyn coming to Korea GIs had this to say, "'Wow, I just gotta see that in the flesh,' said Cpl. Ronald K. Hertz, Holland, Mich. 'I just got see if she looks like that.' Another frontline soldier said his sergeant could march him up one Korean mountain after another if Marilyn led the way. 'With a walk like that, I'd never get tired,' he said…There were only two grumbles from the excited GIs in Korea. Pfc. John W. Reed, Gallup, N.M., said it was too bad DiMaggio had to stay in Japan to help coach Japanese baseball players while his wife came to Korea. 'I would like to see Joe, too,' Reed complained. He said he didn't think Marilyn knew 'center field from third base.' Marine S.Sgt. Orvill A. Metzger, St. Luis, Mo., said his only regret was that Marilyn's visit was coming too late to help his morale. 'I'm going home shortly,' Metzger said. 'And I think she should have come sooner.' But most of the GIs echoed the sentiment of Pfc. Willie Maddox of Spring Hill, Ala, who said the beautiful blonde's visit would be 'the greatest change in scenery we have had here in a long time.'"

Marilyn visits the US Army Hospital in Tokyo on February 5th, and then flies to Kwana, Japan to join Joe who is there to play golf. Before visiting the Hospital, Marilyn visits the base Beauty Salon. She arrived at 11:00 and left at 2:40. She had her hair styled, a manicure, pedicure and a massage. She delayed her scheduled visit to the Hospital over 3 hours getting primped. When asked about Marilyn's beauty treatments a staff physician said he didn't know anything as they wouldn't allow him in because Marilyn was getting her massage. Marilyn had lunch with the patients and enlisted personnel during her visit to the hospital. Marilyn commented about her new hairstyle to Lee Benedict. "Her hair is cut shorter, cut, while she was in Korea and Japan, and she's leaving it that way because, as Marilyn said, 'I'm wearing it like that in my picture—and besides, my husband likes it.'"

While touring the Tokyo Army Hospital Marilyn chatted on the floor with Pvt. Albert Evans, Canton, Ohio. She had to lie on the floor and look up. Evans suffered a broken back in a jeep accident in Korea on Jan. 11th and had been immobilized in a face down position. No matter how famous she would become, Marilyn never lost touch with her humanity.

Marilyn autographed the cast of Cpl. Donald L. Wakehouse of Iowa City, Iowa. Wakehouse was a former prisoner of war who was wounded in the final stages of the war, captured and then returned by the Communists. Marilyn is also photographed with PVT Bill Burres of Stockton, CA, and CPL Allison Ittel of Howard Lake, MN. Marilyn was scheduled to visit the $8167^{th}$ Hospital later.

In a special to the Lowell Sun, on February 6th, Marilyn's visit to the Army Hospital's in Japan was commemorated. "Corp. Frank Tier of Pinehurst, Mass, dazzled by yesterday's meeting with movie beauty Marilyn Monroe, summed up the reaction of his buddies in an Army hospital here to their meeting with the blonde newlywed with 'fine, very fine.' Marilyn had just completed a three-hour visit to the hospital's beauty shop and a tour of the wards leaving a trail of sighs in her wake. Marilyn, called the greatest curative since penicillin, did very little beside shake hands, close her eyes just the slightest bit, and murmur, 'I'm so-o-o glad to meet you.' It was enough. She bestowed one kiss to Pfc. Phillip Loprestri of Long Island City, Queens, NY, who referred to her marriage to baseball hero Joe DiMaggio when he said: 'Hi! Now it's all in the family. We're both Italians!'…Marilyn next went to the seventh floor of the giant Tokyo Army Hospital. GIs were told that she would be in the lounge at 1:30 and any 'ambulatory' patient would be welcome. She was late in arriving there, too, but with her devastating look, her lingering handshake, soft clinging voice and possessive look, she bowled over everyone. Marilyn made it a point to touch every man's hand within reach."

Marilyn, after having taken her Army 'shots,' for her Korean tour, came to Kawana to rest on the 5th. Kawana was a resort town famous for its golf. She was smiling but obviously exhausted on arrival here to join Joe. She was feeling the effects of the inoculations, a nervous stomach upset and the fatigue of celebrity touring. The Army announced that her accompanist would be Cpl. Al Guastefeste, 21, of Uniondale, Long Island, N.Y., who studied classical music as a piano student.

When Joe and Marilyn took a cab to a small fishing village near their hotel in Kawana, the people of the village ignored her and swarmed Joe. Upon arriving at the village a small boy climbed on the back of the cab and yelled, "DiMaggio-san." Marilyn watched in delight as Joe was surrounded by kids for autographs. Photographers take pictures of them strolling along a road, taking in the beauty of a lake and meeting some of the local people. Marilyn is dressed very demurely in a dress and wearing a kerchief on her head.

On February 8th Norma Jeane DiMaggio receives her clearance papers and is issued USO Entertainer Serial #129278. Marilyn will be accompanied on her trip to Korea by Jean O'Doul.

After arriving at the Itazuke Airport in Fukuoka at 7:30 on February 9th their plane is met with a throng of adoring fans.

The *INS* reported the action. "Actress Marilyn Monroe, wearing a tight white sweater and tight black skirt touched off another riot of Japanese movie fans Tuesday when she appeared in her hotel room window in response to the clamor of a crowd of 5,000. Marilyn tossed carnations to her shouting admirers while several fans attempted to climb trees to get closer to her third floor window."

Hundreds of people, this time including many teenage girls, packed the entrance to the Kokusai Hotel where they were staying in room 313. Marilyn is interviewed by a Mr. Kawamura of the Fukunichi Newspaper Co. on February 9th. She is photographed by 3 cameramen in attendance wearing a beret, white sweater, and a tight fitting skirt. She plucks some flowers from a bouquet she was given and sprinkles them over the balcony onto the crowd gathered below. Douglas J. Weber, with the 6107th Air Base Squadron took a lovely photo of Marilyn during the interview.

Later that day she appeared at the US Air Force Troop Carrier Wing at Brady Air Installation in Japan to greet the troops and sign autographs. She rode around for a couple of hours in an open convertible visiting the troops and posing for photographs.

F. E. Raham, CWO USA, Asst. Adj. Gen., writes Marilyn and Jean O'Doul to give them their Invitational Travel Orders on February 9th.

The *UP* gives Marilyn's itinerary for her trip to Korea. "The Army said Marilyn will give shows for seven divisions and at two air bases during her four-day stay in Korea. Scheduled to arrive in Korea from Japan next Tuesday, the film beauty will perform for the First Marine Division and the Seventh, Third, 40th, 25th, Second and 45th Army Divisions over a three-day period. On her final day in Korea, the actress wife of Joe DiMaggio will perform at the Chunchon and Taegu Air Bases."

Marilyn receives some good press in Japan in regards to her tidy hotel room. Back home, accounts of the backseat of her car are not so complimentary. *Albuquerque Journal* newspaper runs this article on February 12th, "Her Just Dues...As much as we deplore all this hero worship of stage, movie, and TV stars--any other stars for that matter--let's give Marilyn Monroe her just dues. It is left to the Japanese room boy for Marilyn and her new husband, Joe DiMaggio, to give the actress her dues. Says he, 'This is the first time I have come across a guest who does not dirty her room. She never fails to empty the ash trays and all scraps of paper in the wastebasket. And unlike Japanese actresses, she is not a snob.' All of which is a mighty high compliment for the curvaceous actress. Thus, Marilyn is creating good will for America in Japan in contrast to the ill will generated by so many of our citizens, particularly famed and temperamental ones, who travel abroad."

On February 12th Marilyn and Joe arrive in Hiroshima from Fukuoka, on Japan's southernmost island, Kyushu. They are accompanied by the O'Doul's and ex-Yankee third baseman who was currently a medical officer for the U.S. Army in Japan, Bobby Brown. The "Blonde Atomic Bombshell" visits the city where the first atom bomb in military history was dropped.

Later in the day Marilyn and Joe visited the scared remains of buildings destroyed in the blast and the Atomic Bomb Casualty Commission. Their host was Dr. Bobby Brown who would eventually become president of the American League. They visited the ABCC because Dr. Brown and Dr. Jack Lewis, an internist at ABCC, were classmates at Stanford University Medical School. They were also welcomed by Dr. William Moloney, Chief of the Department of Medicine. The ABCC Center was constructed by US occupation forces five years after the end of the World War II. Its purpose was to study the irradiated populations of Hiroshima and Nagasaki. They diagnosed radiation illness but did nothing to treat it. Eighty thousand people were chosen to be studied and were followed until their deaths. Candid photos of that visit show the deep concern in Marilyn's face as she views the diorama of Hiroshima after the bomb. It is now understandable that in 1960 she will join SANE, the National Committee for a Sane Nuclear Policy, founded by Steve Allen and Robert Ryan. The group's aim was to urge an effective permanent world-wide ban on the testing of nuclear weapons.

Marilyn created quite a stir when she tries to visit one of Joe's Baseball clinics at a Hiroshima baseball stadium. A radio commentator announced on his news broadcast today that Marilyn had gone to the ball park to watch Joe DiMaggio coach Japanese players. Five thousand radio fans hurried to the baseball park and rushed onto the grounds. Marilyn, dressed in a two-piece brown dress, was roughly pulled and pushed as she tried to make her way behind the net to join Jean O'Doul. Once again, baseball became a side issue, next to the ambulating "Monroe Hurricane," as local newsmen dubbed her. She created such a distraction that she left after 30 minutes.

Marilyn and Jean O'Doul went sightseeing Friday on the scenic island of Miyajima near the atom-bombed city of Hiroshima. In the afternoon Marilyn and Jean went on a boat ride to visit the famed Miyajima shrine and other scenic spots on the island, which is located in the Inland Sea. Marilyn and Joe, along with the O'Doul's and Bobby Brown, were guest at the Ichaen Hotel on the secluded island.

While visiting Hiroshima, Joe and Marilyn also flew to the near-by Iwakuni Air Base on the Southern end of Honshu. Marilyn and Joe were once again swamped by 5,000 screaming fans at the Iwakuni Airport on their arrival. This time the fans included members of a Hiroshima baseball team and American GIs. The Iwakuni Air Base was the home of the 13th Bombardment Division, known as "The Devil's Own Grim Reapers." Lt. Henry W. Purser photographed Marilyn and Joe as they arrived and also later at the Officers Club on Base. On the morning they left Iwakuni, Lt. Purser, who was assigned to the medical corps, was asked to bring Marilyn a couple of aspirin and a good cup of coffee, as she had a headache. Upon bringing her the requested items she visited with him for about 15 minutes, proving that her reputation for kindness was real. Joe will later accompany Marilyn to greet the troops at Itazuke Air Force Base. Their visit is documented in the Base Newspaper on Feb.15. They are photographed in front of a C-199 aircraft. The 187th RCT made some parachute jumps for them to observe.

On February 12th the cast members from the USO show, 'Anything Goes,' fly to Osaka, Japan to prepare for their latest Korean tour. Marilyn will join them on the 14th.

Marilyn and Jean O'Doul travel to Osaka, Japan on February 14th to start rehearsals. Walter Bouillet, coordinator in charge of all operations of the Korean tour, called Pvt. Albert Guastafeste of Uniondale, Long Island, a music instructor at Camp Zama, who had been chosen to be Marilyn's piano accompanist. Given a choice, Marilyn chose to be part of a ten-man package show which had been performing in Okinawa. Guastafeste was instructed to get the band members and come to the hospital auditorium for a rehearsal with Marilyn. She was wearing a long-sleeved black sweater and a pair of tan corduroy pants, with black high-heeled shoes. Marilyn greeted Al and they walked on stage to meet the cast of "Anything Goes" and the band members who would accompany her. The "Anything Goes" show would perform its regular routine and Marilyn would perform her short act, closing the show. Marilyn's introduction would be the song, "There's Nothing Like a Dame," from the Broadway show, *South Pacific*. When the cast revealed the "Dame" they were discussing was Marilyn Monroe, she appeared onstage. This entrance was most effective, never failing to elicit whistles and cheers from the men. Marilyn would sing *Diamonds Are a Girl's Best Friend*, *Somebody Loves Me*, and would close with *Bye, Bye, Baby*. She had included *Do It Again* in her repertoire, but after the first few performances she was asked by military officials to delete the number from her performance as it was unduly arousing the men, and they feared for her safety. Marilyn was sent a Valentine from the 1st Marine Division. It contained a photograph of a fighter jet surrounded by Marines in a heart-shaped configuration. It was signed "Happy Valentine, First Marine Aircraft Wing." Accompanying it was a letter asking her to visit their base and attached to that was a list of signatures from the men, reaching nearly six feet in length.

On the 14th, the *Stars and Stripes* reports of preparations for Marilyn's visit. "Following a recent announcement that the 7th Div. will be the first Army unit to be visited by cinemactress Marilyn Monroe on her tour of Korea, preparations for perhaps the division's biggest entertainment feature got underway at division headquarters. The big event, dubbed 'Operation MM (mm!)' by division Special Services, will also include a talented AFFE all soldier troupe and their show, 'Anything Goes.' Anticipating one of the largest crowds ever gathered at one time in the $7^{th}$, an outdoor theater has been constructed on the parade field for the occasion. Mrs. DiMaggio will perform for an expected crowd of more than 10,000 troops on a portable stage built by Co. D of the $13^{th}$ Engineers. The seating arrangements provided through the efforts of members of Heavy Mortar Co., $31^{st}$ Inf. Regt., will accommodate better than 8,000 men with ample standing room available. Second Lt. Frank T. Nelson, Baldwin, NY, who is in charge of the seating detail from Heavy Mortar Co. expressed his feelings by saying, 'After all this work, I'll probably end up standing anyway.'"

Marilyn rehearses in the morning and in the afternoon for a performance that evening, February 15th, at the Army Hospital in Osaka, Japan. At 7pm the first performance of "Anything Goes," with special guest star, Marilyn Monroe, is presented to the wounded soldiers and hospital personnel. It was, of course, a smashing success. The *INS* reported on the 16th, 'She'll Dance For Yanks…Actress Marilyn Monroe gave a wriggling, breath-taking preview yesterday of the show she will put on in Korea for American GIs and Marines. Curvaceous Marilyn, wearing a low cut purple dress, ran through her song repertoire at the Osaka Army Hospital for an audience of 200 whistling patients."

According to the *AP*, the Army and the Air Force are fighting over Marilyn. "Marilyn is due to land at Seoul city air base Tuesday on a tour of Korea, and it seems the army is eager to get her—a little too eager as far as the air force is concerned. 'I said 'nuts' to that,' declared Air Force Col Elwyn Quinn of Ferth, Idaho. 'The Army was planning on her not being here any time at all,' Quinn protested, 'but she's going to be here a lot longer than that. Everybody on the base wants to get a look at her too.' Quinn said her expects a large crowd and will have about 20 air police on hand to control well-wishers. 'If I had more air police,' Quinn said, 'I'd assign them too—to get a look at her.'"

Cpl. Bob Jennings reported for the *Stars and Stripes* on the $15^{th}$ about Marilyn's impending tour of Korea. "Marilyn Monroe, the glittering blonde cinemactress who will arrive in Korea tomorrow to thaw out the troops, has already halted the frigid mid-winter across the front and aroused unprecedented cries of havoc. The impending arrival of Marilyn, announced here last week, has thrown bunker-weary Yanks into panic-stricken fury with elated shrieks ranging from 'crazy, man,' to an untypical 'who's she?' the platinum-topped bombshell, who rose to fame on a calendar, is scheduled to wiggle off the ramp at Seoul City Airport at 11am, proceeding to the $1^{st}$ Marine Div. for her first show for eager American troops. Across the 155-mile front, Yank soldiers went ga-ga in an almost unanimous display of ecstatic delight with only a few sour notes tempering the general merriment. Monroe scored 100 percent as pin-up cutouts were quickly framed with fancy mother-of-pearl inlaid pine, garnished signs of welcome emerged out of nowhere and lovesick Americans sighed. 'I put in for a three-day pass and enough C-Rations to get front row seats.' That is the way PFC Ivy Way, Millen, GA, Heavy Mortar, Co., 7ith Regt., of the

7th Div. felt about it. Pvt. Donald Franzee, Paloa, KS, B Co., 7 Regt., said, 'It's sure great to have Marilyn visit the Korean Corral. Oh, my aching eyes. This really ought to shape up the troops.' Bobster A/3C Wilbert Jeans, Chicago, of a tactical control Sq., said, 'She goofs me to the utmost.' Jeans will see Mrs. DiMaggio at K-47 next Friday when she performs for the Fifth Air Force. Nearly every marine, soldier and airman agreed that there was no one they would rather see in a strange land so far from home. Waves of gratitude swept the nation over Marilyn's big move, 'I think it is very nice of her to give up part of her honeymoon to entertain us,' gushed A/2C Alfred W. Lupo, Fairmont, NC, of a fighter-bomber wing near Taegu. 'The announcement of her visit to this base has surely boosted morale of everyone, and most certainly me.' Typical marine modesty elicited the cryptic comment of Cpl. Frank Desta, Brooklyn, NY, 1st Marine Div., 'She's the greatest thing to hit Korea since the Inchon landing.' The rags to riches queen will be chauffeured about the 3rd Div. in the general's sedan by M/Sgt. James England, Columbus, GA, who brayed, 'This will be the best cargo I have ever hauled. In my 14 years of Army driving this will be the most curves I've ever taken in one car.' Marnemen will see the famed chassis at 11am Wednesday at the division CP. Cpl. Gordon Calano, Hartford, CN, Hq., 25th Div., who has been in Korea a long, long time, drawled, 'Who's she?'"

On February 16th Marilyn was given a cigarette lighter with an embossed enamel picture of a bee logo of the 21st T.C.H. division, and inscribed Marilyn Monroe. The back was inscribed, "From the officers and airmen of the 21st T.C.H. (H) Tachikawa, Japan 16 February 1954."

And so begins her legendary visit to the fighting men in Korea. On February 16th Marilyn is accompanied to the Itami Airport in Japan by Joe DiMaggio and Lefty and Jean O'Doul. Marilyn and Jean board an airplane, along with the cast members of "Anything Goes" and head to Seoul, Korea. Marilyn is assigned a flight nurse who will accompany her throughout her Korean tour. Her name is Lt. Olive Palmer. The plane landed at Seoul City Airport. She came out of the plane wearing combat boots, pants and a shirt, and could not have look less drab, with her blonde hair framing her smiling face. She scampered down the ramp and remarked to the cheering servicemen, 'I've never seen so many men in my life. I am just sorry Joe couldn't come along.' More newsmen covered her arrival than had covered any event since President Eisenhower visited the war front in 1952. 15 reporters and photographers accompanied Marilyn to document her tour. The group traveled to Yongsan Air Base near Seoul, where they boarded ten helicopters which would fly them to the various sites for the shows along the front and rear lines. The show personnel and equipment occupied three of the helicopters. The remaining six helicopters were occupied by newsmen and photographers. One of the pilots of her helicopter was Army 1st Lt. Charles R. Chapman, Jr., from Syracuse, New York. Even though he received "the Bronze Star for meritorious service, he will probably always be best remembered by his buddies as the fellow who flew the glamorous Mrs. Joe DiMaggio to the troops."

The first stop on the tour was on the Western Front for the thirteen thousand men of the 1st Marine Division who were based in Camp Pendleton, California. They were the first to give her public recognition when in July 1950 they named her "Miss Morale" after she visited them before they left for Korea. Also in February of 1952 Marilyn sang for the Marines at Camp Pendleton. Biographers say this singing debut cinched her role as Lorelei in *Gentlemen Prefer Blondes*. For some of the men, this may have been the second time to see her perform live. At any rate, she was their "California Dream Girl" and it is fitting that she starts with the men of the 1st Marine Division who were there from the beginning for her, living up to their motto Semper Fideles, always faithful.

Marilyn then changed into her purple sequin cocktail dress, designed by Elgee Bove, in a makeshift dressing room backstage. Although, the dress design is usually credited to Ceil Chapman, both Sheilah Graham and Dorothy Kilgallen noted that the dress was by 19 year-old "boy-genius" designer, Elgee Bove. Bove stated in a 1957 newspaper article, "I designed that famous purple dress of hers which created a sensation in Korea. Marilyn is a very clever girl, even though she talks slowly. Like Kim, she doesn't wear foundation garments. But Marilyn just doesn't care about clothes—she only wears them when she has to." In another article he writes about designing for Marilyn, "Since I feel the bustline is the most interesting part of a woman's figure, I have never designed a dress that hides it. In this respect I've had fine cooperation from Marilyn Monroe. It's no secret that Marilyn scorns the use of bras and girdles, but it should be news to her fans that in every Monroe creation I ever made, I've utilized a cupped bodice every time. This blonde goddess wastes no time in explaining how and where she wants her bosom played up. She approaches each suggested design as though it were a blueprint. She can discuss the importance of building in a basic form in any dress as though she was a devout student of architecture. She has admitted to me that she has gotten to know herself thoroughly and intimately, as others see her." In June of 1953 the question was asked, "Who wouldn't change places with a guy who job is to design gowns and fit them to such lovely forms as Marilyn Monroe and Denise Darcel?" Marilyn had a black version with a jacket she had worn on several occasions in 1953. First to the *Redbook* Awards in February, where she wore the matching jacket (Sheliah Graham noted in her column on March 28th that it was black) and then to the Masquers Party for Charles Coburn in June, where she was photographed wearing it by columnist Earl Wilson. Marilyn apparently liked it so much that she had another one made for her in purple.

Jean O'Doul and Lt. Olive Palmer helped Marilyn get dressed and several MP's guarded the area to keep curious Marines away. Some of the Marines had been waiting for seven hours, making sure that they got a front row seat. Five Marine wiremen climbed telephone poles and watched the show hanging by safety belts. After the show, Marilyn visited with the troops from the stage. Many of the Marines had hitchhiked or walked as far as 10 miles to see Marilyn perform. 'I should have brought some C-rations and come earlier,' said PFC Bobby Johnson, 19, of Fargo, ND. 'It sure was nice of her to come over and entertain us, I just wish she could have done more,' said Cpl. William Herly, 21, of Detroit, MI. 'I was so far back I couldn't see her!' The eager Marines were jammed together, shoulder to shoulder, around the open air stage." "'She was everything I expected and a lot more,' said Pfc. Roland Bush, of Dunbar, W VA."

Mike Nechin remembers Marilyn's visit to Korea and to the 1st Marine Division, "I, too, was there the day Marilyn Monroe entertained the troops at the 1st Marines post in Korea in 1954...David Geary's photo is like the ones I and others took (We all carried cameras; the gag at the time was that the Corps issued cameras to all personnel). The excitement Mrs. DiMaggio elicited from the homesick crowd overwhelmed her rendition of 'Diamonds Are a Girl's Best Friend."...I was luckier than most of my comrades. Our Colonel invited Marilyn and her entourage to the Officers' Club after the show. I opened the club, alerted the cooks, and welcomed Marilyn. Our baker brought a huge cake with 'Welcome Marilyn' inscribed. I spoke with her briefly. The pictures I took have been donated to the National Museum of
American Jewish Military History in Washington, D.C."

Marilyn later had this to say about her experience, "I was singing my heart out to all those poor fellows sitting on the ground—singing *Diamonds Are A Girl's Best Friend* because it was a song I knew...but I also sang a Gershwin song, *Do It Again*, because I didn't want the fellows to think they had to give diamonds to the girls back home. The two songs were my whole repertoire--I didn't know any others."

After the show Pfc. Ronald Bush, of Dunbar, WVa, said, "She was everything I expected and a lot more."

The rest of the cast and crew changed into military issue clothing and packed up the equipment. After her show Marilyn posed for pictures and chatted with the Marines. She then changed into an officer's shirt and posed with Brig. General Robert Hogaldoom, Commander of the First Marine Division and Col. William K. Jones, Assistant Commander of the First Marine Division and then enjoyed a meal. She also made a phone call to Joe DiMaggio while at the headquarters, telling him how much she missed him. From the wide grin on her face after hanging up, she must have gotten the response she wanted from Joe. Marilyn also posed in front of the 1st Marines Headquarters with a beaming Marine Col. William K. Jones. Newsreel footage of this particular day exists. Marilyn is show being escorted by Marine Col. Jones. She is absolutely lovely in this footage. One can only imagine the soldier's reaction to seeing her in person. Then the cast and crew finally boarded the helicopters for the next show.

Continuing her rigorous schedule, Marilyn and the cast of "Anything Goes" also performed for the 7th Infantry Division, HQ 17th Regiment. Jesse Fred Godbey drove a jeep in the motor pool and he had the opportunity to drive a jeep with Marilyn as a passenger when she visited Korea. He remembers, "She was pleasant and asked us how we were, etc. She was waving and saying hello to people as we passed. I was taking her to Division HQ, 7th Infantry at the time. My buddies (at HQ & HQ 7th Infantry Regiment)

didn't believe I was going to have Marilyn Monroe aboard; of course, I wanted to prove this to them by driving through the company area so they could see for themselves. Well, that got some waves and whistles from those disbelieving soldiers!"

"Marilyn Monroe sizzled through giant outdoor shows on Korea's cold front and proved to 25,000 Yanks that the world's best known chassis is 'for real!' The fabulous blue-eyed platinum top blonde exploded in song at the Bayonet outfit with the impact of an eight-inch gun. To training–weary Americans 5,000 miles from home, Marilyn was an uncanny phenomenon. Even for the little clans of thinly-clad Koreans that nestled quietly behind the

12,000-man audience, she was like a strange edition of another age brilliantly blazing the quiet of shell-fractured Korea…The girl who rocketed to stardom on a calendar in her birthday suit embarked and giggled, 'These birds are wonderful.' The bombshell was introduced with a rousing assemble version of "There's Nothing Like a Dame," followed by hair-raising, ear-splitting cat calls which brought her—here in the flesh—shimmying to the floor. The hot-eyed calendar girl tossed off kisses and 'thank yous' to the troops, then delayed into a surveyed version of Gershwin's "Do It Again." The point in the lyrics that go, 'You won't regret it. Come and get it,' brought earthshaking hubbas shattering this already electric air…Anti-Monroe fans in Korea became pro-Monroe fans in a matter of seconds for the wet-eyed bombshell startled the most sardonic list with a barrel of charm, poise and a general good nature… 'Were you cold up there?' asked one correspondent. 'I didn't feel anything—except good,' drooled Marilyn. Twenty-five thousand Americans felt the same way."

According to the press there was a mix-up in the dining schedule for Marilyn. The helicopter crew overshot its mark, landing near the Officers' Club of the 7$^{th}$ Division, several miles up the road from her intended destination and a steak dinner with Maj. Gen. R.M. Pate of the 1st Marine Division. He ended up eating the steak dinner alone, and Marilyn downed two cheese omelets at the Officers' Club. "The wall was bare where a week ago hung a huge blowup of that much publicized calendar photograph showing her reclining on a rug an wearing nothing but a smile. 'We thought it might embarrass Miss Monroe if she came here,' a mess attendant explained.

Marilyn and Jean O'Doul had a steak dinner with Maj. General Lionel McGarr of the 7th Infantry Bayonet Division. They all posed for a photograph together. Later Maj. Gen. McGarr sent the photo to Marilyn and inscribed it on the back, "Marilyn, With appreciation and admiration Gen. Mac Korean Bayonet Division 54." A cake was baked in her honor. It was "frosted with a miniature baseball diamond and a miniature Marilyn, wearing shorts. Home plate bore the inscription, 'You made a hit with us Marilyn.' She was presented with a specially tailored GI jacket with every patch and regimental shield of the division sewed on it."

Marilyn's cardboard dinner place card was also sent to her and signed underneath, "To Joe and Marilyn; Gen. Mac 7th Inf. Bayonet Division Lionel McGarr Maj. Gen. USA Korea 54."

Marilyn slept in the 7th Division encampment. Some soldiers made up a sign which read, "Marilyn Slept Here--16 February 1954."

One of the many photographers on hand to capture her performances was Walt Durrell, whose photos were utilized by the *United Press Wire Service*. Ted Russell and Bob Jennings also captured many images of Marilyn's time in Korea.

On the 17th the 'Anything Goes' cast continue to the Central Front to entertain the GIs. Before arriving at the 3rd Division Marilyn was taken to "the sector of the Colombian Battalion, attached to one of the US divisions, and the fighting men from Latin America gave the sloe-eyed actress just as rousing a reception as any she received from their northern GI brethren. Two lines of camera-snapping Colombian soldiers packed a road in a chill, foggy rain for a glimpse—and pictures—of the star as she drove by in an open jeep, smilingly waving to the cheering onlookers. The South Americans drank in the sight of a blonde head and a curvaceous girl clad in a tight black sweater and standard Army trousers." In addition to the Columbian soldiers, Marilyn also met troops from Greece, Turkey, Belgium, Ethiopia, and South Korea.

"A Turkish officer, attached to the 25th division, confessed today that Marilyn Monroe almost got him in trouble in Turkey. As a civilian, Lt. Abi Ipekei PIO of the Turkish Brigade was managing editor of the *Istanbul Express* and also putting out the 25,000 issue weekly supplement on current movies. When the first edition of *Cine-Sports* appeared, the world's best undressed girl was splashed across the cover in four colors. The next day every copy was ordered off the news stands by national police and the district attorney accused Ipekei of 'undermining public morals.'"

Marilyn then made her way to the 3rd Army Division, including the 7th Regiment of the 3rd Division. Maj. Gen. Charles DW Canham, division commander, was too busy to see her show, but encouraged his Marnemen, who had Greek and Belgian troops attached to the units. The men of "The Rock of the Marne," as the 3rd Division was known, provided some of the air crews for the helicopters which carried the tour. A photo of Marilyn sandwiched between two servicemen was captioned, "Marilyn had an enthusiastic greeting she arrived at the 3rd, Rock of the Marne, Div. airstrip. She graciously posed with her arms around PFC John Fenesy, Caldwell, N.J., 3rd Div. air section and Cpl. Dick Armstrong, Williston Park, L.I., 13th Helicopter Co., who was her crew chief aboard the helicopter." The photo was taken by Cpl. Bob Jennings. Marilyn was chauffeured during her visit to the 3rd US Division by Master Sergeant James Endland of Columbus, GA. He commented, "In my 14 years of Army driving this will be the most curves I've ever taken in one car."

*Press Telegram*, Long Beach, California, on February 18th carried an item about Marilyn, "Competition may be the life of trade and one thing that put zest in business, sports and entertainment, but there are times when it's best to toss in the towel and let the other side have the glory. Harold Stassen, U. S. Foreign Operations Administrator, did just that in Korea today. Stassen and Marilyn Monroe visited the same U. S. Division. As you might have expected, poor Harold never had a chance. And he knew it. Stassen, a thorough gentleman always, just kept out of the way and let Marilyn charm the boys. He said, 'I didn't have this much competition when I ran for the Presidential nomination. 'There was competition among the soldiers too. The man with the cleanest jeep got to drive Marilyn around one sector while she was on tour. Pfc. Alexander Mastoras, a Marine from Fresno, stayed up all night washing and polishing his jeep. He placed second and sadly remarked, 'So what did I draw? Some of the correspondents!'"

The show then goes on to perform for the 40th's "Thunderbird" Division and contains the Sunburst Division from California. Marilyn arrived at the stage by riding in a tank. Col. John G. Kelly, 160th Regiment Commander escorted her. Marilyn rode to the Grenadier Palace atop a Patton tank with Kelly. He noted that she was excited about the snow that was falling. "'This still is exciting,' she said. 'I'm from California and I don't get to see too much of it.'" The 160th Regiment must have been especially proud to give Marilyn a ride since they hail from Los Angeles. The hometown girl was proudly driven by "Los Angeles's Own" to the stage area. The tank, #33, USA 30164057, carried a handmade sign welcoming Marilyn to Korea. She left the stage area in a jeep after Col. Kelly put a 40th Division "Sunburst" patch on her shoulder, making her an honorary member of the Regiment.

Marilyn caused a near-riot at the 40th Division when some 10,000 men threatened to trample her military guard causing the show to almost come to an end. Col. John G. Kelly of Bismarck, N. Dak., a regimental commander, had to remind the troops that "You are here to have a good time and there is no sense in anyone getting hurt." His warning went unheeded and the men continued to push and shove even before the show started. When Marilyn wiggled onto the stage, in her purple cocktail dress which she cooed, "Does a little more for me," 10,000 soldiers surged forward for a closer look. They cheered, yelled, whistled and attempted to climb on the backs of their buddies. Col. Kelly had to temporarily stop the show until the men got control of themselves. Marilyn was able to continue and she sang three songs—*Bye Bye, Baby, Diamonds Are a Girl's Best Friend,* and *Do It Again.* The applause was so great she could hardly leave the stage. Marilyn lingered, waving, blowing kisses and posing. She walked back and forth across the stage. Every one of the 10,000 men present appeared to have a camera and shutters snapped in constant lightening of flashbulbs, then when the show was almost over, the soldiers surged toward the stage door to see her walk down the steps. A Patton tank was put at her disposal when soldiers blocked the path. "Marilyn lunched with Brig. Gen. William Bradley, Fireball commander, who greeted her at the chopper strip with assistant unit commander Brig. Gen. John G. Hill, along with 20 handpicked enlisted men were chosen to have lunch, complete with steaks, with Marilyn. In the empty mess, attended by men who were not able to see her perform, Cpl. Wilform Neely, NY, 116 Regt,, sighed as he gurgled down his coffee, 'Just let me sit in the seat that Marilyn Monroe occupied.' He did." Cpl. Robert N. Burkhart of Johnstown, Pa., who was named 160th Regiment soldier of the week, had the place of honor on the actress' right. He said: "Boy! She is all there. And on top of that she has a personality. She wasn't anything like I expected. She was a wonderful, sweet girl." He was also quoted as saying, "Wow! What a Dame!"

The next show was for the men of the 25th Division. The show was performed at night. Marilyn has a slip of memory and forgets some of the words to 'Diamonds Are a Girl's Best Friend.' She gives the men a good view of her backside as she consults with Al Guastafeste on what to do. She returns to the microphone and proceeds with the next verse. The men are more than willing to overlook this mistake and feel quite compensated from seeing Marilyn's lovely derriere. Clp. Gordon Calano of East Hartford, Conn., said, "She's the only weapon this Army needs. Any Communist coming south to see her would desert to our side for sure." Pfc. William Seldon of Nyack, NY, was photographed kissing the outstretched hand of Marilyn during her performance.

Troops in the front rows peered through Bee See scopes as the 10,000-man crowd roared. When Marilyn disappeared, the closing renditions of "Anything Goes" was hopelessly smothered in the uproar of disapproval, only to have the fabulous form wiggled across the stage to oblige photo-fiends. As she performed, snow fell in Monroe Valley. The 100th Regiment troopers changed the name of the show site from Grenadier Valley in honor of Marilyn. California-born Marilyn said she was 'very excited' about the snow.

Carlton Sauder of Grabill, Indiana, was assigned to the Army's 25th Division photo unit. He remembers the experience, "Marilyn would get up in front of an enormous crowd of servicemen and they all just ate it up. She was a great performer and extremely popular with the troops. She was a very nice lady to talk to. We had numerous conversations, and I took some 35-millimeter movies of her. When Marilyn was asked to come to Korea to perform, she and Joe DiMaggio were on their honeymoon in Japan at the time. Despite this, she was nice enough to come and perform for the troops. Joe stayed in Japan, so she had a chaperone escorting her around."

While visiting with the troops, Marilyn is given the 25th Division's "Wolfhounds" scarf by Sgt. Guy Morgan, from Marion, North Carolina. The "Wolfhounds" were the 27th Regiment of the 25th Division. M Sgt. James C. Callahan, San Antonio, TX, is photographed with Marilyn after she had been made honorary member of the 25th Division. Marilyn posed wearing an MP Helmet and M. Sgt James C. Callahan wore the Tropic Lightning patch of the 25th Division on his uniform. She posed with Ernest and Manuel Abril, of Colton, California. They were members of the "Golden Dragons," the 25th Division's baseball team. She gave no batting hints, even though her name was now DiMaggio.

Marilyn was also presented with a certificate from the 25th M.P. Company titling her as an honorary M.P. "Greeting, Know ye, all men, that upon studious and most diligent pursuit, it has been agreed that the person found to be in the best of shape is: Marilyn Monroe. And she is with the deepest reverence--designated an Honorary M.P. of the 25th M.P. Company; Capt. H.P. Vallaw, Company Commander."

On the 18th Marilyn had a 2 hour Jeep ride, escorted by Brig. Gen. John C. Oakes, acting division commander, to the forward bunkers of the 25th Division, Second Division, the 35 Regiment, the 90th FA and the 27th Regiment, in bitter cold temperatures that sank below the 25-degree mark. She bumped in the open jeep over ice-slick trials, lined on both sides with picture-snapping, cheering and hand-waving GIs. Marilyn's jeep stopped on occasion to visit with the men who dotted the road for hours to see her and take her picture. Despite the rough ride, Marilyn stood up frequently in the vehicle, shouting to the boys, 'eeree wa,' a Korean phrase she learned from the soldiers during the first day of her tour. The GIs roared in reply, 'eeree wa,' meaning, 'come here!' Dressed in a high-zippered Air Force flight jacket, blue infantry scarf and olive drab slacks, she started the day with a four-egg breakfast at 25th Division headquarters. She was then was flown by helicopter to the edge of the demilitarized truce area where she had a bird's eye view of some of Korea's historic battlegrounds such as Old Baldy, Pork Chop and T-bone Hills.

Continuing on, the "Anything Goes" show performed for the third time for the men of the Eastern Front in Korea. The first show was for the 2nd Infantry Division at the Bulldozer Bowl. The men of the 35th Regiment and the 90th Field Artillery also saw their dream girl sing and dance for them.

During her show a 2nd Division corporal barged through the soldier mob surrounding Marilyn at a performance today and shouted, "Hey, Marilyn, my name is DiMaggio!" "Come here DiMaggio," said she said. She bent over and shook hands with the corporal. Come to find out, "DiMaggio" was Cpl. Frank Brophy, Elizabeth, N.J.

Marilyn was photographed with Jean O'Doul, Maj. Gen. Barriger, C.G. 2D US Inf Div., and Brig. Gen. Seits, ADC 2D Inf Div., at the Bulldozer Bowl before dining with the 2nd US Infantry Division for lunch. The Army photo was taken by PFC Bernard Bailey, 2D Sig Co US. Marilyn and the cast were formally invited to lunch at the Enlisted Men's Hall and were given a steak dinner. The men of the 2nd Infantry Division even went so far as to have invitations printed up, bearing the Indianhead logo of the 2nd Division. Marilyn's invitation also included a paper with the signatures of the men of the division.

Marilyn donned a tight-fitting knitted dress, from *Gentlemen Prefer Blondes*, and a white chef's hat and served hot rolls to a GI Chow line. She and Jean O'Doul both served on the chow line at the 2nd Division enlisted men's mess. This was Marilyn's first "non-steak meal she ate while on the front, other than yesterday's breakfast at the 25$^{th}$ when she ate four fried eggs." No pretentions for Miss Monroe, she picked up a GI field tray and washed it in boiling water, then fell in behind other waiting GIs. She indulged in portions of everything. She ate with five of the 2nd Division soldiers as her lucky table companions. The luncheon gave Marilyn a midday break in the third busy round of her four-day tour of the Korean front. SFC Harold Crawford of Columbus, OH, was photographed in the chow-line with Marilyn. He reported that her appetite was great, emphasizing, 'she eats everything." PFO Stanley Clostler of Brooklyn, NY, helps Marilyn sample a piece of cake, made especially for her by the 2nd Division, NCO Club. It was decorated with simply, 'Welcome Marilyn Monroe.' PFC Ken Allen, Boston, MA, pins a 2nd Division patch on Marilyn. Marilyn is photographed serving PFC James R. Goggin, Lesterville, MI. and sitting with Corp. Joseph Knapp, Cordova, IL, at the enlisted men's mess. "As she left the mess for the chopper, she called for her escort, Corp. Knapp, 'Corporal, where are you. I can't keep track of you.' A burly white-tasseled, gun-slinging shape rallied with a 'That works both ways, ma'am.'"

Louis T. Corsaletti, of West Pittston, PA, was an Army Tank driver who was assigned to chauffeur duty for Miss Monroe. Mr. Corsaletti worked as a reporter for *The Seattle Times* after the Korean War. He kept a photograph of Marilyn and himself with their jeep during her tour of Korea, on his desk at work.

Leroy Van Dyke, a Special Agent for the U. S. Army Counter Intelligence Corps., and assigned to the 160th Infantry Regiment in the Chor Wan Valley as their regimental agent, was asked by the regimental commander to play his guitar and sing for 15 minutes prior to Marilyn's appearance. He would go on to fame in the country music industry with hits such as "The Auctioneer" and "Walk on By."

Some 6000 impatient soldiers charged the stage later that night when Marilyn sauntered out for an appearance at the 45th Division show. One sight of her in her skin-tight purple cocktail dress was enough, and it caused a riot in which one GI was trampled. His injures looked worse than they were and he was able to return to work the following day. The riot began when the division members got tired of waiting for Marilyn's five-minute act which highlights the 45-minute show. They jeered the performers who were trying to warm up the crowd and followed this up with such a barrage of rocks. Marilyn was hastily rushed onto the stage. Marilyn ran through her songs, barely audible over the cries of the crowd. As she left the stage and hurried to the back stage-door exit, members of the "Anything Goes" show formed a flying wedge around her and someone threw an Army parka over her bare shoulders. She jumped into a waiting Army jeep which drove her away. 'The boys were just a little anxious,' Marilyn said adding she was sorry the unidentified GI was injured.

Marilyn remembers the frightening incident after her chaotic performance for the 45th Division, "I jumped out to say goodbye to men in the 45th Division, which had just been relieved. I was waving and blowing kisses, and was about to shout 'Sayonara!'--the Japanese word for goodbye which I'd learned in Tokyo--when suddenly I heard myself yelling 'Eleewah!'--a Korean word I'd picked up along the way. Within seconds, our jeep was stampeded by men, men and more men. I've never seen so many men in my life. We were besieged, surrounded, overwhelmed by them. After it was all over and MP's had restored order, I asked an officer what had happened. He smiled tolerantly and answered, 'Eleewah, Miss Monroe, means 'Come to me.' Thinking back on the incident, I don't consider it as much of a faux pas as it may have seemed--because subconsciously, I'm sure it was the way I really felt."

She continues, "The 45$^{th}$ Division show was a contrast to her reception at the 2$^{nd}$ Division, where most of the 12,000 soldiers watched blank-faced as she crooned, *Diamonds Are a Girl's Best Friend, Do It Again,* and *Bye Bye Baby*." This was the only show Marilyn didn't take an encore to talk to the men and allow them to take her photo.

Marilyn disclosed to the press on the 18th that she has given up her famous habit of sleeping in the nude and not wearing underwear. After experiencing Korea's frigid weather, she reported that she now wears Army issue long-johns.

The press noticed that her dress was damaged due to her hectic schedule. "Her cocktail dress with the plunging neckline has begun to show the wear and tear of her appearances in seven shows, before some 75,000 service men. The tight-fitting garment has been subjected to such strain by her vigorous onstage walks that bits of beads and spangles are coming loose."

Before proceeding to her next shows on the 19th, Marilyn is taken on a tour of the 45<sup>th</sup> Division in an open jeep. "Soldiers armed with cameras of all descriptions clamored for a shot at the famous Monroe figure as she passed out of the 45<sup>th</sup> Division area. But her admirers were generally disappointed by three layers of heavy clothing which protected her from the intense cold as she rode in the open Jeep.

What they didn't know was that Marilyn was getting sick. Her voice was getting hoarse and she was very tired. Yet, "the buxom movie star, who caused the biggest stir among the bleak Korean hills since the armistice signing, had a winning smile for GIs eager to see her, despite her fatiguing schedule." She was chaperoned by Brigadier General John C. Oakes around Camp Page, in Chunchon. That afternoon Marilyn performed at the K-47 Air Base, also known as Kunsan Air Base. This was the first Fifth Air Base Marilyn performed at while in Korea.

"Marilyn won the hearts of Air Force enlisted men on her last day in Korea by leaving an officer's luncheon party in order to chat with and hug a group of GIs standing outside in the cold. 'Gosh!' cried Sgt. James Bennett, Woodbridge, NJ, 'she's the hottest thing the Air Force has had since napalm.' Bennett was one of 50 shivering enlisted men who stood gawking through a large bay window into the officers' mess building at the 6147 Air Force Tactical Control Group headquarters north of Seoul. Marilyn was inside lunching with Col. William Reed of Houston, TX, and his top aides when she noticed the men peering in at her. The GIs were feverishly motioning for the movie star to come out. The officers were aghast. Suddenly Marilyn waved back and pointed to herself in a gesture meaning, 'who, me?' Stg. 1/c Robert McKeehan, of Dalton, GA, motioned back with a gesture signifying, 'yes, you.' Marilyn stood up from the table, turned her back on the brass and trudged out with her heavy combat boots, tight-fitting black sweater and bright red scarf. The actress 'chinned' and laughed with the GIs, threw her arms around some of them and posed for pictures. After a decent interval, Colonel Reed rushed out, shooed the enlisted men away and retrieved Marilyn for the officers' mess. 'Wow! The tar on the runway started to melt,' Sgt. 1/c McKeehan, exclaimed later. After lunch, Hollywood's 'napalm girl' put on her now-famous 'Anything Goes' act for combined Air Force-Army audience at the base. Later, she flew down to Taegu to give a farewell show for Air Force men, winding up her four-day tour of the truce stilled Korean War Theater."

The last show was put on at Taegu Air Force Base in Korea. Marilyn posed on the wing of a USAF F-84 Thunder jet with 2nd Lt. Gardner H. Snow of Watertown, Mass. The photo was taken by Leonard Rubin. While touring the Taegu Air Base, Marilyn met Vaughn Evans, who was an Air Force gun camera technician. He and his buddies later gave Marilyn a pink silk pajama set and slippers after her show. He photographed her receiving the gift and eventually gave a copy of the photo to the Smithsonian National Portrait Gallery. David Geary, a Navy Medic at the time, also photographed Marilyn as she performed during her show and gave his photographs to the Smithsonian National Portrait Gallery, too. After the final performance, Marilyn posed once again with the cast of "Anything Goes." She signed autographs for cast members, indicating in each her genuine appreciation in being included as part of the USO tour. *Stars and Stripes* reported that, "Marilyn tapered off her morale-boosting swing through Korea with a show which electrified the large audience. She faced it in a form-fitting black, gold-flecked dress, cut like a California hot rod." This is the only description of her dress being black rather than purple. Members of the cast said of Marilyn, "She's great, she's gorgeous, but she's even nicer than she's gorgeous."

A tired, but jubilant Marilyn flew back to Japan and a warm welcome from Joe. As Marilyn stepped from the plane Joe held her by the shoulders and kissed her gently. Only a few Air Force men were on hand. Before leaving Korea Miss Monroe told newsmen 'I never felt like a movie star before--really in my heart--before I came to Korea. I've got the most important thing in my life--Joe,' she told newsmen. 'Now I want to start a family.' Despite rumors that she had lost 10 pounds during her 4 day show, Marilyn told the press, "she might have put on a few pounds in Korea 'because I've been eating everything.' Mrs. O'Doul, who accompanied Marilyn on the Korean trip, reported, 'She eats like a horse. She loves meat. She eats three good meals a day and generally a snack before bed.'"

Marilyn's accompanist, Cpl. Al Guastafeste wrote this interesting article about his time with her. "Cpl. Al Guastafeste, of Uniondale, Long Island, NY, led the five piece band that played for Marilyn Monroe during her Korea performances. Guastafeste describes in the following article just what it was like to accompany Marilyn on the piano before howling audiences of happy GIs…It may sound crazy to most people, but sitting out there on the stage a few feet behind Marilyn Monroe didn't bother me too much. I was mainly interested in the music. She was great, the greatest! The tour with Marilyn as her accompanist resembled nothing else in my experience. During the performances I kept the beat and Marilyn monitored me. While she sang she waved her arms, and those movements got great cheers from the crowds. But she waved her arms to let me know whether we were hitting it too fast or too slow. The arm movements were necessary because she worked over a public address system with the speakers turned toward the crowd and away from the band. One afternoon she tried a new gimmick. She started turning from one side to the other so that we boys in the back got profile views of her—which were pretty terrific. The idea was that we could see her mouth working and catch the part of the song she was in. We got profile views and so did the shutterbugs in the audience whom I sometimes thought would drown out the sound of her singing with the clicking of the cameras. We tried to help her out, especially in the "Diamonds" number, by warning her ahead of time when the bumps were coming up. We told her, 'Here we go, Marilyn,' or 'Here comes the boom, boom.' We didn't know whether she could hear us. But it was great fun to watch when the bumps came up. Now that it's all over, all I can truthfully say about Marilyn Monroe and the whole experience is that it was wonderful, and it was a pleasure to work with her. Marilyn is a real trouper. When we first met her last Sunday at Osaka, we had to argue wither to get her to break up rehearsals for chow. A couple of days before we met and after I found out what was going to happen, I went to see her picture, *Gentlemen Prefer Blondes*. I made my own musical arrangements and we blocked out a routine for her. There were Cpl. Don Obermeyer of Elmhurt, IL, Pvt. Frankie Vayo, Brooklyn, NY, Pfc. Eugene Thompson, New York, and Pfc. David Boucher of San Diego, CA. Pvt. Mickey Carroll of Dover, NJ, worked out the bumps and grinds with Marilyn."

Wood Soanes reported, on February 22nd, "Of all the sticky goo that has cluttered up the wires of the press associations since the discovery of Marilyn Monroe and her fabulous romance and marriage to Joe DiMaggio, nothing has been quite so gummy as their current tour of Japan and Korea. One report of her return from Korea to Japan went in part like this: "DiMaggio calmly walked up to his bride, said, 'Well, how are you,' gave Marilyn a brief kiss and said, 'I've found a place in Osaka that has very good pizza.' The dispatch ends on a very high, not to say illuminating note: Marilyn said the Korea trip had made her feel like a movie star at last. That's the kind of humility Arthur Godfrey would appreciate!"

In Jesse Mae Brown's column on September 9th in the African American newspaper, *The Los Angeles Sentinel*, she commented on Marilyn in Korea. "Speaking of thrills, the weekend found Sammy Flory home from Korea for the first time in a year or two. He told of Marilyn Monroe's visit to the soldiers and had a picture collection to prove just how genuinely friendly she was with the GIs."

An interesting bit of trivia is that Marilyn used baby soap while in Korea. The press tried to make something out of this, but Marilyn told them that the only thing it meant was that the water was hard.

Looking back on her hectic schedule for the USO Tour, beginning with rehearsals on Feb. 14th and going non-stop for the next five days, it is small wonder that Marilyn became ill. The living conditions while in Korea and the weather, coupled with her delicate constitution all conspired to wreck her health. She performed in freezing weather, complete with snow, and toured the icy roads of Korea for hours in an open jeep. While in Korea, Marilyn never once complained or played the Prima Donna. She was always willing to give of her time to the men in uniform. She was a real trooper and fulfilled the old show business adage that "the show must go on."

Marilyn owed a debt to the brave men who had fought in the Korean War. For it was they, more than any other factor, who had helped to create a star out of Marilyn Monroe. Their unwavering support of Marilyn through the early years helped draw attention to her. The studios were forced to acknowledge her appeal when faced with the thousands of letters she received while she was yet an unknown actress.

Marilyn also told Joe Thomas about her feelings of responsibility. "A star has great responsibility. I have learned that through the letters I receive and through other contacts with the public. Most of all, I have learned it through what the servicemen said and wrote to me when I was in Korea and after I returned. It has opened up a whole new world to me that I never before knew existed."

Marilyn had this to say about the GIs in Korea. "Two years ago I flew to the Orient to repay a debt. In the early part of my career I'd had several small roles, without much success. Then letters began pouring in from Korea. My fan mail jumped abruptly from less than 50 letters a week to more than 5,000. My studio was so impressed they began to give me wonderful parts. I felt I owed those boys something for what was happening to me; and I wanted to repay them in the only way I knew how--with a personal appearance tour. There will never be another audience like this one in Korea." Marilyn also told the press, "This trip is the climax to everything in my career. I never felt like a movie star until I came over here. I sort of feel the guys over here were responsible for a lot that happened to me. They are very close to my heart. It was so wonderful to look down and see a fellow smiling at me."

Ben Hecht posed this question to Marilyn, "What's the happiest time you've ever had?" Without hesitation she replied, "It was the time last month when I sang to the soldiers in Korea. There were thousands of them. It was a very cold afternoon, and it was snowing. All the soldiers sat in their winter uniforms. I appeared in a décolleté evening gown, bare back, bare arms. And I was so happy and so excited that I didn't know it was cold or snowing. In fact, the snow never fell on me. It melted away almost before it touched my skin. That was my happiest time—when the thousands of soldiers all yelled my name over and over."

While the men who were fighting a half a world away provided her with an invaluable fan base, she too provided them with something. She gave them a face and body to love, symbolizing to them all the women back home. She had the curious ability to be both a sweet reminder of sisters and friends waiting for them, and a reminder of the women for whom they lusted. Marilyn represented the American woman and became a conduit for each man's fantasy. She was beautiful, sweet and compliant. What a perfect dream for the nightmare that was the Korean War.

Marilyn landed in Kobe, Japan to join Joe. On the 20th Marilyn and Jean O'Doul posed with a group of Japanese Geishas after a 'Sukiyaki' dinner in Kobe. The fete was hosted by the Central League, which was one of Japan's baseball organizations. Left out of the photo was Joe and Lefty. "The party was held in Japanese style with the guests sitting on mats and eating with chopsticks. The newspaper Yomiuri printed a picture of Marilyn eating with 'hashi' (chop sticks). When Marilyn arrived at the restaurant in a mink coat and a black evening dress the staff of the establishment turned out en masse to greet her. For a while the blonde actress could not get out of the car."

While in Kobe, Marilyn and Joe had drinks in the Kobe Oriental Hotel. Kamogawa-san was their bartender.

The DiMaggios returned almost unnoticed on the 21$^{st}$, at the Tokyo International Airport. Reports had them coming back a day later. It was a blessing for them to not be besieged by fans and there were only a couple of newsmen at the airport to question them and take photos. "Some 50 people stood in the airline waiting room watching a wrestling match while the curvaceous film star and her husky husband walked through and boarded a car to take them to their hotel….the shapely blonde looked tired but was still able to flash the smile which endeared her to hearts of servicemen throughout the Far East. 'I feel a little sick,' she said upon landing. Joe had little to say and seemed relieved that there was no crowd on hand at the airport."

Leonard Lyons reported this bon mot from Marilyn on the 22nd. "Hillis Mills, of *Time* magazine, had the good fortune to meet Marilyn Monroe. She was intrigued by his pleasant drawl, and asked if he came from Texas. 'Yes,' said Mills. 'Do you know Texas?' Miss Monroe replied, 'No. I don't. Only Texans.'"

The *INS* reported on the 22$^{nd}$, that the DiMaggios were back in Tokyo. "Marilyn Monroe, back from a tour of Korea, went on a shopping tour in Tokyo today and tried to steer clear of Japanese fans and news photographers. The Hollywood beauty who interrupted her honeymoon with Joe DiMaggio to entertain troops in Korea, said she wanted to rest. She firmly declined all requests for autographs and also refused to pose for photographers who have dogged her steps since she arrived."

Marilyn's hair dresser, Gladys McCallister had recently gotten married, she was now Gladys Whitten. Marilyn brought her back a pinch bottle decanter and a dozen glasses, all laced with sterling silver. To her inner circle of friends, Marilyn was very loyal and kind. Even on her own honeymoon Marilyn thought about her friends. Yet, she will tell Rita Garrison Malloy that, "I didn't get a wedding present from anybody at the studio, or from any player."

Marilyn took ill on the flight back to Tokyo. Marilyn's temperature had reached 104 around 3am Wednesday morning. A doctor diagnosed a mild form of pneumonia. Joe called in his friend, Capt. Bobby Brown, who reported that, "she's got some kind of virus, but we don't know exactly what it is."

Marilyn and Joe leave the land of the rising sun and head for San Francisco on February 22nd. Marilyn, hoarse from her bout with pneumonia whispered to the waiting press, "I just don't feel good." The plane will leave 5 minutes later than scheduled because the once forgotten Joe DiMaggio has finally attracted the attention of the baseball fans in Tokyo and was being besieged by his fans. Marilyn becomes separated from Joe and calls out to him, "Where's my husband? Where's my husband." They are reunited and she was put to bed aboard the Stratocruiser.

The Far East Command awarded Marilyn a silver medallion for entertaining the troops and visiting the sick and wounded, in Japan hospitals. Marilyn and Joe were also presented with engraved, round dog-tags. Marilyn's read, "To Marilyn Monroe, In appreciation for contributing to the entertainment of United Nations Armed Forces personnel in Korea." On the reverse side was inscribed with the Flag of the Far East Command and this inscription, "Far East Command, February 1954." Joe DiMaggio was also given a tag inscribed with thanks and with the cities he had visited while in Japan.

The DiMaggio's were presented with a photo album of their trip by the *Yomiuri Shimbun* Newspaper. The album was covered in purple velvet and embossed with gold letters reading, "Memories of Coaching For Japan Central Baseball League; February 1954; The Yomiuri Shimbun; Tokyo Japan." The album came in a lidded wooden box.

The Osaka newspaper *Sangyo Keizai* said of Marilyn that she was as a "woman who is doing much to deepen the relationship between Japan and the United States."

Precious cargo manager for Pan American Airlines, Kashio Aoki, presents the candid photographs that he took when the DiMaggio's were waiting in the baggage compartment of the plane upon their arrival in Japan. He asked Marilyn to autograph them. Joe allows her to autograph one. They then wave good-bye to Japan and head for the States.

At their stop-over in Honolulu, doctors diagnosed Marilyn with bronchial pneumonia. Upon their return to San Francisco, on February 24th, Marilyn told newsmen, "my doctor ordered me to bed and that's where I am going," Surviving newsreel images show the DiMaggio's deboarding the plane and walking to their car. A beautiful Marilyn is filmed getting into a car wrapped up in her mink coat. They lived with Joe's sister Marie at the DiMaggio Beach St. house in the Marina district. Marilyn suffered an allergic reaction to the Penicillin she had been taking for her pneumonia. She recuperates quietly with Joe's family over the next four days, being tended to by Marie.

After she is sufficiently recovered, Marilyn and Joe, along with Vic and Marie Masi, strolled along the wharf in San Francisco. Marilyn wanted a camera to record the day. Vic went into a camera store and borrowed a camera. The owner agreed only after the DiMaggio's posed for a picture in front of his storefront. After fully recovering from her bout of pneumonia, Marilyn leaves for Los Angeles on March 5$^{th}$.

# Chapter Fifteen
## Becoming "The Girl"

"Star Makes Manhattan Into Isle of Joy...New Yorkers who normally take their celebrities
with a polite head-turn or a cynical stare really flipped out last week. The celebrity producing this
emotional turnabout was Marilyn Monroe, in town to shoot two location sequences
for her new movie *Seven Year Itch*, made from the big Broadway hit."
*LIFE*, September 27, 1954

**O**n February 28th Marilyn writes a letter to Joe, addressed to "Dear Dad," her nickname for him. In the letter she reaffirms her love for him. She apologizes for being late and promises to become a better person. She also declares her hopes of becoming a mother and that she has her heart set on at least two children. She closes by telling him that she misses him and has trouble sleeping if he is not there to cuddle with her. She put the time that she wrote the letter on the top of the page, "Sunday 11:38pm." She also added a "Di" before her monogrammed "M" on her personal stationary. The letter was mailed to Joe at the Madison Hotel in New York City.

*Parade* magazine article by Lloyd Shearer appears on February 28th. Marie DiMaggio, Joe's older sister, gave an interview to Shearer about Marilyn and Joe's marriage. First he got some celebrity opinions on the marriage.
Carry Grant said, "I admire both of them and I think they've made the perfect move. They've really got a lot in common. They're both shy, quiet and retiring."
Jane Russell commented, "This marriage is exactly what they both needed. It will give them security and companionship."
Betty Grable replied, "Marilyn and Joe are two wonderful people. This marriage has got to last. Joe would have to be out of his mind to walk out on that girl and vice versa."
Darryl Zanuck was asked if the marriage had a depressing effect on Marilyn's box office appeal. "This girl is the epitome of femininity. If we can keep putting her in good pictures, she'll be bigger and better than ever. She picked a fine boy in DiMaggio."
Finally, Marie is interviewed.
"Will Marilyn Monroe Stay Married...In San Francisco, Joe's hometown, I spoke with members of the DiMaggio clan after the wedding. Said Marie, Joe's older sister, 'Marilyn's going to make the perfect wife for Joe. They're both the same kind. They like the same things. Joe's idea of a good time is to have a home cooked meal, then lie down on the sofa and watch television. Marilyn's the same way. When Joe first brought her home, we thought maybe she'd be snooty and artificial. Not at all. Around the house she wears pedal pushers or slacks and she washes and sets her own hair. She's the one who always makes the breakfast. She's not a bad cook at all and, of course, she likes television. She and Joe went around together 18 months before they decided to get married. Both of them have been married before and they know what marriage is all about. Joe loves kids and so does Marilyn. I don't think she was kidding when she told reporters she wanted six kids. I know Joe wouldn't object. We DiMaggios are a big family. There were nine of us, five boys and four girls. Eight of us are still living and there are 12 youngsters in the family group. Marilyn is just crazy about them. Take Joe's son, the boy he had by Dorothy Arnold, his first wife. Joey is 12 now and he simply swears by Marilyn. She treats him as if he were her own.' I asked Marie if Marilyn gave the residents of San Francisco the same impression that she so studiously affects for her Hollywood fans--the impression that she's a high-powered, hip-swinging girl whose clothes fit like a sunburn. Marie's answer was: 'In San

Francisco, Marilyn is very demure. She and Joe never go out to night clubs and her clothes always show good taste.'"

The March 1954 issue of *Modern Screen* magazine featured a cover and article, "The Lowdown on Hollywood Women," by Sidney Skolsky. Skolsky revealed the facts around Marilyn's cover shot. She started posing at twelve-thirty and was still going at four p.m. when Sidney left the studio. "Marilyn brought along her favorite hairdresser, Gladys, and her own make-up man, Whitey. She wanted to look her best and these efficient people understand her. Marilyn made several costume changes to get exactly the right pose for *Modern Screen's* cover and when I told her I never realized how much trouble a thing like this was, she said, 'I act when I'm posing. Just as hard as I do when I'm playing a role in front of a movie camera. I think of something for each pose so I'll have the right expression.' (I don't know what she was thinking of for this cover, but *wow*!) I know what Marilyn said is true. When Marilyn is making a picture, she doesn't care to go out. She often forgets to eat and she completely forgets such practical things as time and money. She is almost in a trance. Let me give you a for instance. She telephoned Schwab's to send over some toothpaste, face cream, etc. By the time the boy arrived, Marilyn had forgotten all about it. She was surprised to see him, but she took the package, looked at the bill which amounted to $7.95 and said, 'Wait a minute, I'll give you a check.' When the delivery boy returned to the store. Leon Schwab looked at the check and said to him, 'What's this? The tab is $7.95 and the check is for $2.50. What happened?' The boy said, 'I'm sorry, I never looked at the check. I couldn't take my eyes off Miss Monroe.' So he had to go back for another look and another check. Marilyn told me that when all this happened, she was reading a new script and there was a line in it about two dollars and fifty cents. So she wrote the check out for that amount, naturally."

Louella Parsons reported on March 1st, "Marilyn is staying with Joe DiMaggio's sister in San Francisco. She is still very sick and under the care of a San Francisco doctor, who is keeping her in bed. Joe has to go to New York for a few days and Marilyn will not come to Hollywood until he returns. She could hardly talk over the telephone and has been ordered to rest because she had a slight touch of pneumonia following her appearance before the GI's in Korea in a scanty dress. But, at least she's had her heart's desire--giving a show for the GI's, the one thing she's always wanted to do."

*The Post Standard* newspaper in Syracuse, New York, ran an editorial by Robert C. Ruark, on March 2nd. Mr. Ruark criticizes both Marilyn and the Army's reaction to her visit to Korea. "Would you be getting just a little weary of this bobby-sox army of ours, in which the discipline is slack enough to let some 6,000 GI's stampede a stage in Korea where Marilyn Monroe happened to be appearing? I would at any rate....But back to the storming of Miss Monroe, in the approved fashion of a bobby-sox mob going mad for Sinatra. I think that reflects a very poor fighting force, with the fault starting in Congress and working down to the lowest John. As long as we've got to have a heavy army array, we might as well make it something other than a floor show."

A response was issued on April 12th by PFC David E. White, of the 7th Calvary

Regiment in Korea, "I can't understand how any person, after seeing over 25,000 American boys giving all they had in three years of war, can do an about-face and ask the very people whom these lives were shed for, 'would you be getting just a little bit weary of this bobby-sox army of ours?' You choose as your prime example of 'slack discipline' the welcome given Marilyn Monroe in Korea. Yes, Mr. Rurak 6,000 GIs did storm the stage when she performed because she was the first civilized female star many of them had seen for months and she was there for their benefit. She was great; and they loved her. Perhaps you've watched the changing of the guard at Father Time's post too many times to still appreciate the emotion a girl like Miss Monroe can cause inside a guy. I would not know about that..."

Marilyn returns to Los Angeles on March 5th. She landed at the Burbank Airport from San Francisco on a Western Air Lines flight. Joe's cousin picked her up at the airport and drove her to Beverly Hills. Joe has had to go to New York again. Marilyn checks into the Beverly Hills Hotel under the name of Mrs. J. P. DiMaggio, 2130 Beach St., San Francisco, Calif. She stayed in room 231 at a cost of $16.00 a day, plus charges. Marilyn mails out thank you notes for her wedding. One in particular goes to Mr. and Mrs. Thomas DiMaggio, 3789 Fillmore Street, Apt 4, San Francisco, California. "Dear Lee and Tom, We were so happy to receive your lovely gift. We also thank you for all your moral support we received from you both on January 14th."

Marilyn attends the *Photoplay* Award Dinner on March 8th. She is awarded the Most Popular Actress for *Gentlemen Prefer Blondes* and *How to Marry a Millionaire*. Marilyn is once again escorted by Sidney Skolsky. "Joe told her, 'It's your prize, baby. Go and get your prize and come home to me." Dressed more demurely than last year, she wore the same dress and earrings that she wore to the children's charity event at the Shrine Auditorium on December 4, 1953. Newsreel footage shows her receiving her award from *Photoplay's* editor-in-Chief, Fred Sammis.

Marilyn described her wedding ring to Hedda Hopper reported on March 9th, "'I told Joe I didn't want one, [an engagement ring]' she said, 'My main interest was in a wedding ring. It's white gold--or platinum--with a circle of baguette diamonds. Believe it or not,' said the blonde who sang *Diamonds Are a Girl's Best Friend* in *Gentlemen Prefer Blondes*, 'they're the only ones I have. I didn't have a piece of fur either until Joe game me a mink coat for Christmas.'"

On the evening of March 9th Marilyn appears on Louella Parsons syndicated Radio Show.

Marilyn and Joe meet with Charles Feldman on March 15th in his office to discuss her contract negotiations with Twentieth Century-Fox. These negotiations are the beginning of the end of her old contract with Fox. In the coming months she will consult with Milton Greene about her dissatisfaction with her contract. With Milton Greene's business advice, Marilyn will perfectly maneuver herself out of her old contract. It will take the next 18 months to complete the negotiations and she will end up leaving Hollywood and Joe DiMaggio behind. But for now, Joe had a good head for business and he bolsters Marilyn's confidence to play hard-ball with Fox. Marilyn agrees to these conditions: she will not be involved in the *Girl In Pink Tights* project; an increase in salary; she will be required to do only two films a year; she wants Fox to buy the screen rights to a novel, *Horns of the Devil*, for $225,000.00; and most importantly, Marilyn wanted the right to approve of her scripts, director and cameraman. Feldman didn't think that the executives at Fox would go for Marilyn's demands to approve her scripts, director and cameraman, and as it turns out, he was right.

Harold Heffernan prophetically wrote in his column on February 4th about Joe DiMaggio's influence in her business affairs with Fox. "Who's Managing Marilyn Monroe?...Marilyn Monroe not only got herself a husband, the other week, but what is most pertinent to the company—a sharp, new business manager as well. Recalling Joe's clever handling of his own baseball career as a member of the New York Yankees—his lone and silent holdouts for more money—studio officials were heaving a heavy sigh today and admitting that perhaps, after all, Marilyn is now following a business pattern mapped out for her by the bridegroom. If Joe is masterminding the Monroe career and applying some of his old Yankee pressures, it spells no good for the ailing film business because the practice might become epidemic."

Marilyn and Joe return to Charles Feldman's office on March 18th and he advised her to start working on *There's No Business Like Show Business,* even without a contract, at her old salary of $1250.00 per week. Twentieth Century-Fox agreed that her new salary would be raised to $100,000.00 a picture. Marilyn agreed to play along.

Later that afternoon she and Joe flew back to San Francisco on United Airlines Flight 667 which left at 2:30.

*People Today* article, March 24th, "Keep Your Eye On...Marilyn Tells All...The Lid Is Off For Marilyn Monroe...After her honeymoon she may never return to Hollywood as a full-time star. The mixed up kid has been reported undergoing psychoanalysis in the past year. She has also been telling all the harsh details of her early childhood--including the intimate details of early love problems--to Ben Hecht, the writer biographer, who is writing them on asbestos paper for national publication. The Hecht-Monroe deal will shock Hollywood and the rest of the nation."

Author Ben Hecht ghost-writes an autobiography using Marilyn's personal revelations and stories. The book will be titled, *The Marilyn Monroe Story*. He interviewed her for 10 days while she was in San Francisco at the end of 1953. Although, Marilyn's participation is not as enthusiastic after her marriage to Joe DiMaggio, as it was before. This is only a foreshadowing of trouble to come. Ben Hecht was a co-writer on *Love Happy* and *Monkey Business*.

In April 1954, after spending some time in San Francisco, Joe and Marilyn return to Hollywood and continue to live at the Beverly Hills Hotel until their new home at 508 N. Palm Drive in Beverly Hills is ready. Marilyn gives Grace Goddard's widower, Doc, her bedroom set and several antiques from her Doheny Apartment.

Earlier in her career Marilyn had been in the home that she and Joe will lease on Palm

Drive. They had trouble finding a home that would give them a 6 month lease. Marilyn explained, "We didn't want to be tied down for a year." Barbara Barondess-McLean was the owner. She had been an actress in the 1930s. As her film roles declined she dabbled in Interior design and Fashion design. In the late 1940s and early 50s she had a successful line of sportswear which was carried in Saks Fifth Avenue. During Marilyn's time as a model she had been invited to model Miss Barondess' line and was over at her home at 508 N Palm Drive going over details of the runway, etc. Marilyn told her then that someday she would be a big star and would love to have a home like this one. Little did she know that one day she would live out her dreams of stardom in the very same home on Palm Drive.

On April 6th Marilyn attended the star-studded premier of Danny Kaye's new film, *Knock on Wood*. It was held at the Warners' Beverly Theater. After the show there was a party at the Mocambo where Danny Kaye performed.

On April 8th the press announced that Marilyn had signed a new 7 year contract with 20th Century-Fox. The studio wouldn't comment on her new salary, but a spokesman said, "You can be sure it's one hell of a figure." What the press didn't figure on is that Marilyn will not sign this revised contract.

On April 12th a news conference was held in Marilyn's dressing room/bungalow on the Fox lot upon her return to work on the film, *There's No Business Like Show Business*. In true fashion, Marilyn kept the press waiting 58 minutes. Photographer John Florea was there this day and took several stunning photos of Marilyn which ran in magazines. She also was photographed working on a song with vocal coach Hal Schafer. She announced that she and Joe DiMaggio want to have a family. To which she added, "As soon as possible. I'm not yet, but I want to be. Pregnant, I mean." She said she and Joe will live in his San Francisco home and will rent a house in Hollywood while she working in Hollywood.

A description of Marilyn's dressing room during this time is very interesting. "Marilyn…now has a lavish suite in the ultra-exclusive Star's Building—a suite comprising an outer sitting room or reception room, a spacious main living-dressing room, a kitchenette and bath. The reception room has gray walls, pinkish-red furniture draped in gold and red leaf design, an antique mirrored fireplace with crystal brickettes and crystal candelabra. The walls are decorated with Raoul Dufy's racetrack prints, and a pair of velvet-matted modern comedy plates. The living room is an ensemble of soft green walls, yellow davenport and side chairs, an aqua chair with all blonde wood and a combination radio-phonograph and coffee table with center fern inset. The mirrored makeup table with its special side and overhead fluorescent lighting has a coral leather makeup chair, designed especially for Marilyn. Mirrored wardrobe closets, including shoe, hat and bag racks and shelves, cover one whole wall. The other walls are decorated with original water colors of French countryside scenes. Into the suite Marilyn has brought some of her personal belongings—things like a white woolly Navy goat, a tiny fuzzy toy panda, a vast array of perfume bottles as well as books by the score."

During the press conference, Marilyn also receives the National Movie Poll Award for

Favorite Actress of 1953, Canton, Ohio. It is presented to her by William Wilkerson of the *Hollywood Register*.

Erskine Johnson reported on April 24th, "Hollywords on the Record: Marlene Dietrich on Hollywood's lack of glamour: 'But Hollywood has Marilyn Monroe. She's wonderful. She's the only reason I go to the movies. Marilyn! Ach! 'She's the END, no?'" Marlene might have had a great figure for the 1930s, but Marilyn's fanny had started a new trend. Miss Dietrich, who's derriere was flat and narrow, much like a man's, actually went out and had a foam insert made to give her a more rounded shape.

Charles Feldman called Marilyn on April 26th to tell her that he had talked with Spyros Skouras and Twentieth Century-Fox would be unable to produce *Seven Year Itch*, and thus, she wouldn't be starring in it. This was significant because she had agreed to do *There's No Business Like Show Business* in order to have the opportunity to work with Billy Wilder in *Seven Year Itch*.

Joe and Marilyn move into their rented house at 508 N Palm Drive, Beverly Hills in May of 1954. Before they moved in, it was left a mess by the previous tenants. Inez Melson, Marilyn's business manager, and Marilyn's secretary cleaned the house for Marilyn and Joe. Upon learning of this, Marilyn invited them to stay for the first meal in their new home which she prepared herself. Before moving in Marilyn invited Sidney Skolsky to come see her new home. When they arrived at the house Joe was not there and Marilyn didn't have a key. "Marilyn looked into a side window of the house. A policeman, who had just parked his prowl car in the driveway suddenly approached. He looked sinister. He wanted to know what we were doing. Somehow, I felt guilty. 'This is Mrs. DiMaggio. She was supposed to meet her husband here. They just rented the house and are in the process of moving in.' 'I can't understand what happened to Joe,' said Marilyn softly. It would have won over any cop in a movie. The policeman cased Marilyn, up and down. He gave no sign of recognition. He didn't ask for an autograph. I didn't understand it. He looked me over, too—but quicker. 'This house is on the patrol. We've got it marked unoccupied. Anyone seen around is suspicious. When you two finally move in, please phone the Beverly Hills Police Department so we'll know. We keep a close watch on things. 'That's nice,' said Marilyn. 'Thank you.'…Marilyn discovered the side window wasn't securely locked. She lifted the screen and climbed into her new house. Then she opened the front door for me. 'This won't happen all the time. I'll have a key.'" Joe finally arrived with Vic Masi. They had taken Masi's car to their storage unit to pick up some personal belongings and furniture. As Joe and Vic unload the items from the car Marilyn takes Skolsky on a tour of their new home and gives him advice on marriage that sounds wonderful if you don't remember that they would be divorced after nine months. As he was leaving Marilyn gave this final thought, "Oh, yes, marriage makes a woman less neurotic. Well, anyway, it does when I'm the woman.'"

Marilyn sees the first draft of her new contract on May 5th and she is not happy. Twentieth Century-Fox agreed to everything except her wishes to approve her scripts, director and cameraman. They even refused to allow her to choose her own acting coach or choreographer. She, of course, doesn't sign it. It is about this time that Milton Greene re-enters her life.

Costume Tests for *There's No Business Like Show Business* begin on May 5th. Marilyn is again dressed by Travilla. Marilyn goes into this film thinking that she will not star in Billy Wilder's, *Seven Year Itch*. But as luck would have it, on May 5th Charles Feldman calls with good news. He tells her he finally struck a deal with Twentieth Century Fox and she will star in *Seven Year Itch* after all. Marilyn is too suspicious to be happy.

Lee Benedict tells of Marilyn costume she will wear for the *After You Get What you Want You Don't Want It* routine. "Billy Travilla, her personal designer, outdid himself in costumes *for There's No Business Like Show Business*. Marilyn's much-quoted remark about preferring to stay out of the sun because she likes to feel blonde all over was the inspiration for one outfit she wears in one important scene in *Show Business*. Travilla, who has designed Marilyn's personal and professional film wardrobe for several years, admits he was sitting up nights trying to figure out something that would really be different. 'But this time,' he explained, 'her blondness and her quip about it he me, and that's how this 'blonde-all-over' costume was born.' The costume is made of imported sheer Rodier wool, dyed the exact shade of Marilyn's hair. It's a cover-up dress, sleek and slim of line, but with a deeply-plunging V-neckline. It fits like a second skin. What's more, Marilyn's shoes, stockings, gloves and the long fox stole she wears with it are all dyed the tone of the Monroe tresses."

When Fox executives worried that her blonde-on-blonde gown would get by the censors, Marilyn said, "Why won't it get by? I'm completely covered. You know—with a high neckline like Marlene Dietrich wears. What do you want? Some more beads on the arms or something?"

McLemore reported on May 6th, "Want To Meet Mrs. DiMag?...I had to come home and tell my wife that I had spent most of the afternoon in the dressing room of Marilyn Monroe at 20th Century-Fox lot. No sunshine there. No chance to turn a fast dollar with a customer. Just an afternoon spent listening to Marilyn telling me how hard she was working on the songs in *No Business Like Show Business*, and how she hoped the people would like her in her latest picture, *River of No Return*. Spun all through her conversation on the picture she is making and the one that had just been released, was her talk of Joe. Joe's her husband. Last name DiMaggio. Baseball player. In case you are crazy enough not to have heard of him. It was Joe this and Joe that. If Joe doesn't know it for sure, I'll tell him something right now--he has a real sweet lady, real crazy about him. Yesterday was the third time I had me Miss Monroe. The first time was at lunch at Chasen's when Mary and I sat down with Marilyn and Joe, the second was when she was making *River of No Return* and she sat and talked with Mary, Mary's mother and me in her dressing room. The third time was the first time I had seen her purely as Marilyn Monroe. She wasn't being courted, and she wasn't made up for pictures. She had been rehearsing songs, and her hair was as wild as any Polynesian, no make-up, a four-dollar sweater, and a six-buck skirt. And she was prettier than the girl you see in the movies. I don't think you could make her homely if you put her in a barrel and poured molasses over her head. But there is more to her than her beauty and all the other things that Providence gave her in abundance. It's sweetness. It's solidity. It's genuineness. I have been around too many famous, near-famous and the like not to know when the edge cuts true, or has just been sharpened up for company carving. The publicity end of 20th Century doesn't hover close by when she gives an interview. They know the gal. She told me of Korea, with the boys in the front row looking through binoculars; she showed me her wedding ring with all the pride of a girl who had never heard of a diamond and said, 'Isn't it different? I've never seen one as pretty or like it.' When the cameras crank she is Marilyn Monroe, star. When you talk to her she is Mrs. Joe DiMaggio, solid gal."

Hedda Hopper reported on May 13th, "Marilyn Monroe broke a record by appearing on the dot to be photographed with a makeup mirror given her by the *Detroit Free Press* and delivered by yours truly. I asked why the promptness and she replied. 'Since I married Joe,' those little things I wasted time on are no longer important.' I told Marilyn she looked 18, and she said, 'I wish I felt it.' 'Just keep feeling the age you are,' said I, 'and you will do all right.' The DiMaggios have rented a house for six months, they want to build a French farmhouse later. Marilyn told me she wants a baby, and I suggested that she plan her family like Esther Williams--a baby, a couple of pictures, another baby, more pictures. She opened her baby blue eyes and said, 'But what about nature?' I promised to send her Esther's timetable. Marilyn, incidentally, won't be in *Pink Tights*."

Ben Hecht wrote a letter to Marilyn's attorney, Lloyd Wright, Jr., on May 19th advising him that "The Marilyn Monroe Story" had been sold to *Collier's* magazine. He inquired if Marilyn would agree to edit the book and would she agree to the book's publication by Doubleday? The advantage in doing this, Hecht argued, was to gain her publicity as a literary figure, bringing her a "high and wide-spread type of publicity superior to any she has received."

On May 21st, Marilyn and passenger Joe DiMaggio were involved in a traffic accident on the corner of Sunset Blvd and Beverly Ave, in Beverly Hills, CA. Marilyn rear-ended Bart Antinora's sports car. He was a physical education instructor from Northridge, California. He hired attorney Fred Martino, and proceeded to sue Marilyn and Joe for $3000.00 each. The suit was filed on August 30, 1954. The trial was set for March 28, 1955, but was postponed until August 8, 1955. The case was later settled out of court for $500.

More wardrobe test for *There's No Business Like Show Business* were held on May 23rd. The next day on May 24th Marilyn has a sitting with Milton on the back lot at Fox studios in a French village set from the motion picture, *What Price Glory*. She wears a costume from the movie, *Song of Bernadette*. Milton became so inspired after talking with Marilyn and reading *The Brothers Karamazov*, that he optioned the film rights. He dressed Marilyn in this outfit to try to give her a view of herself as a serious, dramatic actress, a glimpse of Marilyn as Grushenka. For whatever reasons, Marilyn Monroe Productions, Inc. never made the motion picture. It was made in 1958 at MGM with Yul Brenner, Lee J.

Cobb, and Maria Schell, as Grushenka. It is also during this time that Milton captures a rare image of Marilyn holding her picture of Abraham Lincoln in her black Cadillac. Milton said this of photographing Marilyn, "After I photographed her, she asked me about doing a book of pictures on her and we got together. There was a difference in the pictures. She can look great in satin, but she can also look great in an old sweater on a bicycle, too. This series of photos shows her in different character roles. It will stimulate producers and directors to see what she can do."

Shooting begins on *There's No Business Like Show Business* on May 28th. Leon Shamroy, who was the cameraman on her first screen test at Fox, works with her again on this movie. Marilyn stars in this musical with some pretty big guns, Ethel Merman, Dan Dailey, Mitzi Gaynor, Johnnie Ray and Donald O'Conner. All are experienced musical stars. As a result of Marilyn feeling very insecure around such established and talented stars she will impose a ban on non-essential people on the set when she is being filmed. The rumor will be that she is becoming arrogant, but the truth is she is just plain scared. She plays Vicky, an aspiring singer/dancer who has caught the eye of Tim Donahue, played by Donald O'Conner. Marilyn does her best to keep up with the rest of the cast, but this will not be among one of her better films. Marilyn comes down with the flu the first day and wasn't back on the lot until June 5th. It is not unusual for her to succumb to illness when faced with overwhelming stress. She will suffer from colds, the flu, skin rashes and nervous exhaustion during filming, and this will be the first of many sick days to come. Marilyn is still dealing with anemia and is still on a restricted diet. She will tell Paula Walling on the first day of filming, "What I really notice most about my success is that I must watch my health."

In order to keep the peace between Joe and Natasha Lytess, Marilyn hires Cora Bowen as her dialogue coach. Miss Bowen was found on the advice of her hairdresser Gladys Whitten, and she will work with Marilyn at her home. This will make it so that Marilyn will only work with Natasha at the studio, thus avoiding any run-ins with Joe.

Bob Alton choreographed the musical numbers in the film. In a bold move, Marilyn had Alton replaced with Jack Cole for the *Heat Wave* number. Marilyn had gone through the number with Alton's choreography and at the conclusion of the routine she just left the set without saying anything. The next day she demanded that Jack Cole be brought in. She thought Cole would give the number much more interest with his style of dancing. And she was right. Yet she will engender a lot of criticism for her blatant sexual gestures and costume. Bob Alton was no slouch. He was considered one of the best in the business and had been credited with discovering Gene Kelly and Van Johnson. Because Cole had choreographed her numbers for *Blondes* Marilyn felt more secure with him. But just because Cole had broken through Marilyn's reserve and had gained her trust, didn't mean he let her off easy. Cole's dancing involved complicated steps and body movements, but Marilyn stuck by her decision and worked hard to master the choreography. In the finished version on screen she is perfection. She performs the routine like a seasoned pro. She worked tirelessly at learning Cole's exacting dance moves during the day, and then an exhausted Marilyn would go home and study the script for *Seven Year Itch*.

Marilyn also looks to vocal coach, Hal Schaffer, for coaching and a kind heart to listen to mounting problems at home. The cost to him wouldn't fully be realized until the end of July, when he would attempt suicide due to threats by Joe DiMaggio.

Another drama playing out on the set was Marilyn winning the right not to do an Irving Berlin number, written especially for her. It was titled, *The Girl on the Calendar*.

While on the set of *There's No Business Like Show Business* an old acquaintance from Marilyn's modeling days shows up. He is photographer Gene Lester, from *The Saturday Evening Post*. Lester photographed Marilyn during her lean and hungry years. Lester will recount that Marilyn had showed up in a dirty pink sweater and she even had noticeable dirt on the back of her neck. He sent her back to Miss Snively and asked her to make sure Marilyn was clean the next time she was sent to him. Marilyn, upon learning of this, was livid. Despite their history, Marilyn seems to be too preoccupied with other problems to hold a grudge. That will come later. Meanwhile, Lester takes some candid photos of Marilyn on the set. He has with him a small camera, a Minox. Marilyn laughed at him and doubted that the little camera could even take pictures. He took some photographs of Marilyn standing against her dressing room door smoking. After he finished the roll of film. He showed the camera to her, then he carved her initials in it with a pin-knife and gave the camera to her. The small camera would show up in a 1956 sitting he had with her in Beverly Hills to promote the Pete Wilson story about her in *The Saturday Evening Post*. In 1956 she would keep Lester waiting hours for their photo session while she bathed. Maybe she wanted to make sure she was clean enough for him to photograph.

During the filming Eddie Joe, a tour guide for "Holiday in Hollywood" from Niagara Falls, met Marilyn. He was a friend of Johnnie Ray's business manager and was given access to the cast of the film. A party was given in his honor and was attended by all the cast except Marilyn, "whom Eddie says insisted on going to bed every night at 8 o'clock. (Despite a variety of misconceptions about Marilyn, Eddie says, she's a very serious girl and maintains a strict training schedule during movie-making.)…Although, Marilyn Monroe is very strict in enforcing a rule on her own that no one be on the set when she is cutting a scene, Marilyn invited Eddie to watch her perform. She explained that, although she was extremely self-conscious about her signing, feeling that she is only an amateur, she doesn't mind someone else she feels is a friend watching her, which made Eddie feel—Well, how would you feel?"

Despite her perceived "star" demands, Marilyn has a great repore with the cast and crew as illustrated by this story. "Marilyn does have a quiet, almost twinkling kind of humor that pops up at unexpected times and places. Take the day on the sound stage when she was recording one of the two big Irving Berlin songs in the picture she's been making. The song was *After You Get What You Want You Don't Want It*. Marilyn finished the number, got terrific applause from the musicians and everyone else on the set, then drew an extra cheer when she said, demurely, 'You know, that really isn't so.' Or take still another day when Marilyn was chatting with camera operator Irving Rosenberg, and asked Rosenberg how long he'd been working at his trade at 20ᵗʰ. 'Twenty-five years,' Rosenberg said. 'Well, Irving,' Marilyn twinkled, 'play your cards right and this might turn into a steady job.'" When the director Walter Lang wanted Marilyn to wear flat heels because she towered over Donald O'Conner, Marilyn replied, "Don gets higher billing than I do in the picture. Let him wear high heels." Walter Lang directed Marilyn screen-test in 1946 for Twentieth Century-Fox.

A glimpse of Marilyn's relations with the photographers is seen. "Before her marriage, Marilyn was often tense, nervous and on edge when she had to come into the studio portrait gallery for new portraits. But today you see a girl who faces the all-seeing eye of the camera relaxed and happy. While the lights are being arranged, she sings and jokes with the crew. While head portrait photographer Frank Powolny was focusing his camera on her, Marilyn broke up the entire crew when she quipped, 'Imagine! This time they're just going to take pictures of my face!'" She is coy and persuading to another photographer on the set. "'You know,' chuckled the still photographer assigned to Marilyn's picture, 'you can't get angry with Marilyn, no matter how she disappoints you. I complained to her one day on the set that I wasn't getting enough pictures of her. 'I know,' she said, 'but I promise you we'll get them later. And I'll even help you carry your equipment.' 'I told her she didn't have to do that—just stand still long enough for me to get some color shots. 'I promise you we'll get them,' she said, and then she added, 'Here, let's shake on it.' 'So we shook on it,' the photographer said, wryly, 'but I'm still waiting to get the pictures.'"

On May 31ˢᵗ Sheliah Graham gives a hint of Marilyn's interior decorating taste, after Marilyn tells her that she and Joe eventually want to build a home, "...something warm and cozy. Marilyn told me she'll furnish this dream house in Modern Rustic." Miss Graham publishes an article later in the year and gives further information of Marilyn's taste. "'We're going to build our own home in Hollywood. Nothing too large or flashy. Neither of us wants the bother of a huge home.' So I asked what kind of home. 'Maybe a two-bedroom house somewhere in Beverly or Brentwood. Not in the valley. We looked there and it's too hot. We'll probably have a pool, but that's not essential. I'm not very much an outdoor type. But maybe Joe's son would like to swim. How will I furnish it? I know how I won't. I hate early American. Let's say modern rustic. I don't really care what, as long as it's warm and cozy.' Meanwhile Joe and Marilyn have rented decorator Barbara Barondess McClean's fancy two-bedroom-with-pool home in Palm Drive."

During an interview with Sheilah Graham, published on May 30th, Marilyn made this quotable quote, "I like to arrive at a place, but I hate the getting there."

On June 10th Marilyn pinch-hits for columnist Dorothy Kilgallen who is on vacation. She gives advice to women on being married and how to treat your man. "Of the many perquisites of what Hollywood calls 'stardom,' one of the pleasantest is the fan mail which pours in from members of the movie audience who feel free to ask for advice. Before my marriage I noted that many of the letters from women asked the simple question, 'How do you catch a man?' Now that I'm married, the questions are, 'How do you hold him?' and 'Should a married woman be sexy.' Many of the questions imply that there is something tricky or mysterious about being attractive either before or after marriage, and that a woman must be devious and practice secret wiles in order to capture and hold the interest of the man she loves. I think that physical attractiveness is important, since it is the basis of the man-woman relationship but equally important, if something more than a flirtation is desired, is naturalness and honesty. A man may be intrigued by a pretty face or figure, but he falls in love with the real person behind the facade. If he marries one person and discovers he's tied to another, he is bound to become disillusioned and perhaps regret his bargain. My own experience was perhaps different from the normal because before I met Joe DiMaggio I already knew about him as a public figure and had certain preconceived notions as to what he would be like. I rather expected to meet a flashy type, sharply dressed and given to loud conversation. Instead, I met a man who was dressed conservatively. I subsequently learned that he had been named one of the nation's 10 best-dressed men, who was almost shy in his conversation and who preferred quiet talk in out-of-the-way places to the spotlight of nightclubs and public gatherings. I'm sure Joe, in turn, had a mental picture of a theatrical type given to excesses in dress and manner. He was to learn, I think, that actresses have two sides to their make-up--the glamour they strive for in public, and the normality they enjoy when out of public view. In our courtship, then, it became a matter of getting to know each other as we really are. In this we were completely honest and free of artificiality. I know that I fell in love with the real Joe, not the Joe of the headlines, and I think he fell in love with the real Marilyn Monroe, and not the girl of the calendar. I am certainly no authority on the subject, but when someone asks me how to hold a husband, I tell them this: Be yourself, but don't let down. If a man marries a happy girl and one who keeps herself well groomed and desirable, he's entitled to live with that same person and not a frowsy grouch. The big test of marriage is the 'breakfast table' test. Any girl can be attractive in the evening, when she's had time to apply her best cosmetics and wear her best gown and is in a carefree mood. It's how she looks in the morning that really counts--and this isn't a matter of make-up at all. She couldn't dress for breakfast as she would for a night club, because now she's housewife rather than a companion on a date. She can even have her hair up in curlers. But she should remember that a sunny disposition is the best cosmetic of all and she should strive to greet her husband and the new day with a happy smile, rather than a before-coffee expression of grouchiness. Should a married woman be sexy? I think this is a silly question. Sexiness in recent years has taken on a peculiar connotation of physical flamboyance, and what husband wants his wife acting around the house like a temptress in a B-movie? Above all, I think, it is important for a woman to remain feminine. I thoroughly approve of slacks, peddle-pushers and other similar garments, but not as a symbol of who wears the pants in the family. The husband should be the head man and the wife should always remember that she's a woman. The girl who gets her man by virtue of her femininity, and then suddenly turns into a domineering female in the home, is due for trouble. The 'clinging vine' type of wife went out of style years ago and I'm not advocating any such approach, but I do think there should be a clear understanding on the woman's part that she is still a woman. I approached marriage thoughtfully as well as happily. I intend to make mine work by being honest, by being as attractive as I can at all times, and by making a real home when I'm not in front of the cameras."

Hedda Hopper has this update on the continuing Ben Hecht saga. "Marilyn tells me she absolutely did not approve the articles by Ben Hecht that were running in England until her attorney, Lloyd Wright, Jr., had them stopped. 'Mr. Hecht sent me a copy of the script to read,' said Marilyn, 'but he didn't get my approval. I still have the copy I corrected. Legally I'm in the clear. I understand it was not his fault—I hope it wasn't."

On the 15th Hugh French tried to negotiate with Twentieth Century-Fox's general manager, Lew Schreiber, but had no luck swaying him to Marilyn's position. Marilyn was now demanding that Natasha Lytess was to be kept on the Fox payroll with an increased salary. If she couldn't do something for herself, at least she still had the power to get Natasha a raise.

Marilyn met with Twentieth Century-Fox studio chief, Spyros Skouras on June 18th. He arranged a meeting with her again at the Beverly Hills Hotel, in two days. She was hopeful that he would take her side in this dispute, but she forgot that this was a "Boys Club."

Marilyn met with Skouras again on June 20th at the Beverly Hills Hotel. He had obviously been talking with someone from Twentieth Century-Fox, as he now encouraged Marilyn to give in to their demands. She must have been gravely disappointed that she could not find a powerful ally to help her. If she cannot engender support for her viewpoint then she will employ a tactic that always worked to garner her attention, sickness. She would rattle the cages at Fox by costing them money from being absent from the set. It was passive/aggressive bargaining and it put Fox in an untenable position as far as holding her accountable. It was a lesson that came straight from the orphan's playbook in the school of hard knocks. Norman Mailer aptly describes her as, "one of the toughest blondes to come down the pike, there in the concentrated center of her misty blonde helplessness."

On June 23rd Marilyn collapsed on the set while working on *There's No Business Like Show Business*. Dr. S.R. Kennamer sent Marilyn home after her latest collapse. She had collapsed three times in four weeks since the picture started. The doctor said she was run down as a result of having the flu 10 days ago, and she was expected to go back to work on Saturday.

Shelley Winters remembers a story that links Marilyn with another icon of the 50s, James Dean. In July *On the Waterfront*, directed by Elia Kazan and starring Marlon Brando opened at the Astor Theatre in New York City. Before it premiered, Elia Kazan held a private screening for a few invited guests in Los Angeles. Shelley Winters was given two tickets. She invited Marilyn to go with her. They met Jerry Paris, an actor friend, at the Hamburger Hamlet and had dinner before attending the screening. The screening was held at Columbia Studios, in the private screening room of Harry Cohn. This bothered Marilyn, because when she was working at Columbia in 1949 Cohn had referred to her as a, "fat pig," and fired her shortly after she completed *Ladies of the Chorus*. But, she went anyway. Marilyn, Shelley and Jerry sat in the front row with James Dean and director Nick Ray.

After the screening, Nick invited Shelley and Marilyn back to his bungalow at the Chateau Marmont Hotel to discuss the film. While driving back to drop off Jerry at the Hamburger Hamlet to get his car, James Dean began to circle the car in his recently purchased Triumph T-110 motorcycle. By the time they arrived at the Hamburger Hamlet, Dean was nowhere in sight. Jerry left in his car and Marilyn and Shelley continued to Nick Ray's. Out of nowhere Dean blared down the street toward them on his motorcycle, daring them to play "chicken." He followed them into the underground parking garage at the Chateau Marmont. Shelley ended up inviting him to Nick Ray's bungalow. Marilyn was livid at him and annoyed that Shelley invited him. Shelley said that, "Jimmy and Marilyn treated each other like resentful siblings." They spent the evening ignoring each other. Everyone drank Pina coladas and at 11:00pm, Dean turned the television channel to see *Vampira*. The sound was so loud that someone turned the volume completely down. He continued to watch with the sound turned off. Many people would like to think that Marilyn and James Dean would be fast friends, like she and Montgomery Clift. Nothing could be further from the truth. No matter how many artworks are created showing the pair as a couple, they were never even friends.

The July 1954 issue *Picture Scope* magazine article features a photo session between Marilyn and Frank Powolny. "I Want a Girl, Just Like the Girl, That Married Joe DiMaggio...a woman may be only a woman, but if she happens to be Marilyn Monroe, she's an event--custom-built and tailored to sighs...'Marilyn Monroe,' says Frank Powolny, 'is what you might call a camera natural.' Frank, who is in charge of stills on the Fox lot in Hollywood, goes on to explain that Marilyn--unlike many top-flight professional models--needs little coaching or direction once she steps into lens range. While she may--and usually does--show up late, she always has enough ideas of her own as to what would make a worthwhile set of pictures. Twenty shots an hour is about her average pace. This is one photo ever three minutes--or as fast as a still cameraman can work. It is also pretty fast thinking for a gal who climbed to the top rung of the most competitive ladder in the world with 'dumb blonde' roles. But far from being dumb, the beautiful bride of Joltin' Joe DiMaggio is quite well aware of pictures. Twenty shots an hour kind and the blonde kind. 'The wonderful part of Marilyn,' Powolny adds, 'is that success hasn't changed her. She's still just as natural and happy-go-lucky as the first day I met her. If you said she's always aiming to please it would be the understatement of the century. Because she is just naturally built that way.' The pictures you see here, unlike those that have made MM famous, were taken between poses and really point up her naturalism--the kind dear old dad used to rave about."

Erskine Johnson reported on July 3rd, "Marilyn Monroe Stirs Up Feud With Joan Crawford...Behind the Screens: The Joan Crawford-Marilyn Monroe feud touched off when Joan criticized Miss Crazy Hips' famous wiggle, has popped up again--and this time Marilyn strikes back. In Marilyn's spicy life story series running in *London's Empire News*, written by Ben Hecht, she hints that La Crawford's rage may have been inspired by her reluctance to let Joan guide her into the ranks of well-dressed dolls. Joan, relates Marilyn, criticized her for wearing a knitted dress at a dinner party at the home of Joe Schenck and said: 'Will you let me help you with your clothes?' Marilyn agreed to make out a wardrobe list to be approved by Joan but the parted-lips film queen didn't follow through. 'For some reason,' she explains, 'I couldn't tell Miss Crawford that she had seen my wardrobe in full.' Next thing she knew Joan was blasting her tight dress and torso movements in print. 'Maybe,' mused Marilyn, 'she was just annoyed because I had never brought her a wardrobe list for her to approve.'"

Bob Thomas reported on July 6th, "Mae West has some advice for Marilyn Monroe: you'd better win over the ladies, baby…I asked her how she felt about Marilyn Monroe. 'I haven't seen her on the screen,' Mae West said in her nasal voice. 'But folks tell me she is using a lot of the things I do. The walk for instance. They tell me she walks the same way I do. And the humorous things she says. I don't know whether she has said them to herself or not. At any rate, the press boys have done a good job on her. But if she's as great as they say she is, why isn't she saving the studio, the way I did with Paramount? I paid off the mortgage on the place.' Miss West reflected on her own rise to fame and said she 'broke records everywhere' because she didn't alienate the female audience. 'You'll notice in my pictures I never once went after a married man or took a man from another woman,' she said. 'I always treated other women with respect. That was part of my plan to keep the women in the audience happy,'"

On July 9th, Marilyn appears in an article in *Colliers*. Her vocal lessons with Hal Schaefer are written down to let the reader know how hard she works on developing her voice. "Every morning at nine or so, Marilyn slid up to the bungalow in her big new convertible. Hal concentrated first on getting her to relax. 'She's tense when she starts,' says Schaefer, 'because she's determined to become really good singer.' The sessions went like this: 'Think of your stomach,' Hal advised her. 'Breathe from there, not from your chest.' As she practices, Marilyn roamed from piano to sofa to overstuffed chair and back to the piano again. Then, singing into an amplifier, Hal took her to the top of her range—B-flat—coaxed her even higher till she hit a very small D-flat, then down past her normal limit of a low F until she just barely touched a bottom D-flat in a husky whisper. When she'd run through a number a few times, Schaefer turned up the sound-equipment volume high enough for Marilyn to hear herself over her own voice. Then he switched off the amplifier, turned on a recording machine, saying, 'Let's go for the tape,' (which serve as a test for the final recording that's synchronized with the action of the film. Marilyn closed her eyes, moved her hands to the mike, tried the song once more. When she finished, she pounced on the arm of the chair to listen to the playback, singing quietly along with it. Schaefer is pleased with the result. Marilyn herself says, 'I won't be satisfied until people want to hear me sing without looking at me. Of course,' she adds, candidly, 'that doesn't mean I want them to stop looking.'"

During filming Marilyn will also be interviewed by Rita Garrison Malloy for an article that would appear in *Motion Picture* magazine on November. Miss Malloy remembers, "…as we finished talking and just before she stepped into the camera's hot glare, she leaned over and whispered to me, 'Hold a good thought for me.' Better than anyone, she knew how much she needed it. And as much as anyone, I knew how much she deserved it."

Marilyn had just signed with RCA Victor. Her first record from *River of No Return*, she sang *I'm Gonna File My Claim*, sold 75,000 copies during the first three weeks. RCA Victor executive Joe Carlton said of Marilyn voice, "Her voice has a hushed, velvety tone, sort of like a female Nat King Cole.' The company sent out a demo record with no name and a large, red question mark on the label. It passed the test and it was well received. Los Angeles DJ Peter Potter said, "Marilyn sings like she walks."

Marilyn has lessons with Michael Chekhov on July 12th, 15th, and 20th. Despite being in the middle of a movie, she always had time for perfecting her craft.

Earl Wilson devoted his entire column to Marilyn on July 19th. He writes about being on the set during the production of the *Lazy* number. "Marilyn Monroe's now the hardest gal to see in Hollywood…but the nicest there, when you do see her. I wanted to interview her—and take some more pictures of her. 'The picture part is gonna be tough,' Roy Craft of the 20th Century Fox press department said. 'She's been overworked, and has been ill a lot. We've been holding national magazines off. Besides, she's dancing and singing in *Show Business* and whenever we want her, the production department waves that $4,500,000 budget in our face.' One real reason is that Miss Monroe has now become a good singer. Irving Berlin went dizzy with delight when he heard her sing *Lazy*. And it can now be said of Marilyn that when she sings you can't take your eyes off her voice, and you won't be able to listen for looking. This singing takes time. And rest. But when I caught up with her on the set, doing a scene on a red couch, with Donald O'Connor and Mitzi Gaynor dancing around and on the couch, Marilyn was as gay and happy as ever. 'I've got a new camera!' she announced in her out-of-breath way. 'A Canon. When I come to New York in the fall to do *Seven Year Itch* we'll have to take each other's picture.' 'How about some right now?' I asked. I already had out the Rollei, Voigtlander, Super Ikonta and Polaroid. 'All right…but is that color?' It was black and white film. 'Oh that'll make my lips look white,' she said. 'I'll tell you,' she added, accommodatingly, 'I'll wet them.' And she began licking her lips. Marilyn was in black wool jersey, figure-caressing toreador pants. Her famous bosom appears to have grown a half inch or so; her figure in *There's No Business Like Show Business* will be its most sexsational yet. 'Get your B.W. in the picture with me,' Marilyn said as she began posing. Like most Hollywood stars, Marilyn is not permitted by her studio to pose even for a snapshot unless she has gone through the hour to two-hour makeup routine. She doesn't have a permanent, but a cold wave 'that lasts only 20 minutes' and is refreshed by a hairdresser on the set. 'When I come to work in the morning, my hair looks like Joe has combed it with a baseball bat,' she once said…She poses till her bosses got impatient for her to get back to her singing and dancing…Now Marilyn is a good craftsman. For example, director Walter Lang or an aide would blow a whistle when something went wrong in the scene. 'I beat your whistle!' Marilyn exclaimed once when she'd discovered one of her errors before anybody else had." One of Wilson's pictures would be published along with his article in newspapers and the rest were published in

*Movie World* magazine, June 1955, "Earl Wilson Says, 'This is a New Marilyn.'"

Sheilah Graham mentions in her column of July 27th, that she and Marilyn visited the set of *Desiree*. "I talked with Marilyn Monroe and she's fit-as-a-fiddle and much prettier. She proved her good health by walking into a scene and reciting two pages of dialog for one take. We then wandered over to the *Desiree* set and saw Marlon Brando. Marlon in full Napoleon regalia stared at la Monroe. It was just like watching a chemistry experiment about to explode."

Lee Benedict writes about Marilyn's visit to the set of *Desiree*. "Marilyn all but stopped production as she stood and watched on the sidelines. 'I just wanted to see two of my favorite performers,' Marilyn explained. 'They're Jean Simmons and Marlon Brando.' And as she stood there chattering with Brando, once the scene had been filmed, Marilyn found herself embraced in welcome by Merle Oberon and invited in to Jean Simmons' dressing room for tea and some girl talk. These two great stars liked Marilyn; that was obvious. Their friendliness flowed and warmed her."

On July 30th the *Los Angeles Times* newspaper ran an article about Evelyn Nesbit-Thaw. Miss Nesbit-Thaw was, "the Golden Girl of 1906....who at the turn of the century was the showgirl toast of two continents and the prize in a love duel between millionaires....Speaking of a forthcoming art project, a full-size nude statue of a young woman done in clay, she praised the model she had found for this work. 'She's beautiful, a sort of Marilyn Monroe type.' Then she gave a low whistle, in the appropriate accent. 'What a model that Marilyn would make--my!'...There is some talk that Marilyn Monroe will portray me on the screen...That flatters me very much because I think she is very beautiful.'" The movie she referred to was *The Girl in the Red Velvet Swing* and ultimately starred Joan Collins. Miss Nesbit-Thaw was the model for Charles Dana Gibson's famous drawing, *The Eternal Question* and became a model for the iconic Gibson Girl, the romantic feminine ideal of turn of the century advertisers. The movie, *The Girl in the Red Velvet Swing* and the later movie, *Ragtime,* were based on her life. Her millionaire husband Harry K. Thaw shot famed architect of the Madison Square Garden, Stanford White, to death in his penthouse in front of horrified guests. This was heralded as the Crime of the Century, and transfixed the nation.

Marilyn's voice coach Hal Schaefer is found unconscious in his bungalow at the Fox Studio on July 27th. He has taken an overdose of sleeping pills, Benzedrine and typewriter cleaning fluid. He is rushed to the hospital and revived. Marilyn makes frequent visits to his hospital room, despite the jealousy of Joe DiMaggio and his suspicions that Hal and Marilyn had a recent affair.

On August 14th, Marilyn, who was feeling much better, had a shopping spree at one of her favorite stores, Jax. she spent $800 in one afternoon. Marilyn paid Dr. B Sternhill $600 for medical services rendered during her recent illnesses.

Harold Heffernan got a quote from Johnnie Ray about Marilyn in his column on August 14th, "What people don't realize about this girl is that she has a great sense of humor, a lot of talent, which she is constantly striving to improve. One of these days, mark my word, she will be a great actress."

An interview with Joe DiMaggio appeared in the *Boston Globe* on August 22$^{nd}$, "Marilyn Monroe can cook a steak...'My life is dull. I never interfere with Marilyn's work. I don't go to the studios to see her act. It's the same stuff all the time. You see only a little of it. Shoot a scene—and then hang around for the last ones. I wait and see the pictures.' On her days off Marilyn accompanies him to play golf. 'I bought her a set of clubs. She takes a hell of a cut. She hits a long ball when she hits it.' When asked about the rumors that he is envious of Marilyn' renown. 'Are you kidding? She was working hard long before she met me. And for what? What has she got after all these years? Don't think it's easy work, acting in the movies. She works like a dog. It's hard work. When she working she's up at 5 or 6 in the morning and doesn't get through until around 7. Then we eat dinner, watch a little television and go to sleep.' Is she a good cook? 'When she's working she's usually too tired. But she broils a hell of a steak. We're both meat people. We like our steaks....We're people who don't go out much. We don't go to parties. We don't get mixed up in many crowds. Soon as she finishes a picture, we get up to San Francisco. We rent a house in Hollywood. My home is in San Francisco.'"

Marilyn's resolve and sense of purpose for her career didn't keep the detractors from calling her "'unkind, high-handed and big-headed.' Her co-workers in the numbers were less patient when Marilyn asked for odd-hour rehearsals on songs and dances, explaining, rather vaguely, 'This doesn't feel exactly right to me.' Her concern extended to costumes, too, and headaches were epidemic among the designers at 20$^{th}$."

Hedda Hopper commented on the *Heat Wave* number in her column, "I counted 52 people on the set of *No Business Like Show Business*, watching her rehearse her *Heat Wave* number. Some were on business, but most of the visitors came to ogle Marilyn. Marilyn's as popular with her co-workers as she is with Joe DiMaggio. The fellows in the orchestra never took their eyes off her and beamed as she sang *Heat Wave*, which was first sung by Ethel Waters in *As Thousands Cheer*. Now Ethel can belt out a tune, but you haven't heard *Heat Wave* until you watch Marilyn sing it. When Irving Berlin heard her he predicted she'd be a top recording artist." Hedda asked Donald O'Conner to give his opinion of the Monroe. "It's a funny thing about her. She doesn't throw herself around—she's subtle. She's breath-taking."

Marilyn is surprised by another guest who visited the set, her old modeling mentor Emmeline Snively of the Blue Book Modeling Agency. They pose for a picture with Marilyn dressed for her *Heat Wave* number.

Joe DiMaggio, back in town on August 27th, comes to the studio to watch the filming of the *Heat Wave* number. He is so enraged by what he perceives as raunchiness in the routine that he refuses to have his picture taken with Marilyn. Louella Parsons softens the account in her column. "Joe finally took himself to the set of *No Business Like Show Business*. When he was asked to pose with his beautiful wife he said, 'No. I'm not dressed properly.' But he did pose with Irving Berlin, and he watched Marilyn do a song and dance number with pride in his eyes. If Marilyn was hurt because Joe wouldn't pose with her she didn't show it. Later Sidney Skolsky, who was on the set, said that Marilyn was a good sport and told him Joe had only come to the set to see his favorite star, Ethel Merman." Sheilah Graham reported that, "Joe said Marilyn, in her dancing dress, didn't have enough clothes on. So, no picture."

Marilyn also meets Paula and Susan Strasberg on the set that day. She tells them her dream is to one day to study with Lee Strasberg at the Actor's Studio in New York. Marilyn had been introduced to Mr. Strasberg by Sam Shaw when she went to New York in the fall of 1951. They leave without much confidence that her plans will ever come to fruition, unaware of how much determination is underneath her Hollywood veneer. Indeed, in the coming months Marilyn will escape Hollywood and flee to New York. She makes good on her promise to study with Lee at the Actor's Studio by early February 1955. No one is more surprised by Marilyn's dedication to her craft than Paula and Susan.

One of the dancers in the finale was Howard Parker. He received a signed photograph from Marilyn. "To Howard, It's a pleasure to work with you, Marilyn Monroe." Mr. Parker remembers that once the finale was finished and the dancers were dismissed, he was walking back to his dressing room and noticed a crowd gathered around a small canvas tent. He inquired what was happening and was told that Marilyn was inside signing autographs. When he got inside the tent he saw Marilyn standing beside a folding table which was covered with photographs of her. After he selected the photo he wanted, she asked him his name so she could sign a personal autograph. She did this for each cast member who wanted one.

In hind sight, Marilyn hated her performance in *There's No Business Like Show Business*. Writer Del Wrightson wrote about this in an article in 1956. "When she came to New York, a columnist asked her why she had left. She answered, 'To protect myself.' What she meant was that she wasn't having any more roles that made her appear ridiculous. Long before *No Business Like Show Business* was released, she had appraised herself in it, mercilessly. She was furious at herself for having accepted the role. She could take ridicule, but not the kind that might put finis to her career. 'I learned something long before I ever made a movie. Nothing can kill you as a personality as quickly and effectively as ridicule—not even scandal.' She was also angry at herself for not being a good enough actress to overcome the simpering, silly woman she played in that picture. She was playing a caricature, and though she could not prevent it entirely, she felt that if she were an accomplished actress she could have softened the blow."

On August 28th, *The Schnectady Gazette* runs an article about Japan's lingering memories of Marilyn. "'Mon Chan'--that's what the Japanese called Marilyn Monroe--has long since left Japan, but her memory lingers on. In the great seaport of Muji a tempest still rages because Kiichi Swematsu, head of the Municipal Assembly, hung a life-size, scantily-clad picture of 'Honorable Pinup Girl' among the solemn picture gallery of former mayors in the town hall. 'It has made our town hall brighter, friendlier and more relaxing,' Kiichi contends, but angry citizens charge him with outraging their revered ancestors. Meanwhile, crowds fight to see it."

Roy Craft gives the background drama to getting *Seven Year Itch* made. "The studio's contract called for the picture's release to be held up until after the Broadway run of the play. When Marilyn went back to New York for the location shots for *Itch*, the play version was still doing a fair business, but it was approaching the end of its long run. If you bought a seat, the house was only half full. Then Marilyn arrived in New York and shot off publicity sparks and suddenly *The Itch* was S.R.O. signs out again. The result was that it seemed it was never going to stop its stage run; so, after finishing the picture, Fox had to pay out an additional hundred and seventy-five thousand dollars to the owners of the stage property for the privilege of releasing their movie."

Tom Ewell starred in *Seven Year Itch* on Broadway with Vanessa Brown in the part of The Girl. It won a Tony Award in 1953 for Best Play. It was written by George Axelrod.

Marilyn starts to film *Seven Year Itch* immediately after filming *There's No Business Like Show Business*. A Fox publicist describes her hectic schedule. "In the past year she's done the work of ten women. These things don't come easy. It's mental and physical slavery. When they're shooting, she's up at 5:30, on set at 6 for makeup or costumes. She finishes a full day on the sound stage, eats around 7 or 7:30, and goes to her dramatic coach to study the next day's part before she falls into bed so she can be up again at 5:30 looking fresh and lovely. Those cameras are too honest. In straight dramatic pictures, it's not as bad. But those musicals—well there's dancing, singing, music, rehearsals, pre-recording work with the music department, the regulation publicity conferences, still layouts, wardrobe fittings. Everyone's pulling at her a different way. It's the side trips, not the actual work before the cameras that's as wearing. She's in such tremendous demand, everything she says is an item, every magazine wants picture layouts on her. We figured out just before the marriage, that if we worked 30 days at 8 hours a day, we couldn't fill the backlog of requests for interviews and sittings.'"

Without a day of rest, Marilyn is rushed into wardrobe Test for *Seven Year Itch* on August 28th. Billy Travilla once again creates a mythic dress which will forever be associated with Marilyn. It is the white, halter topped dress with a pleated skirt. Simple in its design, in ecru georgette, yet when worn by Marilyn in the film, it forever becomes a symbol of sexual exuberance and sensual abandonment. Marilyn appears clean and cool in comparison to her dingy surroundings, which was exactly the effect Travilla was going for. Marilyn stars as "The Girl," supplying the "Itch" to co-star Tom Ewell. This is the role most closely associated with her legend. The iconic image of her skirt billowing above her creamy white thighs will be forever associated with the American Cinema.

Travilla will later comment on working with Marilyn, "During the 11 pictures I designed for her, Marilyn and I lunched together in the studio café many times. She usually liked to hide away, and we would walk down the far end, not sit up front with the stars, or in the God Room, where stars and directors sat. But she had this fascination—this electric something. No matter how beautiful she looked, or how awful, people froze with forks halfway to their lips to watch her go by. Sometimes she came in straggle-haired, with lanolin greasing her face, looking far from good. Yet everyone stopped talking, eating, smoking, to stare. She had a fetish about eye shadow and lipstick. Even when she wasn't made up, she had a bit of green eye shadow and lipstick. I used to tease her and ask if this was part of a preconceived plan. She would look at me and say, 'Billy, what do you think?' She never really answered. Made-up or not, she was dynamic. With makeup she was sensuously beautiful. Without it she had the face of a child, a cherub. She was two different people, but she always had that magic, whatever you want to call it."

Tom Ewell, her co-star in *Seven Year Itch*, pays her this compliment, "Before they shoot the scene, you wonder if she's going to hold up her end of it. When you see it on screen, she's stolen it from you!" Ewell will say in a later interview, "Marilyn was cooperative, not temperamental. She came to the set prepared, but it took time for her to get organized. She trusted cameramen because the camera gave her all the things she never had as a child—love, illusions. She was fun to be with." When prodded by Hedda Hopper, Ewell gave this touching glimpse of Marilyn. "'I've never met a sweeter, nicer person than Marilyn or one easier to work with. She wanted me in the role. She's a hard worker, but very unselfish, and I've never seen a sign of temperament or temper. She's done a brilliant job and I think she'll be the number one comedienne of the screen when the picture is released.' 'What about her coaches? She generally has Natasha Lytess on the set.' 'She's there, but with a difference this time. Billy tells Natasha what he wants, and she tells Marilyn. What's coming out is not Natasha's idea of the part, its Wilder's.' 'Donald O'Connor told me he had difficulty establishing rapport in a scene with her.' 'You find people as you find them. You have to discover for yourself.'"

Ewell will remember eating lunch everyday with Marilyn on the set. "She would always read the Bible. But she would put a *LIFE* magazine in front of it so no one would know. She told me, 'Every time I turn around people think I'm doing some publicity stunt. I don't want them to think that about reading the Bible.'"

Director Billy Wilder had an artistic appreciation of the unique way Marilyn came across on the screen. "Every movie star has a certain voltage. It is as if one were to hold up a light meter to the screen and certain stars will register more than others. Well, Marilyn has the highest voltage...She never flattens out on the screen. She never gets lost up there. You can't take your eyes away from her. You can't watch any other performer when she's playing a scene with somebody else." Wilder would go on to say about Marilyn, "I don't think there was any danger of Marilyn sinking into oblivion. A thing like her doesn't come along every minute. She has what I call flesh impact. It's very rare. Three I remember are Clara Bow, Jean Harlow and Rita Hayworth. Such girls have flesh which photographs like flesh. You feel you can reach out and touch it. Before we go further, I must tell you that I like the girl, but it's also moot whether you have to be an actor or an actress to be a success in pictures. I'm sure you've heard the theory that there are two kinds of stars—those who can act and those who are personalities. I'll take a personality any time. Something comes down from the screen to you when you see them, in a way that it doesn't always come from the indifferently paid actors, although they may be perfect at their jobs. Right now, as of today, no matter what she thinks, Marilyn's great value is as a personality, not as an actress.

If she sets out to be artistic and dedicated, and she carries it so far that she's willing to wear Sloppy-Joe sweaters and go without make-up and let her hair hang straight as a string, this is not what has made her great to date. I don't say that it's beyond the realm of possibility that she can establish herself as a straight dramatic actress—it is possible—but it will be another career for her, a starting all over."

On September 1st *The Los Angeles Herald Examiner* reports that Marilyn's autobiography, "The Marilyn Monroe Story," which she co-authored with Ben Hecht, was printed in England's *The Empire News* without her permission, Marilyn is threatening to sue. Hecht has voluntarily withdrawn all further publication of the manuscript in magazines and newspapers. He directed his agent to return any profit that was made of the serialization of the manuscript. He even goes so far as to tell his agent to destroy the remaining text of the Monroe manuscript. This seems to satisfy the demands of Marilyn's lawyers.

Hedda Hopper continued to report on this controversial story on September 8th, "Marilyn Monroe, despite stories to the contrary, is no nearer to suing Ben Hecht then she was when I first ran the story months ago. Ben interviewed her for an article to appear in *Ladies Home Journal*, but the stuff was published under her by-line in England, without her consent, and she was furious. I culled a few quotes from the British paper that ran the stories. 'In Hollywood a girl's good name is less important than her hairdo,' said Marilyn. On Hollywood's wolves: 'They seldom get angry or critical of you.' On headline hunters: 'A scandal-made star just can't rest on her old scandals. After 35 getting into romantic hot water is a little difficult. And getting yourself publicized in love triangles and cafe duels over your favorite needs not only a swell press agent but a little miracle to help out.' On the subject of DiMaggio the article said Marilyn didn't want to meet him because she didn't like the way sportsmen and athletes dressed. 'I don't like men in loud clothes with checked suits, big muscles and pink ties. I get nervous...(When I finally met him) he looked like either a steel magnate or a Congressman. My husband winces easily. Many of the things that seem normal or even desirable to me are very annoying to him. Joe is not a success by Hollywood standards. In Hollywood the more important a man is the more he talks. The more successful he is the more he brags.'"

One Hollywood observer of the time said this about Marilyn, "Marilyn's become a national institution, and so far she's delivered the goods, made everybody proud of her. But it hasn't been easy. Look at what she's had to overcome. Not only her nude calendar and reports that she neglected her mother, but more recently her supposedly unauthorized life story carried by an English newspaper. So many copies were sold in the United States that the London publishers had to reprint entire editions, and it was pretty rough on Marilyn. In fact, it was so 'sexsational' that printing the same stuff about anybody else in Hollywood would kill them off immediately at the box office. Marilyn was pretty upset and said she would sue, but the significant thing is that even this bad publicity didn't seem to hurt her. It's almost as if Marilyn has gotten too big for anything to touch her. Yet, it's just not in the cards for her to go on topping herself forever, trying to live up to so many people's expectations of her. The price is too high. When you start off as spectacularly as Marilyn did, the pace gets faster and faster and the physical and emotional demands grow, too. Something has to give, and it's usually one's health. Marilyn knows. She's easily susceptible to colds and respitory disorders and when she's under a work strain, her resistance gets even lower. That's why she had five separate attacks of flu and colds during *No Business Like Show Business* and had to stay in bed. She's always going to have to watch her health. I don't think she'll ever choose to quit or even slow down, but her health may demand it."

Paula Walling of the *Sunday Times* reported on September 5th, "At the party to mark the end of the filming of 20th Century-Fox *Desiree*, Marilyn Monroe arrived in tight blue jeans. She had just walked over from rehearsals on *Show Business*. On her the blue jeans looked good. Marlon Brando, usually Hollywood's worst dressed man, came dressed to kill."

Marilyn leaves for location filming for *Seven Year Itch* on September 9th. The morning Marilyn left for New York, she stopped by Hedda Hopper's home to say goodbye. Joe accompanied Marilyn to the airport inviting much speculation as to why he didn't accompany her to New York. They would be photographed at the Los Angeles International Airport where Joe gave her a goodbye kiss. Marilyn arrives at Idlewild Airport, New York City, on the TWA Champagne Special, to begin filming location scenes for *Seven Year Itch*. She arrives at 8am and was greeted by a throng of reporters and fans, gamely posing for photos.

Roy Craft describes Marilyn's impact on New York. "Another example of the impact she packs: when she went back to New York on the *Seven Year Itch* location. All of a sudden New York was a whistle stop, with the folks all down to see the daily train come in. When Marilyn reached LaGuardia, everything stopped out there. Once columnist said that the Russians could have buzzed the field at five hundred feet and nobody would have looked up. There has seldom been such a heavy concentration of newsreel cameramen anywhere. From then on in, during the days of her stay, one excitement followed another. She was on the front page of the *Herald Tribune*, with art, five days running, which I'm told set some sort of local record."

Another paper reported, "Marilyn Monroe, wearing a form fitting sheer wool dress which borrowed nothing from Paris' new flat chested look, broke up airport routine today when she arrived from Los Angeles. There was not much work done for 45 minutes as some 500 Idlewild employees whistled and shouted approval while the platinum blonde actress posed for photographers on the ramp of her plane. Policemen finally pushed back the crowd which broke through barriers and escorted her to the terminal building. Here to make scenes for a new motion picture, Miss Monroe chatted gaily with reporters. She laughingly admitted that her cooking for her husband, former baseball star, Joe DiMaggio, is so far confined largely to grilling steaks. Asked if she has been taking any current interest in baseball, she hesitated a moment then said, 'Well-yeah.'"

Still another newspaper chimed in about her arrival, "The 'Big City' forgot all the threat of a hurricane named Edna today, being already devastated by a tantalizing twister called Marilyn Monroe who slithered from a plane at Idlewild Airport and, well—you know the results. Clad in a hug-me-tight beige dress that looked as though it had been painted on her, the Hollywood hurricane was stalled in her tracks for 45 minutes while 500 airlines employees and customers sighed like falling trees. And when it was over and Marilyn finally continued on her course, her admirers looked dazed. The whistles and yowls finally subsided, but nobody who had seen her looked quite the same. Marilyn's visit to New York is her first in three years, and by best estimates it will take at least that time to rehabilitate the boys at Idlewild. Accustomed to seeing some of the world's most famous personages and celebrities, her appearance was nonetheless something out of the ordinary for airport workers to reckon with. The crowds raced about the star, toppling wooden barricades and forcing baggage trucks and field tractors off course. The police intervened, but only after they shook off the hypnotism, and Marilyn, finally slinked away for an interview with the press, using just the right gait to prevent her fur-trimmed topcoat from lousing up a single curve. Marilyn, the wife of former 'Yankee Clipper' Joe DiMaggio, flashed a glamorous smile for her admirers during the long ordeal. Finally, in the comparative safety of the terminal building, she consented to some cheesecake pictures. She is in New York only until Sunday, she said, to make film sequences along Lexington Ave. for a Hollywood version of the Broadway hit, *Seven Year Itch*. 'But while I'm here, I want to see everything,' she said. There were lots of volunteers for escort duty, but Marilyn paid no attention. Rescue squads are still trying to revive 'em over at the airport."

*The Courier Mail*, an Australian newspaper, reported on Marilyn's arrival at the airport. "Those terribly sophisticated fellows who work at New York's international airport, and see a foreign countess or a local movie star every other day, went wild today. The reason: Marilyn Monroe came to town. The situation at the airport got out of hand as soon as the actress shimmied down the steps of an airliner from Los Angeles. More than 500 airport employees broke through the police lines--and the police themselves forgot about trying to hold back the crowd. The airport police shrugged his shoulders and explained: 'Well we thought it would be all right cause we assigned only married men with children to this job. We thought their interest would be purely speculative.' More trouble is expected tomorrow and in the early hours of Sunday morning when Marilyn will be standing right in the middle of the sidewalk for all the crowd to see. She has come to New York--for the first time since she became the best known of Hollywood's blondes--to make several street scenes for her forthcoming movie. The New York police chief is planning to assign the married members of his force to put a cordon around Marilyn and the cameramen when she shoots those street scenes."

A photo/essay by Sam Shaw was taken during the while Marilyn was on location in New York City, followed up by scenes at the Twentieth Century-Fox Studio in Hollywood, chronicling the making of *Seven Year Itch*. Shaw collaborated with George Axelrod, author of *Seven Year Itch*, and turned the 6-week photo/essay into a book entitled, *Marilyn Monroe As The Girl: The Making of Seven Year Itch*.

Marilyn was accompanied East by her wardrobe mistress, her hair dresser, her makeup man and Natasha Lytess. She could not talk Joe DiMaggio into accompanying her on this trip.

Newsreel footage of Marilyn being interviewed on September 9th about her visit to New York.

Reporter: Marilyn, what is the reason for coming to New York?
Marilyn: Well, we're here to make *Seven Year Itch*.
Reporter: Location shots on *Seven Year Itch*?
Marilyn: Yes, uh-huh.
Reporter: That's your latest picture, right?
Marilyn: Yes, I'm looking forward to it very much.
Reporter: Joe didn't come along with you, huh?
Marilyn: No.
Reporter: Did he see you off in Hollywood last night?
Marilyn: Oh, yes.
Reporter: You brought your hairdresser, your drama coach and four men from Twentieth Century-Fox. All this and no Joe, huh? I understand there are some fabulous location shots going to be made next Saturday night on Lexington Ave. When you do the "Coney Island Treatment," you know, walking over the subway grate and a gust of wind catches you and so forth. I imagine you'll stop traffic again on Saturday night.
Marilyn: Well, I'm looking forward to working here very much.
Reporter: Do you expect to return here for the World Series?
Marilyn: I wish I could, but I'll be finishing this picture.
Reporter: Uh-huh.
Marilyn: When, uh...
Reporter: When the World's Series are on.
Marilyn: Yes. I've never seen a World Series, but I'd love to, but I just can't seem to fit the schedule together.

That evening, Marilyn attended a Press Conference at the St. Regis Hotel, where she was staying while in New York City. Twentieth Century-Fox had sent out engraved invitations to the cocktail party. Marilyn arrived an hour and a half late. She rubbed shoulders with the likes of George and Joan Axelrod, Samuel Hoffman (father to Hollywood big-wigs, Leonard and Irving Hoffman,) Hy Gardner of the *New York Herald Tribune*, Irving Berlin, and Co-star Tom Ewell. Paul Schumach, George Barris and Earl Wilson took some candid photographs at the party that show Marilyn holding court with the Lords and Ladies of New York. Photographer Philippe Halsman, who was also there, remembers, "I arrived half an hour late and found the room completely filed. I have seldom seen so many celebrities in one room: actresses, composers, writers, producers, directors, mingling with innumerable photographers and flashbulb cameras. Outside in the hall a group of people with autograph books were waiting impatiently. Marilyn was--of course--late. I have seen many receptions where one waited for an important personality to put in an appearance, but I have never witnessed more nervous tension and anticipation. Finally, an hour later, a kind of electric shock went through the crowd. The door opened. Flashbulbs started popping in continuous explosion. In the middle of this electrical storm, a blonde, slightly frightened-looking woman entered--her body trying to free itself from her too-snug-fitting dress, her eyes partly closed, her mouth moist, half-open, breathless. I have seen Marilyn since, but this is the image of her that I would like to keep--the girl whose weakness brought her to the pinnacle of success."

Roxanne, a New York celebrity, made a comment in the press about Marilyn. Roxanne had told Earl Wilson in an interview that, "'Marilyn should take about 15 pounds off of her fanny.' And that she should wear a bra or girdle. After the interview, I phoned Marilyn in Hollywood and asked if she'd comment. She wouldn't. Many months passed. Then by a curious coincidence, Roxanne found herself cast in *Seven Year Itch* also. Roxanne went to a small party for Marilyn. And, as always, Marilyn gave no sign of her real feeling. But later Marilyn asked Roxanne point blank about the statements—and Roxanne tried to deny she'd made them, so Marilyn told me subsequently. Marilyn wasn't bitter, however. 'Oh I get that all the time,' she said. 'The only thing was, it upset Joe. When he read it, he said to me, 'Hey, what about this dame?'"

Earl Wilson had a private interview with Marilyn in her bedroom. He published his story on September 16th in his syndicated column. "Marilyn Says Joe is Before Career...I took a couple of cameras, and $10 worth of film, and went up to have a drink with Marilyn Monroe. Then I asked the greatest female since Cleopatra how things are going with Joe DiMaggio. 'You see...uh...Marilyn,' I stammered--beating around the matrimony bush--'some people are asking whether everything's going smoothly with Joe and you. And whether you might be inclined to put your career above your marriage.' 'You're sweet!' Marilyn said--and I had to admit I was. 'You're saying it much nicer than those other people are saying it. But,' she added, quivering, Jell-O-like, in her low-cut black strapless dress which had some peek-a-boo net up around the top, but not too far up, 'everything's fine with us! A person's life is more important than any career. And when I say 'a person's life'' she went on philosophically, 'I mean whatever a person's life encompasses. That certainly includes marriage. A happy marriage comes before everything.' Thus Marilyn, on the day of her great triumphal entry into New York, served notice on all Hollywood worriers that Joltin' Joe is No. 1, and that her career--fabulous though it is--is No. 2, and not to be cooking up any more rumors. 'You soon have an anniversary, don't you?' I asked. 'Oh, not till Jan. 14!' She quivered prettily again. 'We've confused people about that because we 'went together' so long before we got married.' Marilyn laughed when she used the expression 'went together'--and when Marilyn laughs--well, that's very nice, too. 'Anybody who says anything different about how we're getting along doesn't know,' Marilyn said. 'Who could know? Joe and I rarely see people. He loves TV. I come home and we have dinner. About all we do is fool around the house.' Marilyn said all this and much more up at the St. Regis when she accidentally found herself hostess to a select few of show business' biggest names. Irving Berlin--who discovered she has a voice (he's one of the few men interested in her throat)--dropped in and told her, 'you're beautiful, you're beautiful!' Tom Ewell, who plays opposite her in the movie, *Seven Year Itch*; Elliott Nugent, who took Tom's place in the play of the same name, and RCA Vice-President Mannie Sacks, who wants Marilyn to make more records, were other droppers-in...and Marilyn, after emerging approximately an hour late for her own gathering, had a wonderful time. She rubbed her hand through this reporter's crew cut, for example, and insisted it was fun. 'This is about as far as a girl can go at a cocktail party,' she said. Miss Monroe was asked whether it was true as columnist Mike Connolly of the *Hollywood Reporter* has said, that she has added an inch to her celebrated upper extremities. 'It depends on my weight. If I put on a little weight, that's the first place I put it on,' she replied. 'I'm supposed to be a 36 1/2",' she went on, 'but I did make 37 1/2" once. I never did make 38".' But the way she said it, you felt she might have such a project in mind. While the droppers-in were rhapsodizing about Marilyn, and the titanic reception she got in New York, she was hoping, out loud, that her next picture can be *Guys and Dolls* with Marlon Brando as her leading man. 'Sam Goldwyn wants me for it, and I want it, and now we have to talk my boss, Darryl Zanuck, into it.' she said. Photographers who'd never seen her before used words like 'exotic' and hung around till Hugh French, her agent, asked some of them whether they didn't have a home. Then--having learned that her film shooting schedule here was delayed and that she didn't have to work till the next day--Marilyn decided to go out and see the town. With DiMaggio back home in California, Marilyn went to dinner at Petite Cuvee with photographer Milton Greene and Mrs. Greene, producer Herman Levin, and David Haft, young textile tycoon who is a friend of the Greene's. They then moved on to El Morocco, where Marilyn danced with Milton Greene, and to the Embers, being joined by Billy Rose and Joyce Mathews. Gene Tierney, who was at El Morocco with Greg Bautzer, is a Big Name, but even she didn't reduce the excitement over Marilyn. Producer Levin hastened to clear up the situation concerning being in the party with Marilyn. 'Nobody has a date with anybody,' he said. 'David Haft and I are just sort of sharing the job of being Marilyn's escort. Not that we find it irksome.'"

Leonard Lyons reported about this evening on September 15th, "I shuttled, then settled at Billy Rose's table at the Embers, for his guests included Joyce Matthews, producer Herman Levin, photographer Milton Greene and his wife--and their friend Marilyn Monroe. They had dined, danced at Morocco and Miss Monroc was in the mood for a glass of milk and George Shearling's music before retiring for the night. She devoted most of her attention to the ladies in the party. When she spoke or smiled, the film star--as she does on the screen--moved her lips as if they were her hips. The sultry look was there, or perhaps it's just her nearsightedness. We left early because she said the plane trip and the time difference were catching up with her. On the sidewalk outside the club she removed her shoes, revealing the she doesn't wear stockings either."

Leonard Lyons reported another version of his evening with la Monroe, September 20th,

"A Night With Monroe...She sat in Sardi's wearing a mink coat. It was her Christmas gift from Joe DiMaggio. 'They told me not to bring a mink coat to New York in the summertime,' said Marilyn Monroe. 'But I can always say I don't know any better; it's my first mink coat.' She was flanked by two friends, David Wayne--who had played her husband in four movies--and Milton H. Greene, the photographer. They invited me to join their table. 'This girl,' said Harry Kurnitz, 'is going to bring back table-hopping.' She spoke of her first trip to New York. It was for a movie, *Love Happy*, in which she had only one brief scene. The producers paid her $100 a week to exploit the film. 'In the afternoon, I had a big suite to meet the exhibitors,' said Miss Monroe. 'That night I was moved to a tiny room. I didn't care. I had discovered I could order caviar. Caviar for breakfast, it's the first thing I remember of New York.' Then she came here alone, three years ago, and used to walk to a cafeteria near Grand Central for coffee, alone. The first time she was ever on stage was in Korea last year. The next morning she saw a sign the GIs had made. 'Welcome Marilyn.' She said it was the first time she felt she really was a movie star. Not long ago a minor movie executive who listened to her objections to a film story told her: 'I've been in this business 30 years, and you're gonna tell me about it? What do you know?' Miss Monroe replied: 'I know only that I was born and that I'm still living. That's what I know.' Sam Shaw, the studio cameraman, photographed the table and Sidney Kingsley joined us. Kingsley mentioned his new comedy and his casting problem. He'd been searching for a Marilyn Monroe type, he told her. She smiled and said that when she first went to casting offices she was told they were looking for a Betty Grable type. She said she'd like to do a Broadway show, but her contract might prevent this outside work for pay. 'I would not be allowed to take any salary from you,' she told Kingsley. 'Maybe you'd just have to feed me.' It was time to move on, but she found she couldn't get her shoes back on her feet. We went to Greene's studio on Lexington Ave. to get a pair of his brown loafers for her. She entered the elevator barefoot and with a mink coat. Wayne put her shoes into his briefcase and said: 'I've never had a fetish, maybe this is the start.' We went to the Little Club [Petite Cuvee] for supper, and she spoke of her first Hollywood contract. Ben Lyon, who then was casting director for 20th Century-Fox, had seen her waiting outside his office. He screen tested her that day. 'I discovered Jean Harlow,' he told her, 'You're my second discovery.' When the studio dropped her contract, Lyon protested: 'I brought Jean Harlow to Howard Hughes and he, too, wanted to drop her contract.' The studio signed Miss Monroe again. Joan Castle, the actress, entered the club, saw Marilyn Monroe, and spoke the thoughts of all her sisters: 'It's no use, girls. Tonight we're dead.'"

Marilyn's California Driver's License, #607503, expires on September 9th. She will not get it renewed and that will cost her some legal headaches in the future.

On September 10th Marilyn had a photo-shoot with Richard Avedon for *Harper's Bazaar* magazine. She posed with Billy Wilder for a full page photo captioned, "The Big Buildup," that would be published in the November 1954 issue. This was done to publicize *Seven Year Itch*. *Harper's Bazaar* was the first high fashion magazine to feature Marilyn in its pages. It is also her first sitting with haute couture photographer Richard Avedon. He would come to replace Milton Greene as Marilyn's favorite photographer in 1957. But for now she and Milton are as cozy as two kittens who have caught a mouse, that mouse being 20th Century-Fox. Marilyn will tell Leonard Lyons about being in this magazine, "*Harper's Bazaar*, at last. All my life I've wanted to be in a women's magazine."

Marilyn invited Earl Wilson to come along on the photo shoot. He brought his own Rolleiflex camera. "At the studio she disappeared into the dressing room. We all waited for her outside. Presently somebody called out my name. 'Excuse me,' I said to the others, 'Guess it's a phone call.' The curtain of the dressing room parted. There sat Marilyn in a black slip, making herself up. It was she who had called me. 'Sit down,' she invited. She began chattering of this and that...small talk. Suddenly I got the unspoken message for me to get separate pictures of her. I picked up the bait. 'Do you mind if I take a couple of pictures of you?' I asked. 'Why, of course not,' she said. 'Just as long as you let me see them.' And I went to work! She laughed when I hopped up on a chair and took a shot from above, 'There he goes, up on his perch!' she squealed. She dawdled at her makeup so I could take a lot of pictures. During the fashion shooting, Marilyn demonstrated again her down-to-earthiness. Here she was now, posing for a chic, stylishly snooty, high-fashioned magazine...little Marilyn Monroe. The magazine itself was a trifle surprised at itself for admitting her to its pages. Perhaps it would have to explain to its readers... Marilyn posed in a large chunk of white fur that went up around her ears. She held her head high, looking somewhat aloof. What didn't show in the picture--because it was a head shot--were Marilyn's feet. They were bare! What a shock!"

After the Avedon shoot, Marilyn has a sitting with Milton Greene at his studio on

Lexington Ave., which produced the famous "ballerina" series of Marilyn in a dress supplied by Ann Klein. It is the sumptuous tulle skirt with the ill-fitting bodice, the bareness of her legs and the nonchalance of her expression that gives these photos their power. The "Blue" series is also taken this day. Marilyn sits in a wicker chair, wearing a turquoise top and pedal pushers by Jax. She skillfully uses her drink as a prop as she cuddles and sips it. She is sensuous as she curls up in the chair, world weary in another pose and she gives way to sparkling abandon in another. She will wear this same top for photographer Ted Baron in November.

Marilyn and Milton attended a Broadway production of *The Pajama Game* at the St. James Theatre, starring Carol Haney. Marilyn caused quite a scene during the intermission when it is discovered that she is in the theatre. After the play, she and Milton go backstage and visit with Miss Haney. Marilyn gets into a discussion with Leonard Lyons, a syndicated Broadway columnist. Afterwards, the party adjourns to the 21 Club, for drinks and conversation. Those who attended were Marilyn, Milton, Leonard Lyons, David Wayne, and Pulitzer Prize winning playwright, Sidney Kingsley. Marilyn was shadowed to each of these events by Sam Shaw, who kept snapping photos for his book. The last photo of the day shows an exhausted Marilyn yawning.

Later that night Marilyn finds Joe DiMaggio unexpectedly at the hotel. He spent his evening at Toot Shor's. He said that he came to town to view the upcoming rematch of Rocky Marciano vs Ezzard Charles on September 17th. This was a big fight, as they had fought on June 19th, with Marciano retaining his World Heavyweight Championship Title. The next night, Joe and Marilyn dined at the El Morocco.

Hedda Hopper reported on September 11th, "Marilyn's Buzzing As Joe Tends Hives...Marilyn Monroe, who's attracting crowds wherever she goes in New York, looked like a living doll when she came to my house for an interview just before she planed out to the big city. When she appeared in her traveling outfit--beige from head to foot, she said, 'This is what I mean by looking blonde all over.' Joe DiMaggio and a friend waited in the limousine outside to drive her to the airport, and Joe rapped on the door to warn her it was time to leave. 'Doesn't Marilyn look wonderful?' I asked. He replied, 'She looks nice.' 'Come on, Joe, you can do better than that.' 'I'll try hard,' he grinned. I asked DiMaggio why he didn't go along. Seems to me he would have had a lot of fun showing Marilyn off to all his pals back there. 'I've got the hives,' he explained. 'If I got on a plane and they started bothering me the only thing I could do would be jump.' I could be wrong, but I got the feeling they're foolin'."

Natasha Lytess kept herself busy on September 12th by appearing on the popular game show, *What's My Line*. Four panelist including syndicated columnist Dorothy Kilgallen and Bennett Cerf succeeded in guessing her occupation and that she was Marilyn Monroe's acting coach, although she signed in as Tala Forman, her name before she was known as Natasha Lytess. She ended up winning $35 on the show.

On September 12th Louella Parsons devoted four columns to Marilyn and Joe's Marriage. "Monroe-DiMaggio Discord Rumors Persist...(Editor's Note: Rumors of possible discord in the marriage of Marilyn Monroe and Joe DiMaggio have persisted recently in the face of denials. In the following special article, motion picture columnist Louella O. Parsons, who knows them both, tells what she thinks of the rumors involving one of Hollywood's most dramatic couples). What is the status of the marriage of Marilyn Monroe and Joe DiMaggio? You can't tell me that there is trouble with the number one glamour girl and her famous baseball hero husband, but when Joe failed to appear on the set of *No Business Like Show Business* the gossip mongers started to talk. The fact that Joe refused to play a stage door Johnny while Marilyn was working doesn't mean a thing. Joe never has been one to mix in Marilyn's public appearance or to follow her around like the average Hollywood husband--he is successful and famous in his own right. So much was said, however, that Joe finally took himself to the set of *No Business Like Show Business*. When he was asked to pose with his beautiful wife he said, 'No. I'm not dressed properly.' But he did pose with Irving Berlin, and he watched Marilyn do a song and dance number with pride in his eyes. If Marilyn was hurt because Joe wouldn't pose with her she didn't show it. Later Sidney Skolsky, who was on the set, said that Marilyn was a good sport and told him Joe had only come to the set to see his favorite star, Ethel Merman. Personally, I didn't believe Marilyn was one bit hurt because she and Joe had an understanding when they were married that she would not interfere with his business life, nor he with hers. Marilyn always has been very frank in saying that there are many things she'd rather do than watch a baseball game, and Joe laughs at that. I remember two occasions when Marilyn went all by herself to important business affairs in her life. One was the time she received a magazine award. Joe told her, 'It's yours baby. Go and get your prize and come home to me.' So Marilyn appeared late (as usual) on the arm of a friend of hers and Joe's. Another occasion was a party of celebrities. Marilyn, wearing long black gloves and looking very pretty despite the unbecoming gown selected for her by her studio, whispered in my ear, 'Joe is going to pick me up after the party. There are too many people here. You know he doesn't like all this publicity and he won't get dressed up even for me.'...Marilyn came to see me when she returned from her honeymoon and did a radio show for me and an interview. She said at that time that she wanted to make a go of her marriage more than anything in the world...Marilyn has never forgotten that she was let go at her own studio, and every once in a while when she kicks up her heels I believe this is uppermost in her mind. However, she must be grateful for *Gentlemen Prefer Blondes*, which put her in the star class, and for *How to Marry a Millionaire*. Marilyn suffers from an inferiority complex, despite all her great success and popularity. Once, when she was to be on a radio show with me she became violently ill because she was so frightened...She and Joe waited a long time before they decided on their surprise wedding. Then when Marilyn was put on suspension for refusing to do *Pink Tights*, she took off on a honeymoon telling her studio only a half hour before her marriage. I always thought it was Joe who influenced her to be independent. He was always independent and did as he pleased when he was the big baseball king. I wish Marilyn could be as happy always as she was when she came home from her honeymoon. Although she was suffering from a heavy cold and actually had pneumonia in Korea, she was happier than I have ever seen her. She had entertained the GIs in Korea, something she had wanted to do for a long time. Joe was by her side all the time. As for Marilyn and Joe, I only hope they can enjoy their success without so many disturbing factors. I believe their marriage is stable, and although I could be wrong, I think they will both do everything within their power to keep it successful if only the rumor hounds will let them alone."

Marilyn films her first scene on September 14th. It is the window scene filmed at a brownstone at 164 E. 61 St. Among the photographers who were present to shoot publicity stills were Sam Shaw, George Barris, Gary Winogrand, Elliott Erwitt, Bob Henriques, Earle Dowd and Joseph H. Coudert. Interestingly Mr. Coudert and his wife lived in the 61 St. brownstone next-door to the one where Marilyn was filming in. As he was a professional photographer, Mr. Coudert seized the opportunity to photograph "the girl" in her upstairs apartment. During the photo shoot Mr. Codert stepped into the bathroom to change the film in his camera. When he came out, he learned that all the other photographers had left for the day. With her permission, he continued to photograph Marilyn alone.

Photographer Elliott Erwitt remembered working with Marilyn during *Seven Year Itch*, "...What struck me then was how really funny she was and very bright--extremely bright. I hadn't known this. I had always thought that all those amusing remarks she was supposed to have made for the press had probably been manufactured and mimeographed by her press agent, but they weren't. She was a very bright person, an instinctive type, especially when the situation seemed right. Very rarely does one meet a truly witty woman. Marilyn Monroe was one. Above all, she was funny, an amusing, witty person."

The *Winnipeg Free Press* ran a story about her filming, "A road-block named Marilyn Monroe closed one full block of East 61st Street to traffic for four hours one day this week. The result was almost chaos. All of Miss Monroe's artfully distributed 118 pounds, partially covered by a white terrycloth bathrobe and a mink coat, arrived on 61st Street at 8a.m. Monday to begin work on the motion-picture version of *Seven Year Itch*. Soon thereafter much of the block between Third and Lexington avenues was filled by about 1,000 spectators, including some 500 male students from a nearby High School. During the morning, the favorite day-dream of American males finished two scenes for the movie. Her task in each of them was to lean half of herself--the upper half--out of two different windows in a remodeled brownstone apartment building, while Tom Ewell, the male lead, scurried about the sidewalk....During the scenes, Miss Monroe spoke a total of seven words. In the first scene she said, 'hey!' and tossed a pair of shoes out the window to Mr. Ewell. In the second, she said, 'Hi! I just washed my hair,' as she plied an electric dryer in the window. Constantly helped and advised by her dramatic coach, Miss Natasha Lytess, the platinum blonde actress carried out her duties satisfactorily. The only real problem facing the director and his crew was the uninvited audience. When Miss Monroe was not appearing at the window shouts went up. 'Where's Marilyn' and 'we want Marilyn.' When she came to the window she was greeted with wolf-calls galore."

During filming at the Brownstone Marilyn was greeted by a friend from the past, Roddy

McDowell.

Leonard Lyons reported on a special spectator to Marilyn's filming. "Eleanor Roosevelt left her East Side apartment for a luncheon date one day. She saw a crowd of people on E. 61 St. and stopped to look. 'Guess what?' she later reported to her luncheon companion. 'I saw Marilyn Monroe.'"

After filming, Marilyn retires to her room at the St. Regis, and gets some needed rest. The rest of her stay will be filled with things to do. Later that evening, Marilyn and Joe attend a Broadway production of *The Teahouse of the August Moon*, starring David Wayne. The play was housed at the Martin Beck Theatre.

On September 15th Marilyn filmed the famous "skirt scene" outside the Trans-Lux 52nd St. Theatre on Lexington Ave in New York City, 1:00 to 4:00am. What was supposedly an unpublicized event was attended by hundreds of members of the press and over a thousand fans. Among the photographers present were Milton H. Greene, Sam Shaw, Bill Kobrin a free-lance photographer who was shooting stills for Twentieth Century-Fox, Gary Winogrand, Tom Cunningham, George Zimbel, Bernard of Hollywood, and *Associated Press* Photographer Matty Zimmerman.

Saul Pett described the scene. "It was a chilly night and Marilyn, in a thin dress, had to have her skirts blown up at least 20 times before the scene was done. In the movie, the sequence will consume about 30 seconds, if the censor doesn't cut it out. In the shooting, it took four hours. Each time her skirts went up, the mob howled, whistled, applauded. I asked Marilyn if she minded the crowd. 'Oh, I love it,' she bubbled. 'I love it.'"

Walter Winchell brought Joe DiMaggio to see the spectacle. He had seen Joe and George Solotaire at the King Cole Bar in the St. Regis Hotel around 11:40pm and had talked Joe into coming to watch Marilyn film this classic scene. Joe didn't really want to come. He said he never watches and he didn't want to. Walter Winchell was very persuasive and against his better judgment, Joe went. While watching the men 'oogling' Marilyn, he was heard to say, "Just what the hell is going on here?!" He and George left and went to wait for Marilyn inside the theatre. Amy Greene was there also and witnessed the fury on Joe's face as he watched his wife's panties exposed to the leering crowd.

The scene that was shot this evening was not even used in the film, they later re-shot the scene on a soundstage back in Hollywood. This was just a publicity event designed to rouse public interest in the film. It also helped to make Marilyn an icon.

Earl Wilson brought Gina Lollobrigida by to meet Marilyn. He took a photograph of the two stars "eyeing" each other, then whisked Gina away. A newspaper article from July 26, 1959 recalls the meeting of these two divas. "Gina Vs. Marilyn...At Ciampino, Rome's airport, Gina was asked by reporters whether she would try to outdo a recent sensational arrival at New York's Idlewild airport by Marilyn Monroe. With an angry flash of her brown eyes that nearly gave sunstroke to nearby reporters and--according to one unreliable witness--caused others to fumble in in their pockets for their dark glasses. Gina reported, 'Any competition between Miss Monroe and myself will be confined not to the airfield, but to the field of drama.'...At the American airport she faced a more formidable Press barrage.

She was asked, 'What do you think of Marilyn Monroe?' Says Gina, 'I didn't know what to say.' I looked at Milko. He stared blankly back at me. The reporters were grinning, the camera flashbulbs popping. Finally I blurted out, 'I think we have a little in common.' I couldn't understand why everyone, including Milko, roared with laughter--till a reporter called out, 'Correction, Gina! You mean you have a lot in common!" Director Billy Wilder introduced Marilyn Monroe to Gina. Marilyn wore a very low-cut dress of white-silk jersey. Said Gina, 'How do you do?' Marilyn sighed. There was an embarrassed silence, then Marilyn revealed, 'They call me the Lollobrigida of America.' Responded Gina, 'They call me the Marilyn Monroe of Italy.' Both (being good actresses) managed to look flattered. Reporters argued among themselves about which of them qualified for the 'World Cheesecake' title. Most agreed it was a draw. A woman journalist was heard to observe incredulously, 'It isn't a question of who has the mostest--but how they manage to keep it that way!' (Gina told me, 'I noticed Marilyn was a little bigger than me.') Both gave different theories in separate interviews. Gina, a voracious eater, never diets to keep her 36-22-35 figure (exercise helped her to get back to these measurements after the birth of Milko junior); Marilyn--38 1/2-23-36--diets sometimes ('Nothing drastic. I just concentrate on meat.') She is 5ft, 5 1/2in, half-inch taller than Gina. Both emphasize their charms with a chin-in chest-out posture that delights Guards, drill sergeants--and the rest of the world's male population. In fact, when they are 'on parade' they parade their assets so conscientiously that one reporter claimed he 'thought they were looking down their noses at each other.' Later Gina said to Milko, 'Marilyn is very beautiful--but not very happy.'"

Inside the Trans-Lux Theater, used as the backdrop for the scene, were members of the press and other specially invited guests. John Ringling North stopped by to meet Marilyn. It was a curious meeting, as Marilyn will have one of her biggest publicity coups when she rides a pink elephant in the circus parade next March for the Ringling Bros. Barnum & Bailey Circus. Walter Winchell assisted the press photographers in securing photos of Marilyn while she was in the theater. Earl Wilson was there with his camera shooting photos and having his own photo taken with Marilyn and Gina. Joe DiMaggio was not feeling well. A cake was delivered to celebrate the first anniversary of CinemaScope. Marilyn gamely cut the cake for the photographers. Marilyn participated in 20 or more retakes of the "skirt" scene. By the time it was all over it was almost dawn and Marilyn was exhausted and getting sick.

After filming the skirt blowing scene Marilyn and Joe are heard fighting in their hotel room. According to some reports, Marilyn had bruises that had to be covered with makeup for her photos shoots the next day. These are not the first suspicious bruises Marilyn will have. During the making of *Show Business* writer Rita Garrison Malloy will note, "recently she appeared on the set with black and blue bruises on her arm. When we asked her about it, she giggled and said, 'I bite myself in my sleep.' I think that was a gag. She probably bumped her arm." There was indication that, from her broken thumb on her honeymoon to the bruises during *Seven Year Itch*, Joe DiMaggio didn't hesitate to enforce his anger in a physical manner. It is also a culture and time that sees nothing wrong with "knocking your broad around a bit to keep her in line."

Marilyn had a sitting with Philippe Halsman later that day, which showed no bruises in the photographs. Hollywood makeup could work miracles it seems. Marilyn was wearing a backless top and skirt. He took many portrait photographs to show her range of expressions. He uses these shots as an emotion study. They appear in a later edition of a British magazine, *Picture Post*. There were several head shots used for the "Pick-A-Star" competition. You had to pick six from the gallery. If you won, you were awarded 200 pounds.

Philippe also makes his first "jump" photo with Marilyn. He was a bit puzzled because every time she was photographed jumping she pulled her legs up and you couldn't see them. He finally deduced that she had spent all night posing on the subway grate, with everyone photographing her legs, that it was a natural thing for them to be hidden now. He believed the jump photos revealed the subjects hidden psychological motives. When Marilyn found out, she refused to jump anymore. He was satisfied with her efforts, though, as she was the most famous torso in the world.

Halsman describes Marilyn jumping for the camera. "Since I didn't have any jumping pictures of her, I asked her to jump for me. She did. I was greatly surprised to see the embodiment of sex appeal jump like a small, immature girl. I said to her, 'Will you jump again; I'm not sure you expressed your character the first time.' 'You mean you can read my character from my jump!' she asked. 'Of course,' I replied. She then looked at me with big, frightened eyes and trembled and wouldn't jump anymore.'"

Halsman would go on to say, "Though I have photographed hundreds of actresses, I have never seen one with a greater inferiority complex. I know that a human being is a most complicated creature and that it would be foolish to try to explain all of a person's character by picking one quality. Nevertheless, Marilyn Monroe's inferiority feelings played such a preponderant role in her character that almost everything falls into place if you try to see it from this angle. She always had the feeling that she was not good enough, the she was unworthy; even her sex appeal stemmed from this. When she faced a man she didn't know, she felt safe and secure only when she knew that the man desired her; so everything in her life was geared to provoke this feeling. Her talent in this respect was very great. I remember my experience in her tiny apartment. Her inferiority complex made her spend hour in front of the mirror and be always late for appointments. She was never sure that she looked pretty enough and spent hours correcting—adding a little lipstick, removing a little mascara, and so on. She was late because she was always afraid that after winning over an audience in one place, she would find an unfriendly one in another; and she would do anything to avoid facing the entire struggle over again. The only way she knew to get herself accepted was to make herself desired. Her behavior in this direction was so strong that it even worked with the camera."

Sometime before she left town, Marilyn visited Jean Howard, wife of her agent Charles Feldman, at her East Seventy-seventh street studio in New York. Miss Howard had photographed Marilyn in 1953 on the set of *How to Marry a Millionaire*. Marilyn, true to form, arrived an hour and a-half late. She posed with a birdcage which Tony Duquette had given Miss Howard. Marilyn was wearing what she called her "lucky" dress. It was a black, body-hugging dress with thin spaghetti straps. Miss Howard was interested in taking some different shots other than the usual sexy, posed ones. She gave Marilyn her favorite Hattie Carnegie jacket in black taffeta to wear. In the resulting photo, Miss Howard said, "I found the true spirit and soul of that beautiful, gifted girl." Marilyn and Jean found themselves together at a party given by Gloria Vanderbilt in the fall of 1955. Marilyn announced that Jean had taken the best picture of her she had ever taken.

The DiMaggio's return to California on September 16th. Joe didn't stay after all to attend the Marciano/Charles fight. Obviously, he had done enough fighting of his own with Marilyn. According to Hedda Hopper, Joe checked into a Hollywood hotel under an assumed name. Before she left town, Marilyn found out that she wasn't going to star in *Guys and Dolls* after all. Marilyn was wanting to work with Marlon Brando, although, she would have played the love interest of Frank Sinatra in the film. This might have made up for her refusal to star opposite him in *Pink Tights*, which she felt was an inferior script. Marilyn would have done an excellent job as Miss Adelaide, and the song and dance numbers would have become further legendary images of Marilyn. She was deeply disappointed that Joseph Mankiewicz didn't give her the part of Miss Adelaide in *Guys and Dolls*. Instead, he cast Vivian Blaine, who had starred in the role on Broadway. Marilyn had ambitiously called Samuel Goldwyn himself about wanting to do *Guys and Dolls*, only to be told, "Have you talked to your boss, Darryl Zanuck?" Whether Fox didn't want to loan out their high-powered star or a vendetta against her for not doing *Pink Tights*, once again Fox went overboard to prove that she worked for them and they would decide what movies she made. Marilyn's anger was building against Fox and it wouldn't be long before she rebelled against their tight grip on her career.

Due to illness on September 17th, Marilyn did not go to the studio. According to her doctor, she had the flu. She is to have two more days of rest due to the flu and nervous exhaustion. She also made plans to have her wardrobe fittings at her Beverly Hills home. Plans were in the works to film the much talked-about bathtub scene on Friday.

Edwin Schallert reported on September 17th, "Marilyn Monroe's first scene following her return to Hollywood from New York yesterday with Joe DiMaggio will be in a bathtub. She tries to stop a leaking faucet with her toe, which gets stuck in the outlet. Whereupon Victor Moore as a plumber appears upon the scene to extract the toe. He loses his wrench in the bathtub. It then becomes a problem to rescue this."

Hedda Hopper reported on September 24th, "I was hysterical watching dear, sweet Victor Moore walk into Westmore's to have his pink hair dyed brown for his role as a plumber with Marilyn Monroe and Tom Ewell in *Seven Year Itch*. 'I've never seen anything like the excitement in Sardi's when Marilyn Monroe walked in,' Tom told me. 'The entire place stopped. She took New York like that hurricane, and I don't mean her publicity. Everybody worships this girl.' Tom was amazed when Joe DiMaggio walked over to him while he was waiting to do a scene and said quietly, 'I saw the play and loved your performance.' 'I nearly flipped,' said Tom, 'because Joe ain't a talking man.'"

Hedda Hopper again reported about the bathtub scene on November 9th, "Chosen Few Witness Marilyn's Bath Scene...When Marilyn Monroe made the bathtub scene in *Seven Year Itch* at 20th the gates of the sound stage were locked tight as any atomic project. Billy Wilder had lined up his camera crew for the scene in which Marilyn gets her toe stuck in the faucet and a plumber, played by Victor Moore, is trying to free her. A gallery of males with a sprinkling of make-up women and hairdressers were jockeying for position when Marilyn came on stage wrapped in a huge Turkish towel. A barrage of flashlights from still cameras as she held a whispered consultation with her maid, then a screen was raised while Marilyn dropped the towel and stepped into the tub. A murmur of disappointment at this changed to a delighted 'aaaaaah!' as the screen was pulled back. 'Lots of bubbles,' shouted Wilder and a soapy froth rose like a cloud framing her rosy face and arms, her moongold hair in disarray. 'No soap on the legs and feet,' said Wilder, 'more around the torso.' The bubbleman obliged. Marilyn tucked her toe into the faucet, made a little grimace. 'Get the bubbles off her legs and feet,' said Wilder. Victor Moore obliged with alacrity. Tom Ewell tugged at my jacket: 'I'm here purely in the capacity of a technical adviser,' he grinned. 'Wouldn't miss this for the world.' Next to me stood Cleveland Amory, 'Aren't you playing hooky from Metro?' I asked. 'This is a big moment,' he said, 'this is something to tell my grandchildren. I even met my agent for the first time here,' and he nodded at Charles Feldman. Marilyn flicked her deep-sea eyes at the audience--the barest glance. 'Did you ever see anything like her?' Amory asked. 'That unbelievable childishness...she's unique.' 'Let's run through the lines,' said Wilder. 'When she comes to the cue, Victor, drop the wrench into the tub then grope for it.' Marilyn took on a faraway look: 'Then he lured me to his apartment...' she said in throaty tones. 'He made me sit on the piano bench...he made me play *Chopsticks*...then suddenly he turned on me...his eyes were bulging...he was frothing at the mouth...he was just the *Creature from the Black Lagoon*....' 'Hold it,' said Wilder. 'Victor, you forgot to drop the wrench.' Moore came out of a trance, nodded, and they began again. This time the wrench clattered into the tub and Moore groped. 'Hold it,' said Wilder. 'I'm disappointed in you, Victor. Grope a little higher up.' They began again. This time Victor groped nearer the knee. Wilder nodded, 'okay.' A production man took-over. 'Quiet,' he shouted. 'Let's all get set for a good clean take.' 'Let's have a good one,' said Billy Wilder, 'a clean one it'll never be.'"

Wilder on working with Marilyn in *Seven Year Itch*, "I think she thinks up those funny things for herself. I think also she says those funny things without realizing that they're so funny. One very funny thing she said involves the fact that she has great difficulties in remembering her lines. Tremendous difficulties. I've heard of one director who wrote her lines on a blackboard and kept that blackboard just out of camera range. The odd thing is that if she has a long scene for which she has to remember a lot of words, she's fine once she gets past the second word. If she gets over that one little hump, there's no trouble. Then, too, if you start a scene and say, 'Action!' and hers is the first line, it takes her ten or fifteen seconds together herself. Nothing happens during those fifteen seconds. It seems a very long time. For instance, if she had to say, 'Good morning, Mr. Sherman,' she couldn't get out the word 'morning.' She'd say, 'Good…' and stick. Once she got 'morning' out, she'd be good for two pages of dialogue. It's just that sometimes she trips over mental stumbling blocks at the beginning of a scene."

Marilyn's grip on the interest of the public is well illustrated in this article by Eric Brandeis in *The Bridgeport Telegram,* Conn., newspaper article on September 30th, "My morning paper carried several important stories on the front page. There was an important conference Secretary of State Dulles and Chiang Kai-shek in Taipei, Formosa. A hurricane was threatening our whole New England coast. Thousands of homes might be destroyed. Millions of dollars of damage might be caused. My own home was threatened. In Algeria, there had been an earthquake. More than a thousand people had been killed. Whole towns had been destroyed. The nearby Silver Lakes Dam was damaged and it's waters might flood many other communities and kill thousands more people. But, serenely looking out of my front page there was a picture of Marilyn Monroe, crossing her beautiful legs, sitting on a couch which somehow or other had made its way to the outdoors at Idlewild Airport, happily smiling at the whole world--and at me. And here is part of the accompanying story: 'Five hundred airline employees and everyone else in the vicinity broke through police barriers to howl and whistle and ogle the platinum blonde actress. Jaded mechanics, clerks and porters, who have seen notables and personages come and go and barely turned their heads, lost their aplomb when Miss Monroe, clad in a form-fitting beige wool dress with a matching topcoat trimmed with beige fur over her shoulders stepped from the plane.' I simply could not understand the simplicity of the thousands of intelligent readers of this paper who would read such a silly story as this. Neither could I understand the mentality of all those airport employees who would 'lose their aplomb' over a pretty pair of legs and what other appliances went with them. Then I caught myself. I myself, read every word of that story--and the hundreds more words than those I have quoted. I caught myself looking admiringly at the pictures. There were several other pictures on the front page, all of which I have forgotten by now. I let Dulles, Chiang-Kai-shek and all the other world-shaking events go by the board in order to read all about the arrival of an actress and to bask in the glory of her legs and her sexy smile. My wife saw me read that story. She saw the gleam in my eye, and that faraway look that seemed to tell her that I would have liked to have been one of those who were present at Marilyn Monroe's triumphal arrival at Idlewild. She didn't say anything, though. What is it that makes men make such fools of themselves over a pretty girl? I don't know. When my paper arrived I had been reading a book on philosophy. That certainly didn't give me the answer, although it did say that the three greatest things on earth are Beauty, Goodness and Truth. I wonder how many of these elements are in Marilyn Monroe. I must ask Joe DiMaggio sometime. He ought to know. Oh, by the way, there was still another item on the front page. It said that by the year 2000 men will dress with the elegance of women and will wear lace on their trouser cuffs. They will wear tapering trousers which will reveal the calf, and shoulder lines will puff to emphasize the masculine chest. That's when we men will get even with Marilyn Monroe!"

Marilyn retains famed lawyer Jerry Giesler on October 1st, and has him draw up divorce papers, she also has Joe DiMaggio barred from entering the Twentieth Century-Fox Studio lot. Joe DiMaggio returns home from New York, where he had been covering the World Series, the next day and Marilyn tells him she has filed papers for a divorce. Joe moves from their bedroom to the den downstairs. Neighbors report hearing loud arguments at their home that night, and also report seeing Marilyn out walking for hours late at night.

John Chapman reported on October 3rd, "Lensmen Like Marilyn--But Who Doesn't?...Couple of weeks ago the photographers of this town [New York] were having a busy and happy time. Marilyn Monroe, who probably is the all-time favorite of the fotogs-- and not just because she makes a pretty picture--was making some scenes here for the film version of *Seven Year Itch*, including one in which she gets her skirt blown skyward as she walks over a subway grating. (Practically an impossibility, incidentally. Most sidewalk subway gratings are not directly over the train tracks, but are offset, and a passing train makes no breeze above.)...The reason newspicture men are daffy about Miss Monroe is not that she is such a handsome dish. The men on the airport, ship news and railroad station beats get plenty of photogenic subjects and one more or less isn't going to make them swoon. They like Marilyn because she is a regular guy--never temperamental, never patronizing, never in a hurry and the most expert photographers model in moviedom. One cameraman I know says it is practically impossible to make a bad shot of the lady. Why? Because she almost always keeps her eyes open and her mouth open. He challenged me, 'Did you ever see a picture of Marilyn Monroe with her mouth closed?' Come to think of it I never have.'"

# Chapter Sixteen
## Birth Pains of the "New" Marilyn

"A part of her is totally alone, like a little child in a new school, mystified as to how it got there and passionately looking for a friendly face."
Arthur Miller

Marilyn and Joe set the world tumbling when it is announced that its favorite married couple will divorce after being wed less than a year. It is unbelievable news and it knocks other newsworthy stories off the front pages.

Aline Mosby reported on October 4th, "'Joe Has Struck Out'; Marilyn Monroe Will Divorce DiMaggio... Marilyn Monroe revealed today she will file suit to divorce baseball great Joe DiMaggio tomorrow, and her attorney reluctantly agreed 'Joe has struck out.' The world's favorite blonde dutifully telephoned her studio to announce she and the former New York Yankee star had agreed to a friendly divorce 'because our careers just seemed to get in the way of each other.' Then the shapely film star retired to her bed at home with a 'nervous disorder,' leaving her lawyer, Jerry Giesler, to face a small army of 40 reporters and photographers who crowded on the front lawn. Giesler made it clear the nine-month marriage--the most publicized Hollywood match in a decade--was finished. 'There is no chance of reconciliation,' Giesler, famed for handling celebrity's troubles, told them this was based on general incompatibility with her. The break-up is not sudden, but has been brewing for quite some time. 'She will not seek alimony. The divorce will be filed in Santa Monica Superior Court tomorrow or Wednesday, the charges will be innocuous, probably mental cruelty based on general incompatibility. No community property is involved.' Giesler said he talked to the bosomy blonde in her upstairs bedroom while DiMaggio remained downstairs. Joe did not plan to move out of the house today 'as far as I know,' the lawyer said. Though the DiMaggio's apparently had been under tension during most of their marriage, the separation of the baseball player and the blonde rocked the movie colony. The news shocked not only 20th Century-Fox workers but also most of her closest friends. They had pegged Marilyn and Joe as still happy honeymooners. 'I promised I'd tell you when I got married and I told you I'd call if there was any trouble,' Marilyn told Fox publicist Harry Brand. 'We've agreed to separate because of conflicting career demands.' The only hint that all was not perfect in the DiMaggio's love nest, a large Spanish-style home in Beverly Hills, was that the one-time baseball player had been in New York as much as he's been here during their nine-month marriage. One friend reported the couple been 'bickering' lately, 'but in New York it seemed they had made up.' The film star's work has kept her in Hollywood while DiMaggio has been busy with television and newspaper work in New York. Marilyn always claimed that the couple had not selected a permanent home 'because Joe doesn't know where he wants to settle and our home will be where his work is.' The actress, who soared to fame after revealing she posed nude for a calendar, visited her husband in New York recently when her current picture, *Seven Year Itch*, was shooting there. A studio worker who accompanied the couple reported they were 'affectionate, comfortable, and Joe couldn't have looked happier.' However, a friend pointed out DiMaggio hates the limelight, and Marilyn turned the big city into a small town full of adoring following fans. He was reportedly irritated when Marilyn was filmed standing over a subway air vent with her skirts blowing over her head. The baseball star returned to Hollywood late Saturday night following the end of the World Series and he and his curvaceous wife made a decision to end one of the most publicized marriages in a decade. The actress conferred with famed filmland attorney, Jerry Giesler, yesterday and decided to seek a divorce on grounds of mental cruelty. 'They've talked it over and reached a pleasant understanding,' the attorney said. 'We're going ahead with the divorce to be filed in California. Marilyn told her studio she didn't feel like working today and would meet with Giesler instead. However, she also canceled that appointment and went into seclusion at her home. Marilyn's closest friend, columnist Sidney Skolsky, blamed the break-up on 'a case of conflicting personalities.' Yet, he pointed out, Marilyn and Joe's home life, for the most part, had seemed happy. The couple kept steady company for nearly two years to make sure they wanted to marry. Marilyn had met Joe on a blind date. Despite the fact he didn't like the Hollywood life and she knew nothing about baseball they fell in love. Marilyn then told interviewers, 'If I marry, and I want to, my career would have to work into my marriage or I'd do without the career. You can't curl up with a career on a cold night.'"

Divorce papers are filed by Marilyn's attorney, Jerry Giesler, on October 5th, in the Superior Court of the State of California, in and for the county of Los Angeles; No. S.M.p-12301; Norma Jeane DiMaggio, Plaintiff, vs. Joseph Paul DiMaggio, Defendant. Complaint for divorce on the grounds of mental cruelty.

Hedda Hopper reported on October 5th, "Marilyn Monroe Will Divorce Joe DiMaggio...Marilyn Monroe yesterday decided to divorce Joe DiMaggio. The voluptuous actress instructed her attorney, Jerry Giesler, to file suit today on grounds of mental cruelty. And then she went back to her 'honeymoon house' at 508 N Palm Drive, Beverly Hills, to talk over the separation with Joe. 'They're both indisposed,' a maid told everyone ringing the doorbell. Pigeons billed and cooed under the eaves of the high-pitched English roof and in the jacaranda and juniper trees of the yard, but it was nothing like that with America's No. 1 pinup girl and her husband, one of the greatest baseball players of all time. 'Our careers just seemed to get in the way of each other,' Miss Monroe told Harry Brand, 20th Century-Fox publicity chief. Giesler said the couple 'talked it over' all day and 'reached a pleasant understanding.' The lawyer said the divorce complaint will be filed today in Santa Monica with no specific charges. The actress will not ask for alimony, Giesler stated....Joe and Marilyn drove to my house just before their New York trip. Joe waited in a limousine outside with a friend and then rapped on the door to warn her it was time to leave. I asked him if he didn't think Marilyn looked wonderful. He said, 'She looks nice.' I chided him by saying, 'Joe, you can do better than that." He said, 'I'll try hard.' I asked why he didn't fly back in the same plane with her and he complained of hives...But he boarded a plane for New York that following night. I wrote then that 'I could be wrong,' but I knew it was over. His attitude told the story. She's on top of the heap. He's a great star without a job. They come from two separate worlds--sports and motion pictures. Sports writers have told his story: A lifetime batting average of .325 in 13 seasons with the Yankees, 2214 hits, 361 home runs and 1537 runs batted in. The Yankees paid him a total of $704,761 and before he quit three years ago he was earning $100,000 a year. But somehow his feats like eight World Series homers didn't match up with smash hits she was making in pictures. It would have been different if she had been struggling up the ladder when they were married but she was already a star when the San Francisco judge performed that ceremony last Jan. 14. He went with her to Korea and saw troops stampede every time the Monroe hurricane blew in. After that the great centerfielder never met her halfway. He forgot that she, as well as he, had hit the top. He was just a restaurant boy on Fisherman's Wharf when he began playing baseball. She was an alumna of the Los Angeles Orphanage. Her father died early and her mother had a prolonged illness. She had 12 sets of foster parents before she was 16. She finished school at 16, was married at 17 to Jim Dougherty, a boy in the merchant marine, and divorced at 18 (Dougherty married again and now is a policeman in Van Nuys.) DiMaggio married another actress, Dorothy Arnold, in 1937 and they were divorced in 1944. She has principal custody of their son, Joe II, who is now 12. DiMaggio met Marilyn Monroe on a blind date. At the time they were married, she never had seen a baseball game. She was a model, a famed calendar girl and an actress in the $3500-a-week bracket, with options being snapped up as 20th Century-Fox never has snapped so eagerly before. But Joe would never go to any of the premieres. He skipped the parties that were a must as far as she was concerned. He preferred to stay home and play poker with his friends. I don't think the ages matter too much (he's 39; she's 27) but he has to remember she's on top of the heap and he's out of a job. He has done radio and television work since retiring from baseball, plus newspaper writing on the World Series but he is no longer on the field. During the series in New York he stayed at the Madison Hotel at the suite of George Solitaire, ticket broker. He came back to Los Angeles over the week end. Marilyn missed going to the studio yesterday but she'll return today to the set of *Seven Year Itch*. I keep thinking of that night last month when Joe brought her to my house. He was surly and scowled and said, 'Come on...you'll be late.' And I was warning her that she'd better get a police escort the minute she got to New York. She asked, 'What for?' I told her, 'They'll tear you limb from limb.' And Marilyn looked up at me then with those baby blue eyes and asked innocently, 'Do you think I'll cause a sensation?'"

According to Dorothy Kilgallen on October 5th, Marilyn placed an order with Beverly Hills' top furrier for a new blonde mink coat, reported to have cost $15,000.

Even Marilyn's first husband, James Dougherty, gets in on the act. He is interviewed by George Carpozi, Jr., and it quickly hits the newspapers on the 5th. Marilyn, to her credit, refused to talk about intimate details of her marriage with Jim to reporters. He, on the other hand, did not extend that loyalty to her. He comes off a more than a little bitter in his comments on her. "Only last July, Marilyn had told me on the long-distance phone that she and Joe wanted children. I mentioned that to Jim. 'And you believed her?' he asked. 'You should have asked me,' Dougherty continued. 'I could have told you. Marilyn is a movie star. She doesn't want children. She wants a career. I don't know Joe personally, but I know fellows who are pretty close to him. They told me about his hopes for a large family. No guy in his right mind should marry a gal who runs around town with her skirts up in the air.

That's not the Marilyn I married. The girl I married wasn't that type at all. When I first met her she was going to Union [University] High School here. We were introduced by her foster aunt, and went out together about six months. Then we got married. We were happy together. We had a nice little apartment and she was an average housewife. She liked to stay home and didn't insist on nightclubbing or dancing.' What broke up Jim's marriage to Marilyn was an offer that come out of the blue for her to become a model. 'I was in the Merchant Marine then. She jumped at the chance. And she told me she had to be single to be an actress.' 'Have you talked with Marilyn since your divorce?' I asked. 'Only once—that was four years ago when she called and said that some newspaper reporter would call me for a story about her. She wanted certain facts about her quiet. The reporter never called…I know this gal and I can tell you children are the farthest thing from her mind. Maybe it's because she's got her mind so occupied with becoming an actress—and trying to be on time. She was always late when she was married to me.'"

On October 6th the Press congregates at the DiMaggio home, 508 N Palm Drive, as Joe leaves the residence at 10am and Marilyn and her lawyer, Jerry Giesler, leave together at 10:55am. Marilyn goes to the home of Dr. Khron, and then to 20th Century Fox Studios for a couple of hours, then she returns home and is put to bed.

Newsreel footage captures one of Marilyn's best performances as she waivers and makes her way through the army of waiting press, clinging to the arm of her attorney. She tries to speak, then is overcome with emotion. It is very effective, and the public will have great sympathy for her. Jerry Giesler's gives a statement to the press and physically supports Marilyn as she teeters dangerously close to collapse.
Giesler: Miss Monroe will have nothing to say this morning, and all I can say as her attorney is that this is what we say with a conflict of careers. And as public as it may be, it will have to be presented in the proper place. That's all I can say.
The reporters are trying to get Marilyn to answers questions.
Reporter: The reason for you divorce is a conflict of careers?
Marilyn: Yes.
Giesler: She's not going to answer any questions.
Still, the reporters barrage her with questions.
Reporter: What picture are you working on now?
Marilyn: I'm working...," she staggers back, then mumbles, "On *Seven Year Itch*."
Giesler: Please don't ask her anymore. We're going out to the studio now.
Reporter: Has Joe moved out finally?
Marilyn looks up and then starts to sob.
Giesler: You saw him. You saw him. I don't know if he's moved out or not. You saw him go out. He went out anyway.
Reporter: Marilyn are you going to leave this house?
Giesler: No, I'm not...we're not going to answer that question.
Marilyn: I'm sorry, I have to go. I'm sorry.
They finally make it to Giesler's car and Marilyn is photographed dabbing her eyes with a

handkerchief as they exit the pandemonium. Yet, she cannot be nearly as fragile as she has acted.

Louella Parsons reported on October 6th, "Joe's Jealousy of Marilyn Told In Rift" in which she cites a visit to the hospital with Marilyn's voice coach, Hal Schafer, during which he denies any romance with Marilyn. She also mentions Marilyn's late night walks in her neighborhood.

James Bacon reported on October 7th, "DiMaggio Steals Final Scene...Marilyn, Joe Part Amid Tears, Flashing Cameras... It's back to *Seven Year Itch* for Marilyn Monroe with no Joe DiMaggio to scratch her back. And there is no joy in Fisherman's Wharf today even though the mighty DiMaggio has struck out for there. Barring complications, the blonde blockbuster will report for a 9 a.m. (PST) call on her picture which has been shooting around her during the recent unpleasantness. She slept alone last night in the $1,000-a-month Beverly Hills home that she and Joe rented. DiMaggio left her yesterday in about as final a departure as Hollywood ever has seen. When Joe came out of the house with his bags packed and a grim smile on his face, he seemed to write period for all time on the most publicized marriage since that of Queen Elizabeth and Prince Philip. It may have been Marilyn's greatest performance before the photographers, but Joe stole the scene from his actress wife. About 100 newsmen and photographers chronicled this little bit of movieland history--many more than greeted President Eisenhower's visit here last month. Marilyn, for the first time, lost her composure before the press and had nothing to say. She sobbed almost to the point of collapse. Some cynics called them phony tears, but Marilyn would be the first to admit that she isn't a good enough actress to play the scene the way it was played. Her departure from the house was billed as a return to work but actually it never was intended to be. She wasn't in the mood to play comedy and after a five-minute drive to Lawyer Jerry Giesler's office, she returned home. The exit had accomplished its purpose--a general clearing of the small army of newsmen who had staked out for days on her front lawn. As the real reason for the rift remained unanswered, gossips enjoyed a Roman holiday of speculation. There was talk that Joe was jealous. Of Marilyn's admittedly poor cooking and housekeeping. Of the all-consuming demands of her career. There was even talk of another man or another woman. But insiders who know the couple best quickly pooh-poohed that one. Marilyn has been a one-man woman since she met Joe. And what man would look elsewhere with Marilyn waiting at home? The real reason may never be known if the divorce, as expected, is uncontested. Giesler's legal explanation is conflict of careers. Joe said as he drove off for San Francisco in his Cadillac: 'San Francisco always has been my home.'"

Aline Mosby reported on October 7th, "Breakup of DiMaggio and Marilyn....Marilyn Monroe has admitted she and Joe DiMaggio had their battles, but Marilyn figured she knew how to handle them. 'Marriage is something you learn more about while you live it,' she told a reporter early in the marriage. 'Joe and I quarrel like other couples. You can't outlaw human nature. But there's a way to handle a disagreement. Every wife should know her man. When I sense there's something wrong, I ask, 'What's the matter?' 'Sorry if I did something.' If Joe doesn't answer, I don't push it. There are some men who, when they have trouble, become silent. You have to respect that. Later when what was wrong has worn thin, Joe will say, 'I'm sorry.' I'll say, 'What's there to be sorry about?' You'd be surprised how nice it can be, if done this way.' After their marriage lost the frosting of its honeymoon days, arguments became more frequent. Ten days ago, Marilyn talked to attorney Jerry Giesler about a divorce. She spent last weekend crying on the shoulder of Mary Short, Jane Wyman's sister-in-law. When Joe returned last Saturday night, they agreed to break up. The armchair guessers have countless theories as to why the two didn't get along. Joe's pal, Mark Scott says, 'Joe wanted a wife, not a star. Marilyn would come home at night, too tired for anything but sleep. That would leave Joe looking at the television.' Marilyn's drama coach, Natasha Lytess, calls it a case of conflicting personalities. She thinks Marilyn needs a man 'much more sensitive and understanding. They had different values, different frames of mind. It was a gradual growth of difficulties,' she says. Another coach, Michael Chekhov, says Marilyn told him Joe was a 'sweet guy, but we don't have enough in common.' Yet Marilyn and Joe knew each other well for two years before they carefully decided to wed. She terms 'apple sauce' the report he was jealous of her music arranger, Hal Schaefer. The theory that Joe is an introvert and Marilyn an extrovert also is weak. Marilyn actually is a deeply sensitive person. The theory I prefer comes from a famed psychiatrist, who, though not the one who treated Marilyn for nearly three years, said today, 'I doubt if Marilyn is capable of a lasting relationship with any man. When a woman becomes a big star, it's a sure way of self-destruction. A child must have attention from without. When you grow up you must have something inside to sustain you. A star gets so much from the outside--the applause, the frantic worship--she loses whatever she had inside, particularly if she had an unhappy childhood. She has no sense of values. She is again a child.' That truth lies in what Marilyn told me after she returned from Korea with Joe. Her marriage which she had so carefully planned was doomed when she said, 'In Korea for the first time I felt like a movie star. It was the most exciting thing that has ever happened to me.' In New York recently Marilyn got another taste of that fame. She has only begun to realize the peak of her success. It's too soon--or too late--to give it up."

As reported by Aline Mosby, the press even tried to contact Marilyn's psychoanalyst, Dr. Abraham Gottesman, but he, of course, refused to comment on the current state of her marriage or her.

The next day Marilyn returned to the studio and was reported as saying, "I feel alive for the first time in days." And as Whitey Snyder created her face she said, "I had a wonderful night's sleep, too," She played the scene where she apologizes to Tom Ewell for the potted tomato plant that crashed onto the terrace of his apartment from her balcony. She then films the scene where she comes to his apartment in a pair of pink pongee pajamas. The scenes were filmed on a closed set. Marilyn looks remarkably beautiful and rested, given the personal agony she has just endured.

Joe DiMaggio seemed to have made a remarkable recovery the next day also. He sent word out to newspapermen camped on his doorstep that he'd be glad to talk to them as soon as he was dressed. Finally Joe invited the boys in and posed for pictures in a gray sweater, gray flannel slacks and white shirt. He was in good spirits and told the eager press that he realized that they had to ask about the breakup of his marriage, but that he didn't care to say anything about it now.

H. I. Phillips devoted his syndicated column on October 8th, "The Once Over," to the break-up of Marilyn and Joe. "Cupid To Hymen To Crackup...Did Marilyn Monroe bench Joe DiMaggio? Did the Yankee Clipper release her to the Subway Grating League? Were they both struck out by that famous southpaw 'Fatso' Incompatibility? Did Fats use the beanball on both? Or is it possible that Joe bet on the Giants while Marilyn picked the Indians? These are questions friends of baseball, Hollywood, romance, love, the American fireside, homeruns, and perfect legs are still seeking after the surprising news that both called their marriage in the second inning and went to the showers separately. The world is more saddened by what happened to Joe and Marilyn than by anything that happened in the World Series, for DiMaggio is a public idol. Monroe is the reigning queen of Hollywood and everybody hoped the marriage would go the full nine innings regardless of the weather. But the Yankee Clipper played in a league where cheesecake never kept anybody in the lineup and where no weird street photography could fatten a batting average. A good many folks thought they saw something less than approval in Joe's face as he watched the bride stand over a subway grating, skirts over her head, for a photographers' rodeo a few days back. Marilyn seemingly held that, while a girl's heart may belong to daddy, her legs belong to the public. They were from two different leagues. DiMaggio attained the heights with a high regard for taste, standards and reasonable dignity. He had a fine scorn for circus routines and self-exploitation by high pressure press-agentry. Marilyn found the 'anything goes' publicity routine helpful in a phenomenal rise to stardom from a childhood of poverty. In any phase of life the contrast could threaten happiness, and in the Hollywood world of Marilyn Monroe publicity conquers all, anything is done for a headline, taste is for the birds and the slogan is 'If it's box office it's okay.' Despite this, millions of Americans hoped the marriage would meet no 'knucklers,' no spikings and no unlucky bounces. When it saw the odd inning in New York where the bride stood over a subway grating on a crowded street, 'let the winds blow where they may.' It seemed to us that Joe watched sadly. It was a pretty wild pitch by Marilyn. Most husbands, knowing how they would feel if they came upon their wives in such a street scene, were fairly sure she would get a rebuke in the clubhouse. Joe, we think, scored it as a major error. And perhaps in Marilyn's book the Clipper was too 'slow on the Hollywood bases, lacked the right swing in the Press Agentry League and was too inclined to take a third strike instead of a third photograph.' It was such a short marriage that even the lawyers took the mound without a warmup in the bullpen. Nine months? In the lives of people who really love each other, endure much and try hard to make a go of marriage, this doesn't even give time for batting practice. In the Hollywood atmosphere, however, the career is mightier than the bassinet, the box office gets the nod over home, sweet home and the picture of 'Whistler's Mother' never has a chance against 'Monroe's Legs.'"

October 8th was a busy day for Marilyn as she makes plans to move out of the home she shared with Joe DiMaggio in Beverly Hills. She rented an apartment in the Sunset Strip area.

Marilyn and Joe learn that they were responsible for the damage to the landscaping during the tour de force press conference, and they would be getting a bill from their landlady, Barbara Barondess MacLean. Miss MacLean arrived from New York to inspect the damage to the property after the news conference and to try and find a new lessee. Miss MacLean said she plans to get a better screened tenant who will stay a long time. "'The lawn is a wreck,' she said. 'Sightseers and photographers trampled down the rose bushes." A couple who was interested in leasing the home was singer Vic Damone and his bride, actress Pier Angeli. Yet, they might do well to rent another home. It seems the house was a jinx to love. Barbara Barondess MacLean dissolved her marriage to Douglas MacLean when they lived there, Richard Basehart and Valentina Cortesa almost had their marriage end, and now Joe and Marilyn's marriage ended there.

Marilyn's sister, Berniece Miracle, writes her a letter which was sent in care of Twentieth Century-Fox Studio. "Dear Marilyn, The news about you and Joe came as a shock and we were very sorry to hear it. I know you are lonely--do try and come visit us and it may help you over the cloud. You are very busy and all, but if you could fly down here I'm sure you would feel better. We three are just the same as when you saw us last, except a little fatter and older, ha ha. Mona Rae is very bust in school and loves it. She is trying hard to become a cheerleader for the football team this year. We love you loads and hope to see you soon. Your sister, Berniece."

On October 10th Marilyn wrote a check for $50 to the Anthroposophical Press. The publishing company was located in Great Barrington, Massachusetts and offered books by Rudolf Steiner and related authors on Anthroposophy and the science of spirit.

Marilyn moves into her $450-a-month apartment near swanky Sunset Strip on October 10th. It was beautifully furnished in expensive antiques. The next day the rental agent told the landlady that he had already rented the apartment to a doctor from New York. The physician, a friend of the owner's daughter, had signed a lease, gotten the key and paid the advance rent. The next day the owner had the task of 'evicting' Marilyn Monroe from her new apartment. The owner declared that the incident was, "very distressing and embarrassing to all of us. Marilyn's such a nice girl we would love to have her back when we have a vacancy." Marilyn moved back into the home she shared with Joe in Beverly Hills for a short time. The lease on the home didn't expire until October 22nd. Between October 22nd and November 1st she stayed with friends and even spent a couple of nights in her dressing room on the Fox lot. She would move into an apartment on November 1st.

Leonard Lyons made a shrewd observation in his October 11th column when he was asked if it was true what a press agent described in a magazine about taking credit for Marilyn's publicity during her New York visit. "I never saw any press agent around her. Any press agent who takes credit for promoting Miss Monroe has as much right to take bows as the grocer who sold the bread on which Dr. Fleming discovered penicillin."

On October 13th, the legendary French Showgirl, Mistinguette criticized Marilyn's legs. Mille Mistinguete was known as the girl-with-the-million-dollar-legs and she made legs glorious on the French stage and helped pave the way for the modern pin-up girl. She was now a coquettish lady in her 80s and considered herself an authority on the subject. She blasted Marilyn in the press. "This woman Monroe. Never does she show her legs frankly to the camera. Always one knee is pushing into the other or she is standing with her legs apart and the toes pointed out or her dress is cleverly placed around the legs to hide je ne sais quoi (translation: whatever it is she is trying to hide)."

On October 17th Marilyn is photographed awarding 2nd place trophies to Dean Martin and Nicky Hilton at the 4th Annual Hillcrest Country Club Invitational Golf Tournament.

*Robinson-Hannagan Associates, Inc.* on October 19th, "Marilyn Helps Boys...A big day in the life of 15 year-old Bob Wilson came when Marilyn Monroe presented him with 1) a kiss and 2) one of the sweaters she wears in her new movie, *Seven Year Itch*. The sweater was donated to the 'world's biggest rummage sale,' to be staged at Pasadena Civic Auditorium on October 28th, for the benefit of Boys Republic, 35 miles southeast of Los Angeles, where Bob is a student. Boys Republic offers a high school education and a fresh start in life to teen-age boys who need a second chance."

Joe DiMaggio hired the City Detectives and Guard Service private detective firm to follow Marilyn and Hal Schaffer and to try and catch them in a compromising position throughout the dates of October 20, 1954 thru November 5, 1954 -- The case number was 322-I.D.-54. Marilyn was followed throughout her day to day travels in and around West Hollywood and Culver City. She was noted as going between her apartment on DeLongpre, her Attorney's office, Natasha Lytess's apartment, the Twentieth Century-Fox Studio, and her friend's homes where during one visit she picked up a carload of friends to go to a party in Valley Vista. There was never any evidence of an affair between Marilyn and Mr. Schaffer observed in the report.

Marilyn, Joe and Joe, Jr., have a date to celebrate the boy's 12$^{th}$ birthday. Marilyn gifted him with $25 and his father gave him $20. When asked if there was a reconciliation at hand Marilyn replied, "There is no reconciliation. Joe and I are friends and I hope we'll always be friendly.

Joe DiMaggio and Sidney Skolsky go to Marilyn's home and tried unsuccessfully to talk her into reconsidering the impending divorce the night before she goes to court. The next day, October 27th, Marilyn is granted an interlocutory divorce on the grounds of mental cruelty in the Santa Monica Courthouse, Judge Orlando Rhodes presiding. Her business manager Inez Melson testifies on her behalf. Also, with Marilyn in the courtroom is Mary Short, the sister of Marilyn's old love, Fred Karger.

The accusations made by Joe DiMaggio's first wife Dorothy Arnold in 1944, are similar to the ones Marilyn will make. "Joe rarely took me out and spent his entire life with his men friends. He chose not to talk to me for days at a time. He never acted like a married man. He preferred poker with his friends to coming home, except in season when he rigidly observed all training rules."

Ten years later Marilyn will tell the court, "Your Honor, my husband would give in to moods where he wouldn't speak to me for days. Five to even seven days. Sometimes as many as ten days. When I tried to appeal to him he'd say 'Stop nagging me!' I was permitted to have no visitors at any time. I don't believe I asked more than three times in nine months for a visitor. On one occasion when I was sick he allowed someone but it was under terrific strain. I volunteered to give up my work but it didn't change his attitude at all. I hoped to have out of my marriage love, warmth, affection and understand, but in our relationship there was only coldness and indifference."

The court proceedings took only 15 minutes. Marilyn sat in a filled courtroom while Superior Judge Orlando Rhodes heard two other divorce cases before hers. She wore a black flannel suit by Don Loper, which she would tell reporters waiting outside after her proceedings that she got it wholesale for less than $100 because it was last year's model. When asked how she felt after the divorce, she replied, "I feel numb all over." As to whether she still loved DiMaggio, she answered, "We're still friends, and you might say that I don't know anything about baseball yet." Emily Belser reported that Marilyn told reporters, "There are a lot of things I'd like to find out, a lot of places I'd like to go and a lot of things I'd like to learn."

A truly sad story related to Marilyn's divorce was reported by the *Los Angeles Times* on October 28th, "Divorce Case Spectator Plunges To Her Death...A young Los Angeles woman, mother of two small children, plunged nine stories to her death shortly before noon yesterday from the 10th floor of the 12-story Bay Cities Building in Santa Monica. The victim, Mrs. Selva Lenore Silbert, 28, of 12451 W Beatrice St., landed atop the Bank of America Building adjoining the structure from which she leaped. Her purse was found in a 10th-floor restroom. Her husband Mack Silbert, a Superior Court reporter, told police his wife had accompanied him to Santa Monica Courthouse so that she could hear the Marilyn Monroe divorce proceedings. She was a spectator in the back row of Department A while her husband was working in Department B. Silbert said he had arranged to meet his wife at the Bay Cities Building and they were to have lunch together. He collapsed when he arrived at the scene. Police said they learned Mrs. Silbert has been upset and had attempted on previous occasions to take her life. No notes were found."

One of the loveliest set of photos Marilyn had taken was during this tumultuous time in her life. Marilyn has a sitting with English photographer Nahum "Ted" Baron. Baron had traveled from London to America in order to promote his new book on the ballet. While in America the *London Sunday Graphic*, with the support of *LIFE* magazine, requested that he also arranged to shoot Hollywood's most glamorous women. Baron told Harrison Carroll how he would photograph Marilyn if he got the chance to photograph her. "'If I did Marilyn Monroe I would concentrate on a simple, gentle quality in the girl. She usually is photographed hard and brittle.' I asked Baron to define glamour. He replied, 'It's a mixture of intelligence, sex and mystery, well packaged.'" He expounded on glamour in another article, "Beauty is one thing, and glamour is something quite different. Glamour is a mixture of intelligence, poise, sex appeal and above all, mystery—well packaged. And then there is an added quality of showing off. This makes glamour strictly a theatrical attribute. It is extremely rare to find it in a woman who is not a theatrical performer….There are other things more important—like inner beauty and even outer beauty, that doesn't class as glamour. Anyway, the camera lies. You can make a wonderful person look awful and a plain person look beautiful."

Baron remembers his first impressions of Marilyn. "Before I set eyes on her, Monroe was a big brassy smile and a mass of curves and blonde hair staring at me from the covers of innumerable magazines on bookstands. Then one day a black Cadillac drew up to the Fox Studio administration buildings. I was with a character in the newspaper business who went to the driver and said hello. The driver replied with a greeting and smiled at him, and for some friendly reason she smiled at me--a sweet, cozy look. Someone said, 'That's Monroe,' and I said, 'Nonsense!' But Monroe it was. Next time I saw her was the day before her divorce. She was sitting having luncheon in the Fox dining room. She looked ill and tired. People said Monroe was this or that, but I noticed that everyone was talking about her, and I still wondered why. The blonde with a brassy smile. A few days later I found myself having lunch with her and her friend and agent, Hugh French. She was wearing a towel 'peignoir' and had no makeup on at all. She said 'Hello' or maybe 'Hi' and I replied with a mumbled greeting. She smiled again, and I began to see and to feel the electric touch of Monroe. The smile didn't come from the gaudy covers of magazines--it came from within, and was very warming indeed. Monroe is almost a legend--a remote girl, a smiling, friendly Garbo--in Hollywood. I must eat my words, for I had labeled her without seeing her, a silly thing to do with most people, but with Monroe, high treason.' Baron added to his definition of glamour as 'partly polish acquired by a person who is always in the public eye and partly the projection of the personality beyond the limits of everyday life.'"

In late October Baron finally persuaded Marilyn to pose for him on the last day of his visit to Hollywood. He used the home of his friend, Hollywood columnist and socialite Harry Crocker, at 622 N Bedford Drive in Beverly Hills. Baron was actually staying at Mr. Crocker's home while in Hollywood. Mr. Crocker's home and landscape was designed by noted California architect George McLean. McLean used uncomplicated designs in constructing the garden where Marilyn posed. It was modern and sculptural and created a

Zen-like atmosphere which provided an interesting contrast for Marilyn. How she managed to look so tranquil and self-possessed in these images is a tribute to her skills as a model. As usual, she was almost an hour late. Baron liked to make use of the late afternoon sun and its soft lighting and he feared that he would lose the opportunity to use it. When Marilyn arrived she proved herself a worthy model and wasted no time posing for his camera. This session produces over 50 photos and some of the loveliest portraits of Marilyn ever taken. She has a composed and charming demeanor in these images, making them some of the most coveted photos taken of her. In her posing, gone is the animated pin-up and in its place is a gentle, serene woman. Baron choose a striped dress and sandals, and a red halter jumpsuit to clothe her in. She wore her own Jax blue shantung silk top and candy stripped pedal pushers. She had worn the blue top in photographs by Milton Greene in September when she was in New York.

Of Marilyn, Baron will later say, "When people ask me to name the most colorful personalities in the post-war era, without hesitation I reply Pietro Annigoni, Peter Ustinov, Gilbert Harding and Marilyn Monroe...Marilyn is unique. Nothing about her is affected. Her hips sway when she walks, because she knows no other way to walk. Marilyn, I felt, was one of the most appealing people I had ever met, rather defenseless and rather sad. She does not know how or why she is sexy. She just is. Monroe's success is a triumph of nature rising to the top. Marilyn does everything out of instinct." Baron will later write, "Marilyn was like a cat in the way she moves. As a photographic model I was overawed by Marilyn's ability to automatically flow into a liquid position which no photographer could possibly invent for her. Marilyn seemed to know instinctively when I was not satisfied, and with a fraction of a movement adjust herself to my mood. I didn't even need to say "Hold it". Marilyn just knew. The bond between me and Marilyn was like an electric wire charged with creativity and rhythm." He would also confess about his visit, "The two most exciting camera subjects I ever had photographed in my entire career I found in Hollywood— Marilyn Monroe and Pier Angeli. Monroe has a brassy smile she turns on for the cameras. But if you tell her to stop that, you find a truly amazing girl with great expression, great warmth." In another interview with Elizabeth Toomey, he "dumped a stack of giant-sized glossy prints of Marilyn Monroe on the couch. They were unretouched pictures of the blonde actress as he felt she was—young looking, demure, with a girl-next-door smile. She had her eyes wide open and her mouth closed in several of the pictures."

Photographs from this sitting were featured in many publications during and after Marilyn's lifetime and in a book Baron published titled, *My Life as a Photographer*.

On November 1st Marilyn moves into a duplex at 8336 Delongpre Ave, Hollywood.

Leonard Lyons devoted most of his column to Marilyn and Joe, "Signs of Discord Recalled in Life of Marilyn, Joe...It was late that night in El Morocco, and DiMaggio was talking of the pennant races. Miss Monroe remained silent. She cared nothing about the game. She did mention having glanced at some of his scrapbooks in San Francisco, but the dates and his feats reminded her only of what she had been doing at the time, to make her way. She was curious about new books, new people and expanding her horizons; DiMaggio is shy and retiring, a man content. When she came to New York, she avoided his best friends here, until Joe arrived and brought them home. There was a conflict, too of working hours. A man must feel odd about seeing his wife awakened at 5am to go to work, even if the work is a movie bringing fame and wealth. That night, at Morocco, she mentioned the 5am call. 'I'll stay in another room, so you won't be awakened, too.' she suggested. 'No,' said DiMaggio, 'I'll just roll over.' And then seeing the midnight crowds at Lexington Avenue, cheering when his wife's skirt was blown high. There are always such signs, when you marry electric lights. The night before, at the Little Club, she was told of a magazine article I'd written. She asked what it was about and I told her the title,' Never Marry an Actress.' Miss Monroe's reply was immediate and unequivocal: 'You're right. You're absolutely right.'"

On November 5th Joe DiMaggio engages in a stunt that is straight out of a grade "B" Film Noir and aptly known as "The Wrong Door Raid." Due to misinformation by a private investigator, Joe DiMaggio, Frank Sinatra, Henry Sanicola and Patsy D'Amore, along with private investigators Barney Rudisky and Philip Irwin, go to an apartment building where they believe Marilyn to be with another man, Hal Schaefer. They break the door down to the apartment of Florence Kotz and begin taking photographs of her. Marilyn was having dinner at another apartment in the building at the time of the raid. A friend, Sheila Stewart had made dinner for Marilyn and Hal Schaefer. They had been working at the studio re-recording some songs for *There's No Business Like Show Business*. When Marilyn heard the commotion, she and Hal managed to slip away undetected by Joe DiMaggio and his friends. The Police listed it as an attempted break in, and no one was identified or arrested. In a later suit filed by Florence Katz, involving Joe DiMaggio, Frank Sinatra, Henry Sanicola, Patsy D'Amore, and private detectives Barney Ruditsky and Philip Irwin, she received an out of court settlement for the sum of $7,500. It was not until 1957, when the California State Senate investigated unethical private investigators, that all of this was brought up in court. It was referred to a grand jury, but eventually it just faded away.

On November 5th the Sheilah Graham reported that, "The powers that be are changing Marilyn Monroe's publicity. She was reading The New Testament at lunch the other day. Later, Marilyn posed for ads to raise money to kill the cancer scourge."

Marilyn posed for publicity photos for *Seven Year Itch* during the day on November 6th. That evening she was wined and dined by Hollywood, as the elite of the town turn out for a party in her honor at Romanoff's Restaurant given by director Billy Wilder and her agent Charles Feldman. Marilyn attended the celebration wearing a signature red chiffon gown, which was actually from Fox's wardrobe department. She borrowed her jewels from Mrs. Karger. The jewelry was not the kind that Marilyn owned or liked. They were big and gaudy, but for this occasion they were the perfect choice.

Marilyn was escorted by photographer Sam Shaw. On the way to the party, neither she nor Sam had brought any money with them. The car they were driving in ran out of gas. Marilyn used her charms to obtain gas from a stunned attendant. They finally showed up for Marilyn's party an hour late. Even so, she looked and felt like Cinderella arriving at the ball.

Audrey Wilder had managed to assemble 80 guests from the aristocracy of Hollywood. The powerful, the elite, and even some of the lesser lights in the Hollywood sky, all gathered to pay homage to Marilyn. This was the night when she had finally been accepted as "one of them." The guest list reads like a who's who of Tinsel Town: Twentieth Century-Fox Studio Chief Darryl Zanuck and his wife Virginia, Warner Brothers Studio Chief Jack Warner, MGM Studio Chief Samuel Goldwyn, Humphrey Bogart and Lauren Bacall, Billy and Audrey Wilder, Gary Cooper, Groucho Marx, Clifton Webb, George Burns, Susan Hayward, Jean Howard, Clark and Kay Gable, Loretta Young, Director Charles Vidor, Agent Irving "Swifty" Lazar, Director Jean Negulesco (*How to Marry a Millionaire,*) Columnist Sidney Skolsky, Director Henry Hathaway (*Niagara,*) Evelyn Keys, Agent Ned Marin, French Ballet stars Zizi Jean Marie and Roland Petit, Michael Rennie, David Niven and wife Hjordis Termeden, Claudette Colbert, and Tom Ewell, to name just a few.

After dinner Marilyn joined Audrey Wilder in a duet of "Do It Again." Sam Shaw and *LIFE* photographer Jack Birns captured the evening for Marilyn on film. Jean Howard borrowed Sam Shaw's camera and snapped Marilyn dancing with her childhood idol, Clark Gable. Marilyn met Clark for the first time this evening. Sam Shaw took a photograph of Marilyn kissing Charles Vidor. He requested two copies of the photo, one for him and one for his son at Harvard. The party lasted until 4a.m. Marilyn left with a treasured memento, each guest had signed their signatures on a large portrait of Marilyn. *LIFE* magazine would feature the photographs in its weekly section, "*LIFE* Goes To a Party," in the November 29, 1954 issue. Actor Clifton Webb remembers this about Marilyn, "At the end of the shooting on *Seven Year Itch*, the director, Billy Wilder, gave her a party at Romanoff's. The way the girl went to the various tables showed that she was an absolute perfect hostess. Here was a girl who behaved so much more like a lady than many ladies.'"

Billy Wilder declared of working with Marilyn, "Working with Marilyn is not the easiest thing in the world, but it was one of the great experiences of my life…I have a feeling that this picture helped her in formulating an idea of what she herself is all about."

Wilder also gave these thoughts to working with Marilyn on *Seven Year Itch*. "It's my opinion that she's basically a good girl, but what's happened to her is enough to drive almost anybody slightly daffy, even someone who is armored with poise and calmness by his background and bringing up. You take a girl like Marilyn, who's never really had a chance to learn, who's never really had a chance to live, and suddenly confront her with a Frankenstein's monster of herself built of fame and publicity and notoriety, and naturally she's a little mixed up and made giddy by it all. However, I'd like to go on record with this, I worked with her in *Seven Year Itch* and I had a good time with her. She was seldom on time, but it wasn't because she overslept. It was because she had to force herself to come to the studio. She's emotionally upset all the time; she's scared and unsure of herself—so much so that when I worked with her I found myself wishing that I were a psychoanalyst and she were my patient. It might be that I couldn't have helped her, but she would have looked lovely on a couch. 'You mean that you didn't get annoyed when she was late?' I understood the reasons for it. There was no use getting annoyed. Even at the beginning, when I discovered that I had let myself in for a certain amount of trouble, I found myself liking her. At no time did I find her malicious, mean, capricious or anything but conscientious. There are certain urges and drives in her which make her different, but, as a director, I think it worth combating those things and living with them in order to work with her." When Wilder worked with her on *Some Like it Hot* in 1958, he will come to a totally different opinion of her. He will say of Marilyn, even four years after her death, "She was the meanest woman I have ever met around Hollywood....I have never met anyone as utterly mean as Marilyn Monroe."

On November 7th Marilyn started the day posing for publicity stills at Fox and that afternoon Joe DiMaggio drove her to Cedars of Lebanon Hospital for minor corrective surgery to be performed the next morning, November 8th, by Dr. Leon Krohn her gynecologist. Joe visited her every day, gave her a big bottle of perfume and had John Hall, at the Farmers Market make up attractive baskets of fresh fruit for her. Rumors of reconciliation were rampant in the press.

Louella Parsons on November 9th reports that the affair between Hal Schafer and Marilyn has ended.

When Marilyn left the hospital on November 12th, she took no care for her appearance and tried to slip out through a basement exit. To her surprise she was greeted by a photographer, Gib Brush, of the *Los Angeles Daily News*. He came up with an exclusive and unusual shot of Marilyn with hair awry and sans makeup which won him a $10 prize. Mary Short drove Marilyn home from the hospital on November 12th, as Joe was out of town.

Marilyn's bill totaled $337.42 for her 6 day stay. She made only four outbound calls during this time. She was charged $28.00 a day for her private room #506.

The next day, November 13th, Marilyn, Joe DiMaggio, and his brother Dominic are seen dining at the Villa Capri Restaurant. The *United Press* runs an article on the 15th hinting at reconciliation. They divulge that Joe treated her to Lasagna and Veal Scaloppini at the restaurant where they had their first date, which would be the Villa Nova. Marilyn is quoted as saying, "Joe and I are just friendly, that's all. There's nothing to it."

Marilyn is escorted by Sidney Skolsky on November 19th to hear Ella Fitzgerald sing at the Tiffany Club in Hollywood. Marilyn promises to be there for opening night and for every night of her engagement, and to bring her celebrity friends. This prompted Marilyn and Ella's manager, Norman Grantz, to pressure Charlie Morrison, owner of Macambo's, to hire Ella. Ella will later credit Marilyn for having helped her break into the elite nightclub circuit. It had nothing to do with race and everything to do with proving that Ella could draw a crowd and keep them entertained. Ella was overweight and had no glamorous appeal, or so they thought. She proved once and for all that it was her magnificent voice that could hold court in any venue, and Miss Fitzgerald was actually quite a strudel. The Mocambo had no issue with hiring black entertainers. Marilyn had been to see Eartha Kitt in November of 1953 at the Mocambo. Dorothy Dandridge, Joyce Bryan and Herb Jefferies had all played the stage at the Mocambo in 1952 thru 1953.

Leonard Lyons reported on November 20th, "Re Miss Monroe...The gynecologist who operated on Marilyn Monroe treasures a letter he received from her, on the eve of the operation. It expressed thanks for his care. 'After all,' wrote the star, 'procreation still is a woman's prime function in life.' Miss Monroe still sees Joe DiMaggio, Jr. On the eve of her marriage to his father she told the boy that both of them had heard many stories about stepmothers. 'I can't take the place of your mother, because you have a mother,' she said. 'Can we be friends, good friends?' The boy was delighted, and they remain good friends. In fact, little Joe often calls at her home and sometimes asks to visit her on his way from school. He's popular with his classmates, because he brings them along."

Marilyn receives a ticket for driving without a license on November 21st by Beverly Hills patrolman, H.P. Swantek. Marilyn will allow this ticket to go unpaid and in the future will stir up quite a publicity storm over this traffic violation. It will not be resolved until March of 1956. Dorothy Kilgallen had reported in July that "Marilyn Monroe's uninhibited driving is giving the Los Angeles police a bit of concern. They hope the warnings will help."

Louella Parsons reported on November 22nd, that Marilyn, Shelia Stewart and Mary Short went to hear Ella Fitzgerald sing at the Tiffany Club. Marilyn created a sensation when she wore her mink coat over pedal pushers. Shelia Stewart is the woman in whose apartment Marilyn was during the Wrong Door Raid.

On November 22nd Joe DiMaggio was hospitalized for treatment of a duodenal ulcer that has troubled him in the past. Marilyn said she did not intend to visit him in the hospital even though Joe visited her every day at the hospital during her recent surgery. This was not missed in the press. But, she did call and talk to his doctor about his condition.

Marilyn went to see Charles Feldman at his office on November 22nd. She acted as if she intended to remain as his client and eventually sign with Fox. She listened attentively as he suggested new projects for her. She played the part of the happy client for him, but just the opposite was true. She was angry with him for not getting her the part in *Guys and Dolls*, and for her perception that he did not respect her as an actress. He would come to realize just how angry she was in the next few weeks.

Dorothy Kilgallen reported on November 23rd, "Joe rains posies on Marilyn to prove he still cares. Joe DiMaggio, who used to frown on such sissy stuff, now showers Marilyn with perfume and flowers before each date"

Hedda Hopper reported on November 23rd, "Marilyn Monroe and Joe DiMaggio couldn't stay married, now they can't remain separated. Marilyn, with hair flying, drove up to the Knickerbocker Hotel to pick up Joe and his luggage and drive him to the airport. Truly life is weird, wonderful and surprising in Hollywood."

Before their divorce Marilyn had asked Maureen O'Hara to surprise Joe on his birthday, November 25th. The women had met last year at a party when Miss O'Hara had come up to Marilyn and asked her to meet her brother. Marilyn told her, 'Wait 'til I tell Joe DiMaggio that I met you. You're one of his favorite actresses and he thinks you're beautiful!' Marilyn laughingly told Miss O'Hara she was tired of hearing about Joe's crush on Maureen and she thought of a way to finally give him what he wanted. She asked Maureen to hide in a cake for Joe's upcoming birthday, then pop up and surprise him. Maureen agreed to do this for Marilyn and Joe. Sadly it never came to fruition. Instead Marilyn gave Joe an expensive gold watch engraved with her sentiments. He wore it for years, even after her death.

Marilyn went to the office of Frank Ferguson at Twentieth Century-Fox on November 29th. She wanted copies of all of her contracts, as hers had been misplaced because of the divorce. After she left, he became suspicious and called her lawyer, Lloyd Wright. After Marilyn never mentioned the documents to him, he called Charles Feldman. By the time they realized anything was wrong, Marilyn had sent the documents to New York so that Milton Greene's lawyer, Frank Delaney, could review them. He concluded that Marilyn's 1951 contract with Twentieth Century-Fox was invalid because the studio did not pick up her option in time after her suspension. She had made *Seven Year Itch* without a valid contract.

Marilyn is interviewed by Maria Romero, The Chilean director of the Spanish language magazine *Ecran* on December 2nd. Around five in the afternoon Marilyn arrived at the Polo Lounge in the Beverly Hills Hotel wearing a mink coat, classic Monroe black dress with spaghetti straps and net gloves. At some point in the interview they were joined by a young Robert Wagner. The interview with Marilyn lasted for more than three hours. Miss Romero described Marilyn in these words, "Marilyn is not exaggerated in her gestures. Her voice is soft and musical, and she moves her hands ever so gently. She throws her coat back a little to reveal her sculptural body. The room is softly lit, as most cocktail bars are, and Marilyn's low neckline appears to give off a glow in the middle of the surrounding darkness. Although she has big blue eyes, I can hardly see them, because she half-closes them when she speaks. When she laughs, she shows her beautiful, bright even white teeth, like a child's. A wisp of hair falls across her forehead, and she frequently fixes it in a nervous gesture--the only gesture she shows in relation to her looks. She never touches up her rouge or powders her little nose. She never wears stockings, and her feet are white, soft, with orchid-red nail-polish. Her toes reach just over the wide leather edge of her sandals or pumps. She is absolutely gorgeous. Much more than in the movies." Miss Romero asked Marilyn what she wanted but didn't have. She replied, "Love...I need to be loved. I won't be happy unless I have a home, a bunch of kids...Sometimes I think that maybe asking for a lot of kids is wanting too much. So I ask God to just give me two...two children...That would be enough to make me happy.'"

Sammy Davis Jr.'s publicist, Jess Rand, hosted a party for him at his home on December 2nd. Marilyn, Milton, Jeff Chandler, Tony Curtis, Sammy and a few other people are photographed with Rand. Afterwards, Marilyn, Milton and Sammy attend Mel Torme's show at the Crescendo Club on the Sunset Strip. The group was joined by Jaques Sernas.

Sammy was making his first public appearance since his automobile accident on November 19, 1954 In 1955, *TV Fan* magazine would run an article on Sammy Davis, Jr., and would feature a photograph of Marilyn, Mel Torme', Milton Greene and Sammy Davis, Jr., captioned, "Just a couple of weeks after he lost his eye, Sammy was back in circulation, visiting Hollywood's Crescendo where pal Mel Torme' was singing. Two got together with ringsiders, Marilyn Monroe and Milton Greene, who's doing a special photographic record of Marilyn. Sammy wanted to go back to work in his eye-patch, but doctors made him wait for an artificial eye."

The African-American newspaper, *The Pittsburgh Courier*, also carried the pic, captioned, "Sam Can See—There's no doubt about it, Sammy Davis, Jr. can see well enough out of that good eye to note that he's in the good company of Marilyn Monroe, Milton Greene (Miss Monroe's escort), and Mel (the Fog) Torme. The quartet was snapped at Hollywood's Crescendo night club." The next day the newspaper would announce, "S. Davis Sues for $150,000…Davis, who was seen the previous night sharing a table with Marilyn Monroe and her escort, filed action in Superior Court…" The African-American newspaper, *The Chicago Defender* also ran the captioned picture of Davis, Marilyn, Greene, Torme and Jacques Cernas, on the 18th.

After Torme's show Milton asked if Sammy wanted to come back to his place for drinks. Sammy said he wanted to hit the town with them. They ended up at Ciro's, and then finished up the night at The Mocamabo.

Biographer Will Haygood wrote, "Whenever Sammy found himself in a photo with Monroe, he would soon begin denying rumors that they were having an affair. The denial was Sammy's way of titillating the tabloids--inasmuch as the rumor found a life only in Sammy's breathless denial of it."

An example of which is this article from *The New York Amsterdam News*, an African-American newspaper, had Alvin Chick Webb reporting on December 11th, "Sammy Davis, Jr., currently enjoying dinner and luncheon engagements with no less than the fabulous Marilyn Monroe confirms a pet theory of this pillar--to wit, that the lads who are 'short, dark and TALENTED' are positive threats to those who are 'tall, dark and handsome.'"

Bob Farrell reported on December 13th that Marilyn had been told by 20th-Fox to stay out of the late night bistros. This was possibly in relation to all the press she had gotten being seen with Sammy Davis, Jr.

Mel Torme' remembers this time in Marilyn's life, "I was playing the Crescendo on the Sunset Strip and my marriage to Candy was in serious trouble. One night there, two significant events took place. For his first appearance in public after losing an eye in an automobile accident, Sammy Davis, Jr. came to see me. With him, first time out in public and after her grossly publicized divorce, was Marilyn Monroe, escorted by photographer Milton Greene…Marilyn began to call me at the club. I was slightly uneasy about her attention, but I was also flattered by her calls. She never announced herself as Marilyn Monroe, of course. She would ask for my, saying, 'Tell him it's Sadie.' I had gotten into the habit of calling her that…We began to meet late at night. She loved Delores' Drive-In hamburgers. Several nights we sat in my car, recklessly, in plain sight, eating those tasty hamburgers and talking--about everything. I am still surprised that our not-so-clandestine rendezvous was never discovered by the press. We went to the movies. A few times we met at the home of a friend...She told me she liked me because I made her laugh. When we stopped, we stopped. She had things to do with her life. I had a marriage in disrepair that I thought I should try to salvage. We both got a little misty, that final night we say each other. She assured me of her boundless affection. I promised her if she ever needed anything--anything at all--she could send up a flare and I would come running. I kissed her and that was that. The 'slovenly,' not-very-bright, temperamental, profligate woman described by so many writers was a Marilyn Monroe I never met. The woman-child I knew for an all-too-brief period of time was a nice, reasonably intelligent, eager-to-better-herself individual. She was also insecure, slightly cynical, and opinionated. Her face was always scrubbed, her hair attractively windblown or set. Her language could be salty, but, like Ava Gardner's, her beauty and impishness allowed her to spew forth the most outrageous expletives and get away with them. She was, far and away, the sexiest-looking lady I ever knew."

Edward Schallert reported on December 4th that Marilyn went to a party given by Gladys Robinson, wife of Edward G. Robinson, to introduce the new paintings that they had added to their remarkable collection.

Hedda Hopper reported on December 6th, "Milton Greene, well-known New York photographer, is here shooting Hollywood fathers--among them Dean Martin and Jerry Lewis. He took time out to dine with Marilyn Monroe and Sammy Davis, Jr. Sammy now has eye patches in every color of the rainbow. Dean and Jerry called up stars to get things to auction off at a Bel Air luncheon for Muscular Dystrophy. They asked Marilyn Monroe for something personal--anything close to her. What they got was a copy of Tolstoy's *War and Peace* autographed by Marilyn."

Marilyn attends a birthday party for Sammy Davis, Jr. at his home on December 8th. At her side was Milton Greene, her constant escort in December of 1954. Others in attendance included Frank Sinatra, Tony Curtis and Jeff Chandler.

Marilyn was photographed with Charlie Farrell in the Bamboo room at the Racquet Club in Palm Springs. Milton Greene also accompanied her on this trip. While in Palm Springs, Milton and Marilyn take photos at a desert ranch. Marilyn is photographed sitting on bales of hay, standing near the corral and on horseback, looking over her shoulder. Milton, of course, had to also be on horseback to capture such an image. No small accomplishment for a boy from Brooklyn.

Dorothy Kilgallen reported on December 11th, "Insiders say some of the greatest pictures of Marilyn Monroe ever taken are the experimental ones Milt Greene shot just for curiosity after a formal sitting. Endeavoring to establish just how powerful the Monroe glamour really is, he had her remove all her makeup and pose first in a beat-up slicker, then in the concealing robes of a nun."

Marilyn has lunch with Charles Feldman on December 11th. She once again acted in such a way as to relieve any suspicions that she was not happy. Feldman was promising to acquire *Harlow* for Marilyn. In the meantime, Marilyn and Milton Greene were busy trying to acquire it themselves for the recently organized Marilyn Monroe Productions, Inc.

Marilyn sent a letter on December 11th to the Famous Artists Corporation where Charles Feldman worked. It is Marilyn's formal termination letter and it would send Hollywood reeling.

Marilyn attended a birthday party for Gene Kelly's wife, Betsy Blair on December 11th. Also in attendance were Milton Greene and his wife Amy.

*The New York Amsterdam News*, an African-American newspaper praised Marilyn's singing style in the film *There's No Business Like Show Business* on December 12th, "Monroe steals the show with a specialty number called *After You Get What You Want, You Don't Want It*. Groomed by vocal coach Phil Moore (the expert in the exploitation of pulchritude) the lady literally proves that hard work and persistence pay off."

Another vocal coach of Marilyn's who goes largely unrecognized and uncredited is the great jazz pianist Gerald Wiggins. He also worked with Marilyn on her vocal numbers for her movies. To show her appreciation she autographed a photo for him, "For Gerry, I can't make a sound without you. Love you, Marilyn." Wiggins was known for his "musical sensitivity and his ability to accompany featured artists and singers." "It was his skills as a vocal teacher that brought him the pleasure of working with Marilyn Monroe. 'Marilyn was such an adorable human being,' Wiggins said. 'She was a professional actress, who really could sell herself on stage. I taught her some licks, but unlike many others, Marilyn could really get the job done.'" Like Phil Moore, he had worked with some of the best singers in the business like, Lena Horne, Kay Starr, Nat King Cole, Lou Rawls, Jimmy Witherspoon and Eartha Kitt.

The press reported that Marilyn and Joe DiMaggio dined together at a Malibu restaurant at 27400 W Pacific Coast Highway, and that they left the restaurant at 9:30pm. The article stated that, "less than a month ago Miss Monroe and DiMaggio went to an Italian restaurant where they first dined after they met."

On December 13th Charles Feldman received a letter from Marilyn, dated December 11th, firing him as her agent. The letter stated, "Gentlemen: I hereby cancel and terminate all of my existing agency contracts with you for good and sufficient cause. Kindly do not hold yourself out as my agent or representative in any capacity whatsoever from this date forward. Your authority to endorse my checks is hereby revoked. Thank you for your past services. Yours very truly," (signed) Marilyn Monroe. Underneath her signature was "c/o Frank Delaney 60 East 42nd Street, New York 17, New York."

Shortly after sending Feldman the letter Marilyn makes a half-hearted attempt to go into hiding at the residence of longtime acquaintance Anne Karger, Voltaire Apartments, 1424 N Cresent Heights Blvd, West Hollywood. It wouldn't be long before she was spotted by the press.

Marilyn did not attend the premier for *There's No Business Like Show Business* on December 16th. The *Chicago Defender*, an African-American newspaper, hailed it as a benefit performance for the Negro Actors Guild and other allied organizations of the Actors Fund of America.

Erskine Johnson reported on the 17th "Marilyn Monroe's blushing about moving to a new apartment and refusing to give the address to the Fox studio publicity department. She finally met one of her neighbors--the studio's assistant publicity director."

Hedda Hopper reported on December 18th that while Frank Sinatra was out of town, "he has lent his home to Marilyn Monroe and that's where she's entertaining Joe DiMaggio."

Marilyn Monroe Productions quietly files for charter on December 20$^{th}$ for Marilyn Monroe Productions, Inc. The Certificate of Incorporation was filled in the office of the Secretary of State in Albany, New York.

Jimmie Fidler wrote on December 21st, "Marilyn Monroe is getting around again--or, at least oftener than when she and Joe were man and wife. The glittering blonde is being seen in night clubs and name restaurants, with groups and in two-somes. She went to Gene Kelly's birthday party for his wife Betty, accompanied by Milton Greene, *Look* photographer. Marilyn attracted more than the usual attention. She was wearing a skin-tight, white knit dress that set off the Monroe lines to unusual advantage. Meantime, I hear that Milton has made more shots of Marilyn than any other cameraman since she became a movie star."

In late December Twentieth Century-Fox sends Marilyn a telegram saying that they need her to do retakes on *Seven Year Itch* in 5 days. Frank Delaney tells the studio that she is sick and unable to do it now. Lew Schreiber notifies Marilyn's lawyer that the re-takes have been postponed until January 3, 1955. Delaney tells the studio that Marilyn needs more time to recover her health, so the re-takes are scheduled for January 10, 1955 instead.

Harrison Carroll reported on December 23rd, "Marilyn Monroe was alone at the Devonshire Inn to see pianist Dilson Petrey, whom she met in New York." In New York in 1951 Dilson Petrey stroked the keys at the cafe bar in the Sherry Netherland Hotel where Marilyn stayed during her trip to see *Gentlemen Prefer Blondes*.

A fitting word for Marilyn would be Sprezzatura. It means "to practice in all things a certain Sprezzatura so as to conceal all art and make whatever is done or said appear without effort." Marilyn would have appreciated that it came from the Book of the Courtier, Baldassare Castiglione, 1528. She certainly achieved this manner of presenting herself to the world.

The first half of Marilyn's story is one of the American Dream. A girl from the wrong side of the tracks rising from obscurity and poverty, and by her own hand, reinventing herself as the brightest star in Hollywood. By the end of 1954 she was indisputably the most famous woman in the world. She built her image on a foundation of beauty and in-your-face sexuality. In the coming years she would try to replace that salacious foundation with one of culture and intellect. But for now, she gave to the post World War II world an image of freedom from old restraints and the idea that anything is possible in America. Her open mouthed smile and come-hither sexuality forced open a debate about old mores and standards in this post-war adolescent America that was just now flexing its new morals.

Diana Trilling comes the closest to describing the ineffable gift that Marilyn had. "None but Marilyn Monroe could suggest such a purity of sexual delight. The boldness with which she could parade herself and yet never be gross, her sexual flamboyance and bravado which yet breathed an air of mystery and even reticence, her voice which carried such ripe overtones of erotic excitement and yet was the voice of a shy child—these complications were integral to her gift. And they described a young woman trapped in some never-never land of unawareness."

Ben Hecht offers this fitting description of Marilyn:
"The truth about Marilyn was that she was a sort of evangelist. She peddled a dream to a preoccupied atom age. Her fervor was that of the missionary with happy tidings. Her happy tidings were her luscious figure, her inviting mouth. She looked for no romance for herself. Her happiness lay in her missionary work for others. She lived in the midst of her fame as if she were more a poster than a woman."

# Source Materials

## Chapter One
### A Foundling in the City of Angels
**Quote**—W.H. Auden
**Mortensen, spelled with an "e"**—*Marilyn, The Passion and the Paradox,* Lois Banner, Bloomsbury, 2014
**Norma Jean Cohen, Kentucky**-- 1.15.2003, *Leo Weekly,* Louisville, KY archives, Ward Harrison
**Earl Theisen, knew Gladys; money taken up while pregnant**-- *Marilyn Monroe,* Maurice Zolotow, Hartcourt, Brace, 1960
**Slept in dresser drawer**—*My Sister Marilyn, A Memoir of Marilyn Monroe,* Berniece Miracle, Mona Miracle, 1995, Orion
**Red Car Line**-- Wikipaedia, Pacific Electric; 1.31.2013, *Huffington Post,* Pacific Electric Red Car Line
**MM Quote about memory at six months**-- *This Week Magazine,* 12.11.60, Marilyn Monroe Talks About Herself, Joe Hyams
**Ida Bolender**—*Hello Normal Jeane,* Corey Levitan, fearandloathing.com
**Norma Jeane and Lester**—http://strickertfamily.com/Marilyn_Monroe_Connect.html
**Masturbation story**—*Fragments: Poems, Intimate Notes, Letters, Marilyn Monroe,* Bernard Comment, Farrar, Straus, Giroux, 2012
**Consolidated fire**—11.2.29 Centralia, OH, Blast Wreaks Film Laboratory, no by-line; 11.3.29, *INS,* Where $50,000,000 went up in smoke; 11.4.29, *UP,* Wreckage Caused by Film Blast; vitaphone BlogSpot, 3.1.2007
**Julian Arnold Smith** – viewed information on *eBay*
**Evelyn Gawthrop** – *Hello Normal Jeane,* Corey Levitan, http://fearandloafing.com/features/marilyn.txt
**Sunrise Chorus Hollywood Bowl**—03.13.32, *Los Angeles Times,* Easter Sunrise Plan Complete, no by-line; 3.20.32, *Los Angeles Times,* Easter Sunrise Throngs Will Hail Risen Lord, no by-line; 3.22.32, *Los Angeles Times,* Thirty Thousand Expected to be at Bowl Easter, no by-line; 3.26.32, *Los Angeles Times,* Throng in Lily Procession, no by-line; 3.26.32, *Los Angeles Times,* Easter Sunrise Opens Worship, John Albert Eby, D.D., General Secretary Church Federation of Los Angeles; 5.28.32, *Los Angeles Times,* no by-line; *Collier's,* 1951 Model Blonde, 9.51, Robert Cahn

## Chapter Two
### Life With Mama
**Quote**—*Marilyn, Her Tragic Story,* George Miller, 1962
**Ben Hecht quote**—*Australian Women's Weekly,* 1.12.55, This is My Story, Marilyn Monroe
**Info on Car**—Roy Turner Papers, access provided by Dr. Lois Banner, PhD
**Lester Bolender trip to Catalina**— viewed information on *Everlasting Star*
**Catalina Quote**—6.6.36, *Los Angeles Times,* Steamship Schedule to and From Catalina Island; Catalina Island, Webb-Herrick, Elizabeth, 1935; *Curious California Customs*—Los Angeles Edition, Pacific Carbon & Printing Company, Los Angeles, CA
**Gays Lion Farm**—Brochure, my collection
**Movies quote, sinful**—*American Weekly,* The Truth About Me, 11.16.52, Marilyn Monroe, Liza Wilson; *Australian Women's Weekly,* 1.12.55, This is My Story, Marilyn Monroe; *The Saturday Evening Post,* 5,5,56, The New Marilyn Monroe, Pete Martin
**MM Quote—dreaming of being a movie star**—*My Story,* Marilyn Monroe, Ben Hecht, Stein and Day, 1974
**Strike at studio**— *My Sister Marilyn, A Memoir of Marilyn Monroe,* Berniece Miracle, Mona Miracle, Orion, 1995
**Ben Hecht quote on Arbol home**— *Australian Women's Weekly,* 1.12.55, This is My Story, Marilyn Monroe
**Arbol Street info**—10.21.20, *Los Angeles Times,* Burglar Robs Residence; 10.16.27, *Los Angeles Times,* 6826 Arbol Drive, auction of home; *The Legend of Marilyn Monroe,* John Huston narrator, Terry Sanders, David L. Wolper, Ezra Goodman producers, 1966; Personal Research with Dr. Lois Banner, PhD;
**Reference to Photo of Arbol home**-- *The Legend of Marilyn Monroe,* John Huston narrator, Terry Sanders, David L. Wolper, Ezra Goodman producers, 1966
**Quotes on Arbol home by mm**— *Australian Women's Weekly,* 1.12.55, This is My Story, Marilyn Monroe
**Skolsky on piano**—*Modern Screen,* 10.53, I Love Marilyn, Sidney Skolsky

**Berniece quote about piano**— *My Sister Marilyn, A Memoir of Marilyn Monroe*, Berniece Miracle, Mona Miracle, Orion, 1995
**Amy Greene quote about piano**-- Norman Mailer Files at the Harry Ransom Center, University of Texas, Austin; Files for Norman Mailer's books, *Marilyn*, Grosset & Dunlap, 1973; *Of Women and Their Elegance*, Simon & Schuster, 1980; Courtesy of Dr. Lois Banner, PhD
**Harrell's on Arbol Drive**-- 11.5.35, *Los Angeles Times*, When Childish Laugher Rang in a Garden, no by-line; 1.17.37, *Los Angeles Times*, Busy Society Matron Fond Mother, Too
**Mrs. Harrell**-- 10.10.37, *Los Angeles Times*, Mrs. Harrell Busy Hostess
**Madeline Brandeis**; 9.27.25, *Los Angeles Times*, no by-line; 10.17.1933, *Los Angeles Times*, Miss Brandeis Weds, gives address
**MMs fascination with Jean Harlow**--*My Story*, Marilyn Monroe, Ben Hecht, Stein and Day, 1974
**Whitley Heights**—Personal Research with Dr. Lois Banner, PhD
**First day of school quote by mm**-- *Collier's*, 9.51, The 1951 Model Blonde, Robert Cahn; *Photoplay* 3.54, Orphan in Ermine, Jane Corwin; 11.16.52, *The Truth About Me*, Marilyn Monroe and Liza Wilson
**Telling harry Lipton about Jackie's death**—*Motion Picture*, 5.56, Marilyn's the Most! Harry Lipton
**First love quote**— *Australian Women's Weekly, 1.12.55,* This is My Story, Marilyn Monroe;
**Harry C. Wilson quote**—*MM Personal: From the Private Archive of Marilyn Monroe*, Lois Banner, 2011, Harry N. Abrams

# Chapter Three
## It's a Hard Knock Life

**Quote**--*Photoplay*, 11.62, Marilyn Monroe, Aljean Meltsir
**Los Angeles New Year's Flood**-- 1.31.2014, *KNX On Your Corner:* New Year's 1934 Flood; 4.23.2009, *Songs About Los Angeles:* "The New Year's Flood" by Woodie Guthrie, Will Campbell
**Alice Miller quote** -- *The Drama of the Gifted Child: The Search for the True Self*, Alice Miller, Harper Collins, 1980
**Edward Mortensen, contacted to care for NJ**--2.12.81, *The Rock Hill Herald*, MMs Dad Identified; 2.12.81, *AP*, Yardena Arar; 2.12.81, *Omaha World Herald*, *AP*, Miss Monroe's Birth Believed Legitimate; 2.12.81, *Tri City Herald*, *AP*, Star's birth proved legitimate After All; *Marilyn, The Passion and the Paradox*, Lois Banner, Bloomsbury, 2014
**MM on Mortensen**—*Photoplay*, 1.53, Marilyn Monroe Tells the Truth to Hedda Hopper, Hedda Hopper
**MM quote on selling whiskey bottles**; *The Saturday Even Post*, 5.5.56, The New Marilyn Monroe, Pete Martin
**Whiskey bottle babies**—12.52, *Modern Screen*, The True Life Story of Marilyn Monroe, Elyda Nelson
**Reginald Carroll**-- *Marilyn Monroe*, Maurice Zolotow, Hartcourt, Brace, 1960
**MMs quote after Gladys breakdown**— *Australian Women's Weekly*, 1.12.55, This is My Story, Marilyn Monroe
**Quote to Elyda Nelson**--12.52, *Modern Screen*, The True Life Story of Marilyn Monroe, Elyda Nelson
**Grace financial records & Inventory of Estate**—Roy Turner Papers, access provided by Dr. Lois Banner, PhD
**Aunt Ana buying piano**-- Roy Turner Papers, access provided by Dr. Lois Banner, PhD; *The Legend of Marilyn Monroe*, John Huston narrator, Terry Sanders, David L. Wolper, Ezra Goodman producers, 1966
**Grace's friends whisper about caring for NJ**— *Australian Women's Weekly, 1.12.55,* This is My Story, Marilyn Monroe
**Marilyn on being placed in the orphanage**—8.22.62, *Marilyn:* Orphanage To Teen–Age Bride, Theo Wilson
**Accounts of grace Goddard in bakery line and orphanage**— *Australian Women's Weekly*, 1.12.55, This is My Story, Marilyn Monroe
**Grace in Up Pops the Devil**—9.27.35, *Los Angeles Times*, Studio workers to Stage Drama
**LA Orphanage Jam**—10.13.35, *Los Angeles Times*, Ingathering of Orphans Home Society This Week, no by-line; 10.14.35, *Los Angeles Times*, Orphans to Get Shower of Jams and Goodies, no by-line
**Christmas entertainment**—3.12.35, *Los Angeles Times*, Orphans Greet Stage Players, no by-line
**Pearl necklace**—*PIC*, 10.51, PIC Goes Shopping With Marilyn Monroe, Jane Morris
**Jim Henaghan 1952 quote**-- *Redbook*, 6.52, So Far To Go Alone, Jim Henaghan
**Records at orphanage**—*American Weekly, 10.2.55,* Mystery of MM, Zolotow
**Star at RKO quote**—*American Weekly, 11.16.52,* The Truth About Me, *Marilyn Monroe*, Liza Wilson
**Jim Henaghan on crash out**—*Redbook*, 6.52, So Far To Go Alone, Jim Henaghan
**Powder her face**—*Collier's*, 9.8.51, 1951 Model Blonde, Robert Cahn; *Redbook* 6.52, So Far To Go Alone, Jim Henaghan
**No one told me I was pretty**…*Motion Picture and Television*, 8.52, Why Women Hate Marilyn Monroe, Isabel Moore

**Ezra Goodman quote**…*Cavalier* 8.61, The Girl With Three Blue Eyes, Ezra Goodman
**Marilyn visiting orphanage**—information viewed on *Everlasting Star*; *Pix Annual*, Spring 1954, Intimate Facts About the Real Marilyn Monroe, Arthur Everett Scott
**Grace quote by mm—god; aunt grace; Clark gable**— *Australian Women's Weekly*, 1.12.55, This is My Story, Marilyn Monroe
**Final assessment at orphanage**—*Redbook*, 6.52, So Far To Go Alone, Jim Henaghan
**Sleep in bed too small**— 7.9.62, Louella Parsons, *Marilyn Monroe's Hidden Torments*
**Mm quote never happy in grade school; human bean**— *Australian Women's Weekly*, 1.12.55, This is My Story, Marilyn Monroe
**Hedda hopper intvw in 1952**—5.4.52, Hedda Hopper, *The Blowtorch Blonde*
**Gerry Grissman 5th grade quote**—2.5.53, *UP*, Marilyn Monroe, 'Very Plain' in 5th Grade
**Atchinson home**— *Australian Women's Weekly*, 1.12.55, This is My Story, *Marilyn Monroe; Marilyn, The Passion and the Paradox,* Lois Banner, Bloomsbury, 2014
**Ginger Rogers**— *Modern Screen*, 2.51, I was an Orphan, Marilyn Monroe; Julian's auction, Marilyn Monroe Auction 2014, lot 693
**Doc Goddard and the kiss**— *Conversations With Marilyn*, W.J. Weatherby, Robson Books, 1976; *Legend, The Life and Death of Marilyn Monroe*, Fred Lawrence Guiles, 1984; *The Marilyn Scandal*, Sandra Shevey, William Morrow & Co, 1987; *Marilyn Monroe*, Barbara Leaming, Three Rivers Press, 2000; *Marilyn, The Passion and the Paradox,* Lois Banner, Bloomsbury, 2014
**Quotes from schoolmates**—Roy Turner papers, access provided by Dr. Lois Banner, PhD
**Mm quote – at 12**— *Australian Women's Weekly*, 1.12.55, This is My Story, Marilyn Monroe
**Quotes by Ana Lower; not clothes crazy**—*Modern Screen*, 2.51, I was an Orphan, Marilyn Monroe
**Aunt Ana finding Berniece**—*Photoplay,* 1.53, Marilyn Monroe Tells the Truth to Hedda Hopper, Hedda Hopper
**Howell family**—Interview with Cheryl Howell Williams; 4.4.1955, *Los Angeles Times*, Daughter of Howells Engaged, no by-line;
**Mabel Ella Campbell**—*The Legend of Marilyn Monroe*, John Huston narrator, Terry Sanders, David L. Wolper, Ezra Goodman producers, 1966
**Howard Keel**—*Modern Screen*, 9.52, The Secret Life of Marilyn Monroe, Steve Cronin; *Photoplay*, 1.53, Marilyn Monroe Tells the Truth to Hedda Hopper, Hedda Hopper; *Modern Screen*, 9.51, Who'd Marry Me, Marilyn Monroe; *Australian Women's Weekly,* 1.12.55, This is My Story, Marilyn Monroe
**Mm quote on sweater**— *Australian Women's Weekly*, 1.12.55, This is My Story, Marilyn Monroe
**Norma Jeane and the Muirs**—*The National Tattler*, Vol. 18, No. 14, 10.7.73, The Real Teen-Aged Marilyn Monroe, Dorothy Muir
**Doc Goddard**— *Marilyn, The Passion and the Paradox*, Lois Banner, Bloomsbury, 2014
**Jim made blueprints**--*Photoplay*, 3.53, Marilyn Monroe Was My Wife, James Dougherty
**Mm in HS**— *Australian Women's Weekly*, 1.12.55, This is My Story, Marilyn Monroe
**MM and Jim dating**--*Modern Screen*, 12.52, The True Life Story of Marilyn Monroe, Elyda Nelson; *Photoplay*, 3.53, Marilyn Monroe Was My Wife, James Dougherty
**Never been away**—*Modern Screen*, 2.51, I Was an Orphan, Marilyn Monroe
**Engagement, Rev. Lingenfelder, rings, lemon pies**--*Modern Screen*, 12.52, The True Life Story of Marilyn Monroe, Elyda Nelson
**Mm on Jim Dougherty**— *Australian Women's Weekly*, 1.19.55, This is My Story, Marilyn Monroe;
**On being asked**—5.17.56, A Profile of a Phenomenon, A Cynic and Monroe, Article 2, Milton Shulman
**Marriage quote**—*Photoplay* 1.53, Marilyn Monroe Tells the Truth to Hedda Hopper, Hedda Hopper
**Marriage quote**—*The Saturday Evening Post*, 5,5,56, The New Marilyn Monroe, Pete Martin

# Chapter Four
**The Marrying Kind**
**Quote**—*Silver Screen*, 12.62, Death of a Golden Girl, Virginia DePaolo
**Aunt Ana made wedding dress, quote about Aunt Ana**--8.22.62, *Boston Traveler*, Theo Wilson, Marilyn: Orphanage To Teen –Age Bride
**Aunt Ana's book, Marilyn recalls being frightened of sex**—8.21.62, *Boston Traveler*, Theo Wilson, Marilyn Tells 'My Bad Times'; 8.22.62, *Boston Traveler*, Theo Wilson, Marilyn: Orphanage To Teen –Age Bride
**Jim on being "just friends"**— *Photoplay*, 3.53, Marilyn Monroe Was My Wife, James Dougherty
**NJ doesn't throw her bouquet**--*Modern Screen*, 12.52, The True Life Story of Marilyn Monroe, Elyda Nelson

**Jim on NJ as an outdoor girl**--*Photoplay*, 3.53, Marilyn Monroe Was My Wife, James Dougherty
**Letter to Grace Goddard**—Dr. Lois Banner, PhD, collection
**Jim on NJ as housekeeper**--*Photoplay*, 3.53, Marilyn Monroe Was My Wife, James Dougherty
**Didn't like to be teased**--3.53, *Photoplay*, Marilyn Monroe Was My Wife, James Dougherty
**Marilyn quote on finding out she was illegitimate at 15**--8.22.62, *Boston Traveler*, Theo Wilson, Marilyn: Orphanage To Teen –Age Bride; *Cavalier*, 9.61, The Girl With Three Blue Eyes, Ezra Goodman
**Red Rock Dairy, Hemet, CA**—*Parade*, 8.5.73, Marilyn Monroe, Why Won't They Let Her Rest In Peace, Lloyd Shearer
**Natasha attempt to see MMs Father** –*Cavalier* 8.61, The girl With Three blue Eyes, Ezra Goodman
**Robert Mitchum tells of meeting NJ**—*Marilyn*, Sydney Skolsky, 1954
**Mitchum on early MM**– 8.9.62, *Marilyn, A Friend Recalls*, Earl Wilson
**Catalina island Sfc. Robert Lightfoot quote**—8.20.53, *Stars and Stripes*, Europe, 110$^{th}$ Sgt. Was this Close to That Blonde
**Douglas Kirkland, MM watching movies**—*With Marilyn: An Evening 1961*, Douglas Kirkland, 2012, Glitterati Incorporated
**Smell of Glue**--*Australian Women's Weekly*, 1.12.55, My Story, Marilyn Monroe;
**Ethel Dougherty arranges a transfer**-*Modern Screen*, 12.52, The True Life Story of Marilyn Monroe, Elyda Nelson
**Queen of Radioplane**—collection of Maite Minguez Ricart, viewed at *Everlasting Star*
**Jim Dougherty quote**—*The Secret Happiness of Marilyn Monroe*, James Dougherty, Playboy Press, 1976

# Chapter Five
## A Big Slice of Blonde Cheesecake

**Quote**—*American Weekly*, 10.9.55, the Mystery of Marilyn Monroe, Maurice Zolotow quote, "She finally found the lever by which she could move the world and hold on to it from then on."; *USA1*, 7.62, Marilyn, Ed Rees
**Trip to Big Bear**--*Photoplay*, 3.53, Marilyn Monroe Was My Wife, James Dougherty
**MMs quote about not angering the ladies, and her quote to Conover**--*The Saturday Evening Post* 5.5.56, The New Marilyn Monroe, Pete Martin
**Conover**-- *Art Photography* 10.54; *Modern Screen* 7.54, The Secrets of Marilyn's Life as a Model, Emmeline Snivel; *Photoplay* 1.53, defense movies reason for screen test; *People Today* 4.7.54; *The Saturday Evening Post* 5.5.56, The New Marilyn Monroe, Pete Martin; *Finding Marilyn*, David Conover, Grossett and Dunlap; 1981; 5.11.54, *The Star*, Conover credited with discovery of MM
**Conover pic used in The Models Bluebook**-- *The Legend of Marilyn Monroe*, John Huston narrator, Terry Sanders, David L. Wolper, Ezra Goodman producers, 1966
**MM Quote on Conover**—*Marilyn*, Gloria Steinem, Henry Holt & Co., Inc., 1986
**Florabel Muir quote**-- 10.12.1952, *Chicago Daily Tribune*, Marvelous Marilyn Monroe, Florabel Muir
**Sweaters**— *American Weekly*, 10.16.55, the Mystery of Marilyn Monroe, Maurice Zolotow
**Yank, August 2, 1945**--http://www.wartimepress.com/; Dave, Irek, and Mike
**Quote by Fitzgerald**--*Tender is the Night*, F. Scott Fitzgerald, Scribner, 1995
**Living with Ana Lower**—*Modern Screen*, 2.51, I Was an Orphan, Marilyn Monroe
**Billy Wilder**—*USA 1*.7.62, Marilyn, Ed Rees
**Marilyn wearing overalls**-- *Australian Women's Weekly*, 1.12.55, My Story, Marilyn Monroe;
**Emmeline Snively – 5 essentials to be a good model**—3.12.43, *San Antonio Light*, 'Blue Book' Gives Figures and Numbers
**Snively quote**--*Cavalier* 8.61, The Girl With Three Blue Eyes, Ezra Goodman
**Snively, she Was a Round Faced Girl**-- *People Today*, 4.7.54, Exclusive, I Taught Marilyn How, Emmeline Snively
**Instructors at Blue Book**--6.7.62, *Los Angeles Herald Examiner*, Ted Thackery
**Snively to Zolotow**— *Marilyn Monroe*, Maurice Zolotow, Harcourt Brace, 1960
**Snively/heart went out**—*Modern Screen*, 7.54, the Secrets of Marilyn's Life as a Model, Emmeline Snively
**Snively/she first came into my office in Aug 1945**—3.31.54, *Delwin Register*, Iowa, Marilyn's First Teacher Gives Low Down
**Snively—nose too long**—*People Today*, 4.7.54, Emmeline Snively, I Taught Marilyn How;
**Snively, laugh with lower jaw**—*Movie Time*, 12.54, The Marilyn Monroe I Used to Know, Earl Leaf
**Old modeling photos**—11.5.53, Sheilah Graham

**Snively** --4.9.54, *Boston Traveler*, Monroe Never Had Home Life, Kendis Rochlen and Charles Park; 6.7.62, *Los Angeles Herald Examiner*, Ted Thackery
**Paul Parry & Bob Farr quote**—Blowtorch Blonde, 5.4.52, Hedda Hopper; *Modern Screen*, 7.54, The Secrets of Marilyn's Life as a Model, Emmeline Snively…worked w Potter Hueth; *People Today* 4.7.54, Exclusive, I Taught Marilyn How, Emmeline Snively; *Art Photography* 10.54; Hamburgers and Cheesecake, Emmeline Snively; *Redbook*, 6.52, So Far to Go Alone, Jim Henaghan
**Paul Parry Calendar Top**—*NormaJeaneBaker*.Tumbler.com
**Snively pic taken on location/great Dane**—*Modern Screen*, 7.54, The Secrets of Marilyn's Life as a Model, Emmeline Snively
**Losing ring at turkey farm**--*Modern Screen*, 12.52, The True Life Story of Marilyn Monroe, Elyda Nelson
**Wrecking her Ford V-8**--*Modern Screen*, 12.52, The True Life Story of Marilyn Monroe, Elyda Nelson
**John Randolph**—*Art Photography*, 10.54; Hamburgers and Cheesecake, Emmeline Snively
**Hair so frizzy covered it with a bathing cap**— *Modern Screen*, 7.54, The Secrets of Marilyn's Life as a Model, Emmeline Snively
**Kronquist meant to use her**—*Art Photography*, 10.54, Hamburgers and Cheesecake, Emmeline Snively
**Snively—did wonders wither nose**— *Modern Screen*, 7.54, The Secrets of Marilyn's Life as a Model, Emmeline Snively
**Industry on Parade**— *Los Angeles Times*, 9.7.1945, 'Miss Industry to be named Tomorrow, no by-line
**Snively, no beauty contest**—*Art Photography*, 10.54, Hamburgers and Cheesecake, Emmeline Snively
**Snively, she was a wow**—*People Today*, 4.7.54, I Taught Marilyn How, Emmeline Snively
**Snively quote, "she still seemed…"**--6.7.62, *Los Angeles Herald Examiner*, Ted Thackery
**Dr. Gurdin and Dr. Pangman**—11.10. 2013, Julian's Auction, Icons and Idols, lot 1257
**Andre de Dienes on meeting Norma Jeane**-- *Modern Man*, 11.53, "I Knew Her When…" Andre de Dienes; 8.8.62, *Los Angeles Times*, Jack Smith, I Loved Marilyn, 'Started Career,' Mourns Hollywood Photographer
**Andre de Dienes sittings, Nov–Dec 1945**-- *MARILYN, MON AMOUR: The private album of Andre de Dienes, her preferred photographer,* Andre de Dienes, St. Martin's Press, 1985
**Andre de Dienes quotes on Norma Jeane**—*Modern Man*, 11.53, "I Knew Her When…" Andre de Dienes; 8.8.62, *Los Angeles Times*, Jack Smith, I Loved Marilyn, 'Started Career,' Mourns Hollywood Photographer
**How de Dienes photographs models**—*Parade,* 7.19.53, He Calls This Hard Work
**Jim's growing jealousy**-- *Modern Screen*, 12.52, The True Life Story of Marilyn Monroe, Elyda Nelson ; *Photoplay*, 3.53, Marilyn Monroe Was My Wife, James Dougherty
**Snively on hair, really intend to go places**— *Modern Screen*, 7.54, The Secrets of Marilyn's Life as a Model, Emmeline Snively
**Straight permanent**— *Modern Screen*, 7.54, The Secrets of Marilyn's Life as a Model, Emmeline Snively
**Zolotow, saw it worked**—*Marilyn Monroe,* Maurice Zolotow, Harcourt Brace, 1960
**Carved out of ice cream**—*USA1*, 7.62, Marilyn, Ed Rees
**Barnhart, Sylvia**—viewed information at *Everlasting Star*
**Jasgur photo shoots**—*The Birth of Marilyn: The Lost Photographs of Norma Jean*, Joseph Jasgur, 1991, St. Martin's Press
**Frank Powolny on Pin-Ups**—*Parade*, 10.10.54, Who Is She? Who'll take their place?
**Snively, Jasgur thought her too skinny**—*Art Photography*, 10.54 Hamburgers and Cheesecake, Emmeline Snively
**MM, sex with photographers**—*Hollywood Close Up*, 5.17.74, Jaik Rosenstein
**Richard C. Miller**—Richard Miller internet site; *Art Photography*, 10.54 Hamburgers and Cheesecake, Emmeline Snively
**Moran, Jasgur taking photo**—information viewed on *Everlasting Star*
**Norma Jeane was overexposed**—*Art Photography*, 10.54 Hamburgers and Cheesecake, Emmeline Snively
**Helen Ainsworth**—*Modern Screen*, 7.54, The Secrets of Marilyn's Life as a Model, Emmeline Snively; *Art Photography* 10.54, Hamburgers and Cheesecake, Emmeline Snively; *Motion Picture*, 5.56, Marilyn's the Most, Harry Lipton
**Harry Lipton, makeup spilled**— *Motion Picture*, 5.56, Marilyn's the Most, Harry Lipton
**Harry Lipton, calling at midnight**— *Motion Picture*, 5.56, Marilyn's the Most, Harry Lipton
**Gladys visit with Miss Snively**--6.7.62, *Los Angeles Herald Examiner*, Ted Thackery
**Cover with lamb Family Circle quote**—*Family Circle*, May 1953, What Caused Marilyn Monroe, Harry Evans
**William Carroll**—5.7.2001, *Santa Fe New Mexican*, Photo Exhibit Offers Look at Innocence of Norma Jeane; *Marilyn Monroe 1945 (Norma Jeane Dougherty),* William Carroll, Coda Publications, 2008
**Helldorado**—5.18.46, *Reno Evening Gazette*

**Lazlo Willinger quote, ripe peach--** *Movieland* 12.52, The Uncensored Marilyn Monroe Story; *Art Photography* 10.54, Hamburgers and Cheesecake, Emmeline Snively
**Mailer quote** *–Marilyn*, Norman Mailer, Grosset & Dunlap, 1973
**Jim cuts off allotment--***Photoplay*, 3.53, Marilyn Monroe Was My Wife, James Dougherty
**Bill Purcel**—*Marilyn Monroe, Private and Confidential*, Michelle Morgan, 2012, Skyhorse Publishing
**MM quote, child widow--** *Australian Women's Weekly*, 1.12.55, My Story, Marilyn Monroe
**MM, 'Hello Bill'--** *Photoplay*, 3.53, Marilyn Monroe Was My Wife, James Dougherty
**MM on modeling career**—*The Saturday Evening Post*, 5.5.56, The New Marilyn Monroe, Pete Martin
**Sidney Skolsky on Beerman photographing MM**— *Modern Screen*, 10.53, I Love Marilyn Monroe, Sidney Skolsky
**Whitey Snyder on MM as a model**—*Screen Life* 7.54, An Open Letter to Joe DiMaggio, Joe Thomas
**Bruno Bernard**—2.4.61, *Winnipeg Free Press*, Marilyn Once Was A Sweet Little Teenager, Jim Anderson

# Chapter Six
**The Hardest Working Starlet in Town**
**Quote**—*Marilyn*, 1954, Sidney Skolsky; *Modern Screen* 3.54, The Lowdown on Hollywood Women, Sidney Skolsky
**Harry Lipton Quote**—*Cavalier* 8.61, The Girl With Three Blue Eyes, Ezra Goodman
**MM quote on what she wore to Fox, looked the coolest of them all**—7.9.56, Leonard Lyons
**Ben Lyon on seeing MM in his office**—*The Marilyn Scandal*, Sandra Shevey, William Morrow & Co, 1987
**Ben Lyon quote, Louella Parsons natural blonde**—7.8.62, Louella Parsons, *Film Star Lives in State of Fear*
**Ben Lyon quote--**5.17.56, *A Profile of a Phenomenon, A Cynic and Monroe*, Article 2, Milton Shulman
**Bill Purcel information**— *Marilyn Monroe, Private and Confidential,* Michelle Morgan, 2012, Skyhorse Publishing
**Snively quote about Howard Hughes**— *People Today* 4.7.54, I Taught Marilyn How, Emmeline Snively; *Modern Screen*, 7.54, The Secrets of Marilyn's Life as a Model, Emmeline Snively; *Art Photography*, 10.54, Hamburgers and Cheesecake, Emmeline Snively; *Movie Time* 12.54, The Marilyn Monroe I Used to Know, Earl Leaf; *Cavalier* 8.61, The Girl With Three Blue Eyes, Ezra Goodman
**Marilyn pic to Ben Lyon NBLSB**—9.12.54, Louella Parsons, *Gossip Perils Marilyn-DiMag Marriage*
**Leo Caloia and Emmeline Snively films**—viewed photos of brochure and video on *Everlasting Star*, eBay and YouTube; *The Legend of Marilyn Monroe*, John Huston narrator, Terry Sanders, David L. Wolper, Ezra Goodman producers, 1966
**Leon Shamroy quote, first meeting**—*Collier's*, 9.51, The 1951 Model Blonde, Robert Cahn
**Leon Shamroy quote—She is Jean Harlow**—*Coronet*, 10.52, The Story Behind Marilyn Monroe, Grady Johnson
**Leon Shamroy, curls edges of film**—*Screen Guide*, 12.51, Mighty Marilyn, no by-line; *Motion picture* 3.53, Too Much Fire, Julie Paul
**Leon Shamroy, MM not good looking--***Cavalier* 8.61, The Girl With Three Blue Eyes, Ezra Goodman
**Whitey Snyder on MMs makeup**— *This Week Magazine*, 12.11.1960, Marilyn Monroe Talks About Herself, Joe Hyams
**Mailer, coven**— *Marilyn*, Norman Mailer, Grosset & Dunlap, 1973
**Bill Purcel waits at Aunt Ana's**— *Marilyn Monroe, Private and Confidential*, Michelle Morgan, 2012, Skyhorse Publishing
**Snively, set new record**—*Art Photography,* 10.54 Hamburgers and Cheesecake, Emmeline Snively
**Snively, how she got there--***Cavalier*, 8.61, The Girl With Three Blue Eyes, Ezra Goodman
**Grace signing Marilyn's contract**—viewed information on *Everlasting Star* and *eBay*
**Marilyn's Publicity Number**—Lasse Karlsson, Everlasting Star
**Earl Theisen**— *Marilyn Monroe*, Maurice Zolotow, 1960, Harcourt Brace, 1960
**Ed Clark on MM**—*LIFE* internet site; *Ed Clark, Decades, A Photographic Retrospective,1930-1960* Publisher at Yardleyville; *The Fredricksburg Post*, MD, 9,10,1983, Getting Familiar, The Clarks—family portrait of photographers, Joy Pittman Gurley (tomato quote)
**Tommy Zahn--** *Goddess: The Secret Lives of Marilyn Monroe*, Anthony Summers, MacMillan Publishing Company, 1985; 9.19.2007, *Corsair*, Volume 94, Number 3, SMC Alumnus, Former Lifeguard and Professor Discusses Recently Published Historical Work, Amber Rae Smith; *Marilyn, The Passion and the Paradox,* Lois Banner, Bloomsbury, 2014; *The Surfboard: Art, Style, Stroke*, Ben Marcus, MVP Books, 2007
**Photo of Marilyn at luau--** *Marilyn, The Passion and the Paradox,* Lois Banner, Bloomsbury, 2014; Los Angeles County Lifeguard Association; Surfing Heritage Foundation; Everlasting Star, Marilyn At a Surfer's Party in Malibu 1947, Marilyn and Tommy Zahn, posted by Joan Newman;

**Women Family Dinner; Signing Divorce Papers; Free Love**—*The Secret Life of Marilyn* Monroe, J. Randy Taraborrelli, Grand Central Publishing,2009; Photoplay, 3.53, Marilyn Monroe Was My Wife, James Dougherty; *My Sister Marilyn, A Memoir of Marilyn Monroe,* Berniece Miracle, Mona Miracle, Orion, 1995; *Marilyn, The Passion and the Paradox,* Lois Banner, Bloomsbury, 2014

**Andre de Dienes jealous**--8.8.62, *Los Angeles Times,* Jack Smith, I Loved Marilyn, 'Started Career,' Mourns Hollywood Photographer; *MARILYN, MON AMOUR: The private album of Andre de Dienes, her preferred photographer,* Andre de Dienes, St. Martin's Press, 1985

**Andre de Dienes sitting Sept. 46**-- *MARILYN, MON AMOUR: The private album of Andre de Dienes, her preferred photographer,* Andre de Dienes, St. Martin's Press, 1985

**Santa Claus Lane Parade**; **Jasgur; Alan Young**-- *Los Angeles Times,* 9.16.1946, Stars Parade to open Santa Claus Lane, no by-line; 11.19.1946, *Los Angeles Times,* Santa Claus Lane Parade Opens With Parade of Stars, no by-line

**Alan Young—** 2.6.53, Earl Wilson; *Motion Picture* 1.55, On Again, Off Again, Earl Wilson; *Mister Ed and Me and More*! Alan Young, 2007, Gordie Press;

**Darrin Motor Car**—Viewed photos and information on *eBay*

**Last meeting of MM and Jim Dougherty**-- 3.53, *Photoplay,* Marilyn Monroe Was My Wife, James Dougherty

**Martha Raye**— *12.17.46, Los Angeles Times,* Martha Raye to star in Autobiography, Phillip Schurer

Jantzen "Double Dare and "Temptation" swimsuits—3.11.47, Times Picyune, LA, Double Dare ad; 5.25.47, Idaho Statesman, Double Dare and Temptation ad;

**Andre de Dienes end of affair**--Jan 47--8.8.62, *Los Angeles Times,* Jack Smith, I Loved Marilyn, 'Started Career,' Mourns Hollywood Photographer; *MARILYN, MON AMOUR: The private album of Andre de Dienes, her preferred photographer,* Andre de Dienes, St. Martin's Press, 1985

**Quote by de Dienes**—*Cavalier* 8.61, The Girl With Three Blue Eyes, Ezra Goodman; *Tab* 5.53, Who Made Marilyn, no by-line; *Art Photography* 10.54 Hamburgers and Cheesecake, Emmeline Snively; *US Camera* 6.54, Marilyn Monroe, no by-line

**Jet Fore on MMs early fox bio**—*The Rock Hill Herald,* 2.12.1981, MMs Dad Identified; *AP*, 2.12.1981, Yardena Arar; *Los Angeles Times,* 8.2.12, Michael Seiler, Father of Film Star Dies; *Omaha World Herald,* 2.12.81, *AP,* Miss Monroe's Birth Believed Legitimate; *Tri City Herald,* 2.12.1981, Star's birth proved legitimate After All, *AP*; *Silver Screen,* 12.56, She Made a Piker of Cinderella, John Maynard

**Daddy sitter quote by mm**—*The Saturday Evening Post,* 5.5.56, The New Marilyn Monroe, Pete Martin

**They worried if a girl has cleavage**—*The Saturday Evening Post,* 5.19.56, the New Marilyn Monroe, Blonde Incorporated, Pete Martin

**American Legion's annual ceremony honoring "Studio Starlings."**—3.22.2001, Butterfields, Marilyn Monroe: The Red Velvet Images

**Mabs of Hollywood "Hourglass" swimsuit**—5.9.47, Times Picyune, LA , Mabs of Hollywood Hourglass ad

**Actors Lab**— *Marilyn Monroe,* Maurice Zolotow, 1960, Harcourt Brace, 1960

**Phoebe Brand**-- *Marilyn Monroe,* Maurice Zolotow, 1960, Harcourt Brace, 1960

**"Eye-Catcher" by Catalina**—470604, Iowa City Press, Catalina ad

**MM and S. Skolsky, early in MMs career**—*Marilyn,* 1954, Sidney Skolsky

**Helena Sorrell**—9.15.43, *Milwaukee Observer, UP,* Beauty, Personality May Help, but Not Sufficient for Box Office Success,

**Bill Burnside**—5.6.84, *The Observer,* Darling You're Too Fat, Bill Burnside

**Helena Sorrell**— *Marilyn Monroe,* Maurice Zolotow, Harcourt Brace, 1960; 5.6.84, *The Observer,* Darling You're Too Fat, Bill Burnside

**Las Vegas trip**— *Marilyn Monroe, Private and Confidential,* Michelle Morgan, 2012, Skyhorse Publishing; *Los Angeles Times,* 7.24.1947, Free Air Taxi to Las Vegas

**Orphanage quote**—10.2.55, *American Weekly,* the Mystery of MM, Zolotow

**Frank Borzage motion picture golf tournament**—470802, *Los Angeles Times,* Motion Picture Golf Tourney on Tomorrow; 470813, *Los Angeles Times,* Movie Golfers Compete Today in Tournament

**Lucille Ryman..Florabel Muir**—*Chicago Daily Tribune,* 10.12.1952, Marvelous Marilyn Monroe, Florabel Muir

**Mm quote—pose for stills**—*The Saturday Evening Post,* 5.5.56, The New Marilyn Monroe, Pete Martin

# Chapter Seven
## A Pretty Panhandler
**Quote**-- *Australian Women's Weekly,* 1.19.55, This is My Story, Marilyn Monroe;

**MM quote, unphotogenic**—*Australian Women's Weekly*, 1.19.55, This is My Story, Marilyn Monroe, Ben Hecht
**Harry Lipton**…MM quote "case of supply and demand", video intvw; Also transcribed in *The Secret Life of Marilyn Monroe*, J. Randy Taraborrelli, Grand Central Publishing, 2009
**MM quote**—pulling myself up and slipping back---*Coronet*, 10.52, The Story Behind Marilyn Monroe, **Grady Johnson**; *Movie Spotlight*, 8.51, What Makes a Glamour Girl?, no by-line
**Realized Mm was only 20**—*Motion Picture*, 5.56, Marilyn's The Most!, Harry Lipton
**MM quote—epiphany…actress must act**— *Filmland*, 1.53, Failure Was My Spur, Marilyn Monroe; *Filmland*, 4.52, mmmm—It's Marilyn, no by-line
**MM quote—vague notions about motion picture business**—*Movieland*, 5.51, Lessons I've Learned in Hollywood, Tex Parks
**Dreaming in colors**— interview with Dr. Joseph Meador, PhD, Austin, Texas; *Australian Women's Weekly*, 1.19.55, This is My Story, Marilyn Monroe
**The ability to act; fell in love with herself**—*Australian Women's Weekly*, 1.19.55, This is My Story, Marilyn Monroe
**Fred Harris on MM**—*Screen*, 11.56, Now Marilyn Can Talk, Fred Harris
**Florabel Muir on wolves**-- *Chicago Daily Tribune*, 10.12.52, Marvelous Marilyn Monroe, Florabel Muir
**Audition for Glamour Preferred**—*Marilyn: Her Life and Legend,* Susan Doll, Omnibus Press, 1990
**Quote by Clifton Webb**—*Inside Hollywood Annual*, 1955, A Sad Ending to a Short Love Story, no by-line; *Picturegoer*, UK, 6.11.55, You Don't Really Know Monroe…, Clifton Webb interviewed by Ernie Player
**Donna Hamilton and Paris Gazette**—11.3.64, Earl Wilson
**Harry Lipton—break in story—Pics for Burbank paper**-- *Redbook*, 6.52, So Far To Go Alone, Jim Henaghan;
**How She Met Police Officer,** *Motion Picture*, 1.53,Wolves I Have Known, Florabel Muir; *Joy*, 7.53, Men In My Life, Marilyn Monroe; *Motion Picture*, 5.56, Marilyn's the Most!, Harry Lipton
**MM was asked not to press charges**--*National Police Gazette*, 3.56
**Florabel Muir, Lucille Ryman quote on mm**— 10.12.52, *Chicago Daily Tribune*, Marvelous Marilyn Monroe, Florabel Muir
**Lucille Ryman quote kitten exterior**—*Cavalier*, 8.61, The Girl With the Three Blue Eyes, Ezra Goodman
**Glamour Preferred**-- *Marilyn: Her Life and Legend,* Susan Doll, Omnibus Press, 1990
**Penny Wise**—12.5.47, *Los Angeles Times*, 'Penny Wise', by Katherine Von Blon;
**Schenck on Schenck**—*Cavalier* 8.61
**Mm on Schenck**—6.6.54, *Empire News*
**Louella parsons on Schenck**—7.8.62, Louella Parsons, Marilyn Monroe's Hidden Torments
**mm on Schenck**-- *Marilyn Monroe*, Maurice Zolotow, Harcourt Brace, 1960
**George Seaton quote on mm and Schenck**— Norman Mailer Files at the Harry Ransom Center, University of Texas, Austin; Files for Norman Mailer's books, *Marilyn*, Grosset & Dunlap, 1973; *Of Women and Their Elegance*, Simon & Schuster, 1980; Courtesy of Dr. Lois Banner, PhD
**Orson Welles on mm**—*Who the Hell's In It*, Peter Bogdanovich, Knoph, 2004
**Louella Parsons meeting MM at Scheck's home**—*Modern Screen*, 7.53; 5.31.53, Sunday Pictorial Review, *Boston Advertiser*
**Marilyn on greed of rich men**-- *Australian Women's Weekly*, 1.19.55, This is My Story, Marilyn Monroe
**Fifty cents for your soul**—*Australian Women's Weekly*, 1.19.55, This is My Story, Marilyn Monroe
**Flea on a girdle—Lipton**— *Norma Jean*, Fred Lawrence Guiles, McGraw Hill Book Co., 1969
**Artichoke festival**—12.8.89, *The Artichoke Queen*, compiled by Ausonio, Andy, and adapted by Whitmore, Paula, Office Manager for the Castroville Artichoke Festival, Inc., Castroville, California
**Marilyn being hired at Columbia**; *Screen World*, 11.53, The Private Life of Marilyn Monroe, Natasha Lytess
**Mailer quote about Schenck**—*Marilyn*, Norman Mailer, Grosset & Dunlap, 1973
**Edwin P. Hoyt on MM at Columbia**—*Marilyn, The Tragic Venus*, Edwin P. Hoyt, Duell, Sloan & Pearce, 1965
**Natasha on MM**—*Marilyn Monroe*, Maurice Zolotow, 1960, Harcourt Brace; *Norma Jean*, Fred Lawrence Guiles, McGraw Hill Book Co., 1969
**Natasha Lytess quotes –first meeting and that voice**—*Screen World*, 11.53, The Private Life of Marilyn Monroe, Natasha Lytess
**MM had it, has it**— *Family Circle*, 6.53, What Caused Marilyn Monroe, Harry Evans; *Photoplay*, 1.55, Don't Blame Yourself, Marilyn, Lilla Anderson
**Wiggled into office not wearing a bra**—*The Marilyn Scandal*, Sandra Shevey, William Morrow & Co, 1987
**I was not impressed—inhibited and cramped**—11.25.52, Aline Mosby, Marilyn Monroe's Screen Voice Recalled; *Goddess: The Secret Lives of Marilyn Monroe*, Anthony Summers, MacMillan Publishing Company, 1985

**Say things freely**—*Goddess: The Secret Lives of Marilyn Monroe*, Anthony Summers, MacMillan Publishing Company, 1985
**Dire need of what I had to offer**—*Photoplay,* 7.57, Marilyn at the Crossroads, Alex Joyce
**NL quote 1953**—*Family Circle*, 6.53, What Caused Marilyn Monroe, Harry Evans
**Natasha quotes…success with acting**— *Photoplay*, 1.55, Don't Blame Yourself, Marilyn, Lilla Anderson
**Fred Karger acetate disc**—Viewed information on *eBay*
**Bruno Bernard, Lilly St. Cir**— *Marilyn, The Passion and the Paradox*, Lois Banner, Bloomsbury, 2014
**Aunt Ana inscription in The Potter**—*Screen Fan*, 10.52, Skyrocket, A Star is Born, no by-line
**MM quote on Aunt Ana**— *Motion Picture*, 11.54, Marilyn, Oh, Marilyn, Rita Garrison Malloy
**MM on Aunt Ana's death**—*Modern Screen*, 2.51, I Was an Orphan, Marilyn Monroe
**Letter to Berniece Miracle, c 1948**-- 8.28.2005, *Santa Fe New Mexican*, Monroe Letter Provide Rare Look at Star, Rosemary McKittrick
**Anne Karger**— *Marilyn, The Tragic Venus*, Edwin P. Hoyt, Duell, Sloan & Pearce, 1965
**Mary Karger**— Marilyn, The Passion and the Paradox, Lois Banner, Bloomsbury, 2014
**Action, April 1948**— Information from the collection of Dr. Lois Banner, PhD,
**Hair Fashion show at Wilshire Ebell**— *Los Angeles Times*, 4.8.1948, Hair Fashion Show at Wilshire Ebell
**Rand Brooks quote**—3.9.2003, *Santa Barbara News Press,* Rand Brooks Obituary
**James Bacon introduced to MM**—12.27.73, James Bacon, Hollywood Hotline
**Rose Marie Reid Plaid** –48.05.06, Cleveland Plain Dealer, captioned photo of MM in suit; 48.05.27 *Cleveland Plain Dealer*, Rose Marie Reid ad; *Rose Marie Reid: An Extraordinary Story,* Covenant Communications Inc., 1995
**Emperors Waltz**— *Los Angeles Times*, 5.27.1948, 'Emperor Waltz' Elegant Extravaganza, Edwin Schallert
**George White Scandals**— *Los Angeles Times*, 6.8.1948, Holm Trouble, no by-line; *Toledo Blade*, 6.14.1948, Seeing Stars Everywhere, Premier of GWS, Jackie Coogan, Donald O'Conner, Mrs. O'Conner, Mrs. Coogan
**Lend an Ear**— *Los Angeles Times*, 6.14.48, 'Lend and Ear' to Premiere, no by-line
**Clarice Evans**—*11.21.54,* I Was Marilyn Monroe's Roommate, and 11.28.54, Why Marilyn and Joe Broke Up, Clarice Evans, as told to Leslie Lieber; Appeared in newspaper Sunday inserts around the country
**Dr. Taylor dentist**—2.11.35, *Los Angeles Times,*; 1.14.36, *Los Angeles Times*, Fist Fight Loser Also Second in Court Bout; 2.9.46, *Los Angeles Times*, Dentist Hunted in Turf Brawl, no by-line; 2.10.46, *Los Angeles Times*, Dentist gives Self Up in Vase Assault Case, no by-line; 2.15.46, *Los Angeles Times*, Horse Trainer Won't Press Suit, no by-line; 3.24.48, *Los Angeles Times*, Former Dancer Divorces Dentist, no by-line
**Stage Door**— *8.22.48, Los Angeles Times*, Ad for Stage Door, Bliss-Hayden Theatre; another ad on 8.12.48; *Marilyn: Her Life and Legend,* Susan Doll, Omnibus Press, 1990
**Purcel, Grunion Run, Madame butterfly**— *Marilyn Monroe, Private and Confidential*, Michelle Morgan, Skyhorse Publishing, 2012
**Mm quote, pulling myself up and slipping back**—*Filmland*, 1.53, Failure Was My Spur, Marilyn Monroe
**Meeting with executives a Columbia**— *Filmland*, 1.53, Failure Was My Spur, Marilyn Monroe
**Mm on wanting to act**—Silver Screen, 10.51, Love is My Problem, Marilyn Monroe
**Anne Karger, go to church**—*Legend: The Life and Death of Marilyn Monroe*, Fred Lawrence Guiles, Stein and Day, 1984
**Natasha quote on being dropped**—*Movieland*, 9.53, The Marilyn I Know, Natasha Lytess
**Natasha quote on Columbia dropping her**—*Family Circle*, 6. 53, What Caused Marilyn Monroe, Harry Evans
**Being fired from Columbia**— *Filmland*, 1.53, Failure Was My Spur, Marilyn Monroe; *Screen World*, 11.53, The Private Life of Marilyn Monroe, Natasha Lytess
**Tom Kelley**—*Modern Man's Annual, Hunting Edition,* 1956, I Photographed Marilyn Monroe in the Nude, Tom Kelley; *Marilyn Monroe, The Red Velvet Images*, Butterfields Auctioneers Corp., 2000; *American Weekly*, 10.16.55, The Mystery of Marilyn Monroe, Maurice Zolotow

# Chapter Eight
## Paying Her Dues
**Quote**—5.20.50, *Daily Independent Journal*, San Rafael, CA
**Groucho quote**—*The Legend of Marilyn Monroe*, John Huston narrator, 1966
**Groucho Quote**—2.6.56, Erskine Johnson
**Pacific Coast Antiques Show, 1948**--11.4.48, *Sausalito News*

**November 5, 1948 Lester Cowan writes a letter to Mr. Grad Sears** —viewed information at the Margaret Herrick Library, Lester Cowan Files
**LIFE mag J.R. Eyerman photos**—*Time LIFE* site
**Phil Moore quote by Steve Cronin**—*Modern Screen*, 9.52, The Secret Life of Marilyn Monroe, Steve Cronin
**Zolotow quote about Moran**--M*arilyn Monroe*, Maurice Zolotow, 1960, Harcourt Brace
**Newspaper blurb about Marilyn**—11.20.48, *The Evening Star*, Washington, D.C., Jay Carmody; 11.20.48, *The Bakersfield Californian*, Monroe, United's Newest, Hits Cinderella Highway;
**letter from Sam Kerner to Lester Cowan**-- viewed information at the Margaret Herrick Library, Lester Cowan Files
**Joe Kirkwood, Jr.** – 2.6.49, *Wisconsin Journal*, Star in Your Eyes, Edith Gwynn; Dr. Lois Banner, PhD, collection; *Marilyn Monroe: Private and Undisclosed*, Michelle Morgan, Carroll & Graf, 2007
**February 8th, Lester Cowan wrote a letter to Groucho Marx**-- viewed information at the Margaret Herrick Library, Lester Cowan Files
**Benny Goodman**-- 9.12.52, Louella Parsons
**MM met Johnny Hyde in Palm Springs**--*Untold Secrets*, 10.61, The Men Who Made Marilyn, no by-line
**MM on Johnny Hyde**—*Untold Secrets*, 10.61, The Men Who Made Marilyn, no by-line
**Arthur Hornblow, Jr.**--*Untold Secrets*, 10.61, The Men Who Made Marilyn, no by-line
**Not a Svengali**—*American Weekly*, 10.16.55, The Mystery of Marilyn Monroe, Maurice Zolotow; *Untold Secrets,* 10.61, The Men Who Made Marilyn, no by-line
**Edwin P. Hoyt quote**— *Marilyn, The Tragic Venus*, Edwin P. Hoyt, Duell, Sloan & Pearce, 1965
**Al Tamarin of United Artist was sent a letter from Bill Chaikin**-- viewed information at the Margaret Herrick Library, Lester Cowan Files
**MM quote on Halsman**—*Cosmopolitan*, 5.53, The Fabulous Story of Hollywood's Biggest Build-Up: Marilyn Monroe, Robert L. Heilbronner; *Photography*, 6.53, Shooting Marilyn, Philippe Halsman; *Popular Photography*, 1.66, Marilyn Monroe, The Image and the Photographers, Ralph Hattersly
**March 14th Lester Cowan sends a telegram to Bill Chaikin**-- viewed information at the Margaret Herrick Library, Lester Cowan Files
**Kelley on MMs appearance**—1.10.54, *The Sun Herald*, Australia, Miss Monroe's Doctrine
**Nude calendar shoot**— 4.1.51, *Los Angeles Times*, Ad Lensman Kelley's Methods in Creating Pictures Explained, no by-line; *Modern Man's Annual, Hunting Edition*, 1956, I Photographed Marilyn Monroe in the Nude, Tom Kelley; *Marilyn Monroe, The Red Velvet Images*, Butterfields Auctioneers Corp., 2000; *American Weekly*, 10.16.55, The Mystery of Marilyn Monroe, Maurice Zolotow; 3.22.2001, Butterfields, Marilyn Monroe: The Red Velvet Images
**Calendar Appearance**— *Marilyn Monroe*, Maurice Zolotow, Hartcourt, Brace, 1960; *Tom Kelley's Studio*, Peter Doggett, Tom Kelley, Jr., Reel Art Press, 2014
**John Baumgarth on the nude calendar**—2.10.55, *Los Angeles Times*, Calendar Maker Strikes it Rich on $50 paid to Marilyn Monroe
**Advise to girls posing nude**—8.23.59, Earl Wilson, Marilyn Gets Some Advice
**Shot seen round the world**—12.13.73, *Los Angeles Times*, Jim Stingley, Shot Seen Round the World
**Studies of the nude figure**—*Studies of the Nude Figure*, The John Baumgarth Co., 1955
**Clark Gordon**—*YouTube* video
**Barney Rossen sends Al Tamarin of United Artist a telegram** —viewed at the Margaret Herrick Library, Lester Cowan Files
**Reasons for Choosing Rockford**—5.24.49, *The Freeport Journal Standard*, 3 Hollywood Actresses to Attend Premier of Film in Rockford
**Rockford, IL newspapers**—6.7.49, *Rockford Register Republic*, captioned pic; 6.13.49, *Rockford Register Republic*, Movie Starlet Shuns Coffee, no by-line; 6.13.49, *Rockford Register Republic*, Love Happy at State Tuesday, no by-line; 6.13.49, *Rockford Register Republic*, captioned pic of Marilyn w Orphans; 6.14.49, *Rockford Morning Star*, Marilyn Monroe is "Wow" Girl to Star Interviewer, no by-line, captioned pic accompanies article, Movie Starlet Goes for Walk in Rain with "Harpo"; 6.14,49, *Rockford Register Republic*, captioned picture of Marilyn, Today Being Flag Day; 6.14.49, *Rockford Register Republic,* State Offers "Love Happy"; 6.15.49, *Rockford Morning Star*, Big Crowds Greet Star "Love Happy", captioned picture with article, Vivian Johnson with Marilyn; 1.11.52, *Rockford Register Rockford Morning Star*, Hal Nelson; *Rockford Register Republic*, Clifton Webb Coronado Star; 6.18.49, *Rockford Morning Star*, "Love Happy" Plays State; 6.19.49, 6.19.49, *Rockford Morning Star*, Photo Highlights of the Week in Rockford, It's "Swim Health Week"
**Florabel Muir quote, rely on myself**--10.12.1952, *Chicago Tribune, Grafic Magazine,* Marvelous Marilyn Monroe, Florabel Muir

**Caviar**—*Photoplay*, 1.55, Don't Blame Yourself, Marilyn, Lilla Anderson
***Photoplay* editor Adele Whitely-Fletcher**—*Photoplay*, 9.65, So That the Memory of Marilyn Will Linger On, Adele Whitley Fletcher
**2.2.56 Fleur Cowles and Adele Fletcher quote**-- *Photoplay*, 9.65, So That the Memory of Marilyn Will Linger On, Adele Whitley Fletcher
**Warrensburg newspaper quote**—6.23.49, Warrensburg, NY, Mrs. MacAllister Accepts Key to Dream House Before 500
**Earl Wilson quote about Fred Joyce/Marilyn interview**—8.20.58, Earl Wilson
**Earl Wilson quote Shorehaven Beach Club**—11.14.75, Earl Wilson, Nobodies Become Somebodies
**Earl Wilson quote on MM interview**—*Silver Screen*, 4.53, M-m-m-my Marilyn; 8.9.62, Earl Wilson, Blonde Starlet Nobody Knew Remembered
**Sherry Netherland Hotel**-- *Marilyn, The Tragic Venus*, Edwin P. Hoyt, Duell, Sloan & Pearce, 1965
**Henry Rosenfeld**— *Goddess: The Secret Lives of Marilyn Monroe*, Anthony Summers, MacMillan Publishing Company, 1985
**Slave bracelet quote by mm**-- *This Week Magazine*, 12.11.60, Marilyn Monroe Talks About Herself, Joe Hyams
**de Dienes at Jones Beach w MM**-- *MARILYN, MON AMOUR: The private album of Andre de Dienes, her preferred photographer,* Andre de Dienes, St. Martin's Press, 1985
**Sexiest pic I've ever taken by de Dienes**—*Screen Album*, winter 53
**Film stars world series baseball game**—Colin Glassborow collection, marilynmonroe-photos.com
**Gus Zernail quote on MM**—7.20.2007, Gus Zernail, One of the Best Baseball Players No One Remembers, www.associatedcontent.com
**Roddy McDowell, Ricketts Restaurant**—Colin Glassborow collection, marilynmonroe-photos.com
**Tony Weitzel/Visit to Detroit**—8.21.77, Along the Trail, Tony Weitzel
**John Ahlhauser and Milwaukee Journal visit**—8.6.62, *Milwaukee Journal*, Marilyn's Milwaukee Visit Was Early in Her Career, Raymond E. McBride; 10.28.2012, *Journal Sentinel Online*, Kodak's Diminished Role Disappears in a Flash, Meg Jones
**Erskine Johnson…mm in love happy**—8.5.52, Erskine Johnson, Marilyn Monroe, Blonde, Saucy and Sexy
**Ken Murray**—12.05.52, Erskine Johnson; *Movies*, 6.55, If You Were Marilyn Monroe's Friend, Jack Holland; *Life On a Pogo Stick; Autobiography of a Comedian*, Murray, Ken, John C. Winston, Co., 1960
**Marie Wilson to Sheilah Graham**—4.15.54, Sheilah Graham
**Mary loos quote on MM, had all the wrong things to be a star**—
**Lionel Newman**— *Marilyn, The Tragic Venus*, Edwin P. Hoyt, Duell, Sloan & Pearce, 1965
**Ticket to tomahawk pants fell down prank**—10.11.74, Earl Wilson, Some Memories of Marilyn; *Blonde Heat: The Sizzling Career of Marilyn Monroe*, Richard Buskin, Billboard Books, 2001
**Ann Baxter on MM**—*Intermission*; Baxter, Ann; Putnam; 1976
**Barbara Berch Jamison**, ---7.12.53, Body and Soul: A Portrait of Marilyn Monroe Showing Why Gentlemen Prefer That Blonde, Barbara Berch Jamison
**Mm quote, skin of her teeth**— *My Story*, Marilyn Monroe, Ben Hecht, Stein and Day, 1974
**Lucille Ryman quote to convince Huston to cast MM**— 10.12.52, *Chicago Daily Tribune*, Marvelous Marilyn Monroe, Florabel Muir
**Dumb**—11.21.52, *American Weekly*, The Truth About Me, Marilyn Monroe, Liza Wilson
**Guilaroff quote AJ**— *Crowning Glory: Reflections of Hollywood's Favorite Confidant*, Sydney Guilaroff, Cathy Griffin, 1996, General Publishing Group
**James Bacon, Arthur Hornblow quotes**—8.6.62, James Bacon, No Peace of Mind for Famous Blonde
**Huston taking out falsies**—6.19.73, James Bacon, Hollywood Hotline
**Tom Davidson**—*Modern Screen*, 2.51, I Was an Orphan, Marilyn Monroe
**Julie Paul** – *Motion Picture*, 3.53, Too Much Fire, Julie Paul
**Guilaroff**—*Crowning Glory: Reflections of Hollywood's Favorite Confidant*, Sydney Guilaroff, Cathy Griffin, 1996, General Publishing Group
**Dana Andrews quote on mm**—*Hollywood Enigma: Dana Andrews*, Carl Rollyson, University Press of Mississippi, 2012
**Mm, Rooney, Jasgur**— *The Birth of Marilyn: The Lost Photographs of Norma Jean*, Joseph Jasgur, St. Martin's Press, 1991
**Skolsky on his friendship w/MM**—*Marilyn*, pg. 33, Sydney Skolsky, 1954

**Edith head …extremely knowledgeable about fit and fabric**—9.4.84, *Boston Herald*, Edith Head, Marilyn Monroe a Free Spirit Harnessed
**Edith head…Persian kitten**—*News Palladium*, Benton Harbor, Mich., That Look of Softness…
**Saroyan quote**—*TV and Movie Screen*, 3.55, I'll Always Be Alone, no by-line; 3.25.50, *Los Angeles Times*, Bill Saroyan Tells Theme of New Play, Philip K. Scheuer; 3.31.50, *Los Angeles Times*, Circle Players Premier William Saroyan's 'Son', Edwin Schallert
**Guilaroff**— *Crowning Glory: Reflections of Hollywood's Favorite Confidant, Sydney Guilaroff*, Cathy Griffin, General Publishing Group, 1996
**Mankiewicz on mm reading Rainier Marie Rilke**-- *Marilyn, The Tragic Venus*, Edwin P. Hoyt, Duell, Sloan & Pearce, 1965; *Legend: The Life and Death of Marilyn Monroe*, Fred Lawrence Guiles, Stein and Day, 1984
**Natasha intro to Rilke**—*Cavalier*; 8.61, The Girl With Three Blue Eyes, Ezra Goodman
**Natasha books; de Saint-Exupery**—*Photoplay*, 7.57, Marilyn at the Crossroads, Alex Joyce
**Mm to Florea about reading**—*Screen Stars*, 11.54, Things They Never Told About Marilyn, Alice Craig Greene
**MM on reading**—*Movieland*, 5.55, Marilyn: Will Her Big Gamble Pay Off, no by-line
**George Sanders on MM**—*Australian Women's Weekly*, 6.29.60, Marilyn So Longed For Love, George Sanders
**Fox Publicity Machine**—*The Saturday Evening Post*, 5.5.56, The New Marilyn, Pete Martin
**Julian Myers** – internet article
**Roy Craft mms studio bio**—*Movie Stars Parade*, 3. 53, The Row About Marilyn Monroe, Merry Louis; *Silver Screen*, 12.56, She Made a Piker of Cinderella, John Maynard; *Marilyn Monroe*, Maurice Zolotow, Hartcourt, Brace, 1960
**Craft on publicity in 1952**-- *Marilyn Monroe*, Maurice Zolotow, Hartcourt, Brace, 1960
**Roy Craft on publicity**— *The Saturday Evening Post*, 5.5.56, the New Marilyn Monroe, Pete Martin
**Roy Craft on MM**—8.13.62, *The Oregonian*, Roy Craft, Paper's Editor Recalls Marilyn in Early Years of Stardom
**Roy Craft on MM**—9.13.77, *The Seattle Times*, Rick Anderson, Not Marilyn, but now she's Farrah-st; 9.14.80, *The Seattle Times*, Rick Anderson, Who Knew Her? Each Man's Fantasy: Only He Understood Marilyn Monroe
**Marilyn on publicity**—*Movie Play* 3.54, The Row About Marilyn, Merry Louis

# Chapter Nine
## The Making of a Star
**Quote**—*Untold Secrets*, 10.61, The Men in Marilyn's Life
**Natasha quote, walked over corpses**—*Family Circle*, 6.53, What Caused Marilyn Monroe, Harry Evans
Mm quote—to Zanuck…should have been fired—4.1.51, Louella Parsons, Marilyn Monroe From Orphanage to Stardom
**Zanuck quote to Marilyn**—*Legend: The Life and Death of Marilyn Monroe*, Fred Lawrence Guiles, Stein and Day, 1984
**Marilyn quote about Zanuck**—7.29.62, Bob Thomas, quoted from interview from May 19, 1962
**MM quote to Earl Leaf**—*Movie Time*, 12.54, The Marilyn Monroe I Used to Know, Earl Leaf
**Anthony Beauchamp**-- *Focus On Fame*, Beauchamp, Anthony; Odham's Press Limited, 1958; *Australian Women's Weekly*, 9.15.71, Mother and Son
**MM on investing in herself**—*Movieland*, 7.51, Are Budgets Necessary? Movieland Forum
**Shooting MM Beauchamp**—530815, *Niagara Falls Gazette*, Beauchamp shooting MM
**Ed Clark**—*Time/LIFE* website
**Danny Kaye's party for Mr. Sir**-- *Elia Kazan: A Life*, Elia Kazan, Da Capo Press, 1997
**Engstead**—*Star Shots, Engstead*, John; Dutton; 1978
**Mme Renna on MM**—*Cavalier*, 8.61, The Girl With Three Blue Eyes, Ezra Goodman
**Constance Bennett quote**—8.25.74, Earl Wilson
**All About Eve cape auctioned off**—12.15.50, *Calgary Herald*
**Peter Lawford at Malibu Beach**—*Newsweek*, 8.19.2002, Gidget Girls; Everlasting Star, Marilyn At a Surfer's Party in Malibu 1947, Marilyn and Tommy Zahn, Joan Newman post
**Thanksgiving Pilgrim Photo**—3.31.2012, Julian's Auctions, Hollywood Legends, lot 458
**Henaghan, mm on JH**---- *Redbook*, 6.52, So Far To Go, Jim Henaghan
**MM on JH**—*Movieland*, 5.51, Lessons I've Learned in Hollywood, Tex Parks
**MM on JH**-- *Marilyn Monroe*, Maurice Zolotow, 1960, Hartcourt, Brace
**Liza Wilson**--, *American Weekly*, 11.16.52, The Truth About Me, Marilyn Monroe, Liza Wilson

# Chapter Ten
## Stalled On the Launching Pad
**Quote**— *My Story*, Marilyn Monroe, Ben Hecht, Stein and Day, 1974
**Miss Buxley**—08.05.84, *Pacific Stars and Stripes*; 09.03.2000, *Logansport Pharos Tribune*, IN, Beatle Bailey at 50, Denise Lavoie
**Miller and Kazan in Hollywood**— *Elia Kazan: A Life*, Elia Kazan, Da Capo Press, 1997
**Natasha on MM talking about meeting Miller**—*Hot Times: True Tales of Hollywood and Broadway*, Earl Wilson, Contemporary Books, 1984
**Miller on recommending Abraham Lincoln**-- *Norma Jean*, Fred Lawrence Guiles, McGraw Hill Book Co., 1969
**Kazan's Letter to Marilyn**--3.22.2001, Butterfields, Marilyn Monroe: The Red Velvet Images
**Shelly Winters**—*Shelley Also Known as Shirley*, Shelley Winters, Harper Collins, 1981; *Shelley II: The Middle of my Century*, Shelley Winters, Simon & Schuster, 1989; *Best of Times, Worst of Times*, Shelley Winters, Frederick Muller, Ltd, 1990
**UCLA**—*Collier's*, 9.51, The 1951 Model Blonde, Robert Cahn; *Movie Life*, 3.52, Wotta Co-Ed; *UCLA Yearbook, Southern Campus*, 1952; *Photoplay*, 4.52, Temptations of a Bachelor Girl, Marilyn Monroe; *Movies*, 8.52, Keeping Up With Marilyn, no by-line; *Screen Album*, Summer 1952, Marilyn Monroe: Love Will Have to Wait, no by-line; *Movieland*, 12.52, The Uncensored Marilyn Monroe Story, no by-line; *Movie Stars Parade*, 5.53, Marilyn Monroe Off Guard, no by-line; *Photoplay*, 1.55, Don't Blame Yourself, Marilyn, Lilla Anderson; *Modern Screen*, 10.55, The Very Private Life of Marilyn Monroe, William Barbour; *Marilyn Monroe: Private and Undisclosed*, Michelle Morgan, Constable Publishing, 2007
**Zolotow quote on UCLA**-- *Marilyn Monroe*, Maurice Zolotow, Hartcourt, Brace, 1960
**Marilyn walking at the studio in negligee**— *Collier's*, 9.51, 1951 Model Blonde, Robert Cahn; *The Saturday Evening Post*, 5.5.56, The New Marilyn Monroe, Pete Martin
**MM on Zanuck, Freak**—11.19.60, The Real Monroe, 'The Public Was My Way Out,' Maurice Zolotow
**Jane Greer on veteran's hospital visit**-- *Screen Guide*, 12.51, Mighty Marilyn, no by-line
**Luncheon at Café de Paris**—*Collier's*, 9.51, 1951 Model Blonde, Robert Cahn
**Trick of making an entrance**—*Australian Women's Weekly*, 1.19.55, This is My Story, Marilyn Monroe
**MM quote on studio bosses**--11.19.60, The Real Monroe, 'The Public Was My Way Out,' Maurice Zolotow
**MM quote on the Public**—*Untold Secrets*, 10.60, The Men in Marilyn's Life, no by-line; 11.19.60, The Real Monroe, 'The Public Was My Way Out,' Maurice Zolotow
**Johnny Hyde quote**—*Cavalier*, 8.61, The Girl With the Three Blue Eyes, Ezra Goodman
**Russell Birdwell quote**—*Brief*, 3.53, Why Marilyn Monroe, Dan Jenkins
**lack of publicity**—3.8.51, Toledo Blade
**Bill Tusher quote on publicity**—*Movie Stars Parade*, 6. 53, The Mystery Man in Marilyn's Life, Bill Tusher
**Grady Johnson quote on publicity**—*Coronet*, 10.52, The Story Behind Marilyn Monroe, Grady Johnson
**Quote by Roy Craft**—*Movie Stars Parade*, 6. 53, The Mystery Man in Marilyn's Life, Bill Tusher
**Photographers on MM**—*Motion Picture*, 11.53, Marilyn Monroe Loveable Fake, Jim Henaghan
**Robert Cahn quote on MMs growing appeal**—*Collier's*, 9.51, 1951 Model Blonde, Robert Cahn
**Red Cassini dress**—*Movieland*, 10.51, Why Women Hate Marilyn Monroe, no by-line; *Modern Screen*, 7.52, Am I Too Daring? Marilyn Monroe
**Letters to Arthur miller**—*Timebends: A Life,* Arthur Miller, Grove Press, 1987; *Norma Jean*, Fred Lawrence Guiles, McGraw Hill Book Co., 1969
**Tearing dress at academy award…Television & Screen Guide**, 8.51, Home Life of a Hollywood Bachelor Girl, no by-line
**Bill Tusher radio intvw with MM**… *Movie Stars Parade*, 6.53, The Mystery Man in Marilyn's Life, Bill Tusher; 8.5.2002, *the Seattle Times*, Erik Lacitis, My Love and Thanks Forever, Marilyn
**Josefa**—Heritage Auctions, Lot 4617, A Marilyn Monroe Group of Black and White Snapshots of Her Chihuahua, "Josefa," 1953
**Renie**—viewed information on *eBay*
**Contract with Fox, William Morris, 7 year contract**—*Marilyn Monroe*, Barbara Leaming, Three Rivers Press, 2000
**Kazan on MM, legs parted**-- *Elia Kazan: A Life*, Elia Kazan, Da Capo Press, 1997
**Cameron Mitchell on MM**—12.9.60, Pin-Ups Put Marilyn in Direct Line for Contract, Part 6, Maurice Zolotow
**David Wayne on MM**—6.21.56, Earl Wilson, Close Look at Marilyn Monroe

**David Wayne on MM**—*Screen Guide*, 12.51, Mighty Marilyn, no by-line
**With Kazan to preview of Streetcar**— Elia Kazan: A Life, Elia Kazan, Da Capo Press, 1997
**Party w Kazan at Charlie Feldman**— *Elia Kazan: A Life, Elia Kazan*, Da Capo Press, 1997
Jack Paar to Hy Gardner; 11.16.81, *Field Newspaper Syndicate*, Glad You Asked That!, by Marilyn and Hy Gardner, All About Jack Paar's movie career
**MM at Brownsville set of viva Zapata**— *The Joy of Marilyn In The Camera Eye,* Shaw, Sam; Exter Books; 1979; *Marilyn Among Friends*, Rosten, Norman and Shaw, Sam; Henry Holt & Co.; 1987; *Marilyn the New York Years*, Sam Shaw, Lardon Media, 2004
**Anthony Quinn quote**—*One Man Tango, Anthony Quinn*, Daniel Paisner, Harper Collins, 1995
**Quote on Shaw, Kazan and MM**—*Marilyn: Among Friends, Sam Shaw*, Norman Rosten, Henry Hold & Co, 1988
**Sam Shaw on Marilyn**—Runnin' Wild, No 9, January 1993, Shutterbugs, Sam Shaw
**Jody Lawrence quote, Ezra Goodman**--*Cavalier*, 8.61, The Girl With Three Blue Eyes, Ezra Goodman
**Kazan, party at Feldman house**-- *Elia Kazan: A Life, Elia Kazan*, Da Capo Press, 1997
**Dental work for Natasha**—viewed information on eBay
**7 year studio contract details**— *Marilyn Monroe*, Barbara Leaming, Three Rivers Press, 2000
**MM on dating and Bings little French boy**—*Movie People*, 5.54, The Men in Marilyn's Life, Michael Sheridan
**Jet Fore**—8.5.82, *AP*, Two Photos That Made a Difference
**Calendar meeting with Hy Gardner**—8.8.62, *New York Herald Tribune,* Hy Gardner
**Hy Gardner, 1st meeting MM**—1.21.80, *Field Newspaper Syndicate*, Glad You asked That! Marilyn and Hy Gardner, Hy Recounts the first time her met Marilyn (Monroe, that is!)
**Pete Martin, mm quote abt. Fox executives**—*The Saturday Evening Post*, 5.5.56, The New Marilyn, Pete Martin
**Phil Moore quote**—*Dorothy Dandridge,* Bogle, Donald, Armistad Press, Inc, 1997
**MacDonald Carey quote**-- *The Days of My Life*; Carey, MacDonald; St. Martin's Press; 1991; *Screen Guide*, 12.51, Mighty Marilyn, no by-line;
**Sydney Skolsky, Jerry Wald/MM**—*Marilyn*, Sydney Skolsky, 1954
**Richard Widmark, knocked off the screen**—*Marilyn Monroe*, The Biography, Donald Spoto, Harper Spotlight, 1993
**Frog Men, USS Benham**—viewed information on *Everlasting Star*
**Roy Craft, Long Beach Harbor**—08.07.62, *Los Angeles Times*, Ex-Press Agent Recalls Monroe's Magic Appeal; 08.05.02, *The Seattle Times*, Erik Lacitis, My Love and Thanks  Forever, Marilyn
**Sheilah Graham quote**—*Modern Screen*, 9.54, Marilyn Talks About Joe and Babies, Sheilah Graham
**New York, August 1951**— *Marilyn, The Passion and the Paradox*, Lois Banner, Bloomsbury, 2014
**Marlon Brando quote on trip**--10.10.54, *Baltimore Sun*, Louis Berg, Marilyn Meets Brando
**Sam Shaw**— *Marilyn, The Passion and the Paradox*, Lois Banner, Bloomsbury, 2014; *Marilyn: Among Friends,* Sam Shaw, Norman Rosten, Henry Hold & Co, 1988; *Theosophical Society* website
**Joe DiMaggio meeting MM harness track**— *DiMaggio, Setting the Record Straight*, Morris Engelberg, Marv Schneider, Motorbooks International, 2003
**Lilla Anderson on 1951 trip to NY, seeing JdM**—*Photoplay*, 1.55, Don't Blame Yourself, Marilyn, Lilla Anderson

# Chapter Eleven
## Heavenly Body

**Quote**— *Australian Women's Weekly*, 2.2.55, This is My Story, Marilyn Monroe;
**Dec. 1950 release of calendar**-- *Marilyn Monroe*, Maurice Zolotow, Hartcourt, Brace, 1960; *The Marilyn Scandals*, Sandra Shevey, William Morrow & Co, 1987
**James Bacon on nude calendar**—The Marilyn Scandals, Sandra Shevey, William Morrow & Co, 1987
**Natalie Kelley quote**—*Movie Stars Parade*, 7.53, I was There When Marilyn Posed, Natalie Kelley Grasco
**Nude Calendar**—Heritage Auctions, Lot 46001, A Marilyn Monroe Rare Signed Nude Calendar, Circa 1952
**Earl Wilson Autographed calendar**—8.9.72, Earl Wilson, What Happened to Monroe Photos; 8.7.73, Earl Wilson, Monroe Magic Still Crackles
**Robert Ryan quote**—1.6.63, Sheilah Graham
**Bacharach quote, "…can of lard"**—8.12.47, *UP*, Screen Photo Ace Bemoans Figure Cuts;
**Jack Palance**—*Norma Jean, Fred Lawrence Guiles*, McGraw Hill Book Co., 1969
**Chekhov**—*To the Actor*, Michael Chekhov, 1953
**Chekhov home**— *4.21.83, Los Angeles Times*, California bungalow of 1940s is not just another house for sale, Martha L. Willman

**All about eve quote**—*Marilyn*, 1954, Sidney Skolsky; *Modern Screen*, 3.54, The Lowdown on Hollywood Women, Sidney Skolsky
**Joan Caulfield on Chekhov**—4.13.55, *Los Angeles Times*, Joan Caulfield's Acting Given Lift by TV Role
**Roy Craft on Stanislavski**—*Movie Stars Parade*, 6.53, The Mystery Man in Marilyn's Life, Bill Tusher; *Screen Stars* 11.54, Things They Never Told About Marilyn, Alice Craig Greene
**Anthroposophy quote**— *Anthroposophical Society in America;* Rudolf Steiner at www.rudolfsteinerweb.com
**Mabel Elsworth Todd**—*The Thinking Body*, Mabel Elsworth Todd, Gestalt Journal Press, 2008
**Ralph Roberts**—*Mimosa*, Ralph Roberts unpublished memoir of Marilyn Monroe
**Charlie Chaplin, Jr.**—*Mimosa*, Ralph Roberts unpublished memoir of Marilyn Monroe
**Chekhov Cherry Orchard**—*Look*, 10.23.51, Marilyn Monroe…a Serious Blonde Who Can Act, Rupert Allan; *Redbook*, 8.62, Alan Levy, A Good Long Look at Myself; *My Story*, Marilyn Monroe, Ben Hecht, Stein and Day, 1974; *Conversations With Marilyn*, W.J. Weatherby, Ballentine, 1976
**Erotic freak** – *Family Circle*, 5.53, What Caused Marilyn Monroe, Harry Evans
**Jean Negulesco…sell sex all the time--** *Marilyn Monroe*, Maurice Zolotow, Hartcourt, Brace, 1960
**Bob Willoughby, energy field**—*Hollywood, A Journey Through the Stars*, Bob Willoughby, Assouline Publishing, 2001
**Ralph Roberts, blue-whiteness**—*Marilyn and Me, Sisters, Rivals, Friends*, Susan Strasberg, Time Warner Paperbacks, 1992
**Saul Bellow…incandescence under the skin**—*Saul Bellow, Letters*, Penguin Classics, 2010
**Yul Brenner--**6.22.59, *Chicago Daily Tribune*, Yul Looks for 'Simple Femininity,' Arlene Dahl
**Kundalini Yoga**—Joseph Meador, PhD, Austin, TX, interview
**Gems from Collier's**—*Collier's*, 9.8.51, 1951 Model Blonde, Robert Cahn
**Norman Mailer quote--** *Marilyn*, Norman Mailer, Grosset & Dunlap, 1973
**Harriet Parsons quote**—*Modern Screen*, 3.62, Marilyn Monroe's Hidden Fears, Louella Parsons
**Jane Russell quote--15 year old girl; Nick Ray--** *Silver Screen*, 8.53, What I Think of Marilyn, Jane Russell
**MM journal**— *Fragments: Poems, Intimate Notes, Letters, Marilyn Monroe*, editor, Bernard Comment, Farrar, Straus and Giroux, 2010
**MM Quote about bus trip**—5.4.52, Hedda Hopper, Blowtorch Blonde
**MM Quote about not forgetting**—*The Marilyn Scandal*, Sandra Shevey, William Morrow & Co., 1987
**Stanwyck quote**—*Stanwyck: A Biography*, Al Diorio, Coward Mc Cann, 1984
**Ernest Bacharach** –8.12.47, *UP*, Screen Photo Ace Bemoans Figure Cuts
**MM Quote, I'm a bookworm and proud of it!**—4.28.52, Erskine Johnson
**Theisen quote…Look shoot**—*Movie Stars Parade*, 6.53, The Mystery Man in Marilyn's Life, Bill Tusher
**Theisen quote**… *Marilyn Monroe*, Maurice Zolotow, Hartcourt, Brace, 1960
**Annie Lebowitz quote**—3.10.2010, *Santa Fe New Mexican*
**MM Quote, Looking in a mirror**—*Conversations With Marilyn*, W.J. Weatherby, Robson Books, 1976
**Philippe Halsman on photographing MM**—*Popular Photography*, 1.66, Marilyn Monroe: The Image and Her Photographers, Ralph Hattersly
**Abraham Gottsman**—Personal Research with Dr. Lois Banner, PhD; *The American Weekly*, 10.2.55, The Mystery of Marilyn Monroe, Maurice Zolotow; *Modern Screen*, 1.55, Why Joe Let Her Go, William Barbour
**Beverly Carlton**—*Screen Guide*, 12.51, Mighty Marilyn, no by-line
**MM Quote, Dumb blonde**—*Screenland*, 8.52, Marilyn Doesn't Believe in Hiding Things
**MM quote on her intelligence**— *Modern Screen*, 9.54, Marilyn Talks About Joe and Babies, Sheilah Graham
**Lotte Goslar**—*What's So Funny? Sketch's From My Life*, Lotte Goslar, Routledge, 1998;
**MM studying pantomime, body freedom--**4.27.52, Marilyn Monroe, Louella Parsons
**MM Quote on Goslar**—*Screenland*, 8.52, Marilyn Doesn't Believe In Hiding Things, Michael Sheridan
**Nick Ray quote to Jane Russell**— *That Girl Marilyn*, 1953, Jane Russell
**Roy Baker quote**—*The Marilyn Scandal*, Sandra Shevey, William Morrow & Co, 1987
**MM Quote to Pete Martin about calendar**— *The Saturday Evening Post*, 5,5,56, The New Marilyn Monroe, Pete Martin
**Phil Moore Quote about Calendar--** *Dorothy Dandridge*, Bogle, Donald, Amistad Press, Inc., 1997
**Widmark quote on MM**—7.8.2002, *The Telegraph*, UK, Michael Shelden
**Jim Backus quote on MM**—6.19.73, James Bacon, Hollywood Hotline
**Zanuck on Svengali Natasha Lytess**—memo dated 12.10.52
**MM Quote on Whitman Chocolates**—*Family Weekly*, 2.10.74, Ask Them Yourself, Arlene Dahl
**Edith Gwynn African Queen party**—*Photoplay*, 2.52

**James Bacon New Year's Eve**-- *Goddess: The Secret Lives of Marilyn Monroe*, Anthony Summers, MacMillan Publishing Company, 1985
**Elizabeth Toomey intvw** -- 2.9.55, Marilyn doesn't live up to her flamboyant screen personality, Elizabeth Toomey
**Red dress**— *Movieland*, 10.51, Why Women Hate Marilyn Monroe, no by-line; 4.10.52, Aline Mosby, 'Teach Marilyn Monroe How to Dress' Columnist Chorus; *Modern Screen*, 7.52, Am I Too Daring?, Marilyn Monroe;
**Hildegard Knef on MM at Henrietta Awards**—*The Gift Horse*, Hildegard Knew, McGraw Hill, 1970
**Bra and panties**—*Modern Screen*, 7.52, Am I Too Daring? Marilyn Monroe
**April Look Party, quote on I owe no apologies**—*Photoplay*, 4.52, The Temptations of a Bachelor Girl, Marilyn Monroe; *Modern Screen*, 7.52, Am I Too Daring?, Marilyn Monroe; *Motion Picture and Television*, 8.52, Why Women Hate Marilyn Monroe, Isabel Moore
**USO show at El Toro**— *Coronet*, 10.52,The Story Behind Marilyn Monroe, Grady Johnson; *Leatherneck*, 12.52, Monroe Doctrine, SSgt. Robert A. Suhosky, photos by MSgt. J.W. Richardson; *The Saturday Evening Post*, 5.5.56, The New Marilyn Monroe, Pete Martin
**Bob Hope on MM**—*Larry King Live,* Transcripts, 0308;
**Pete Rendina seeing MM at Camp Pendleton**--
http://www.kwp.org/html/comm.cfm?com_url=2004_marine_bbs_2&threadid=636&MARINES_MESSAGES=5&TANGO=266.63.21.90.176.254.63.21.90.176.245.443.63.21.90.176.287.332.63.21.90.176.476.122
**Jerry Wald on MM**—*Motion Picture and Television*, 5.52, What is Sex, Who Are Hollywood's Most Sexy Stars, Jerry Wald
**Wald Quote; Zolotow Quote**—10.16.55, *American Weekly*, The Mystery of Marilyn Monroe, Maurice Zolotow;
**Wald quote**--5.20.56, A Profile of a Phenomenon, A Cynic and Monroe, Article 5, Milton Shulman
**Travilla burlap sack**— *Screen Life*, 7.54, An Open Letter to Joe DiMaggio, Joe Thomas
**Roy Craft on potato sack**—5.2.2008, *The Seattle Times*, Erik Lacitis, My Love and Thanks Forever, Marilyn;
**MM on meeting JdM**—8.7.62, *Los Angeles Times*, Ex-Press Agent Recalls Monroe's Magic Appeal, Paul Weeks; 8.13.62, *The Oregonian*, Roy Craft, Paper's Editor Recalls Marilyn in Early Years of Stardom
**Liza Wilson, MM and JdM**—12.6.53, *The American Weekly* magazine, Liza Wilson
**Louella Parsons…mm and JdM**—5.31.52, Louella Parsons, Love Can Wait
**Norman Brokaw…mm and JdM**—*DiMaggio, Setting the Record Straight*, Morris Engelberg, Marv Schneider, Motorbooks International, 2003
**JdM…Edward Bennett Williams**-- *DiMaggio, Setting the Record Straight*, Morris Engelberg, Marv Schneider, Motorbooks International, 2003

# Chapter Twelve
## Riding the Publicity Rocket
**Quote** -- *Eye*, 3.52, Cinema's Sexiest Starlet, no by-line
**MM & Aline Mosby calendar caper**—3.13.52, Aline Mosby; 6.6.62, Aline Mosby, *Santa Monica Evening Outlook*; *Marilyn Monroe*, Maurice Zolotow, Hartcourt, Brace, 1960
**John Baumgarth quote on realizing the model was MM**--5.17.56, A Profile of a Phenomenon, A Cynic and Monroe, Article 2, Milton Shulman
**Distributed by Western Lithograph Co**—*Modern Screen*, 9.52, The Secret Life of Marilyn Monroe, Steve Cronin; *Redbook*, 6.52, So Far To Go Alone, Jim Henaghan
**Kneblecamp displeasure**— *Marilyn Monroe, Private and Confidential*, Michelle Morgan, 2012, Skyhorse Publishing
**Billy Wilder quote on Calendar**—*The Saturday Evening Post*, 5.5.56, The New Marilyn Monroe, Pete Martin
**Sheilah Graham quote on calendar**— *Modern Screen*, 9.54, Marilyn Talks About Joe and Babies, Sheilah Graham
**William Bruce, Calendar**—*Movieland*, 11.54, Meet the New Marilyn Monroe, William Bruce
**Roy Craft quote on calendar**--11.19.60, The Real Monroe, 'The Public Was My Way Out,' Maurice Zolotow
**Hollywood Stars vs Major League all-stars benefit baseball game for the Kiwanis club**—3.8.51, *Los Angeles Times*, Kiwanis Cut-ups
**Elia Kazan…marry JdM**—*Elia Kazan: A Life*, Elia Kazan, Da Capo Press, 1997
**Post academy award party Kazan**— *Elia Kazan: A Life*, Elia Kazan, Da Capo Press, 1997
**Billy Holiday, 5-4 Club, Fox Angry**-- *Australian Woman's Weekly*, 11.5.69, There's Marilyn--For Remembrance; Travilla Style blogspot, Eric Woodard, 2.4.2013
**Travilla and Memorable Dress**—*Australian Woman's Weekly*, 11.5.69, There's Marilyn--For Remembrance

**Natasha Lytess in Once Upon a Honeymoon**—12.19.42, *Los Angeles Times*, Reviews of Previews; 12.24.42, Andrew R. Kelley;
**Mm's hair by Gladys McCallister**-- *Marilyn Monroe*, Maurice Zolotow, Hartcourt, Brace, 1960
**Snyder on mms makeup routine**-- *Marilyn Monroe*, Maurice Zolotow, Hartcourt, Brace, 1960
**Isabel Moore, publicity**—*Motion Picture & Television*, 8.52, Why Women Hate Marilyn Monroe, Isabel Moore
**Quote by Cary Grant**—8.3.52, earl Wilson
**Vic Masi** —viewed information on *Everlasting Star*, French magazine, other ephemera
**Roller skating**—*Screen World*, 11.53, The Private Life of Marilyn Monroe, Natasha Lytess
**Nico Minardos**— *Goddess: The Secret Lives of Marilyn Monroe*, Anthony Summers, MacMillan Publishing Company, 1985
**Sidney Skolsky letter**—3.31.2012, Julian's Auctions, Hollywood Legends, lot 427
**Roy Craft quote** –8.7.62, *Los Angeles Times*, Ex-Press Agent Recalls Marilyn's Magic, Paul Weeks
**Halsman on MM**—*Cosmopolitan*, 5.53, The Fabulous Story of Hollywood's Biggest Build-Up: Marilyn Monroe, Robert L. Heilbronner; *Popular Photography*, 1.66, Marilyn Monroe, The Image and the Photographers, Ralph Hattersly; *Photography*, 6.53, Shooting Marilyn, Philippe Halsman
**Harold Lloyd**— *3-D Hollywood*, Suzanne Lloyd Hayes, Harold Lloyd, Simon & Schuster, 1992
**Roy Craft nude in LIFE**—8.7.62, *Los Angeles Times*, Ex- Press Agent Recalls Monroe's Magic Appeal; 8.5.02, *The Seattle Times*, Erik Lacitis, My Love and Thanks Forever, Marilyn;
**Signing copies at Rexall Drug**—4.6.52, *INS*, Puts Up Brave Front at Publicity; 4.17.52, Aline Mosby
**Western Litho hired 5 people**—4.18.52, *Boston Evening American*
**Gladys Eley**— *Marilyn, The Passion and the Paradox*, Lois Banner, Bloomsbury, 2014
**MM Quote on romance**— *Screenland*, 8.52, Marilyn Doesn't Believe In Hiding Things, Michael Sheridan
**Talisman to MM from Natasha**—*Photoplay*, 7.57, Marilyn at the Crossroads, Alex Joyce
**Grace Goddard and Gladys**— *Marilyn, The Passion and the Paradox*, Lois Banner, Bloomsbury, 2014
**MM on cheesecake to acting**—*Screenland*, August 1952, Marilyn Doesn't Believe in Hiding Things, Michael Sheridan
**MMs Bel Air Address**-- *Hometown Girl: A Chronological Photo Guide of Marilyn Monroe Related Los Angeles Area Addresses From 1923 to 1962*, Eric Monroe Woodard, David Marshall, HG Press, 2004
**Eleanor Parker coming to MMs defense**—*Photoplay*, 11.52, I Want Women to Like Me, Marilyn Monroe
**Guilaroff MMs hair Niagara**— *Crowning Glory: Reflections of Hollywood's Favorite Confidant*, Sydney Guilaroff, Cathy Griffin, General Publishing Group, 1996
**Jack Carroll**—*Falling for Marilyn*; Carroll, Jack; Friedman/Fairfax Publications; 1996
**Park Hotel**—10.24.72, *Niagara Falls Gazette*, Fire Guts old Lockport Hotel, Gen Hammond;
**Whitey Snyder photos**—viewed on *Everlasting Star*
**Joseph Cotten cocktail party**— *Vanity Will Get You Somewhere*; Cotten, Joseph; Mercury House; 1987
**Smoking for Niagara; bad habits**— *Photoplay*, 1.53, Marilyn Monroe Tells the Truth to Hedda Hopper, Hedda Hopper
**Drake hotel**—10.24.72, *Niagara Falls Gazette*, Fire Guts Old Lockport Hotel
**MM and Hy Gardner interview**-- *Falling for Marilyn*; Carroll, Jack; Friedman/Fairfax Publications; 1996
**Channing 200 Word Telegram**—7.20.66, *Niagara Falls Gazette*, B. Thomas; 8.18.66, WNS, Carol Channing on GPB;
**Trial—newspaper**; *Confidential*, 3.55, When A Cop Tried to Blackmail Marilyn Monroe, Howard Rushmore;
**Blackmail**—*Confidential*, 3.55, When a Cop Tried to Blackmail Marilyn Monroe, Howard Rushmore; *Silver Screen*, 3.53, Marilyn's Love Problem! Michael Sheridan
**Channing not to test for blondes**—6.29.52, *INS*, Channing Ducks Test in Blondes
**San Francisco press conf**—*San Francisco Examiner* photographs viewed on *eBay*
**Ray Anthony party**—8.8.52, Aline Mosby, Best Seen by Helicopter; 9.21.52, *Lowell Sun*, captioned pic;
**Willoughby quote**-- *Hollywood, A Journey Through the Stars*, Bob Willoughby, Assouline Publishing, 2001
**I had the radio on quote**-- *The Saturday Evening Post*, 5.12.56, The New Marilyn, Here She Talks About Herself, Pete Martin; 5.17.56, A Profile of a Phenomenon, A Cynic and Monroe, Article 3, Milton Shulman
**Roy Craft on blonde all over**—*Movie Stars Parade*, 6.53, The Mystery Man in Marilyn's Life, Bill Tusher; *Screen Life*, 7.54, An Open Letter to Joe DiMaggio, Joe Thomas; *The Saturday Evening Post*, 5.12.56, The New Marilyn Monroe, Here She Talks About Herself, Pete Martin; 5.2.80, *The Seattle Times*, Erik Lacitis, My Love and Thanks Forever, Marilyn;
**Blonde all over quote**-- *Screen Stars*, 11.54, Things They Never Told About Marilyn, Alice Craig Greene
**MM on her quotes**--5.17.56, A Profile of a Phenomenon, A Cynic and Monroe, Article 3, Milton Shulman
**Henry Hathaway quote**—12.7.62, Hedda Hopper
**Alice Craig Greene quote**— *Screen Stars*, 11.54, Things They Never Told About Marilyn, Alice Craig Greene

**Clara bow on MM**-- 7.8.62, Louella Parsons, Marilyn Monroe's Hidden Torments, part 1;
**Saalfield publishing contract**—Viewed information on *eBay*
**Wolf story**—*Joy*, 7.53, Men in my Life, Marilyn Monroe
**Slatzer in Buffalo, Niagara**—*Pix Annual*, Spring 1954, Arthur Everett Scott
**Ken Murray quote**— *Life On a Pogo Stick; Autobiography of a Comedian*; Murray, Ken; John C. Winston, Co.; 1960
**Mm Leap year quote**—8.22.52, *Fresno Bee*, Star Hollywood Actresses Want Leap Year Abolished
**Mel Torme**—*It Wasn't All Velvet, An Autobiography*; Mel Torme, Viking Press, 1988
Roy Craft on NY trip, MM sick--8.13.62, *The Oregonian*, Roy Craft, Paper's Editor Recalls Marilyn in Early Years of Stardom
**Mm on dressing for the opposite sex**—*Movie Life*, 4.53
**Betty Bacharach home**—www.bachrach.org
**Spyros Skouras home**— *Marilyn, The Passion and the Paradox*, Lois Banner, Bloomsbury, 2014
**Earl Holliman at Wil Wrights**—12.7.2007, *Exotic Gardening Thoughts*, Peonies, Jane Withers and James Dean Festival, Sheri Ann Richerson
**Atlantic city schedule**— *The Saturday Evening Post*, 5.12.56, The New Marilyn Monroe, Here She Talks About Herself, Pete Martin
**MM in Atlantic city parade** – *The Saturday Evening Post*, 5.12.56, The New Marilyn Monroe, Here She Talks About Herself, Pete Martin
**Gladys at Bernice home FL; back to Grace**— *Marilyn, The Passion and the Paradox*, Lois Banner, Bloomsbury, 2014
**Sid Ross Quote**—*Parade*, 10.12.52, How Marilyn Monroe Sees Herself, Sid Ross
**Ben Ross Quote**—*US Camera*, 5.53, A Photo Date With Marilyn, Ben Ross
**Michael Sean O'Shea quote**—8.7.64, Michael Sean O'Shea in for Dorothy Kilgallen
**Miss America contestants with MM**—9.2.52, *Canton Repository*, Carol Jean Given Warm Welcome in Atlantic City; 9.2.52, *Cedar Rapids Gazette*, Carolyn and Marilyn; 9.2.52, *Lubbock Avalanche Journal*, Connie Wray Misses Meeting Parade Marshal Marilyn Monroe; 9.2.52, *The Daily Plainsman*, It's a Big Day in Life of Sandra Kay Hart as Final Competition Nears; 9.3.52, *News Palladium*, Benton Harbor, MI, B.H. Entry in Miss America Contest Poses With 'Hurt' Movie Star; 9.4.52, *Nevada State Journal*, Screen Star; 9.4.52, *Reno Evening Gazetter*, Miss Nevada and Screen Star; 9.5.52, *Billings Gazette*, Miss Montana is Congratulated; 9.6.52, *Cedar Rapids Gazette*, Carolyn and Marilyn; 9.7.52, *Boise Idaho Sunday Statesman*, ID, Screen Star Marilyn Monroe; 9.7.52, *Minneapolis Sunday Tribune*, Beauties Chat;
**Jane Russell, round one**—*Silver Screen*, 8.53, What I Think of Marilyn, Jane Russell
**MM on her intellect** – *Screenland Plus TV Land*, 7.53, Helping Hand For Marilyn, Peter Sherwood
**MM quote on Ceil Chapman dress**—9.2.52, *AP*, Marilyn Leads Parade;
**Roy craft on dress debacle**—5.17.56, A Profile of a Phenomenon, A Cynic and Monroe, Article 3, Milton Shulman; *The Saturday Evening Post*, 5.12.56, The New Marilyn, Here What She Talks About Herself, Pete Martin
**Roy craft on MMs shrewdness**—8.7.62, *Los Angeles Times*, Ex-Press Agent Recalls Monroe's Magic Appeal, Paul Weeks; 5.17.56, A Profile of a Phenomenon, A Cynic and Monroe, Article 3, Milton Shulman
**Milton Schulman comment**— 5.17.56, A Profile of a Phenomenon, A Cynic and Monroe, Article 3, Milton Shulman
**Roy Craft comment about the photo**--5.17.56, A Profile of a Phenomenon, A Cynic and Monroe, Article 3, Milton Shulman
**Roy Craft on apology from Pentagon**--8.13.62, *The Oregonian*, Roy Craft, Paper's Editor Recalls Marilyn in Early Years of Stardom; 9.3.82,*The Seattle Times*, Marilyn, Military, Media Add Up to Classic Case, Paul Andrews
**Connie Wray Hopping, Miss Texas on MM**—9.2.52, *Lubbock Avalanche Journal*, Fred W. Schwarz
**Mm curt to reporters at airport in LA**—9.4.52, *Los Angeles Times*, Marilyn Monroe Banned Army Photo Dress
**I am an American day**—9.14.52, *Los Angeles Times*, Throngs Jam Bowl for Patriotic Fete
**Outpost estates, 2393 Castilian Dr.**—*Hometown Girl*, Eric Woodward Monroe & David Marshall, HG Press, 2004
**Out of this world series baseball**—Program, personal collection; 9.14.52, *Los Angeles Times*, Charity Tilt Set for Tomorrow
**MM to Kilgallen on Thomas Wolfe**—8.3.54, Dorothy Kilgallen
**MM to William Bruce on Thomas Wolfe**—*Movieland*, 11.54, Meet the New Marilyn Monroe, no by-line
**Sydney Skolsky on Jane and MM**—*Modern Screen*, 10.53, I Love Marilyn Monroe, Sidney Skolsky
**Howard Hawks Quote**—5.24.70, Los Angeles Times, Filmdom's Gray Fox is Back on Job Again, Wayne Warga
**Howard Hawks**—*Family Circle*, 5.53, What Caused Marilyn Monroe, Harry Evans
**Jane Russell on MM**—*Silver Screen*, 8.53, What I Think of Marilyn, Jane Russell
**Miss Snow**—viewed information on *eBay*
**Publicity**—11.26.52, Jimmy Fidler

**Nico Minardes and Thanksgiving at Karger's**--*Goddess: The Secret Lives of Marilyn Monroe*, Anthony Summers, MacMillan Publishing Company, 1985
**Hedda Hopper intvw about sister-in-law**—*Photoplay,* 1.53, Marilyn Monroe Tells the Truth to Hedda Hopper, Hedda Hopper
**Modern Screen Award**—*Modern Screen*, 2.53, Modern Screen's Party of the Year
**MMs Quote on Diamonds song**—9.13.53, The Sunday Tribune, Albert Lea, Minn, Owns No Diamonds Says Marilyn Monroe
**MM response to Zsa Zsa**— *The Saturday Evening Post*, 5.5.56, the New Marilyn Monroe, Pete Martin
**Travilla on diamonds bikini and new pink gown**—*Australian Women's Weekly*, 11.5.69, There's Marilyn—For Remembrance, William Travilla
**Daryl Zanuck**—*Modern Screen*, 5.55, The Storm About Monroe, Steve Cronin
**Max Reinhardt on MM auction win**—*Hartford Courant*, 1.5.1965, worth $50,000, no by-line
**Roy Craft on Reinhardt collection**--5.19.56, A Profile of a Phenomenon, A Cynic and Monroe, Article 4, Milton Shulman
**Natasha Lytess on Reinhardt auction**--5.19.56, A Profile of a Phenomenon, A Cynic and Monroe, Article 4, Milton Shulman
**Russell on Working with Jack Cole**—*Dance Magazine*, 1.83, The Legacy of Jack Cole: Rebel With a Cause, Glenn Loney; *Unsung Genius: The Passion of Dancer, Choreographer Jack Cole*, Glenn Loney, Franklin Watts publisher, 1984

# Chapter Thirteen
## Sex Bomb

**Quote**--everything that girl does is sexy, Joseph Cotten
**Edith Sitwell** –*Australian Women's Weekly*, 4.6.55, Marilyn Becomes Protégée of English Poet; Bill Strutton
**George Chakiris on MM**— *Blonde Heat: The Sizzling Career of Marilyn Monroe*, Richard Buskin, Billboard Books, 2001
**NJ's upbringing; Gladys stayed with Bolenders before going into Rest Haven; MM called**—*Cavalier*, 8.61, The Girl With the Three Blue Eyes, Ezra Goodman
**Hal Schafer, Jack Cole and MM**— *Unsung Genius: The Passion of Dancer, Choreographer Jack Cole*, Glenn Loney, Franklin Watts publisher, 1984; 8.9.2009, *Los Angeles Times*, Jack Cole Made Marilyn Monroe, Debra Levine
**Debra Levine Quote on Cole directing; Coaching dance numbers**-- *Dance Heritage Coalition*, Jack Cole, Debra Levine, 2012
**Peter Matz Quote**-- *Unsung Genius: The Passion of Dancer, Choreographer Jack Cole*, Glenn Loney, Franklin Watts publisher, 1984
**Jack Cole Baby Doll quote**— *Silver Screen*, 8.53, What I Think of Marilyn, Jane Russell
**Debra Levine quote on Jack Cole's style**-- *Dance Heritage Coalition*, Jack Cole, Debra Levine, 2012
**Gladys Rockhaven**— *Marilyn, The Passion and the Paradox*, Lois Banner, Bloomsbury, 2014
**Powolny on MM**—*Screen Guide*, 12.51, Mighty Marilyn, no by-line
**Travilla on MMs gold gown**-- *Australian Women's Weekly*, 11.5.69, There's Marilyn—For Remembrance, William Travilla
**Gold gown quote**— *9.5.77, Los Angeles Times*, Juggling Movie Figures, David Chierichetti
**Charles LeMaire on Gold Gown**—7.13.61, James Bacon, Dresses for Jayne, Marilyn Pose Problem
**Ladies of the Chorus quote**—*Movie Fan*, April 53, Marilyn Monroe, That Soul Doesn't Belong in That Body, Hank Fardell
**Natasha Lytess…dead man needs a coffin**— *Cavalier*, 8.61, The Girl With the Three Blue Eyes, Ezra Goodman
**Andre de Dienes, another model, not MM**--*Parade*, 7.19.53, He Calls This Work; 8.8.62, *Los Angeles Times*, Jack Smith, I Loved Marilyn, 'Started Career,' Mourns Hollywood Photographer
**Martin and Lewis radio show, Jerry to MM**--*Marilyn*, Sidney Skolsky, 1954,
**Martin and Lewis show**—*Motion Picture*, 11.53, Marilyn Monroe, Lovable Fake, Jim Henaghan
**Sheilah Graham quote on Redbook** –*Photoplay*, 11.53, Hollywood's Lost Ladies, Sheilah Graham
**Just breathe good and heavy**—*Screen Album*, Spring 1954, Marilyn Monroe, Her Soul Doesn't Belong in That Body, no by-line
**Easter parade fashion show**—4.4.53, *Cleveland Plain Dealer*, Film Stars Shine in Easter Finery
**Easter service with Nico Minardos**— *Goddess: The Secret Lives of Marilyn Monroe*, Anthony Summers, MacMillan Publishing Company, 1985

**MM Quote, "I Just Hate Careless Men"**—*Trinity and Beyond, The Atomic Bomb Movie;* 1999, Goldhill Home Media, Peter Kuran Director, narrated by William Shatner
**William Powell quote**—*Modern Screen*, 7.53, Joan and Marilyn Talk to Louella Parsons, Louella Parsons
**David Wayne** –6.24.56, Earl Wilson
**David Wayne, MM inexperienced**—8.13.75, *Oakland Tribune*, Remembering Marilyn Monroe, Nancy Anderson
**David Wayne** – 6.24.56, Earl Wilson
**David Wayne on MM being shy**—*Movie Life*, 11.54, Marilyn and Joe, Gretchen Field
**Betty Grable on MM**—11.16.53, Aline Mosby
**Grable on MM**—7.24.55, Sheilah Graham
**Sydney Skolsky quote and MM quotes about B. Grable**—*Modern Screen*, 10.53, I Love Marilyn Monroe, Sidney Skolsky
**Lauren Bacall on MM**—10.08.54, Bob Thomas, *Marilyn Monroe Heart-Broken Over Difficulties with Her Joe*
**Frank worth quote**-- *Worth Exposing Hollywood, Frank Worth's Glamorous and Unpublished Hollywood Photographs 1939-1964*, Mutti-Mewse, Austin and Mutti-Mewse, Howard, Cinemage Limited, 2002
**Ed McMahon**—*For Laughing Out Loud*, Ed McMahon, Grand Central Publishing, 2001
**Walter Winchell, 1953 Press Club**—*Photoplay*, 11.62, the Midnight World of Walter Winchell
**Walter Winchell party, quote by Grable**— *Screen Life*, 7.54, An Open Letter to Joe DiMaggio, Joe Thomas; **Focus**, 10.28.53, Pinch-Hitting for DiMaggio, no by-line
**Deeco, Mischa Pelz**—viewed information on *eBay* and *Everlasting Star*
**Louella Parsons, Coconut Grove**—*Modern Screen*, 3.62, Marilyn Monroe's Hidden Fears, Louella Parsons; 5.6.53, Louella Parsons
**Grace Goddard staying with MM**— *Marilyn, The Passion and the Paradox*, Lois Banner, Bloomsbury, 2014
**Nunnally Johnson on MM in Millionaire**—*The Saturday Evening Post*, 5.5.56, The New Marilyn, Pete Martin; *The Saturday Evening Post*, 05.19.56, The New Marilyn Monroe, Blonde, Incorporated, Pete Martin; 10.16.55, *American Weekly*, The Mystery of Marilyn Monroe, Maurice Zolotow;  Nunnally quote on Dust Jacket, *Tragic Venus*, Edwin P. Hoyt, Duell, Sloan & Pearce, 1965; *USA1*, 7.62, Marilyn, Ed Rees
**Jean Negulesco on MM**— *Screen Life* 7.54, An Open Letter to Joe DiMaggio, Joe Thomas
**Negulesco quote, mashed potatoes**—10.16.55, *American Weekly*, Maurice Zolotow
**Whitey Snyder on MM**— *Screen Life*, 7.54, An Open Letter to Joe DiMaggio, Joe Thomas
**Mike DiMaggio's death**—6.4.53, Louella Parsons
**Using sex to her advantage**—*Movie Fan*, 4.53, Marilyn Monroe, Her Soul Doesn't Belong in that Body, Hank Fardell
**Eisenstadt**—*Eisenstaedt's Celebrity Portraits: Fifty years of Friends and Acquaintances*; Alfred Eisenstaedt; Random House; 1984; 11.23.1978, *Boston Globe*
**Mm golf clubs**—*American Weekly* 12.53, Liza Wilson
**Vic and Marie Masi**—viewed information on Everlasting Star
**Charles LeMaire on MM**—8.29.81, *Los Angeles Times*, Charles LeMaire, 40 Years of Creating Costumes for the Stars, David Chierichetti
**James Bacon & Whitey Snyder**—*Goddess: The Secret Lives of Marilyn Monroe*, Anthony Summers, MacMillan Publishing Company, 1985
**Elgee Bove**—6.8.53, *Brooklyn Eagle*, Marilyn, Ava, Denise Putty in Hands of Dress Designer, 18, Leslie Hanscom
**Stanley Rubin on MM**—*The Marilyn Scandal*, Sandra Shevey, William Morrow & Co, 1987
**Preview of GPB w/Skolsky**—*Modern Screen*, 10.53, I Love Marilyn Monroe, Sidney Skolsky; *Photoplay*, 5.54, Marilyn Monroe's Honeymoon Whirl, Sidney Skolsky
**Guilaroff did hair for diamonds**— *Crowning Glory: Reflections of Hollywood's Favorite Confidant*, Sydney Guilaroff, Cathy Griffin, General Publishing Group, 1996
**Ed Wynn joke**—*Movie People*, 5.54, The Men in Marilyn's Life! Michael Sheridan
**Guilaroff did hair for handprint**— *Crowning Glory: Reflections of Hollywood's Favorite Confidant*, Sydney Guilaroff, Cathy Griffin, 1996, General Publishing Group
**Five disc jockey charity show**—7.8.53, *Los Angeles Times*, Array of Stars to Aid Hospital Show in Bowl; 7.9.53, *Los Angeles Times*, Farmers Market Today…With Mrs. Fred Beck; 7.10.53, *Los Angeles Times*, St. Jude Child Aid Event Set in Bowl Tonight; 7.10.53, *Los Angeles Times*, Video-Radio Briefs
**Robert Q's Waxworks**—7.12.53, *New York Times*, On the Radio This Week
**MMs Apartment described**--4.6.54, *Boston Traveler*, Kendis Rochlen and Charles Park, Story of Joe and Marilyn
**Dr. Elliot Corday diet**—*Motion Picture*, 11.54, Marilyn. Oh, Marilyn, Rita Garrison Malloy
**Puerto Penasco**—information viewed on *Everlasting Star*

**MM on Robert Mitchum**—5.30.54, Sheilah Graham
**Ray O'Neil**-- *Saturday Night*, Volume, 115, No. 6, 6.3.2000, Marilyn in the Rockies; Finkle, Derek
**Seattle-Tacoma Airport**—*Vancouver Sun*, 7.25.53
**Marilyn in Jasper**-- *Saturday Night*, Volume, 115, No. 6, 6.3.2000, Marilyn in the Rockies; Finkle, Derek
**MM quote in 1956**—*The Saturday Evening Post*, 05.19.56, The New Marilyn Monroe, Blonde, Incorporated, Pete Martin
**Jane Russell on MM**—*Screen Stars*, 12.53, Let's Talk About Marilyn Monroe, Jane Russell
**Joe and MMs hurt ankle**—4.6.54, *Boston Traveler*, Kendis Rochlen and Charles Park, The Story of Joe and Marilyn
**Marilyn, Joe and her ankle**—*Marilyn*, Sidney Skolsky, 1954
**Auction**—8.16.53, *Boston Sunday Herald* ad
**Julian Arnold smith**—information viewed on eBay
**Milton and MM; sex w mm**— Norman Mailer Files at the Harry Ransom Center, University of Texas, Austin; Files for Norman Mailer's books, *Marilyn*, Grosset & Dunlap, 1973; *Of Women and Their Elegance*, Simon & Schuster, 1980; Courtesy of Dr. Lois Banner, PhD
**Jack Benny show**-- *Sunday Nights at Seven: The Jack Benny Story*; Benny, Jack, Benny Joan, Burns, George, Warner Books, 1990
**Milt Josefsberg Jack Benny show**— *The Jack Benny Show, The Life and Times of America's Best-Loved Entertainer*, Josefsberg, Milt, Arlington House Publishers, 1977
**Elsie Lee quote about women and MM aft JB appearance**—*Screenland Plus TV Land*, 7.54
**Grace and Doc helping MM with business**-- *Marilyn, The Passion and the Paradox*, Lois Banner, Bloomsbury, 2014
**Marilyn and the Knebelcamps**-- *Marilyn Monroe, Private and Confidential*, Michelle Morgan, Skyhorse Publishing, 2012
**Negulesco painting of MM**—*Screenland Plus TV Land*, 5.54, Peeking in On Marilyn As a Housewife, Bea Maddox
**Halloween at Marilyn's**—11.6.53, Hedda Hopper; *Goddess: The Secret Lives of Marilyn Monroe*, Anthony Summers, MacMillan Publishing Company, 1985
**Oil rig on fox**-- 11.4.53, *AP*, Glamor Oil Well Drilled On Film Lot
**Clement Jones**—11.4.53, Clement D. Jones
**MM getting ready for Premier**—11.15.53, *San Antonio Express*, The Great White Hope Attends Premier
**Nunnally Johnson on mm**— *Marilyn Monroe*, Maurice Zolotow, 1960, Hartcourt, Brace
**Note from Adele Fletcher**-- *MM Personal: From the Private Archive of Marilyn Monroe*, Lois Banner, 2011, Harry N. Abrams
**Eartha Kitt & Johnnie Ray**—Marilyn, Sidney Skolsky, 1954 ppg 65 & 66; 11.12.53, *Los Angeles Times*, Skylarking With James Copp, Johnny Ray at Ciro's; 11.14.53, *Los Angeles Times*, Skylarking with James Copp, Eartha Kitt at Mocambo; 11.18.53, *Los Angeles Times*, Show Not Too Risqué, Say King and Queen; 11.19.53, *Los Angeles Times*, Skylarking With James Copp, Eartha Kitt knocking 'em dead at Mocambo
**King and Queen of Greece—MM late**—*Marilyn*, Sidney Skolsky, 1954; Action! Around the Lot, December 1953
**MHG coffee pot**—10.17.53, Sheilah Graham, *10 Most Fascinating Men to Marilyn Monroe*
**Ben Ross Shoot, Goldberg Quote**—*American Masters*, Marilyn Monroe Still Life, Thirteen/WNET New York, 7.19.2006
**Norman Mailer Quote**--*Marilyn*, Norman Mailer, Grosset & Dunlap, 1973
**General Dean**—12.17.53, *Long Beach Press Telegram*; 12.17.53, *Edwardsville Intelligencer*; 12.21.53, Sheilah Graham; 12.23.53, *Stars and Stripes, Europe*, Marilyn Joins Salute to Dean; 12.27.53, *Breckenridge American*, "General" Gayety
**Bebe Goddard birthday**—6.1.91, *Los Angeles Times*, Dean E. Murphy, Marilyn Monroe's Star Shines Brighter Than Ever
**Mm quote goose that lays golden eggs** -- *My Story*, Marilyn Monroe, Ben Hecht, Stein and Day, 1974

# Chapter Fourteen
## Mrs. DiMaggio and the Boys
**Quote**—9.30.62, *Family Weekly*, The Truth About Marilyn, Ben Hecht
**EB Sharp, honeymoon Paso Robels**—1.17.54, Hedda Hopper; 1.17.54, *UP*, Joe, Marilyn Spend Nuptial Night in Hotel
**Honeymoon Idyllwild**—*Modern Screen* 4.54, The Only Complete Story of Marilyn Monroe's Honeymoon, Alive Hoffman; *Modern Screen*, 5.54, Who Turned Love's Dream Into a Free-For-All, no by-line
**MMs passport**—viewed information on *Everlasting Star*

**Greene's on MM's broken thumb**— Norman Mailer Files at the Harry Ransom Center, University of Texas, Austin; Files for Norman Mailer's books, *Marilyn*, Grosset & Dunlap, 1973; *Of Women and Their Elegance*, Simon & Schuster, 1980; Courtesy of Dr. Lois Banner, PhD

**San Francisco Airport**—1.30.54, *AP,* Marilyn and DiMaggio on Their Way to Japan; 1.30.54, *PNA News*, Marilyn, Joe Fly to Japan on Baseball-Honeymoon Trip; 2.1.54, *Abilene Reporter-News*, Tokyo Bound Stars, captioned picture; 2.1.54, *AP Wire photo*, Tokyo Bound; 2.1.54; *NEA Telephoto*, Joe and Marilyn Leave for Tokyo; 2.1.54, *Winnipeg Free Press*; Wire Photo, Newlyweds Marilyn Monroe and Joe DiMaggio…; 2.3.54, *International Wire photo*, Joe and Marilyn Off For Japan; 2.3.54, *Pacific Stars and Stripes, INP,* Joe, Marilyn Shift Honeymoon to Japan

**Hawaii** –1.30.54, *AP*, Big Welcome for Marilyn, Joe in Oahu; 1.31.54, *AP*, Hulas Greet Marilyn, Joe, no by-line; 1.31.54, *UP*, Joe, Marilyn Visit Hawaii on Way West; 1.31.54, *AP*, Marilyn, Joe Leave Honolulu for Tokyo, no by-line; 1.31.54, *UP*, DiMaggio's Leave Hawaii For Japan; 2.1.54, *AP*, Marilyn and Joe Given Warm Welcome En Route; 2.1.54, Howard K. Janis, DiMaggio, Marilyn Get Ovation From Japanese; 2.1.54, *INS*, Marriage Now Marilyn's Main Career; 2.1.54, *Pacific Stars and Stripes*, Marilyn, Joe Due in Tokyo From Honolulu; 2.1.54, *UP*, Marilyn, Joe Leave Hawaii for Japan

**Arrival in Tokyo**—2.1.54, *AP Wire photo*, Marilyn And Joe In Tokyo; 2.1.54, Frank Jordan, Marilyn, Joe Mobbed by Japs; 2.1.54, *Ogden Evening Standard*, Japanese Mob Marilyn, DiMaggio, no by-line; 2.1.54, *The Daily News, Huntington*, PA, DiMaggio's Almost Killed With Kindness at Tokyo; 2.1.54, *UP Press Photo,* Flowers For the DiMaggio's; 2.2.54, UP, 'Wolf-Whistling' Japanese Mob Marilyn Monroe, DiMag; 2.2.54, *Chicago Daily News Service*, Howlin' Mob Greets Marilyn Monroe, Joe DiMaggio On Arrival in Japan, no by-line; 2.2.54, *Pacific Stars and Stripes*, Far East News, Chilling Wind, Cheering Mob Greet Marilyn, Joe in Tokyo, PFC Don Towles; 2.2.54, *Europe Stars and Stripes*, Fans in Tokyo Mob DiMaggio, Marilyn; 2.5.54, *INS Radiophoto*, Marilyn and Joe in Tokyo

**Tokyo, as visitors**—2.11.54, *INS Radiophoto*, Marilyn Sees Joe Turn on Charm; 2.11.54, *The Boston American*, Front Page Captioned Photo, The Honeymooners

**Earl Moran**— *Modern Screen*, 7.54, The Secrets of Marilyn's Life as a Model, Emmeline Snively; 2.1.54, *Daily Mail*, Hagerstown, MD, International Exclusive; Marilyn Redated; 2.3.54, The News of the Day in Pictures, *International Radiophoto*, This Eye-Catcher; 2.6.54, *INS Radiophoto*, Joseph Jasgur, You May Have Seen; 2.18.54, *INS*, Joseph Jasgur photo, You May Have Seen

**GIs in Korea**—2.1.54, *INS*, GIs Wild to See Marilyn as Bride; 2.2.54, *INS*, Marilyn Declines GI Bid to Visit Korea; 2.2.54, *Boston Evening American*, Marilyn Switches Plan to Visit Korea, no by-line

**Keyes beech article**—2.1.54, Keyes Beech, Jap Fans Crowd Airport to View Double Feature

**Kashio Aoki**—viewed information and photographs on *Everlasting Star*

**Maid**—6.1.87, *AP*, Marilyn Remembered

**Press Conference**—2.2.54, *AP*, Marilyn Confesses She's Never Seen a Ball Game, no by-line; 2.2.54, *AP*, Marilyn Says She's Not a Baseball Fan; 2.2.54, *AP*, Shinn Higashi, Marilyn Never Saw a Ball Game; 2.2.54, *UP,* Marilyn Monroe Tells Japs How to Keep Beauty; 2.2.54, *UP*, Marilyn Dominates Jap Press Parley; 2.2.54, *AP* Wire photo, Marilyn Meets the Mob; 2.2.54, It's Your World, *Long Beach Press Telegram*, no by-line; 2.2.54, *Ogden Standard Examiner*, Names in the News; 2.3.54, *AP Wire photo*, Marilyn Poses; 2.3.54, *Pacific Stars and Stripes*, Monroe Sidesteps Queries On Tour, Family, Lingerie

**Wire photo signing autographs**--2.3.54, *International Radiophoto*, Marilyn Busy Autographing; 2.4.54

**Massage**—3.7.57, *Stars and Stripes*; Roamin' Around, A/2C Marvin B. Scott; Got a Bad Case of Nerves? The Shiatsu's Thumb May Be a Cure

**Boston newspaper on 3rd** --2.3.54, *Boston Evening American*, Marilyn to Korea Alone, no by-line

**Purpose of Honeymoon, Baseball Clinic**—2.4.54, Alan Ward, Tribune Sports Editor

**Korea, Before Trip**—2.4.54, *AP*, Marilyn Cleared for Korean Visit; 2.4.54, *INS*, Korea GIs Plan Big Welcome For Shapely Marilyn Monroe; 2.4.54, *UP*, Monroe Rests for Journey to Korea; 2.4.54, *AP*, Soldiers in Korea Await Marilyn Monroe; 2.12.54, Mexia, TX, *NEA Wire photo*, Going to Korea; 2.12.54, *Newport News*, Joy in Korea

**Hospital Visit** --2.5.54, *UP*, Last Yank Repatriate on Way Home, Robert Vermillion; 2.5.54, *AP*, Marilyn Brings Marilyn to Ailing GIs; 2.5.54 *AP Wire photo*, Marilyn Puts Autograph on Iowa GI; 2.5.54, *El Paso Herald Post*; 2.5.54, *INS,* Marilyn Monroe Keeps First GI 'Date' In Far East; 2.5.54, *INS*, Marilyn Ready to Tour Army Hospital in Japan; 2.5.54, *Pacific Stars and Stripes,* inset in Monroe-Service Show Set; 2.6.54, *INS*, Marilyn Thrills GI Patients in Tokyo; 2.6.54, *Lowell Sun*, Special to the Sun, Pinehurst Soldier Describes Tokyo Meeting With Marilyn; 2.9.54, *AP Wire photo*, Marilyn talking to paralyzed GI; 2.9.54, *INP photo*, by Ichiru Fujimuro, Marilyn with GI in hospital; 2.10.54, *San Antonio Express*, The 'Up' Look **Marilyn's shorter hair**—*Movie Stars Parade*, 10.54, What Joe Did For Marilyn, Lee Benedict

**Brady AFB**—2.17.54, *AP Wire photo*, Marilyn Meets Non-Coms

**Korea, Show Details**—2.5.54, *Pacific Stars and Stripes*, Monroe-Service Show Set; 2.11.54, *INS*, Marilyn to see Most U.S. Units

**Kawana**—2.5.54, *El Paso Herald Post*; 2.6.54, *AP*, Marilyn Rests Before Trip to Korea to Sing; 2.6.54, *AP*, Marilyn Monroe Rests at Jap Resort Before GI Performances In Korea; 2.8.54, *INS*, Marilyn Leaves Joe's Fans Cold; 2.12.54, *CPC Wire photo*, Honeymooning DiMaggio's Go Visiting in Japan
**Camp Zama**— 2.9.54, *Pacific Stars and Stripes*, Zama to Open New Workshop with Big Show; *A Different View of Marilyn*, Al Carmen Guastafeste, Trafford Publishing, 2003
**Fukuoka**--2.9.54, *UP*, Marilyn and Joe Reach Fukuoka; 2.10.54, *INS*, Add Riots Over Marilyn; 2.10.54, *UP*, Jap Cops Rescue Joe, Marilyn From Fans; 2.11.54, *INS*, Marilyn's Room Boy Wins Fame
**Backseat of MMs car**—*Motion Picture*, 11.54, Marilyn, Oh, Marilyn, Rita Garrison Malloy
**Hiroshima**—2.14.54, *INS*, Japanese Ignore Clinic; Prefer Marilyn Monroe; 2.13.54; *INS*, Marilyn Monroe Goes Hiroshima Sightseeing
**Korea, GIs Getting Ready For Marilyn**—2.14.54, *Pacific Stars and Stripes*, 7$^{th}$ Div. Set For Marilyn; 2.15.54, *AP*, Army, Air Force Not Agreed on Marilyn Monroe; 2.15.54, *Pacific Stars and Stripes*, Cpl. Bob Jennings, Blonde Bomb Due; Korea Rocks Already
**Osaka**—2.15.54, *INS*, Marilyn Gives Preview; 2.16.54, *INS*, Monroe Show Ready, She'll Dance For Yanks;
**Arriving in Seoul**—2.16.54, *UP*, Marilyn Monroe Visiting Korea
**Elgee Bove**—6.8.53, *Brooklyn Eagle*, Marilyn, Ava, Denise, Putty in Hands of Dress Designer, 18, Leslie Hanscom; 3.15.54, Sheilah Graham, Elgee Bove designed MMs purple Korea dress; 3.29.54, Phyllis Battelle, MM owns most expensive Elgee Bove gown; 8.24.55, Dorothy Kilgallen, Elgee Bove designed MMs Korea dress; 7.19.56, Dorothy Kilgallen, MM on architecture of dress; 11.14.57, *WNS*, Barbara Rabin, Designed MMs Korea Dress
**Korea, Day One**—2.16.54, Jim Becker, Marilyn Monroe Starts Four-Day Tour in Korea; 2.16.54, *Charleston Gazette*, Charleston, 'Model' GIs Ignore Steaks, Devour Delectable Marilyn; 2.16.54, *INS*, 11,000 Marines Cheer GI-Togged Marilyn; 2.16.54, *INS*, GIs Go Wild Over Marilyn; 2.16.54, *UP*, Marilyn in Purple Wows GIs; 2.16.54, *UP*, 10,000 Marines Mesmerized by Joe's Marilyn Monroe; 2.17.54, *AP Wire photo*, Cynosure of All Eyes; 2.17.54, *AP Wire photo*, Boys Get Eyeful; 2.17.54, *AP*, Marilyn Monroe Wows GIs on Korean Front; 2.17.54, *AP*, 30,000 GIs Whistle to Marilyn; 2.17.54, *AP*, Marilyn's Neckline Uplifts 30,000 GIs; 2.17.54, *UP*, Morale Mounts on Korean Front as Marilyn Makes Appearance; 2.17.54, *INS*, Marilyn's All He Expected; 2.17.54, *Pacific Stars and Stripes*, Blonde Bomb Sizzles, Heats Huge Throngs Along Cold Korea Front; 2.17.54, *NEA Radio-Telephoto*, Marilyn with men of 1st Marine Division; 2.17.54, *INS*, Area GI Says Marilyn's All He Expected; 2.17.54, *UP* Telephoto, Marines Cluster; 2.17.54, *UP*, Monroe Entertains Troops; 2.18.54, *AP* Wire photo, Marilyn Entertains Seventh Division in Korea; 2.18.54, *INS Radiophoto*, After Effect, Marilyn Slept Here Sign; 2.18.54, *UP* Wire photo, GI's Turn Out to Greet Marilyn; 2.19.54, *AP Wire photo*, That Dress Again; 2.19.54, *AP* Wire photos , Marilyn Wows 'Em in Korea; 2.19.54, *AP Wire photo*, Marilyn Peps Up Korean GIs; 2.19.54, *Daily Herald*, Utah, Marilyn Has Landed; 2.22.54, *INS Wire photo*, Marilyn Makes a Direct Hit on This Tank
**Korea, Day Two**--2.17.54, *AP*, Army Approves Curves; 2.17.54, Jim Becker, Shivering Marilyn Monroe Big Hit With GIs in Korea; 2.17.54, Jim Becker, Marilyn Monroe Captivates Three More U.S. Divisions; 2.17.54, *AP*, Marilyn Gets On With Korean Tour; 2.17.54, *AP*, Marilyn Thinks Snow Exciting; 2.17.54, Sanford Socolow; Marilyn Disregards Snow, Cold And Makes Scheduled Visits to GI Units; 2.17.54, Sanford Socolow, Thousands of GI's In Korea Greet Marilyn; 2.17.54, *UP*, 'Anything Goes' for Troops; 2.17.54, *UP*, Marilyn Monroe Causes Near Riot in GI Visit; 2,17,54, *UP*, Marilyn Sets Off Near Riot; 2.17.54, *UP*, Mrs. DiMaggio's curves Cause Near-Riot; 5.18.54, *Daily News*, Mount Union, PA, Monroe is Big Hit With Johnstown GI; 2.18.54, *Pacific Stars and Stripes*, Bob Jennings, 25$^{th}$ Roaring Thousands Greet Singing, Slinking Blonde Bomber; 2.18.54, *UP*, Curves Cause Near Riot; 2.19.54, *AP*, Marilyn Ends Tour in Korea; 2.19.54, *INS*, Marilyn Monroe Stops US Army in Korea; 2.19.54, *Pacific Stars and Stripes*, 6,000 Thunderbirds Riot, Mob Stage to See Marilyn, Cpl. Bob Jennings; 2.20.54, *AP Wire photo*, A Day to Remember; 2.21.54, *AP Wire photo*, A Day to Remember; 2.21.54, *Pacific Stars and Stripes*, Photo by Cpl. Bob Jennings, Anything Goes
**Korea, Day Three**—2.18.54, *UP*, GI Trampled As Unruly Soldiers Mob Marilyn; 2.18.54, Jim Becker, Soldier Injured In Unruly Rush at Marilyn; 2.18.54, *AP*, Korea Conquered, Marilyn Moves on to New Territory; 2.18.54, *AP*, Marilyn Monroe Invades Eastern Front In Korea; 5.18.54, *AP*, Soldier Trampled by Army Throng Rushing to View Marilyn Monroe; 2.18.54, *INS Radiophoto*, Gives the Boys an Eye Full; 2.18.54, Robert Pennell, Marilyn Monroe Forced to Flee From Mob of Unruly GIs; 2.18.54, *INS*, Marilyn Serves GI Chow Line; 2.18.54, *San Antonio Light*, Marilyn Escapes Mob of GIs; 2.18.54, *UP*, 6,000 Riot Over Marilyn; 2.18.54, *UP*, Infantryman Trampled in Mad Rush to See Marilyn Monroe Act in Korea; 2.18.54, James Morrissey, GIs Riot as Marilyn Gives Show; 2.18.54, James Morrissey, Marilyn Brings Early 'Thaw' To Frozen U.S. GIs; 2.18.54, *UP*, Marilyn Warms Up Korean Front for the 3$^{rd}$ Day; 2.19.54, *AP*, In-the-Flesh Marilyn Starts GI Stampede; 2.19.54, *INS*, Marilyn Shows Heels to 6,000 Surging GIs; 2.19.54, *Pacific Stars and Stripes*, Cpl. Bob Jennings, 6,000 Thunderbirds Riot Mob Stage to See Marilyn; 2.19.54, James Morrissey, Marilyn Gives Up Sleeping Raw; Longies 'Fog' Lenses; 2.19.54, *AP*, Movie Queen 'Stampedes' 45 Division; 2.20.54, *INS*

*Radiophoto*, Everything was under control; 2.20.54, *Pacific Stars and Stripes,* Cpl. Bob Jennings, 6,000 Thunderbirds Stampede Mob Stage to See Marilyn; 2.22.54, *AP Wire photo*, An Autograph For the Boys
**Korea, Day Four**—2, 19.54, *AP*, Marilyn Ends Tour in Korea; 2.19.54, *INS*, Monroe Winds Up 4-Day Tour of Korea Area; 2.19.54, *Pacific Stars and Stripes,* Cpl. Bob Jennings, 6,000 Thunderbirds Riot Mob Stage to See Marilyn; 2.20.54, *INS*, Marilyn Deserts Officers for GI Visit; 2.20.54, *Pacific Stars and Stripes*, M.M. Ends Korea Swing; 2.22.54, Mansfield News, Mansfield, OH, Lucky Flier wire photo; 2.22.54, *Pacific Stars and Stripes*, M.M. Ends Korea Swing Amid Flashbulb Farewell, captioned wire photo, Meets Marnemen
**Marilyn on Korean Tour**—2.19.54, *AP*, Korea Conquered, Marilyn Leaving; 2.19.54 AP, Marilyn Ends Tour in Korea; 2.19.54, James Morrissey, Marilyn Monroe Says Korean Trip Made Her Feel Like Star for First Time; 2.19.54, *UP*, Marilyn Says She Owes Her Success to GIs; 2.19.54, *UP*, Marilyn Says She Has Movie Star Feeling; 2.20.54, *INS*, Star Touches High Point in GI Show; 2.21.54, *Pacific Stars and Stripes*, Marilyn Lauds Yanks, Heads For Tokyo
**Al Guastafeste**—2.20.54, Cpl. Al Guastafeste, Marilyn's Accompanist Interested in Music; *A Different View of Marilyn*, Al Carmen Guastafeste, Trafford Publishing, 2003
**Korea, general info and photos**—2.22.54, *AP*, Marilyn Monroe Has Busy Day in Korea
**Happiest**—*Family Weekly*, 9.30.62, the Myth About Marilyn, Ben Hecht
**Kobe**—2.21.54, *INS*, Marilyn Attends Jap Style Show
**Tokyo**—2.22.54, *INS*, Marilyn Monroe Back in Tokyo
**Shopping**—*Movie Stars Parade*, 10.54; 2.22.54, *Pacific Stars and Stripes*, DiMaggio's 'to Shop' in Tokyo Before Return Flight to US; 2.23.54, *UP*, Korea Appearance Sidelines Marilyn
**Texas Quote**—Leonard Lyons 2.21.54
**Japanese Press Laud Marilyn**—2.22.54, *INS*, Japanese Press Lauds Marilyn For Friendship

# Chapter Fifteen
## Becoming "The Girl"
**Quote**—9.27.54, *LIFE*
**Dear Dad letter to JdM**—viewed information on *Everlasting Star*
**MMs return to Burbank from SF**—3.6.54, *Los Angeles Times*, Mrs. DiMaggio Back in Town Without the Mr.
**Thank you not to Lee and Tom**—viewed information on *Everlasting Star*
**MM at Photoplay, JdM quote**—9.12.54, Louella Parsons, *Gossip Perils Marilyn-DiMag Marriage*
**Contract negotiations with MM and JdM**-- *Marilyn Monroe*, Barbara Leaming, Three Rivers Press, 2000
**6 months lease & haystack**—*Photoplay*, 8.54, 260,000 Minutes of Marriage, Sidney Skolsky
**Barbara Barondess-McLean**—video interview; *Los Angeles Times*, 5.25.36, Actress Refuses to Pay Divorced Spouse's Rent, no by-line; 5.13.48, Early Screen Comic Divorced by Third Wife, no by-line; 7.23.51, Suit Charges Neighbor With Razing Trees, no by-line; *Los Angeles Times*, 5.29.53, Husband divorced as Too Critical, no by-line; 3.7.57, Barbara M'Lean's Jewelry Stolen, *UP*
**Danny Kaye, Knock on Wood**—4.7.54, *Los Angeles Times*, Star-Studded Group Greets Kaye Film
**Press conference**—4.46.54, *Los Angeles Times*, Wants to Be a Mother, Says Marilyn Monroe; 4.17.54, *Coshocton Tribune*, Welcome Back; 4.17.54, *The News, Newport*, RI, Wants to Be a Mother, Says Marilyn; 4.25.54, *Progress Index*, Petersburg, VA, Welcome Back
**Description of MMs dressing room**—*Movie Star Parade*, 10.54, What Joe Did For Marilyn, Lee Benedict
**Dietrich foam buttocks**— 9.5.80, *Los Angeles Times*, David Chierichetti, Juggling Movie figures
**Cora Bowen dialogue coach**—*Motion Picture*, 11.54, Marilyn. Oh, Marilyn, Rita Garrison Mallory
**Going into new home; Joe and Masi**--*Photoplay*, 8.54, 260,000 Minutes of Marriage, Sidney Skolsky
**Travilla NBLSB**—Movie Stars Parade, 10.54, What Joe Did For Marilyn, Lee Benedict
**MM on blonde on blonde gown**—*Movieland*, 12.54, Too Hot Not to Cool Down, no by-line
**Marilyn on set of NBLSB**—*Movie Stars Parade*, 10.54, What Joe Did For Marilyn, Lee Benedict
**Donald O'Conner quote**—*Movieland*, 12.54, Too Hot Not to Cool Down, no by-line
**Photographer quote**—*Movie Stars Parade*, 10.54, What Joe Did For Marilyn, Lee Benedict
**Sheilah Graham intvw**—*Modern Screen*, 9.54, Marilyn Talks About Joe and Babies, Sheilah Graham
**Traffic accident with Bart Antinora**—9.2.54, *AP*, Marilyn Monroe Sued
**Milton Greene**—The Archives; 1.14.55, Aline Mosby, *Photographer Organized 'New' Marilyn*
**Skin rash**—7.7.54, Sheilah Graham
**Anemia**—6.13.54, *Marilyn Monroe's Liver*, Paula Walling

**Alton replaced with Cole**—*Movie Life*, 11.54, Marilyn and Joe, Getchen Field; *Movie Life*, 11.54, The Chatterbox; *Modern Screen*, 5.55, The Storm About Monroe, Steve Cronin; *Movieland*, 5.55, Marilyn: Will Her Big Gamble Pay Off, no by-line
**The Girl on the Calendar**—5.30.54, *Progress Index*, Petersburg, VA, Marilyn Monroe Wins Fight on "Calendar Girl" Number
**Gene Lester and camera; modeling story**— *When Hollywood Was Fun! (Snapshots of an Era);* Lester, Gene; Birch Lane Pr., 1993
**Del Wrightson on show business role**—*Movie Secrets*, 8.56, Marilyn Monroe Says, I Don't Owe Hollywood a Thing, Del Wrightson
**Publicity on films**— *Screen Stars*, 11.54, Things They Never Told About Marilyn, Alice Craig Greene
**Norman Mailer on MMs fragility**    *Marilyn*, Norman Mailer, Grosset & Dunlap, 1973
**Hedda on Hecht**—6.15.54, Hedda Hopper
**Shelley Winters on MM and James Dean**—*Best of Times, Worst of Times,* Shelley Winters, Frederick Muller, Ltd, 1990
**Hal Schaefer and MM lessons on set**—*Collier's*, 7.9.54, Marilyn Monroe Hits a High Note, Robert Cahn
**RCA Victor and Peter Potter**—*Collier's,* 7.9.54, Marilyn Hits a High Note, Robert Cahn; *Screen Stars*, 11.54, Things They Never Told About Marilyn, Alice Craig Greene, Robert Cahn
**MM on set of Desiree**—*Movie Stars Parade*, 10.54, What Joe Did For Marilyn, Lee Benedict
**Eddie Joe**—8.14.54, *Niagara Falls Gazette*, Charles Dineen
**Hedda Hopper on *Heat Wave* and Don. O'Conner**—6.15.54, Hedda Hopper
**Joe, *Heat Wave***—9.12.54, Louella Parsons, *Gossip Perils Marilyn-DiMag Marriage*; 8.31.54, Sheilah Graham
**Howard Parker**—viewed information on *eBay*
**Roy Craft quote, 75,000 to play**—*The Saturday Evening Post*, 5.12.56, The New Marilyn Monroe, Here She Talks About Herself, Pete Martin
**Roy Craft quote, MM in NY for Itch**—*The Saturday Evening Post*, 5.12.56, The New Marilyn Monroe, Here She Talks About Herself, Pete Martin
**MM at Airport, NYC**—9.9.54, *AP*, Marilyn Lands, Airport Routine Goes Phooey
**Hurricane MM**—9.10.54, *Boston Evening American*, Hurricane Marilyn Hits NY
**Joseph H. Coudert**—12.9.2004, *Washington Post*, An Enduring Portrait of Marilyn; *PRWeb*, 6.1.2005, Austin Man Releases Unpublished Photos of Marilyn Monroe's Dress Scene From *The Seven Year Itch* On Movies 50th Anniversary
**Elliott Erwitt quote on MM**—Popular Photography, 1.66, Marilyn Monroe: The Image and Her Photographers
**Tom Ewell quote—stolen it from you**—5.17.59, *Chicago Tribune Sunday Magazine*, She's No Dumb Blonde, William Leonard
**Tom Ewell Quote on working with MM**—2.10.74, *Dallas Morning News*, John Neville, Tom Ewell Comes to Dinner
**Tom Ewell interview with Hedda Hopper**—12.12.54, Hedda Hopper
**Tom Ewell Quote on MM reading the Bible**—8.8.82, Bob Thomas, Marilyn—the Sex Goddess Lives On
**Working with MM on Itch**—*Modern Screen*, 5.55, The Storm About Monroe, Steve Cronin
**Billy Wilder quote—voltage; can't take eyes off her**— *Marilyn Monroe*, Maurice Zolotow, Hartcourt, Brace, 1960
**Billy Wilder Flesh Impact; meanest woman**—*The Saturday Evening Post*, 5.5.56, The New Marilyn, Pete Martin; *The Saturday Evening Post*, 5.12.56, The New Marilyn, Here She Talks About Herself, Pete Martin
**Marilyn's an institution**—*Movieland*, 12.54, Too Hot Not to Cool Down, no by-line
**Roxanne**—*Motion Picture*, 1.55, On Again, Off Again, Earl Wilson
**MM to L. Lyons**—1.3.55, Leonard Lyons, *Dream Comes True for MM: She's in Harper's Bazaar*
**Earl Wilson on Avedon sitting**— *Motion Picture*, 1.55, On Again, Off Again, Earl Wilson
**Saul Pett quote on skirt scene**—9.18.54, Saul Pett, for Hal Boyle, *Miss Monroe Doesn't Mind the Mob—Even at Skirt Blowing*
***Trans-Lux Theater***—9.20.54, *Springfield Union*, Hometowner in Gotham—At Ringside for Filming, Wally Beach
**Bruises on her arm**—*Motion Picture*, 11.54, Marilyn. Oh, Marilyn, Rita Garrison Malloy
**Philippe Halsman quote**—*Hollywood Dream Girl* , 1955, Three Encounters With a Love Goddess, Philippe Halsman; *Photography*, 6.53, Shooting Marilyn, Philippe Halsman; *US Camera*, 7.53, How Philippe Halsman Works, John Baird; *US Camera*, 6.54, Marilyn Monroe, You First Saw Her On The Cover of U.S. Camera, no by-line; *Popular Photography*, 1.66, Marilyn Monroe, The Image and the Photographers, Ralph Hattersly
**Jean Howard**— *Jean Howard's Hollywood: A Photo Memoir*; Howard, Jean; Harry N. Abrams; 1989
**Goldwyn, Guys and Dolls**—*Movieland*, 11.54, Meet the New Marilyn, William Bruce; *Movieland*, 12.54, Too Hot Not to Cool Down? no by-line

"**Meanest Woman in Hollywood**"--*Boston Globe*, 11.6.1966, Marjory Adams, Billy Wilder, the Unpredictable;
**John Chapman**—10.3.54, *Chicago Daily Tribune*, Lensmen Like Marilyn—but Who Doesn't?

# Chapter Sixteen
## Birth Pains of the "New Marilyn"
**Quote**—*USA1*, 7.62, *Marilyn*, Ed Rees
**I feel alive**—10.8.54, *UP*, Marilyn, Now Back At Work Begins 'To Feel Alive Again'
**Jim Daugherty intvw/George Cap**—10.5.54, *Boston Evening American*, George Capozi, Jr, Marilyn Didn't Want Family, Says Ex-Mate
**Miss MacLean; yard is a mess**—541009, Sheilah Graham; 541111, Harrison Carroll; 541117, Harrison Carroll
**House unlucky for love**—10.12.54, Sheilah Graham
**Dr. already rented apt/MM had to move**—10.16.54, Aline Mosby, Rental Mixup Puts Marilyn Out of Apartment in Hurry
**Mistinguette quote**—10.13.54, *Los Angeles Times*, Why, Marilyn! Monroe Legs Criticized by Mistinguette
**4th Annual Hillcrest Country Club Invitational Golf Tournament**—10.14.54, *Los Angeles Times*, Team Scores 64 at Hillcrest; 10.17.54, *Los Angeles Times*, Martin, Hilton in Hillcrest Lead; 10.18.54, *Los Angeles Times*, San Gabriel Twosome Wins Hillcrest Title
**Joe, Jr.s 12th birthday**—11.5.54, *AP*; 11.6.54, Aline Mosby, *Joe Tries to Patch Up Marriage to Marilyn*
**Dorothy Arnold quote**— *Motion Picture*, 11.54, Marilyn. Oh, Marilyn, Rita Garrison Malloy
**MM court testimony**—*Modern Screen*, 11.54, The Two Worlds of Marilyn Monroe, Jack Wade; 10.23.55, The Mystery of Marilyn Monroe, Maurice Zolotow
**Don Loper dress for court; I feel numb; baseball**—10.28.54, *The Springfield Union*, Marilyn Monroe
**A Lot of Things quote**—10.26.54, Emily Belser, Marilyn Denies 'Mysterious' Actions
**Ted Baron's quotes**— 11.12.54, Harrison Carroll; 11.14.54, Elizabeth Toomey, Marilyn Monroe, Pier Angeli Head Britisher's Glamor List; *Australian Women's Weekly*, 4.6.55, Hollywood's Loveliest Women, Baron; 11.16.54, *UP*, Photographer Claims Glamorous Girls Few, no by-line
**Marilyn, unique, rather sad, Baron**-- *Australian Women's Weekly*, 5.1.57; 11.16.54, *UP*, Photographer Claims Glamorous Girls Few, no by-line
**George MacLean architect**—12.01.54, *Los Angeles Times*, G. MacLean; LA Architect, Land Developer
**Wrong door raid**—*Confidential*, 9.55, The Real Reason For Marilyn Monroe's Divorce! J.E. Leclair
*LIFE* **party Karger jewels**--*Marilyn: Among Friends,* Sam Shaw, Norman Rosten, Henry Hold & Co, 1988
**Clifton Webb quote**—11.54, *LIFE*, LIFE Goes to a Party
**Billy Wilder on working w/MM**— *The Saturday Evening Post*, 05.19.56, The New Marilyn Monroe, Blonde, Incorporated, Pete Martin
**Joe D gave MM gifts while in hosp**—11.8.54, *Brooklyn Eagle*, Marilyn in Hospital with Joe at the Door
**Hospital Records**—viewed information on eBay
**Villa Capri**—11.15.54, *UP*, Joe and Marilyn Are Dating Like a Couple of Romancers;
**Ella Fitzgerald**— *Los Angeles Times*; *Jet*, 8.13.53, Herb Jefferies; *Jet*, 12.12.53 Eartha Kitt; *Jet* 11.12.53 Joyce Byran; DDandridge— *Los Angeles Times*
**MMs Driving**—7.19.54, Dorothy Kilgallen
**Joe in Hospital/MM didn't visit**—11.22.54, *AP*, Ulcer 'Acts Up'; Puts DiMaggio in Hospital; 11.29.54, Hedda Hopper
**Maureen O'Hara**— *'Tis Herself: An Autobiography*, Maureen O'Hara, John Nicoletti, Simon & Schuster, 2005; *Movie Pix*, December 1953
Gerald Wiggins vocal coach—allaboutjazz.com, Gerald Wiggins; 9.11.96, *Corsair*, Volume 72, Number 2, Solidarity at SMC, Bruno Pokas;
**Eating in Malibu**—12.13.54, *Los Angeles Times*, DiMaggio and Marilyn Dine Together
**Contract dispute/MM requesting copies**— *Marilyn Monroe*, Barbara Leaming, Three Rivers Press, 2000
**Maria Romero intvw**—*Marilyn Monroe in Spain: A Life Documented,* Frederic Cabanas, Edicons, 2007
**Sammy Davis, Jr**--*In Black and White: The Life of Sammy Davis, Jr.,* Will Haygood, Knopf, 2003
**MM to stay out of nightclubs**—12.13.54, Bob Farrell
**MM and JdM at Malibu restaurant**—12.13.54, *AP*, Joe and Marilyn Have Date Again
**Mel Torme quotes**— *It Wasn't All Velvet, An autobiography*; Mel Torme, Viking Press, 1988

**Sprezzatura**—*Book of the Courtier*, Baldassare Castiglione, 1528
**Diana Trilling quote**—*Claremont Essays*, Diana Trilling, Harcourt, Brace & World, Inc., 1963
**Ben Hecht quote**—*Australian Women's Weekly*, 1.19.55, Marilyn Monroe

# About the Author

STACY EUBANK was born in Lubbock, Texas to Joe and Norma Meador. She was a member of the Class of 1978 at Olton High School. She graduated with an Associate of Arts degree in psychology from South Plains Jr. College in Levelland, Texas. She now lives in Las Vegas, Nevada. She is married to Bruce Eubank, who is a teacher and coach at Bonanza High School and a minister at South Valley church of Christ. They have a son, Bobby, who lives and coaches in Austin, Texas.

Miss Eubank is an accomplished artist and has had her artwork included in *Marilyn in Art* by Roger Taylor. She served as research assistant to Dr. Lois Banner, PhD, with both of her books on Marilyn Monroe...*MM Personal: From the Private Archive of Marilyn Monroe*, and *Marilyn, the Passion and the Paradox*.

 Holding a Good Thought for Marilyn

Ed: 2005-2015

Made in the USA
Lexington, KY
25 June 2015